HANDBOOK OF PROFESSIONAL DEVELOPMENT IN EDUCATION

Handbook of
Professional Development
in Education

*Successful Models and Practices,
PreK–12*

EDITED BY

Linda E. Martin
Sherry Kragler
Diana J. Quatroche
Kathryn L. Bauserman

Foreword by Andy Hargreaves

THE GUILFORD PRESS
New York   London

This volume evolved out of our years of consulting in schools, as administrators and teachers implemented new programs that were meant to help their students learn. Working with them has guided us to read and reflect on what is known about how adult learning takes place, as well as how successful school reform happens. Therefore, this book is dedicated to the educators who work with children across the grades and the scholars across the decades who have examined the issues that our schools and teachers face.

© 2014 The Guilford Press
A Division of Guilford Publications, Inc.
370 Seventh Avenue, Suite 1200, New York, NY 10001
www.guilford.com

Printed in the United States of America

This book is printed on acid-free paper.

Last digit is print number: 9 8 7 6 5 4

Library of Congress Cataloging-in-Publication Data
Handbook of professional development in education : successful models and practices,
PreK–12 / edited by Linda E. Martin, Sherry Kragler, Diana J. Quatroche, Kathryn L.
Bauserman
    pages cm
  Includes bibliographical references and index.
  ISBN 978-1-4625-1521-9 (hardback)
  1. Teachers—In-service training—United States—Handbooks, manuals, etc.
2. Teachers—Training of—United States—Handbooks, manuals, etc.   3. Professional
learning communities.   I. Martin, Linda E.
  LB1731.H197 2014
  370.71′1—dc23
                                                          2013038779

About the Editors

Linda E. Martin, EdD, is Professor of Elementary Education at Teachers College, Ball State University, where she serves as Director of Doctoral Programs for the Department of Elementary Education. For over two decades, she has worked with teachers across grades to develop effective literacy practices. Dr. Martin served for 7 years as a professional development liaison for Ball State, and helped to implement two large grants focused on teachers' literacy instruction in urban schools in the Midwest. Her research interests include students' development of reading and writing strategies, teachers' implementation of effective instructional strategies across grades, content-area reading and materials across grades, and issues that affect teachers' professional development.

Sherry Kragler, PhD, is Associate Professor of Childhood Education and Literacy Studies at the University of South Florida. Before becoming a university professor, she was a classroom teacher, curriculum specialist, and Title I reading teacher/coordinator. Through two federal grants, Dr. Kragler spent 2 years working with primary-grades teachers to improve their reading instruction. She has conducted professional development programs on content-area reading, comprehension instruction, portfolio assessment, and other areas. Her research interests include comprehension development of young children, issues that impact professional development of teachers, literacy development of young readers, and using content texts in the primary grades.

Diana J. Quatroche, PhD, is Professor and Chair of the Department of Elementary, Early, and Special Education in the Bayh College of Education at Indiana State University. In addition to her classroom teaching experience, she has supervised school reading programs and coordinated Title I reading programs. She served for 6 years as a professional development liaison for Indiana State University, and developed the first professional development school while a faculty member at Southeast Missouri State University. Dr. Quatroche has received grants to support professional development for classroom teachers in Indiana, Missouri, and Pennsylvania. Her research interests include the role of graduate programs in preparing reading specialists as literacy leaders and the effect of professional development on teacher practice and student learning.

Kathryn L. Bauserman, PhD, is Associate Professor in the Department of Elementary, Early, and Special Education in the Bayh College of Education at Indiana State University. She has cowritten and codirected five different 2-year grant projects in Indiana that focus on graduate-level teacher professional development through workshops for teachers. Workshop topics have included developing writing using the arts as a tool, increasing higher-level thinking skills in content-area literacy, differentiating reading instruction, using writing to teach comprehension skills across content areas, and enhancing disciplinary literacy through technology and formative assessment.

Contributors

Kathryn H. Au, PhD, SchoolRise LLC, Honolulu, Hawaii

Kathryn L. Bauserman, PhD, Department of Elementary, Early, and Special Education, Bayh College of Education, Indiana State University, Terre Haute, Indiana

Rita M. Bean, PhD, Department of Instruction and Learning, School of Education, University of Pittsburgh, Pittsburgh, Pennsylvania

William G. Brozo, PhD, Graduate School of Education, George Mason University, Fairfax, Virginia

Emily F. Calhoun, EdD, The Phoenix Alliance, St. Simons Island, Georgia

Jason A. Chen, PhD, School of Education, College of William and Mary, Williamsburg, Virginia

Sarah K. Clark, PhD, School of Teacher Education and Leadership, Emma Eccles Jones College of Education and Human Services, Utah State University, Logan, Utah

Laura M. Desimone, PhD, Graduate School of Education, University of Pennsylvania, Philadelphia, Pennsylvania

William A. Firestone, PhD, Department of Educational Theory, Policy and Administration, Graduate School of Education, Rutgers, The State University of New Jersey, New Brunswick, New Jersey

Douglas Fisher, PhD, Department of Educational Leadership, San Diego State University, San Diego, California

Angela Joy Fortune, MEd, Department of Curriculum and Instruction, College of Education, University of Illinois at Chicago, Chicago, Illinois

Nancy Frey, PhD, Department of Educational Leadership, San Diego State University, San Diego, California

Claudia Galindo, PhD, Language, Literacy, and Culture Program, College of Education, University of Maryland Baltimore County, Baltimore, Maryland

James R. Gavelek, PhD, Department of Curriculum and Instruction, College of Education, University of Illinois at Chicago, Chicago, Illinois

Priscilla L. Griffith, PhD, Department of Instructional Leadership and Academic Curriculum, Jeannine Rainbolt College of Education, University of Oklahoma, Norman, Oklahoma

Thomas R. Guskey, PhD, Department of Educational, School, and Counseling Psychology, College of Education, University of Kentucky, Lexington, Kentucky

Andy Hargreaves, PhD, Department of Teacher Education, Lynch School of Education, Boston College, Boston, Massachusetts

Lawrence Ingvarson, PhD, Australian Council for Educational Research, Camberwell, Victoria, Australia

Jennifer Jacobs, PhD, Department of Childhood Education and Literacy Studies, College of Education, University of South Florida, Tampa, Florida

Ann Jaquith, PhD, Stanford Center for Opportunity Policy in Education, Stanford University, Stanford, California

Bruce R. Joyce, BA, Booksend Laboratories, St. Simons Island, Georgia

Susan J. Kimmel, PhD, Center for Early Childhood Professional Development, College of Continuing Education, University of Oklahoma, Norman, Oklahoma

Brian Kissel, PhD, Department of Reading and Elementary Education, College of Education, University of North Carolina at Charlotte, Charlotte, North Carolina

Sherry Kragler, PhD, Department of Childhood Education and Literacy Studies, College of Education, University of South Florida, Tampa, Florida

John Lane, MA, Educational Policy Program, College of Education, Michigan State University, East Lansing, Michigan

Ann Lieberman, EdD, Stanford Center for Opportunity Policy in Education, Stanford University, Stanford, California

Richard Long, EdD, Literate Nation, Washington, DC

Melinda M. Mangin, PhD, Department of Educational Theory, Policy and Administration, Graduate School of Education, Rutgers, The State University of New Jersey, New Brunswick, New Jersey

Linda E. Martin, EdD, Department of Elementary Education, Teachers College, Ball State University, Muncie, Indiana

Jennifer Merriman, PhD, The College Board, Newtown, Pennsylvania

Lynne Miller, EdD, Educational Leadership Program, University of Southern Maine, Gorham, Maine

Maryann Mraz, PhD, Department of Reading and Elementary Education, College of Education, University of North Carolina at Charlotte, Charlotte, North Carolina

Leah Nellis, PhD, Department of Communication Disorders and Counseling, School, and Educational Psychology, Bayh College of Education, Indiana State University, Terre Haute, Indiana

Diana J. Quatroche, PhD, Department of Elementary, Early, and Special Education, Bayh College of Education, Indiana State University, Terre Haute, Indiana

Taffy E. Raphael, PhD, Department of Curriculum and Instruction, College of Education, University of Illinois at Chicago, Chicago, Illinois

D. Ray Reutzel, PhD, Emma Eccles Jones College of Education and Human Services, Utah State University, Logan, Utah

Ruth L. Rohlwing, EdD, School of Education, Saint Xavier University, Chicago, Illinois

Jiening Ruan, PhD, Department of Instructional Leadership and Academic Curriculum, Jeannine Rainbolt College of Education, University of Oklahoma, Norman, Oklahoma

Mavis G. Sanders, PhD, Department of Education and Language, Literacy, and Culture Program, University of Maryland Baltimore County, Baltimore, Maryland

Maureen Spelman, EdD, School of Education, Saint Xavier University, Chicago, Illinois

Jennifer Stepp, MEd, Hardman Center for Children with Learning Disabilities, Jeannine Rainbolt College of Education, University of Oklahoma, Norman, Oklahoma

Daniel Stuckey, PhD, Graduate School of Education, University of Pennsylvania, Philadelphia, Pennsylvania

Allison Swan Dagen, PhD, Department of Curriculum and Instruction/Literacy Studies, College of Education and Human Services, West Virginia University, Morgantown, West Virginia

Ruth Sylvester, PhD, Department of Middle Childhood Education, School of Education, Cedarville University, Cedarville, Ohio

Marilyn Tallerico, PhD, Educational Leadership Program, Graduate School of Education, Binghamton University, State University of New York, Binghamton, New York

Megan Tschannen-Moran, PhD, School of Education, College of William and Mary, Williamsburg, Virginia

Jaime Madison Vasquez, MEd, Department of Curriculum and Instruction, College of Education, University of Illinois at Chicago, Chicago, Illinois

Shelley B. Wepner, EdD, School of Education, Manhattanville College, Purchase, New York

Diane Yendol-Hoppey, PhD, Department of Childhood Education and Literacy Studies, College of Education, University of South Florida, Tampa, Florida

Peter Youngs, PhD, Department of Curriculum, Instruction, and Special Education, Curry School of Education, University of Virginia, Charlottesville, Virginia

Foreword

Six Sources of Change in Professional Development

ANDY HARGREAVES

INTRODUCTION

After years of being undervalued and out of fashion, teachers' professional development and professional learning in the United States are on the rise again. Ever since the introduction of the No Child Left Behind (NCLB) legislation, the improvement of teaching has been treated more and more as a matter of compliance with imposed training in prescribed methods and content, backed up by the high-stakes force of standardized testing and its often punitive consequences. To increase excellence and equity, one state department after another set out to impact classroom learning directly by bypassing the leadership and the professional judgment of the teacher, and going straight to the student through closely prescribed and intensively paced pedagogy. The teacher no longer counted. Student performance and results measured by test scores were all that mattered. No excuses. No escape. That has been the theory of action.

But in the second term of the Obama administration, educational reform strategies are starting to change, and so are the attitudes and approaches to developing the nation's teachers. There are at least six reasons for this shift and its impact on the changing landscape of teachers' professional development:

- The exhaustion of existing reform strategies and their limited conception of professional development.
- The policy impact of international comparisons of educational achievement and the attention they have drawn to the central role of positive strategies for professional development in high-performing systems.
- The reemergence and acknowledgment in policy and research of teacher quality as the main in-school determinant of student achievement.

- The development and widespread adoption of sophisticated Common Core State Standards and the demands they are placing for a more highly qualified and capable teaching force.
- The new pathways for professional learning that are being created by the impact and spread of digital technologies.
- The ubiquitous availability of metrics concerning learning, performance, and effectiveness and the need for teachers' professional community to be able to process and make sense of these data in ways that will lead to improved practice and outcomes.

These six shifts signal new opportunities and renewed possibilities for professional development and they also manifest themselves in the chapters in this comprehensive compendium of leading thinkers and researchers in the professional development field.

THE END OF NCLB

It has become increasingly apparent to the public as well as the profession that while NCLB might have initially heightened the nation's sense of educational urgency and focused its efforts more sharply on educational equity for all categories of students in every school, in practice, the legislation's targets, timelines, and implementation strategies have had quite damaging effects (Nichols & Berliner, 2007).

At first, the drive to make adequate yearly progress (AYP) in proficiency levels for all students, on a timescale defined by the federal government, led to greater focus and heightened effort, and many schools that made the cut or that turned around after failing to do so celebrated with pep rallies (Hargreaves & Shirley, 2009). But as the targets ascended every year for every child until everyone, everywhere was supposed to be proficient by 2015, a set of perverse incentives to avoid failure at almost any cost started to corrode and then corrupt the system (Bird et al., 2005; Campbell, 1976). More and more teachers were told to prep students for their tests, instead of actually teaching them. The curriculum became a narrower and narrower bottleneck of basics where easily memorized content in literacy and mathematics was all that most urban schools now had to offer. Measured rates in reading proficiency appeared to be on the rise, but rates of reading for pleasure actually declined. Teachers were pressed to concentrate more and more of their efforts on "bubble" students just below the passing mark at the expense of other struggling learners who wouldn't yield the desperately needed quick returns in test results that would keep schools in line with AYP (Booher-Jennings, 2005). State departments redesigned their tests so they became easier to pass. And in places such as Atlanta, Georgia, educators up to the very highest level simply cheated ("Former Atlanta Schools Superintendent," 2013). The drive to raise the bar of performance drove out the most basic principles of professional learning and professionalism itself.

The United States shouldn't have been so surprised. Under the first-term government of Tony Blair in the late 1990s, England and Wales had seen it all before.

A highly controversial program of prescribed literacy and numeracy had lifted results on the government's own measures of proficiency, but the gains were hotly disputed, with some critics pointing out that the upward trends preceded the government's action (Tymms, 2004). The results also hit a plateau once all the huffing and puffing of extra effort rather than higher-quality teaching had reached its limit. Moreover, on independent measures of student performance such as the international PISA results of student achievement (Organisation for Economic Cooperation and Development [OECD], in press), where teaching to the test was not possible, England's performance continued to lag far behind that of many other countries, including the United States. Finally, the prescriptive and highly pressured nature of the literacy and numeracy reforms inflicted considerable collateral damage on the teaching profession, with widely reported problems of teacher recruitment, retention, and demoralization being the result. In response to these challenges, the second-term Blair government turned its attention to renewing the teaching profession, improving teachers' working conditions, and investing in improved professional learning for teachers and school leaders. As if it were following the British playbook, the second-term Obama government now appears to be cautiously adopting a similar course.

THE ONSET OF INTERNATIONAL COMPARISONS

In the past 5 years or so, U.S. educational performance, as well as the nation's reform strategies, has been put in perspective by the high-profile publicity assigned to international comparisons of educational achievement. On OECD's widely disseminated international PISA results of student achievement, for example, the United States has been positioned somewhere between 17th and 31st in relation to other countries, depending on the subject being tested (OECD, in press). According to the developmental stages of school system improvement defined by McKinsey and Company, the United States is also neither great nor excellent but struggles even to be merely "good" (Mourshed, Chijioke, & Barber, 2010).

Crucially, analyses of the reasons for high performance in the world's leading school systems by international organizations such as OECD and McKinsey and Company, as well as in the firsthand research that Dennis Shirley and I have reported in *The Fourth Way* and *The Global Fourth Way* (Hargreaves & Shirley, 2009, 2012), point to the importance that these systems attach to attracting, retaining, developing, and connecting high-quality teachers and leaders. These systems, in other words, invest in, accumulate, and circulate the professional capital of their teachers in order to generate strong returns in teaching and learning (Hargreaves & Fullan, 2012).

Consider a few examples. Teachers in Finland are selected from the highest echelons of the university graduation range, applicants to teacher preparation programs have less than a 10% chance of being accepted, and all members of these programs have to undergo rigorous theoretical and practical preparation through a full-time master's program. Once they are teaching, Finnish teachers are expected to create curricula together with their colleagues in each school district, and they spend proportionately more time than teachers in any other country out of class, away from their students, to work with their colleagues on improving their practice together (Sahlberg, 2011).

In Singapore, teachers are paid as much as engineers when they take up their profession, they receive mentoring to support their development along personalized pathways as they progress through their careers, and they collaborate extensively with colleagues within and across schools as they seek to "teach less" so students can "learn more" in an increasingly innovative curriculum (Tucker, 2011).

In South Korea, teachers' pay, status, and security have become firmly established through government reforms and union negotiations following the 1990s economic collapse. These have made teaching an attractive career prospect for the country's academically highly qualified graduates. South Korean teachers also collaborate extensively with their colleagues, especially through online interaction and sharing of files related to lesson planning (Seo, in press).

Last but not least, on the United States's northern border, the world's highest English-speaking performer in education, Canada, also invests heavily in its teachers. In the province of Alberta, for example, the Alberta Teachers' Association, the province's teacher's union, spends around 50% of its resources on research, policy advocacy, and professional development, compared to around 2% in the case of U.S. teacher unions. It has also collaborated closely with government in supporting teacher-designed innovations, shared across schools with 2% of the government education budget, and has worked tirelessly with other partners to bring an end to all high-stakes standardized testing by 2015 (Hargreaves & Shirley, 2012).

Within the United States, outliers of higher performance are also characterized by strong support for various forms of teacher professional development. McKinsey and Company, for example, draw attention to the teacher residency program for new teachers developed in the Boston public school system, and to the strong emphasis that the school system in Long Beach, California, has placed on collaborative professional engagement in the development of its reforms (Mourshed et al., 2010). Meanwhile, in *The Global Fourth Way* (2012), Dennis Shirley and I describe the success of the California Teachers' Association in taking responsibility for turning around hundreds of the state's lowest-performing schools.

In light of the inescapable evidence of professional development practices in higher-performing countries, the United States has finally begun to attend to the issue of elevating the teaching profession, although the way in which it is doing that is not yet consistently aligned with best practice in these other systems.

THE CREATION OF TEACHER QUALITY

With the resurgence of respect for teaching have come defining contributions from leading economists about the value that teachers create for economic outcomes and student results. The good news is that these economists have confirmed the long-term findings of school effectiveness researchers—that within the school, the most important contributor to student achievement is not curriculum standards, assessment, or even governance or leadership, but the quality of teaching. High-quality teaching adds value to student outcomes and is one of the strongest predictors of a child's economic future as an adult. In terms of the cumulative added value that teachers provide for students, it has been argued (see Center for American Progress & the Education Trust, 2011) that three or four good teachers in a row can set a student up for life, whereas a sequence of weak ones can ruin a child's prospects forever.

Renewed respect for teaching hasn't translated into respect for teachers and the teaching profession in general, though. The emphasis of economists and policymakers on human capital is interpreted as individual teacher characteristics and performances that correlate with and can be recorded according to measured student achievement (Hanushek & Rivkin, 2012). This has led to and justified a strategy of rewarding effective individual teachers who have high human capital and removing teachers whose human capital is weak.

In one of the defining papers underpinning this strategy, Hanushek and Rivkin (2012) claim that the only truly reliable indicator of teachers' performance is in the results teachers get with their students as measured by those students' test scores. Even here, they argue, correlations between teacher quality and student outcomes in the broad middle ranges of performance are weak. Therefore, the argument continues, it is better to concentrate performance incentives at the extremes of competence and incompetence, where the evidence is more compelling—using performance management to reward "star" teachers through recognition and increased remuneration and to discipline and eventually dismiss the poorest performers who persistently fail to improve.

One of the prime strategies for improving teacher quality has therefore been to impose performance management systems that rely heavily on student test scores and have high-stakes consequences attached. This strategy of increasing human capital by concentrating on individual teacher performance through extrinsic sanctions and rewards, however, is what Michael Fullan (2011) calls a "wrong driver" of educational change. Historically, the strategy has been a proven and persistent failure. Motivationally, teachers, like other professionals doing complex work, are, beyond a baseline of satisfactory compensation, driven more by the intrinsic satisfaction and stimulation of the work rather than by the extrinsic incentives attached to it (Pink, 2009). And in social as well as statistical terms, the competence of most teachers cannot be calculated with accuracy separately from the degree of support they receive from leaders and colleagues, and from how well or badly they work together as a team.

In other words, more important than human capital is social capital—the capital of trust, collaboration, and collective responsibility that a community is able to create and circulate together. In a key study, University of Pittsburgh Professor Carrie Leana (2011) calculated the effects of human and social capital, respectively, on the mathematics outcomes of 5,000 fifth-grade students in New York City. Her findings are compelling. Perhaps as expected, they revealed that increases in either human capital or social capital each contribute to growth in student achievement.

However, more surprising is the finding that whereas the high human capital of a few individuals will not raise the overall social capital of a community, strong social capital will raise individual human capital, whatever its preexisting level. The implications are clear: while it is always important to attract and retain strong individual human capital, it is improvement in social capital among existing teachers as professional communities that will yield the greatest and most immediate returns.

There is one final point. In our book that introduces the idea of professional capital, Michael Fullan and I argue that there is a third kind of capital that affects teacher quality, in addition to human and social capital (Hargreaves & Fullan, 2012), what we call *decisional capital*. Decisional capital concerns people's capacity to make professional judgments in circumstances where the objective evidence is not incontrovertible. In teaching, as in other professions, it takes most people between 4 and 8 years to develop their abilities to make these daily judgments effectively at a highly expert level. The implication is that we cannot and should not be bringing in young, idealistic, and inexpensive teachers and then moving them on when their costs rise or they become burned out, before our investment in coaching and mentoring them has started to yield high returns. Professional development, in this sense, is and should be a long-term professional commitment, not a short-term training fix.

RAISING STANDARDS

Untrained or undertrained teachers working largely on their own may, for a while, be able to cope with or even excel at whole-class teaching with the help of ring-binders of strategies, regular test preps, a set curriculum script, and a brisk management style. However, frustrated by the number of states that lowered their standards in response to NCLB targets, and fearful of being economically overtaken by Asian economic competitors who have educationally outstanding results, the overwhelming majority of U.S. states have committed their schools to implementing a set of demanding Common Core standards for student learning.

These standards do not lend themselves to factual memorization or easy test prep. They are geared to higher-order thinking, questioning, and investigation, as well as applications of knowledge to unfamiliar problems. This is the kind of innovative curriculum now being embraced by countries such as Singapore and China, it is the sort of knowledge that is measured by the Programme for International Student Assessment of OECD, and it is a set of standards for which there is no suitable binder of easy-to-deploy strategies, nor any given curriculum script.

The challenge for Americans is no longer whether to have Common Core standards. It is how to implement them successfully—how to bring them to life for every student in every school. And there is a challenge in doing so with a teaching force that in its early career is often underprepared to deliver high-level learning outcomes in complex, differentiated classroom environments, and that in midcareer is often required to overturn the ingrained habits of compliance and standardization that have been enforced for years by much of NCLB.

Common Core standards will require high-caliber professional learning for all members of the profession. A few half-day training courses here and there will not be enough. Without a massive commitment to professional learning that adheres to the best practices long advocated by Learning Forward in terms of being embedded, continuous, and collaborative, and that is supported by effective leadership and appropriately allocated time, the admirable ambitions of the standards will be dashed upon the rocks of insufficient implementation. The public and the profession cannot face another failed reform without risking terminal disillusionment with America's ability to see all its students succeed and all its teachers reach the standard that these students deserve. This is a key moment for the future of professional development and for the future of America's children who depend on it. It is a moment that must be seized by everyone.

TURNING TO TECHNOLOGY

The commitment cannot be made cheaply, though. It costs money to bring in trainers, coaches, and consultants. It takes time, support, and substitute or supplementary staffing to enable teachers to work alongside each other in the classroom, or to plan together within the school day. The United States is already a high spender on education in costs per student, so where is the extra investment going to come from?

There are always philanthropic resources to draw on, of course, but while additional support is always welcome, these resources are typically temporary, targeted, and uneven in their application across the system. Other policy shifts can, over time, also redirect resources back to having a direct impact on teachers, students, and classrooms. These include reducing rates of special education identification and the resources attached to one-to-one support by creating more inclusive classrooms and curricula; cutting the budgets for school transportation by making every local school a good school and by using social housing policies to create more diverse residential communities; and bringing expenditures on high-stakes testing down to the level of higher-performing countries by following their practices of testing students in one or two subjects and one or two grades rather than on almost everything they are taught, every year.

In the meantime, securing sufficient levels of support for effective professional development in a system striving to attain higher standards of learning will remain challenging. So emerging opportunities afforded by new technologies are undeniably attractive. Digital platforms are now enabling teachers to download lesson plans, view excellent or simply interesting exemplars of practice, connect with other classrooms, study courses and gain certification online, and join colleagues in various kinds of discussion forums.

There are many risks in these developments, including reduced quality, absence of face-to-face interaction, and exploitation of teachers' out-of-school time. The greatest temptation in responding to new professional standards, though, will be the expectation in some quarters that teachers can and should access online professional learning individually, at low cost, in their own time.

Technologically delivered professional development can be highly collaborative in nature. Collaborative professional learning in professional communities is not the only valuable form of professional development, but it is, in general, the most effective one. However, this does not rule out the potential added value of digitally driven professional development. Online platforms can give teachers access to colleagues and practices that are not immediately available in their own physical working environment. The most locally accessible person is not always the most expert one. Teachers in other schools, systems, and countries may exemplify many alternatives that are not available nearby.

And then there is the intriguing possibility that child care issues, which sometimes lead modestly paid teachers to leave their workplace as soon as their contracted in-school hours permit so they can collect and care for their own children, may become turned into an asset for teacher recruitment, not a perceived liability of the system, with the support of technological flexibility. Need to collect your children promptly after school rather than pay additional costs out of your salary? Then come to an agreement with colleagues to leave school early but reconnect with them later in the evening through technology, once you have put your own children to bed. In combining family flexibility with technological access to a professional community, teaching can become an increasingly attractive career for highly qualified candidates who also want to be supportive parents. It's not the only solution, or even the main one, but it can make a real contribution to the powerful social capital that is contained in strong professional communities.

DATA-DRIVEN DEVELOPMENTS

The final factor that is turning people's attention back toward professional development as a key component of successful school reform is data. "Big Data" are redefining our lives—the ways we shop, the steps and calories that we count, and the information that underpins sports coaches' decision making (Schönberger & Cukier, 2013). And now Big Data are everywhere in education too—in how schools pay increasing attention to test scores, graduation rates, behavior incidents, and absences, to mention just a few.

When Big Data are deployed thoughtfully, with due respect to the strengths and limitations of the data, they provide educators with valuable feedback on their students' progress and difficulties that can inform decision making and even lead to changes in practice.

The best organizations set shared targets for improvement that are owned by everyone, not simply imposed from on high. In places such as Ontario, Canada— one of the highest-performing English-speaking educational systems in the world— many leaders enable all teachers to assume collective responsibility for all students' achievement, across grades and between special education and regular classroom teachers. In these settings, data are collected and organized to stimulate purpose-ful collective discussions and to inform real-time interventions for students who are also known well by their teachers (Hargreaves & Braun, 2012).

However, the continuing U.S. emphasis on narrowly defined, high-stakes mea-sures based on student test scores creates perverse incentives for too many educa-tors to allocate their efforts disproportionately to those students who are likely to yield the quickest test score gains, rather than to those who may have the greatest needs. It also contributes to an adversarial school climate, rather than one of collec-tive responsibility and collective action. This is not only contrary to best practices in other countries, but also detrimental to improvement and accountability.

So the challenge of professional learning communities in a data-driven world is for teachers to be the drivers of change, not the driven (Datnow & Park, 2014). Expertise has no algorithm. Wisdom is not manifest on a spreadsheet. It's the judg-ment, expertise, and sense of collective responsibility that teachers bring to all kinds of data—not just defined by numbers or confined to test scores—that lead to sustainable improvements in practice.

THE HANDBOOK OF PROFESSIONAL DEVELOPMENT IN EDUCATION

A field-defining, state-of-art collection by some of the best scholars in the field of professional development, this book describes the ups and downs of the field over the past half-century. It articulates the connections between professional develop-ment on the one hand and policy, research, and the impact of standards on the other. It carefully identifies the contours of successful practice in teachers' com-munities, in coaching and mentoring, in relationships with districts and commu-nities, and in engagements with culturally diverse populations. The book reviews the contributions of teacher research and action research to effective professional development. It points to the value of partnerships that schools and teachers can develop with universities and with one another. It's a comprehensive, cutting-edge book. It's a book for the profession and a book for these times.

Teachers' professional development is on the radar of educational change once more. Yet, by being employed thoughtlessly or deployed cheaply, it could so very easily be forgotten again. This book provides a vital, accessible, and well-supported resource in the struggle to ensure that this does not become the field's fate—a fate that the students of the nation and the teachers who teach them do not deserve.

REFERENCES

Bird, S., Cox, D., Farewell, V., Goldstein, H., Holt, T., & Smith, P. (2005). Performance indi-cators: Good, bad and ugly. *Journal of the Royal Statistical Society: Series A, 168*(Pt. 1).

Booher-Jennings, J. (2005). Below the bubble: "Educational triage" and the Texas Account-ability System. *American Educational Research Journal, 42*(2), 231–268.

Campbell, D. T. (1976). *Assessing the impact of planned social change*. Kalamazoo: Evaluation Center, College of Education, Western Michigan University.

Center for American Progress & the Education Trust. (2011, February 23). *Essential elements of teacher policy in ESEA: Effectiveness, fairness, and evaluation*. Washington, DC: Author.

Datnow, A., & Park, V. (2014). *Data-driven leadership*, San Francisco: Jossey-Bass

Former Atlanta schools superintendent reports to jail in cheating scandal. (2013, April 3). *CNN*. Retrieved from *edition.cnn.com/2013/04/02/justice/georgia-cheating-scandal/*.

Fullan, M. (2011). *Choosing the wrong drivers for whole system reform* (Seminar Series 204). East Melbourne, Victoria, Australia: Centre for Strategic Education.

Hanushek, E., & Rivkin, S. (2012). The distribution of teacher quality and implications for policy. *Annual Review of Economics, 4*, 131–157.

Hargreaves, A., & Braun, H. (2012). *Leading for all: A research report of the development, design, implementation and impact of Ontario's "Essential for Some, Good for All" initiative*. Oakville, ON, Canada: Council of Ontario Directors of Education.

Hargreaves, A., & Fullan, M. (2012). *Professional capital: Transforming teaching in every school*. New York: Teachers College Press.

Hargreaves, A., & Shirley, D. (2009). *The fourth way: The inspiring future for educational change*. Thousand Oaks, CA: Corwin Press.

Hargreaves, A., & Shirley, D. (2012). *The global fourth way: The quest for educational excellence*. Thousand Oaks, CA: Corwin Press.

Leana, C. R. (2011, Fall). The missing link in school reform. *Stanford Social Innovation Review*, pp. 29–35.

Mourshed, M., Chijioke, C., & Barber, M. (2010). *How the world's most improved school systems keep getting better*. London: McKinsey & Company. Retrieved May 30, 2013, from *www.mckinsey.com/client_service/social_sector/latest_thinking/worlds_most_improved_schools*.

Nichols, S., & Berliner, D. (2007). *Collateral damage: How high-stakes testing corrupts America's schools*. Cambridge, MA: Harvard Education Press.

Organisation for Economic Co-operation and Development. (in press). *Strong performers and successful reformers in education: Lessons from PISA for the United States*. Paris: Author.

Pink, D. H. (2009). *Drive: The surprising truth about what motivates us*. New York: Riverhead Books.

Sahlberg, P. (2011). *Finnish lessons: What can the world learn from educational change in Finland?* New York: Teachers College Press.

Schönberger, V., & Cukier, K. (2013). *Big data: A revolution that will transform how we live, work, and think*. Boston: Houghton Mifflin Harcourt.

Seo, K. (in press). Professional learning of observers, collaborators, and contributors in a teacher-created online community in Korea. *Asia Pacific Journal of Education*.

Tucker, M. (2011). *Standing on the shoulders of giants: An American agenda for education reform*. Washington, DC: National Center on Education and the Economy.

Tymms, P. (2004). Are standards rising in English primary schools? *British Educational Research Journal, 30*(4), 477–494.

Preface

This handbook shares successful models and practices of teacher professional development and learning, along with suggestions for sustaining professional development. Traditionally, teacher growth was provided in various staff development initiatives through local school districts. However, through the years, research indicated that short staff development sessions did not provide enough of the information teachers needed to refine their craft. Because of this situation, the field of professional development began to emerge. Research in the field highlighted various aspects that made for successful teacher growth and subsequent instructional change in the classroom. Recently, though, various state departments of education have initiated policies that in effect mandate professional development programs for teachers. Consequently, many teachers and others are facing professional development programs that do not fit their needs and that may affect positive student growth. In fact, in some cases, teachers are expected to implement practices that are contrary to current research in their fields.

RESEARCH

Five characteristics of successful professional development have emerged from the research:

- Professional development is instructive. It supports teachers as they gain content knowledge and acquire instructional strategies (Long, 2012).
- Professional development is reflective. Teachers need to reflect deeply over time (Donnelly et al., 2005), focused on theory-based practice (Brooke et al., 2005; Kedzior, 2004).
- Professional development is active. Teachers are thinkers and intellectuals. They should be engaged in the learning process (Donnelly et al., 2005).

- Professional development is collaborative. Collaboration challenges teachers to expand their thinking (Hurd & Licciardo-Musso, 2005; Mahn, McMann, & Musanti, 2005).
- Professional development is substantive. It should be extensive (not less than 6 and, for a greater impact, as many as 35 or more hours per focus or topic), while continuously focusing on specific topics (Kedzior, 2004; Long, 2012).

CURRENT ISSUES

In today's schools, as in the past, teachers' professional development has been framed and implemented, for the most part, by the educational policies that affect our schools (Long, Chapter 2, this volume; Valencia & Wixson, 2004; Wilkinson & Son, 2011). At the same time, scholars have examined how teachers learn in order to make changes mandated by policies. Even though these two fields of research (educational policy and professional development) do agree in some instances, often there is conflict. A closer examination of both fields may help us understand how to ensure positive professional learning of teachers.

Schools with effective teachers produce better situations for students' learning (Darling-Hammond, 2009–2010; Dillon, O'Brien, Sato, & Kelly, 2011; Guskey, 2003; Hill, 2009; Rose, 2010). Because of this, scholars in the fields of professional development and educational policy should support quality instruction for teachers sustained by research (Rose, 2010). Thus, both educational policy and professional development fields place teachers at the center of any change that may occur in their schools (Kragler et al., 2008; Quick, Holtzman, & Chaney, 2009; Semadeni, 2010). If professional development is successful, the result is an environment that is highly motivational (Friedrich & McKinney, 2010). However, changing a school's learning environment and instructional routines is a complex process, and it takes time, generally many years, for new teaching behaviors to become a permanent part of teachers' routines (Guskey, 2003; Guskey & Yoon, 2009; Rose, 2010; Taylor, Pearson, Peterson, & Rodriguez, 2005).

According to Spillane, Reiser, and Reimer (2002), the complexity of any change imposed on schools may be affected by various issues: (1) Teachers' perceptions of a policy may not align with the intent of the policy, so the policy implementation may be different; (2) teachers may lack the background, experience, or skills and resources to implement a new policy; and (3) teachers need to understand the value that a new policy will have on their classrooms, which may prompt them to inquire and implement a new practice. This is expected even though the daily routines that encompass teachers' lives in the workplace are complex (Fullan, 2000; Knapp, Bamburg, Ferguson, & Hill, 1998; Knight, 2009). Furthermore, each school is somewhat different depending on the community that supports it. Thus, to meet the learning requirements of students and teachers, one also has to meet the needs of the school, as well as of the community (Sarason, 1996, 2004).

Both fields understand that effective instructional practices are important; however, they differ in two important ways. First, educational policy and professional development are grounded in very different theories. Educational policy is grounded in institutional theory and sense-making theory. Coburn (2001) relates institutional theory, a more cultural approach, in an attempt to examine the multilevel needs of a school's faculty and of the children who are taught. Data (scores and classroom practices) gathered from a school environment are examined for patterns or norms in classroom practices, which could lead to concerns and could evolve into formal policy to reform the educational environment (Coburn, 2001, 2006). Sense-making theory describes how teachers within their school environment interpret and adapt a message from outside the school, which includes policies. As a result, the beliefs of the school staff—that is, the principal and the teachers—will affect how they perceive any new messages of reform and will affect classroom practices, as well as the school as a whole. Normally, teachers collectively reshape messages (new practices) to fit their schools and classrooms. On the other hand, professional development aligns with adult learning theory, which recognizes that adults bring a variety of life experiences to learning and approach learning differently because they are at different stages of their development (Knowles, 1970: Merriam, 2001). In this respect, learning is a personal and constructive process (Desimone, 2011; Knowles, 1970; Merriam, 2001). To develop professionally, teachers should be provided opportunities to reflect on their instruction and to examine various methods of instruction.

Another difference in how professional development and educational policy view reform is in the ways in which teacher learning is planned and implemented. Based on professional development research, teachers should to be able to set individual learning goals according to their own professional needs, as well as their students' needs. They may also act collectively (Bandura, 1977) with their peers to support shared school goals. But, even when acting collectively, teachers may perceive new policies differently as they adapt them to their classroom practices. Basically, Guskey (2003) asserts that teachers should believe that the new instructional practice is worth the effort and will benefit their students. While educational policy supports a learning environment for teachers, the focus of any topic will be based on economics and competition, which most often includes mandated test scores to determine teacher effectiveness. Often the goals are broad and based on the beliefs of those in charge rather than on relevant research (Coburn, 2006).

These differences are well documented; however, educational policies (local, state, and federal) are not going away anytime soon. Therefore, educators at all levels need to be actively involved in the decisions that affect them, their students, and their school communities (Allington, 2009; Long, Chapter 2, this volume; Smit, 2005). Within this handbook, scholars and educators share various experiences that describe successful professional development and learning opportunities for teachers and school leadership.

OVERVIEW OF THE BOOK

This handbook, intended to address professional development issues for PreK–12 educators in all content areas, forges a balance between policy issues and theoretical frameworks and presents recommendations for best practices in professional development. It is meant to become a source for graduate programs, school district leaders, classroom teachers, politicians, and officials in state departments of education in providing effective, sustainable professional development for teachers and school leaders. The *Handbook* is divided into four parts: (I) Professional Development, Past and Present; (II) The Complexity of Professional Development in Today's Schools; (III) Developing Solutions for Effective Professional Development; and (IV) Pulling It Together. Each section begins with a quote from a teacher or administrator reflecting on his or her experiences with professional development. The *Handbook* also includes an appendix highlighting schools in national and international settings that have implemented effective professional development.

Part I begins with Chapter 1, by Ann Lieberman and Lynne Miller, who provide a historical context for professional development, along with the theoretical frames and changes in the terminology over time. In Chapter 2, Richard Long explores how federal mandates and the allocation of federal funding have affected schools and led to changes in how professional development is implemented. In Chapter 3, Allison Swan Dagen and Rita M. Bean present a comprehensive overview of research-based best practices in professional development, along with a discussion of coaching and the importance of teacher leaders and learning communities.

In Part II, D. Ray Reutzel and Sarah K. Clark (Chapter 4) address the impact of legislative and business issues on professional development initiatives in the schools. In Chapter 5, Ann Jaquith discusses how policy influences teacher behavior and professional development. In Chapter 6, Mavis G. Sanders and Claudia Galindo explore the community issues that may affect schools. Marilyn Tallerico, in Chapter 7, describes issues that affect professional development initiatives at the district and school building levels. Taffy E. Raphael, Jaime Madison Vasquez, Angela Joy Fortune, James R. Gavelek, and Kathryn H. Au (Chapter 8) describe the multiple ways in which professionals learn and grow over time, considering sociocultural approaches. The last three chapters in Part II present examples of sustained models of professional development at different levels of schooling for students: Maryann Mraz and Brain Kissel explore the current delivery of professional development in early childhood school settings, as well as the importance of a long-term commitment to professional development in maintaining change (Chapter 9); Priscilla L. Griffith, Jiening Ruan, Jennifer Stepp, and Susan J. Kimmel explore the delivery of professional development within the context of their logic model in an elementary setting (Chapter 10); and Douglas Fisher and Nancy Frey describe some of the practical issues that need to be considered when planning and implementing professional development programs in secondary settings (Chapter 11).

Part III begins with Chapter 12, by Ruth L. Rohlwing and Maureen Spelman, who present the significance of adult learning when working with teachers and the characteristics that influence how they respond to professional development. In Chapter 13, Megan Tschannen-Moran and Jason A. Chen discuss the concepts of self-efficacy and collective efficacy as influences on the success of professional development efforts at the school and district levels. William G. Brozo, in Chapter 14, describes the success he has had in working at the state level to bring about change in individual districts and schools through a systems approach to professional development. Chapter 15, by Peter Youngs and John Lane, demonstrates how meeting the actual needs of teachers can have a positive impact on the success of professional development efforts. Jennifer Jacobs and Diane Yendol-Hoppey, in Chapter 16, review how teachers can use the results of action research in their own classrooms to inform their professional learning. William A. Firestone and Melinda M. Mangin follow with a discussion of the importance of leadership when planning a coherent professional development program (Chapter 17). A strong school and university partnership can foster professional development in different ways, as described by Shelley B. Wepner in Chapter 18. Jennifer Merriman examines teacher effectiveness as demonstrated by the connections between teachers' content knowledge and instructional expertise in Chapter 19. In Chapter 20, Lawrence Ingvarson discusses an international perspective on teachers meeting high-level standards and being involved in professional learning through the national board certification process. Bruce Joyce and Emily F. Calhoun, in Chapter 21, describe the importance of considering how technology can be utilized in classrooms as teachers are learning. Diana J. Quatroche, Kathryn L. Bauserman, and Leah Nellis, in Chapter 22, present a variety of external resources that can support teachers' professional growth.

Part IV focuses on approaches to sustain professional learning of teachers and school leaders. In Chapter 23, Thomas R. Guskey describes ways to measure the effectiveness of teachers' professional development. Laura M. Desimone and Daniel Stuckey, in Chapter 24, clearly outline how to maintain sustainability of professional development. In the final chapter, Chapter 25, Sherry Kragler, Linda E. Martin, and Ruth Sylvester describe some of the lessons learned about teachers' professional development over time.

REFERENCES

Allington, R. (2009). Literacy policies that are needed: Thinking beyond "No Child Left Behind." In J. V. Hoffman & Y. M. Goodman (Eds.), *Changing literacies for changing time: An historical perspective on the future of reading research, public policy, and classroom practices* (pp. 247–265). New York: Routledge.

Bandura, A. (1977). *Social learning theory.* New York: General Learning Press.

Brooke, R., Coyle, D., Walden, A., Healey, C., Larson, K., Laughridge, V., et al. (2005). Finding a space for professional development: Creating third space through after-school writing groups. *Language Arts, 82,* 367–377.

Coburn, C. (2001). Collective sensemaking about reading: How teachers mediate reading policy in their professional communities. *Educational Evaluation and Policy Analysis, 23*(2), 145–170.

Coburn, C. (2006). Framing the problem of reading instruction: Using frame analysis to uncover the microprocesses of policy implementation. *American Educational Research Journal, 43*(3), 343–379.

Darling-Hammond, L. (2009–2010). America's commitment to equity will determine our future. *Phi Delta Kappan, 91,* 8–14.

Desimone, L. M. (2011). A primer on effective professional development. *Phi Delta Kappan,* *92*, 68–71.

Dillon, D. R., O'Brien, D. G., Sato, M., & Kelly, C. M. (2011). Professional development and teacher education for reading instruction. In M. L. Kamil, P. D. Pearson, E. B. Moje, & P. P. Afflerbach (Eds.), *Handbook of reading research* (Vol. 4, pp. 627–660). New York: Routledge.

Donnelly, A., Morgan, D., DeFord, D., Files, J., Long, S., Mills, H., et al. (2005). Transformative professional development. *Language Arts, 82,* 336–346.

Friedrich, L., & McKinney, M. (2010). Teacher inquiry for equity: Collaborating to improve teaching and learning. *Language Arts, 87,* 241–251.

Fullan, M. (2000). The three stories of education reform. *Phi Delta Kappan, 81,* 581–584.

Guskey, T. R. (2003). What makes professional development effective? *Phi Delta Kappan, 84,* 748–750.

Guskey, T. R., & Yoon, K. S. (2009). What works in professional development. *Phi Delta Kappan, 90,* 495–500.

Hill, H. C. (2009). Fixing teacher professional development. *Phi Delta Kappan, 90,* 470–476.

Hurd, J., & Licciardo-Musso, L. (2005). Lesson study: Teacher-led professional development in literacy. *Language Arts, 82,* 388–395.

Kedzior, H. (2004). Teacher professional development. *Education Policy Brief, 15,* 1–6.

Knapp, M. S., Bamburg, J. D., Ferguson, M. C., & Hill, P. T. (1998). Converging reforms and the working lives of frontline professionals in the schools. *Educational Policy, 12,* 397–418.

Knight, J. (2009). What can we do about teacher resistance? *Phi Delta Kappan, 90,* 508–513.

Knowles, M. (1970). *The modern practice of adult education: Andragogy versus pedagogy.* Englewood Cliffs, NJ: Prentice Hall/Cambridge.

Kragler, S., Martin, L. E., & Kroeger, D. C. (2008). Money down the drain: Mandated professional development. *Journal of School Leadership, 18,* 528–550.

Long, R. (2012). Professional development and education policy: Understanding the current disconnect. *Reading Today, 29*(3), 29–30.

Mahn, H., McMann, D., & Musanti, S. (2005). Teaching/learning centers: Professional development for teachers of linguistically and culturally diverse students. *Language Arts, 82,* 378–387.

Merriam, S. B. (2001, Spring). Andragogy and self-directed learning: Pillars of adult learning. *New Directions for Adult and Continuing Education, 89,* 3–14.

Quick, H. E., Holtzman, D. J., & Chaney, K. R. (2009). Professional development and instructional practice: Conceptions and evidence of effectiveness. *Journal of Education for Students Placed at Risk, 14*(1), 45–71.

Rose, M. (2010). Reform: To what end? *Educational Leadership, 67*(7), 6–11.

Sarason, S. B. (1996). *Revisiting the culture of the school and the problem of change.* New York: Teachers College Press.

Sarason, S. B. (2004). *And what do you mean by learning?* Portsmouth, NH: Heinemann.

Semadeni, J. (2010). When teachers drive their learning. *Educational Leadership, 67*(8), 66–69.

Smit, B. (2005). Teachers, local knowledge, and policy implementation: A qualitative policy-practice inquiry. *Education and Urban Society, 37,* 292–306.

Spillane, J. P., Reiser, B. J., & Reimer, T. (2002). Policy implementation and cognition: Reframing and refocusing implementation research. *Review of Educational Research, 72,* 387–431.

Taylor, B. M., Pearson, P. D., Peterson, D. S., & Rodriguez, M. C. (2005). The CIERA school change framework: An evidence-based approach to professional development and school reading improvement. *Reading Research Quarterly, 40,* 40–68.

Valencia, S. W., & Wixson, K. K. (2004). Literacy policy and policy research that makes a difference. In R. B. Ruddell & N. J. Unrau (Eds.), *Theoretical models and processes of reading* (5th ed., pp. 69–92). Newark, DE: International Reading Association.

Wilkinson, I. A. G., & Son, E. H. (2011). A dialogic turn in research on learning and teaching to comprehend. In M. L. Kamil, P. D. Pearson, E. B. Moje, & P. P. Afflerbach (Eds.), *Handbook of reading research* (Vol. 4, pp. 359–387). New York: Routledge.

Contents

PART I

PROFESSIONAL DEVELOPMENT, PAST AND PRESENT

For years, teachers were required to continue their education, either with college courses and/or workshops that interested them as well as ones they felt would improve their teaching. Teachers are now required to take inservice of the administration's choice, whether it is pertinent to them or not. Teachers are then asked to implement the new "learning" with no additional support and many times lack of materials. Teachers need to be able to choose an inspirational workshop that reminds them that what they do each day is important, especially to that struggling, forgotten child.

—KARIN HUTTSELL
National Board Certified first-grade teacher
Eel River Elementary School
Fort Wayne, Indiana

CHAPTER 1

Teachers as Professionals
Evolving Definitions of Staff Development

ANN LIEBERMAN
LYNNE MILLER

- The histories of staff development and school reform are intrinsically related. They demonstrate the enduring tension between top-down federal reform policies and bottom-up whole-school reform initiatives and the types of staff development each promotes.
- Competing models of staff development have developed alongside each other over time. Although the *training model of inservice teacher education* continues to hold sway in many schools and districts, it is challenged by the *growth-in-practice model of professional learning* in settings inside and outside of school.
- Networks and partnerships provide opportunities for professional learning outside of school. They are "boundary-crossing" organizations that connect educators regionally and nationally around common interests and concerns.
- Professional learning communities provide opportunities for small groups of teachers to meet regularly and engage in collaborative inquiry into their own and each other's teaching practice. They usually exist within schools but reach beyond those boundaries as well.
- Advances in multimedia and new technologies are emerging as powerful tools for teacher development. While they provide opportunities for teachers through courses and workshops in the training model, they also pioneer ways for networks, partnerships, and communities of practice to occur in new environments.

Our task in this chapter is to provide a framework for understanding the history and definition of staff development. Our framework is informed by both research and practice, and it explores how shifts in approaches to school reform and the development of new knowledge about learning have influenced policy and practice over time. We organize our discussion around the five understandings just listed.

A SHORT HISTORY OF SCHOOL REFORM AND PROFESSIONAL DEVELOPMENT

The pressure to reform schools and improve teaching has been a constant drumbeat in American education and has been the result of federal policies. Larry Cuban (2011) identified the recurring cycles of federal efforts to reform schools. This cycle reflects a consistent theme in how federal policy has defined and driven the content and form of teacher staff development. Each cycle begins with an event or problem that is pressured by social, economical, political, or demographic changes in the larger society. "Opinion elites" discuss the problem with each other, talk with the media, and point to the schools as being a part of the problem, arguing for reforms in school curriculum, teacher preparation, and continuing education. According to Cuban, then, what begins as a social problem quickly morphs into a teaching problem in need of a solution. The opinion elites who first identified the problem, now self-identified as reformers, lobby legislators and policymakers to adopt and implement the reforms they propose. When the reforms prove difficult to implement or simply wrongheaded, the reformers blame educators and their unions, as well as flawed professional development schemes, for the failure of the reform to produce improved outcomes. As outside events change, the cycle begins again, and each time new efforts to improve teaching and teachers are at the center.

FEDERAL REFORMS AND STAFF DEVELOPMENT

With each new reform strategy come ideas about how to "fix" teachers and teaching. Here we consider three examples of federal school reform policies and how they influenced the history and definition of staff development. We begin with the launch of *Sputnik* by the Soviet Union in 1957, which undermined the United States in its efforts to dominate the new frontier of space. The response was palpable; opinion leaders and the media made *Sputnik* a crisis of epic proportions, one that challenged our safety and position in the world. This was the beginning of the Cold War, and the Soviets seemed to have gained an upper hand by way of their advances in science and technology. America's schools were held culpable as being largely to blame for not paying enough attention to the teaching of science and mathematics. Within a year, President Eisenhower signed into law the National Defense and Education Act (NDEA), which originally aimed to improve the quality of teaching in science and mathematics and later included foreign languages, social sciences, and English. Teacher institutes that enrolled K–12 teachers were formed as summer programs held on university campuses and taught by university faculty. Although the structures, formats, and pedagogies of the institutes varied, they were all based on the assumption that teachers did not have a clear grasp of the disciplines they taught and that the best way to correct this deficit was through exposure to practicing academics who were expert in their content areas. The theory was that if school science teachers could learn how to think like scientists, they could teach their students to do the same, and the result would be a generation that could rival their Soviet counterparts in scientific knowledge and skill. However, the institutes were not as successful as hoped. Their unavailability to teachers limited their prospects of transforming science and math education in general, and research by the General Accounting Office concluded that they had no effect on science and math learning (Michelli & Earley, 2011, p. 9).

Almost 30 years after the launch of *Sputnik*, the United States faced a new threat to its standing in the world. This time the threat was economic, and the focus was on Japan. Leaders in the business world and opinion makers in the media viewed Japan's spectacular economic growth with alarm and as a harbinger of our own decline. Again, the focus quickly shifted to the schools. In response, *A Nation at Risk* was published in 1983 by the National Commission on Excellence in Education, a federally authorized body, and fueled the flames. In words reminiscent of the *Sputnik* era, it stated:

> If an unfriendly foreign power had attempted to impose on America the mediocre educational performance that exists today, we might well have viewed it as an act of war.... We have, in effect, been committing an act of unthinking, unilateral educational disarmament. (p. 8)

Lest there be any doubt about what motivated this statement, the report said, "Our once unchallenged preeminence in commerce, industry, science, and technological innovation is being overtaken by competitors throughout the world" (p. 7).

The report's recommendations focused on curriculum reform for the "new basics," which included (1) 4 years of math, science, English, and social studies and a mandatory one-semester course in computer science; (2) more stringent requirements for grade-to-grade promotion, high school graduation, and college entry; (3) career ladders and differentiated pay scales for teachers; and (4) an increased emphasis on standardized testing. The report returned to the recommendations of *A Nation at Risk* and stated, "We call upon university scientists, scholars, and members of professional societies, in collaboration with master teachers, to help in this task, as they did in the post-Sputnik era" (p. 25). And as was the case in the *Sputnik* era, school districts depended on outside experts to conduct workshops for classroom teachers on how to implement the practices the report recommended.

We see a similar cycle in play with the reforms included in the No Child Left Behind (NCLB) legislation. President George W. Bush signed the No Child Left Behind Act of 2001 into law with the support of two groups that were not natural allies, civil rights activists and the Business Roundtable. The civil rights activists saw the legislation as a continuation of the *Brown* decision of 1954 that desegregated schools, whereas business leaders saw it as a way to make America a more competitive force by applying to education the outcome measures usually reserved to industry. At root, the bill was about accountability; it proposed the use of state-developed tests to measure school and teacher effectiveness and advocated scientifically based staff development approaches that focused on linking student achievement, teacher knowledge and skills, and standards and assessments. As with previous federal reforms, the NCLB view of staff development was limited and technocratic and based on a deficit model. It focused on the implementation of policies and practices that were aimed at raising student scores on the mandated state tests. The result was more teacher workshops, more prescribed skills and content, more scripted curriculum, more activities geared to teaching to the test, and a continued use of a training approach.

The newest U.S. Department of Education initiative, the Common Core State Standards (CCSS), is yet another example of the cycle of reform. Building on NCLB's advocacy of standards-based curriculum, teaching, and assessment and also acknowledging its central flaw, having 50 different state standards and assessments, the National Governors Association called for the establishment of a uniform set of learning standards and urged state legislatures to adopt them in place of the existing standards. The CCSS have now been adopted in 45 states, and plans are in place to develop two common assessment systems from which states can choose. Like NDEA, the "new basics," and NCLB before it, the Common Core was developed in response to an outside threat: the standing of U.S. students in international comparison of academic achievement. Fueled by a fear on the part of business and several foundations, the Common Core has inspired the development of new training modules, workshops, and courses for teachers—all designed to ease implementation.

WHOLE-SCHOOL REFORMS AND STAFF DEVELOPMENT

Alongside the federal, top-down reforms described previously, a different sort of reform has emanated from the school level. These reforms called for "whole-school change" and "school restructuring" and linked changes in teaching to changes in school culture. According to this view, improving teaching is a complex affair that requires major changes in the norms, behavior, and values of schools. Seymour Sarason (1971) was perhaps the first to articulate this view in his iconic book, *The Culture of the School and the Problem of Change.* He made the case that it was not just the "what," or the content, of the reforms that mattered; it was the "how" of the reforms, the ways people interacted and connected to new ideas that mattered. His now-famous maxim "the more things change, the more they remain the same" was an indictment of federal top-down reforms based on technocratic strategies that did not consider the social, cultural, and organizational arrangements of schools and what they meant for teachers.

Staff development for whole-school change involved teachers in reculturing their schools at the same time they were reculturing their classrooms. These new school cultures had to provide opportunities for teachers to foster collegial relationships and to learn from each other; they had to encourage and support full participation of all members of the staff and also find a balance between institutional and individual needs and concerns. Team teaching and planning, collective curriculum writing and assessment development, peer observation, and teacher study and work groups were some of the staff development approaches that restructuring schools embraced. The emergence of teacher leadership also played a major part in these efforts. Teacher leaders were pivotal in reconstructing relationships, changing conditions of teaching and learning, and professionalizing teaching. These school-based reforms offered teachers the opportunity to expand their knowledge and to build repertoires that deepened their practice. Although these approaches are not always valued in the current reform environment, they point to what may be the future in school reform and staff development.

COMPETING MODELS OF STAFF DEVELOPMENT

Our discussion of the top-down federal school reform initiatives describes a view of staff development based on the assumption that teachers need direct instruction about how to improve their skills and master new strategies. The early term "inservice education" connoted an extension of the preservice education that prospective teachers experienced in college. The change in terms, from "inservice" to "staff development," that occurred in the 1970s was perfunctory at best, having little impact on adopting a training model for improving teaching. The NDEA Institutes of the 1960s and 1970s, the staff development workshops on the "new basics" of the 1980s, and NCLB are clear examples of this idea. In recent years, the term "professional learning" has gained credence as a better descriptor of the kind of staff development that best serves teachers and their students.

THE TRAINING MODEL

In their synthesis of findings from 30 years of staff development research, Showers, Joyce, and Bennett (1987) concluded that effective inservice/staff development followed a specific workshop design, with onsite coaching recommended. In this model, trainers followed a series of steps: (1) presentation of the theory, (2) expert demonstration of the strategy or skill, (3) opportunities for participants to practice what had been demonstrated, and (4) feedback from the trainers to the participants on how they had performed the new skill or strategy. The researchers concluded, "It doesn't seem to matter where or when training is held, and it doesn't really matter what the role of the trainer is. . . . What does matter is the training design" (p. 106). This last statement captures the essence of what Little (1993) described as the training model of staff development: that in which teachers are presented with small pieces of knowledge or skill in a prescribed workshop and are expected to implement the new skill in their classrooms regardless of context, content, or changes that they would have to make. Much of the staff development that teachers have been and continue to be exposed to at the district and school levels appears to follow that training model.

PROFESSIONAL LEARNING AS GROWTH-IN-PRACTICE

As might be expected, several researchers (Lambert, 1989; Lieberman, 1995; Little, 1993) found that the training model—with its formal workshop designs, prescribed practices, detachment from classroom practice, and disregard for adult learning—was not a good fit for the ambitious reforms of the whole-school change/restructuring movement. Shulman's (1986) notion of "pedagogical content knowledge" described the complexity of teaching and provided a strong rationale for those who advocated for another model of staff development. Shulman proposed that content and pedagogy were not independent of each other, that the mastery of content was attached to and dependent on the way it was taught, and that improvement efforts would have to consider not only how to improve teacher content knowledge but also how to connect content to teaching and teaching to learning. Elmore and McLaughlin's (1988) research supported this view. In their study of the long-term effects of staff development, they found that teachers got better at their craft by engaging in "steady work" that is inclusive, broad based, and grounded in the day–to-day realities of school life. Lieberman and Miller (1999) added to the conversation by identifying the shifts in the social realities of teaching that would require a shift to a different paradigm for staff development (see Figure 1.1).

Policy researchers such as Darling-Hammond and McLaughlin (1995) stressed the importance of the changing conception of teaching and proposed creating organizational structures that fostered collaboration and promoted ways of thinking about collaborative inquiry. They recommended that districts develop policies with a "learner-centered" view of teaching. Taken together, these forces joined in a concerted effort to move away from the training model of inservice and staff

individualism and privatism	→	collegiality and community
classroom concerns	→	whole-school concerns
teaching at the center	→	learning at the center
technical work	→	intellectual work/inquiry into practice
managed/controlled work	→	leadership for accountability
weak knowledge base	→	expanding knowledge base

FIGURE 1.1. Shifts in the social realities of teaching. From Lieberman and Miller (1999, p. 19). Copyright 1999 by Teachers College Press. Reprinted by permission.

development and toward a growth-in-practice model. This alternative model is best described as *professional learning* and is distinguished from inservice education and staff development in the following important ways (Lieberman & Miller, 2000, 2007; Little, 2006; McLaughlin & Talbert, 1993; Talbert, 2010):

- Professional learning is steady, intellectual work that promotes meaningful engagement with ideas and with colleagues over time; inservice/staff development is primarily technical, skills-based work that promotes the application of prescribed skills and occurs in fragmented pieces.
- Professional learning involves teachers in knowledge creation through collaborative inquiry into practice; inservice/staff development involves teachers most often in knowledge consumption through the transfer of knowledge by way of direct instruction.
- Professional learning relies on both inside teacher knowledge and outside expert knowledge; inservice/staff development relies on outside expert knowledge.
- Professional learning focuses on specific problems of practice and takes into account the experience and knowledge of teachers; inservice/staff development focuses on general problems of implementation of new programs and policies and tends toward a "one size fits all" approach.
- Professional learning assumes that teachers will actively engage in reflection, analysis, and critique; inservice/staff development assumes that teachers will passively comply with the delivery of content.

Professional learning, then, requires a commitment to a different way of thinking. Despite the present emphasis on the training model we see in inservice/staff development approaches, the notion of professional learning is being kept alive and flourishing in venues both inside and outside of school in networks and partnerships and in professional learning communities. Next we describe these settings and their basic assumptions and practices.

PROFESSIONAL LEARNING IN NETWORKS AND PARTNERSHIPS

Networks, coalitions, and partnerships are venues for professional learning that sidestep traditional institutional roles, hierarchies, and bureaucracies. As "boundary-crossing" organizations, they provide a neutral space for teachers from different settings to meet for the sole purpose of collaborative work and to learn from each other. Although they are not uniform in either form or focus, they share some common characteristics. Allen Parker (1979) identified some of these commonalities in his study of 60 active networks; they included a strong sense of commitment to an idea or innovation, a sense of shared purpose, a mixture of information sharing and psychological support, leadership by an effective facilitator, voluntary participation, and equal treatment of members. Lieberman and Grolnick (1996) added to the knowledge base in their study of 16 school-reform networks and identified attributes that included agendas that were more challenging than prescriptive, learning that appeared to be more indirect than direct, formats for work that were more collaborative than individualistic, work that was more integrated than fragmented, leadership that was more facilitative than directive, and structures that were more movement-like than organization-like. They found that members had a compelling reason to participate, used collaborative tools to build consensus and commitment, developed ongoing relationships, and made a special effort to keep values visible.

Writing in 1973, organizational sociologist and network theorist Mark Granovetter introduced the idea of the "strength of weak ties" to describe the unique dynamic that undergirds complex, voluntary organizations such as networks and how they manage to connect people who do not know each other well in common work and commitments. He wrote, "Weak ties provide people with access to information and resources beyond those available in their own social circle" (p. 209). Unlike strong ties, in which people know each other too well to step out of their ascribed roles and break with tradition, weak ties encourage people to try on new roles, to experiment with new ideas, and to move more quickly toward innovation. Weak ties are what hold networks together. Next, we describe three long-lived networks.

Coalition of Essential Schools

The Coalition of Essential Schools (CES) is a school-reform network that has been in existence since 1984. Beginning with 12 schools as members, it has grown to include hundreds of schools, organizations, and individuals who share a common vision of "an educational system that equips all students with the intellectual, emotional, and social habits and skills to become powerful and informed citizens who contribute actively toward a democratic and equitable society" (Coalition of Essential Schools, 2012). The network is open to schools, organizations, and individuals who pay an annual fee for membership. It is a complex organization that is governed by an executive board and carries out its work through the national organization and through regional centers.

Founded by Ted Sizer, a former high school teacher, principal, college professor, and dean, CES is based on his powerful vision of schooling that is reflected in the "CES Common Principles" (Coalition of Essential Schools, 2012):

- Learning to use one's mind well: Schools have a central intellectual purpose.
- Less is more, depth over coverage: Schools focus on the mastery of a limited number of essential skills and knowledge.
- Goals apply to all students: Schools have common goals for all students and meet them through uncommon means.
- Personalization of teaching: Student–teacher ratios are low, so that teachers can make appropriate decisions about curriculum, instructional materials, and pedagogies.
- Student-as-worker, teacher-as-coach: Teachers act as coaches who help students learn how to learn and to teach themselves.

- Demonstration of mastery: Students are assessed on their performance of real tasks using multiple forms of evidence; graduation is based on "exhibitions" of mastery to an authentic audience.
- A tone of decency and trust: The feeling tone of the schools is one of "unanxious expectation."
- Commitment to the entire school: The principals and teachers are committed to the whole schools as educational generalists first and content specialists second.
- Resources dedicated to teaching and learning: Budget targets focus on teacher loads and time for collaborative planning and phase out or reduce services that don't add to personalization.
- Democracy and equity: The schools model democratic practices, honor diversity, build on the strength of its communities, and challenge all forms of inequity.

CES activities include an annual Fall Forum, where members meet with each other and with leading thinkers to share ideas, concerns, insights, and practices; a monthly digital newsletter that provides information about the network and access to publications and products relevant to the CES mission; a quarterly journal and a website that demonstrates mentor sites; and access to 15 affiliate centers that provide school coaching, professional learning opportunities, technical assistance development, and technical assistance on a regional basis. In addition, CES advocates policies that support its view of schooling at the local, state, and national levels.

National Writing Project

The National Writing Project (NWP) is a national network dedicated to the improvement of writing and writing instruction. First established in Berkeley, California, in 1974 as the Bay Area Writing Project by James Gray, a local high school teacher and teacher educator, and his colleagues, it is a network of approximately 200 university-based sites across the country. Based on the idea that teachers are the best teachers of teachers, the NWP "envisions a future where every person is an accomplished writer, engaged learner, and active participant in a digital, interconnected world" (National Writing Project, 2012). Although the sites function autonomously, they share core principles of professional learning:

- Teachers at every level—from kindergarten through college—are the agents of reform; universities and schools are ideal partners for investing in that reform through professional development.
- Writing can and should be taught, not just assigned, at every grade level. Professional development programs should provide opportunities for teachers to work together to understand the full spectrum of writing development across grades and across subject areas.
- Knowledge about the teaching of writing comes from many sources: theory

and research, the analysis of practice, and the experience of writing. Effective professional development programs provide frequent and ongoing opportunities for teachers to write and to examine theory, research, and practice together systematically.

- There is no single right approach to teaching writing; however, some practices prove to be more effective than others. A reflective and informed community of practice is in the best position to design and develop comprehensive writing programs.
- Teachers who are well informed and effective in their practice can be successful teachers of other teachers, as well as partners in educational research, development, and implementation. Collectively, teacher leaders are our greatest resource for educational reform (National Writing Project, 2012).

The centerpiece of the NWP is the Summer Invitational Institute, facilitated by a site director and a cadre of teacher leaders, who are called "teacher consultants." Lieberman and Wood's (2003) case studies of summer institutes at two different sites—a rural and an urban site—uncovered social practices that resonated with Etienne Wenger's (2012) ideas about the interplay of social participation, a sense of social belonging, and professional learning. These practices included honoring teachers' knowledge, turning ownership over to learners, sharing leadership, promoting an inquiry stance, and encouraging a reconceptualization of professional identity linked to professional community. In the summer institute, teachers taught each other about their practice, wrote and had their writing critiqued by others, read research and discussed it, and took turns being leaders and audience. In the process, they came to understand that much of what they were experiencing could be transferred to their own classrooms. Some became teacher consultants who facilitated learning for others on a continuing basis, whereas others joined local writing project sites and formed their own networks.

Southern Maine Partnership

The Southern Maine Partnership (SMP) is a regional network that links school districts with their local university in support of educator and student development in southern Maine. Established in 1985 as an original member of John Goodlad's National Network for Education Renewal, the partnership's major goal is to find common ground between the culture of schools and the culture of the academy and to leverage change in both. That requires the creation and maintenance of a third culture with a distinct identity and set of norms, as well as expectations that support open conversation, critique, and—when called for—joint action (Miller, 2001). Member districts pay a small sum to belong to the partnership, and the university supports one-fourth of a faculty load to provide support. Members sign on to share information, practices, and insights and to maintain their connections with each other over time.

The partnership is a loosely governed alliance that responds to local needs as they arise. Its centerpiece consists of role-alike or agenda-specific groups that function autonomously; they form, change direction and membership, dismantle, and form again as needs arise. These groups usually meet at least once a month over a meal, a tradition that has become known as "dine and discuss." Groups have emerged for superintendents, principals, K–8 math and literacy teachers, high school English, math, and social studies teachers and department heads, curriculum directors, assessment coordinators, team leaders, and middle school educators, to name a few.

As a regional network based on school–university collaboration and reciprocity, the SMP has characteristics that distinguish it from national networks such as the CES and NWP. Although the latter is housed in a university, its goals do not rest on building a joint collaborative culture. The SMP's place-bound nature limits its membership to educators who live in close proximity and can regularly meet face-to-face with little difficulty. Although it is sensitive to and aware of national reforms, it focuses on their local implications. It is especially responsive to state policies and mandates and, as a result, forges relationships with state agencies; these vary from being congenial to oppositional in nature. Finally, it focuses on several agendas simultaneously and does not promote a specific reform or subject area.

The university's commitment to the partnership is essential. In recent years, that commitment has waned, and the power of the SMP as a network for professional learning has been diminished. In its stead, member districts have created smaller regional alliances and based them on the premises and practices of the SMP. Dine-and-discuss meetings have become routine; role-alike groups meet regularly; there are group responses to state policies and initiatives. What is missing is the connection to the university and the university's connection to the schools. Fortunately, that is changing, and a revitalized Southern Maine Partnership is emerging.

Networks represent a viable alternative to traditional inservice/staff development programs and embody many of the principles of professional learning. They engage members in steady intellectual work, promote innovation, and value teacher critique and dissent; they honor the knowledge and skills of members and connect to larger educational issues, as well as local practice. Whether regional or national, they view teachers as thinkers and doers.

PROFESSIONAL LEARNING COMMUNITIES

Professional learning communities are defined by Lieberman and Miller (2008) as "ongoing groups of teachers who meet regularly for the purpose of increasing their own learning and that of their students" (p. 2). Professional learning communities also provide arenas for the enactment of professional learning. Unlike networks that tend to be larger in scale and involve large numbers of people, sites, and organizations, they are small and intimate social arrangements. They create strong (rather than loose) ties among members and use those ties to strengthen capacities to talk honestly, to inquire critically into practice, to develop deeper understandings about teaching and learning, to share work publicly, and to assume mutual responsibility for student learning.

The Big Ideas behind Professional Learning Communities

Three big ideas underpin professional learning communities: (1) *reflective practice*, as described by Don Schön (1983); (2) *communities of practice*, as defined by Etienne Wenger (1998, 2012); and (3) *inquiry as stance* as defined by Marilyn Cochran-Smith and Susan Lytle (1993, 2009).

The idea of *reflective practice* originated with Don Schön in his seminal work, *The Reflective Practitioner* (1983). He introduced the terms "reflection-in-action" and "reflection-on-action" to describe how professional architects think about what they do, refine their actions, and develop theories that guide their practice. He made the distinction between reflection-in-action and reflection-on-action; both contributed to the development of enacted theories of action that inform and guide practice. Reflection-in-action occurs during an action; it is "thinking on one's feet." That is what teachers do all the time within their individual classrooms. As they teach, they generate hypotheses that inform their next course of action. Reflection-on-action occurs after an action has taken place. It can be in the form of writing things up or engaging in conversation with a colleague. This is what happens in professional learning communities; collegial conversation leads to questions and further inquiry into practice. During the process of reflection, practitioners develop mental maps that they use to identify and solve problems. When they work collaboratively, they develop shared maps; these maps become what Schön calls "theories in use" that they apply to their work.

The second big idea originated in the work of Jean Lave and Etienne Wenger (1991). Like Schön, they studied professionals outside of the realm of education—in this case novices who were enrolled in an apprenticeship program and were learning to become full members of a guild. They coined the term "communities of practice" to describe groups of people who, like the apprentices, come together to share a common passion and a desire to learn from each other. Wenger (2012) has since expanded on this idea and characterized members of a community of practice as being practitioners who "develop a shared repertoire of resources, i.e., experiences, stories, tools, ways of addressing recurring problems." He further elaborated on the idea and identified 13 attributes of communities of practice:

- Presence and visibility: A community needs to have a presence in the lives of its members and make itself visible to them.
- Rhythm: Communities live in time, and they have rhythms of events and rituals that reaffirm their bonds and value.
- Variety of interactions: Members of a community of practice need to interact in order to build their shared practice.
- Efficiency of involvement: Communities of practice compete with other priorities in the lives of their members. Participation must be easy.
- Short-term value: Communities of practice thrive on the value they deliver to their members and to their organizational context. Each interaction needs to create some value.
- Long-term value: Because members identify with the domain of the community, they have a long-term commitment to its development.

- Connection to the world: A community of practice can create value by providing a connection to a broader field or community that its members care to keep abreast of.
- Personal identity: Belonging to a community of practice is part of one's identity as a competent practitioner.
- Communal identity: Successful communities have a strong identity that members inherit in their own lives.
- Belonging and relationships: The value of belonging is not merely instrumental but personal as well: interacting with colleagues, developing friendships, building trust.
- Complex boundaries: Communities of practice have multiple levels and types of participation.
- Evolution: maturation and integration: Communities of practice evolve as they go through stages of development and find new connections to the world.
- Active community building: Successful communities of practice usually have a person or core group who takes some active responsibility for moving the community along.

The third big idea, *inquiry as stance*, came out of work directly related to education. It was originally defined and later developed by Marilyn Cochran-Smith and Susan Lytle (1993, 2009), two teacher educators who wanted to find a middle ground between the formal knowledge lodged in universities and the practical knowledge that preservice and experienced teachers carry with them. They proposed that teacher inquiry was that middle ground and that it led to the creation of "knowledge of practice." They explained:

> Rather implicit in the idea of knowledge-of-practice is the assumption that through inquiry, teachers across the professional life span—from very new to very experienced—make problematic their own knowledge and practice as well as the knowledge and practice of others and thus stand in a different relationship to knowledge. (1993, p. 49)

In effect, Cochran-Smith and Lytle developed a new paradigm of knowledge that challenged that which defined knowledge production as the sole province of universities and knowledge use as the province of teachers and placed inquiry at the center of professional learning.

Getting Inside Professional Learning Communities

Some professional learning communities exist within larger networks. The CES created "critical friends groups" in which 8–12 educators meet monthly to look at their own practice, using structured protocols to guide the discussion. In the NWP, the summer institute serves as a temporary learning community that also provides participants with the skills to initiate and lead such communities in their home settings. In the Southern Maine Partnership, small groups of educators come together as "leaders for tomorrow's schools" for 4 years to deepen their understandings about teaching, learning, and leadership.

Most professional learning communities, however, take place within a particular school. Grossman, Wineburg, and Woolworth (2001) convened a group of 22 social studies teachers in a traditional high school with the purpose of developing an interdisciplinary curriculum. They had, in their own words, "created a community of learners by declaration" and placed themselves in the dual roles of facilitators and researchers, intending to document the group's development over 18 months. Although the Humanities Group never solidified as a real community of learners, it did provide insights into the challenges that such communities face. The first of these is the challenge to form a group identity; the second involves navigating the fault lines that exist among different groups and perspectives and learning how to manage conflict; the third concerns negotiating the tensions that emerge when trying to reconcile issues of both teacher and student learning; and the fourth involves taking responsibility for one's own growth and the growth of others. Although this group had difficulties in developing a genuine learning community, the study revealed the complexity and challenges that school cultures would inevitably face.

The Algebra Group is a successful school-based professional learning community that has existed for some time at East High School with a very strong math department that has long engaged in collective curriculum development while controlling its own hiring by seeking teachers who want to work in the collaborative environment the department offers. Teacher-initiated and based on volunteer participation, the Algebra Study Group meets weekly and has existed for several years. Described by Horn (2005), who participated in and studied the group, its members "shared a rigorous common curriculum, had an active commitment to students, took on teaching as a collective enterprise, and used innovative instructional practices" (p. 207).

Algebra Group meetings last 2 hours; each begins with a "check-in" during which someone frames a problem of practice or brings in an idea for the group to consider. Group members make use of the meetings to replay past classroom events, give and receive feedback, and rehearse new responses. In so doing, they analyze their teaching, reflect on their practice, and develop common standards of pedagogy in an environment of honesty and trust. Because the group is so well established and has such clear norms and expectations, it is easy for new members to enter and participate. As this example shows, professional learning communities can be powerful arenas for professional learning. But they take time and commitment to develop and endure. They require both strong passions and disciplined inquiry; they balance content and process; and they combine an unwavering commitment to purpose with flexibility and improvisation. They forge new identities for community members, who contribute and enrich each other's practice and together learn to find ways to disavow compliance with bureaucratic norms that surround them. They value knowledge grounded in practice and practice grounded in knowledge, and, above all, they value teachers as professionals who can take charge of their own learning.

MULTIMEDIA, TECHNOLOGY, AND THE FUTURE
OF PROFESSIONAL LEARNING

With new media and technologies have come new opportunities for teacher learning and development. Interactive websites provide opportunities for teachers to share their work. For example, the Making Teaching Public website (*www.tcrecord.org/ makingteachingpublic/*) presents a series of exhibitions of teacher work, along with commentary by developers and space for feedback from visitors. *YouTube* provides teacher-made videos of their classrooms, as well as captured lectures and presentations. The *Teaching Channel* is a website, a television series, and a YouTube presence. It is a collection of videos in which teachers showcase their practices. The website provides a clear classification system that lets visitors access videos by grade, subject, and topic and also click onto tips, techniques, resources, and documented lesson plans. The channel now has 120,000 members, some of whom are members of an online community that provides a forum for conversation, guidance, and support.

Online Learning

Online learning is perhaps the most widely known use of technology in teacher development. The motivation for this approach is often based on economies of scale and efficiency. A recent article (Davis, 2009) in *Education Week* reported, "Schools facing budget cuts and higher demand for professional development are turning to online offerings to lower their bottom lines and increase access to opportunities for teachers striving to improve their skills." One director of technology explained that "Once a training course or a workshop is developed it can be reused multiple times and that's where the cost savings come from" (Davis, 2009). The key phrase here, "a training course or a workshop," might lead one to believe that these programs are totally in line with the training model. But it is more complex than that. These programs, offered for a fee by nonprofit and for-profit organizations to teachers and/or schools and districts, have also incorporated the language and some of the practices associated with professional learning.

As an example, the Educational Development Corporation's *Ed Tech Leaders Online* (2012) provides educators and institutions with "more than 70 high-quality professional development courses for teachers, administrators or other educational staff that are research-based and aligned to national and Common Core State Standards." That sounds like the training model associated with efforts to teach how to implement a reform. However, *Ed Tech Leaders Online* also supports something closer to the idea of professional learning. Its website describes its Peer Connection Network, which is "a community of educators—coaches, mentors, teachers, and others—who come together to share ideas and resources and learn from each other" (Education Development Corporation, 2012). The websites for other online professional development programs are also sprinkled with such terms as "professional learning communities" and "communities of practice." However, under closer inspection, it becomes clear that these communities are more "contrived" than authentic, more directed than self-governing. One might ask whether online discussions and interactions are the stuff of communities and whether there is a confusion of talk with deep collaboration and true collegial connections.

Using Technology to Promote Authentic Professional Learning

There is a growing body of evidence from both research and practice that authentic professional learning can be promoted through online networks and learning communities. *Tapped In* is a Web-based online network that was initiated in 1997 with support from the National Science Foundation. It offers educational organizations, which it calls "tenants," the ability to set up spaces, called "rooms," where they can create and manage their activities, which include threaded discussion, shared files, mentoring, text chats, and other collaborative activities. The number of online educational networks is growing rapidly. There are online networks that focus on subject matter teaching, grade-level teaching, using technology, visual mapping, special education, and college transitions. Facebook hosts 14 teacher networks; other social media support some as well.

In addition, there is a drive to create platforms to support authentic communities of practice. Wenger (1996), who originated the idea, is now deeply involved in conceptualizing what those platforms might look like. He envisions them including an array of applications on one site that would include, but not be limited to, the following: instant messaging; community calendars; synchronous events, such as teleconferences, virtual conferences, and online meetings; invitations; minutes of recent events made available quickly afterward; hot topics; e-mail and discussion boards; tours of new activities; archiving of interactions, synchronous lectures, and large meetings; mechanisms for asking questions; databases of answers; access to experts; forums for getting help with problems; brainstorming facilities; repositories for artifacts; taxonomies; search mechanisms; discussion and updating of learning agendas; spaces for practice-development projects, new developments, and new technologies; and reference materials. The U.S. Department of Education (2011) is currently supporting research to develop a framework for online communities of practice in education with the goal of improving teaching and learning, assessment, learning, and school structures. According to the plan, "This community of practice work will connect teachers, district leadership, education technology professionals, educational researchers, state and local data management personnel, and the special needs community with data, resources, content, and support" (U.S. Department of Education, 2011). It is clear that technology is very much the future of teacher development and has the potential of moving the professional learning agenda to the forefront.

PROFESSIONAL DEVELOPMENT THAT MATTERS

Our contribution to this book intends to make clear the tensions involved in teacher learning and development. Reform efforts push particular ideas, international comparisons make schools in the United States look poorer than their counterparts elsewhere despite the differences in context, and new pressures for teachers to know more and do more to enter the 21st century continue unabated. Yet, despite these pressures, teacher knowledge, professional learning communities, growth in practice strategies, inquiry into practice, expanded teacher leadership roles, and continued knowledge about how adults learn continue to grow as well. Professional learning for teachers and those who work at it must continually negotiate the pressures that emanate from these two distinctly different views of development—the pressures to change and the social realities of teacher learning and development—which must be considered. Many look for the silver bullets that do the job quickly, but the evidence shows that teacher involvement in creating knowledge, help in leading the change, participation in outside as well as inside groups, and learning from others must be a significant part of professional learning.

QUESTIONS FOR DISCUSSION

For Teachers

1. What is the nature of professional development in your school? To what degree is it based on the inservice training model? To what degree is it based on the growth-in-practice model? To what degree is it teacher-driven?

2. How is your school or district connecting the Common Core and other externally driven initiatives with professional development?

3. What networks, collaborations, or partnerships are available to you? How could you use them to deepen your practice? What networks do you want to know more about?

4. Do you have access to school- or district-level professional learning communities? What kind of community would you choose to join if you had the choice?

5. What challenges do you face in your teaching and how are you addressing them?

For Principals and District Administrators

1. How are you facilitating regular professional learning during the school year? What models of professional learning do you provide or advocate?

2. How do you help teachers respond to and navigate federal and state mandates?

3. Do teachers take (or share with you) leadership in professional learning?

4. How are you continuing to enhance your own learning? Are there opportunities for administrative leaders in your district or region to learn from each other? Networks for leaders?

5. What challenges do you face in your leadership and how are you addressing them?

For Policymakers

1. What policies are in place to support teacher learning?

2. What are the sources of knowledge and the influences that drive your policymaking in terms of professional learning?

3. What professional learning policies exist in your jurisdiction that you would like to change? What policies would you like to add?

4. Who is or should be involved in making professional learning policy?

5. What challenges do you face in your role as a policymaker and how are you addressing them?

REFERENCES

Coalition of Essential Schools. (2012). The CES common principles. Retrieved from *www.essentialschools.org/items/4*.

Cochran-Smith, M., & Lytle, S. (1993). *Inside/outside: Teacher research and teacher knowledge*. New York: Teachers College Press.

Cochran-Smith, M., & Lytle, S. (2009). *Inquiry as stance: Practitioner research in the next generation*. New York: Teachers College Press.

Cuban, L. (2011). The inexorable cycles of school reform [Web log post]. Retrieved from *http://larrycuban.wordpress.com/2011/01/18/the-inexorable-cycles-of-school-reform/*.

Darling-Hammond, L., & McLaughlin, M. W. (1995). Policies that support professional development in an era of reform. *Phi Delta Kappan, 76*(8), 597–604.

Davis, M. R. (2009, March 13). Online professional development weighed as cost-saving tactic. *Education Week Digital Directions*. Retrieved from *www.edweek.org/dd/articles/2009/03/13/04ddprofdev.h02.html*.

Education Development Corporation. (2012). Building capacity through online learning. Retrieved from *http://edtechleaders.org*.

Elmore, R., & McLaughlin, M. (1988). *Steady work: Policy, practice and the reform of American education*. Santa Monica, CA: Rand Corporation.

Granovetter, M. S. (1973). The strength of weak ties. *American Journal of Sociology, 78*(6), 1360–1380.

Grossman, P., Wineburg, S., & Woolworth, S. (2001). Toward a theory of teacher community. *Teachers College Record, 103*(6), 942–1012.

Horn, I. S. (2005). Learning on the job: A situated account of teacher learning in high school mathematics departments. *Cognition and Instruction, 23*(2), 207–236.

Lambert, L. (1989). The end of an era of staff development. *Educational Leadership, 47*(1), 78–81.

Lave, J., & Wenger, E. (1991). *Situated learning*. Cambridge, MA: Cambridge University Press.

Lieberman, A. (1995). Breaking the mold: From in-service to professional learning. *Phi Delta Kappan, 76*(8), 591–596.

Lieberman, A., & Grolnick, M. (1996). Networks and reform in American education. *Teachers College Record, 98*(1), 8–14.

Lieberman, A., & Miller, L. (1999). *Teachers: Transforming their world and their work*. New York: Teachers College Press.

Lieberman, A., & Miller, L. (2000). Teaching and teacher development: A new synthesis for a new century. In R. S. Brandt (Ed.), *Education for a new era* (pp. 47–66). Alexandria, VA: Association for Supervision and Curriculum Development.

Lieberman, A., & Miller, L. (2007). Transforming professional development: Understanding and organizing learning communities. In W. D. Willis & D. L. Rollie (Eds.), *The keys to effective school: Educational reform as a continuous improvement* (pp. 74–85). Thousand Oaks, CA: Corwin Press.

Lieberman, A., & Miller, L. (2008). *Teachers in professional communities: Improving teaching and learning.* New York: Teachers College Press.

Lieberman, A., & Wood, D. R. (2003). *Inside the National Writing Project: Connecting network learning and classroom teaching.* New York: Teachers College Press.

Little, J. W. (1993). Teachers' professional development in a climate of reform. *Educational Evaluation and Policy Analysis, 15*(2), 129–151.

Little, J. W. (2006). *Professional community and professional development in the learning-centered school.* Washington, DC: National Education Association.

McLaughlin, M. W., & Talbert, J. (1993). *Contexts that matter for teaching and learning.* Palo Alto, CA: Stanford Center for Research on the Context of Secondary School Teaching.

Michelli, N., & Earley, P. (2011). Teacher education policy context. In P. Earley, D. G. Imig, & N. Michelli (Eds.), *Teacher education policy in the United States: Issues and tensions in an era of evolving expectations* (pp. 1–13). London: Taylor & Francis.

Miller, L. (2001). School–university partnerships as a venue for professional development. In A. Lieberman &, L. Miller (Eds.), *Teachers caught in the action: Professional development that matters* (pp. 102–117). New York: Teachers College Press.

National Commission on Excellence in Education. (1983). *A nation at risk: The imperative for educational reform.* Washington, DC: U.S. Government Printing Office.

National Writing Project. (2012). NWP core principles. Retrieved from *www.nwp.org/cs/public/print/doc/about.csp.*

Parker, A. (1979). *Networks for innovation and problem solving and their use for improving education: A comparative review.* Washington, DC: Dissemination Process Seminar IV.

Sarason, S. (1971). *The culture of the school and the problem of change.* Boston: Allyn & Bacon.

Schön, D. A. (1983). *The reflective practitioner.* New York: Basic Books.

Showers, B., Joyce, B., & Bennett, B. (1987). Synthesis of research on staff development: A framework for future study and a state of the art analysis. *Educational Leadership, 45*(3), 77–87.

Shulman, L. (1986). Those who understand: Knowledge growth in teaching. *Educational Researcher, 15*(2), 4–14.

Talbert, J. (2010). Professional learning communities at the crossroads: How systems hinder or engender change. In A. Hargreaves, A. Lieberman, M. Fullan, & M. Hopkins (Eds.), *Second handbook of educational change* (pp. 555–571). London: Springer.

U.S. Department of Education. (2011). The promise of communities of practice. Retrieved from *www.ed.gov/oii-news/promise-communities-practice.*

Wenger, E. (1998). *Communities of practice: Learning, meaning, and identity.* Cambridge, UK: Cambridge University Press.

Wenger, E. (2012). Communities of practice: A brief introduction. Retrieved January 14, 2012, from *www.ewenger.com/theory.*

CHAPTER 2

Federal Investments in Professional Development

What Do 50 Years of Experience Tell Us about What It Takes to Make a Difference?

RICHARD LONG

- The federal government has attempted to support professional development in various ways.
- The federal government's support affects how teachers receive professional development.
- The goals of various education programs become a mandate for specific types of professional development.

One of the most interesting, least understood, and poorly implemented federal education initiatives has been in the area of professional development, and it is one of the most critical to get right. This is a role that has seen major initiatives, beginning with the federal response to *Sputnik* in the late 1950s, that are still being debated during the first two decades of the 21st century (see Table 2.1). Yet the key issue remains: Should the federal government be in the professional development business, and if it is, how can it be effective?

The traditional role of the federal government in education has been to ensure equal access to a basic education. When the Elementary and Secondary Education Act (ESEA) was first passed by the Congress in 1964, many of the leaders who fought for it thought education for our nation's disadvantaged children would be changed simply by adding funds to school districts that lacked resources to provide a quality education. The money would mean that kids growing up in these communities, which had essentially no tax base for schools, would now attend schools with well-educated teachers, library books, and the auxiliary learning materials

TABLE 2.1. Major Federal Legislation with Professional Development

Date	Event	Implication
1957	*Sputnik* launched—U.S. public sees Soviet threat	Math/science professional development
1965	Formula programs launched: Elementary and Secondary Education Act/Higher Education Act; Bilingual Education	Federal funds for disadvantaged—beginning of process of general professional development for schools with low-performing students.
1972	Right to Read	Passage of federal program that provided support for reading at many age and skill levels, with professional development for specific programs
1976	Education of the Handicapped Act	Dedicated professional development program using federal funds to expand specific disciplines
1982	Nation at Risk	Federal commission launches new reform movement in education with first-time emphasis on teacher education
1985	Dwight D. Eisenhower Mathematics and Science Education Act	Money for professional development for math and science teachers, first for middle and high schools, then expanded to elementary level, and finally expanded to reach all disciplines to support professional development
1989	National Summit, National Education Goals	Teachers and teacher knowledge part of national purpose
1994	Improving America's Schools Act	New era of federal involvement in teaching and education
1997	Comprehensive School Reform Demonstration Act/Reading Excellence Act	Feds start defining instruction
2002	No Child Left Behind (NCLB)	Defines professional development—see Figure 2.1
2002	Reading First	While part of NCLB has separate definitions and requirements for reading instruction, professional development and scientifically based reading research
2010	American Recovery and Reinvestment Act	Provides massive funding for schools with an emphasis on professional development but little or no data to date

that make a difference in many learners' lives. Sam Halperin, then a senior aide to Francis Keppel, the commissioner of education in the old Department of Health, Education, and Welfare, said:

> In 1965, everyone had a naive view of education. We felt, in the words of Senator Wayne Morse, educators were all good people and that all you needed to do was give them some tools and some dollars and good things would happen. They didn't need a lot of specifics. (cited in Cross, 2010, p. 29)

By 1968, with the first rewriting of this landmark act, policymakers had learned that just providing resources alone was not going to make the difference. Much more needed to be done. Over the next several reauthorizations, sections were added, revised, and added again that focused on teachers' professional development, second-language learners, the Right to Read Act, and other concerns. These sections on the professional knowledge of teachers were being changed with almost every reauthorization. Even though with each reauthorization the funding formula was stable, the federal government found it difficult to have an impact on what is actually practiced in a classroom. Some policy observers have said that more time has been spent writing the sections on teachers than the sections involved with the actual distribution of the funds. The consensus among policymakers who were interviewed is that this is a difficult policy to get right in order to show any effect.

Although neither the U.S. Department of Education nor the Congress has ever created a bureau of professional development or funded an initiative to ensure the ongoing improvement of teachers, it is in the business of supporting professional development. Theses bodies have, however, used other tools to influence how professional development is defined and implemented. Generally, the federal government has five basic methods of influencing the ways education programs, including professional development, are structured:

1. Maintenance programs: the large-scale programs, such as Title I (ESEA), that provide money to a large number of schools to run a specific program
2. Capacity development: wide-ranging programs, such as the Dwight D. Eisenhower Mathematics and Science Education Act (1988), that provide funds to a large number of schools to develop the capacity to improve a service
3. Demonstration: small programs (e.g., Right to Read, 1974) for which a school would apply for funding to show how something would work
4. Research/dissemination: sharing of information on what works with the expectation that practice will change
5. Goal setting/bully pulpit: placing pressure on the school districts to change by raising awareness among important constituencies, including the public, education leaders, and the media.[1]

---

[1] The idea that federal programs consist basically of maintenance, demonstration, and capacity development was the conclusion drawn from a discussion in 1978 with the then head of the National School Board Association's government relations program, August W. Steinhilber, and his assistant, Michael A. Resnick, with Richard Long.

Because there are other issues at play in classrooms and schools across the nation, each one of the aforementioned tools has been tried and has failed to systematically improve instruction.

One issue is the idea of how much (money, time, effort, regulation) is needed to make a difference. Sometimes, this idea is called "dosage," which is then translated at the school level into the amount of professional development needed to be effective. For instance, should a professional development program be run for 20 hours over a year, or for 250 hours over 5 years? What amount of time, money, and energy makes a difference? Next, in addition to the problem of determining how much professional development is needed is the issue that education policy is always being changed by either the political leadership or the newly hired (and frequently changing) professional leadership at the state and district levels. According to Michael Fullan (2006), the link between education reform and political attention requires that attempted education changes must show results by the end of the current election cycle. Fullan is commenting on the maddening tendency of education change/improvement/reform to be attempted at the school-building, district, state, and federal levels, only to be stopped and changed whenever a new president comes into office with a "new and better way" to make a difference.

To compound the difficulty in developing long-term policy that schools can implement, the education policy system is almost always in a state of change. Federal involvement in professional development is affected by everything from a shift in political and educational philosophies to pure partisan politics:

1. Some members of one political policy believe that federal funds for teacher professional development are going to support their political opposition. They believe money accessible to teacher organizations at the building level will end up supporting the teacher union, which may support their political opposition.
2. Some members of Congress haven't supported the idea of professional development because they view the federal funding of professional development as taking money away from the specific instruction of high-needs children. This group believes the purpose of federal funds is to improve access to equitable instruction and that it is a state or local responsibility to provide quality teachers.
3. Others are suspicious of any federal involvement because they believe that the federal government should not be deciding whether math is needed over reading or whether reading improvement will occur if more emphasis is placed on vocabulary development than other topics.

How, then, can we decide whether the federal government has created mandates that have affected professional development? To conduct this analysis, other areas must be reevaluated, including the goals of the program under consideration. For example, the goal of Title I is to improve reading and mathematics abilities of students so they can catch up to children who are not living in poverty and can learn content just as well as their peers. However, the reality is that the long-term goal of the program has been replaced with the short-term goal of scores on the annual reading and/or mathematics tests, which were originally designed to be a check as to whether the program was going in the right direction. Now programs are continued or cut depending on the short-term measure. The "goal" has defined what professional development would be supported and what would not be supported. This is an important issue. If the federal government were to support teacher education and professional development generally, they would have an effect simply by the amount of time over which they supported such an endeavor. However, the government does not routinely do that; rather, they support professional development that is linked to specific programs through the legislation that supports funding to have an impact on specific groups of people. Therefore, the primary impact of federal support for professional development is found in how it is used to support the goals of programs such as Title I, Title III (formally Title VII), and the Individuals with Disabilities Education Act (IDEA). These programs are implemented by states and local districts in a variety of ways: (1) through teacher inservice days that are part of the rhythm of the school and classroom; (2) through conferences held by the ever growing professional societies (e.g., the International Reading Association, the National Council of Teachers of Mathematics, and other similar groups); and (3) through rewarding teachers for spending more time in university classrooms gaining master's degrees (and beyond). Rarely has the federal government sponsored professional development sessions conceptualized as something ongoing and linked, or, for that matter, those concerning new ideas about human learning. Mainly, the government is focused on improving instruction in very specific parts of those disciplines that are part of a program funded in the schools.

This, then, leads to other questions: Has the federal involvement in professional development become the definer of professional development as both a practice and a field? By funding specific programs, does the federal government promote one method over another, either by intent or by the consequences of its actions?

THE HISTORY OF FEDERAL INVOLVEMENT
IN PROFESSIONAL DEVELOPMENT

The U.S. government has a long history of involvement in education that has been changing with the passing decades, with changing definitions of education, and with the demands of society. As far back as the Northwest Ordinance in 1787, the national government has been involved by creating land and resources for schools. In the 1800s, the federal government supported the development and creation of land-grant colleges and basic education for newly freed slaves in the Freedmen's Bureau. By the early part of the 1900s and America's entry into World War I, new recruits were found wanting in significant and important skills, which resulted in the federal law to support vocational training. In 1953, the government's involvement changed with the acknowledgment that separate-but-equal education resulted in neither equality nor education. The civil rights movement became a major driver of the American education policy, but what really generated direct federal involvement was the launch of a grapefruit-sized satellite that sent out a beep heard round the world. *Sputnik*'s success was directly responsible for the passage and funding of the federal National Defense Education Act and, with it, a major push to improve instruction by already hired and trained teachers. Professional development became a tool of national policy. However, even so, this tool had a mixed purpose (see Table 2.1). For some federal leaders in Congress and in the Department of Health, Education, and Welfare, the funding for teacher training activities in mathematics and science was to improve instruction; but in practice it had a different effect. Funds for professional development supplemented their local salaries and kept them in the classrooms.

In 1964, Congress changed the course of the nation's education system with the passage of the ESEA, which was signed into law as Public Law 89-10 by President Lyndon Johnson on April 11, 1965. This act put into place the policy that every child had a right to a basic education regardless of his or her economic condition. This section became known as Title I. Another title (IV) included the training of teachers. Within 3 years of enactment of this law, it was amended to include sections for the education of children with disabilities or children who were English language learners. Now in place were the three key areas of federal involvement: children with economic disadvantages, children with disabilities, and children who do not speak English. As a result, funds were now available to schools to provide for the education of these children.

At the same time, Congress passed the Higher Education Act (1965), which created a federal grants program to help the children of low-income families to go to college and others to gain access to low-cost student loans. In addition, this act also provided funding to teacher education programs to support the expansion of the number and quality of teachers for the nation's high-need K–12 schools. Although these funds were always significantly less than what was thought to be needed, the act did begin the flow of federal funds to expand the number of teachers available to school districts.

When Richard Nixon became president in 1969, many thought he would sweep away the programs Lyndon Johnson and the Congress had enacted. Even though Nixon did not eliminate the programs, he did change the focus of some of the programs and tried to influence their funding streams. There were already questions about how well underresourced states and districts would be able to provide high-need students with quality teachers.

Reading instruction had already been identified as a critical area, and there was a vigorous debate taking place on what constituted good instruction. To provide school districts with information and examples of effective instructional practice, the 1974 ESEA amendments included the Right to Read Act. This measure provided grants to school districts (which applied and passed review) to incorporate specific training for teachers in schools in how to teach reading. It is important to note that these were the high-need schools and that the professional development being done in the schools with these funds was linked to Title I and its purposes. Title I defined what was supported and what constituted effective reading instruction.

In creating the National Right to Read program, the administration made a choice to focus specific and limited resources on the area the federal government defined as being critical for education. In addition, it used all of its power and leverage. Billboards were seen around the nation supporting reading. Questions were asked at state and district levels about the focus of reading instruction. It is important to note that reading improvement itself became the goal, not improvement in how well students did in their content classes or how soon they graduated from high school. Once again, a proxy measure became the goal reported to the federal government, state governments, and the press.

By the mid-1970s, the emphasis on reading became even more refined. Marshall "Mike" Smith, the director of the U.S. Department of Education's Office of Policy and Planning, held a series of meetings and commissioned a series of papers considering where the focus should be placed and decided, after much study and review, that the emphasis should be on vocabulary instruction (personal communication, August 1, 2010). This meant that federal research dollars, federal dissemination of information on instruction dollars, and training dollars began to be channeled to improve vocabulary instruction. The reasoning for this decision was pretty clear. Vocabulary was thought to represent intelligence and was used to demonstrate how well a student was able to perform in specific areas of learning. It was also linked to performance on the job site as well. Knowledge of specific words could be monitored, and teachers could directly help a child to learn specific vocabulary. It was the variable that, if mastered, could create the cascade effect of change, or so it was thought. It could be the subject of specific training for teachers across the nation. This became one of the significant measures for Title I effectiveness in tests such as the Nelson–Denny Vocabulary Test and others.

This wasn't the only major change in federal policy that affected professional development. By 1976, the nation's handicapped citizens had a new tool. The Education for All Handicapped Act was changed in a rewriting decades later to the IDEA. Unlike the earlier ESEA, this act contained explicit and specific sections for professional development. Now, instead of an inferred link of federal programs to professional development, there was a major act that was designed to provide enough funds (and in this case, legal requirements) for programs to be run in every school to inform teachers and administrators of the needs of students who were disabled in their schools (a maintenance program). Furthermore, it provided specific elements to build the capacity of the program, teacher education, and professional development (a capacity development program). The act had research and dissemination elements; it was the complete package.

This act also created the legal category of learning disabilities. In so doing, it then created a policy of educating children who were significantly different from the "general" education population. The advocates, who supported the need for a distinct category for children who had learning disabilities, had a body of research, learning theories, and intervention techniques to be used with these children. Without the federal government's legal definition of learning disabilities, the entire group of ideas, interventions, and the professional development required to make those interventions would have become only a small percentage of the overall education system's tools.

By the late 1970s, it became clear that the Elementary and Secondary Education Act was really the Elementary Education Act. To offset this emphasis, the Carter administration invested itself in the creation of a basic skills secondary education act. They held meetings in the White House, with Vice President Walter Mondale in the lead, built coalitions, and gave out grants to various education groups to get their "buy-in" to the program. This proposed annual $2 billion program, which was going to send money to school districts for maintenance at the high school level, would emphasize reading. To create this emphasis, the act was going to distribute professional development funds to further high school teachers' knowledge of teaching reading. The concern was that America would not be economically competitive in the ensuing decades unless more people graduated from high school with basic skills. The emphasis was on basic skills, not on a wider sense of literacy (reading and writing at levels needed to be successful in society). Although this act failed to pass the Congress, the idea of having older students learning basic reading as a part of vocational or career training took hold. High school and career-tech teachers would now be expected to use their vocational classes to build their students' vocabularies and to help their students learn how to learn from manuals.

With the election of President Ronald Reagan, education policy was again to change. Unlike the Democrats, who created the separate cabinet-level U.S. Department of Education, the Republicans thought the increased role of the federal government was both unwelcome and counterproductive. The expectation was that the Reagan administration would seek to withdraw the Department of Education from the cabinet. The appointee to the Secretary of Education position was Terrell Bell, the former U.S. Commissioner of Education and chief state school officer of Utah. Bell initially hired a staff that included Alan Cohen, who had chaired the coalition to create the separate cabinet-level Department of Education. Bell worked to refocus the federal role and commissioned a national panel to look at U.S. education and make recommendations. This panel, the National Commission on Excellence in Education, produced a report that is still seen as the bedrock of education change. *A Nation at Risk: The Imperative for Education Reform* (1983) called for significant change. Of note is that almost all of their 38 recommendations were focused on higher education, with some significant exceptions in the area of K–12 teaching. The panel's recommendations could be organized into five major categories; professional development of teachers was one of the categories. The panel made a key point that teacher knowledge was critical for improving America's schools.

The significance of this report is that it focused on all teachers, not just teachers of children with disadvantages or disabilities and English language learners. The report was also a catalyst for a change in federal involvement. It effectively moved the federal involvement in education from access and equity to access, equity, and quality. From here on, the debate on education was about educational quality, and this included teachers and their ability to teach well.

SPECIFIC FEDERAL INVOLVEMENT
IN PROFESSIONAL DEVELOPMENT

By the mid-1980s, the period of emphasis on mathematics and science that was ignited by *Sputnik* had passed. Although the National Science Foundation continued to fund small projects and there was a $20 million dollar graduate fellowship program for mathematics and science education, little was being spent at a national level; therefore, a new crisis was emerging. *A Nation at Risk* (1983) linked education and economic development, but how change was to come about was not addressed by the report. The report neither authorized nor appropriated any funds. It changed no laws, regulations or requirements, but its influence was widespread and pervasive because of the bully pulpit.

The math and science education community began to push for the funding of a pipeline that would create a flow of new engineers. The National Council of Teachers of Mathematics (NCTM) began collecting data on the lack of new graduating mathematics teachers (Stanic & Kilpatrick, 2003). Some states were reporting two and three new teachers graduating from teacher training programs in their respective states with degrees to teach mathematics. Federal policy shifted once again. This time it was to create programs to increase the numbers of students graduating from college with degrees in engineering, the sciences, and mathematics education by looking to improve instruction in the high school, then middle school and the elementary school. To do this, the federal government supported intensive professional development activities that were designed to improve instruction to interest more children in staying in these subject areas. This directly affected the nation, as schools tried to create the mathematics programs to meet the challenges outlined in the *Nation at Risk* report (1983), which called for every student to take 3 years of mathematics. To support this expansion, the Congress enacted the Eisenhower Mathematics and Science Education Act in 1985 and then again reauthorized it in 1988 (Dwight David Eisenhower Mathematics and Science Education Act, 1988). This act was designed to provide money to all school districts based on a formula for a maintenance program. Unfortunately, the funding level first set by the appropriators was so low that some school districts concluded that it would cost more to implement (and be in compliance with its provisions) than they would get in funds.

Eventually, and after several reauthorizations, the Eisenhower program was used for elementary school professional development in math and science because research was pointing to decisions being made by students earlier and earlier in their academic careers about these critical areas. Girls and minorities were found to be especially sensitive to bias in the early grades that led them to see themselves as not mathematically oriented. Note that Malcolm Gladwell (2008) defines this self-talk in terms of whether or not person believes he or she has a "math gene."

As seen, there was a growing political awareness that education was the key to a nation's economic development, and the United States was facing a greater awareness that progress was not being made. The National Assessment of Educational Progress (NAEP), referred to as the "nation's report card," was showing no progress, as the scaled score for 17-year-olds had moved only 5 scale points, from 285 in 1971 to 290 in 1988 (NAEP, 2013). The nation's schools were undergoing a massive change as more language-minority children, children with disabilities, and others with significant challenges were in school and staying in school. The implications of this situation were getting the attention of more than just economists and education policy leaders; they were getting the attention of political and government leaders. In 1989, then President George H. W. Bush called together the nation's first (and only) meeting of the chief executives of every state in the nation to meet with him in Charlottesville, Virginia. Out of this summit came the national education goals and the National Education Goals Panel (1990), enacted into law in as part of the Goals 2000: Educate America Act (1994). Different from the *Nation at Risk* report (1983), this document pushed public policy more in the direction of K–12 education.

The eight National Education Goals, defined by the governors and Congress to improve learning and teaching in the nation's education system, helped provide a national framework for education reform and promoted systemic changes to ensure equitable educational opportunities and high levels of educational achievement for all students. The goals are as follows:

- Goal 1: Ready to learn
- Goal 2: School completion
- Goal 3: Student achievement and citizenship
- Goal 4: Teacher education and professional development
- Goal 5: Mathematics and science
- Goal 6: Adult literacy and lifelong learning
- Goal 7: Safe, disciplined, and alcohol- and drug-free schools
- Goal 8: Parental participation (National Education Goals Panel; see *http://govinfo.library.unt.edu/negp/page3-9.htm*)

For our purposes let's take a look at Goal 4: the goal focused on teacher education and professional development. The 1989 national summit's goals became the centerpiece of the 1994 legislation. By the year 2000, the nation's teaching force was to have access to programs for the continued improvement of their professional skills and the opportunity to acquire the knowledge and skills needed to instruct and prepare all American students for the next century. The following objectives were set:

- All teachers will have access to preservice teacher education and continuing professional development activities that will provide such teachers with the knowledge and skills needed to teach to an increasingly diverse student population with a variety of educational, social, and health needs.
- All teachers will have continuing opportunities to acquire additional knowledge and skills needed to teach challenging subject matter and to use emerging new methods, forms of assessment, and technologies.
- States and school districts will create integrated strategies to attract, recruit, prepare, retrain, and support the continued professional development of teachers, administrators, and other educators, so that there is a highly talented work force of professional educators to teach challenging subject matter.
- Partnerships will be established, whenever possible, among local educational agencies, institutions of higher education, parents, and local labor, business,

and professional associations to provide and support programs for the professional development of educators. (National Education Goals Panel Goal 4;
see *www2.ed.gov/legislation/GOALS2000/TheAct/intro.html*)

Now professional development was clearly a top-level item in thinking about
improving America's schools—all of them. Although the national goals clearly
mention the traditional high-need populations—students with disadvantages and
disabilities and language-minority students—these goals apply to all schools. The
goals were put into statute law by the Goals 2000: Educate America Act, which was
enacted in 1994. The effect was as much moral as practical in that it didn't require
specific changes in education practice, but it did change how education programs
were discussed. It also linked up with the push for education standards that was
initiated in 1989 by the NCTM in the publishing of *Curriculum and Evaluation
Standards for School Mathematics.* These standards were seen by many, including
President Bush, as the national glue to link states together and improve instruction.
The NCTM standards were created by the mathematics education profession with
the intent of informing policymakers, educators, and others what students need to
know and be able to do. By 1992, this was being seen as a model of change, and
the government was providing grants to professional education societies to generate discipline-by-discipline standards that the states could then use to create state
curricula.

These sets of federal standards became the yardstick for almost all of the state
standards that were developed. In turn, the generated curriculum necessitated pur-
chases of new textbooks and accompanying professional development to go with
those products. Federal programs, such as Title I of the ESEA, required the use
of state-based standards. Most states used these discipline-based standards even
when they were surrounded by controversy, such as the International Reading Asso-
ciation/ National Council for Accreditation of Teacher Education (IRA/NCATE)
English Language Arts Standards. As Alan Farstrup, codirector of the English Language Arts Standards, said, " The English Language Arts Standards were used by
many states to generate their own standards in addition to the use of assumptions
that were used to build the NAEP frameworks" (personal communication, September 5, 2012). The Improving America's Schools Act (IASA) was a significant change
for ESEA; it was written to take the ideas of the education goals and the developing
standards and required states to change their instructional practices by using these
new standards.

During this time period, several questions were beginning to be asked about
the effectiveness of federal programs that had professional development objectives.
As P. David Pearson, former dean of the University of California Berkeley School
of Education, said, "We used to believe that if we provided teachers and principals
with research-based information that they would change their practice" (personal
communication, August 13, 2010). He found that just providing information to
practicing professionals did not result in a change in practice.

What was changing was how professional development would be supported
by the federal government. Consequently, the federal government was not just

changing its approach to providing resources and monitoring for compliance; it was also looking at the relationship of the federal government to the states, to the districts, to the schools through a much different lens. Equity, access, and quality were now to be defined by the federal government. One of the first programs to do this was a small program, the Comprehensive School Reform Demonstration Act (1997). It was never formally authorized; rather, it was annually defined through an appropriations bill managed by David Obey (D-WI) and John Porter (R-IL). Politically, this was an important relationship for education, as it represented a bipartisan push to reform education, and it did not come from the usual source, the authoring committee. Most believe that Congressman Obey, the ranking Democrat on the committee, had been working with Bob Slavin, a Johns Hopkins University professor and researcher, who developed a program of school change that used professional development as a critical tool. But unlike other methods, this was highly coordinated with the curriculum being used and had a mentor/leader in the school building to maintain focus on the elements of the program.

With the enactment of the Comprehensive School Improvement Demonstration Act, federal support for professional development entered the realm of specifying requirements for how instruction was being conducted. The Reading Excellence Act (1998) took it a step further. This program had been enacted by the Congress independent of the regular rewriting of the ESEA. The Reading Excellence Act provided funds to states to improve reading instruction. But it created a big change in how decisions were made. First, states had to submit applications, which were reviewed for content in a much more rigorous manner. Then states distributed funds to school districts that would train teachers in scientifically based reading research (SBRR), which was defined as follows:

The term "scientifically based reading research"—

(A) means the application of rigorous, systematic, and objective procedures to obtain valid knowledge relevant to reading development, reading instruction, and reading difficulties; and
(B) shall include research that—
  (i) employs systematic, empirical methods that draw on observation or experiment.
  (ii) involves rigorous data analysis that are adequate to test the stated hypotheses and justify the general conclusions drawn.
  (iii) relies on measurements or observational methods that provide valid data across evaluators and observers and across multiple measurements and observations
    and
  (iv) has been accepted by a peer-reviewed journal or approved by a panel of independent experts through a comparably rigorous, objective, and scientific review. (Reading Excellence Act, Section 2252)

Taking both of these legislative actions together, it is clear that the Congress was expanding the role and tools of the federal government to influence what teachers were being taught and how it was to be used. Never before had the federal government defined what would be considered appropriate to be taught in a reading program, nor had they defined what the mix of elements would be for a successful building-level school change. The federal government was now in the business of defining not just what would be the level of work in reading and in school reform but what was to be used to create a quality outcome.

No Child Left Behind

By the 2000 election, it became clear that the NAEP scores were not moving. National goals, state selected standards, voluntary compliance with IASA, and a host of smaller programs were not having the impact that policymakers, politicians, and the public expected. During the committee hearings of the late 1990s, especially in the House of Representatives Committee on Education and the Workforce, the now majority Republicans were voicing frustration with the lack of change in the NAEP test scores. In meetings at the U.S. Department of Education, in preparation for the rewriting of IASA, education leaders were calling on the U.S. Department of Education to maintain the path of the federal law to allow time for the existing reforms to take hold and work. But this was not to be. Now education was understood to be an important part of government and the future economy, and it was also part of the public's view of what was important. Education became a top-rated public policy item in repeated *USA Today* polls (Benedetto, 1996). The result was stunning.

Almost as soon as George W. Bush assumed the presidency, he announced that his number one domestic policy agenda item was the passage of a new Elementary and Secondary Education bill. He brought in a Democrat from Texas to oversee this effort and to begin holding public meetings on the need to make a change. Almost all of the drafting of what was to become the No Child Left Behind Act (NCLB; U.S. Department of Education, 2002) was done in secret by four members of Congress: Senators Edward Kennedy (D-MA) and Judd Gregg (R-NH), with House members John Boehner (R-OH) and George Miller (D-CA). These four and their staffs decided that a new approach was needed, and they focused on accountability as their main lever for change. However, that was not their only tool.

The rewriting of the ESEA into NCLB created several initiatives focused on professional development. Professional development is mentioned 197 times in the 630-page bill. The largest of these was actually Title I, but the most public was the Reading First program. Reading First was the successor to the Reading Excellence Act and, unlike Reading Excellence, it had more "teeth." First on the requirement side, Reading First dollars were not to be used instead of state and local dollars to provide teachers with professional development in reading. Federal monies were to be used with state and local dollars to support reading instruction, but the federal monies had to follow more specific requirements.

The U.S. Department of Education's political leadership appointed a leader to the Reading First program who had a very specific idea of what needed to be done and how it should done. The statute was also to incorporate the work of the National

Reading Panel (NRP) to define the focus of beginning reading instruction. The NRP reviewed thousands of reading studies looking for what the experimentally designed studies reported as being critical. They found five major areas: phonemic awareness, phonics, vocabulary, fluency, and comprehension. They stated that they had no time to focus on other important areas of reading.

Like a lens focusing light into a powerful force, Reading First focused on reading professional development. This program required state governments to write plans for professional development around the five areas identified by NRP, with a greater focus on phonemic awareness and phonics. Reading First also had a separate accountability requirement to use approved tests, and almost all schools had to use the Dynamic Indicators of Basic Early Literacy Skills (DIBELS) assessment. DIBELS focused on fluency, which was assumed to be a proxy for all five areas. The assumption was that if students could demonstrate their ability to read easily, then they must have a sense of what the passage and words mean. It was also cheap, easy to administer, and quick. Unfortunately, it also became proxy for the entire program.

The program was mired in controversy almost from the start. The U.S. Department of Education was accused of: (1) promoting specific programs of instruction and professional development that supported that instruction, (2) requiring states to hire specific consultants to write their state plans, (3) hiring specific personnel to manage the implementation, and (4) requiring the local schools to use programs only from a specific list. The list was labeled a federal list, but it was a list of programs that had been reviewed by Oregon University and posted on their website. Their work had been supported with federal dollars and was being enforced by federal suggestions.

However, this was not the only intervention by NCLB in defining professional development. The act also stated that no longer would federal money be used to support 1-day workshops or attendance at professional education conferences. Bethany Little, former education counsel to Senate Education Committee Chairmen Ted Kennedy (D-MA) and Tom Harkin (D-IA), made several significant observations about professional development and how the professional education public policy community viewed it. First, in general the education public policy community believed that professional development is critical for the success of any school reform. Second, it hasn't worked. Little observed that federal education public policy requirements are in essence a "blunt instrument" for change. Yet she observed that Reading First had something different; it had a specific set of goals and a specific accountability measure. Although the program certainly had some issues in "how it was administered," there are states in which these problems were managed with positive results (Little, personal interview, 2012).

The reality was that there was not the ability for enforcement as there was in Reading First, but there was noticeable change. The core idea was that 1-day (now described as "drive-by") professional development was not an effective way of improving teacher knowledge or instruction. In addition, linking specific research to a specific practice was now viewed as an important element of any professional development. There was a greater awareness of the standards for professional development that had been created by the former National Staff Development Council (now Learning Forward), which emphasized much more participation by staff in setting the agenda for professional development and the increased level of participation in the actual program.

However, the largest change to federal funding of professional development is found in Section 9101 of NCLB, in which it defines professional development (see Figure 2.1).

The reason for this section having a greater impact on professional development is that it changed the nature of professional development by putting in place a federal definition of what the process of professional development would be. In the past, teachers could go to a conference and select sessions that would best reflect their needs for improvement; now their needs for improvement would have to be defined by the need of the school to meet the goals of a program.

Beyond NCLB

When the Obama administration structured its approach to education, it seemed to be continuing many of the practices of Secretary of Education Margaret Spellings's tenure. Its regulatory approach seemed similar to NCLB. But that was changed with the stimulus package known as the American Recovery and Reinvestment Act (ARRA) of 2009. ARRA provided over $10 billion in funds to schools to hire new teachers and for teacher improvement through professional development. While data are still unavailable, it is hard to determine how much money was actually

---

The term "professional development"—

(A) includes activities that—

  (i) improve and increase teachers' knowledge of the academic subjects the teachers teach, and enable teachers to become highly qualified;

  (ii) are an integral part of broad schoolwide and districtwide educational improvement plans;

  (iii) give teachers, principals, and administrators the knowledge and skills to provide students with the opportunity to meet challenging State academic content standards and student academic achievement standards;

  (iv) improve classroom management skills;

  (v)

    (I) are high quality, sustained, intensive, and classroom-focused in order to have a positive and lasting impact on classroom instruction and the teacher's performance in the classroom; and

    (II) are not 1-day or short-term workshops or conferences;

  (vi) support the recruiting, hiring, and training of highly qualified teachers, including teachers who become highly qualified through State and local alternative routes to certification;

  (vii) advance teacher understanding of effective instructional strategies that are—

    (I) based on scientifically based research. . . .

FIGURE 2.1. Definition of "professional development" in No Child Left Behind.

spent on professional development versus teacher salaries. It is also hard to determine whether money spent made an impact on professional development.

Race to the Top, a smaller program, made available over $3.5 billion for professional development. The money from this program was used to fund more specific types of professional development. It is defined as follows:

> Job-embedded professional development is professional learning that occurs at a school as educators engage in their daily work activities. It is closely connected to what teachers are asked to do in the classroom so that the skills and knowledge gained from such learning can be immediately transferred to classroom instructional practices. Job-embedded professional development is usually characterized by the following:
>
> - It occurs on a regular basis (e.g., daily or weekly);
> - It is aligned with academic standards, school curricula, and school improvement goals;
> - It involves educators working together collaboratively and is often facilitated by school instructional leaders or school-based professional development coaches or mentors;
> - It requires active engagement rather than passive learning by participants; and
> - It focuses on understanding what and how students are learning and how to address students' learning needs, including reviewing student work and achievement data and collaboratively planning, testing, and adjusting instructional strategies, formative assessments, and materials based on such data.
>
> Job-embedded professional development can take many forms, including, but not limited to, classroom coaching, structured common planning time, meetings with mentors, consultation with outside experts, and observations of classroom practice. (U.S. Department of Education Office of Elementary and Secondary Education, June 2010, revised)

As can be seen, this definition and the funding level were distinct changes from previous general policy about professional development. It basically defined what would be and would not be considered professional development. In so doing, it excluded professional development as a long-term improvement of knowledge and practice. The purpose and structure were now both tied to the immediate goal of education reform and change.

RECOMMENDATIONS AND FUTURE DIRECTIONS

Federal involvement in professional development has a record of general programs that have failed to register a significant difference. Why is this? The brief review in Table 2.1 finds several critical elements in the mix. These include several types of programs. One set of programs consists of those with goals that are general with little or no evaluation linked to them. Another set consists of programs that do have an effect that seems to be linked to goals, procedures, and evaluations that are more specific. The combination of both has resulted in modest overall gains that can be attributed to supporting professional development. However, a significant impact on how decisions are made about instruction, teacher knowledge, and even the very structure of professional development remains unclear. From the days of the nation's response to *Sputnik* to the emerging struggle to implement college- and career-ready standards, support for professional development has been part of that debate. Unfortunately, federal education policy seems to be lacking in the tools to evaluate its requirements and how to improve it. Still, with the high rate of teacher turnover, especially in schools servicing high-need populations, it is critical to get professional development right.

The next big opportunity to learn from the past is here, as professional development is factored into the federal policy that will be part of the implementation of the college- and career-ready standards, such as the Common Core State Standards (CCSS). The standards have dimensions to which most teachers have had little exposure in their teacher prep programs. For example, whereas many teachers have been taught how to teach narrative writing, fewer have been taught how to teach other forms of writing. In addition, many teachers have had little training in how to teach writing that is specific to content areas, such as science, math, and history (Miller, McCardle, & Long, 2014). In addition, few teachers have had the term "text complexity" presented to them before the publication of the CCSS. The challenge is that there are no dedicated resources for such training.

There are two ways that the federal government could send money to state and local school districts for professional development. One is through some sort of general aid package in which professional development is an option. Historically, this type of funding stream is called a block grant. Education block grants tend to be focused on a theme, and the funding is automatic to states and schools. Everyone gets a share and must send in a report. However, a general block grant for education is not likely because it is not focused on any specific area of improvement.

In contrast to the block grant is the prescriptive approach, which means that funds are provided under specific conditions and must be spent in a required manner. In a sense, Reading First and the Eisenhower programs are examples of this approach. In these programs, funds are for a specific targeted discipline and are distributed either by formula or by taking applications from states. This is not the approach that will be taken.

What is likely to happen is that the federal government is going to continue along the lines of making agreements with states and local districts that will be based on a competitive and negotiated process. This will also allow the federal government to see professional development as part of a more complex process of ongoing reform. This reform will be modulated by either control of how the inputs are structured (what quality of teacher, which populations, are trying to achieve which specific goals) or by outcomes. The outcomes will be measured by some specific change in student performance.

This, then, becomes the question of the chapter. Although there are clearly federal mandates for how professional development is structured and implemented, most federal involvement in professional development has been influenced by the specific goal or goals of a program. The most recent example is the funding for professional development in the education stimulus program. The goal of NCLB was to close the achievement gap as measured by reading and math scores. Therefore, one result is that most Title I funding for professional development is targeted at helping teachers improve reading and math scores, as measured by tests. Consequently, professional development is focused on specific areas of reading and math.

Furthermore, ideas such as professional learning communities, which support building-level, longer-term instructional improvements, are rarely supported, and the same is true for professional development by graduate program study and short-term conferences. Graduate programs are seen as education that will have little direct application to the "problem" at hand. One-, 2-, or 3-day conferences are similarly seen as having little impact on changing the school building problem. The goal of the federal program becomes the purpose of professional development.

An interesting case in point on professional development can be seen in how the federal government has been supporting technology and instruction. Generally speaking, the federal government has been trumpeting the use of technology as one of the key ways that instruction will change. Over the years, the federal government has supported and held conferences, structured specific grant programs, and directed resources. The federal programs have allowed the purchase of equipment, but they have also had a major emphasis on professional development. Two major federal K–12 programs, Title I and IDEA, have both been used to buy hardware and software and for professional development to help teachers and administrators learn how to use these tools to change instruction. The results have been mixed. Although there are whiteboards in many classrooms, few teachers use these tools as anything more than a chalkboard. Again, the federal government has been supporting professional development and demanding specific paths to be followed, but it is usually linked to the goal of the overarching program. It is neither long term nor structured by those who are participating in the professional development.

The response has been to stop funding technology as a stand-alone program and to create a different type of public policy initiative. The U.S. Department of Education has decided not to fund the Title II–A (ESEA) technology fund but rather to require all spending programs to include technology as a part of their grant funding. Professional development will likely go the same way. Stand-alone funding will no longer be supported, but reform programs will be required to include technology with very specific requirements. The question will then be: What are the specific requirements and how will they be measured?

In summary, the future will find the federal government still struggling with professional development. Although any new legislation will be encouraging flexibility, the implementation will see the states and school districts creating goals that will be measured. The use of these measurements will have one significant new function: They will link student performance with professional evaluations of teachers and principals. A secondary outcome will be linked to professional development and how teachers and principals will have input in deciding how they can improve their practice as it relates to student outcomes. What will be lost is developing concepts, such as professional learning communities. Professional learning communities is an idea and practice that has a longer-term horizon and is more about teachers being in control of their own learning and making it a part of their work week.

Federal mandates pertaining to professional development programs are linked to the specific federal goals. In addition, the federal government's linkage of professional development to specific elements results in short-term goals and short-term means to meet those goals. Rarely does the federal government develop programs that will take years to produce solid gains. Consequently, because of the federal mandates, professional development techniques are developed for short-term gains.

This new push is likely to be continued at the federal level. Unfortunately, this focus on short-term gains has rarely resulted in desired improvements. By focusing on the short term, the federal government has crippled most professional development outcomes to the point of ineffectiveness. One critical lesson to be learned from the history of federal involvement is that professional development needs to be longer term, with a high degree of focus and insightful assessments.

QUESTIONS FOR DISCUSSION

1. Why have some of the federal attempts at professional development been more effective than others?

2. Looking at the more than 50 years, should the federal government be in the professional development business? Is it an effective tool of federal education policy?

3. Is federal education policy focused enough to have an effect on the knowledge of content and instructional practice of teachers?

REFERENCES

American Recovery and Reinvestment Act. (2009). Retrieved from *http://thomas.loc.gov/home/h1/Recovery_Bill_Div_B.pdf.*

Benedetto, R. (1996, January 10). Keys to '96 campaign: Education, for 1st time, is top voter concern. *USA Today*, p. A1. Retrieved from *http://global.factiva.com.mutex.gmu.edu/ha/default.aspx.*

Comprehensive School Reform Demonstration Act, Public Law No. 105-78, § 111, Stat. 1467 (1997).

Cross, C. (2010). *Political education: National policy comes of age* (updated ed.). New York: Teachers College Press.

Dwight D. Eisenhower Mathematics and Science Education Act, Public Law No. 100-297, § 1001, Stat. 219 (1988).

Fullan, M. (2006). Centre for Strategic Education Seminar Series Paper: Vol. 157. Change theory: A force for school improvement. Retrieved from *www.catalyst-chicago.org/sites/catalyst-chicago.org/files/michael_fullen_change_theory.pdf.*

Gladwell, M. (2008). *Outliers: The story of success.* Boston: Little, Brown.

Goals 2000: Educate America Act. (1994). Retrieved March 26, 2013, from *www2.ed.gov/ legislation/GOALS2000/TheAct/intro.html*.

Miller, B., McCardle, P., & Long, R. (2014). *Together and apart: Reading and writing in the 21st-century classroom*. Baltimore: Brookes.

National Assessment of Educational Progress. (2013). The nation's report card: Long-term trend. Overall average reading scores higher in 2008 than in 2004 for students at all three age groups. Retrieved from *http://nationsreportcard.gov/ltt_2008/ltt0003. aspx?subtab_id=Tab_3&tab_id=tab1#chart*.

National Council of Teachers of Mathematics Commission on Standards for School Mathematics. (1989). Curriculum and evaluation standards for school mathematics. Reston, VA: Author. Retrieved from *www.standards.nctm.org/index.htm*.

National Education Goals Panel. (1990). Goal 4: Teacher education and professional development. Retrieved November 24, 2012, from *http://govinfo.library.unt.edu/negp/ page3-9.htm*.

Reading Excellence Act, 8 U.S.C. § 2252 (1998).

Right to Read, Pub. L. No. 93-380, § 402 Stat. (1974).

Stanic, G. M. A., & Kilpatrick, J. (Eds.). (2003). *A history of school mathematics* (Vol. 1). Reston, VA: National Council of Teachers of Mathematics.

U.S. Department of Education. (1983). *A nation at risk: The imperative for educational reform*. Washington, DC: U.S. Government Printing Office.

U.S. Department of Education. (2002). No Child Left Behind Act. Retrieved March 26, 2013, from *www2.ed.gov/policy/elsec/leg/esea02/107-110.pdf*.

U.S. Department of Education, Office of Elementary and Secondary Education. (2010, June). Guidance on school improvement grants under section 1003(g) of the Elementary and Secondary Education Act. Available at *http://www2.ed.gov/programs/sif/ sigguidance05242010.pdf*.

CHAPTER 3

High-Quality Research-Based Professional Development

An Essential for Enhancing High-Quality Teaching

ALLISON SWAN DAGEN
RITA M. BEAN

- Evidence about professional development as a key factor for improving teacher practices and student learning has increased.
- Characteristics of effective professional development include adequate time, study of content and pedagogical learning, active learning activities appropriate for adults, and follow-up support.
- Professional development can be more effective when it occurs within a culture of collaboration in schools.
- Literacy coaching combines many of the features or characteristics of effective professional development.
- The establishment of professional learning communities in schools requires a different way of approaching leadership in the school (i.e., requiring that teachers function as instructional/teacher leaders).

Research evidence over the past several decades has made it clear: Teacher quality is important. Teachers must have the knowledge and skills that enable them to address the challenges of the 21st-century classroom, which means they must have an understanding of their specific content and how to teach it to meet national, state, and local standards; know how to use technology to promote high-level learning; and be prepared to teach in ways that enable all students to be "college or career ready" (Darling-Hammond, Wei, Andree, Richardson, & Orphanos, 2009). Although education changes as the demands of the classroom, school, or society change, the importance of teacher effectiveness has been a constant. As stated by Sir Michael Barber and Mona Mourshed, "the quality of an education system cannot exceed the quality of its teachers" (2007, p. 16).

And although teacher preparation programs have a responsibility to send well-prepared teachers into the schools, these novice educators have much to learn in their beginning years and will need ongoing professional learning experiences that help them meet the demands of a specific group of students in a specific context. Likewise, experienced teachers who have been in the system for a period of time understand the importance of ongoing learning as times change, and with them students, materials, and research findings that promote new and different ways of teaching. Moreover, at the present time, we have additional evidence that calls for new ways of supporting teacher learning (Blank & de las Alas, 2009; Bryk, Sebring, Allensworth, Luppescu, & Easton, 2010; Silva, 2008).

Over a 7-year period, Bryk and colleagues (2010) studied 100 elementary schools in Chicago that had improved and 100 that had not. Among other factors contributing to improvement was professional development. They summarize as follows:

> Our results affirm that quality professional development is a key instrument for school change. Most maximum leverage is achieved...when this professional development occurs within a supportive professional work environment where teaching is grounded in a common, coherent, and aligned instructional system. (p. 134)

In their longitudinal evaluation of the Eisenhower Professional Development Program, Desimone, Porter, Garet, Yoon, and Birman (2002) identified six key features or characteristics of professional development in improving teaching practice. The structural features include: design or organization of the activity; duration, including contact hours and span of time; and collective participation of the groups (vs. individuals). The core features include teacher engagement and active learning, coherence with school standards and goals, and content focus (in this review, mathematics and science). Desimone and colleagues concluded that most school-supported professional development projects did not successfully address these six elements.

In this chapter, we first define professional development, introducing what we call "the third wave." We then describe landmark large-scale studies that provide important evidence about the status of professional development, identify features or characteristics of effective professional development, and follow this with a discussion of standards for professional development. Finally, we describe three research-based approaches to professional development—literacy coaching, teacher leadership, and professional learning communities. We close with some major conclusions about the current research and make several recommendations for improving professional development.

WHAT IS PROFESSIONAL DEVELOPMENT?

During recent years, efforts have been made to define and describe effective professional development. For example, in their review of professional development literature, Anders, Hoffman, and Duffy (2000) present a list of six criteria that should be considered when designing professional development initiatives: (1) intensive/extensive commitment, (2) coaching/clinical model, (3) teacher reflection, (4) deliberation, dialogue, and negotiation, (5) voluntary participation, and (6) collaboration.

Then, in 2005, the American Educational Research Association (AERA) published a brief in which two waves of professional development are described. The first wave, beginning in the 1960s, focused on generic teaching skills—that is, helping teachers understand how to group students, hold their attention, allocate instructional time, and so forth. In the 1990s, research was focused on student learning, for example, how students reason and problem-solve. This second wave put the emphasis on content-matter knowledge as important in professional development programs for improving student achievement. In this brief, four important notions about professional development are described: (1) a focus on the subject matter being taught; (2) professional development aligned with teachers' classroom work, using actual materials and assessment tools; (3) sufficient time and extended opportunities to learn; and (4) the importance of evaluating professional development, focusing on both teacher practices and student learning (AERA, 2005).

We propose a third wave, a recognition of the importance of the culture within which teachers work and the need for distributed leadership that helps teachers focus on the goal of improving student learning. Thus we define professional learning as those *experiences that take place within a collaborative culture of shared leadership, that increase educators' knowledge about content and pedagogy and enable them to use that knowledge to improve classroom and school practices that improve student learning.* In other words, although we recognize the importance of professional growth of individual teachers, our primary goal is to discuss professional learning as it affects the collective ability and capacity of teachers in a school to address challenges and solve problems that enable the organization to become more effective in its most important endeavor—improving student learning. Although collaboration in schools has been mentioned in earlier studies (Anders et al. 2000; Bryk et al., 2010; Desimone et al., 2002) as a key feature of effective professional development, an emphasis on systematic approaches to developing such collaborative efforts has intensified in recent years.

PROFESSIONAL DEVELOPMENT: A SUMMARY OF KEY RESEARCH

In this section, we summarize the results of key research findings that provide an update about the status of professional development and criteria important to its success. Three major reports of teacher professional learning opportunities conducted by Learning Forward and the Stanford Center for Opportunity Policy in Education in the United States have provided substantial information about the status of professional development in the United States. In the first report, Wei, Darling-Hammond, Andree, Richardson, and Orphanos (2009) evaluated the status of professional development in the United States in relation to professional development in other countries. The researchers found that between 2000 and 2004 there was a decrease in the number of learning opportunities that allowed for regular collaboration of teachers (e.g., regularly scheduled collaboration, observations of teaching in other schools). Teachers most often engaged in workshops and conferences (90%) versus coaching (46%) and observations of peers (22%). The report found that teachers desire more professional learning experiences concerning students with disabilities, subject matter/content, classroom management, and use of technology. They indicated that professional development that is disconnected from classroom practice has little impact. Finally, the authors cite the limited pool of rigorous research studies available about professional development (Wei et al., 2009).

In Phase 2 of this research study, Wei, Darling-Hammond, and Adamson (2010) addressed trends and challenges for professional development in the United States. The report, which uses several large datasets, indicated that a great majority of new teachers participate in some type of induction program (75%) and are mentored (80%). Most professional development projects studied focused on learning-specific content. Furthermore, the report states that teachers had fewer opportunities to participate in professional development activities that are sustained over time (e.g., more than 8 hours' duration) and that short-term workshops were still the norm. Last, teachers reported lack of access to professional development that focuses on at-risk learners (e.g., those with disabilities and special needs, English language learners [ELLs]).

In the Phase 3, Jaquith, Mindich, Wei, and Darling-Hammond (2010) provided an in-depth analysis of the policies of four states in which there was active teacher involvement in professional development and student achievement was improving. According to this report, state policies and systems are key to improving professional development for teachers. Specific features of state involvement include: standards for professional development; accountability and monitoring of professional development efforts; various intermediary offices that provide the infrastructure and support for professional development in districts; and resources that schools and districts can use to enhance professional development efforts.

Although these three reports provide important information about trends and challenges overall, only a few studies have focused specifically on the relationship between professional development and teacher practices or student achievement. Yoon, Duncan, Lee, Scarloss, and Shapley's (2007) synthesis of studies was an attempt to determine how professional development affects student achievement. Their sample size of more than 1,300 studies was reduced to 9 after applying evidence standards from the What Works Clearinghouse. All nine studies were situated in elementary schools and addressed reading, language arts, math, or science.

All studies had positive student outcomes and shared similarities in design elements; for example, professional development generally consisted of a workshop format. Similarities of these workshops included implementation of research-based instructional practices, an active learning component, and opportunities for teachers to adapt to meet the needs of the learners in their classrooms. Furthermore, the studies that showed positive student outcomes were also led by outside experts and were not in-house or site-based. These experts not only presented information to the teachers but also facilitated the implementation. The analysis also indicated that initiatives reviewed consisted of at least 30 contact hours and did include a significant amount of follow-up that was job-embedded and specific to the teachers' classrooms. Again, many of the features identified by others (Anders et al., 2000; Darling-Hammond et al., 2009; Desimone et al., 2002) were integral parts of the studies described by Yoon and colleagues (2007).

Blank and de las Alas (2009) also investigated the effects of teacher professional development (K–12) on student achievement in math and science and, in addition, identified the characteristics of professional development that best explained the degree of effectiveness. Their meta-analysis of 16 studies that met their established criteria revealed modest effects between professional development and student achievement in mathematics from the professional development program (12 of 16 studies focused on math). Features that were common across studies included strong focus on specific subject and pedagogical content and follow-up support, such as coaching, mentoring, networking, and so forth, that often included support for mentors and colleagues in their schools. Given that the individual studies in this investigation included both school-level work and studies for which individual teachers enrolled or volunteered, there was mixed evidence of the importance of teachers' collective participation.

In the most recent *Handbook of Reading Research*, Dillon, O'Brien, Sato, and Kelly (2011) discuss the research in professional development and teacher education for reading instruction. Although the primary focus of the chapter is preservice education, they do cite the need for additional professional development studies that examine direct observation of changes in classroom practices and student outcomes. They highlight literacy coaching as an important professional development model, although they also indicate that the effects of coaching on changing teacher practices or on student learning remains limited. They also emphasize the need for more longitudinal work, studying teacher practices for several years beyond the first year. They recommend formative experimental research, suggesting that new technologies will enable researchers to study geographically mobile teachers at multiple points in time.

In sum, the recent research has validated the importance of features such as focused content, active learning, duration, and ongoing support. But, in addition, it has emphasized a new feature, that of collaborative learning—that is, the importance of the organization in which the teacher works. Thus the "third wave" does not negate features identified as important; rather, the third wave adds another dimension that can be helpful in building capacity and ultimately improving student learning in the school. In other words, it is difficult to separate the various features that are necessary in any effective professional learning program; rather, effective professional development would encompass as many of those features as appropriate for a specific professional development initiative.

STANDARDS FOR PROFESSIONAL DEVELOPMENT

In the publication *Standards for Staff Development* (2001), the National Staff Development Council (NSDC) identified three important elements of effective professional development: content, context, and process. These standards were influential in helping educators, as well as researchers, think about features such as the content being addressed, the characteristics of the teachers, students, and schools in which the professional development was being offered, and the activities that would help ensure active engagement on the part of the participants. In 2011, Learning Forward (previously known as NSDC) released its new *Standards for Professional Learning*, which provided a more analytical overview for educators. Learning Forward made the decision to use the phrase "professional learning" rather than "professional development" to signal an increased emphasis on educators taking an active role in their own learning. The standards now include seven dimensions: learning communities, leadership, resources, data, learning design, implementation, and outcomes (*www.learningforward.org*). Learning Forward also indicates that professional learning by itself will not address all challenges that educators face and identifies four prerequisites for effective professional learning: (1) educators' commitment to all students; (2) educators' receptivity to professional learning; (3) importance of collaborative inquiry to enhance both individual and collective performance; and (4) respecting the difference in educators' learning needs. These standards, as well as those of other professional organizations, such as the International Reading Association (2010), the Council for Exceptional Children (2009), the American Speech–Language–Hearing Association (2010), and the Interstate Teacher Assessment and Support Consortium (2011), can be helpful for designing policies and shaping practice for professional learning and for evaluating the effectiveness of these efforts.

RESEARCH-BASED PRACTICES FOR PROFESSIONAL DEVELOPMENT

We begin with a discussion about what is called the "third wave," building on the two-wave model described by the AERA (2005). The third wave focuses on the importance of the culture of the organization as an important ingredient in effective professional development initiatives (see Figure 3.1). Then we describe three approaches to professional development that, based on research, include many of the features described earlier and also build capacity in the school by promoting collaboration, teacher leadership, and shared decision making.

Improvement in overall student learning requires collective participation and collaboration among all educators in the school. Such participation means that

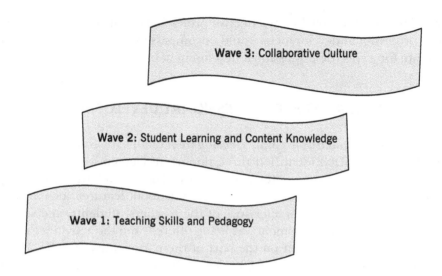

FIGURE 3.1. Waves of professional development.

there is shared leadership in the building by which all educators have a role in facilitating literacy learning. In other words, the culture of the organization is important. Although Joyce and Showers (2002), for example, continue to emphasize ideas found in previous editions of their book *Student Achievement Through Staff Development* (e.g., coaching), in the present edition, there is even more emphasis on the importance of the organizational infrastructure, the need to create communities in districts and schools, and the role of leadership. Joyce and Showers state that educators involved in a staff development effort must function as a community of professionals who study together, apply what they are learning, and share results.

Evidence from both the educational field (Bryk et al., 2010; Marzano, 2003) and the corporate world (Collins, 2001) speaks to the impact that the culture in an organization has on those who work there and on its ultimate success. Specifically, what matters is how the members of that organization interact with one another, that is, the collegiality among members (Marzano, 2003). As cautioned by Fullan and Hargreaves (1996), however, such collegiality does not come about by mandate (e.g., that teachers *will* meet and plan together, that they are *required* to coach each other). Furthermore, collaboration does not mean that teachers interact socially; rather, the conversations among teachers must be focused on improving instruction in the classrooms. Too often, there are structural changes that provide opportunities for teacher conversations, but there is little that helps teachers understand how to work meaningfully with others.

Leana and Pil (2006) provide solid evidence about the importance of school culture or climate. In their study of a large urban district, they distributed questionnaires to teachers in many of the schools—elementary through high school—and analyzed the relationship between teacher responses and student achievement. What they found was that having a trusting climate in the school, that is, strong social capital, was more important in predicting student achievement scores than other factors such as teacher experience or certification, generally known as human capital. Moreover, the patterns of responses were similar, regardless of level or type of school. In schools that exhibit strong social capital, "teachers talked to each other, shared the same norms, and had strong agreement in their descriptions of the culture of the school" (Leana, 2010, p. 18). In a later study of social capital in New York City schools, they asked teachers to identify the colleagues with whom they talked if they were having difficulties. Most often (a ratio of 2:1), teachers reported that they talked to their peers. As Leana (2010) stated, "They don't talk to experts. They don't talk to the coaches. They don't talk to the principal....they talk to one another" (p. 19). Leana does not negate the importance of human capital, the capacity and ability of teachers, but indicates that social and human capital are "inextricably intertwined" (p. 19). One must have both to have good classrooms and a good school. She makes a plea for recognizing the collective efforts of teachers, one that recognizes that teachers in a school have a shared destiny and a shared purpose.

The following three research-based approaches show promise in that they include many features found to be essential in effective professional development programs, including the importance of a collaborative culture. What is even more promising is that all three of these can be incorporated into a school professional learning plan–that is, a school can employ coaches to help lead professional learning communities. Such a school can also draw on the resources of its teachers to serve as instructional leaders. These three approaches all address both social and human capital/capacity. They involve teachers, what they know, who they are, and how they function with others (not in isolation as door closers) as a critical variable in the design of the approach. Moreover, any one of these, to be successful, requires an organizational structure in which there is a common vision and common goals and in which teachers work collaboratively to achieve those goals.

Coaching

Coaching is a good example of a key approach that has multiple feature of effective professional development in that it requires adequate time or duration and activities that build knowledge and theory and in that it provides for ongoing support and feedback. Moreover, it operates more effectively when teachers are receptive or ready for coaching; that is, when they recognize the importance of learning from others and trust the coach to work with them in a supportive, collegial fashion. Coaching frequently requires working with teachers in collaborative groups (e.g., analyzing data, lesson study, study groups) (Bean & Swan Dagen, 2012). Such activities can be most effective when the climate is one in which teachers share a common vision and have common goals for student learning (Vescio, Ross, & Adams, 2008).

A study by Biancarosa, Bryk, and Dexter (2010) provides an excellent example of an extended professional learning program, based on a train-the-trainer model, that builds knowledge of participants and provides for ongoing support and feedback over an extended period of time. The study was conducted in 17 schools with second-grade students who were assessed with the Dynamic Indicators of Basic Early Literacy Skills (DIBELS) and the TerraNova test. Literacy Collaborative, a school reform program designed to improve students' reading, writing, and language skills, provides a graduate-level program for literacy coaches selected by their schools; coaches at the same time are teaching students at their schools. The program includes theory, content, and pedagogical knowledge about how to teach literacy, as well as how to work with teachers through site-based professional development and coaching. After the initial year, coaches spend half of their time working with teachers in their schools and also continue to teach students for the remainder of the time. The coaches during this second year facilitate a 40-hour course for their teachers and also work with their peers one-on-one, modeling, observing, and in general supporting teachers in their implementation efforts. The authors used an accelerated longitudinal cohort design to determine effects of the program on student learning. Results indicate significant gains in student literacy learning beginning in the first year of implementation, with larger gains during each subsequent year of implementation (Biancarosa et al., 2010, p. 27). Biancarosa and colleagues hypothesize that the increase in effects over time may speak to the fact that coaches may need several years to grow into their position and, in addition, to establish the relationships with teachers that enable them to work well together.

Neuman and Cunningham (2009) conducted a study in which they provided professional development intervention to early childhood educators; participants were randomly selected for one of three groups, including (1) coursework at a local community college, (2) coursework plus weekly coaching, and (3) a control group. These researchers found that professional development plus coaching was related to significant increases in teacher knowledge and practice; coursework alone had no effects, and results in this group were similar to those in the control group. Neuman and Wright (2010) conducted a study in an effort to examine the effects of coaching *or* coursework on the language and literacy teaching practices of prekindergarten teachers. In this study, 148 teachers from six urban cities were randomly assigned to one of three groups: a coursework-only group, an onsite coaching group, or a control group. Participants in group 1 attended a 30-hour program, whereas those in group 2 received onsite individualized coaching and those in group 3 received no professional development. Results indicated no significant gains between groups on their knowledge of early language and literacy. In other words, neither treatment condition appeared to improve teacher knowledge of early language and literacy. However, those in group 2, the coaching group, made statistically significant improvements in the literacy environment in their classrooms, as determined with the Early Language and Literacy Classroom Observation (ELLCO; Smith & Dickinson, 2002), an observational tool that assesses the environment and literacy activities. Although participants in group 1 appreciated the course they attended, they had difficulty transferring what they were learning to their classrooms, with some indicating that the literacy demands were too high and concepts too abstract. According to the authors, the results indicate that coursework may need to be adapted to meet the needs of adult learners and that coaching promotes application to practice. Coaching gave these teachers the ongoing support they needed to implement important language and literacy practices in their own classrooms with their own students. Several limitations of this study are discussed: There was no measure of the effect of teacher learning on student learning, the professional development was developed and conducted by an external group, and participants were volunteers.

Matsumura, Garnier, Correnti, Junker, and Bickel (2010) summarize the results of a longitudinal randomized field trial of a literacy coaching program with 73 fourth- and fifth-grade teachers in 32 elementary schools with high teacher mobility. The 73 teachers were recruited midway through the program's implementation as replacements for teachers who had left their school or grade. The focus of the literacy initiative was effective reading comprehension, based on Questioning the Author (QtA), developed by Beck and McKeown (2006) as an approach for supporting meaningful discussions to promote and deepen reading comprehension. Professional development was provided for coaches; they studied the QtA framework, saw trainers model the approach, and were then given opportunities to practice teaching QtA lessons and provided with feedback. They also observed other coaches teaching such lessons. In addition, coaches had opportunities to build their coaching skills using notions of content-focused coaching (CFC; West & Staub, 2003).

Coaches then met with teachers to discuss the theories underlying effective reading comprehension and to help them plan QtA lessons. These coaches then met with teachers individually to help them implement QtA in their classrooms. Results indicated that there was an increase in participation in coaching for the CFC teachers relative to teachers in comparison schools, and more of the CFC teachers viewed their coaching experience as useful; however, few teachers participated in coaching at the level expected by program developers. Researchers also found significant average gains on the state test for the CFC schools, with ELLs scoring higher than ELLs in the comparison schools. There was not a significant effect for all students, although the trend was in a positive direction for the CFC schools. Matsumura and colleagues (2010) suggest that the fact that the coaching program was an established one—that is, that coaches had experience with the reform initiative and with coaching techniques—was a key factor in their ability to work with teachers new to the school and also had a positive effect on the student results.

In each of the preceding studies, there is a specific framework for instruction, based on theory and research in the field—in these cases, literacy instruction—and there are also opportunities for support of teachers as they attempt to implement these new instructional practices. In all these instances, the reform initiative is one that has been developed by an external agent or agency and, in addition, built on researched practices. Yet not all evidence about coaching as a follow-up approach to any instructional change effort is positive.

Walpole and McKenna (2009) discuss the fact that there is "mixed" evidence about coaching as a tool for changing teacher practices. They cite the results of the Garet and colleagues (2008) study, in which there were three treatments: professional development only, professional development plus coaching, and a control group. Specifically, teachers in both treatment groups scored higher than the control group on knowledge measures, and there was no difference between the professional development-only and professional development-plus-coaching groups. Furthermore, there were no effects on student achievement. Yet Walpole and McKenna indicate that coaching still provides one of the important options for the future and cite the need for studies that address more specifically the various nuances of coaching. According to these authors, researchers must develop studies that recognize the multifaceted dimensions of coaching, including differences in the coach, what the coach does, and the context in which coaching occurs. In other words, coaching is not a "monolithic" construct (p. 31). They in fact provide their own definition of coaching, "a strategy for implementing a professional support system for teachers, a system that includes research or theory, demonstration, practice, and feedback" (McKenna & Walpole, 2008, p. 1). In other words, again, the professional development includes the development of knowledge based on theory, opportunities for modeling, practicing, and feedback. The researchers also identify questions important for both those interested in implementing coaching as an integral part of professional development and those involved in studying coaching:

1. How do models of coaching direct coaching efforts?
2. To what extent are coaching efforts mediated by characteristics of districts and schools?
3. How can coaches work with administrators to optimize their efforts?
4. How can coaching be differentiated to meet the needs of all teachers?
5. What personal characteristics tend to be shared by effective coaches? (McKenna & Walpole, 2008, p. 26)

Although coaching has shown great promise, coaching positions are often eliminated when schools face budget difficulties. Therefore, there have been efforts to investigate technology as a means of providing cost-efficient and effective coaching. Gentry, Denton, and Kurz (2008), for example, synthesized peer-reviewed studies on technology-mediated mentoring for teachers and found that teachers were positive about their experiences; however, they indicated that there was a need for more rigorous research on this type of coaching.

In sum, there is increasing evidence that coaching includes specific elements known to be important aspects of effective professional development: adequate time; opportunities to develop knowledge, both content and pedagogical content; and follow-up activities that help teachers understand how to implement effectively what they are learning. In addition, coaching appears to be most effective when it operates in a context that provides for the support of coaches and coaching and recognizes the importance of coaches as instructional leaders who can work collegially with teachers.

Teacher Leadership

York-Barr and Duke (2004) define teacher leadership as "the process by which teachers, individuals or collectively, influence their colleagues, principals, and other members of school communities to improve teaching and learning practices with the aim of increased student learning and achievement" (pp. 287–288). Commonalities among descriptions of school-based teacher leaders include educators who:

- Influence peers and school community through collegial interactions (Danielson, 1998; Fullan & Hargreaves, 1996; Lambert, 2003);
- Work in classrooms and the overall school system (Katzenmeyer & Moller, 2009);
- Concentrate their efforts on school improvement, specifically student growth and achievement (Crowther, Ferguson & Hann, 2009; Donaldson, 2006; York-Barr & Duke, 2004); and
- Engage in formal and informal leadership responsibilities (Danielson, 2007).

This overview of teacher leadership is congruent with research on distributed leadership, which Spillane (2005) defines as "a system of practice comprised of a collection of interacting components: leaders, followers and situation" (p. 150). That is, distributed leadership is *stretched* across various personnel (principal, teachers, and specialists) within a school. The distributed notion reflects teacher leadership as an organizational element within a school.

There is a strong link between professional development and teacher leadership (Poekert, 2012), one in which the culture or organization is a vital backdrop for professional learning. Teacher leadership can be developed as a form of ongoing professional development, and in many schools teacher leaders are responsible for planning and implementing professional development (Swan Dagen & Nichols, 2012). Teacher leaders plan and facilitate these experiences but are also colearners in the process. So not only do they learn content, but they also grow professionally from their leadership experience. Therefore, professional development is "both a cause and an outcome of teacher leadership" (Poekert, 2012, p. 170). In this model, teacher leadership takes the form of job-embedded professional development.

Professional development/professional learning is just one of seven domains presented in the Teacher Leader Model Standards (TLMS) developed and released by the Teacher Leadership Exploratory Consortium (2011). The purpose of the standards is to "stimulate dialogue" about what constitutes the knowledge, skills, and competencies that teachers need to assume leadership roles. Domain 3, "promoting professional learning for continuous improvement," addresses job-embedded professional development aligned with school improvement goals. The standards indicate that teacher leaders should collaborate with peers and administrators; be knowledgeable about adult learning theories; facilitate peers' learning; use technology to promote learning; collect, analyze, and disseminate data on the effects of professional learning; advocate for time and support for job-embedded professional development; provide feedback; and remain current on emerging trends in education.

As highlighted in the TLMS standards, collaborating with peers is a critical element of teacher leadership, as it seems to improve teaching (Sparks, 2004), Teachers who work in isolation rarely change their practice (Greenwood & Maheady, 2001). Furthermore, Fuchs and Fuchs (2001) assert that classroom teaching becomes more effective when peers and administrators collaborate and use student data as a backdrop to their decision making and planning. Collaboration is a key function of teacher leaders. Collaboration, as a form of teacher leadership, can transform schools as places of learning (Bean & Swan Dagen, 2012). This transformation, however, takes time and cannot be mandated or required for authentic learning and growth to occur. However, not all activities that take place between peers in schools can or should be labeled collaboration.

Little (1990) describes three layers of collaboration that are low intensity–low risk; they include: (1) collegiality through storytelling, which is mainly anecdote-based; (2) responding to peers' requests for help and assistance (when asked); and (3) material, idea, and strategy sharing. Authentic collaboration, which Little calls "joint work," is the most effective form of collaboration and includes activities such as team teaching, planning, observing, mentoring, and action research. For this type of high-level collaboration to be successful, the following school variables need to be considered: active support from principal and colleagues, available time and resources within the school schedule, and authentic opportunities to collaborate (York-Barr & Duke, 2004). Only when these elements are in place do schools have the potential to develop into places for professional/adult learning.

The *MetLife Survey of the American Teacher: Collaborating for Student Success* (2010) addressed collaboration opportunities of U.S. teachers. They reported that participating teachers on average spent 2.7 hours a week collaborating. These collaborating activities consisted mainly of team meetings or as participants in student-centered meetings. On the other hand, in the technical report called *Professional Learning in the Learning Profession*, Wei and colleagues (2009) reported on teachers in parts of Europe and Asia who have less direct contact with students and who spend more time planning and collaborating with peers. The authors report that in some instances these two activities are equal in duration (e.g., 15–20 hours teaching, 15–20 hours collaborating). Examples of collaborating activities include coplanning lessons, observing peers, evaluating student assessment and progress, developing curriculum, and participating in study groups.

Many have conducted research and published articles on such topics as how schools find time for teacher collaboration (Dearman & Alber, 2005), cultivating a culture by creating opportunities for teachers to pursue collaborative leadership (Mongiello, Brady, Johnson, & Berg, 2009), designing comprehensive professional development plans highlighting teacher collaboration (Kennedy & Shiel, 2010), and strategies to get teachers involved in collaborative efforts (Allen, 2006). However, very few empirical studies currently exist on the relationship between teacher leadership and its impact on teacher or student learning.

Colbert, Brown, Choi, and Thomas (2008) present the results of research studying the changes teachers made when they were given autonomy, responsibility, and funding to work with peers and select, plan, design, and implement their own professional development experiences. Teams of these teachers were solicited to apply for a $30,000 professional development budget to be used for a 2-year cycle. The teams were required to examine their own needs for professional development, and options for professional development activities included travel to conferences, coursework, implementing and evaluating curriculum, and bringing in experts from the field into schools and classrooms. All teachers (100%) reported moderate to major benefits—empowerment, efficacy, self-confidence, and professionalism; 96% felt that participation had a moderate to major impact on their subject matter knowledge; 100% reported that participation had a moderate to major impact on their feelings of self-efficacy; 96% felt that they were engaged in a moderate to major amount of teamwork; and 83% reported the project had resulted in improving student learning. Through in-depth interviews, the researchers learned about the reflective experiences of a team of teachers from a Los Angeles elementary school. These teachers focused their professional development on nonfiction writing and decided to attend a workshop at New York's Teachers College. Once there, the team of California teachers met a second group of teachers, from New York, who were also attending the workshop. However, unlike the team of teachers who selected this opportunity, the New York group was disheartened about attending because the content did not match their professional needs. The California teachers felt that designing their own professional development experiences had resulted in a meaningful experience. One of the limitations of this study was that it did not address the effects on actual classroom practices or student achievement; rather, data were obtained using teacher self-perceptions.

Lieberman and Wood (2002) shared their research about the National Writing Project (NWP), one of the most successful teacher networks in the United States. The NWP project, which began in 1974, currently oversees nearly 200 university-based sites in all 50 states. Teachers participate in summer institutes and then continue collaborative work throughout the school year. Lieberman and Wood studied two NWP implementation sites in two states from 1997 to 1999. Through site visits, document analysis, interviews, focus groups, and classroom observations, they identified two key features responsible for the success of this project: (1) group social practices that build community and (2) ongoing networks (of teachers) in which relationships are supported and sustained. Lieberman and Wood identified the critical social practices that resulted in transformations in the NWP participants: treating everyone as a contributor; teaching other teachers; sharing, discussing, and critiquing in a public forum; turning ownership over to the learners; situating learning in practice and relationships; providing multiple entry points into learning communities; reflecting on teaching by reflecting on learning; sharing leadership; adopting a stance of inquiry; and rethinking professional identity and linking it to professional community. Also, Lieberman and Wood followed six teachers at various points in their careers and found that participation had had an impact on their teaching practices.

Hunzicker (2012) studied teachers who assumed informal leadership roles in their schools. The participants in this multiple case study were eight elementary teachers who were enrolled in a science, technology, engineering, and math (STEM) master's program. In this program teachers completed coursework, action research projects, and a teacher leadership portfolio. Self-reported data were collected for this multiyear project through focus groups, questionnaires, and narrative reflections. Hunzicker concluded that there were three project variables that cultivated leadership: exposure to research-based practices (e.g., action research tied to coursework and school initiatives); increased self-efficacy (e.g., through student-centered instructional approaches such as data-driven decision making); and serving beyond the classroom (e.g., leading professional development, collaborative decision making). Through the project, aimed at improving teaching, teachers gradually developed leadership capacity. Effective professional development paired with job-embedded collaboration helped nurture these teachers into leaders. Exposure to these high-quality project experiences took place within the context of the project, and the teacher leadership skills of the eight teachers grew gradually over time.

In sum, developing teacher leaders requires time, administrative support, and authentic opportunities that focus on a teacher's work in school. Although leadership abilities can be innate or developed by an individual teacher, fulfilling the potential in this role requires a supportive collaborative school culture. The research evidence to this point has generally been based on self-report and focused on teacher responses or reactions to their experiences.

Professional Learning Communities

One of the prominent approaches to enhancing collaboration is the notion of developing a school as a professional learning community (PLC). But what is a professional learning community, and what evidence is there that the existence of such a community makes a difference in teacher practice and student learning?

Defining a PLC is not easy; various terms have been used to describe such initiatives— for example, "critical friends," "community of practice," and "community of learners." However, the five characteristics identified by Newmann and his colleagues (1996) are helpful in thinking about essential components of any PLC; these include (1) shared values and norms; (2) a focus on student learning rather than teaching; (3) opportunities for reflective dialogue; (4) collaboration as the norm; and (5) teaching made public. Too often, the term "professional learning community" is used to describe an organizational culture in which only one or two of these components exist (e.g., teachers have opportunities to collaborate). As cautioned by DuFour (2004), however, just labeling one's school as a PLC is not enough. For example, teachers can be given opportunities to meet frequently, but unless those meetings are focused on student learning, unless they provide opportunities for reflection, and so forth, they do not meet the criterion that defines a PLC.

What evidence exists about the value of professional learning communities for teacher practice and student learning? One of the key studies is that of Vescio and colleagues (2008), who reviewed 11 studies, published and/or peer reviewed, that provided empirical evidence about the effectiveness of PLCs. Their goal was to focus on these 11 studies rather than on the many others available that highlighted the self-perceptions of teachers who appeared to value such initiatives. Vescio and colleagues found that in organizations with well-developed PLCs, there was a positive impact on classroom practices and student learning. They were able to identify the following as essential characteristics of the PLCs in their reviewed studies: (1)

collaboration, which includes opportunity for reflection and open dialogue about teaching practices; (2) an emphasis on student learning; (3) teacher decision making, or what they called teacher authority; and (4) opportunities for continuous teacher learning. They also indicated that, although some of the studies did not identify specific changes in teacher practices, they did provide evidence of changes in the professional culture of the school. Vescio and colleagues call for more rigorous research to help educators understand exactly what it means to implement PLCs in schools in ways that enhance student learning.

A 5-year quasi-experimental study conducted by Saunders, Goldenberg, and Gallimore (2009) also supports the importance of teamwork as a means of improving student achievement. Saunders and colleagues compared two groups of schools, nine in which grade-level teams were given time to work collaboratively using protocols to think about student learning, and a matched group of six schools. During the first 2 years (Phase 1), they provided training to principals only, and during the final 3 years (Phase 2), training was provided for both principals and teacher leaders. In addition, the researchers provided explicit protocols for the grade-level meetings during Phase 2. These researchers found no differences in achievement between the two groups of schools in Phase 1, but achievement at the experimental schools improved at a faster rate and showed greater growth during Phase 2. Saunders and colleagues indicate that the addition of schoolwide leadership and structured support—that is, providing specific and explicit protocols focusing on meeting students' learning needs—were essential in building effective teacher teams. They conclude that time to learn to work collaboratively and structured support, in this case from external collaborators, are key elements leading to changes in student learning. They state, "time for collaboration itself, even when administratively supported, is unlikely to improve achievement unless additional conditions are in place that structure its use" (p. 1028). Saunders and colleagues indicate that the nine schools in the study were volunteers and that there is a need for evidence about whether such collaborative work will be successful if mandated by a district or school. They also highlight difficulties that schools might face because of multiple and competing initiatives.

The Saunders and colleagues (2009) study reflects some of the findings of Wood (2007), who analyzes one district's efforts to institute learning communities in its schools. She found that although there were many successes, there were also many difficulties, and district support and leadership is needed if such an initiative is to succeed. In this case study report, Wood, an outside researcher, collected data, including interviews, focus groups, observations, and surveys, over a 2½-year period from educators in an urban district struggling with changing demographics and an achievement gap between middle class and poor students. With support from a foundation, and using a professional development design of the National School Reform Faculty (NRF), the superintendent of the district began her efforts to establish learning communities in five district schools, including three elementary schools, one middle school, and one high school. Wood identifies several factors that limited the effectiveness of learning communities as a means of building capacity. First, many teachers failed to see a connection between their collaborative work and student learning; that is, they enjoyed the community-building efforts, using protocols in group work, but did not delve deeply enough to engage in critical inquiry focused on improving teaching practices. There was also tension created by high-stakes accountability policies that competed with the agendas developed by those leading learning community efforts. Moreover, other curricular or assessment demands, especially those that came from the district, that forced changes in the agendas of the learning communities led participants to question the purpose of these communities. Wood concludes that for learning communities to be effective, "districts must invest greater authority and autonomy in participants as well as adequate time and support" (p. 2).

In sum, although the notion of "professional learning communities" seems to have the potential for changing school culture, teaching practices, and student learning, there is a need for more research about how such initiatives can be successfully established in schools, specifically, what conditions need to exist if they are to be effective. What is clear is that professional learning communities are not a "quick fix" but that establishing them in schools requires structured experiences, a long duration, and effective shared leadership.

CONCLUSIONS

Our work has led us to draw four key points about professional development in the schools.

1. We know a great deal about professional development and have substantial evidence that the most effective professional learning occurs when it is job-embedded, that is, when it relates to what teachers are doing in their classrooms and helps them to understand in more depth the subject they are teaching. Such professional development respects teachers as active learners who recognize the need for ongoing learning for improving instructional practices.

2. Professional development is a journey, not a single event, and it is based on the belief that effective teaching can occur only when there are opportunities for ongoing and active learning. Such professional development calls for teachers who understand and value the opportunity to continue to learn; at the same time, it highlights the need for professional development that is focused on the needs and goals of the schools. Therefore, it requires that school professional development initiatives should be focused and enable teachers to study in depth what they are learning. Too often, the multiple initiatives of schools create confusion and limit teachers' ability to implement with integrity what they are learning.

3. Enabling teachers to actualize what they are learning—that is, to use it in the classrooms—requires ongoing support and feedback, often through coaching or mentoring. Peers can also provide such support informally as they help each other understand the initiative being undertaken.

4. Professional development can be more effective if it occurs in a collaborative culture that emphasizes the importance of teacher as learner and schools as places of learning for both students and teachers.

RECOMMENDATIONS AND FUTURE DIRECTIONS

- There is still much to learn about what type of professional learning works best for whom and in what conditions. We need more information about coaching, how it may differ at elementary versus secondary levels, how structured it should be, and so forth. We also need additional information about the ways that technology can be helpful in promoting teacher learning in a cost-efficient and effective manner.

- We must continue to evaluate the professional development efforts that occur in schools. Although funded projects often require an evaluation component, schools and/or districts that implement professional development initiatives should also consider ways that they can evaluate the impact of these efforts. Such evaluative efforts can provide the information that schools need to better guide their school change or reform efforts; moreover, it will help them answer questions of accountability often asked of school personnel. Guskey's (2000) five-level model for evaluating professional development can be a helpful tool for those responsible for evaluation efforts. The model is one that is arranged hierarchically, from simple to more complex, and generally success at one level is necessary for success at the following levels. The five critical levels include: participants' reactions, participants' learning, organizational support and change, participants' use of new knowledge and skills, and student learning outcomes.

- There is a need for more rigorous and empirical research about professional development. Such research should address significant questions about the impact of professional development models on teacher practices and student learning. Longitudinal research on changes over time can provide important information about the impact of professional development.

QUESTIONS FOR DISCUSSION

1. How do the standards for student learning, developed at the state or district level, influence the professional learning experiences of teachers in a school? What supports are necessary from the state or district to enhance such professional development?

2. The chapter describes three specific research-based collaborative strategies for professional development. Which model(s) would be a "best fit" for the school where you work? What would be the barriers to implementation?

3. The theme of collaboration is highlighted throughout this chapter. What are the barriers to such collaboration in your school and how might you address them?

REFERENCES

Allen, J. (2006). *Becoming a literacy leader.* Portland, ME: Stenhouse.

American Educational Research Association. (2005). Teaching teachers: Professional development to improve student achievement. Retrieved from *www.aera.net/Publications/ResearchPoints/tabid/10234.*

American Speech–Language–Hearing Association. (2010). Roles and responsibilities of speech–language pathologists in schools. Retrieved from *www.asha.org/policy/PI2010-00317.*

Anders, P., Hoffman, J., & Duffy, G. (2000). Teaching teachers to teach reading: Paradigm shifts, persistent problems, and challenges. In M. Kamil, P. Mosenthal, P. D. Pearson, & R. Barr (Eds.), *Handbook of reading research* (Vol. 3, pp. 721-744). Mahwah, NJ: Erlbaum.

Barber, M., & Mourshed, M. (2007). *How the world's best-performing school systems come out on top.* London: McKinsey.

Bean, R. M., & Swan Dagen, A. (2012). Schools as places of learning: The powerful role of literacy leaders. In R. M. Bean & A. Swan Dagen (Eds.), *Best practices of literacy leaders: Keys to school improvement* (pp. 355–378). New York: Guilford Press.

Beck, I. L., & McKeown, M. G. (2006). *Improving comprehension with Questioning the Author: A fresh and expanded view of a powerful approach.* New York: Scholastic.

Biancarosa, G., Bryk, A. S., & Dexter, E. (2010). Assessing the value-added effects of Literacy Collaborative professional development on student learning. *Elementary School Journal, 111*(1), 7-34.

Blank, R. K., & de las Alas, N. (2009, June). *Effects of teacher professional development on gains in student achievement: How meta-analysis provides scientific evidence useful to education leaders.* Washington, DC: Council of Chief State School Officers.

Bryk, A. S., Sebring, P. B., Allensworth, E., Luppescu, S., & Easton, J. Q. (2010). *Organizing schools for improvement: Lessons from Chicago.* Chicago: University of Chicago.

Colbert, J., Brown, R., Choi, S., & Thomas, S. (2008). An investigation of the impacts of teacher-driven professional development on pedagogy and student learning. *Teacher Education Quarterly, 35*(2), 135-154.

Collins, J. (2001). *Good to great: Why some companies make the leap...and others don't.* New York: HarperCollins.

Council for Exceptional Children. (2009). *What every special educator must know: Ethics, standards, and guidelines for special education.* Arlington, VA: Author.

Crowther, F., Ferguson, M., & Hann, L. (2009). *Developing teacher leaders: How teacher leadership enhances school success* (2nd ed.). Thousand Oaks, CA: Corwin Press.

Danielson, C. (1998). *Teacher leadership that strengthens professional practice.* Alexandria, VA: ASCD.

Danielson, C. (2007). The many faces of leadership. *Educational Leadership, 65*(1), 14–19.

Darling-Hammond, L., Wei, R. C., Andree, A., Richardson, N., & Orphanos, S. (2009). *Professional learning in the learning profession: A status report on teacher development in the United States and abroad.* Palo Alto, CA: Stanford University.

Dearman, C., & Alber, S. (2005). The challenging face of education: Teachers cope with challenges through collaboration and reflective study. *Reading Teacher, 58*(7), 634–639.

Desimone, L., Porter, A. C., Garet, M., Yoon, K. S., & Birman, B. (2002). Effects of professional development on teachers' instruction: Results from a three-year study. *Educational Evaluation and Policy Analysis, 24*(2), 81–112.

Dillon, D. R., O'Brien, D. G., Sato, M., & Kelly, C. M. (2011). Professional development and teacher education for reading instruction. In M. Kamil, D. Pearson, E. Birr Moje, & P. Afflerbach (Eds.), *Handbook of reading research* (pp. 629–660). New York: Routledge.

Donaldson, G., (2006). *Cultivating leadership in schools: Connecting people, purpose, and practice.* New York: Teachers College Press.

DuFour, R. (2004). What is a professional learning community? *Educational Leadership, 61*(8), 6–11.

Fuchs, D., & Fuchs, L. (2001). One blueprint for bridging the gap: Project practice. *Teacher Education and Special Education, 24,* 304–314.

Fullan, M., & Hargreaves, A. (1996). *What's worth fighting for in your school?* (2nd ed.). New York: Teachers College Press.

Garet, M. S., Cronen, S., Eaton, M., Kurki, A., Ludwig, M., Jones, W., et al. (2008). *The impact of two professional development interventions on early reading instruction and achievement* (NCEE 2008-4030). Washington, DC: National Center for Educational Evaluation and Regional Assistance, Institute of Education Sciences.

Gentry, L. B., Denton, C. A., & Kurz, T. (2008).Technologically-based mentoring provided to teachers: A synthesis of the literature. *Journal of Technology and Teacher Education, 16*(3), 339–373.

Greenwood, C., & Maheady, L. (2001). Are future teachers aware of the gap between research and practice and what should they know? *Teacher Education and Special Education, 24,* 333–347.

Guskey, T. (2000). *Evaluating professional development.* Thousand Oaks, CA: Corwin Press.

Hunzicker, J. (2012). Professional development and job-embedded collaboration: How teachers learn to exercise leadership. *Professional Development in Education, 38*(2), 267–289.

International Reading Association. (2010). *Standards for reading professionals: A reference for the preparation of educators in the United States.* Newark, DE: International Reading Association.

Interstate Teacher Assessment and Support Consortium. (2011). *Model core teaching standards.* Washington, DC: Council of Chief State School Officers. Retrieved from *www.ccsso.org.*

Jaquith, A., Mindich, D., Wei, R. C., & Darling-Hammond, L. (2010). *Teacher professional learning in the U.S.: Case studies of state policies and strategies: Summary report.* Dallas, TX: Learning Forward and Stanford University. Retrieved from *www.learningforward.org.*

Joyce, B., & Showers, B. (2002). *Student achievement through staff development* (3rd ed.). Alexandria, VA: ASCD.

Katzenmeyer, M., & Moller, G. (2009). *Awaking the sleeping giant: Helping teachers develop as leaders* (3rd ed.). Thousand Oaks, CA: Corwin Press.

Kennedy, E., & Shiel, G. (2010). Raising literacy levels with collaborative on-site professional development in an urban disadvantaged school. *Reading Teacher, 63*(5), 372–383.

Lambert, L. (2003). *Leadership capacity for lasting school improvement.* Alexandria, VA: ASCD.

Leana, C. (2010). Social capital: The collective component of teaching quality. *Voices in Urban Education, 27*, 16–23.

Leana, C., & Pil, F. K. (2006). Social capital and organizational performance. *Organization Science, 17*(3), 353–366.

Learning Forward. (2011). Standards for professional learning. Retrieved from *www.learningforward.org/standards#.UlQkcvvD85v.*

Lieberman, A., & Wood, D. R. (2002). *Inside the National Writing Project: Connecting network learning and classroom teaching.* New York: Teachers College Press.

Little, J. (1990). The persistence of privacy: Autonomy and initiative in teachers' professional relations. *Teachers College Record, 91*(4), 509–536.

Marzano, R. J. (2003). *What works in schools.* Alexandria, VA: ASCD.

Matsumura, L. C., Garnier, H. E., Correnti, R., Junker, B., & Bickel, D. D. (2010). Investigating the effectiveness of a comprehensive literacy-coaching program in schools with high teacher mobility. *Elementary School Journal, 111*(1), 35–62.

McKenna, M. C., & Walpole, S. (2008). *The literacy coaching challenge: Models and methods for grades K–8.* New York: Guilford Press.

MetLife Survey of the American Teacher: Collaborating for student success.(2010). Dallas, TX: MetLife.

Mongiello, P., Brady, D., Johnson, G., & Berg, J. (2009). Strength training: Institutes pump up teachers' roles as instructional leaders. *Journal of Staff Development, 30*(4), 20–22.

National Staff Development Council. (2001). *Standards for staff development.* Oxford, OH: Author. Retrieved from *www.nsdc.org.*

Neuman, S. B., & Cunningham, L. (2009). The impact of a practice-based approach to professional development: Coaching makes a difference. *American Educational Research Journal, 46*(2), 532–566.

Neuman, S. B., & Wright, T. (2010). Promoting language and literacy development for early childhood educators: A mixed-methods study of coursework and coaching. *Elementary School Journal, 111*(1), 63–86.

Newmann, F. M. (Ed.). (1996). *Authentic achievement: Restructuring schools for intellectual quality.* San Francisco: Jossey-Bass.

Poekert, P. (2012). Teacher leadership and professional development: Examining links between two concepts central to school improvement. *Professional Development in Education, 38*(2), 169–188.

Saunders, W. M., Goldenberg, C. N., & Gallimore, R. (2009). Increasing achievement by focusing grade-level teams on improving classroom learning: A prospective quasi-experimental study of Title I schools. *American Educational Research Journal, 46*(4), 1006–1033.

Silva, E. (2008). *Measuring skills for the 21st century.* Washington, DC: Education Sector. Retrieved from *www.educationsector.org/usr_doc/MeasuringSkills.pdf.*

Smith, M., & Dickinson, D. (2002). *Early language and literacy classroom observation.* Baltimore: Brookes.

Sparks, D. (2004). Look for ways to ignite the energy within: An interview with Jane Dutton. *Journal of Staff Development, 25*(3), 38–42.

Spillane, J. P. (2005). Distributed leadership. *Educational Forum, 69*, 143–150.

Swan Dagen, A., & Nichols, J. (2012). Teachers as literacy leaders. In R. M. Bean & A. Swan Dagen (Eds.), *Best practices of literacy leaders: Keys to school improvement* (pp. 21–42). New York: Guilford Press.

Teacher Leadership Exploratory Consortium. (2011). Teacher Leader Model Standards

(TLMS). Retrieved from *www.teacherleaderstandards.org/downloads/TLS_Brochure.pdf*.

Vescio, V., Ross, D., & Adams, A. (2008). A review of research on the impact of professional learning communities on teaching practice and student learning. *Teaching and Teacher Education, 24*(1), 80–91.

Walpole, S. & McKenna, M. (2009). Everything you've always wanted to know about literacy coaching but were afraid to ask: A review of policy and research. In K. Leander, D. Rowe, D. Dickinson, M. Hundley, R. Jimenez, & V. J. Risko (Eds.), *58th yearbook of the National Reading Conference* (pp. 23–33). Oak Creek, WI: National Reading Conference.

Wei, R., Darling-Hammond, L., Andree, A., Richardson, N., & Orphanos, S. (2009). *Professional learning in the learning profession: A status report on teacher development in the United States and abroad.* Dallas, TX: National Staff Development Council. Retrieved from *www.learningforward.org*.

Wei, R. C., Darling-Hammond, L., & Adamson, F. (2010*). Professional development in the United States: Trends and challenges.* Dallas, TX: National Staff Development Council. Retrieved from *www.learningforward.org*.

West, L., & Staub, F. C. (2003). *Content-focused coaching: Transforming mathematics lessons.* Portsmouth, ME: Heinemann.

Wood, D. (2007). Teachers' learning communities: Catalyst for change or a new infrastructure for the status quo? *Teachers College Record.* Retrieved from *www.tecrecord.org/PrintContent.asp?ContentID=12829*.

Yoon, K. S., Duncan, T., Lee, S. W.-Y., Scarloss, B., & Shapley, K. (2007). *Reviewing the evidence on how teacher professional development affects student achievement* (Issues & Answers Report No. REL 2007-NO. 033). Washington, DC: U.S. Department of Education. Retrieved from *ies.ed.gov/ncess/edlabs*.

York-Barr, J., & Duke, K. (2004). What do we know about teacher leadership? Findings from two decades of scholarship. *Review of Educational Research, 74*(3), 255–231.

PART II

THE COMPLEXITY OF PROFESSIONAL DEVELOPMENT IN TODAY'S SCHOOLS

Twenty years ago, professional development was a moment in time . . . static, not fluid. It was embedded in a workshop you attended or a packaged program that was delivered to you. Today, facing increased demands for accountability with fewer financial resources, teachers must embrace professional development in order to stay current, informed, and renewed. We must also be realistic about the challenges our students face, waiting for their interests to be piqued, their talents to be identified, and their learning to be engaging. We owe them that much!

—MELANIE S. BEAVER
Seventh-grade language arts teacher
West Vigo Middle School
Terre Haute, Indiana

CHAPTER 4

Shaping the Contours
of Professional Development, PreK–12
Successful Models and Practices

D. Ray Reutzel
Sarah K. Clark

- All professions assert that continuous professional learning is key in increasing the practitioner's knowledge and performance.
- Reform movements over the past several decades have adopted a "social efficiency" view of the purposes, values, and outcomes of U.S. education.
- All professions have suffered, to one degree or another, from an inability to secure practitioner compliance with evidence-based practices.
- Assuming that educational practitioners are knowledgeable about evidence-based practices appears unwarranted and unwise, especially in the implementation of the Common Core State Standards.
- Standards and tests are poor substitutes for rich, coherently designed curricula that specify content and skill-based learning sequences sufficiently well to inform the nature of lessons to be developed and taught by educational practitioners.

A standard assertion made in many professions, that professional capacity improves when practitioners add to their knowledge and skills, is not new. Professional development in the education profession, however, is a relative newcomer, emerging principally in the latter part of the late 20th century (Roskos & Vukelich, 1998; Sykes, 1999). Professional development is the means by which teachers receive continuing education to update and refine the knowledge and skills they acquired in their initial training. The ostensible purpose, then, of professional development is to help teachers to remain current in their knowledge, as well as to increase the effectiveness of their instructional practices. As with other professionals, it is expected that teachers will pursue continuing education to update and refine their knowledge and skills in ways that will result in an increase in student motivation and achievement in schools.

In the educational community, the term "professional development" has been used to describe a wide variety of activities, such as teacher induction, university credit for courses/degrees, workshops, conferences, and observational teaching visits (Wei, Darling-Hammond, Andree, Richardson, & Orphanos, 2009). Professional development activities, however, have been criticized for their cost, vague purposes, and lack of meaningful data to justify continuation or implementation of further professional development pursuits. Thus, in many contemporary circles, the term "professional development" has become passé at best or closely associated with inadequate outcomes at worst. It has been largely replaced by the less pejorative term "professional learning." What has led to the current skepticism about past claims made for professional development? To answer this question, one must delve into the historic forces, including legislative and business influences, that have shaped the current contours of professional development in education.

EDUCATIONAL REFORM IN RECENT U.S. HISTORY

In the 1980s, President Ronald Reagan's Secretary of Education Terrell Bell commissioned a blue-ribbon panel to examine the status of U.S. education. This panel issued a widely disseminated report titled *A Nation at Risk* (National Commission on Excellence in Education, 1983). In this report, the status of education in the United States was found to be at risk—equated with a threat to national security. The report ominously warned:

> The people of the United States need to know that individuals in our society who do not possess the levels of skill, literacy, and training essential to this new era will be effectively disenfranchised, not simply from the material rewards that accompany competent performance, but also from the chance to fully participate in our national life. (National Commission on Excellence in Education, 1983, p. 2)

Public suspicion resulting from the publication of *A Nation at Risk* began to call into question the credibility of the U.S. education establishment. Based on a model of social efficiency, concerns among corporate and government officials began to surface about the ability of the education community to rise to the challenge of fixing what was perceived as a system in dire need of reform. As a result of this report, many recommendations were made to improve teacher quality and ultimately the educational system. Though not fully implemented, some of these recommendations included higher standards for teacher preparation programs, competitive teacher salaries, 11-month salaries to allow for more curriculum and professional development, career ladders to reward teachers based on experience and skill, and mentoring and induction programs for beginning teachers. Clearly, the emphasis of school reform at this stage was centered on improving teacher quality and teacher development.

In the early 1990s, George H. W. Bush and William Jefferson Clinton met at the University of Virginia, along with other governors of U.S. states, to discuss national goals in anticipation of the upcoming millennial year, 2000 (Sweet, 2004). One of the most enduring outcomes of this meeting was the finding that third-grade reading scores were among the best predictors for planning future prison facilities into the next millennium. As Fielding, Kerr, and Rosier (1998) explained:

> The most expensive burden we place on society is those students we have failed to teach to read well. The silent army of low readers who move through our schools, siphoning off the lion's share of administrative resources, emerge into society as adults lacking the single prerequisite for managing their lives and acquiring additional training. They are chronically unemployed, underemployed, or unemployable. They form the single largest identifiable group of those whom we incarcerate, and to whom we provide assistance, housing, medical care, and other social services. They perpetuate and enlarge the problem by creating another generation of poor readers. (pp. 6–7)

As a result, the ability to read and read well became a powerful "tool" for measuring the success of schools and a means to achieve national economic and social goals. In fact, teaching students to read was seen as a remedy for curing a host of social and economic ills. Adding to this the number of those who have the ability to read but choose not to (called *aliteracy*), the size and scope of the problems associated with reading failure were only some of several examples of educational failure shaping the educational reform agenda of the past three decades.

After his inauguration as U.S. President in 1994, President Clinton led the effort to operationalize the plans of the National Governors Convention as embodied in national legislation called the Goals 2000: Educate America Act (1994). In addition, President Clinton not only strongly supported and urged implementation of a nationwide testing program in reading and mathematics to assess whether the nation's goals of improved education were being reached but also requested and received from Congress increased funding for professional development for educators. Simultaneous with these other educational reforms, the Congressionally funded National Assessment of Educational Progress (NAEP, 1995) released its reading report card showing that a statistically significant decline in fourth-grade reading scores had occurred across the nation. Teachers were encouraged to seek local professional development opportunities to better understand how to prepare students to perform well on the NAEP assessment, but efforts to provide meaningful professional development activities were not addressed. School reform at this point was centered on assessment (Ravitch, 2010).

By the mid-1990s, public opinion and policymakers in Washington, D.C., had determined that educational reform was no longer a luxury to be managed by the educational establishment but rather a social and economic necessity that would only succeed with external intervention. Fortunately or unfortunately, government leaders and global corporations had finally come to recognize the power of education to transform lives, address social maladies, and bolster sagging economies. As such, education reform had become a tremendously powerful and popular political tool in the hands of federal and state governments. Add to this scenario the complaints of many corporate leaders that workers entering the marketplace were unprepared to successfully engage in a range of increasingly complex, technologically based job-related tasks required in a rapidly changing and increasingly competitive national and global economy (Friedman, 1999). Taken together, the conditions in the mid-1990s led to a perfect storm of national legislative actions aimed at dramatically reforming the educational system.

At or near the same time, research studies began to highlight the importance of the quality of the teacher in the classroom. For example, several studies showed that the quality of the classroom teacher had more impact on student performance than did class size (Hanushek & Rivikin, 2010; Sanders & Horn, 1994; Sanders & Rivers, 1996). In fact, Sanders and Rivers (1996) found that teacher effects were long term, showing that students who had high-quality teachers several years in a row demonstrated greater achievement gains than did those students who were assigned to less effective teachers. Clearly, the data were indicating that teacher quality *did* matter and that teachers *do* make a difference in and have an impact on the academic outcomes of their students.

These findings led to the inevitable question, "Isn't every child deserving of a highly qualified teacher?" The answer was—of course! Yet study after study continued to find that students living in poverty were more likely to be taught by the least prepared and least qualified teachers (Darling-Hammond, 1996; Darling-Hammond & Sykes, 2003; Hanushek, 2010; Peske & Haycock, 2006). For example, it was found that African American students were almost two times more likely than others to be assigned to the least qualified teachers (Sanders & Rivers, 1996).

After the election of George W. Bush in 2000, educational reform policy already well ensconced in bipartisan efforts within the U.S. Congress was furthered with the passage of Senator Edward Kennedy's and President Bush's joint efforts to reauthorize the Elementary and Secondary Education Act of 1964 into the sweeping legislative reform of public education known as No Child Left Behind (2002). The No Child Left Behind (NCLB) legislation passed with one of the largest bipartisan affirmative vote margins on record since 1964. This federal intervention into state and local education provided significant funds to states, along with a long menu of unfunded mandates, to cement the educational reforms begun in the mid- to late 1990s.

After the passage of NCLB, factions within and external to the education community seized on this new legislation as an unwelcome federal intrusion into states' rights. Adversaries of the law cited the fact that all functions of government not expressly assigned to the federal government in the U.S. Constitution were to be left to the states, and this most certainly included education policy. NCLB defined professional development activities funded in this law as not to be "one-day or short-term workshops or conferences." Nested within Part B of NCLB (2002), a multibillion-dollar test of professional development known as Reading First was funded for K–3 reading teachers in low-achieving, high-poverty schools. Reading First was to be a particularly potent form of professional development cemented in the educational reforms passed in NCLB (2002; see Figure 4.1). As a result of these efforts, teachers in many of the schools with the greatest proportions of minority, limited English proficient, and low-income students reported significantly higher rates of participation in professional development activities (Wei et al., 2009).

As time went on, the Reading First program was tainted by the scandalous actions of specific individuals operating within the U.S. Department of Education, as revealed in a report of the Office of the Inspector General (2006; Stern, 2008). In 2008, after years of mixed implementation effectiveness across the nation and billions of tax dollars expended, the Institute of Education Sciences, the research division of the U.S. Department of Education, issued a report showing that students attending schools in Reading First reform programs performed no better on a standardized, norm-referenced subtest of reading comprehension than did students who were not attending Reading First schools (Gamse, Jacob, Horst, Boulay, & Unlu, 2008). As a consequence, funds to support Reading First and efforts to provide professional development to classroom teachers of students in high-poverty, low-performing schools were canceled in the U.S. Congress.

In 2005, Friedman's book *The World Is Flat: A Brief History of the 21st Century* soon became recognized as the most influential case made since *A Nation at Risk* (National Commission on Excellence in Education, 1983) for school reform. Friedman's book declared that the United States no longer had privileged status in the global economy and that the economic playing field had been flattened through the convergence of technologies, new ways of doing business, and the removal of economic and political barriers (Petrilli, 2006). Friedman (2005) put reforming of the educational system in the crosshairs, claiming that U.S. schoolchildren were no

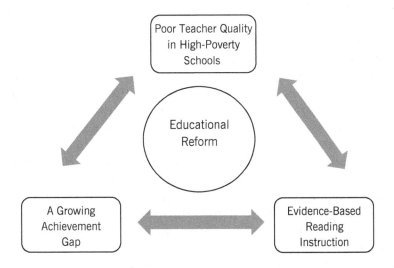

FIGURE 4.1. Three forces driving current educational reforms.

longer competitive on international tests of reading, math, and science. Friedman reported that 44% of the eighth graders in Singapore, 38% of the eighth graders in Taiwan, and only 7% of the eighth graders in the United States scored at the most advanced levels of mathematics. Simply stated, Friedman asserted that teachers in the United States were preparing students for jobs that were irrelevant and/or disappearing.

The events of the historic presidential election of 2008 swept Barack Obama's change agenda into the White House and into the halls of political power. But in terms of any hope for real change in the utilitarian, social efficiency view of education as a means to solve pragmatic, social, and economic problems in the United States, nothing was forthcoming. To illustrate the point that education is continuing to be seen as an economic tool, we use the words of President Obama as he described the achievement gap in education as "morally unacceptable and economically untenable" (Darling-Hammond, 2010, p. 3).

Under the leadership of Obama's U.S. Secretary of Education, Arne Duncan, educational reforms have pitted state against state in a rigorous competition for new funds attached to a federal initiative called Race to the Top. In order to receive funding from this federal initiative, states must submit an educational reform plan that includes state takeover of failing local schools, reconstitution of the failing schools' administrations and faculties, increased testing and accountability, and longitudinal databases used to ensure that teachers are effectively preparing students for competition in a global economy (Brill, 2011; Friedman, 2005; Friedman & Mandelbaum, 2011). Thus education reform continues to be viewed by policymakers as a powerful political and economic tool in a race to economic supremacy and international competitiveness.

Under the direction of the Council of Chief State School Officers and the National Governors Association, efforts to spearhead broad education reforms with a renewed emphasis on raising standards and expectations to ensure that U.S. schoolchildren are college and career ready by the time they graduate from high school were initiated at the state level. In July 2009, representatives from higher education, K–12, and the research community began work on creating a set of standards in mathematics and English language arts. Feedback was sought from a wide variety of educators, business, and community members. By June 2010, the final version of the Common Core State Standards (CCSS) was released with the hopes that they would raise standards, contribute to curricular alignment across state boundaries, revise assessment practices, and inform parents about the knowledge and skills necessary for their students to succeed. But once again, the federal government intruded into what was initially a state process. Using the carrot of federal funds, states were given incentives to adopt the CCSS standards in order to effectively compete for federal Race to the Top grants. To date, 45 of the 50 states have adopted the CCSS and have aligned themselves with two major consortiums funded by federal dollars to design new assessments to measure student achievement of the CCSS.

Thus we see that educational reform in the United States continues to be viewed by policymakers as serving a utilitarian, socially efficient purpose that promotes education primarily as a potent political and economic tool in a no-holds-barred race toward economic supremacy and international competitiveness. Furthermore, these more recent educational reform efforts, either intentionally or unintentionally, no longer emphasized or supported the role of professional development as an integral part of school reform, but rather focused on establishing national standards and the development of new assessments to determine whether schools, teachers, and students were achieving the lofty new goals associated with the adoption of the CCSS by 90% of the states in the United States as of this writing.

FUTURE DIRECTIONS: CAVEATS AND RECOMMENDATIONS FOR PROFESSIONAL LEARNING IN EDUCATION

As scholars, journalists, corporate executives, and policymakers continue to decry the failures of public education to adequately prepare U.S. students for a global economy that is increasingly competitive, the crucial role that professional learning can play in the eventual success or failure of U.S. education reform becomes equally apparent. In reality, education reform in its most basic form *is* professional learning. Yet the concept of professional learning in the education community continues to be marred with missteps and misunderstandings. In this section, we discuss several caveats that should give pause to those engaged in planning for and providing professional learning in the second decade of the 21st century.

Caveat 1: Standards and Accountability Are Necessary but Insufficient Educational Reforms

Diane Ravitch (2010), in *The Death and Life of the Great American School System: How Testing and Choice are Undermining Education*, laments the use of standards to drive the construction of new testing systems without first putting into place carefully developed, coherent, and rich curricula to support the teaching of new standards. Ravitch writes, "Tests should follow the curriculum. They should be based on the curriculum. They should not replace it or precede it" (p. 16). Ravitch warns that "we should attend to the quality of the curriculum—that is, what is taught. Every school should have a well-conceived, coherent, sequential curriculum. A curriculum is not a script but a set of general guidelines. . . . The curriculum is the starting place for other reforms" (p. 231).

Other nations' educational systems, to which that of the United States is often compared, have diligently labored to develop excellent curricula that specify the progressions of what students are supposed to be learning. Standards are not curriculum. Tests are not curriculum. A curriculum is intended to specify not only what is taught but also the sequence of what is taught along a clearly demarcated pathway of learning development or progressions from simple to complex. For example, a quality curriculum answers such questions as, What does mastering the skill of *getting the main idea* look like when progressing from reading easy to complex texts? Or, What does mastering the ability to solve word problems look like when progressing from performing simple to complex mathematical functions? An understanding of the learning progressions needed to adequately support student learning is needed by classroom teachers in order to teach to achieve the new standards and to help students successfully pass new tests on these standards. These aspects of a high-quality curriculum are missing from the recent reform efforts associated with the CCSS. Put rather bluntly, classroom teachers will need significant ongoing professional development within the context of a professional learning community to acquire new knowledge, develop curricula, design and refine lessons, diligently apply evidence-based practices, and study student data obtained from performance assessments to ultimately succeed in their assigned duties to prepare a career- and college-ready group of high school graduates to meet the new standards.

In order to measure the effectiveness of professional learning activities and the influence they have on student achievement, a well-established curriculum is essential. It is the bridge between what teachers do and what students need to learn. Therefore, it is recommended that school leaders take the time to determine what the CCSS intend as far as specific objectives and learning processes. Most of this work will likely take place locally in professional learning communities (PLCs) in schools. Over the past decade, educators have looked to PLCs as the best place for these types of discussions and trainings to occur. As the newest form of professional learning, PLCs are intended to build upon teachers' knowledge and skills in a collaborative environment (Chappuis, Chappuis, & Stiggins, 2009). In order to be optimally effective, however, PLCs need to be structured in ways that utilize the extant evidence and elements of effective professional learning activities for teachers. In a recent review of effective elements of professional learning, Desimone (2009) noted that professional learning needs to focus on using active learning and collective participation to learn content. Research has also indicated that professional learning is effective only when it occurs over an extended period of time and is sharply focused on learning subject matter content and on acquiring the content pedagogical knowledge needed to meet the diverse needs of today's students (Dopplet, Schunn, Silk, Mehalik, Reynolds, & Ward, 2009; Yoon, Duncan, Lee, Scarloss, & Shapley, 2007).

Caveat 2: The Unwarranted Assumption of Adequate Teacher Knowledge

The significance of the teacher's specialized knowledge about effective instruction must not be underestimated. Research indicates that teachers' content, or subject-matter, knowledge has potential to influence their instructional decisions, such as the extent to which certain concepts are taught and mastered or which concepts are deemed as irrelevant and are eliminated from the curriculum, as well as which materials are selected for instruction (Kolis & Dunlap, 2004; Valencia, Place, Martin, & Grossman, 2006). But for schoolteachers, the amount of knowledge necessary to adequately instruct their students has grown exponentially. Darling-Hammond (2010) states:

Knowledge is expanding at a breathtaking pace. It is estimated that five exabytes, equivalent to five quintillion bytes, of new information (500,000 times the volume of the Library of Congress print collection) was generated in 2002, more than three times as much as in 1999. Indeed, in the 3 years from 1999 to 2002, the amount of new information produced nearly equaled the amount produced in the entire history of the world previously. (p. 4)

Although most want to honor the knowledge, skills, and professionalism of our teachers, we cannot afford to stick our heads into the proverbial sand with respect to how much and how complex the knowledge is that the typical schoolteacher must have to be effective in preparing students for a brave new, unknown, world.

In Gawande's book *The Checklist Manifesto: How to Get Things Right* (2009), he tells the story of the failed maiden flight of Boeing's legendary B-17 bomber in World War II. After the fiery demise of this first flight, an investigation into the causes of the crash yielded a startling finding. The new Boeing bomber was deemed by one newspaper as "too much airplane for one man to fly." The work of today's teachers seems to have entered its own B-17 bomber phase. In other words, in multiple fields, including education, the job has become too much airplane for one man or individual to fly. Gawande notes that in many fields, today's jobs have become so complex that increasing specialization is the necessary outcome. So, to illustrate this caveat, we highlight the case for the depth of teacher knowledge needed to teach the most foundational skill of all learning—reading.

Strickland, Snow, Griffin, Burns, and McNamara (2002) found that typical primary-grade teachers took an average of 1.3 courses in the teaching of reading as preservice teacher candidates, with a recent survey indicating a slight increase to 2.2 courses. These researchers state: "Even with the slight increase, the total time spent on preparing to teach reading is entirely inadequate" (p. 21). The situation is no better for inservice teachers. Somewhere between a one-quarter and one-third of inservice teachers are receiving professional development in effective, evidence-based reading instruction in "one-shot" sessions. And we know that this type of professional development is not highly effective. The effects of the economic recession beginning in 2007 have also resulted in massive budget cuts in educational funding across the nation. These budget cuts have, in turn, radically reduced the amount of professional learning available in the teaching of reading for almost all inservice teachers in recent years at a time when teacher knowledge and effectiveness is coming under increasing scrutiny.

In the movie and book *Waiting for "Superman,"* Eric Hanushek (2010) notes that some teachers are simply much more knowledgeable, skilled, and effective than others. The magnitude of the differences among teachers in effectiveness is quite simply stunning. In a single academic year, an effective teacher will get 1.5 years of grade-level growth from students, whereas a less effective teacher will get only 0.5 years of grade-level-equivalent growth (Hanushek, 2010). In fact, Hanushek explains that the differences among teacher effectiveness *within* schools are much greater than the differences *between* schools. Without opportunities for professional learning, both at the preservice and inservice levels of teaching, to ensure that teachers have access to current knowledge about evidence-based teaching practices and expanding content knowledge across a wide variety of disciplines taught in the nation's elementary and secondary schools, continued failure of the system seems quite likely. As Friedman and Mandelbaum (2011, pp. 79–80) explain, "So this is the world we are in. This is where every conversation about how we must fix our economy and transform our schools has to start.... There is only one way to square this circle: more innovation powered by better education for every American," including our teachers. Thus professional learning for teachers is seen as a vital ingredient in reducing national achievement and international competition gaps.

Darling-Hammond and Rothman (2011) provide three specific recommendations on the topic of ensuring that teachers are better trained and equipped through professional learning to meet the challenges in today's classrooms. First, they recommend cutting the amount of time novice teachers spend in instruction during their first few years of teaching. For example, teachers in Finland spend only 60% of the time that U.S. teachers spend teaching students. This allows more time during the day to consult with and learn from other teachers, to meet with students and parents, and to plan and discuss lessons. Second, they recommend systematic approaches to ongoing professional learning. In Singapore, Darling-Hammond and Rothman found that teachers are guaranteed up to 20 hours a week in ongoing training and professional learning activities. Finally, teachers continue to be trained and are taught to create their own evidence of success. Teachers in Finland are encouraged to seek graduate degrees, whereas teachers in Singapore are trained in lesson study and action research to further develop their teaching skills. These systematic reforms move teachers from isolated practitioners in a single classroom to groups or teams working together to improve student learning. Moreover, these recommended reforms provide teachers with necessary knowledge and support to diligently implement evidence-based teaching practices into their instruction.

Mentoring and induction-related professional learning activities are yet another way to boost the knowledge and ongoing professional learning that teachers need. Feiman-Nemser (2001) explains that "new teachers have two jobs—they have to teach, and they have to learn to teach. No matter how good a preservice program may be, there are some things that can only be learned on the job" (p. 1026). Collaboration is important for educators, and it allows for camaraderie and synergy. Wong, Britton, and Ganser (2005) explain that a variety of activities should be considered when establishing collaborative experiences, including lesson observations, teaching demonstrations, discussions among colleagues, and feedback with constructive critique.

Kouzes and Posner's (2008) work on transformational leadership highlights the critical role that local school leaders play in ensuring that teachers receive adequate mentoring and support. Transformational leadership requires leaders who are willing to remove roadblocks that often prevent these professional development interactions. They also describe those transformational school leaders as those individuals with the ability to "enable others to act." A school administrator can organize and create the school structures necessary for teacher learning to occur.

Effective school leaders understand the long-term benefits associated with investing both time and resources in their teachers and supporting instructional staff. Local school administrators can also play a significant role in resolving many of the challenges inherent in learning to teach and, by so doing, can stave off the chronic problem of teacher attrition (Ingersoll, 2002).

Though the practice of teaching is not new, the context wherein teaching occurs continues to rapidly evolve. Friedman (2005) articulated the importance of working together in the 21st century. He explained, "We've been here before. Each century, as we push out the frontiers of human knowledge, work at every level becomes more complex, requiring more pattern recognition and problem solving" (pp. 372–373). The more complex the issue, the more leadership is needed to ensure that individuals join together to share knowledge and to create solutions.

Caveat 3: The Universal Problem of Practitioner Compliance

One of the most perplexing and pernicious pitfalls that professional development in the 21st century must address is the perpetual problem of practitioner compliance. When provided with evidence of best practices, do teachers comply? When teachers receive training and professional learning opportunities, do they in turn use this information to change teaching practices? We turn, for an illustration of the problem of practitioner compliance, not to education, but rather to medicine. In 1847, long before the discovery of germs, Dr. Ignaac Semmelweis introduced hand washing with chlorinated lime solutions to address the unusually high incidences of puerperal fever, childbirth fever, in a Vienna, Austria, hospital. The introduction of this effective practice immediately reduced the incidence of fatal puerperal fever from 10 to 1–2%. Many years later, in the 21st century, no one disputes the efficacy of hand washing in stopping the spread of infectious disease.

Atul Gawande's (2007) book *Better: A Surgeon's Notes on Performance* reports a study of his hospital's infectious-disease control team whose full-time job it was to control the spread of infectious disease. The focus of this study was on the well-established and evidence-based practice of hand washing and the continuing failure to get modern-day medical practitioners to adequately disinfect their hands. The disease control team tried everything. They repositioned sinks and had new ones installed. They bought $5,000 "precaution carts" to make washing, gloving, and gowning easy and efficient. They posted admonishing signs and issued hygiene "report cards." They even gave away free movie tickets as an incentive for cleaning up. Nothing worked!

Gawande (2007) laments:

> Compliance rates for proper hand hygiene improved substantially from 40 percent to around 70 percent. But—and this is the troubling finding—hospital infection rates did not drop one iota. Our 70 percent compliance just wasn't good enough. If 30 percent of the time people didn't wash their hands, that still left plenty of opportunity to keep transmitting infections. Indeed, rates of resistant Staphylococcus and Enterococcus infections continued to rise. (p. 19)

In the end, this meant that doctors and nurses washed their hands about one-third to one-half as often as they should. What should be the "take away" message for reform-minded educators and professional developers from this study of medical practitioners? The issue of practitioner compliance in education, like medicine, suggests that the difficult problem of getting educational practitioners to apply evidence-based practices diligently in their teaching practice must be addressed. Failure to overcome this known pitfall will most likely result in continuing decreases in the value of and support for professional learning opportunities.

In order to successfully address the concern regarding practitioner compliance in education, one must first understand to what the practitioner is expected to be compliant. This is especially important in any professional learning context. Guskey and Yoon (2009) explain:

> Practitioners at all levels must demand better evidence from consultants and purveyors of new strategies and practices. Stories about what happened at one time in a single school or district may be interesting, but they do not justify broader implementation. (p. 498)

Guskey and Yoon further recommend that educators avoid the phrase, "Research says..." as justification or credibility for any program or training. The federal government has attempted to address these misconceptions about what are considered empirically valid practices through the What Works Clearinghouse (*http://ies. ed.gov/ncee/wwc/*) sponsored by the Institute of Education Sciences. Although this website is a great starting place, Guskey and Yoon also recommend that educators and administrators make a concerted effort to ensure that any professional learning activities that are initiated in their schools or districts are measured for their effectiveness. Guskey and Yoon explain: "those responsible for planning and implementing professional development must learn how to critically assess and evaluate the effectiveness of what they do" (p. 500).

FINAL THOUGHTS

In today's complex world, nearly every occupation has become too specialized and complex for any single person to know all he or she needs to know to perform competently, and teaching is no exception. Professional learning opportunities that are long-term, coherently designed, and continuously assessed to ensure practitioner compliance hold the key to successful implementation of new and higher standards. If our students are to become globally competitive in their academic and career preparation, then their teachers will require world-class support in learning and applying evidence-based practices and developing team-based problem-solving skills. Continuing failure to provide professional learning support for our nation's teachers will likely lead to further erosion of U.S. student performance. We simply must invest in professional learning for our nation's teachers, including the unambiguous expectation that teachers will diligently comply with use of evidence-based practices, if we expect educational outcomes to significantly improve.

QUESTIONS FOR DISCUSSION

1. Based on the recent history of education reform provided in this chapter, in what ways can education reform emphasize or deemphasize the role of professional learning in schools?

2. Can you think of examples of educational policy that have directly or indirectly influenced professional learning and practice?

3. How can school administrators provide the "transformative leadership" needed to ensure that meaningful professional learning occurs at the local school and classroom levels?

4. What recommendations would you make for administrators and coaches seeking to create the curricula needed to support the CCSS and the subsequent assessment? How would you design professional learning opportunities to support these new curricula and assessments?

5. How can teachers be proactive in the area of practitioner compliance? Identify teacher practices, strategies, and techniques that should be included on a teacher checklist for evidence-based practices in the classroom.

REFERENCES

Brill, S. (2011). *Class warfare: Inside the fight to fix America's schools*. New York: Simon & Schuster.

Chappuis, S., Chappuis, J., & Stiggins, R. (2009). Supporting teacher learning teams. *Educational Leadership, 66*(5), 56–60.

Darling-Hammond, L. (1996). *What matters most: Teaching for America's future*. New York: Columbia University, Teachers College, National Commission on Teaching and America's Future.,

Darling-Hammond, L. (2010). *The flat world and education: How America's commitment to equity will determine our future*. New York: Teachers College Press.

Darling-Hammond, L., & Rothman, R. (Eds.). (2011). *Teacher and leader effectiveness in high-performing education systems*. Washington, DC, and Stanford, CA: Alliance for Excellent Education and Stanford Center for Opportunity Policy in Education.

Darling-Hammond, L., & Sykes, G. (2003). Wanted: A national teacher supply policy for education: The right way to meet the "highly qualified teachers" challenge. *Educational Policy Analysis Archives, 11*(33). Retrieved September 25, 2012, from *http://epaa.asu.edu/epaa/v11n33/*.

Desimone, L. M. (2009). Improving impact studies of teachers' professional development: Toward better conceptualizations and measures. *Educational Researcher, 38*(3), 181–199.

Dopplet, Y., Schunn, C., Silk, E., Mehalik, M., Reynolds, B., & Ward, E. (2009). Evaluating the impact of a facilitated learning community approach to professional development on teacher practice and student achievement. *Research in Science and Technology Education, 27*(3), 339–354.

Feiman-Nemser, S. (2001). Helping novices learn to teach: Lessons from an exemplary support teacher. *Journal of Teacher Education, 52*(1), 17–30.

Fielding, L., Kerr, N., & Rosier, P. (1998). *The 90% reading goal*. Kennewick, WA: New Foundation Press.

Friedman, T. L. (1999). *The lexus and the olive tree.* New York: Farrar, Straus, & Giroux.

Friedman, T. L. (2005). *The world is flat: A brief history of the twenty-first century.* New York: Farrar, Straus, & Giroux.

Friedman, T. L., & Mandelbaum, M. (2011). *That used to be us: How American fell behind in the world it invented and how we can come back.* New York: Farrar, Straus, & Giroux.

Gamse, B. C., Jacob, R. T., Horst, M., Boulay, B., & Unlu, F. (2008). *Reading First Impact Study Final Report* (NCEE 2009-4038). Washington, DC: U.S. Department of Education, Institute of Education Sciences, National Center for Education Evaluation and Regional Assistance. Retrieved from *http://ies.ed.gov/ncee/pubs/20094038.asp.*

Gawande, A. (2007). *Better: A surgeon's notes on performance.* New York: Picador/Henry Holt.

Gawande, A. (2009). *The checklist manifesto: How to get things right.* New York: Metropolitan Books.

Goals 2000: Educate America Act, Pub. L. No. 103-227 (1994).

Guskey, T. R., & Yoon, K. S. (2009). What works in professional development? *Phi Delta Kappan, 90*(7), 495–500.

Hanushek, E. (2010). The difference is great teachers. In K. Weber (Ed.), *Waiting for "Superman": How we can save America's failing public schools* (pp. 81–100). New York: Public Affairs Press.

Hanushek, E. A., & Rivikin, S. G. (2010). Generalizations about using value-added measures of teacher quality. *American Economic Review, 100*(2), 267–271.

Ingersoll, R. (2002). The teacher shortage: A case of wrong diagnosis and wrong prescription. *NASSP Bulletin, 86,* 16–30.

Kolis, M., & Dunlap, W. P. (2004). The knowledge of teaching: The K3P3 model. *Reading Improvement, 42*(2), 97–107.

Kouzes, J. M., & Posner, B. Z. (2008). *The leadership challenge.* San Francisco: Jossey-Bass.

National Assessment of Educational Progress. (1995). *The nation's report card: Fourth-grade reading highlights 1994.* Washington, DC: U.S. Department of Education, National Center for Educational Statistics.

National Commission on Excellence in Education. (1983). *A nation at risk: The imperative for education reform.* Washington, DC: U.S. Department of Education.

No Child Left Behind Act of 2001, 20 U.S.C. § 6319 (2002).

Office of the Inspector General. (2006). *The Reading First program's grant application process: Final inspection report.* Washington, DC: U.S. Department of Education.

Peske, H., & Haycock, K. (2006). *Teaching inequality: How poor and minority students are shortchanged on teacher quality.* Washington, DC: Education Trust.

Petrilli, M. (2006). If the world is flat: Why does American education go in circles? *Education Next, 6*(1), 73.

Ravitch, D. (2010). *The death and life of the great American school system: How testing and choice are undermining education.* New York: Basic Books.

Roskos, K. A., & Vukelich, C. (1998). How do practicing teachers grow and learn as professionals? In S. B. Neuman & K. A. Roskos (Eds.), *Children achieving: Best practices in early literacy* (pp. 250–271). Newark, DE: International Reading Association.

Sanders, W. L., & Horn, S. P. (1994). The Tennessee Value-Added Assessment System (TVAAS): Mixed-model methodology in educational assessment. *Journal of Personnel Evaluation in Education, 8*(3), 299–311.

Sanders, W. L., & Rivers, J. C. (1996). *Cumulative and residual effects of teachers on future academic achievement.* Knoxville: University of Tennessee, Value-Added Research and Assessment Center.

Stern, S. (2008). *Too good to last: The true story of Reading First.* Washington, DC: Thomas B. Fordham Institute.

Strickland, D. S., Snow, C., Griffin, P., Burns, M. S., & McNamara, P. (2002). *Preparing our teachers: Opportunities for better reading instruction.* Washington, DC: John Henry Press.

Sweet, R. W. (2004). The big picture: Where we are nationally on the reading front and how we got here. In P. McCardle & V. Chhabra (Eds.), *The voice of evidence in reading research* (pp. 13–44). Baltimore: Brookes.

Sykes, G. (1999). Introduction: Teaching and learning profession. In L. Darling-Hammond & G. Sykes (Eds.), *Teaching as the learning profession: Handbook of policy and practice* (pp. xv–xxiii). San Francisco: Jossey-Bass.

Valencia, S. W., Place, N. A., Martin, S. D., & Grossman, P. L. (2006). Curriculum materials for elementary reading: Shackles and scaffolds for four beginning teachers. *Elementary School Journal, 107*(1), 93–121.

Wei, R. C., Darling-Hammond, L., Andree, A., Richardson, N., & Orphanos, S. (2009, February). *Professional learning in the learning profession: A status report on teacher development in the United States and abroad: Technical report.* Dallas, TX: NSDC. Retrieved from *www.nsdc.org/stateproflearning.cfm.*

Wong, H. K., Britton, T. & Ganser, T. (2005, January). What the world can teach us about new teacher induction. *Phi Delta Kappan, 86*(5), 379–384.

Yoon, K. S., Duncan, T., Lee, S. W.-Y., Scarloss, B., & Shapley, K. (2007). *Reviewing the evidence on how teacher professional development affects student achievement* (Issues & Answers Report No. REL 2007-No. 033). Retrieved October 8, 2012, from *http://ies. ed.gov/ncee/edlabs/regions/southwest/pdf/REL_2007033.pdf.*

CHAPTER 5

Changing the Relationship between Professional Development Policy and the Practitioner's Role

ANN JAQUITH

- The broad purpose of professional development policy is to improve teaching and learning, but for various reasons policies do not penetrate into classrooms in uniform ways.
- Professional development policies exist at the national, state, and local levels, and these policy environments are multilayered.
- The design of professional development policy has changed over time, as has the way policy researchers have studied the relationship between policymaking and its implementation.
- How a professional development policy actually is implemented in a district and a school has a great deal to do with who the particular implementers (e.g. teachers and administrators) of the policy are and the particular conditions in that school and district. Implementing policy requires learning.
- Local educational leaders—principals and district administrators—have significant influence on how professional development policies are interpreted and enacted in schools and shape to a considerable degree the extent to which professional development policy is able to achieve its intended goals.

This chapter offers a short history of the evolution of implementation policy research and how the field has traditionally conceptualized and studied the impact of professional development policies on practice. I begin with an overview of what professional development policies are, what we have learned thus far from implementation research, and where the field is currently heading. Next, I describe recent changes in the federal, state, and local policy environments and what current research is teaching us about the relationship between policy and practice. A description of the complex and multilayered policy environments in which today's professional development policies are created, interpreted, and then either adopted, adapted, or rejected provides a backdrop for exploring the relationship between recent accountability policies at the federal, state, and local levels and practitioners' implementation of those policies. Recent examples from the research literature provide evidence of new directions that the field is moving in to study and make sense of this complicated relationship between policy, professional development programs, and contexts and their effects on learning. Researchers are beginning to design studies to illuminate how multilayered policy environments intersect. Research that shows how actors of various types, located at different levels of the system, interact with and influence the policy environment in ways that benefit as well as constrain learning are briefly described in this chapter. Studies that illuminate the complexity of policymaking and implementation merit further attention.

WHAT DO WE KNOW ABOUT THE IMPACT OF PROFESSIONAL DEVELOPMENT POLICY ON PRACTICE?

In order to consider the impact of professional development policies on practice, we need to first know the intended purpose of these policies. In broad terms, these policies are intended to improve the quality of teaching and learning in our nation's schools. National, state, and local professional development policies exist. At the national level, professional development policies fall under the Elementary and Secondary Education Act of 1965 (ESEA), which has undergone numerous reauthorizations and in 2001 was reauthorized as the No Child Left Behind Act (NCLB).

NCLB is the largest federally funded education act and has become an important source of funding for school districts. The overall purpose of NCLB is "to ensure that all children have a fair, equal, and significant opportunity to obtain a high-quality education and reach, at a minimum, proficiency on challenging state academic achievement standards and state academic assessments" (No Child Left Behind Act, 2002). Policy levers are embedded in NCLB, such as the use of achievement standards aligned to a state system of assessments, the expected use of "scientifically based instructional strategies" intended to improve teaching and learning, and the expectation to provide "high-quality professional development." The Education for Economic Security Act of 1983 (EESA), also known as the Eisenhower Program, is an example of a past national professional development policy. In the 1980s and 1990s, the Eisenhower Program allocated federal funds "to improve elementary, secondary and postsecondary education in mathematics and science" by allocating federal dollars for teacher professional development (Koppich, Toch, & Podgursky, 2000, p. 266). It was replaced by Title II, Part A, in the reauthorization of ESEA as part of NCLB.

Under Title II, ESEA supports a broader array of professional development in all core subject areas, not just in math and science. Title II provides approximately $3 billion annually to support state- and district-level activities to improve teacher and principal quality. Allowable uses for these funds distributed to districts through "Improving Teacher Quality State Grants" include recruiting and retaining highly qualified teachers; offering professional development in core academic areas; promoting growth and rewarding quality teaching through mentoring, induction, and other support services; testing teachers in academic areas; and reducing class size (Office of Elementary and Secondary Education [OESE], 2013). Districts have discretion over how they choose to use these funds. According to an annual government survey that collected data from a national sample of 800 districts, stratified by district size and poverty level, more districts allocated Title II funds for professional development for teachers (66%) in 2011–2012 than for reducing class size (46%). In addition, the 2011–2012 survey shows that 89% of the nation's 2.37 million teachers who teach in core academic content areas participated in professional development programs. The most common topics for their professional development included using effective instructional strategies and increasing core academic content knowledge. Thus policy tries to impact teaching and learning, as these examples suggest, by controlling inputs, such as teachers' professional learning experiences, class size, course curricula, content standards, and assessments.

State education agencies also make professional development policies. Until recently, education was governed almost exclusively by states. State professional development policies take the form of statutes, rules, funding allocations, sanctions, and incentives (Jaquith, Mindich, Wei, & Darling-Hammond, 2010). For instance, the state of Missouri passed legislation to fund a statewide network of regional professional development centers to support professional learning for teachers and leaders. Other states, such as New Jersey and New Mexico, have used state policy to create teacher licensure boards that oversee the licensing and professional advancement of teachers (Darling-Hammond, 2012; Jaquith et al., 2010). Many states have policies that establish target levels for student performance with consequences for schools or districts that do not meet these targets. In these states, consequences for schools can be as severe as a state takeover or closing of its underperforming schools.

At the local level, professional development policies take the form of school board policies, rules, funding allocations, sanctions, and incentives. For example, some local school districts have established policies focused on instructional improvement, such as instituting a peer assistance and review (PAR) program to work with struggling or novice teachers (Darling-Hammond, 2012, pp. 34–35). Other district policies can include early release days to secure additional time for teachers' planning and professional learning. These policies typically involve negotiations with the local teacher's union. As with state and national policies, the intention undergirding local professional development policies is to improve students' learning outcomes by strengthening the overall quality of teaching, usually by focusing on what policymakers can easily control: time, materials, access to and enrollment in professional development programs, and the granting of licenses and credentials.

Given that the aim of professional development policy is to strengthen teaching and learning, there are at least five ways that such policies can affect practice:

1. By increasing the opportunities for and participation in particular (e.g., content-focused and "high-quality") professional development programs through incentives or regulations.
2. By providing professional learning resources to the field in the form of curriculum, materials, assessments, and professional development programs—and by ensuring equitable access to these resources or giving preferential access to districts according to some established criteria.
3. By regulating the quality of system "inputs," such as the quality of teachers or principals entering the profession, which is typically accomplished through licensure or credentialing programs and/or by requiring teacher mentoring programs for teachers newly entering the profession.
4. By stimulating the creation of new organizational structures and/or mechanisms—such as standards boards or professional development committees—to support professional learning.
5. By framing a particular way of thinking about teaching and learning.

Any or all such policy effects might stimulate changes in leaders' behavior and teachers' instruction in ways that positively influence student learning. However, there is no guarantee that such policy effects will cause teachers to learn or to change their instructional practice (Cohen & Barnes, 1993b; Koppich et al., 2000; O'Day, 2002). This is why some policymakers, practitioners, and researchers are interested in changing the relationship between policymaking and its implementers. Some indications that this relationship is changing are offered.

Increasing Opportunities for Professional Development

States and local districts can and do incentivize participation in professional learning experiences in a variety of ways—for example, requiring professional development hours for licensure renewal, requiring new teachers to participate in mentoring programs, requiring struggling teachers to enroll in PAR programs, and offering a stipend for obtaining National Board certification all provide incentives for participating in professional development (Jaquith et al., 2010). Increasingly, states are designing policies to promote teachers' participation in professional development programs.

Providing Professional Development Resources

Policies can provide resources, particularly money, aimed at improving teaching and learning to states, districts, and schools, often according to needs-based criteria. For example, the 1994 reauthorization of the Eisenhower Program "altered, to some extent, the way in which state and local funds [were] distributed" (Koppich et al., 2000, p. 274) by using a funding formula that calculated the state's Title I funds and the total number of students within a state in an effort to ensure that the most underserved communities received resources. It also included a cost-sharing provision to encourage continued local investment in professional development, particularly after federal dollars were discontinued (Koppich et al., 2000, pp. 274–275). More recently, the U.S. Department of Education awarded School Improvement Grants (SIG) to the persistently lowest achieving school districts across the country (OESE, 2013). In the current climate of shrinking state resources, federal funds provide the lion's share of professional development resources in many states and districts. Therefore, policies regarding how such money is distributed can also affect practice.

Regulating Inputs and Creating New Organizational Structures

State policy can create infrastructures to support teacher learning. For example, New Mexico established a standards-based teacher licensure program in 2003 that was linked to compensation and based on an independent review process for teachers (see Darling-Hammond, 2012, pp. 8–9). This particular policy stimulated the creation of a variety of organizational structures and mechanisms at both the state and local levels to support teachers' learning and advancement from one licensure level to another. In Missouri, progressive state legislatures passed legislation that invested in the professional learning of teachers through the Excellence in Education Act of 1985 and the Outstanding Schools Act of 1993. This legislation established a statewide regional network of professional learning, through the creation of regional professional development centers (RPDC), and established school-based professional development committees, which are local decision-making bodies that determine how funds earmarked for professional development are spent (Jaquith et al., 2010, p. 49).[1] Through the creation of the RPDCs, Missouri built a statewide professional development infrastructure that school districts, and increasingly the state, relied on to provide targeted, on-the-ground professional learning to schools.

Framing a Particular Way of Thinking about Teaching and Learning

Finally, there is accumulating evidence that the way a policy frames problems of teaching and learning can and does influence practice, although not always as intended. Policies do this, in part, by focusing attention on particular aspects of teaching and learning. For example, the Eisenhower Program brought increased attention to science and math. NCLB framed the teaching and learning problem as one of achievement and brought national attention to the uneven achievement of students from different racial and economic backgrounds. By requiring student test score data to be disaggregated by students' socioeconomic and demographic characteristics, NCLB made inequities in the system more transparent. Public reporting of state, district, and school test score data made the achievement gap salient and

---

[1] For more information on Missouri's professional development policymaking, see "Building a Statewide Infrastructure to Support Professional Learning: A Coherent System within Reach" (Jaquith et al., 2010, pp. 45–71).

helped reveal consequential patterns of inequity in how educational resources have been historically distributed (e.g. Darling-Hammond, 2010). Visibility into such inequities, coupled with sanctions for insufficient "student improvement" on state assessments, put pressure on educators at all levels of the system to examine which students were not learning and focused attention on how to address this "achievement gap." NCLB also had the unwanted effect of focusing educators' attention on "the test" in some districts in perverse ways that distracted attention from creating meaningful learning experiences. For example, the emphasis on state standardized test scores focused practitioners' attention in some schools on narrow conceptions of math and English language arts, as represented by test items, to the exclusion of focusing on conceptual understanding or on other subject matter. In many districts, the threat of sanctions stimulated local policymaking that increased regulation of curricula and monitoring of teaching performance in ways that decreased practitioners' ability to exercise professional judgment and make decisions regarding instruction.

Overall Impact of Professional Development Policy on Practice

If the ultimate measure of success of a professional development policy is to strengthen the quality of teachers' instruction to improve student learning, professional development policy has not been terribly successful. Policy levers remain a fairly blunt instrument for effecting the specific changes to instruction that are necessary to improve student learning on any given day by a specific teacher who is teaching particular subject matter to a group of students. Therefore, it is not surprising that policy analysts traditionally have found little evidence to show that such policies have had an impact on teachers' classroom practice as intended (Cohen & Barnes, 1993b; Koppich et al., 2000; O'Day, 2002). Because teaching well involves complex operations, judgment, and nuanced decision making, professional development policy alone is probably ill suited to improve teaching practice in such fine-grained ways (Cohen & Barnes, 1993b; Darling-Hammond, 2009; Elmore, 2000; McLaughlin, 2006).

FINDINGS FROM POLICY IMPLEMENTATION RESEARCH

Federal, state, and local policies have been the subject of scholarly study over many decades, beginning in the 1950s. In order to understand the impact of policy on practice, it is helpful to know how research on professional development policy, particularly at the federal and state levels, has been conceptualized and undertaken and how it has evolved over time. Early studies of the effects of federal legislation, such as ESEA, focused primarily on what was implemented in order to understand successes and failures in implementation (Honig, 2006b; Smylie & Evans, 2006). These policies were the "first significant federal-level attempts to stimulate change in local education practices" (McLaughlin, 1990, p. 11), and policy designs at this time were top-down and assumed to have a relatively direct link to practice. Researcher Meredith Honig (2006b) points out that these early policies were intended to improve local educational practices "based on assumptions that policy-makers *should* develop policies for implementers to carry out and monitor imple-menters' compliance" (p. 5). Evaluations of these policy implementations typically found that "schools and districts tended not to put programs in place in ways that faithfully resembled policy designs" (p. 5). Therefore, analysts concluded that pol-icy implementation was a failure.

Such findings are not surprising given what we now understand about imple-menting policy. In the words of two policy researchers: "[policy implementation] is fraught with uncertainty and unpredictability. It is a process that is difficult to control and prone to failure" (Smylie & Evans, 2006, p. 187).

Milbrey McLaughlin has pointed out that policy researchers of that era brought a perspective to the research that both shaped and limited its findings. In a retro-spective look at the important RAND Change Agent Studies, which were under-taken from 1973 to 1978 to evaluate the success of a planned educational change effort, McLaughlin (1990) commented:

> We assumed that the structure most relevant to teachers was the policy structure—federal, state and local policies—that eventuated in classroom practice. Had we made those assumptions problematic, rather than taken them as givens, we would have seen that although we as policy analysts were chiefly concerned with the pol-icy system, it was not always relevant to many teachers on a day-to-day basis. (p. 14)

This observation points to the importance of knowing the research design, includ-ing how the impact of policy is conceptualized, to fully understand the research findings.

Researching the Policy–Practice Relationship

The RAND Change Agent Study (Berman & McLaughlin, 1976) was important because it reshaped the way analysts looked at how policy influences practice. Over-all, the study found that federal change agent policies had a major role in prompt-ing local school districts to undertake projects that were in line with broad policy goals (McLaughlin, 1990). Among the study's findings were that "project resources did not predict outcome" and "the active commitment of district leadership was essential to project success and long-run stability" (McLaughlin, 1990, p. 12). Impor-tantly, the study also "demonstrated that the nature, amount, and pace of change at the local level was a product of local factors that were largely beyond the control of higher-level policymakers" (McLaughlin, 1990, p. 12). These findings endure today. The critical role of local leadership in districts and schools cannot be overstated given the importance of creating conditions in the implementation environment that are conducive to learning and change (Rorrer & Skrla, 2005; Sun, Penuel, Frank, Gallagher, & Youngs, 2013) and given the institutional need for guiding a thoughtful process of "mutual adaptation."

As a result of such studies, researchers began to realize that professional development policies should not simply be regulatory in nature, and they began to recognize that implementation sites and actors mediate policies. Over time, analysts viewed policy environments as increasingly complex and multilayered (Chrispeels, 1997; Honig, 2006b; McLaughlin, 2006; O'Day, 2002). McLaughlin (2006) has since described policy implementation as a "multilayered phenomenon" in which "each layer or level acts on the policy as it interprets intention, resources and regulatory frameworks" (p. 212).

Today, it is widely recognized that policies do not make change—people do (Honig, 2006b; McLaughlin, 1990, 2006; O'Day, 2002; Smylie & Evans, 2006)—and that the contexts in which policies are taken up (or not) and the manner in which policies are made sense of (or not), as well as the extent to which implementation is monitored, if at all, matter. In addition to understanding that there are multiple levels to the policy environment, we recognize that each of these levels can function as its own site for policy implementation (McLaughlin, 2006). And we recognize that these implementation environments are complex and dynamic, as well as mutually influencing, making policy implementation anything but straightforward (Honig, 2006b; Jaquith et al., 2010; O'Day, 2002). Nevertheless, we continue to use policy levers to try to improve teaching and learning—such as through high-stakes accountability under NCLB or by allocating federal dollars to stimulate the creation of professional programs through legislation—and we continue to see mixed or minimal results from these policy efforts, depending on how policymakers and analysts conceptualize policy outcomes (Cohen & Barnes, 1993a, 1993b; Koppich et al., 2000; O'Day, 2002).

Realizing the limits of policy to improve teaching and learning, coupled with accumulated field knowledge about the complexity of teaching all students well, has led some policy analysts to propose a different policy solution to this problem: the need to develop a new kind of policy called "professional policy" (Darling-Hammond, 2009). The key idea of "professional policy" is that policymakers hand over some policy levers to the profession itself (L. Darling-Hammond, personal communication, May 23, 2013). Proponents of this approach point out that professions such as law and medicine do this through the creation of standards-setting boards made up of professionals who can develop and enforce professional standards by accrediting preparation programs and granting licenses and certification to practitioners (Darling-Hammond, 2009, p. 15). Linda Darling-Hammond, who has helped state policymakers develop professional policies for education, explains the rationale for this sort of policy:

> The assumption is that, because knowledge is always growing and its appropriate application is contingent on many different factors, the process of developing and transmitting a complex knowledge base and ensuring its appropriate use is better managed by members of the profession [rather than through state regulation]. (2009, p. 15)

Although such professional policies, as described, have not taken root in most states, the logic model makes sense. Professional policies are one way to productively link the macro-policy environment to actors who must work to accomplish broad policy goals in complex, dynamic, and varied contexts. Through such enabling policies, policymakers, for example, can use policy to create the conditions for establishing and enforcing professional standards, which Darling-Hammond asserts is "a major lever for profession-wide transfer of knowledge and continual improvement of practice" (p. 15) in organized professions.

In addition to standard-setting and the oversight of teachers and principals to ensure a more expert teaching work force in all of our schools, the field would also benefit from standards and oversight of professional development and its providers. An industry of professional development providers and school improvement vendors has sprung up on the educational landscape—partially in response to increases in federal and state money earmarked for professional development. These professional development providers, of course, vary enormously. Most make claims about their own merit that are often unsubstantiated by research. In this diffuse and growing marketplace of ideas about instructional improvement, professional development providers and vendors peddle their school improvement wares and reform approaches to districts and principals. School leaders, however, have little way of knowing beyond their own judgment which professional development providers, which products, or which approaches will best meet the learning needs of teachers and administrators or can be counted on to deliver results. In the absence of professional policies that "hold the profession accountable for developing shared expertise among all of its members" (Darling-Hammond, 2009, p. 15), the field—including professional developers, teachers, and school leaders—will not be able to accumulate knowledge or develop reliable mechanisms to ensure quality learning experiences for students, for teachers, or for their leaders.

AN EMERGING TENSION BETWEEN ACCOUNTABILITY POLICIES AND FIELD KNOWLEDGE ABOUT QUALITY IMPLEMENTATION

The reauthorization of ESEA in 2002 as NCLB signaled a significant change in accountability mechanisms that traveled through each level of the system. Policy analysts, such as the Consortium for Policy Research in Education, have analyzed various components of what they termed the "new accountability" in education: "the emphasis on student outcomes as a measure of adult and system performance, a focus on the school as a basic unit of accountability, public reporting of student achievement, and the attachment of consequences to performance levels" (O'Day, 2002, p. 294). These accountability components of NCLB mark a period in our history of increased and unprecedented federal and state regulation of schooling in an attempt to assert more control over the system to improve student learning. According to institutional scholar W. Richard Scott, regulatory processes—in the form of more rule setting, monitoring, and sanctioning activities—are an attempt to influence future behavior (Scott, 2001). In this regard, NCLB attempts to decrease inequities in our education system and to increase the focus on student learning outcomes. As a consequence of this legislation, the macro-environment now has more regulatory processes—federal regulations have spurred increased regulatory activity by states, which have similarly affected local environments—in the name of school improvement. All this regulation, however, can make the local environment in which districts and schools operate seem like a morass of rules and regulations for local actors to comply with and navigate.

In the context of increased regulations and controls at each level of the system, reconsidering the relationship between the macro-environment and micro-influences can be instructive. Although we now recognize complexity in the macro-environment with its multilayered levels, each functioning as policy implementation sites, the fundamental observation that Milbrey McLaughlin and Paul Berman (1975) made four decades ago remains helpful: Implementation occurs on at least two levels—a macro- and a microlevel. McLaughlin and Berman stated the "microproblem" this way: "[local practitioners] must learn to implement new ideas and practices effectively" (p. 1). This micro-problem of policy implementation, which McLaughlin and Berman framed as a problem of learning, still exists. Through their analysis, McLaughlin and Berman concluded four microprocesses were critical to effective implementation of federal change policies:

- Implementation—rather than the adoption of technology, the availability of information, or the infusion of money—dominates the outcomes of innovations.
- Effective implementation of significant change is characterized by the process of mutual adaptation.
- Effective implementation depends on the receptivity of the institution setting to change.
- Local school systems vary in their capacity to implement significant change. (p. 2)

Their conclusions about the microprocesses that matter for *effective* implementation hold true today and can provide helpful guidelines for policymaking at all levels of the system, but particularly at the local level.

An alternative perspective to policy implementation values fidelity of implementation. If fidelity of implementation means following a script rather than exercising professional judgment, then those who ascribe to a sociocultural view of learning and see knowledge as a socially constructed activity will object to a mechanistic and compliance orientation to school improvement. They will doubt that such an approach could effect significant or sustainable change. And research has shown that having a deep understanding of the core principles of a change effort is critical for effecting significant change (McLaughlin & Mitra, 2001). [2] Understanding these principles enables local actors to exercise prudent judgment and adapt policies to meet the needs of the local context while maintaining fidelity to the broad policy goal.

---

[2] See McLaughlin and Mitra (2001) for a discussion of what constitutes "first principles" of theory-based change and the necessity that teachers and leaders understand these principles in order to take up these ideas and implement them.

Significantly, recent research has documented how current regulation of the educational system, with its severe and punitive consequences, can have the opposite and unintended effect of diverting attention away from improving teaching and learning in some schools and districts (O'Day, 2002). These accountability policies do not foster the development of deep understanding by practitioners about how to change instructional practice and improve learning outcomes for all students. In a recent address to Congress, Secretary of Education Arne Duncan acknowledged some of these limitations when he promoted allowing state waivers to NCLB as a way to grant states more flexibility to pursue new and better ways to prepare students (Brenchley, 2013). Duncan said that one of the unintended consequences of NCLB is that it provided incentives in some states to lower standards and that "there was far too much focus on a single test score" (Duncan, as quoted in Brenchley, 2013). In some districts, schools, and/or classrooms, the focus was on complying with requirements (O'Day, 2002), which effected surface-level changes but failed to make deep or lasting change. One reason for this may be that achieving the purpose underlying NCLB requires learning; some learning and education is always required to achieve any new purpose (Cohen & Barnes, 1993b).

Policy analyst Jennifer O'Day (2002) offers additional reasons for surface-level changes. She examined the complexity of the school context and identified three significant tensions (or problems) that emerge when districts try to use policy and its regulatory mechanisms to improve teaching and learning at the school level. These tensions are (1) the relationship between collective accountability and individual action; (2) the operating assumption that external forces can positively influence what happens inside of schools in order to improve student learning; and (3) the essential and problematic nature of information, which is essential to school improvement but, as O'Day points out, is inadequate for learning in both its specificity and frequency. Inherent in these tensions that O'Day identifies and analyzes is the relationship between the broader policy environment and the local implementation context, as well as the problem of learning.

In her analysis of the accountability system in the Chicago Public Schools, O'Day (2002) found that accountability policies "helped focus attention throughout the system on student outcomes and provided data that can be used for targeting resources and assistance" (p. 314), but she also found significant shortcomings in the district's bureaucratic approach to accountability. For example, O'Day described how patterns of interaction within schools were negatively affected when "bureaucratic school accountability mechanisms serve to maintain interaction patterns that foster compliance and hierarchy over system learning" (p. 311). In such contexts, information flows were typically top-down, partnerships focused on "whether people [were] carrying out prescribed tasks," and collective problem-solving sessions, such as planning for school improvement, tended toward a symbolic exercise of responding to formulaic requirements rather than providing a context for thoughtful learning and problem posing by the staff (p. 311). Such behavior is mechanistic in nature and compliance-oriented and is not characterized by a process of mutual adaptation, which fundamentally requires sense making. This accountability context, with its punitive sanctions, created an implementation environment in some schools and districts in which complying with regulations dominated local actions and prevented local sense making. Such an implementation approach is counter to the process of "mutual adaptation" that McLaughlin and Berman (1975) found characterized effective policy implementation in the RAND Change Agent study. Policy goals must be fitted to the particular needs of those within the implementing environment. This requires that users of policy assume agency in its interpretation and in establishing feedback mechanisms to monitor how the enactment of policy influences teaching and learning in classrooms and schools. When this occurs, we see evidence of accountability being used in a manner to effect productive change. In a collection of state case studies of teacher professional learning in Vermont, Colorado, New Jersey, and Missouri, examples are given of how states make effective use of federal policies to promote teacher learning (Jaquith et al., 2010). These case studies provide evidence of states' using and interpreting federal policy to design state policy frameworks and strategies to effectively support teacher learning. Although the four states differed in both their approaches to professional development and the levels of control they asserted over professional learning, we found that these states shared the ability to "address federal mandates and accountability requirements in constructive ways" (Jaquith et al., 2010, p. vi). These states were able to leverage "federal policy productively to support high-quality learning in collegial contexts, without restricting their focus to narrow types of instructional improvement defined only by basic skills test scores" (p. vi). We found they shared some common strategies, which included developing standards to guide accountability, monitoring quality, requiring induction and mentoring programs, leveraging collegial strategies for professional learning, partnering with professional organizations, and skillfully marshaling resources (p. vi). Most important, these states created a vision for professional development through their creative use of standards to guide licensing and school planning and through the creation of state infrastructures to support the implementation of their visions.[3]

One lesson that we can draw from these examples of how local and state practitioners interact with accountability policies is that organizations and individuals are able to learn when policy structures enable actors to make sense of policies and encourage practitioners to do so while also paying attention to outcomes. What, then, are some of the mechanisms that can broker a productive and educative relationship between the macro-environment of policymaking and the local, micro-influences that operate in schools and districts?

BUILDING POLICY FROM PRACTICE: NEW DIRECTIONS, NEW ACTORS, AND NEW ROLES

There are a variety of existing organizational and policy structures that are facilitating a more productive relationship between the broader policy environment

---

[3]For more information about how these states established a vision for professional learning and built local capacity, see Jaquith et al. (2010).

and the needs of local contexts.[4] A more productive relationship between policy-makers and practitioners assumes a shared understanding of the broad policy goal and is characterized by two-way communication, attempts to learn by both parties, and a more equitable distribution of decision-making power. Three examples of structures that can facilitate a more productive and educative relationship include: (1) the process of policymaking itself, such as the creation of "professional poli-cies," described earlier; (2) intermediary organizations, which come in all sizes and shapes but exist outside of the formal educational system and can act as brokers between the two parties; and (3) district structures or infrastructures that encour-age leaders to assume a sense-making stance toward policy and act as policy brokers to mediate between the local needs of teachers and students on the one hand and broad policy goals on the other.

Policy Design

Analysts have written about the need for policy designs to be more cognizant of the practitioner. An evocative set of ideas along these lines was offered by David Cohen and Carol Barnes (1993a), who articulated: (1) a need for policymakers who are committed to reforming teaching and learning to recognize how challenging it is to change instructional practice; (2) to take the education of teachers and lead-ers seriously in policy formation; and (3) to therefore reimagine "the processes in which policy is made and enacted" (p. 251). Ultimately, Cohen and Barnes pro-pose that "educational policy should be deeply educational for those who enact it" (p. 257). The sort of educative policymaking they seemed to envision in 1993 is akin to the "professional policies" suggested by Darling-Hammond and others. Cohen and Barnes call for policymakers to treat teachers as "active and interesting think-ers [who are] central in policymaking" rather than "acting as though teachers were empty vessels to be filled" (p. 257). Twenty years later, there are some signs indicat-ing change in these directions, albeit often initiated outside of the policymaking realm.

Intermediary Organizations and Professional Organizations

Intermediary organizations can sometimes facilitate learning between policymak-ers and practitioners. As an organizational type, intermediaries are flooding the educational landscape. Although they vary considerably in their missions, organi-zational structures, and theories of change, intermediaries are typically nonsystem actors that often function as brokers or connectors (Jaquith & McLaughlin, 2010, p. 86). Some intermediary organizations, such as the RPDCs in Missouri, mediate by design between state educational agencies and regional districts and schools. The Missouri RPDCs often acted as brokers, translating the needs of one envi-ronment to the other, in order to build capacity for school improvement in both macro- and micro-environments (Jaquith et al., 2010, pp. 62–64). As the state began

---

[4]The four state case studies described earlier offer examples of such structures at the state level.

to assume more control over educational governance, corresponding to changes in the national educational policy landscape, the RPDCs began to fulfill a new role in the state accountability context, which included helping district and school leaders make sense of and respond productively to Missouri's accountability system (Jaquith et al., 2010, pp. 49–59). During this period, the RPDCs tried to assist the state in better understanding the local needs of schools, which vary considerably between the state's urban and rural contexts, in order to help states better serve schools' varied and particular needs. In addition, RPDCs have looked for ways to provide professional learning programs to complement and strengthen federally funded state programs, such as Response to Intervention, and the state-sponsored professional learning communities program. By mediating between federally funded state initiatives and the needs of the local school district, the RPDC was able to provide customized support to schools and districts to facilitate the enactment of policies on the ground. The RPDC network also leveraged professional development resources across the state, including the spread of ideas and practices about how to use scarce resources most effectively (Jaquith et al., 2010, pp. 66–69).

Other professional organizations, such as Learning Forward, can also work in an intermediary capacity. Learning Forward's mission is to "advance educator effectiveness and student results through standards-based professional learning" (Learning Forward, 2013). It recently made "affect[ing] the policy context" (Islas, 2010, p. 6) a strategic priority of the organization. "Advocacy and policy" is one of the three named priority areas in its 2012 strategic plan. Its leading advocacy and policy goal states: "By 2020, 100,000 individuals will advocate for or change policies and practices that advance effective professional learning" (Learning Forward, 2013). This goal illustrates the organization's advocacy stance toward policymaking. Unwilling to wait for policymakers to discover what practitioners' particular needs are, organizations such as Learning Forward are becoming more activist-minded and insisting on having a voice in policymaking about professional learning. This activist approach illustrates the agency that more and more nonsystem actors are beginning to display in the policymaking arena.

A third example of an influential, nonsystem actor that also functions as an advocate for the needs of teachers and leaders and that brokers knowledge between policymakers and practitioners is the National Board for Professional Teaching Standards. The mission of this organization is "to advance student learning and achievement by establishing the definitive standards and system for certifying accomplished educators, providing programs and advocating policies that support excellence in teaching and leading" (National Board for Professional Teaching Standards [NBPTS], 2013). Teachers' experiences and knowledge have historically guided the development of the NBPTS. This organization "actively works with Congress, the U.S. Department of Education and other federal agencies to shape education policy that advances teaching and learning." The NPTS also assumes an activist stance toward policymaking, and it serves as an important conduit for communicating practitioners' needs to policymakers. Policymakers, in turn, also call upon National Board Certified Teacher (NBTC) networks to share their ideas and perspectives and to help educate policymakers.

New Roles for Principals as Policy Brokers, Interpreters, and Advocates

As discussed previously, policy analysts have delineated the micro-influences on implementing policy in various ways, and they agree it is the implementer and the local context that defines the manner in which a policy is implemented. Whereas external policy demands contribute to the context of the classroom and school, they do not change schools uniformly because school contexts are different and "local forces within a school retain some agency in selecting classroom practices" (Sun et al., 2013, p. 2). Whether or not and how districts and principals use this agency matters. Andrea Rorrer and Linda Skrla (2005) argue that district and school leaders can act as "policy mediators" and reframe the meaning of accountability required by NCLB. Like other policy analysts, they assert that "local actors maintain considerable discretion over how any policy is perceived, enacted, ignored, misappropriated or integrated" (p. 60). They describe how principals in Texas and North Carolina cultivated relationships with their faculties and built trust, such that they were able to "reculture" their schools by developing new norms and values about student learning. Rorrer and Skrla found that these principals were able to "integrate and align school and district purposes, goals, policies and practices to support the achievement of all children" (p. 55). Other studies (Camburn, Rowan, & Taylor, 2003; David & Talbert, 2012; Hemmings, 2012; Sun et al., 2013) have similarly found that school and district leaders can play a critical role in changing the culture of underperforming schools to raise the achievement of all students and to begin to close achievement gaps by using federal and state accountability policies as a tool for local reform.

This conception and enactment of instructional leadership at the local level stands in contrast to the sort of leadership that Jennifer O'Day (2002) described as broadly enacted in the Chicago Public Schools under its bureaucratic, outcomes-based school accountability system. The model of principal as "policy mediator" offers an image of local leaders with a shared vision, a sense of agency, and a willingness to learn and develop the skills needed to interpret, broker, and advocate for particular policy goals related to instructional improvement. This approach to leadership appears to distinguish schools and districts that effectively adapt accountability policies to their local context from those that are not able to generate learning and make productive change. This observation, grounded in the research literature, reaffirms the finding from the RAND Change Agent Study (McLaughlin, 1990, p. 12) that "the active commitment of district leadership was essential to project success and long-run stability," and it further specifies the sort of leadership that is needed. Leadership focused on building a school's instructional capacity for improving learning seems to be necessary for implementing policy effectively and in a manner that remains true to the overarching policy goals.[5]

The role of local leadership emerges as particularly important when the complexity of the local context is illuminated. One way to think about a context's

---

[5]For more on what instructional capacity is and what leaders can do to build instructional capacity, see Jaquith (2013a, 2013b).

complexity is in terms of the sociocultural conditions in the implementing environment, which are typically difficult to see and complicated to measure. In addition, sociocultural conditions vary considerably from one context to the next. This realization has led some scholars to conclude that variation in policy implementation, rather than uniform implementation, is desirable, as well as inevitable (Honig, 2006b; McLaughlin, 2006). Sociocultural conditions include the degree to which social capital and trust exist in an environment (Bryk & Schneider, 2002; Smylie & Evans, 2006) and the type of formal and informal leadership structures and practices that operate within a given school (Camburn et al., 2003; Sun et al., 2013). For instance, Mark Smylie and Andrea Evans (2006) describe how "social relations in school organization function to promote or impede implementation and change" (p. 188). They also show that the sort of leadership that exists within a school influences how organizational structures are used to promote or impede the development of professional community.

Another sociocultural dimension of schools that matters for implementing policy is whether or not teachers have a shared repertoire of instructional practice. A shared repertoire of instruction and beliefs about what effective instruction is often ensues when organizational structures and routines for professional interaction are in place within the school to support teaching as a joint enterprise (Coburn & Stein, 2006). Principals often play an important role in creating these school conditions that nurture and grow the development of communities of practice and shared instructional repertoires. Evidence is growing that the leadership structure in schools matters in creating such learning conditions for teachers. In a recent study, Min Sun and colleagues (2013) show how "in the enactment of external reforms, leadership is distributed across multiple actors within a school" (p. 2). They found that a distributed leadership structure in schools composed of both formal leaders (defined as those with the authority to allocate resources) and informal leaders (defined as those who share the same context as other classroom teachers) was an effective mechanism for implementing external reforms. They show how the relationship between formal and informal leaders influenced teachers' instructional practices in complementary ways that cohered with the aims of a national reading policy. From their analysis, they recommended that policymakers attend to the intraorganizational processes of implementation through multiple sources of school leadership.

Some districts have paid attention to the intraorganizational processes that promote learning for instructional improvement. These districts, such as the ones Rorrer and Skrla (2005) studied, recognize that local policy can promote a stance toward the practitioner's role in policy implementation. In some districts, local policymakers have created mechanisms to encourage or enable leaders to take a sensemaking stance toward policy. These districts appear to value practitioner knowledge and experiences in the creation of more effective local policies aimed at improving student outcomes. Sanger Unified School District, a successful "turnaround district" (David & Talbert, 2012) located in California's Central Valley, where the child poverty rate is two to three times the national average, is such a district. It made significant improvement in students' performance. As Jane David and Joan Talbert have documented, improvement in this district has occurred slowly and steadily over the past decade by "sustaining a singular focus on student learning and nurturing the implementation of a small number of keystone practices over many years" (2012, p. 4). Over time, the district was able to shift its culture from a top-down approach to one that embraced "reciprocal accountability" (David & Talbert, 2012, p. 55).

This culture shift was instantiated through several structures and practices, such as the *principal summits*, which the district described as "an opportunity for principals to present their school's past and current level of student achievement, their plans for improving achievement, and to receive feedback/suggestions from their peers" (David & Talbert, 2012, p. 57). District leaders in Sanger approached accountability from a perspective of learning: "rather than relying on negative labels and sanctions, they focused on building the leadership capacity of principals as well as central office staff and the instructional capacity of teachers" (p. 56). In other words, Sanger adopted a learning orientation to meeting state policy goals for improving student achievement. It rejected a compliance-oriented approach. Instead, Sanger created various structures to enable, support, and insist upon practitioner learning. For example, at the recommendation of Superintendent Marc Johnson, the board adopted goals for the district that centered on increasing student achievement, deepening a culture of collaboration, and empowering parents to serve as partners in the process (personal communication, July 10, 2013). In addition, Johnson suggested to the board that his evaluation ought to be tied to a *superintendent summit*, in which he would present evidence to the board of how he has worked to accomplish the board-adopted district goals.

As these structures, such as the principal and superintendent summits, were put into use, Sanger district leaders were able to identify new practices and policies to support the goal of improving student learning in the district. In an implementation study of school–community partnerships, Meredith Honig documents the importance of developing "new learning relationships between the central office and [school] sites" (2006a, p. 137) in order to build policy from practice. The structure of the principal summits—their learning orientation, purpose, and attendees—and the superintendent summit provided the context for these sorts of learning relationships to develop between district policymakers and practitioners.

In another successful "turnaround" district in California, Chula Vista, district leaders also created an approach to accountability and a system of supports that promoted learning and shared responsibility for student outcomes by leaders at all levels of the system: school board members, district administrators, principals, and teachers. As in Sanger, leaders in Chula Vista created a system of supports with an important role for school principals. Chula Vista developed a practice similar to the Sanger principal summits, in which principals annually present the learning status of their schools, largely in the form of student achievement data, to the local school board. School board meetings are public events, and so school leaders are held publicly accountable for their school's performance and for their leadership. If a school is struggling, school board members typically want to know what the principal plans to do next. If a school is succeeding, the question becomes "what did you do to see these results?" (E. Sanchez, personal communication, May 16, 2013).

In this way, learning and being held accountable for learning has become a culture-changing practice in the district that has stimulated the creation of a districtwide system of instructional improvement.

In addition to these annual reviews, Chula Vista has established small professional learning communities for principals that are led by "sitting" principal coaches. In principal cohorts, principals are supported to continuously learn and develop the leadership skills they need to effectively lead their schools. According to one district administrator, the district is always asking, "how can we continue to move forward?" Investing in principals' and teachers' learning through the creation of enabling structures and policies that simultaneously focus on instructional improvement and the continuous development of knowledge and skills that leaders and teachers need (and that they themselves often identify) is part of the answer to improving instruction. Local policymakers can and should develop such "enabling" policies that build local instructional capacity by promoting and teaching "professional accountability," by creating mechanisms for developing and enforcing common standards of practice, and by developing a shared repertoire for instruction, instructional leadership, and the use of instructional materials.

CONCLUSION

This chapter describes how the broad purpose of professional development policy is to improve teaching and learning, and it illuminates the various reasons that policies do not penetrate into classrooms in uniform ways. Some reasons for this include the multilayered policy environments that exist at the national, state, and local levels, as well as the variation that exists among dynamic implementation contexts in which professional development policy ultimately is interpreted, ignored, or in some way enacted. Therefore, this chapter suggests a more promising approach to policymaking that stands a better chance to improve teaching and learning. This approach involves (1) creating mechanisms for two-way communication between policymakers and implementers, (2) establishing "professional policies" that give practitioners some responsibility for monitoring the quality of teaching, learning, and professional development, and (3) developing "enabling" policies at the local level that create mechanisms to gather information and build local policy from practice.

QUESTIONS FOR DISCUSSION

For Teachers

1. What professional development policies exist in your district?

2. How do professional development policies (local, state, or national) affect how you plan and how you teach? And to what effect?

3. What, if any, opportunities do you have to provide feedback to leaders or local policymakers about how professional development policy affects your teaching and student learning?

For Administrators

1. What professional development policies exist in your district? What is the purpose of these professional development policies, and what are the anticipated outcomes?

2. What is your district's stance toward accountability policies? How does this stance affect your leadership, professional learning, and student performance?

3. Does your district or state have any "professional policies" in place? If so, how do these policies affect you and your role? If not, what would be the advantages and/or disadvantages of such policies?

For Policymakers

1. What do you see as the purpose of professional development policy? What outcomes do you want and/or expect to result from these policies?

2. In what ways do you see professional development policy enabling and/or constraining learning?

3. What do you see as the relationship between policymaking and policy implementation? What do "professional policies" enable and constrain?

REFERENCES

Berman, P., & McLaughlin, M. (1976). Implementation of educational innovation. *Educational Forum, 40*(3), 345–370.

Brenchley, C. (2013, February 7). Duncan to Congress: Giving states flexibility is working. *Homeroom* [Web log post]. Retrieved April 12, 2013, from *www.ed.gov/blog/author/cbrenchley/*.

Bryk, A. S., & Schneider, B. (2002). *Trust in schools: A core resource for improvement.* New York: Russell Sage Foundation.

Camburn, E., Rowan, B., & Taylor, J. (2003). Leadership in schools: The case of elementary schools adopting comprehensive school reform models. *Educational Evaluation and Policy Analaysis, 25*(4), 347–373.

Chrispeels, J. H. (1997). Educational policy implementation in a shifting political climate: The California experience. *American Education Research Journal, 34*(3), 453–481.

Coburn, C., & Stein, M. K. (2006). Communities of practice theory and the role of teacher professional community in policy implementation. In M. I. Honig (Ed.), *New directions in education policy implementation: Confronting complexity* (pp. 25–46). Albany: State University of New York Press.

Cohen, D. K., & Barnes, C. A. (1993a). Conclusion: A new pedagagy for policy. In D. K. Cohen, M. McLaughlin, & J. Talbert (Eds.), *Teaching for understanding:Challenges for policy and practice* (pp. 240–275). San Francisco: Jossey-Bass.

Cohen, D. K., & Barnes, C. A. (1993b). Pedagogy and policy. In D. K. Cohen, M. McLaughlin, & J. Talbert (Eds.), *Teaching for understanding: Challenges for policy and practice* (pp. 207–239). San Francisco: Jossey-Bass.

Darling-Hammond, L. (2009). Securing the right to learn: Policy and practice for powerful teaching and learning. *Journal of Education, 189*(1/2), 9–21.

Darling-Hammond, L. (2010). *The flat world and education: How America's commitment to equity will determine our future.* New York: Teachers College Press.

Darling-Hammond, L. (2012). *Creating a comprehensive system for evaluating and supporting effective teaching.* Palo Alto and Stanford, CA: Stanford Center for Opportunity Policy in Education.

David, J., & Talbert, J. (2012). *Turning around a high-poverty school district: Learning from Sanger Unified's success.* Palo Alto and Stanford, CA: Bay Area Research Group and Center for Research on the Context of Teaching.

Elmore, R. F. (2000). *Building a new structure for school leadership.* Washington, DC: Albert Shanker Institute.

Hemmings, A. (2012). Four Rs for urban high school reform: Re-envisioning, reculturation, restructuring and remoralization. *Improving Schools, 15*(3), 198–210.

Honig, M. I. (2006a). Building policy from practice: Implementation as organizational learning. In M. I. Honig (Ed.), *New directions in education policy implementation: Confronting complexity* (pp. 125–148). Albany: State University of New York Press.

Honig, M. I. (2006b). Complexity and policy implementation: Challenges and opportunities for the field. In M. I. Honig (Ed.), *New directions in education policy implementation: Confronting complexity* (pp. 1–23). Albany: State University of New York Press.

Islas, M. R. (2010). The federal policy landscape: A look at how legislation affects professional development. *Journal of Staff Development, 31*(6), 10–17.

Jaquith, A. (2013a, April). *Developing system capacity to support principals as instructional leaders.* Paper presented at the annual conference of the American Educational Research Association, San Francisco.

Jaquith, A. (2013b). Instructional capacity: How to build it right. *Educational Leadership, 71*(2), 56–61.

Jaquith, A., & McLaughlin, M. (2010). A temporary, intermediary organization at the helm of regional education reform: Lessons from the Bay Area School Reform Collaborative. In A. Hargreaves, A. Lieberman, M. Fullan, & D. Hopkins (Eds.), *Second international handbook of educational change* (Vol. 1, pp. 85–103). London: Springer.

Jaquith, A., Minich, D., Wei, R., & Darling-Hammond, L. (2010). *Teacher professional learning in the United States: Case studies of state policies and strategies.* Oxford, OH: Learning Forward.

Koppich, J., Toch, T., & Podgursky, M. (2000). The federal role in teacher professional development. *Brookings Papers on Education Policy* (pp. 265–305). Washington, DC: Brookings Institution Press.

Learning Forward. (2013). Strategic plan. Retrieved May 27, 2013, from *www.Learningforward.org.*

McLaughlin, M. (1990). The RAND Change Agent Study revisited: Macro perspectives and micro realities. *Educational Researcher, 19*(9), 11–16.

McLaughlin, M. (2006). Implementation research in education: Lessons learned, lingering questions and new opportunities. In M. I. Honig (Ed.), *New directions in education policy implementation: Confronting complexity* (pp. 209–229). New York: State University of New York Press.

McLaughlin, M., & Berman, P. (1975, June). *Macro and micro implementation.* Paper presented at the IMTEC Training Course "Towards a New Secondary School–Problems of Implementation," Federal Republic of Germany.

McLaughlin, M., & Mitra, D. (2001). Theory-based change and change-based theory: Going deeper, going broader. *Journal of Educational Change, 2,* 301–323.

National Board for Professional Teaching Standards. (2013). Advancing the teaching profession [Web log post]. Retrieved May 29, 2013, from *www.nbpts.org/federal-policy.*

No Child Left Behind Act of 2001, Pub. L. 107-110 C.F.R. (2002).

O'Day, J. (2002). Complexity, accountability, and school improvement. *Harvard Educational Review, 72*(3), 293-329.

Office of Elementary and Secondary Education. (2013). Improving teacher quality state grants (Vol. 2013). Retrieved from *www2.ed.gov/programs/teacherqual/guidance.pdf.*

Rorrer, A. K., & Skrla, L. (2005). Leaders as policy mediators: The reconceptualization of accountability. *Theory into Practice, 44*(1), 53-62.

Scott, W. R. (2001). *Institutions and organizations.* Thousand Oaks, CA: Sage.

Smylie, M., & Evans, A. (2006). Social capital and the problem of implementation. In M. I. Honig (Ed.), *New directions in education policy implementation: Confronting complexity* (pp. 187-208). New York: State University of New York Press.

Sun, M., Penuel, W., Frank, K., Gallagher, A., & Youngs, P. (2013). Shaping professional development to promote the diffusion of instructional expertise among teachers. *Educational Evaluation and Policy Analysis, 35*(3), 344-369.

CHAPTER 6

Communities, Schools, and Teachers

MAVIS G. SANDERS
CLAUDIA GALINDO

- Two definitions of community—as neighborhoods and as social networks—relate to students' education outcomes.
- Three factors have changed the composition and structure of U.S. communities.
- There are benefits and challenges with school–community collaboration.
- Teachers can become agents for community responsiveness in schools.

Children develop and learn within complex systems that include their families, schools, and communities (Bronfenbrenner, 1994). Epstein (2011) contends that when there is overlap between and among caring adults in students' families, schools, and communities, or "spheres of influence," students' learning and development are enhanced. This theory has been supported by over two decades of research showing the quantitative and qualitative impact of family and community engagement on students' learning and achievement (Galindo & Sheldon, 2011; Henderson & Mapp, 2002; Sanders & Sheldon, 2009). In this chapter, we focus specifically on the relationship between communities and schools, which has been an enduring topic in the field of education. It was central in the work of Dewey (1976) and remains a critical component in constructivist approaches to learning and in reform initiatives such as integrated services in schools (Sanders & Hembrick-Roberts, 2013). We also describe how teachers can serve as agents for community responsiveness within schools through collaborative and inclusive professional practices.

This chapter first defines community and discusses key theories and studies linking communities to education and related outcomes. It then describes the impact of immigration, deindustrialization, and increasing economic inequality on U.S. communities. The third section discusses the school as a vital community institution and the benefits of and barriers to school–community collaboration. The fourth section describes ways in which teachers can engage in community-responsive instruction in order to create effective school environments for all children and youth. The concluding section highlights the main ideas of the chapter and suggests future directions for the preparation and professional development of community-responsive teachers.

FRAMING COMMUNITY

The term "community" can refer to bounded geographic locations, as in the case of neighborhoods, or alternatively to the relationships or networks among individuals with similar interests and goals, which can include or transcend geographic boundaries. Both of these definitions have been the focus of scholarship within education and related fields. In this section we discuss the theory and research on how each of these definitions of community directly and indirectly relates to students' education outcomes.

Communities as Neighborhoods

Interest in the impact of neighborhoods on children and adolescents dates back nearly 70 years (Leventhal & Brooks-Gunn, 2000). Neighborhood studies have generally compared youth outcomes in economically distressed and more affluent communities. With few exceptions, these studies report that children and adolescents residing in low-income neighborhoods show lower rates of school readiness and achievement (Catsambis & Beveridge, 2001; Chase-Lansdale, Gordon, Brooks-Gunn, & Klebanov, 2000); more behavioral and emotional problems (de Souza Briggs, 1997); higher incidents of delinquency (Kingston, Huizinga, & Elliott, 2009) and school dropout (Aaronson, 1997); lower grades (Dornbusch, Ritter, & Steinberg, 1991); and lower levels of educational attainment (Garner & Raudenbush, 1991) than their more affluent counterparts.

Over time, several theories have been posited to explain how high-poverty neighborhoods affect these outcomes. Prominent approaches include social disorganization or structural theories, contagion or epidemic theories, and environmental theories. According to social disorganization theories, structural factors in neighborhoods explain incidents of antisocial behaviors among youth. More specifically, theorists within this tradition posit that neighborhoods with high levels of poverty, residential instability, single-parent households, and ethnic heterogeneity produce high rates of delinquency and school dropout through their negative impact on community cohesion and order (Sampson & Morenoff, 1997; Sampson,

Morenoff, & Gannon-Rowley, 2002; Shaw & McKay, 1969). Sociologist Julius Wilson (1996) argues that neighborhood disorganization disproportionately affects children and youth of color who are more likely to be segregated in high-density, low-income communities.

Empirical support for social disorganization theory includes studies using census and neighborhood survey data. For example, Sampson and Groves (1989) found that higher incomes and residential stability were negatively associated with crime and delinquency, whereas ethnic heterogeneity and urbanization were positively associated with crime and delinquency. In a more recent study, Kingston and colleagues (2009) also found support for the social disorganization theory. Based on parent and youth data from 44 neighborhoods in Denver, the researchers found that indicators of social disorganization, specifically poverty and ethnic and racial heterogeneity, predicted delinquency rates and lower rates of social control, respectively. Importantly, the study also found a strong relationship between delinquency rates and youths' perceptions of limited opportunities for their futures. The researchers concluded that students in high-poverty neighborhoods with low levels of social control lack optimism about their future opportunities. They are thus more vulnerable to delinquent and antischool behaviors, as well as association with peers engaged in such behaviors.

Similarly, epidemic or social contagion theories argue that neighborhoods affect youth outcomes through a process of peer influence (Crane, 1991; Jones & Jones, 2000). These theories contend that youth from disadvantaged neighborhoods are more likely than others to drop out of school, make poor grades, and not attend college because they are exposed to peers who exhibit or encourage such behaviors. This peer group influence can occur either directly through imitation or indirectly through the internalization of norms and attitudes antithetical to school success (South, Baumer, & Lutz, 2003). In a study using longitudinal data from 1,128 respondents in the National Survey of Children, South and colleagues (2003) examined factors contributing to higher rates of school dropout and lower rates of high school graduation in socioeconomically distressed communities. The authors found that approximately one-third of the observed effect of community socioeconomic disadvantage on school dropout could be explained by the educational behaviors of peers, a result consistent with epidemic models of neighborhood effects.

Other theorists and researchers focus on what can loosely be categorized as environmental factors to explain the impact of neighborhoods on children and youth. Berliner (2006, 2009), for example, argues that neighborhood characteristics, such as "collective efficacy," or community members' shared sense of having control over their environments and lives, affect educational outcomes (2009, p. 31). According to Berliner, limited collective efficacy in low-income communities, along with other conditions associated with poverty, such as environmental pollutants and poor housing and health care, are related to physical, sociological, and psychological problems that children often bring to school. Consequently, poor children are not as likely as more affluent children to succeed in school without significant efforts to ameliorate their living conditions.

Berliner (2006) points to decades of census tract data showing the negative influence of low-income communities on a host of educational, behavioral, and emotional outcomes to support his thesis. He observed:

> It does take a whole village to raise a child, and we actually know a little bit about how to do that. What we seem not to know how to do in modern America is to raise the village to promote communal values that ensure that all our children will prosper. We need to face the fact that our whole society needs to be held as accountable for providing healthy children ready to learn as our schools are for delivering quality instruction. (p. 988)

Communities as Social Networks

Other theorists have focused on communities as networks of individuals and institutions, such as families, schools, and faith organizations, that provide members with resources and support. These networks can reside in neighborhoods or extend beyond them. The resources and support embedded within these networks that facilitate purposeful action are referred to as *social capital* (Coleman, 1988; Lin, 2001). Theory and research show that social capital can protect individual children and youth from the risk factors and negative outcomes associated with low-income communities.

Social capital has both "bonding" and "bridging" functions. The function of bonding social capital is to create stronger ties between members of a social network in order to build community cohesion. The function of bridging social capital is to build connections across communities to expand access to important (or potentially important) human and material resources (Halpern, 2005). Through bonding and bridging social capital, individuals within communities can access resources needed to achieve individual and collective goals. For example, studies of Latino neighborhoods reveal strong social ties among community members even under conditions of economic scarcity (Small, 2004). These community ties provide families with social support and informal services through trusting and reciprocal relationships often defined by shared kinship, language, and ethnic identity (Coleman, 1988; Portes, 1998). Such social networks may be particularly important for childbearing mothers when other agents of support are scarce (Small & McDermott, 2006).

Communities need certain characteristics in order to be high-quality sources of social capital. The quality of the social capital available through communities largely depends on the degree of trust and obligations among network members (Coleman, 1988). Close networks facilitate the flow of resources or social capital within the group. Group control mechanisms constrain or reinforce actions to ensure that individuals' well-being is monitored and a common culture and set of orientations are created (Coleman, 1988). In addition, a sense of collectivism, rather than individualism, within the community facilitates feelings of reciprocity and mutual benefit—values that are related to better disposition for sharing resources (Coleman, 1988; Kao, 2004).

Bonding and bridging capital within low-income communities have been found to increase positive social, developmental, and educational outcomes for children and youth (Coleman, Hoffer, & Kilgore, 1982). Whereas parental social capital has been found to have more direct influences on students' academic achievement, community social capital has been found to have significant and primarily indirect effects on school achievement and attainment through its effects on students' peer groups and school-related attitudes and behaviors (Israel, Beaulieu, & Hartless, 2001; Perna & Titus, 2005).

A study of 827 African American adolescents in an urban school district, for example, found that students' involvement in community-based organizations, such as the African American church, indirectly influenced academic achievement through its positive and significant influence on their academic self-concept. A subset of these students was interviewed to enhance the interpretation of the survey data. Focal students reported that church provided them with opportunities to engage in a number of activities that required school-related skills, such as public speaking and reading and analyzing texts, in a supportive, nurturing environment. The social capital garnered through relationships between these youth and caring, encouraging adults provided them with the positive motivation and conception of self that are necessary for academic success (Sanders, 1998).

Similar findings based on high school data from the National Educational Longitudinal Study led Israel and colleagues (2001) to conclude:

> Access to adults outside the immediate family has a positive effect on these students.... The role of community social capital may not directly influence high school students' educational performance, but it may exert indirect effects through the variety of programs, organizations, and activities available in a locality. By these means, citizens can convey the importance of high educational performance to children. (pp. 62–63)

School-based social networks can also play a fundamental role in the well-being of families and children (Horvat, Weininger, & Lareau, 2003; McNeal, 1999). For instance, within the school context, if parents are able to form a sense of community, they can be mutual sources of information, can monitor each other's children, and can respond collectively to resolve school issues (Horvat et al., 2003). School personnel can also expand and strengthen children's social networks, helping them to successfully meet the demands of their environments. In addition to teachers and coaches acting as mentors, confidantes, and role models for children, Spilsbury (2005) found that other school personnel also play significant roles. For example, his study in Ohio neighborhoods found that school crossing guards play critical roles within children's social networks. In addition to helping children negotiate busy streets, crossing guards protected them from bullies, provided them with mittens, hats, and scarves during the winter months, buttoned their coats, wiped their noses, and provided emotional support after difficult school days. Other studies (see Stanton-Salazar, 2001) have reported similar findings and underscore the significance of schools and their personnel for the well-being of students and their families.

Thus communities, whether conceived as neighborhoods or social networks, influence educational, social, and emotional outcomes for children and youth. These influences are both direct and indirect and can serve as either risk or protective factors for young people. Economically distressed neighborhoods are associated with a variety of negative child and youth outcomes. Some theorists attribute these outcomes to high levels of social disorganization, others to peer contagion, and still others to the environmental risks and lack of collective efficacy that characterize many communities with high levels of poverty. Yet these neighborhoods also include resources embedded within and across social networks that can minimize and ameliorate the negative effects of poverty. For educators, being able to understand communities in their complexity, including the potential risk and protective factors that exist across socioeconomic strata, is essential for meeting the needs of all students. Equally important is recognizing the dynamic nature of communities and factors contributing to their continual change.

CHANGING U.S. COMMUNITIES

Three macrolevel trends have generated important changes in U.S. communities: immigration, deindustrialization of urban cities, and economic inequality. These trends have had important consequences for the types of student populations that schools currently serve and will serve in the foreseeable future.

Immigration

Perhaps one of the most important demographic changes affecting U.S. communities is the significant increase of immigrants, particularly from Latin America and Asia. According to the 2010 U.S. Census, self-identified Latinos and Asians accounted for 16% and 5%, respectively, of the total population, with over 50.5 million Latinos and 14 million Asians living in the United States (Humes, Jones, & Ramirez, 2011). Latinos and Asians experienced a higher population growth (43% for both groups) between 2000 and 2010 than whites and blacks (6% and 12%, respectively; Humes et al., 2011). Based on population projections, by 2050, one in three individuals in the United States will be Latino or Asian, compared to one in five in 2010 (Martin & Midgley, 2010). This trend is due to increased immigration to the United States and higher fertility rates among some ethnic groups. Latinas, for example, had a fertility rate of 2.73 children in 2009, in comparison to 1.99 for white females and 2.06 for black females (Martin et al., 2011). These population changes are having and will continue to have a significant impact on the cultures, practices, and lifestyles of communities in this country.

Most immigrants live in California, Texas, New York, Florida, Illinois, and New Jersey, with California, New York, and New Jersey having the highest concentrations. However, immigrant settlement patterns are rapidly becoming more dispersed throughout the United States. States such as Nevada, North Carolina, and Georgia, which are not among the most common receiving states, have experienced a steady increase of immigrants in the past 20 years. The number of immigrants in these states more than tripled (Beavers & D'Amico, 2005). Living in geographical areas with high (or low) concentrations of immigrants has important consequences for their adaptation and adjustment.

Diversity among immigrants is also reflected in their poverty levels and English language skills. Although the 2010 poverty rate for the foreign-born population was 19%, immigrants from Latin America and Africa were more likely to be poor (23% and 21%, respectively) than foreign-born Asians (14%). Poverty rates were even higher for foreign-born children (31%), with Mexican and African children having poverty rates of 46% and 37%, respectively (Grieco et al., 2012). Nationally, 18% of U.S.-born children and 72% of immigrant children spoke a language other than English at home (Hernandez, 2004). Moreover, in 2000, about 25% of children in immigrant families lived in households in which no one age 14 or older spoke "English only" or spoke "English very well." Although prior studies suggest that most children of immigrant parents prefer to use English, retention of a native language has varied by country of origin (Portes & Hao, 1998). Children from Latino backgrounds have been most likely to maintain their native language.

Immigrants, as a diverse group, bring important cultural and social assets to the United States. Immigrant parents tend to cultivate and rely on strong ethnic communities and social networks, participating in ethnic organizations that encourage positive outcomes (Small, 2004). Being part of a strong ethnic community yields possibilities for valuable information about jobs and educational opportunities, helpful social contacts, or financial support (Zhou & Bankston, 1998). Cohesive ethnic communities also facilitate social control among adolescents, affirm cultural values, and may provide exposure to positive role models (Coleman, 1988). As such, these communities house protective factors that can counterbalance the economic disadvantage many immigrant children experience (Portes, 1998).

Communities in the United States, then, are becoming more diverse as a result of current immigration and fertility trends. Although there are commonalities among immigrants, they differ in their national origins, cultures, languages, educational and social backgrounds, and relocation experiences, which have consequences for the communities where they reside. In addition to immigration, deindustrialization has also significantly changed how communities in the United States are organized and function.

Industrialization/Deindustrialization and Urbanization/Suburbanization

The proportion of individuals living in urban, suburban, and rural areas has been historically influenced by periods of industrialization and deindustrialization. The rapid expansion of industries and subsequent increasing labor demand and economic growth during the early 20th century was accompanied by a significant period of urbanization. Cities such as Detroit, Chicago, Philadelphia, Cleveland,

and Newark experienced important economic and population growth during the first half of the 1900s, in some cases until the late 1960s. These cities were niches for economic prosperity that also provided some economic opportunities for racial and ethnic minorities, especially because labor demands could not be filled solely by the white population. The expansion of cities during this time period also coincided with the largest voluntary migration of African Americans from the South to northern cities, known as the Great Migration (1915–1970; Wilkerson, 2010). Thus, during this time period, the population in cities not only grew, but its racial and ethnic makeup also changed.

Between 1950 and 2000, the population of the United States increased from 152 to 272 million, although some large cities began to experience a negative growth rate (Smith & Allen, 2008). After World War II, in the 1950s, suburbanization in the United States intensified. Economic prosperity after the war, governmental incentives to lower housing costs in suburbia, and the decentralization of industry facilitated growth of the suburbs. At this point, cities began to experience "white flight," the large-scale and rapid outmigration of individuals of European descent from the city to the suburbs (Jackson, 1987). The outmigration of whites had negative consequences for the prosperity and well-being of the cities, mainly due to the exodus of economic resources. Cities rapidly became financially debilitated and experienced significant funding cuts for several public services, including education and social welfare. With increasing residential mobility, the economic health of cities continued to decline. More homes became vacant, housing values decreased, and revenue from property taxes tumbled. The departure of businesses and shopping facilities also had a negative impact on urban economies (Hanlon & Vicino, 2007).

As cities have experienced racial residential segregation and economic crises, indicators of well-being such as health and safety have been negatively affected (Williams & Collins, 2001). Moreover, education indicators, such as test scores, attendance, and graduation rates, reflect the problems that are commonly found in schools serving inner-city children and youth. Many of these schools are plagued with larger student enrollments and fewer resources compared with their suburban and, to a lesser degree, rural counterparts (Kozol, 1992; Lippman, Burns, & McArthur, 1996), and these circumstances present obstacles to students' learning and development (Anyon, 2005).

It is important to note that suburbanization is not only a white phenomenon. Although whites began exiting cities first (Garnett, 2007), racial and ethnic minorities were responsible for the significant population increases in suburban communities during the 1990s (Frey, 2003). Some racial/ethnic minorities and immigrants viewed owning a home in the suburbs as a symbol of integration into the United States or a sign of prosperity (Garnett, 2007). Most moved into what is currently referred to as inner or first-ring suburbs. Inner or first-ring suburbs are those that lie just outside of cities, while those that are farther away are known as the outer suburbs. In terms of prosperity, there is a fundamental distinction between inner or first-ring suburbs and outer suburbs (Garnett, 2007). Indeed, Puentes (2001) has argued that some inner suburbs experience similar or worse problems than cities as their populations have increased in racial and ethnic diversity and wealthier residents have moved to the more affluent outer suburbs (Madden, 2000).

Increasing Economic Inequality

The third important trend that has had important consequences for U.S. communities is the increasing economic inequality that has occurred since 1965 (Reich, 2008). Sawhill and McLanahan (2006) define a society with economic opportunity as one "in which all children have a roughly equal chance of success regardless of the economic status of the family into which they were born" (p. 3). Similarly, a society has strong social mobility opportunities when the position of individuals within the economic structure is a function of their own merits and does not depend on their family background or inheritance. In other words, all children in such societies have equal chances of success, and correlations between parents' and children's incomes or occupations are small or nonexistent (Jenks & Tach, 2005).

The notion of the United States as the land of opportunities and social mobility is a fundamental element of the "American dream" (Hochschild & Scovronick, 2003). However, it is well known that the likelihood of transforming the "American dream" into reality varies significantly as a function of race, ethnicity, and socioeconomic status. In contrast to popular beliefs, income inequality in the United States has grown steadily since the late 1970s, with a major widening of the income gap between the middle and upper classes. Income has been increasing and taxes have been decreasing for the wealthy more than any other group in society (Knowledge Economy Network, 2012).

Beyond the global economic recession experienced since 2007 and historical events such as the Great Depression and several major wars, there are three key factors that have had important consequences for income inequality in the United States. First, the structure of the economy has significantly shifted from manufacturing and goods production to service provision, which brings along standardization of procedures, use of advanced technologies, and increasing demands for highly skilled workers (Clark & Clark, 2011). Second, the United States economy, described as an "hourglass," has been characterized by the expansion of high-skill and high-income jobs and low-skill and low-income jobs, along with a decline of middle-level jobs, which has significantly reduced economic mobility. Moreover, patterns of job expansion are racialized (Wright & Dwyer, 2003). Whites are concentrated at the upper level of the structure, whereas blacks and Latinos are concentrated at the bottom of the employment structure. Third, with globalization and increasing trade agreements with low-wage countries, the routine part of production or services (e.g., keypunch operators, routine data processing) is transferred to countries where labor is cheaper. As a result, good-paying routine jobs in the United States are decreasing (Reich, 2008). These three characteristics of the U.S. economy have contributed to a steady increase in income inequality.

In sum, the three macrolevel factors that are generating important changes in U.S. communities are immigration, deindustrialization and suburbanization, and increasing economic inequality. These factors have affected communities throughout the United States, resulting in greater ethnic heterogeneity, residential mobility, and economic insecurity. Schools, in collaboration with individuals and other institutions in students' communities, can help to address these conditions and lessen their impact on the learning and development of children and youth. In the following section, we discuss the benefits and challenges of school–community collaboration.

SCHOOL–COMMUNITY COLLABORATION

Schools, at their best, are institutions intricately linked to the stability and well-being of their surrounding communities (Tatian, Kingsley, Parilla, & Pendall, 2012). Schools can realize this potential by strategically partnering with individuals and organizations to enhance the social capital available to students, families, community members, and school personnel. In this section, we define school–community partnerships and describe their benefits, as well as challenges to their successful implementation.

Defining School-Community Partnerships

School–community partnerships refer to connections between schools and individuals, businesses, organizations, and institutions within or beyond the geographic boundaries of neighborhoods. Within the theoretical literature, there are a number of rationales for school–community partnerships. Proponents emphasize their importance for effective school functioning, arguing that such collaboration can provide underresourced schools with human, financial, and material resources to operate more effectively (Waddock, 1995). Proponents also argue that school–community partnerships, specifically those that involve businesses and universities, are critically important because leaders, managers, and personnel in business and higher education are uniquely equipped to help schools ensure that students are college and career ready (Nasworthy & Rood, 1990). Others argue that through mentoring, tutoring, and other volunteer programs, school–community partnerships can increase the number of caring adults available to children and youth and committed to their learning and well-being (Merz & Furman, 1997). Still others view school–community partnerships as integral to school reform and broader efforts to improve community health and development (Mediratta, Shah, & McAlister, 2009).

School-community partnerships fall along a continuum from simple to complex. On the left end of the continuum are simple partnerships that require very little coordination, planning, or cultural and structural shifts in school functioning. Consequently, they are relatively easy to implement, especially for schools that lack the experience needed for more complex partnerships. For example, a school might partner with a local business to procure refreshments for an event or prizes for an incentive program. When well implemented, the impact of simple partnerships is likely to be positive, albeit limited. As school–community partnerships move right along the continuum, they increase in complexity. On the far right end are long-term partnerships characterized by bidirectional or multidirectional exchange, high levels of interaction, and extensive planning and coordination. Community schools that offer onsite integrated health, counseling, and recreational services to students and families are examples of complex partnerships.

In addition, school–community partnerships may have multiple foci. Activities may be student-centered, family-centered, school-centered, or community-centered. Student-centered activities include those that provide direct services or goods to students, for example, mentoring and tutoring programs, contextual learning and job-shadowing opportunities, as well as the provision of awards and scholarships to students. Family-centered activities are those that have parents or entire families as their primary focus. This category includes activities such as parenting workshops, general educational development (GED) and other adult education classes, parent/family incentives and awards, and family fun and learning nights. School-centered activities are those that benefit the school as a whole, such as beautification projects and the donation of school equipment and materials or activities that benefit the faculty, such as staff development and classroom assistance. Community-centered activities have as their primary focus the community and its citizens, for example, charitable outreach, neighborhood art projects, and community service and revitalization activities.

Schools can collaborate with a variety of community partners to plan and implement partnership activities. These partners include (1) large corporations and small businesses, (2) universities and educational institutions, (3) faith-based organizations, (4) government and military agencies, (5) health care organizations, (6) national service and volunteer organizations, (7) social service agencies, (8) charitable organizations, (9) senior citizen organizations, (10) cultural and recreational institutions, (11) media organizations, (12) sports franchises and associations, (13) other groups such as sororities and fraternities, and (14) community volunteers that can provide resources and social support to youth and schools (Sanders, 2006).

Research has documented the benefits of well-planned and implemented community partnerships. Community–school collaborations focused on academic subjects have been shown to enhance students' attitudes toward these subjects (Clark, 2002). Mentoring programs established through such partnerships have been found to have significant and positive effects on students' grades, school attendance, and exposure to career opportunities (McPartland & Nettles, 1991; Thompson & Kelly-Vance, 2001). Partnerships with businesses and other community organizations have provided schools with needed equipment, materials, and technical assistance and support for student instruction (Mickelson, 1999; Scales et al., 2005). Documented benefits of more complex school–community partnerships, such as community schools' offering integrated services, include behavioral and academic gains for students and greater access to needed services, and reduced stress and increased engagement in their children's education for parents (Sanders & Hembrick-Roberts, in press).

Challenges to School–Community Partnerships

School–community partnerships are not without challenges. Planning, designing, implementing, evaluating, and maintaining school–community partnerships take time, funding, leadership, and committed school and community members (Epstein et al., 2009). When any of these components are missing or insufficient, partnership activities fail to achieve the outcomes previously described (Sanders, 2006). Whether or how schools address these challenges depends largely on their organizational cultures.

As normative environments, schools are governed by patterns of behavior regarded as typical more than by clear rules or guidelines. These collective patterns constitute the school culture. Although cultures within schools and classrooms differ, there are some commonly observed norms that can impede effective school-community collaboration. Two such norms are isolation and autonomy. Mutually reinforcing, these cultural norms establish defined boundaries around classrooms and teacher practice (Lortie, 2002) that often extend to the school as a whole. That is, to maintain their ability to carry out their core functions—effective teaching and learning—schools may rationally feel the need to isolate themselves from "outsiders." This isolation also provides a degree of professional autonomy that educational leaders and practitioners value (Pearson & Moomaw, 2005) but that severely restricts community engagement.

Two additional norms that affect how schools conceptualize their roles and relationships with their surrounding communities are order and control. Schools are characterized by a high degree of population density and a nonselective and sometimes unwilling population. To carry out their core responsibilities, schools must coordinate and control students' behaviors. Consequently, one measure of school and teacher effectiveness is the extent to which schools can maintain acceptable levels of order and control. By definition, collaborating with individuals and organizations in the community requires that schools relinquish or share some of the control exercised by teachers and administrators. Consequently, many schools may resist partnership efforts, especially when they threaten to penetrate organizational planning and decision making (Shatkin & Gershberg, 2007).

Yet research shows that with a clear understanding of the benefits of partnerships; strong leadership that models, provides professional support for, and rewards collaborative practice; and persistence and time, schools can develop transformative cultures that challenge norms that impede community engagement (Comer, 1995; Epstein, 2011). Teachers, through their efforts in the classroom, school, and community, can play an essential role in achieving this cultural transformation.

TEACHERS AS AGENTS OF COMMUNITY RESPONSIVENESS

Recognizing the role of teachers in developing collaborative classrooms and schools, this section describes how teachers can engage in professional practice that is responsive to students' communities. The community-responsive teaching strategies that we describe include collaboration with community-based organizations and individuals to enhance students' learning; incorporation of families' funds of knowledge into classroom lessons; and the development of community-based service learning projects to encourage civic engagement. Although not exhaustive, these practices illustrate how teachers can overcome norms of isolation and control to facilitate stronger school–community ties that promote students' learning and development.

Collaborating with Community-Based Organizations

Principles of universal design for learning and multicultural education highlight the importance of making instructional styles and classroom content relevant to students in order to enhance learning and reduce disruptive behaviors (Banks, 2001; Hackman, 2008; Nieto, 1999). One way that teachers can create more relevant and engaging learning opportunities is by increasing the role, visibility, and presence of community individuals and institutions in students' formal education. For example, teachers can identify individuals from community organizations to serve as guest speakers, provide demonstrations, deliver performances, and provide hands-on learning opportunities. When linked to the school curriculum, this outreach can boost students' enjoyment of and engagement with subject matter content. History can come alive as local citizens recount their life experiences, ratios and proportions can be made more meaningful as students work with local artists to paint a community mural, and lessons about changing seasons can be enhanced by community walks led by local leaders. These activities are just a few of the ways that teachers can connect communities and schools.

To successfully implement these and similar activities, teachers must become knowledgeable about the community surrounding the school. Because many teachers, especially those in urban schools, live outside the neighborhoods where they teach, this requires intentional effort. Freiberg and Driscoll (2000) use the term "advance work" to describe what teachers do to get to know their students and school communities. Regarding the latter, Frieberg (2002) suggests that teachers can shop in the neighborhoods where they teach, attend and volunteer for community events, eat at local diners and restaurants, and borrow books from the local library. To identify potential resources to support classroom instruction, teachers can also drive, walk, or take a bus through the neighborhood, noting the businesses, social service agencies, faith-based organizations, health care facilities, and educational institutions within a 5-mile radius of the school (Sanders, 2006). Through this "advance work," teachers can establish authentic, supportive, and academically challenging learning environments theoretically and empirically linked to higher student achievement (Marks, 2000).

Funds of Knowledge

To develop stronger relationships with students' families, teachers can incorporate their "funds of knowledge" into educational practice. Funds of knowledge refer to the sociocultural and economic knowledge and traditions manifested in daily activities that are also situated in the historical evolution of families (Moll, Amanti, Neff, & Gonzales, 1992). All families, regardless of their socioeconomic status, immigrant origin, ethnicity, or language, have strengths and resources deriving from their life experiences that can enrich the school environment. Teachers and schools working within this framework incorporate their students' family traditions and experiences in the curriculum, classroom activities, and assignments to enhance learning (Gonzalez, Moll, & Amanti, 2005) and overcome cultural differences between the school and the home (Warren, Hong, Rubin, & Uy, 2009).

Accessing families' funds of knowledge requires that teachers systematically gather information about their interests, experiences, and lives. This information is often gathered through classroom assignments or ethnographic interviews at students' homes. Teachers can work with university researchers and faculty and school colleagues to develop appropriate interview questions, analyze the data, and brainstorm strategies to incorporate their findings into classroom instruction (Genzuk, 1999). Genzuk (1999) describes how this process allowed one teacher to move from a deficit to a strengths-based approach when working with Mexican American youth.

Indeed, there are several benefits of using strategies such as "funds of knowledge" to develop strong partnerships with communities. First, it helps to create trusting and respectful relationships with families because schools show that they know, respect, and value their cultures and traditions regardless of how different they are from the mainstream. Given the history of oppression and discrimination that many minority groups have experienced (Spring, 2010), some families may feel alienated by the school system. Incorporating families' "funds of knowledge" into the school and classroom could be an important first step in building stronger connections between students' homes and the school.

Second, it can help strengthen parents' sense of efficacy as partners in their children's education. Some parents may feel that they don't have the experience and know-how to help their children with their schoolwork or navigate the school system. However, these negative perceptions could be neutralized if parents realize that schools are validating and acknowledging their experiences and traditions as relevant for their children's learning. Third, incorporating family-based knowledge into the classroom helps to make students' learning experiences more meaningful. Learning is situated in a familiar social context and is conceptualized as reciprocal when the knowledge that students bring to the classroom is also recognized as relevant.

Service Learning Projects

Advocates of service learning argue that although educational and intellectual achievement are necessary aspects of public education, equally important is a focus on community and civic participation. Writing two decades ago, Ruggenberg (1993) argued that without the balance of both, "we give students the impression that acts of courage, compassion, duty, and commitment are rare, and surely done by extraordinary people; people much different from them" (p. 13). Service learning projects provide students with opportunities to assist individuals or agencies in addressing social and environmental problems or community needs. Field experiences can include working with emotionally or physically disabled children, planting community gardens, or organizing voter registration drives. The goals of service learning include building stronger neighborhoods and communities, creating more active and involved citizens, and invigorating classroom instruction.

Careful planning that includes teachers, administrators, and supervisors of the field experiences is required to successfully incorporate students' service learning projects into the school curriculum. The curriculum should be adapted to include opportunities for students to reflect on their service learning experiences, tie them to academic content, and analyze the consequences of their work (Halsted & Schine, 1994; Ruggenberg, 1993). Studies suggest that when tied to coursework, service learning helps students to gain a more comprehensive understanding of academic subjects and positively affects their reflective judgment (Eyler, 2002). At the same time, involvement in service learning has been linked to stronger self-efficacy and civic engagement attitudes (Morgan & Streb, 2001).

There are a variety of resources that teachers can draw on to help them design and evaluate effective service learning projects. One of these is a handbook developed through a collaboration between the University of San Diego and the San Diego Unified School District (2010). The handbook, designed specifically for teachers of elementary school students, describes the underlying principles of service learning, provides examples of service learning projects for different academic subjects, and provides reflection and evaluation exercises for students. The National Service-Learning Clearinghouse (2012) is another useful resource for teachers at all grade levels; it offers a database titled Service-Learning Ideas and Curricular Examples. The database contains hundreds of service learning lesson plans, syllabi, and project ideas that are submitted by educators and service learning practitioners. Teachers can filter the entries by student and school demographics, type of service, and theoretical approach. Through the use of such resources, teachers can create learning opportunities that are responsive to both student and community needs.

CONCLUSION

School–community collaboration matters for children and youth. It is a mechanism to enhance the social capital available to students, families, community members, and school personnel. As such, school–community collaboration can improve school functioning, facilitate community development, and enhance students' learning and well-being. By engaging in community-responsive practices, teachers play a key role in creating school cultures that support and sustain effective community partnerships.

To be effective as agents of community responsiveness in schools, teachers require professional development (Epstein & Sanders, 2006). Ideally, teachers' professional preparation for collaboration would begin during the preservice stage of teacher training so that they enter schools and classrooms with a clear understanding of the benefits and rewards of collaboration, as well as a working knowledge of strategies for successful collaboration. It also would be an ongoing theme of the inservice professional development of educators so that the day-to-day reality of teaching and classroom management would not cloud their view of themselves as partners in the development of children and youth.

In addition to a greater emphasis on collaboration, preservice teachers also require professional development to build their capacities to work with diverse populations. Growing diversity in U.S. communities is providing a broad set of opportunities for enriching the learning experiences of all students. Yet this same diversity poses challenges to schools and teachers. Stress and conflict can emerge between communities and school personnel if differences in cultural lenses, norms, and expectations regarding the ways of educating and socializing children exist (Lawrence-Lightfoot, 1978, 2004). Being able to cross borders of difference is critical for meaningful and sustained connections between educators and the families and communities they serve. Thus teachers need opportunities to enhance their skills as border crossers (Sanders, 2009).

The first decade of the 21st century suggests that our society and schools are becoming more diverse and complex. Teacher educators must ensure that their graduates are prepared to meet the needs of PreK–12 students in these challenging times. This is no easy task given limited credit hours and national and state standards and requirements. Nevertheless, teacher professional development programs must find ways to prepare teachers to be critical, innovative, and collaborative thinkers and strategists, as well as pedagogical and subject matter experts. Integrating key themes such as family and community engagement, collaborative decision making, and diversity into methods and content courses, action research projects, and internships is one way to begin to meet this challenge. Theory and research suggest that we should attend to these themes, and our increasingly diverse schools and communities demand that we do so.

QUESTIONS FOR DISCUSSION

1. Which of the theories explaining the impact of neighborhoods on student outcomes do you find most compelling? Explain.

2. Do you think school–community partnerships are important for students regardless of socioeconomic status? Why or why not?

3. What can teachers and administrators do to ensure that social networks within schools are inclusive of diverse populations?

4. What skills, knowledge, and dispositions do teachers need in order to successfully implement the community-responsive teaching strategies described? What courses and experiences are needed to prepare teachers for community-responsive teaching?

5. Many schools pull students from a variety of neighborhoods. What does this mean for school–community partnerships and community-responsive teaching? Explain.

REFERENCES

Aaronson, D. (1997). Sibling estimates of neighborhood effects. *Neighborhood Poverty, 2,* 80-93.

Anyon, J. (2005). *Radical possibilities: Public policy, urban education, and a new social movement.* New York: Taylor & Francis Group.

Banks, J. A. (2001). *Cultural diversity and education.* Boston: Allyn & Bacon.

Beavers, L., & D'Amico, J. (2005). *Children in immigrant families: U.S. and state-level findings from the 2000 Census.* Baltimore and Washington, DC: The Annie E. Casey Foundation and the Population Reference Bureau.

Berliner, D. (2006). Our impoverished view of educational reform. *Teachers College Record, 108*(6), 949–995.

Berliner, D. (2009). *Poverty and potential: Out of school factors and school success.* Boulder, CO: National Education Policy Center. Retrieved September 1, 2012, from *http:// nepc.colorado.edu/publication/poverty-and-potential.*

Bronfenbrenner, U. (1994). Ecological models of human development. In T. Husen & T. N. Postlethwaite (Eds.), *International encyclopedia of education* (2nd ed., Vol. 3, pp. 1643–1647). Oxford, UK: Pergamon.

Catsambis, S., & Beveridge, A. A. (2001). Does neighborhood matter? Family, neighborhood, and school influences on eighth-grade mathematics achievement. *Sociological Focus, 34*(4), 435–457.

Chase-Lansdale, P. L., Gordon, R. A., Brooks-Gunn, J., & Klebanov, P. K. (2000). Neighborhood and family influences on the intellectual and behavioral competence of preschool and early school-age children. *Neighborhood Poverty, 1,* 79–119.

Clark, C., & Clark, E. A. (2011). America's response to globalization and financial crisis: The "high road" and "low road" alternatives. *International Journal of Contemporary Sociology, 48*(2), 305–332.

Clark, R. (2002). Ten hypotheses about what predicts student achievement for African American students and all other students: What the research shows. In W. R. Allen, M. B. Spencer, & C. O'Conner (Eds.), *African American education: Race, community, inequality, and achievement: A tribute to Edgar G. Epps* (pp. 155–177). Oxford, UK: Elsevier Science.

Coleman, J. S. (1988). Social capital in the creation of human capital. *American Journal of Sociology, 94,* S95–S120.

Coleman, J. S., Hoffer, T., & Kilgore, S. (1982). *High school achievement: Public, Catholic, and private schools compared.* New York: Basic Books.

Comer, J. (1995). *School power: Implications of an intervention project.* New York: Free Press.

Crane, J. (1991). The epidemic theory of ghettos and neighborhood effects on dropping out and teenage childbearing. *American Journal of Sociology, 96,* 1226–1259.

de Souza Briggs, X. (1997). Moving up versus moving out: Neighborhood effects in housing mobility programs. *Housing Policy Debate, 8*(1), 195–234.

Dewey, J. (1976). *The school and society* (J. A. Boydston, Ed.). Carbondale: Southern Illinois University Press.

Dornbusch, S. M., Ritter, P. L., & Steinberg, L. (1991). Community influences on the relation of family statuses to adolescent school performance: Differences between African Americans and non-Hispanic Whites. *American Journal of Education, 99,* 543–567.

Epstein, J. (2011). *School, family, and community partnerships: Preparing educators and improving schools* (2nd ed.). Boulder, CO: Westview Press.

Epstein, J. L., & Sanders, M. G. (2006). Prospects for change: Preparing educators for school, family, and community partnerships. *Peabody Journal of Education, 81*(2), 81–120.

Epstein, J. L., Sanders, M., Sheldon, S., Simon, B., Salinas, K., Jansorn, N., et al. (2009). *School, family and community partnerships: Your handbook for action* (3rd ed.). Thousand Oaks, CA: Corwin Press.

Eyler, J. (2002). Reflection: Linking service and learning—Linking students and communities. *Journal of Social Issues, 58*(3), 517–534.

Freiberg, H. J. (2002). Essential skills for new teachers. *Educational Leadership, 59*(6), 56–60.

Freiberg, H. J., & Driscoll, A. (2000). *Universal teaching strategies* (3rd ed.). Boston: Allyn & Bacon.

Frey, W. H. (2003). Melting pot suburbs: A study of suburban diversity. In B. Katz & R. E. Lang (Eds.), *Redefining urban and suburban America: Evidence from Census 2000* (Vol. 1, pp. 155–163). Washington, DC: Brookings Institution Press.

Galindo, C., & Sheldon, S. (2011). School efforts to improve parental involvement and effects on students' achievement in kindergarten. *Early Childhood Research Quarterly, 27*, 90–103.

Garner, C. L., & Raudenbush, S. W. (1991). Neighborhood effects on educational attainment: A multilevel analysis. *Sociology of Education, 64*(4), 251–262.

Garnett, N. S. (2007). Suburbs as exit, suburbs as entrance. *Michigan Law Review, 106*(2), 277–304.

Genzuk, M. (1999). Tapping into community funds of knowledge. In *Effective strategies for English language acquisition: Curriculum guide for the professional development of teachers, grades kindergarten through eight* (pp. 9–21). Los Angeles: Los Angeles Annenberg Metropolitian Project/ARCO Foundation. Retrieved from *www-bcf.usc.edu/~genzuk/Genzuk_ARCO_Funds_of_Knowledge.pdf.*

Gonzalez, N., Moll, L. C., & Amanti, C. (2005). *Funds of knowledge theorizing practices in households, communities, and classrooms.* Mahwah, NJ: Erlbaum.

Grieco, E. L., Acosta, Y. D., de la Cruz, P. G., Gambino, C., Gryn, T., Larsen, J. L., et al. (2012). The foreign-born population in the United States: 2010. *American Community Survey Report.* Suitland, MD: U.S. Census Bureau. Retrieved from *www.census.gov/prod/2012pubs/acs-19.pdf.*

Hackman, H. W. (2008). Broadening the pathway to academic success: The critical intersection of social justice education, critical multicultural education, and universal instructional design. In J. L. Higbee & E. Goff (Eds.), *Pedagogy and student services for institutional transformation: Implementing universal design in higher education* (pp. 25–48). Minneapolis: University of Minnesota Center for Research on Developmental Education and Urban Literacy.

Halpern, D. (2005). *Social capital.* Cambridge, UK: Polity Press.

Halsted, A. L., & Schine, J. C. (1994). Service learning: The promise and the risk. *New England Journal of Public Policy, 10*(1), 22.

Hanlon, B., & Vicino, T. (2007). The fate of inner suburbs: Evidence from metropolitan Baltimore. *Urban Geography, 28*(3), 249–275.

Henderson, A., & Mapp, K. (2002). *A new wave of evidence: The impact of school, family, and community connections on student achievement.* Austin, TX: Southwest Educational Development Laboratory.

Hernandez, D. J. (2004). Demographic change and the life circumstances of immigrant families. *The Future of Children, 14*(2), 17–48.

Hochschild, J., & Scovronick, N. (2003). *The American dream and the public schools.* New York: Oxford University Press.

Horvat, E. M., Weininger, E. B., & Lareau, A. (2003). From social ties to social capital: Class differences in the relations between schools and parent networks. *American Educational Research Journal, 40*(2), 319–351.

Humes, K. R., Jones, N. A., & Ramirez, R. R. (2011). *Overview of race and Hispanic origin 2010. 2010 Census briefs.* Suitland, MD: U.S. Census Bureau. Retrieved from *www. census.gov/prod/cen2010/briefs/c2010br-02.pdf.*

Israel, G. D., Beaulieu, L. J., & Hartless, G. (2001). The influence of family and community social capital on educational achievement. *Rural Sociology, 66*(1), 43–68.

Jackson, K. (1987). *Crabgrass frontier: The suburbanization of the United States.* New York: Oxford University Press.

Jones, M. B., & Jones, D. R. (2000). The contagious nature of antisocial behavior. *Criminology, 38*(1), 25–46.

Jenks, C., & Tach, L. (2005) Would equal opportunity mean more mobility? In S. L. Morgan, D. B. Grusky, & G. S. Fields (Eds.), *Mobility and inequality: Frontiers of research in sociology and economics* (pp. 23–58). Redwood City, CA: Stanford University Press.

Kao, G. (2004). Social capital and its relevance to minority and immigrant populations. *Sociology of Education, 77,* 172–175.

Kingston, B., Huizinga, D., & Elliott, D. S. (2009). A test of social disorganization theory in high-risk urban neighborhoods. *Youth and Society, 41*(1), 53–79.

Knowledge Economy Network. (2012). Trends of income inequality in the United States (Weekly Brief No. 27). Retrieved from *www.knowledge-economy.net/uploads/documents/2012/briefs/KEN%20Brief,%20No.%2027,%20Year%202.pdf.*

Kozol, J. (1992). *Savage inequalities: Children in America's schools.* New York: Harper Perennial.

Lawrence-Lightfoot, S. (1978). *Worlds apart: Relationships between families and schools.* New York: Basic Books.

Lawrence-Lightfoot, S. (2004). *The essential conversation: What parents and teachers can learn from each other.* New York: Ballantine Books.

Leventhal, T., & Brooks-Gunn, J. (2000). The neighborhoods they live in: The effects of neighborhood residence on child and adolescent outcomes. *Psychological Bulletin, 126*(2), 309.

Lin, N. (2001). *Social capital: A theory of social structure and action* (Vol. 19). Cambridge, UK: Cambridge University Press.

Lippman, L., Burns, S., & McArthur, E. (1996). *Urban schools: The challenges of location* (NCES Publication No. 96-184). Washington, DC: U.S. Department of Education.

Lortie, D. C. (2002). *Schoolteacher: A sociological study.* Chicago: University of Chicago Press.

Madden, J. F. (2000). Jobs, cities, and suburbs in the global economy. *Annals of the American Academy of Political and Social Science, 572,* 78–89.

Marks, H. M. (2000). Student engagement in instructional activity: Patterns in the elementary, middle, and high school years. *American Educational Research Journal, 37*(1), 153–184.

Martin, J. A., Hamilton, B. E., Ventura, S. J., Osterman, M. J. K., Kirmeyer, S., Mathews, T. J., et al. (2011). Births: Final data for 2009. *National Vital Statistics Reports, 60*(1), 1–72. Retrieved from *www.cdc.gov/nchs/data/nvsr60/nvsr60_01.pdf*

Martin, P., & Midgley, E. (2010). *Immigration in America 2010: Population Bulletin Update.*

Washington, DC: Population Reference Bureau. Retrieved from *www.prb.org/pdf10/ immigration-update2010.pdf.*

McNeal, R. B., Jr. (1999). Parental involvement as social capital: Differential effectiveness on science achievement, truancy, and dropping out. *Social Forces, 78*(1), 117–144.

McPartland, J. M., & Nettles, S. M. (1991). Using community adults as advocates or mentors for at-risk middle school students: A two-year evaluation of project RAISE. *American Journal of Education, 99,* 568–586.

Mediratta, K., Shah, S., & McAlister, S. (2009). *Community organizing for stronger schools: Strategies and successes.* Cambridge, MA: Harvard Education Press.

Merz, C., & Furman, G. (1997). *Community and schools: Promise and paradox.* New York: Teachers College Press.

Mickelson, T. (1999). International business machinations: A case study of corporate involvement in local educational reform. *Teachers College Record, 100*(3), 476–512.

Moll, L. C., Amanti, C., Neff, D., & Gonzalez, N. (1992). Funds of knowledge for teaching: Using a qualitative approach to connect homes and classrooms. *Theory into Practice, 21*(2), 132–141.

Morgan, W., & Streb, M. (2001). Building citizenship: How student voice in service-learning develops civic values. *Social Science Quarterly, 82*(1), 154–169.

Nasworthy, C., & Rood, M. (1990). *Bridging the gap between business and education: Reconciling expectations for student achievement* (Critical Issues in Student Achievement Paper No. 4). Austin, TX: Southwest Educational Development Lab.

National Service-Learning Clearinghouse. (2012). Service-learning ideas and curricular examples (SLICE). Retrieved September 1, 2012, from *www.servicelearning.org/slice.*

Nieto, S. (1999). *The light in their eyes: Creating multicultural learning communities.* New York: Teachers College Press.

Pearson, L. C., & Moomaw, W. (2005). The relationship between teacher autonomy and stress, work satisfaction, empowerment, and professionalism. *Educational Research Quarterly, 29*(1), 38–54.

Perna, L. W., & Titus, M. A. (2005). The relationship between parental involvement as social capital and college enrollment: An examination of racial/ethnic group differences. *Journal of Higher Education, 76*(5), 485–518.

Portes, A. (1998). Divergent destinies: Immigration, the second generation, and the rise of transnational communities. In P. Schuck & R. Munz (Eds.), *Paths to inclusion: The integration of migrants in the United States and Germany* (pp. 33–57). Oxford, UK: Berghahn Books.

Portes, A., & Hao, L. (1998). E pluribus unum: Bilingualism and the loss of language in the second generation. *Sociology of Education, 71*(4), 269–294.

Puentes, R. (2001). First suburbs in the Northeast and Midwest: Assets, challenges, and opportunities. *Fordham Urban Law Journal, 29*(4), 1468–1491.

Reich, R. B. (2008). Why the rich are getting richer and the poor, poorer. In L. Weis (Ed.), *The way class works* (pp. 13–24). New York: Routledge.

Ruggenberg, J. (1993). Community service learning: A vital component of secondary school education. *Moral Education Forum, 18*(3), 13-19.

Sampson, R. J., & Groves, W. B. (1989). Community structure and crime: Testing social-disorganization theory. *American Journal of Sociology, 94*(4), 774–802.

Sampson, R. J., & Morenoff, J. D. (1997). Ecological perspectives on the neighborhood context of urban poverty: Past and present. *Neighborhood Poverty, 2,* 1–22.

Sampson, R. J., Morenoff, J. D., & Gannon-Rowley, T. (2002). Assessing "neighborhood effects": Social processes and new directions in research. *Annual Review of Sociology, 28,* 443–478.

Sanders, M. (2006*). Building school–community partnerships: Collaboration for student success*. Thousand Oaks, CA: Corwin Press.

Sanders, M., & Hembrick-Roberts, J. (2013). Leadership for service integration in schools. In L. Tillman & J. Scheurich (Eds.), *Handbook of research on educational leadership for diversity and equity* (pp. 476–493). London, UK: Routledge/Taylor & Francis.

Sanders, M., & Sheldon, S. (2009). *Principals matter: A guide to comprehensive programs of school, family, and community partnerships*. Thousand Oaks, CA: Corwin Press.

Sanders, M. G. (1998). The effects of school, family, and community support on the academic achievement of African American adolescents. *Urban Education, 33*(3), 385–409.

Sanders, M. G. (2009). Teachers and parents. In L. J. Saha & A. G. Dworkin, *International handbook of research on teachers and teaching* (pp. 331–341). New York: Springer.

San Diego Unified School District. (2010). Learn and serve San Diego. Retrieved September 1, 2012, from *www.sandi.net/cms/lib/CA01001235/Centricity/Domain/62/Current%20CRD%20Web%20Docs/Elementary%20Handbook%20Revised%20July%2010.pdf.*

Sawhill, I. V., & McLanahan, S. (2006). Introducing the issue. *The Future of Children, 16*(2), 3–17.

Scales, P. C., Foster, K. C., Mannes, M., Horst, M. A., Pinto, K. C., & Rutherford, A. (2005). School–business partnerships, developmental assets, and positive outcomes among urban high school students: A mixed-methods study. *Urban Education, 40*(2), 144–189.

Shatkin, G., & Gershberg, A. I. (2007). Empowering parents and building communities: The role of school-based councils in educational governance and accountability. *Urban Education, 42*(6), 582–615.

Shaw, C. R., & McKay, H. D. (1969). *Juvenile delinquency and urban areas: A study of rates of delinquency in relation to differential characteristics of local communities in American cities*. Chicago: University of Chicago Press.

Small, M. L. (2004). *Villa Victoria: The transformation of social capital in a Boston barrio*. Chicago: University of Chicago Press.

Small, M. L., & McDermott, M. (2006). The presence of organizational resources in poor urban neighborhoods: An analysis of average and contextual effects. *Social Forces, 84*(3), 1697–1724.

Smith, F., & Allen, S. (2008). Urban decline (and success) in the United States. In R. Whaples (Ed.), *EH.Net Encyclopedia*. Retrieved from *http://eh.net/encyclopedia/article/Smith.Urban.Decline.doc.*

South, S. J., Baumer, E. P., & Lutz, A. (2003). Interpreting community effects on youth educational attainment. *Youth and Society, 35*(1), 3–36.

Spilsbury, J. C. (2005). Children's perceptions of the social support of neighborhood institutions and establishments. *Human Organization, 64*(2), 126–134.

Spring, J. (2010). *Deculturalization and the struggle for equality: A brief history of the education of dominated cultures in the United States* (6th ed.). New York: McGraw-Hill.

Stanton-Salazar, R. D. (2001). *Manufacturing hope and despair: The school and kin support networks of U.S.-Mexican youth*. New York: Teachers College Press.

Tatian, P. A., Kingsley, G. T., Parilla, J., & Pendall, R. (2012). *Building successful neighborhoods*. Washington, DC: Urban Institute.

Thompson, L. A., & Kelly-Vance, L. (2001). The impact of mentoring on academic achievement of at-risk youth. *Children and Youth Services Review, 23*(3), 227–242.

Waddock, S. A. (1995). *Not by schools alone: Sharing responsibility for America's education reform*. Westport, CT: Praeger.

Warren, M. R., Hong, S., Rubin, C. L., & Uy, P. S. (2009). Based relational approach to parent engagement in schools. *Teacher College Record, 111*(9), 2209–2254

Wilkerson, I. (2010). *The warmth of other suns: The epic story of America's great migration*. New York: Vintage Books.

Williams, D. R., & Collins, C. (2001). Racial residential segregation: A fundamental cause of racial disparities in health. *Public Health Reports, 116*, 404–416.

Wilson, J. (1996). *When work disappears: The world of the new urban poor*. New York: Knopf.

Wright, E. O., & Dwyer, R. E. (2003). The patterns of job expansions in the USA: A comparison of the 1960s and 1990s. *Socio-Economic Review, 1*, 289–325.

Zhou, M., & Bankston, C. L. (1998). Networks of social relations: Support and control. *Growing up American: How Vietnamese children adapt to life in the United States* (pp. 93–107). New York: Russell Sage Foundation.

CHAPTER 7

District Issues

Administrators at All Levels Involved in Teachers' Professional Development

MARILYN TALLERICO

- There are three main ways that PreK–12 administrators influence student learning.
- A critical leadership role is to streamline school priorities.
- The knowledge base on professional development helps leaders focus.
- Administrators shape working conditions and processes key to professional development effectiveness.
- Examples of how to make time for collaboration can inform professional development leadership.

This chapter centers on the importance of PreK–12 administrators in supporting and sustaining teachers' professional development. Several premises underlie our approach to this topic. First, student learning is the goal; that is, the desired end. Ongoing teacher growth is but one of several means toward that goal. Other means that could be considered yet that are beyond the scope of this chapter include, for example, rigorous curricula, engaged parents and caregivers, and assessment practices that provide educators with timely and actionable information.

Our second premise is that leadership at all levels matters. Other chapters in this *Handbook* elaborate teacher-led models and the best practices, studies, or theories undergirding them. Here we synthesize the research on administrative leadership, with particular emphasis on applications to adult and student learning.

FIRST THINGS FIRST: CONNECTIONS TO STUDENT LEARNING

In U.S. public education, school size and district communities vary enormously, from small rural environments to sprawling urban systems, with innumerable combinations of unique variables in between (Mizell, 2010; Wirt & Kirst, 2005). Accordingly, much of the theorizing about effective leadership underscores context-dependent, situational differences and demands (Firestone, 2009; Murphy, Elliott, Goldring, & Porter, 2006). Clearly, it's wise to avoid overgeneralizations about relationships as complex as those between administrative leadership and student learning.

That said, comprehensive studies of schools, districts, and administrators have found that at least three broad categories of leadership practices appear to be effective regardless of context. These sets of practices capture how school and district administrators influence children's learning in indirect yet significant ways (Leithwood, Louis, Anderson, & Wahlstrom, 2004; Leithwood & Riehl, 2005). They are: (1) setting directions; (2) developing people; and (3) structuring workplace conditions.

Although the "developing people" finding may seem most obviously relevant to the topic at hand, we organize this chapter around all three aspects of leadership practice. Why? Because their potential to positively influence student learning derives from their synergy. That is, each is valuable, yet insufficient, by itself. Instead, it is the combination and mutual reinforcement among them that can result in positive outcomes for children (Wahlstrom, Louis, Leithwood, & Anderson, 2010).

In this chapter, we interpret and apply this trifaceted framework (Leithwood et al., 2004; Leithwood & Riehl, 2005). Although space limitations preclude illustration of every aspect of the framework, the examples included are intended to highlight administrators' roles specific to supporting and sustaining teachers' professional development (Tallerico, 2005).

SETTING DIRECTIONS

Direction setting means collaboratively establishing priorities that focus educators' collective work (Marzano, Waters, & McNulty, 2005). At the district level, those priorities are typically articulated in annual or multiyear statements of goals resulting from data analyses, varied constituencies' input, and endorsement by the governing board. In parallel fashion at the building level, improvement plans are often generated by teachers, parent representatives, and principals to determine where school staffs' shared efforts should be aimed. School improvement planning is intended to connect to and support district goals while simultaneously addressing particular local factors (e.g., student demographics that may be different from those of other schools in the district; unique circumstances; language diversity).

DuFour (2002) underscores a critical point for increasing the odds that such direction setting will be motivating to teachers' collective work:

> Schools stumble when their leaders cannot identify priorities, or when they seem
> to say, "Pay attention to everything; everything is important." . . . Six school
> improvement goals are not better than one. Meaningful substantive changes in
> schools occur through focused, concentrated efforts. (pp. 60–61)

Similarly, after carefully investigating the ways school systems address the problem
of limited time for teachers' professional development, Watts and Castle (1993)
conclude that "Sometimes it is better to slow down, accomplish more by attempting
less, and accept the fact that you can't do it all" (p. 309).

What does "accomplishing more by attempting less" mean for adult-learning
direction setting? It is better to address a few carefully selected professional development priorities deeply and well than to scatter limited resources of time, funding,
and human capital. Moreover, it is wiser to sustain those few priorities over time
rather than spread investments across multiple shorter-term initiatives. Michael
Fullan's extensive research on change in educational organizations illuminates the
serious downsides of the latter:

> The greatest problem faced by school districts and schools is not resistance to
> innovation, but the fragmentation, overload, and incoherence resulting from the
> uncritical acceptance of too many different innovations. (1991, p. 197)

In contrast to conventional wisdom about resisters or blockers of leaders' directions, Fullan's insights shift attention from change-averse teachers to the broader
working conditions in which changes are introduced. This is a different way of
thinking about why the improvements that administrators embrace may not take
hold school- or districtwide. Fullan's perspective suggests that resistance to change
is more likely a *symptom* than a *cause* of systemic problems. Fragmentation, disori-
entation, and dilution of focus can easily creep into the adult work environment
when well-intended improvement efforts accumulate over years.

School and district administrators occupy key vantage points for reviewing
and making sense of the bigger picture of cumulative changes. As precursors to
new direction setting, opportunities for coherence making can begin by mapping
out the recent history of professional development expectations for teachers in the
form of a graphic organizer or spreadsheet. If the graphic demonstrates that teachers are being pulled in myriad directions (as Fullan's research suggests it likely will),
tough decisions must be faced about which initiatives to discontinue and which to
extend and strengthen over time.

Help in making streamlining decisions can be found in studies of factors that
contribute to professional development effectiveness (Birman, Desimone, Porter,
& Garet, 2000; Darling-Hammond, Wei, Andree, Richardson, & Orphanos, 2009;
Desimone, 2009; Garet, Porter, Desimone, Birman, & Yoon, 2001). Taken together,
this research suggests that professional development should emphasize deepening
teachers' content knowledge. That means subject-matter or disciplinary knowledge,
as contrasted with knowledge of generic instructional strategies such as Socratic
teaching, cooperative learning, or integrating technology in the classroom. As Birman and colleagues explain:

> Focusing on content means targeting a staff development activity on a specific subject area or on a subject-specific teaching method, such as increasing teachers' understanding of motion in physics or of the way elementary students solve story problems in mathematics. (2000, p. 30)

This research finding is consistent with the increased expectations for student learning reflected in Core Curriculum standards. For example, national and state standards expect higher-level thinking of students and abilities to apply, rather than simply recall, information. Accordingly, educators require deeper understanding of particular curriculum content and how students best learn that content. When the latter becomes central to professional development, teachers' knowledge and skills increase (Birman et al., 2000; Darling-Hammond et al., 2009; Desimone, 2009; Garet et al., 2001).

Essentially, then, direction setting necessitates answering the question: What should be the focus of teachers' professional development? In shortest terms, the answer is straightforward: the curriculum. The more specific answer is those parts of the curriculum that students struggle with most. To define and target professional development to those struggles, effective administrators organize, examine, and consider patterns of student achievement data over several years. As important, they also tap into teachers' qualitative judgments and firsthand observations of children's responses to taught curricula (Tallerico, 2005, 2012).

Thus administrative direction setting at all levels involves:

- Taking stock of recent professional development for teachers
- Streamlining to fewer professional development priorities
- Focusing on deepening teachers' pedagogical content knowledge in selected curriculum areas

DEVELOPING PEOPLE

Although direction setting is one of three main ways that administrators can have a positive impact on student achievement, such prioritizing helps primarily with determining professional development *substance*. However, adult growth requires more than wisely chosen content (i.e., substance). Administrators at all levels must also facilitate and ensure sound *processes* through which teachers engage with those thoughtfully streamlined substantive foci. Adults differ in their strengths and preferences regarding how they learn best (Knowles, Holton, & Swanson, 1998). Therefore, school and district administrators need to understand and foster varied means of addressing targeted professional development content.

Although scores of particular professional development processes and formats have appeared over time, all correspond fundamentally to one of five models categorized conceptually decades ago (Sparks & Hirsch, 1997; Sparks & Loucks-Horsley, 1990) and summarized briefly as follows.

Individually Guided

This model is built on the premise that teachers can be trusted to address school- or district-defined content priorities through independent study. Processes encompassed by individually guided professional development (York-Barr, Sommers, Ghere, & Montie, 2001) include reading, reflective journaling, writing for publication, videotaping and analyzing one's own classroom instruction, constructing portfolios that demonstrate growth, or completing an online course. Although this model of adult learning can be highly motivating to self-starters, administrators need to build in checkpoints to ensure that the self-selected activities contribute to advancing the school's or district's collective priorities.

Collaborative Problem Solving

In contrast to individually guided approaches, this model involves small groups of teachers thinking and working together around targeted priorities. This approach capitalizes on learning from each other, motivates social learners, and can promote teamwork and collective responsibility for school or district priorities. It is grounded in strong faith in teachers' expertise, willingness to address issues beyond their own classrooms, and daily proximity to the curriculum content that students struggle with most. For collaborative problem solving to work, administrators need to model skillful group facilitation themselves or provide teacher groups with facilitators or training in productive group dynamics. Study groups and critical friends groups are examples of collaborative problem solving. So are currently popular "professional learning communities" (PLCs). Importantly, though, PLCs also involve whole-school cultural shifts, from teachers working in isolation to routine and deep collective work sustained over time.

Observation and Assessment of Teaching

This model also hinges on teacher collaboration. However, it relies primarily on pairs of teachers rather than small groups. It focuses specifically on reciprocal observations in each other's classrooms. The underlying premise is that much can be learned about a targeted priority by having teachers serve as second sets of eyes and ears for one another. Potential learning derives from subsequent joint reflection on student engagement and responses, teacher thinking and actions, and dialogue to imagine possible improvement for the future. Sometimes this model is referred to as peer coaching or collegial supervision (Sullivan & Glanz, 2009). Administrators need to honor the fact that this model is intended to provide exclusively formative, nonthreatening, growth-inspiring opportunities, completely separate from teacher evaluation and summative assessment by superordinates.

Action Research

This option is variably referred to as inquiry, teacher research, practitioner research, or reflective action (Dana & Yendol-Silva, 2003; Sullivan & Glanz, 2009). One way to differentiate this model from those described earlier is to think of it as teachers conducting mini-experiments in their classrooms, then changing some practice as a result of what is learned from the experiment. The changed practice is what makes this action-oriented research. Its teacher-directed aspects distinguish it from more formal educational research wherein teachers are more likely to be the subjects, rather than the initiators, of empirical studies. Action research may be an independent, small-group, or whole-school professional development activity. As such, it shares characteristics of the individually guided and collaborative problem-solving models. Although action research can take a variety of forms, three steps are common. One or more educators: (1) identify a question or area of interest; (2) collect relevant data through active experimentation; and (3) change what they do on the job, based on their interpretation of results. Appropriate administrative roles involve stimulating teachers' curiosity, supporting risk taking even when teachers' experimentation falls short, and building in checkpoints similar to those in individually guided professional development.

Training

This model sometimes looks like large-group direct instruction or expert lecturing. However, informed school and district administrators understand that there are actually four components necessary for training to result in effective acquisition of new teaching skills *and* transfer of those skills to routine classroom use (Joyce & Showers, 2002):

1. *Theory.* Presentation of the rationale or theory that defines the value, importance, and use of the skill. This is the telling or describing portion of training that can look like a lecture.
2. *Demonstration* or modeling of the skill, typically by an experienced trainer.
3. *Practice.* Opportunities for learners to practice the skill, both while under the direction of experts and over time, in more natural work settings.
4. *Follow-up* or *coaching.* Long-term guidance and assistance so that what was practiced in training sessions or other simulations is transferred to the actual work setting.

In practice, skill training for teachers is often incomplete. It may include one or two of the elements required to be effective, but not all four. Multiple opportunities for practice with feedback, as well as follow-up, are frequently neglected or absent. Consequently, anticipated change in teachers' instructional repertoire does not occur.

Administrators at all levels need to understand that effective training is an expensive, long-term investment. Partial implementation may entertain, inspire, or raise awareness of an unfamiliar strategy or skill, but it will not result in changed classroom practice. Wise educational leaders question whether skills training should be initiated if it is known in advance that resources will not permit execution and support of all four necessary components of this model.

Administrators' Roles in Developing People

Part of the complexity of leading professional development in today's schools has been its limited research base historically (Guskey, 2003). For example, similar to enduring ambiguities about "what works best" in classroom teaching, there are no clear formulas for when to employ which model. Instead, such decisions require consideration of professional development goals and history in a given context, as well as leadership judgment about the adult learners in a particular school or district (Tallerico, 2005).

Several more recent studies of teacher learning suggest that traditional training in the form of workshops or institutes, as well as multiple variations of any of the other four models summarized previously, all can be effective. Potential effectiveness derives not from the model but from features that cut across design, including (1) focus on content knowledge, (2) coherence, (3) duration, (4) collective participation, and (5) use of active learning strategies (Birman et al., 2000; Darling-Hammond et al., 2009; Desimone, 2009; Garet et al., 2001). Because our prior discussion of direction setting included focus on content knowledge, we turn next to the other four features, framed in terms of leadership responsibilities.

Enhance Coherence

In this context, synonyms for *coherence* are *connection, complement,* and *fit*. But what should teachers' professional development complement, fit, or be connected to? Coherence involves two elements:

- Curriculum content identified as top priority directions
- The substance of previous professional development initiatives, so that adult learning is experienced as a cumulative and recursive enhancement of prior knowledge

Just as strong teachers link their current instruction to what came before and what is expected to follow on children's learning paths, strong leaders ensure that the foci of adults' development opportunities are logically consistent with one another. In this respect, professional learning coherence is similar to the vertical alignment schools work hard to achieve in curricula for children. Both require keen awareness of, and attention to, connecting today's learning to yesterday's and to what is anticipated for tomorrow's. Both also require enough content overlap to be *reinforcing*, but not so much as to become redundant.

Increase Duration

Longer duration contributes to professional development effectiveness in two ways. First, duration increases opportunities to digest, try out, and reflect upon new learnings. Second, increased duration facilitates the incorporation of other effectiveness features; for example, *depth* of subject-matter knowledge and *reinforcement* of coherence. The value of longer duration applies to the professional development activity itself and the time span during which follow-up is supported and integrated with other improvement initiatives. This finding parallels the research on time on task for students: More is better than less, assuming, of course, that what learners spend their time on is high quality.

The latest multiyear studies published by Learning Forward (formerly the National Staff Development Council) and led by scholars from Stanford University shed additional light on time, timing, and professional development results. For example, Wei, Darling-Hammond, and Adamson (2010) find that professional development "that is sustained over time and includes a substantial number of contact hours on a single professional focus" is most effective (p. 2). They define "substantial" as ranging from an average of 49 to a high of 100 contact hours per single focus.

Their data also illuminate notable changes in the broader context of time for adult learning in education:

> Unfortunately, in this regard, U.S. trends are going in the wrong direction. The data reveal that there has been a dramatic shift in the last decade away from [professional development] of a modest duration of 9–16 hours to [professional development] of 8 hours or shorter in length. (Wei et al., 2010, pp. 2–3)

Foster Collective Participation at the School Level

Professional development has also been found to be more effective when teachers participate in it with grade-level or subject-area colleagues from their schools. Such participation contrasts with staff development structures in which teachers from different schools participate individually (in districtwide staff development, offsite institutes or academies, college course taking, etc.). Instead, school-based collective participation can beget sharing and problem solving around common concerns, goals, students, and curriculum.

Collective participation centered on shared hopes and challenges can also enrich school culture more broadly. This positive by-product relates directly to contemporary aspirations that schools function less like bureaucracies and more like PLCs (DuFour, Eaker, & Burnette, 2002). Such communities shift development goals from emphasis on individual growth to increased *school capacity* for improvement and renewal.

Use Active Learning Strategies

Complementing strong subject-matter focus, enhanced coherence, increased duration, and collective participation, effective professional development practice is also characterized by opportunities for teachers' active learning. This finding is consistent with research on training that demonstrates that hands-on practice is essential for the transfer of new skills to classroom use. Examples of active adult-learning strategies include discussion, application exercises, simulations, reviewing student work together, role playing, observing or being observed teaching, joint planning, reciprocal mentoring, peer coaching, and team-created presentations, demonstrations, or other written products.

Additional Implications for Administrators: Affect

We return to and extend earlier discussion of the importance of professional development *duration* because administrative support at all levels is so critical to sustaining continuation over time. Prior research from decades of study indicates that it takes at least 20–25 practice trials over approximately 8–10 weeks to transfer even moderately complex new teaching skills and strategies appropriately and consistently into routine use (Joyce & Showers, 1995, 2002). Moreover, it takes 3–5 years to implement changed educational practices school- or districtwide (Corcoran, Fuhrman, & Belcher, 2001; Hall & Hord, 2001; Wagner et al., 2006). Momentum plateaus, dips in performance, conflict, confusion, and reluctance to continue are inevitable parts of such extended processes (Fullan, 1991, 2001).

Even if key facilitators change during that time, leadership support throughout the entire process must be maintained. This often means that new principals will need to pick up where their predecessors left off, to build upon the efforts resulting from prior direction setting. Without such continuity, overburdened teachers' rationale for nonparticipation because "this too shall pass" will be validated. The antidote to such arguments is the *demonstration* of ongoing support for the professional development focus.

Later in this chapter, we detail means of finding and making time for professional development priorities. Our emphasis here is on the *affective* side of leadership. For example, administrators at every level need to communicate frequently and enthusiastically about the continuing importance of the initiative. Similarly, they need to provide personalized encouragement to the teachers and teacher leaders who were the early adopters, turnkey trainers, and department- or grade-level facilitators of small-group implementation, practice, or feedback components of professional development. They also need to celebrate any positive outcomes related to the change (e.g., improved student performance, outside recognition, increased grant funding).

Address Conflict Directly

Administrators also need to bring differences out into the open so that they can be resolved (Janas, 1998). Teachers should be invited to voice and negotiate issues by addressing together questions such as: Where are we in the process? Where do we want to end up? How will getting there help us meet our top priorities for student learning? What is impeding us from getting there?

Such one-on-one and small-group discussions can be guided by the collaborative direction setting addressed earlier. After all, the purpose of that prior work was to clarify and refine shared directions for school improvement. If part of motivational and momentum plateaus stem from having veered from agreed-upon priorities or from feeling undersupported in pursuing them, then school and district leaders should want to hear about how, where, when, and why.

Openly airing concerns and differences can provide administrators at all levels with valuable information about emerging conflicts and frustrations before they become overwhelming barriers to progress. For example, teachers may "legitimately resist change required by a [professional development or curriculum] program that is poorly designed, underfunded, or focused on unnecessary activities" (Janas, 1998, p. 11). Hearing out staff members is essential to eliciting this kind of feedback. Additionally, this example illustrates that opportunities to articulate the underlying reasons for conflict or resistance can serve constructive purposes.

Counteract Stories of Failure

Diminished motivation is often perpetuated in the negative anecdotes that are shared among staff members about "the last time we tried something like that" or in comments criticizing forms of teacher learning other than trial-and-error in one's own classroom (Peterson, 2002). How can administrators help prevent such accounts from dominating the school or district's culture? By "finding examples of success to counteract stories of failure...and replacing negative stories of professional development with concrete positive results" (Peterson, 2002, p. 15).

Again, careful listening is the first step. Administrators' antidotes will be more effective if they address the specifics of the toxic account. For example, if the essence of the negative anecdote is that "teaming never works around here," principals need to have at the tip of the tongue several current examples of which departments or grade levels are collaborating successfully. Wherever possible, illustrations of how teamwork helped students or contributed to other school improvement priorities should be included.

The point is not to disparage any individual's interpretation of history, nor to pretend that missteps have not occurred. Rather, the goal is to maximize communication about productive efforts and positive outcomes to ensure that balanced and hopeful stories predominate in the broader narrative that is a school or district's context.

Model Hopefulness

Educational leaders' language, actions, and attitudes are constantly on display. Administrators can capitalize on that high visibility among teachers by consciously modeling openness to improvement. For example, principals' reactions to state mandates or district directives will be easily observed by staff. If they frequently demonstrate opposition, or routinely lament "what's coming from central office," they might be serving as the perfect role models for resisters in their own buildings. In contrast, when administrators search for the common ground among state, district, and building initiatives and exhibit receptivity to all sources of potential improvement, they are modeling the constructive attitudes expected of students and staff.

Of course, critical thinking is also an important part of strong leadership. Administrators can sometimes increase their credibility by refraining from exclusively "Pollyannaish" stances. In fact, change leaders "reflecting publicly and straightforwardly on their own doubts and resistance to change may...give other stakeholders a chance to identify with someone going through the difficult process of change" (Janas, 1998, p. 12).

Again, balance is key. Overall, school and district culture will be enhanced by its administrators' positive worldviews. Leaders' modeling of hope, energy, and "opportunity thinking" rather than "obstacle thinking" can be another way of fostering teachers' dispositions to persist.

Understand Efficacy

This personalized, human side of leadership for developing people derives largely from research and theory on efficacy (Bandura, 1997a, 1997b, 1982). Wahlstrom and colleagues (2010) succinctly explain Bandura's key concepts:

> Efficacy is a belief about one's own ability (self efficacy) or the ability of one's colleagues (collective efficacy) to perform a task or achieve a goal. Efficacy beliefs are central to people's ability to get things done. They affect the choices people make about which activities to engage in, and they affect coping efforts once activities have begun—determining, for example, how much effort people will expend and how long they will persist in the face of failure or difficulty. (p. 15)

Principals' actions to support and encourage staff individually, to model hopefulness, to address conflict directly, and to counteract stories of failure can help motivate teachers to persist and sustain efficacy beliefs that "together we can achieve this goal." Similarly, central office administrators "are able to influence teaching and learning, in part, through the contributions they make to positive feelings of efficacy on the part of school principals" (Wahlstrom et al., 2010, p. 15). The latter reminds us that building-level leaders require support of their affective needs in order to sustain motivation and efficacy beliefs, just as teachers and students do.

STRUCTURING WORKPLACE CONDITIONS

Thus far, we have elaborated two main ways that administrators influence student learning: setting direction and developing people. However, streamlined priorities for professional development directions and careful attention to the various contributors to professional development effectiveness (summarized previously) are insufficient by themselves. Administrators must also put into place structures for increasing the odds of attaining adult learning goals. Because creating time for teachers' collaboration and professional development are keys to structuring enabling workplace conditions, we address this topic next.

Making Time to Collaborate

How can administrators at all levels find or make more time for professional development? Watts and Castle's (1993) comprehensive syntheses of five options remain relevant today. We draw primarily from that seminal work here, while updating with examples from more recent resources (e.g., Bowgren & Sever, 2010; Johnston, Knight, & Miller, 2007; Khorsheed, 2007; Lauer & Matthews, 2007; Richardson, 2007; Sever & Bowgren, 2007; Tienken & Stonaker, 2007; White & McIntosh, 2007). Though overlap exists among the five options, we illustrate each separately to facilitate understanding.

Schedule Common Planning Time

One strategy for structuring within-school-day time for professional development centers on synchronizing the preparation periods of grade-level, department, interdisciplinary, or other targeted groups of teachers. This approach is grounded in the premise that local school traditions or collectively bargained agreements allot specified amounts of teacher planning/preparation time without student contact each day or week.

At the secondary level, job-embedded common time for teacher work groups may be built into the master schedule of course offerings. In elementary settings, such scheduling typically involves coordinating when children are *pulled out* of "regular" classrooms to participate in physical education, music, other arts, library, computer labs, or additional specialized curricula. In some instances, common planning periods can be extended by selectively connecting them to other, noninstructional times (e.g., recess or lunch periods every 2 weeks), if teachers or unions agree to such an option for creating more within-school opportunities for collective efforts.

A variation of the common planning time model is used in the Papillion–La Vista, Nebraska, public schools. That district fosters different ways of providing weekly professional collaboration time at its 16 component schools (Johnston et al., 2007). Some principals help extend teacher team meetings that start a half-hour before students arrive by organizing literacy coaches or other staff to lead activities to begin the students' day. Sometimes multiple classes are combined for these beginning-of-day lessons and activities. In secondary schools that start with a homeroom session, some principals arrange for similar coverage to free up selected teachers' time for professional development that amplifies before-school contracted time. This district's examples incorporate elements of a second approach, summarized next.

Reduce Teachers' Contact Time with Students

A variety of methods have been used to release selected teachers from some instructional duties to carve out time for periodic collaboration during the work day while maintaining traditional school-day start and dismissal times for students. Most involve enlisting other adults to substitute-teach classes or otherwise supervise children's learning activities during the time for which targeted collaborators are freed up from classroom instruction. Replacements may include existing paid or nonpaid personnel, such as teaching assistants, other support staff, college interns, administrators, community partners, volunteers, or members of teaching teams.

Sometimes, educational programming that can accommodate large groups of students with fewer adult supervisors can free up selected teachers' time. Examples include student assemblies of various kinds, theater performances, or special presentations by older students, business volunteers, or community groups.

Secondary schools with vocational internships, school-to-work apprenticeships, or community service expectations may be able to use the time set for students' off-site field experiences as opportunities for teacher professional development time. For example, if such off-campus activities could be scheduled for the same hours or part of day each week, teachers' classroom instructional responsibilities might be eliminated for regular blocks of time.

Although the methods noted so far maintain children's usual school arrival and departure times, other options for freeing up professional development time for all school personnel involve releasing students early or starting school late on designated days. For example, the Findlay City School District in Findlay, Ohio, used a 2-hour delay in the start of classes to enable teachers to work together from 7:00–9:00 A.M. once each quarter (White & McIntosh, 2007, p. 32). Similarly, the Carman–Ainsworth Community Schools in Flint, Michigan, collectively bargained an agreement to start school an hour later than usual each Wednesday morning to free up time for teacher collaboration by grade level or subject area (Richardson, 2007). And in Loveland, Colorado, students are dismissed early each Wednesday, as, by contract, "some of these afternoons are designated for teachers to work on their professional goals, others are for district-wide curriculum alignment, and the remaining are for site-based staff development" (Lauer & Matthews, 2007, p. 39). The Maine–Endwell school district in upstate New York dismisses students 2 or 3 hours early for teachers' professional collaboration on a differentiated schedule shared well in advance with parents: six times a year for its two elementary schools, four times for the middle school, and three times for the high school (Sever & Bowgren, 2007).

Early-release and late-start approaches are appropriate only for schools that already exceed minimum instructional hours/days mandated by different states. For those that do not, the following modification may be a better alternative.

Bank Teachers' Contact Time with Students

Banking minutes and hours is a strategy for creating blocks of time for professional development without diminishing students' total instructional time with their regular teachers in any given week. This approach can take varied forms. The commonality among them is that not every school day begins and ends at the same time. Sometimes, extended instructional time on 4 days of the week is "saved up" ("deposited," in banking terms), so that it can be "expended" (i.e., "withdrawn") on a 5th day, when students either arrive later or exit school earlier than the other 4 days. The deposited and withdrawn minutes leave the weekly balance of instructional time for students even.

For example, the Papillion–La Vista district in Nebraska considered feedback from teachers and found that adding 10 minutes of daily instructional time fell within collectively bargained agreements (Johnston et al., 2007). By extending each school day in this way, they were able to bank time to create six professional development days for teachers, spread across the school year.

Richardson (2002) shares the illustration of Addison Elementary School in Marietta, Georgia. There, the school day starts 10 minutes earlier and ends 10 minutes later than it had in the past for 4 days a week. Those 80 minutes of banked instructional time were exchanged for releasing students from school at 1:30 A.M. on Wednesdays, so that teachers could work together each Wednesday afternoon. Some high schools follow similar banking models but schedule later arrival times (rather than early release) for students on the fifth day.

Buy Additional Time

More expensive ways to create professional development collaboration time involve hiring substitutes or other support staff to free up teacher time, as well as compensating regular teachers for hours dedicated beyond the contracted work day or year. Historically, for example, much professional development work has been accomplished during summer months by paying stipends to teachers who volunteered, who were selected by colleagues, or who were tapped by administrators. Sometimes, weekends and breaks during the school year have been used for similar purposes, if sufficient numbers of teachers are willing to trade personal time for remuneration.

Bowgren and Sever (2010) describe a substitute roll-through model designed to minimize disruption to regular classroom instruction while enabling professional collaboration during the school day. This model requires hiring sufficient numbers of substitutes to cover one grade level, department, or other identified group of teachers at a time. The cohort of substitutes teaches for 1 or 2 hours while the specified grade level, department, or other group of teachers works together. The first group of released teachers then returns to teach the rest of the day, while the substitute cohort "rolls" to the next set of classrooms. Thus within just a few days (depending on school size), all teachers in a school can gain additional time to collaborate with other adults in their school.

Capitalize on Existing Time

When funding, substitutes, or other time-generating options are not available, using existing time wisely becomes even more important. That often entails organizing and focusing faculty, grade-level, and department meetings to be as productive and learning-centered as possible. It can also involve taking full advantage of the noninstructional work days included in teacher contracts.

For example, the public school district of Monroe Township, New Jersey, reorganized time for professional development by shifting from two teacher preparation days to one immediately prior to opening day for students (Tienken & Stonaker, 2007). The second day without students was moved to a month later in the fall for additional adult learning and collaboration time. The district also timed several student early-release days throughout the year so as to meet state requirements for instructional days without adding work hours to teachers' contractual work days. The latter also contributed to more adult collaboration time. The Monroe Township example illustrates the idea of spreading teacher collaboration days across the calendar to provide more frequent, shorter school-based professional group work opportunities.

Khorsheed (2007) suggests rethinking student grouping as another means of freeing up small teams of teachers to work together during the regular school day. She shares an example at Garfield Elementary School in Livonia, Michigan. There, three first-grade classes of 20 students each were reorganized into two groups of 30 students for music and physical education, followed by recess. "In this way, three classes were covered by two specialist teachers, and three classroom teachers were able to collaborate for at least an hour" (p. 45).

Practical Considerations in Restructuring Time

Of course, challenges and downsides accompany the benefit of increasing time for professional development. Some entail financial costs, modifications to bus schedules, and irregular school start–dismissal times that may be confusing or inconvenient to parents and caregivers. Others involve treating specialty subject teachers (e.g., the arts, computer lab, physical education) differently from regular classroom teachers. Some result in decreased individual teacher planning time and increased teaching by substitute personnel. Many necessitate negotiations with unions or professional associations.

What are some steps administrators can take to generate support for changed staff or student time in school? Richardson's (2002) suggestions remain relevant today:

• Give teachers a strong voice in exploring options and planning any changes. Share with them the possibilities described earlier and the examples of actual schools that have implemented different strategies for making time. Invite them to brainstorm other possibilities that might work for a particular school or district. Involve teacher associations, unions, and collective bargaining leaders early in the process.

• Negotiate directly which trade-offs faculty, staff, and administrators are open to—and which they are unwilling to touch—in order to gain time for professional development.

- Involve parents and other community caregivers in discussions, particularly if plans are likely to affect teacher contact time with children or altered school start and dismissal times. Be prepared with clear explanations of how your school's professional development goals are tightly linked to student learning priorities. Provide examples of how students are likely to benefit from teacher growth.

- Pilot any new plans for at least a year prior to committing to them. Where possible, piloting several different approaches within the same school district can produce valuable insights and comparisons of costs and benefits.

SUMMARY

This chapter drew connections between studies of how educational administrators influence student learning and the conditions that foster teachers' professional development. Three main research findings were addressed: direction setting (content), developing people (process), and structuring the workplace (context).

Content

Administrators at all levels can help by working with teacher leaders to identify the parts of the curriculum students struggle with most. Professional development directions should derive from those priority areas and focus on deepening educators' subject-area knowledge and subject-specific teaching methods. Such focus is critical to ameliorating the overload and ineffectiveness that result from scattering attention across multiple and varied professional development initiatives. Setting clear directions also allows greater investment in just a few priorities that can be sustained over time.

Process

Whereas professional development content priorities need to be focused and few, adult learning pathways benefit from differentiation. Accordingly, this chapter recapped five distinct options that administrators can make available to teachers: individually guided professional development, collaborative problem solving, observation and assessment of teaching, action research, and training. Research on professional development suggests that the effectiveness of any design can be increased by longer duration, coherence with prior efforts, collective participation at the school level, and reliance on active learning strategies.

Process also refers to how administrators at all levels influence staff motivation and persistence via the affective side of leadership. Teachers' sense of individual and collective efficacy may be enhanced by school and district leaders' personal encouragement, communication of values, recognition of successes, hopefulness, and willingness to address conflict directly.

Context

On the one hand, who administrators are and what they stand for as people influence the tone, "feel," and culture of schools and districts in innumerable subtle and amorphous ways. On the other, teachers' working conditions and, thereby, professional development accessibility are concretely shaped by how time is structured and used in schools. This chapter summarized five main ways that administrators can find or make time for professional development, with examples from schools and districts across the United States. They included scheduling common planning time for teachers, reducing teachers' contact time with students, banking teachers' contact time with students, buying additional time, and capitalizing on existing time.

RECOMMENDATIONS AND FUTURE DIRECTIONS

We conclude with two recommendations for future investigation and analyses. First, the departmentalized structure of universities sometimes results in research silos, wherein those who study teaching and educate current and prospective teachers operate largely separately from those who study and educate administrators. As this chapter has attempted to demonstrate, much can be learned when findings from one specialty area (e.g., administrators' influence on student learning) are considered and applied to another specialization (e.g., teachers' professional development). Perhaps additional insights might result from more frequent boundary-spanning connections and analyses.

Second, although this chapter focused on ideas and actions relevant to administrators at all PreK–12 levels, the structural and interpersonal relationships between building and central office leadership warrant additional study. For example, the school-to-district relationship is often characterized by tensions between autonomy and coordination, flexibility and consistency. These tensions point to unanswered questions amenable to future research, such as: Under what circumstances should principals and teacher teams be free to determine their school's professional development directions, preferred designs, and time structuring? Alternately, when should those determinations be standardized across multiple schools within a district? Similarly, although current theory, professional consensus, and expert thinking cohere around the value of job-embedded, school-centric professional development, to what degree are such practices realistic when scarce resources press districts to enact efficiencies of scale?

QUESTIONS FOR DISCUSSION

1. For teachers: Revisit the five models discussed in this chapter's section on developing people while reflecting on how you typically learn best. Then think about a current

professional development initiative in which you are being required or encouraged to participate. If a mismatch exists between how you think you learn best and the current initiative's format, propose a different model for addressing the same school or district priority. Develop your proposal in either a written format that could be respectfully forwarded to relevant administrators or as a set of talking points that could be discussed in person with your principal. (You might be pleasantly surprised by what such introspection and research-informed advocacy might lead to, for yourself and others at your school.)

2. For administrators: Which, if any, of the time-making strategies have you implemented in your school or district in the past? Which might be discussed with teacher and union leaders as you move forward with a streamlined set of priorities for professional development directions?

3. For policymakers: Make a list of the policies you have enacted or revised in the past 5 years that have required new learning or changed practices by schools or school districts. Discuss that list in light of the research finding quoted in this chapter that "the greatest problem faced by school districts and schools is not resistance to innovation, but the fragmentation, overload, and incoherence resulting from the uncritical acceptance of too many different innovations" (Fullan, 1991, p. 197).

REFERENCES

Bandura, A. (1997a). *Self-efficacy: The exercise of control.* New York: Freeman.

Bandura, A. (1997b). Self-efficacy: Toward a unifying theory of behavioral change. *Psychological Review, 84*(2), 191–215.

Bandura, A. (1982). Self-efficacy and mechanism in human agency. *American Psychologist, 37*(2), 122–147.

Birman, B., Desimone, L., Porter, A., & Garet, M. (2000). Designing professional development that works. *Educational Leadership, 57*(8), 28–33.

Bowgren, L., & Sever, K. (2010). *Differentiated professional development in a professional learning community.* Bloomington, IN: Solution Tree Press.

Corcoran, T., Fuhrman, S., & Belcher, C. (2001). The district role in instructional improvement. *Phi Delta Kappan, 83*(1), 78–84.

Dana, N., & Yendol-Silva, D. (2003). *The reflective educator's guide to classroom research.* Thousand Oaks, CA: Corwin Press.

Darling-Hammond, L., Wei, R. C., Andree, A., Richardson, N., & Orphanos, S. (2009). *Professional learning in the learning profession: A status report on teacher development in the United States and abroad.* Dallas, TX: National Staff Development Council.

Desimone, L. (2009, April). Improving impact studies of teachers' professional development. *Educational Researcher, 38*, 181–199.

DuFour, R. (2002). One clear voice is needed in the din. *Journal of Staff Development, 23*(2), 60–61.

DuFour, R., Eaker, R., & Burnette, R. (2002). *Reculturing schools to become professional learning communities.* Bloomington, IN: National Education Service.

Firestone, W. (2009). Culture and process in effective school districts. In W. Hoy & M. DiPaola (Eds.), *Studies in school improvement* (pp. 177–203). Charlotte, NC: Information Age.

Fullan, M. (1991). *The new meaning of educational change*. New York: Teachers College Press.

Fullan, M. (2001). *The new meaning of educational change* (2nd ed.). New York: Teachers College Press.

Garet, M., Porter, A., Desimone, L., Birman, B., & Yoon, K. (2001). What makes professional development effective?: Results from a national sample of teachers. *American Educational Research Journal, 38*(4), 915–945.

Guskey, T. (2003). What makes professional development effective? *Phi Delta Kappan, 84*(10), 748–750.

Hall, G., & Hord, S. (2001). *Implementing change: Patterns, principles, and potholes*. Boston: Allyn & Bacon.

Janas, M. (1998). Shhh, the dragon is asleep and its name is resistance. *Journal of Staff Development, 19*(3), 10–12.

Johnston, J., Knight, M., & Miller, L. (2007). Finding time for teams. *Journal of Staff Development, 28*(2), 14–19.

Joyce, B., & Showers, B. (1995). *Student achievement through staff development* (2nd ed.). White Plains, NY: Longman.

Joyce, B., & Showers, B. (2002). *Student achievement through staff development* (3rd ed.). Alexandria, VA: Association for Supervision and Curriculum Development.

Khorsheed, K. (2007). Four places to dig deeper to find more time for teacher collaboration. *Journal of Staff Development, 28*(2), 43–45.

Knowles, M., Holton, E., & Swanson, R. (1998). *The adult learner*. Newton, MA: Butterworth-Heinemann.

Lauer, D., & Matthews, M. (2007). Teachers steer their own learning. *Journal of Staff Development, 28*(2), 36–41.

Leithwood, K., Louis, K. S., Anderson, S., & Wahlstrom, K. (2004). Review of research: How leadership influences student learning. Retrieved June 29, 2012, from *www.wallacefoundation.org/KnowledgeCenter/KnowledgeTopics/CurrentAreasofFocus/EducationLeadership/Pages/HowLeadershipInfluencesStudentLearning.aspx*.

Leithwood, K., & Riehl, C. (2005). What we know about successful school leadership. In W. Firestone & C. Riehl (Eds.), *A new agenda: Directions for research on educational leadership* (pp. 22–47). New York: Teachers College Press.

Marzano, R., Waters, T., & McNulty, B. (2005). *School leadership that works: From research to results*. Alexandria, VA: Association for Supervision and Curriculum Development.

Mizell, H. (2010). The central office must evolve. *Journal of Staff Development, 31*(3), 46–48.

Murphy, J., Elliott, S., Goldring, E., & Porter, A. (2006). Learning-centered leadership: A conceptual foundation. Retrieved June 24, 2012, from *www.wallacefoundation.org/wallace/learning.pdf*

Peterson, K. (2002). Positive or negative. *Journal of Staff Development, 23*(3), 10–15.

Richardson, J. (2002, August–September). Think outside the clock: Create time for professional learning. *Tools for Schools Newsletter*, pp. 1–7.

Richardson, J. (2007). Bargaining time. *Learning System Newsletter, 2*(6), 1, 6.

Sever, K., & Bowgren, L. (2007). Shaping the workday. *Journal of Staff Development, 28*(2), 20–23.

Sparks, D., & Hirsch, S. (1997). *A new vision for staff development*. Oxford, OH: National Staff Development Council.

Sparks, D., & Loucks-Horsley, S. (1990). Models of staff development. In R. Houston (Ed.), *Handbook of research on teacher education* (pp. 234–250). New York: Macmillan.

Sullivan, S., & Glanz, J. (2009). *Supervision that improves teaching: Strategies and techniques* (3rd ed.). Thousand Oaks, CA: Corwin Press.

Tallerico, M. (2005). *Supporting and sustaining teachers' professional development: A principal's guide.* Thousand Oaks, CA: Corwin Press.

Tallerico, M. (2012). *Leading curriculum improvement: Fundamentals for school principals.* Lanham, MD: Rowman & Littlefield.

Tienken, C., & Stonaker, L. (2007). When every day is professional development day. *Journal of Staff Development, 28*(2), 24–29.

Wagner, T., Kegan, R., Lahey, L., Lemmons, R., Garnier, J., Helsing, D., et al. (2006). *Change leadership: A practical guide to transforming our schools.* San Francisco: Jossey-Bass.

Wahlstrom, K., Louis, K. S., Leithwood, K., & Anderson, S. (2010). Investigating the links to improved student learning: Executive summary of research findings. Retrieved June 16, 2012, from *www.wallacefoundation.org/KnowledgeCenter/KnowledgeTopics/CurrentAreasofFocus/EducationLeadership/Pages/learning-from-leadership-investigating-the-links-to-improved-student-learning.aspx.*

Watts, G., & Castle, S. (1993). The time dilemma in school restructuring. *Phi Delta Kappan, 75*(4), 306–311.

Wei, R., Darling-Hammond, L., & Adamson, F. (2010). *Professional development in the U.S.: Phase 2.* Oxford, OH: National Staff Development Council.

White, S., & McIntosh, J. (2007). Data delivers a wake-up call: Five-year plan unites teachers into a collaborative culture. *Journal of Staff Development, 28*(2), 30–35.

Wirt, F., & Kirst, M. (2005). *The political dynamics of American education* (3rd ed.). Richmond, CA: McCutchan.

York-Barr, J., Sommers, W., Ghere, G., & Montie, J. (2001). *Reflective practice to improve schools.* Thousand Oaks, CA: Corwin Press.

CHAPTER 8

Sociocultural Approaches to Professional Development
Supporting Sustainable School Change

Taffy E. Raphael
Jaime Madison Vasquez
Angela Joy Fortune
James R. Gavelek
Kathryn H. Au

- Sociocultural approaches to professional development create opportunities for teachers to appropriate, transform, share publicly, and make part of everyday practice what has been learned.
- Sociocultural approaches to professional development position teachers as empowered agents of change.
- Meaningful learning occurs when teachers engage in dialogue that addresses their own situated problems of practice.
- Successful professional development is systemic, sustained, and sustainable over time.

In contemporary professional practice—teaching, nursing, engineering, architecture, and so forth—the importance of professional development is widely recognized. With that recognition comes the associated investment of time, resources, and effort to provide effective professional development (Webster-Wright, 2009). However, effectiveness, or the degree to which professional development is considered to be successful, can vary depending on its purpose. In professional development designed to improve the quality of literacy teaching and learning, for example, goals can range from improving individual participants' understandings to the degree to which the professional development builds capacity for sustainable improvement in teaching and learning (Raphael, Au, & Popp, 2013). The very construct of professional development suggests professional learning beyond simply being trained to use programs and processes faithfully. Webster-Wright (2009), however, argues that the construct of professional development ignores the importance of situating the professionals' learning in authentic problems of practice to be solved and recognizing that there are multiple ways that professionals can learn and grow, "from formal PD programs, through interactions with work colleagues, to experiences outside work, in differing combinations and permutations of experience" (p. 705). She offers the term "continuous professional learning" for the "learning of practicing professionals." Regardless of label, our work is focused on how professionals—in this chapter, literacy educators—invest in a full array of activity in ways that lead to sustainable improvements through developing new and deep understandings of their field.

Within literacy education, our particular focus is professional development that supports sustainable school change. Like many scholars (e.g., Bryk, Sebring, Allensworth, Luppescu, & Easton, 2010; Hubbard, Mehan, & Stein, 2006; Lai, McNaughton, Amituanai-Toloa, Turner, & Hsaio, 2009; McLaughlin & Talbert, 2006), we recognize both its importance and its challenges. Sustainability presents significant challenges, as it requires coordinated support at institutional (e.g., cultural shifts, infrastructure support) and individual (e.g., disciplinary knowledge, pedagogical practices) levels. As past decades have demonstrated, there is "no quick fix" (Allington & Walmsley, 1995; Darling-Hammond, Wei, Andree, Richardson, & Orphonos, 2009; Desimone, 2009; Long, 2011) to ensure sustainable improvement. Today's professional development faces challenges, from outmoded conceptions of knowledge to issues related to evaluation, control, and overall uncertainty in the face of complex change (Webster-Wright, 2009). In literacy, educators have been frustrated by the relatively controlled, top-down mandates that have not led to positive, sustained change, such as those associated with No Child Left Behind (Meier & Wood, 2004) and curriculum-driven reforms characterized by comprehensive school reform initiatives (Correnti & Rowen, 2007). However, there is hope, as seen in the relatively few examples of successful professional development initiatives that demonstrated positive and sustainable changes (see Taylor, Raphael, & Au, 2011, for examples). Many of these positive examples were based in principles consistent with sociocultural theory.

SOCIOCULTURAL THEORY AND PROFESSIONAL DEVELOPMENT

Social or sociocultural theories of mind can be interpreted narrowly (i.e., referring only to Vygotsky's [1978] original theory) or more broadly to include other theories (e.g., situated cognition, sociolinguistics, cultural historical activity theory) consistent with the underpinnings of Vygotsky's original work. From our perspective, the essential point is that what is learned emerges from, but is not reducible to, interactions with others. Key constructs within this family of theories (e.g., systems orientation, emphasis on dialogical experience solving meaningful problems) provide hope for building capacity collectively within institutions, as well as individually, to lead to sustainable improvements in our schools. Sociocultural approaches to professional development instantiate five principles consistent with the theory.

The first principle of professional development in literacy teaching and learning grounded in sociocultural theory is the importance placed on *teacher agency*. Professional development begins by engaging teachers and results in their ownership, agency, and shared understandings (i.e., intersubjectivity) of the processes and products of the professional development (Au, 2013; Johnston-Parsons, 2012). The second principle is that professional development is *situated* as participants address meaningful problems of practice (e.g., teaching to high standards, curriculum integration between the language arts and disciplinary learning, evidence-based teaching; Florio-Ruane, Berne, & Raphael, 2001; Florio-Ruane & Raphael, 2004; Goatley et al., 1994).

The third principle emphasizes *dialogical* practice. Participants have the opportunity for meaningful conversation (i.e., dialogue) as they assume increasing responsibility for appropriating, adapting, and enacting new ideas independently (Johnston-Parsons, 2012; Pearson, 1985; Routman, 2012). Fourth, participants engage in work that takes a *systemic* view (Bryk et al., 2010; DuFour, DuFour, & Eaker, 2008; McNaughton, 2002), embedded in a sustainable infrastructure (Advanced Reading Development Demonstration Project [ARDDP], 2008; Dutro, Fisk, Koch, Roop, & Wixson, 2002). Fifth, professional development activities are *sustained* across time, as teachers engage in knowledge development about subject matter and pedagogical practices and significantly develop a strong infrastructure for high-functioning collaborative work groups (Fisher & Frey, 2007; McLaughlin & Mitra, 2001; McLaughlin & Talbert, 2006; Weber & Raphael, 2013).

Success depends on customizing professional development in light of agreed-upon goals that the work is designed to achieve and that participants recognize in the learning cycle. Some have characterized the process as one of universal design (e.g., Chappuis, Stiggins, Chappuis, & Arter, 2011; DuFour et al., 2008; Stiggins, 2007). Others have linked it to design-based research (e.g., Reinking & Bradley, 2008). Similarly, the professional development approach we describe in this chapter favors ownership over compliance, conversation over transmission, deep understanding over enacting rules and routines, and goal-directed activity over content coverage. We use the Vygotsky space, introduced by Harré (1983), elaborated by Gavelek and his colleagues (Gavelek & Raphael, 1996; McVee, Dunsmore, & Gavelek, 2005), and applied to educational reform by Gallucci (2008), to illustrate five principles in a sociocultural model of professional development. We find this model helpful for illustrating how dialogue, activity, and the nature of professional development changes as members of the professional learning community mature in their knowledge and understanding.

We build on Taylor and colleagues (2011), who distinguish between "curriculum-driven" and "professional development-driven" approaches, arguing that the latter have a stronger potential for sustainability relative to episodic (Raphael et al., 2013; Webster-Wright, 2009) school change efforts. We begin by describing the Vygotsky space, introducing key terms that capture the process of learning within a sociocultural lens. We then focus on the five principles that underlie and support successful movement among the quadrants of the Vygotsky space as participants engage in professional development that leads to learning and to the potential for sustainable school change.

THE VYGOTSKY SPACE

Harré (1983) introduced the Vygotsky space to represent two critical dimensions for learning. The first is the continuum from social to individual learning activity; the second is the range from public to private displays of learning. When these two dimensions are integrated (see Figure 8.1), they create four quadrants (QI–QIV) that capture "a process through which cultural practices are internalized by individuals, transformed in the context of individual needs and uses, then externalized (shared) in ways that may be taken up by others" (Gallucci, 2008, p. 7).

Activity within and movement across quadrants is characterized by particular language and activity practices to support teachers' learning, and the cycle through these quadrants is iterative, rather than linear or cyclical.

Public Spaces

Above the horizontal axis (QI, QIV), language and activity are public—that is, shared among participants in ways that can be easily observed. However, language and activity between these public quadrants differ in nature. Typically in QI, a more knowledgeable other has the goal of introducing new constructs or pedagogical tools. Participants are responsible for making sense of this new information and understanding it, with the goal of enacting the ideas in their own practice. In pedagogical terms, language and activity in QI reflect what Duffy and his colleagues (1986) refer to as explicit explanation. It is observable because the activity involves public displays of information, often involving a more knowledgeable leader with expertise in the to-be-learned constructs, materials, or approaches. The more knowledgeable other (e.g., the leader of the professional development session) is responsible for supporting teachers' acquisition of the new content. The participants' responsibility is to engage with the new ideas until they are clearly understood. In isolation from the rest of the Vygotsky space, QI comes closest to the all-too-common one-shot or one-off workshop (Ball & Cohen, 1999; Kelleher, 2003).

In QIV, the other public space, the roles of participants and more knowledgeable other shift. The emphasis is on participants' sharing their adaptations and transformations of the formerly new, now tried–tested–adapted–transformed, concepts as enacted in ways that meet the needs of their particular situations. In contrast to QI, leadership and sharing are driven by the participants; ideas may reflect a range from how ideas were enacted with little change (e.g., using a template for teaching students to use response journals) to major transformation (e.g., moving from templates to teachers' and students' creating new forms of responses to use in students' journals).

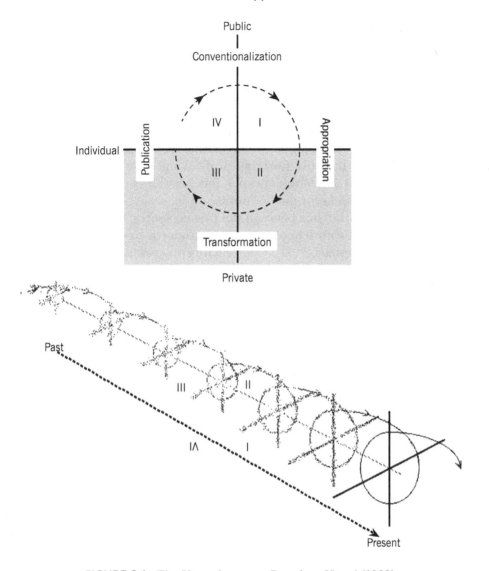

FIGURE 8.1. The Vygotsky space. Based on Harré (1983).

Private Spaces

Below the horizontal axis, language and activity are assumed to be private. That is, individual participants draw on what was learned in QI and make it work for them in their own settings. QII and QIII, the two quadrants in the private spaces, differ in terms of the degree to which the uptake of what was learned in QI parallels what was introduced, or is adapted and transformed. In QII, learning is both social and private. Similar to the construct of near transfer, participants have the opportunity to practice what they've learned through social interactions in QI in their individually situated contexts. QIII is private and individual, where participants make new discoveries by applying the content to their individual settings and transforming what they have learned and now practiced. QIII is a unique and powerful distinction for sociocultural approaches to professional development, a distinction that transforms teacher learning to meet the needs of their students, schools, and communities. New insights gained during QIII play a critical role in the iterative process of learning. In QIV, teachers go public with their individual experiences and transformations, influencing and shaping the conventionalization of practices that move the school improvement efforts forward in a sustainable way. Of course, this influence and resulting conventionalization cannot be assumed. It depends on the type of feedback given by those fostering professional development and by one's peers in the professional development experience, as well as the uptake of feedback by those offering their ideas for public consideration.

We illustrate the difference between the private spaces, QII and QIII, with an example from our work with schools using the standards-based-change (SBC) process (Au, 2013; Au & Raphael, 2011). Constructing an evidence system for tracking student progress toward year-end goals and providing formative assessment data to teachers to inform instruction toward those goals are among the core components of the process. Co-construction of the system provides an opportunity for teachers to build shared understanding of assessment while developing a practical and powerful tool. Much of the discussion in QI helps develop shared understandings of what counts as "worthy" evidence, the nature of tasks that will lead students to generate products that can provide the worthy evidence, and the scoring tools and anchor pieces that allow teachers to engage in consistent evaluation among all classrooms within a grade-level team. Teachers are taught a particular form for a rubric, consisting of three categories of features to evaluate and three levels (working on, meeting, exceeding) to capture where students fall on the continuum toward success.

Some teachers follow the system very closely, creating 3-by-3 rubrics with specific numbers of bullet points as recommended in the professional development session. This is typical of QII—appropriating what was learned in the social and public setting of QI. In contrast, some teachers use the fundamental principles underlying what was presented as part of QI activity but adapt or transform them for their own settings. Some adaptations are minor, such as using four levels instead of three to align with their district's system. Some are more transformative (indicating movement to QIII), maintaining similarity of principles but perhaps using student-generated evaluation systems rather than teacher-generated ones or alternative scoring tools that fit their needs better than the rubric would.

Movement among Spaces

As participating teachers move from QI to QII and QIII, they engage with one another to *appropriate* or to *transform* new ideas (i.e., take ideas up as introduced, for use in specific contexts, characteristic of QII; transform for use in new setting, characteristic of QIII), and interaction with others is critical. Those with more knowledge, through language and activity, introduce concepts and ideas with the goal of helping participants to appropriate particular ways of thinking.

Movement from QI or QII to QIII reflects the individual participants' learning as they *transform* new ideas, adapting them for their particular contexts. Transformation may happen in small units of change, such as changes to individual lesson plans or development of new formative assessments. It may occur in larger units of change, such as adapting an instructional unit to integrate literacy instruction and disciplinary learning or restructuring the classroom environment to facilitate inquiry-based learning with multiple texts. It also is reflected in the decisions made by teachers working together in grade-level teams, departments, and other collectives within the professional learning community. Such decisions include working together to establish a new collective identity and associated cultural practices that reflect values promoted by new standards (e.g., reading for understanding over fluency as an end goal) and to achieve the ultimate goal of improved student outcomes, including engagement, achievement, and independence.

The private learning that occurs in QII and QIII may be shared with colleagues and peers in various settings, characterizing movement to QIV. Thus movement from QII and QIII to QIV represents the process of *making public* those appropriations and transformations in cultural practices, often through dialogue or actions, sometimes in written forms (e.g., sharing lessons with colleagues, sharing an experience through publication in a professional journal). Publication of ideas may lead to new ways of thinking and working becoming a part of the community's discourse practices—the process of *conventionalization*. Conventionalization marks the acceptance of what was once a new concept as part of the cultural practices of the professional community, practices that will be shared for further appropriation (e.g., by induction-year teachers or teachers new to the school or district) as part of the process of continual learning. This reflects changes to the discourse and activity in QI as ideas, now conventionalized, are conveyed to members of the community. Or the discourse in QIV may involve learning that leads participants back to work in QII or QIII for further refinement.

The Vygotsky Space: An Illustration

This cycle, represented in the Vygotsky space, was illustrated in a recent meeting of the READI Teacher Network, a component of the Reading for Understanding research project at the University of Illinois at Chicago (Goldman, Lee, Britt, Greenleaf, & Brown, 2009). Across the school year, about 30 participating teachers meet within and across three disciplinary (history, literature, science) teams. Participating teachers teach at middle through high school grade levels. During the 2012–2013 school year, teams focused on creating a staircase curriculum (described by Au & Raphael, 2011, as consisting of learning goals and an assessment system to inform instructional decision making) in their disciplinary areas with a particular emphasis on argumentation. The emphasis on argumentation is consistent with the project's overall focus on high-level thinking and has the practical benefit of aligning with Common Core State Standards (Common Core State Standards Initiative, 2010). Using a process based on Au's (2013) work with the SBC process in high schools, each team of teachers created a vision of the excellent graduating scientist, historian, or literary thinker. They crafted a set of strands within which they organized what students needed to learn at each grade level or within each course to ensure that all students could achieve that vision. Each strand shared the theme of developing students' ability to understand, engage in, and create strong arguments using multiple sources of evidence within each disciplinary domain. Teachers crafted specific learning goals within each strand for three grade bands: 6–8, 9–10, and 11–12. To test the usefulness of the strands and learning goals for instruction, they each created and taught a lesson set—one to a few lessons in which argumentation played a central role—using multiple texts.

During the quarterly meetings, the interactions within QI involved a range of professional development activities, from formal presentations to collaborative work in pairs, small groups, and disciplinary teams. Opportunities were frequent for cross-disciplinary, whole-group sharing for critique, feedback, identifying common themes and unique features associated with specific disciplines, and celebration. Teachers engaged in reflective writing, as well as writing to create their staircased curriculum goals. In short, the public and social spaces in which initial work occurred provided support necessary to develop content knowledge about argumentation, Common Core, learning goal construction, and so forth. The lesson development to test the usefulness of this work for individual classroom instruction moved teachers from QI to QII/QIII. Individually, teachers worked between meetings reviewing the strands and their definitions, considering the vision of the graduate, creating and teaching their planned lesson(s), examining the student work that resulted from the set of lessons, and planning for sharing what they thought was significant about the lesson, student product, and their analyses when they returned for the next network meeting. The sharing during the network meetings reflected a return to the quadrants above the horizontal axis, where work engaged in as individuals (i.e., private) is made public.

During the March 2013 session, teachers spent a good part of the morning within disciplinary teams sharing their lessons and discussing implications for their current working drafts of their vision, strands, and learning goals, as informed by the results of their lesson enactment and analysis. This reflected discourse of QIV, where ideas (the QII and QIII individual/private activity) that were made public had the potential to become conventionalized (moving from QIV to QI) through revisions to the working drafts or to cause reexamination of how the ideas were appropriated by individual teachers (moving from QIV to QII or QIII).

The teachers then returned to the whole group to share across disciplines what they had discussed within their individual teams. The science team shared the story of a very productive conversation that made visible a key difference in understandings about argumentation in science within the group. This difference had been largely invisible throughout their earlier shared work (QI), benefiting from the private activity (QII and QIII) of the lesson component. One group of science teachers had created lessons that framed argumentation for their students in terms of using scientific understandings to construct an argument for taking a stand on social issues (e.g., climate change, the importance of funded space exploration). From their perspective, based on transcripts of their discussion, learning goals for teaching argumentation centered on "understanding and using evidence about a scientific phenomenon."

A second group of teachers had framed argumentation in terms of "confirming a scientific phenomenon through text evidence" (e.g., arguing the critical features that lead to volcanic eruption). When sharing across disciplinary areas, Eli[1] indicated his struggle to create an appropriate balance so all students could achieve the vision of the excellent graduating science student. He stated:

> "I don't know where to reconcile that because I would say what ours was, was science, and I think pretty interesting for the kids, but wasn't necessarily them arguing scientific phenomenon and finding evidence to support that—it was [arguing about a] social issue through using scientific evidence. I'm not sure where we're at on that or if we need to change that at all within our lesson because they're not arguing about scientific phenomena."

Reframing Eli's comments in the language of the Vygotsky space makes visible the five principles that underlie this example of a sociocultural approach to professional development. To paraphrase Eli:

> We spent a great deal of time in QI discussing our vision of the graduating science student and establishing clear strands of work that our students would need to learn to be successful in achieving that vision. We also spent time in QI laying out learning goals for each grade band so that in developing our course content and specific lessons, we would have a shared understanding of what we should be teaching when. When we moved from QI to the more private work of developing, teaching, and analyzing a lesson, we anticipated appropriating the goals [QII] to create these lessons based on our work in QI and returning in several weeks to share publicly [QIV] our various iterations of lessons designed to accomplish our shared goal. We did not anticipate engaging in transformation [QIII]. What a surprise! It turns out we did not have the shared understanding we thought. By making our thinking public, though, we came to realize the dual meaning of argumentation in science. That is the definition that we will have in mind as we continue our curriculum work [conventionalization]. As we move forward and mentor new colleagues, we will describe argumentation in science [QI] in these terms.

This example reflects relationships among appropriation, transformation, publication, and conventionalization concerning the definition of argumentation and its implications for science instruction for this team of teachers. It also underscores the complexity and challenges of effective professional development when the criterion for success is sustainable change. In the next section, we discuss how the

---

[1] All names are pseudonyms, with the exception of the example from Chicago Public Schools. Erin Koning's name and the name of the project were used with permission.

five core principles guide professional development that supports the interactions detailed in the Vygotsky space. For teachers to be able to appropriate and transform new ideas, the professional development must emphasize their individual and collective agency, provide opportunities to engage in dialogical practices that support learning, focus on problems of practice that are situated within their day-to-day professional lives, focus on the system in which teachers work, and be sustained over time.

In the remaining sections, we discuss each principle. Although we recognize that these are inextricably integrated in successful professional development initiatives, for analytical purposes we shine a spotlight on each in turn. For each, we contrast the typical approach to professional development and the approach that research in general and our own experiences suggest is more likely to lead to sustainable change, illustrating how this occurs with examples from our work with the SBC process (Au, 2005, 2013; Au & Raphael, 2011; Raphael, 2010). We conclude with comments and recommendations for future research on professional development from a sociocultural perspective.

AGENCY IN SOCIOCULTURAL APPROACHES TO PROFESSIONAL DEVELOPMENT

The first principle of our sociocultural approach to professional development is the importance of teacher ownership and agency in the change process. Teachers must believe that, through their actions, they can influence their students' learning and that they have the power to make decisions necessary to effect improvements. Agency is not inherent in the individual but, rather, inextricably linked to "the social context and the cultural tools that shape the development of human beliefs, values, and ways of acting" (Lasky, 2005, p. 900).

Teaching without Agency

Professional development related to the social context (e.g., federal and state policies, district mandates and expectations) and cultural tools (e.g., high-stakes tests, instructional materials, required pedagogical approaches) can either promote or undermine teacher ownership and agency. For example, when cultural tools of teaching are packaged programs and assessments, professional development emphasizes management and fidelity to the materials. In researching the effects of one such initiative, Valli and Buese (2007) describe how teachers' roles shifted from that of professional educators using their knowledge to support students' learning to data managers and analysts, even when asked to collect data that they ultimately did not trust. At one point, teachers attempted to modify the curriculum to better meet the needs of their students. After the state test had been administered, and only for those students who showed competency in reading, they asked to emphasize writing instruction instead of the packaged reading intervention program. The petition was rejected on the grounds that writing was not assessed on the state test.

Research on the effects of program- or assessment-driven initiatives and associated professional development has not shown significant, sustainable impact on improving student literacy achievement (Crocco & Costigan, 2007), though this is not unique to literacy. Similar findings have emerged in the study of mathematics reform (Desimone, Smith, & Phillips, 2013; Valli & Buese, 2007) and in secondary school reform in Canada (Lasky, 2005), as well as in literacy. Taking away teachers' agency, diminishing their professional knowledge by removing opportunities to make pedagogical decisions based on students' needs, and ignoring the importance of teacher ownership of the basics of reform are steps that create severe problems. There is no justification for these steps, which lead to a deprofessionalized and discouraged teaching force. Research has found no increase in student engagement or achievement that might warrant such approaches.

Teaching with Agency: An Alternative Model

Taylor and colleagues' (2011) review of research on professional development-driven reform efforts identified shared features of seven successful programs (e.g., Fisher & Frey, 2007; Lai et al., 2009; Taylor, Pearson, Peterson, & Rodriguez, 2005; Timperley & Parr, 2007). Central to the projects was teacher ownership of the reform effort. This played out in terms of a collaborative and high-functioning professional learning community with a shared vision of both the successful graduate and the school change process to help students achieve that vision.

Teachers' agency through ownership of the reform effort is at the heart of an initiative in a small three-school, K–8 district in the Chicago metropolitan area. The district serves diverse students, primarily African American, with approximately 50% of the students eligible for the federal free lunch program. The superintendent and assistant superintendents for professional development and curriculum are striving to meet all the demands of the Illinois Flex waiver and Race to the Top, a large component of which is enacting the Common Core. Though the Common Core initiative was externally driven by federal and state policies and introduced by the district, the key leaders paid careful attention to teacher ownership from the beginning. Common Core documents were positioned as professional resources, as a new wave in a long history of standards-based reform, with a welcomed focus on higher-level thinking. Professional development focused on exploring three questions: (1) What knowledge should students develop from kindergarten through grade 8? (2) What are the expectations for knowledge development within grade levels? (3) What are the implications for teaching this knowledge across subject areas? Each component of professional development was anchored in teachers' consideration of their own practices, the degree to which they reflected Common Core content, and new directions and content they needed to learn.

Teachers across the three schools started by creating a common vision of their excellent graduate, drawing on knowledge of and expectations for their students and community. Teacher ownership surfaced in reflections such as, "I am very excited to see what changes will take place as this work has allowed teachers to share a common vision for our students." Using a backward design process, they constructed visions of the excellent graduating writer for each school. These served as each school's end goals for developing their staircase curriculum or road map for each grade level's instructional focus.

In creating strands and learning goals for their staircase curriculum, teachers were asked to "think their own thoughts first," using their professional expertise and knowledge, with Common Core as a professional resource. One teacher reflected that the time to "brainstorm and develop our own ideas in our own words" deepened their understanding of the standards, and another noted that the approach was "an excellent example of giving us ownership and honoring our experience simply by asking us first what we know and think before just telling us and giving us something to go do."

Teacher agency, in which teachers gain opportunities to take up new and socially mediated ideas or practices (QI; e.g., practice of developing vision of the graduate, common core standards) and internalize them through application to individual contexts (QII; e.g., developing grade-level curricular strands and student learning goals), enables transformations and enacting new ways of thinking (QIII). Individual transformation of existing ideas and practices to best meet needs of students, grade levels, departments, schools, and communities has the potential for ownership of the change process as individual learning is externalized and shared publicly (QIV), through language and activity, with other members of the community of learners. Depending on their reception by the community, shared ideas and practices have the potential to become conventionalized as individuals take them up in their own practices and/or the community adopts them as part of their conventional practice.

THE SITUATED PRINCIPLE IN SOCIOCULTURAL APPROACHES TO PROFESSIONAL DEVELOPMENT

Sociocultural approaches to learning have long recognized the centrality of meaningfulness for success (Brown, Collins, & Duguid, 1989; Robbins & Aydede, 2009), a logical extension of the agency principle. We use the term *situated* to capture the idea that sociocultural approaches to professional development support teachers in addressing problems of practice they identify as important. An unintended consequence of our history of top-down, mandated, transmission models of professional development is that the content is often decontextualized from participants' perceived needs (Kerr, Marsh, Ikemoto, Darilek, & Barney, 2006; Wood, 2007a). *Situated* reflects two key ideas in sociocultural approaches to professional development. First, it is an extension of the agency principle, underscoring the importance of teacher ownership of the goals of professional development. Second, it is consistent with the research on learning within communities of practice (e.g., Brown et al., 1989; Clancey, 1997; Lave & Wenger, 1991; Robbins & Aydede, 2009; Schatzki, Cetina, & von Savigny, 2001). This research emphasizes the importance of situating activity and interaction within ongoing practice—the cycle captured by the variation in the way language functions within the quadrants of the Vygotsky space.

Situated, Not Compliance

QI activities focus on developing shared understandings, so a key decision is framing and connecting professional development to participants' needs. Two case studies provide insights into the importance of this connection. Kerr and colleagues' (2006) research examined variations in how schools developed their school improvement plans (SIP), the official shared understandings of a school's core activities. SIPs supposedly serve as a school's road map, with clear, coherent goals to guide the work of school administration (e.g., in allocating resources), faculty (in pedagogical goals), and staff (in allocation of support time). As such, the content of professional development for any given year is reflected in the SIP document, and the likelihood of success of the professional development depends on the degree of buy-in, ownership, and agency of the participating teachers. When not situated in the immediate needs of the faculty, or when time is not allotted to build shared understandings of these goals, professional development is less likely to be effective.

In one of the schools Kerr studied, the content of the SIP grew out of dialogue among all stakeholders to collectively identify school goals based on internal expertise and understanding of the students' needs. In two other schools, SIP content was externally driven rather than situated within perceived needs of teachers and staff. In schools that were engaged in a process that helped them identify school and classroom needs, teachers described the SIP document as more meaningful than in the past and more useful in guiding their practice. In the other two schools, the SIP was viewed as a compliance document. Professional development associated with compliance suffers from the same problems noted in the agency principle section. Professional development associated with a collectively designed SIP, situated within the needs teachers have identified collectively as critical to students' success, increases teacher ownership and, in turn, increases the likelihood of long-term, sustainable school change.

A case study contrasted two approaches to professional development, one general (monthly school meetings not situated to address immediate problems of practice), the other situated within grade-level teams with professional development aligned to their immediate pedagogical needs (Wood, 2007a). The contrast between the two approaches was notable in the way in which the situated work developed capacity for a sustainable school change effort. More teachers participated more enthusiastically and authentically, raising problems of common interest within the group and drawing on expertise and judgment within the group to address problems. Protocols used during professional development were viewed as tools for appropriation and transformation, not prescriptions with which to comply. Leadership and facilitation rotated within the grade-level teams, building capacity within the group and a deep bench of leaders so that work could continue across years without fear of losing momentum from loss of a key leader. In the example that follows, we highlight one school's professional development initiative, situated in the immediate needs of the teachers, designed to improve writing teaching and learning.

Situated Professional Development: An Example from the Pacific Northwest

The curriculum coordinator of a small semirural district outside a large metropolitan area in the Pacific Northwest attended a conference and learned of an opportunity to begin a multiyear initiative to improve writing teaching and learning schoolwide. She had a specific school in mind, one that had continually struggled to make adequate yearly progress (AYP) despite much energy and effort on the part of the administration and staff. The district coordinator thought the opportunity would be a good fit but recognized that the school staff needed (1) to own the work and not see it as a district mandate and (2) to engage with the work as part of their everyday practice. In short, she knew the importance of situated practice for long-term success.

The multiyear support was a joint project of Regie Routman (2012) and two of us (Taffy Raphael, Kathryn Au). To situate the work in the context of the school's needs, the team conducted a needs assessment to: (1) identify key issues from the school community and (2) begin building the relationship among the professional development providers, school leaders (administrative and curriculum), teachers, and resource staff. A major theme that emerged was that teachers reported a lack of consistency in their writing instruction. Teachers and administrators described their curriculum as "all over the map," with too many differing programs. Their desire for coherence was used to situate the work as an opportunity to tackle a meaningful problem in their writing instruction practice. Related themes included inconsistency in how they used professional meeting time and need for an internal staff member to have time allocated to lead the initiative, collaborating closely with the external consultants, both issues associated with capacity building to sustain the initiative over time.

The professional development plan was collaboratively constructed, again situating it in authentic needs of the school but based on findings from the external consultants' analyses of the needs assessment data. They created a three-part plan: (1) infrastructure changes, (2) knowledge building, and (3) creating their staircase curriculum with their learning goals and assessment system to inform instructional decision making. First, professional development support focused on helping the administration create an infrastructure to support a sustainable professional development project. This included time for teachers to create their own professional norms and the administrative leadership allocating a curriculum leader's time to the initiative. It included professional development to support the creation of a leadership team with teacher representation from each grade level, as well as professional development for the leadership team in guiding the writing reform initiative. And it included structural changes, such as the use of some of the early release days for grade-level and vertical teams to work on the initiative. Second, it included knowledge building about writing instruction and the writing process through onsite residencies, with Routman modeling and guiding teachers' writing instructional practices (QI–QIII activity). It included formal analysis and annotations of writing samples (both typical and exemplary) of student work across the year and over multiple years to evaluate collectively improvements in pedagogical practices and their results on students' written products (QII–QIV activity). Third, it included a focus on identifying their vision of the excellent graduating writer and learning goals for each grade level that formed the steps to achieving that vision. They aligned the learning goals internally to ensure smooth building from one grade level to the next, as well as aligning their learning goals to key external documents, including the Common Core State Standards in writing and the district's writing assessment system.

As the school's work with the external consultants evolved to minimal support, the writing initiative was a part of their everyday work, conventionalizing the structures, norms, and the practice of whole-school assessments three times per year of student writing and subsequent sharing within and across grade levels and throughout the school.

THE DIALOGUE PRINCIPLE IN SOCIOCULTURAL APPROACHES TO PROFESSIONAL DEVELOPMENT

The third principle underlying our sociocultural approach to professional development underscores the importance of dialogue as a means for engaging in inquiry. Through dialogue, learning occurs (Johnston-Parsons, 2012), engaging participants, such as the teachers in the previous examples, in ways that help them move beyond initial understandings and commitments (Burbules, 1993) as they come to common understandings. Dialogue within varying group structures is the basis for movement among the four quadrants of the Vygotsky space. Successful professional development creates a range of opportunities for dialogue among members of the professional learning community, guiding them through the appropriation, transformation, publication, and conventionalization of ideas. This contrasts with one-shot (i.e., insufficient time allotted for dialogical inquiry), transmission (i.e., unidirectional) models of professional development that have dominated for decades (Curry, 2008).

Transmission over Dialogue

The form that discourse takes in professional development can support or undermine teacher learning. For too many years, professional development has taken the approach of unidirectional delivery of information, likely based on the assumption that "professionals are in need of 'training' or 'developing' through knowledge being 'delivered' to them" (Webster-Wright, 2009, p. 713). Webster-Wright even cautions against the use of the term *professional development* if it simply moves the emphasis from the "knowledge-deficient" professional to the "knowledge-possessing provider" (p. 713).

In terms of the Vygotsky space, conventional training models tend to focus on the kinds of activity and talk characteristic of QI. The function of language is univocal (Wertsch & Toma, 1995), with information directed from the speaker to the participants. Teachers attend professional development so they will "have" the information they need. The term *teacher training* reflects the emphasis in transmission models. Teachers' responsibilities are to attend training to "get" the information, and evaluation focuses on their fidelity of implementation (e.g., Rowan, Camburn, & Barnes, 2004; Shanahan & Barr, 1995; Slavin & Madden 2001). As Seymour and Osana (2003) note, however, training approaches to professional development result in superficial understandings reflected in "lethal mutations" that render evidence-based practices ineffective.

Dialogue over Transmission

Dialogical underpinnings of a sociocultural approach to professional development are characterized by joint construction of meaning and customizing the language and activity to the needs of the participants. This dialogical approach is influenced by Voloshinov's (1973) description of a word as a "two-sided act" (p. 86), emphasizing the goal-directed interaction, mutual commitment, and reciprocal roles of both the speaker and listener in constructing meaning and understanding (Bakhtin, 1986). It reflects the talk that supports appropriation and transformation of what has been shared. It provides opportunity for publication of what has been learned, adapted, and transformed such that other participants may take up new practices. Professional learning, change, and the associated language and activity occur in the context of the professional learning community (Nelson, Slavit, Perkins, & Hathorn, 2008; Wood, 2007a, 2007b), where ideas are appropriated and transformed through ongoing interactions with colleagues and ongoing practice with students (McVee et al., 2005).

Our earlier example of Eli and his science teacher colleagues illustrated how dialogue among high school teachers in collaborative work groups lead to intersubjective agreement (i.e., conventionalization) on their vision of the graduating learner (i.e., the science student) and the student learning outcomes they would target to ensure students' progress toward that vision. Here, we illustrate how multiple contexts and support systems allow teachers time to appropriate and transform new ideas. We have worked with Erin Koning and her colleagues from the Chicago Public School Department of Literacy on their Common Core Early Adopters project. In a district that had historically relied on a trainer-of-trainer transmission model of professional development, this project engaged the entire language arts teaching staff of approximately 30 lead schools and representatives from each grade of approximately 25 support schools. Koning and her team were committed to creating multiple opportunities for teachers to engage in dialogical inquiry. The inquiry was guided by introducing relevant concepts within whole-group settings in ways that could be useful to teachers' individual schools and classrooms. Teachers then met in teams to consider how they could appropriate, adapt, and transform the concepts to meet the needs of their diverse learners. The teacher teams were then asked to make their appropriations and transformations public (i.e., to the whole group of participants) for possible conventionalization within their own schools or across sites.

Structurally, Koning and her team needed a context in which consistent and coherent information could be shared across participating schools. So the overall context involved four rounds of professional development each year, each round consisting of consecutive days on which teachers at a particular grade level met. That is, all first-grade teachers met on Tuesdays, second-grade teachers on Wednesdays, and so forth. The agenda reflected variation in groupings reflective of different dialogical opportunities. For example, during the first hour to two of the day, dialogue consisted of "turn-and-talk" or "pair-square" interactions embedded within a formal presentation (characteristic of QI) made by one of the Department of Literacy specialists.

The bulk of the middle part of the day consisted of "table conversations" supported by a table facilitator. Participants were sometimes from a single school (e.g., a school's grade-level team), whereas other groups were formed by mixing teachers from the same grade level across schools. Dialogical inquiry about content shared in the opening presentation was shaped by engaging in and discussing collaborative tasks (e.g., unpacking standards, constructing assessment system tools, developing units of instruction; characteristic of QII and QIII). By pairing table facilitators with the grade-level teams and by sometimes mixing teachers from different schools, conversations included insider and outside perspectives. Through dialogue, teachers began the process of appropriation or transformation, but with a clear sense that the process needed to continue in grade-level and vertical team meetings when they returned to their schools.

The end of the day involved reconvening in a larger group form to share across teams, providing opportunities for teachers to share ideas publicly with one another to gain new ideas, as well as for feedback and critique. Participants' comments reflect the shift in emphases and collaboration across the sessions. Following Session 1, teachers' comments emphasized individual learning and the challenges of engaging in dialogical inquiry: "I never realized how many components are packed into each standard. Talking them through was helpful, but hard!" Following Session 2, typical reflections emphasized the value of cross-talk and an openness to feedback/critique: "It was so helpful to get feedback from someone at another school. This is so new that it's nice to see how other teams are thinking about it." Following Session 3, we saw an increased sense of agency and understanding: "I'm not a curriculum expert, but I *can* do this. It's finally starting to make sense to me." By the end of Session 4, teachers increasingly sought out the consultation and collaboration of colleagues on their work in order to extend their own learning and reflection.

Through dialogue, both teachers and professional development leaders can engage in systematic analysis of curriculum, instructional practices, and student work, together contributing to the content of the learning. With each party coming to understand the meaning of the other, the possibility exists for resolving disagreements and achieving consensus.

THE SYSTEMIC PRINCIPLE IN PROFESSIONAL DEVELOPMENT

The fourth principle underpinning our sociocultural approach to professional development is that it is systemic in nature. A systemic approach focuses on the same goals or constructs for all stakeholders, building shared understanding through professional development that delivers consistent messages throughout the initiative (McLaughlin & Talbert, 2006; Talbert, 2009; Wood, 2007b). Systemic professional development effectively brings about change as participants are supported in collaborative work, coordinating their efforts to achieve common goals (Bryk et al., 2010; Horn & Little, 2010) that, in education, usually relate to improving student achievement (Taylor et al., 2005).

In a systemic approach, careful consideration is given to the level of institutional participation. Research by Au (2005) and Raphael (2010) found that the most promising unit is the school (vs. smaller units such as a grade level or larger units such as a district). Au and Raphael (2011) suggest that professional development at the school level focus on curriculum coherence (Newmann, Smith, Allensworth, & Bryk, 2001) to engage all teachers in improving student achievement.

Coherence develops as teachers engage in a form of backward design that Au and Raphael refer to as the "to do cycle." The first phase involves school staff members in constructing a common vision of the excellent graduate in general, then in the focal curricular area (e.g., reading, writing, critical thinking, literate thinking). Teachers in each grade level or department define their step in the staircase by identifying end-of-year student learning goals. Each step in the staircase builds on the learning goals of the previous step and leads to the learning goals of the following step, with goals at the highest step matching the vision. Although conceptually simple and straightforward, such work is socially complex and demands a systemic approach to the professional development that supports and guides the process.

Nonsystemic Professional Development

Too often, professional development efforts lack any systemic orientation, confining the work to a single part of the system. Or pursuing a more-is-less method can result in a "Christmas tree" or "grab bag" approach to professional development (Raphael, Gavelek, Hynd, Teale, & Shanahan, 2001). The ineffectiveness of such approaches can be traced to two faulty assumptions. The first is that improvements in a single part of the system will produce the desired results. For example, reading improvement efforts for over a decade focused on K–2 teachers, despite research demonstrating the importance of ongoing reading instruction, particularly for comprehending disciplinary texts (Schoenbach, Braunger, Greenleaf, & Litman, 2004). Such initiatives have shown mixed results at best (Beck, 2010; Hurry & Sylva, 2007; Venezky, 1998).

The second faulty assumption is that providing support to only a part of the whole will somehow have an effect on the school's entire professional community. Instead, this kind of partial or piecemeal approach sends unintended messages to faculty members about whose expertise is most valued. For example, focusing professional development at K–2 can send upper-grade teachers the message that their role in reading improvement efforts is unimportant. It should not be surprising that, after a decade or more of such messaging, upper-grade teachers view reading improvement as the responsibility of primary grade teachers and are skeptical, if not reluctant to participate, when professional development is eventually offered. In our own work in more than 100 schools in the past decade alone, we have seen this piecemeal approach occur repeatedly, undermining the school community and frustrating teachers across grade levels.

Systemic Professional Development

In contrast, systemic professional development involves all key participants (i.e., all grade levels or departments, resource teachers) from the start (Louis, Marks, & Kruse, 1996). It creates a common purpose and shared responsibility for reaching concrete goals, such as improved student achievement through enacting a staircase curriculum. It uses multiple coordinated activity settings, including whole-school, grade-bands, department, and grade-level meetings to provide opportunity for dialogue, from public and social to private and individual, reflecting all four quadrants of the Vygotsky space.

Later stages of professional development focus on curriculum construction, starting with the creation of a vision of the excellent graduate, as well as the graduate within the focal curriculum area. This vision was developed by one of our participating schools: *The excellent graduate is a critical problem solver who enhances and sustains the world in which he or she lives.* The activity settings here consisted of movement among whole-school (QI, building shared understanding and common language for moving from the general vision to the vision related to the curriculum) and grade-level teams (QII, QIII). In a school creating its reading curriculum, each grade-level team identified characteristics of the excellent graduating reader and how those characteristics contributed to a vision of the graduating excellent reader. In terms of the Vygotsky space, these smaller teams engaged in social and private discourse that would eventually become public (QIV) when shared within the entire school. Teachers then looked for common themes that would be converted into the vision of the graduating reader, which, after revision, became conventionalized as part of the identity of the school. This vision of the graduating reader reflects the shift from the general vision—*Our school aspires to graduate motivated, engaged, and confident readers with the ability to apply their passion for literacy to a variety of contexts, leading to a greater understanding of themselves, their communities, and the world*—to that of a graduate in a specific curricular area.

These activity settings, supporting dialogical interaction appropriate to the quadrants, recur throughout effective professional development (Gallucci, 2008). In our work within the SBC process, more advanced activity focuses on creating the learning goals and the assessment system to inform teachers' instructional decision making throughout the year. The work is systemic in that it includes all stakeholders in the process, eventually including students and their families. It is systemic in that it follows a research-based process—the Seven Levels to Success—that builds capacity among the individuals and teams of educators (Raphael, Au, & Goldman, 2009). It is systemic in that the model of learning—the Vygotsky space—provides experience to teachers, serving as a model for effective instructional practice within their own classrooms. It is in the making public of ideas and practices (Q4) that the real work of building consensus necessary for a systematic approach takes place. This iterative process requires continuing opportunities for teachers to coordinate their instruction.

SUSTAINED PROFESSIONAL DEVELOPMENT

The fifth principle in sociocultural approaches to professional development is that they are sustained, in two senses of the word. The first sense relates to the fourth principle. To be systemic, professional development must be sustained over time (Cambone, 1995; Collinson & Cook, 2001; Darling-Hammond et al., 2009; Garet, Porter, Desimone, Birman, & Yoon, 2001). As described, systemic professional development requires an ongoing process of alternation between whole-group and small-group sessions (Kruse & Louis, 1997). This process of alternation must be sustained or continued over a sufficiently long period of time for the common goal to be achieved (i.e., the entire cycle represented in the Vygotsky space can recur multiple times). In general, the loftier or more ambitious the common goal, the more time must be dedicated to its accomplishment.

The second sense of "sustained" refers to the extent to which professional development contributes to the sustainability of improved practice and positive results (Birman, Desimone, Porter, & Garet, 2000; Coburn, 2003) over a multi-year period. Professional development approaches cannot be considered successful when they yield fleeting results. In terms of the Vygotsky space, the goal is conventionalization, or the institutionalizing of improved practices and, therefore, improved results. For example, teachers' long-term use of improved instructional practices can lead to increased student achievement at a school, with large-scale test scores rising and remaining significantly higher than baseline scores. "Sustained" in this second sense relates to the notion of capacity building, so that participants are able independently to carry out the improved practices gained through professional development and even to lead others in carrying out these practices (Stoll, Bolam, McMahon, Wallace, & Thomas, 2006).

Episodic Professional Development

Typically, professional development is episodic, or short-lived. One-shot workshops are common, as is the absence of follow-up coaching that would enable participants to apply new knowledge in the context of their endeavors (Ball & Cohen, 1999; Kelleher, 2003). In episodic professional development, session topics tend to shift rapidly. Organizers often focus on covering, or even rushing through, the content and seldom assess participants' ability to apply the material or the extent to which participants' practices have been improved in the situations and settings targeted for application. When episodic professional development becomes the norm, it is not situated in the needs of the participants, and as a result, they no longer expect professional development sessions to be connected or meaningful to their practice. As a result, participants become cynical and begin going through the motions during professional development sessions, perhaps brushing tasks aside or completing tasks with minimal thought and effort.

Sustained and Sustainable Professional Development

We discussed the first sense of "sustained" in the previous section in term of its importance in allowing systemic change to take hold (Newmann et al., 2001; Smith, Smith, & Bryk, 1998). The second sense of "sustained" refers to the degree to which professional development contributes to the long-term sustainability of improved practices and positive results. Sustainability depends on professional development participants' ownership over the change effort and long-term commitment to it, relating to the first principle, agency. If the principle of agency has been observed, participants will find their contributions to be meaningful and effective (Scribner, Sawyer, Watson, & Myers, 2007). What may have begun as an externally driven change effort can become internally driven, carried forward by professional development participants.

Our experiences in the multiple schools we've supported in building a staircase curriculum illustrate this principle. For example, during the process of alternating between whole-group sharing sessions and small-group (grade level or department) coaching sessions, teachers come to value their work and seek ways to strengthen their contributions. We have frequently observed adjacent grade-level teams request time to meet together (e.g., seeking release time or after-school support from their principal) so they can better coordinate their steps in the school's staircase curriculum.

Sustainability across years requires capacity building (Darling-Hammond, 1993). When executed well, capacity building emphasizes professional development that enables key individuals to lead change efforts with less and less external support. That is, the key leaders learn to create opportunities for and to support dialogue relevant to each quadrant at the appropriate time in the process. To support our schools' work in creating their staircase curriculum, professional development sessions are conducted with the principals, key curriculum leaders, and teacher leaders. These sessions are designed to engage school leaders in simulations of the whole- and small-group professional development activities to be carried out later with the entire faculty.

Leaders learn how to set objectives and draft agendas for workshops. They provide feedback about the design of activities and the nature of the background knowledge and support the faculty will need to be successful. After whole-school professional development sessions, leaders debrief participants about what went well, what could be improved, and what follow-up support or intervention is needed.

As time goes on, leaders learn to conduct parts of the professional development sessions themselves, such as giving a short presentation or facilitating a small-group discussion.

Over time, teacher leaders have become increasingly committed to leading whole-school sessions on their own, rather than asking their external consultants to do so. Teacher leaders have made comments such as, "this change process is about our school, not about [external consultant's company] and we need to take charge of it." Using such a model reduces the amount of time required for schools to create their staircase curriculum in subsequent subject areas, in our experience. Whereas the first staircase typically takes approximately 3 years to achieve sustainability, the subsequent ones often can be accomplished in 2 years, a 33% savings in time.

To return to the Vygotsky space that underlies this principle, the ongoing nature of professional development over an extended period of time plays a critical role in building capacity for sustainable change. Teachers need sustained time and continuous opportunities to alternate between constructing new knowledge through social interaction and appropriating that learning in individual and small-group contexts to gain ownership of the change process. It is over a sustained period of time and through these ongoing opportunities that teachers are able to internalize, transform, and externalize new ways of thinking that lead to a systematic conventionalization of improved practices in a community of learners.

CONCLUDING COMMENTS

In this chapter, we have explained the theoretical underpinnings of our sociocultural approach to professional development, highlighting examples from our school improvement work with teachers. These theoretical underpinnings center on the Vygotsky space and five principles: that professional development should (1) give agency to participants, (2) be situated in actual settings and problems of practice, (3) involve participants in dialogical learning, (4) be systemic, and (5) be sustainable. We close by highlighting three broad themes in professional development growing from a sociocultural perspective.

First, we argue for consideration of what the term *professional* should mean when used to modify *development*. The very construct of *professional* has been lost in initiatives that view the process as one of transmitting knowledge from an external expert to the participants. In our view, the term *professional* in education and other fields should be linked to expert performance that requires knowledge, practice, and judgment with a human element beyond that which can be captured in a flow chart or programmed on a computer. For example, today's teachers are challenged with educating students for a rapidly changing world, with policies in developed countries increasingly focused on students' proficiency in processes of high-level thinking, such as the comprehension of texts with complex disciplinary content. Given this situation, we believe that transmittal models of professional development will show a continued failure to help teachers address the challenges they face. We argue that teachers must be provided with professional development, based in sociocultural theory, that gives them ample opportunity to engage in high-level thinking, paralleling the emphasis that is desirable for them to follow in their own teaching.

Second, in a sociocultural approach, the focus of professional development is on teamwork and collaborative accomplishment rather than on individual achievement alone. A corollary to the concept of teachers as change agents is that the system in which they work must build their capacity and facilitate their collaborative work as members of a unified professional learning community, such as a schoolwide professional learning community. In our examples from the field of education, we have demonstrated the effectiveness of a shared vision of the excellent student and teachers working together to build their schools' own staircase curriculum, coordinated across grades and departments. The more complex the learning required of students, the greater the need for consistent instruction across the years. Although the value of collaboration may seem self-evident, leaders who value collaboration can find this position challenging to maintain. In education, for example, the current political climate lends momentum to competitive models, including approaches to strategic teacher compensation that potentially pit teachers against one another.

Finally, any sociocultural approach to professional development takes the long view, leveraging participants' increasing expertise to put sustainable solutions in place. As our examples imply, professional development should be guided by models that provide road maps for moving toward solutions, such as Raphael and colleagues' (2009) Seven Levels to Success or Fisher and Frey's (2007) work in the San Diego schools. Road map models serve as frameworks for moving participants forward in applying knowledge gained through professional development to address problems of practice. These models are necessary to establish a clear focus and purpose for whole- and small-group discussions. They take the discussions from talk to action by requiring specific accomplishments at specific points in time. Ownership and a sense of agency are maintained because participants construct the product to be completed (such as a staircase curriculum) or decide on the action to be taken (such as implementation of new instructional strategy). With a road map model in place, leaders can be more confident that the considerable time and resources set aside for dialogical learning will indeed result in progress toward desired outcomes.

In our view, a sociocultural vision for professional development has profound implications for research, practice, and policy. The existing base of studies for understanding the nuances of sociocultural approaches and the nature of dialogue across activity settings is relatively thin, thus offering investigators of adult learning, professional discourse, systems analysis, and other topics a wealth of opportunities for research. We hope this chapter has made clear not only the theoretical foundations for sociocultural approaches to professional development but also their potential benefits to participants and those they seek to serve. These approaches offer the promise of moving from transmission models of teaching, learning, and service to transformative models consistent with promotion of the kinds of creative, insightful thinking needed to address the complex issues facing society today.

QUESTIONS FOR DISCUSSION

1. How have current professional development initiatives allowed and encouraged teachers to appropriate, transform, and make public their learning, or discouraged them from doing these things? What changes in structure and framing are necessary for this to happen?

2. How can leaders of professional development balance the tension of external accountability while empowering teachers to be agents of change in their own schools and classrooms?

3. What kinds of structures and protocols can be embedded within a professional development structure to promote dialogue among all stakeholders about meaningful problems of practice?

4. How can professional learning communities use components of the school's infrastructure and clear goals (both for the learning community and the students) to effect sustained and systemic change?

ACKNOWLEDGMENT

The examples related to disciplinary literacy professional development were drawn from PROJECT READI, a multidisciplinary, multi-institution collaboration for research and development to improve complex comprehension of multiple forms of text in literature, history, and science. The work is supported, in part, by the Institute of Education Sciences, U.S. Department of Education (Grant No. R305F100007) to the University of Illinois at Chicago. The opinions expressed are those of the authors and do not represent views of the Institute or the U.S. Department of Education.

REFERENCES

Advanced Reading Development Demonstration Project. (2008). Partnerships for improving literacy in urban schools. *Reading Teacher, 61*(8), 674–680.

Allington, R. L., & Walmsley, S. A. (1995). *No quick fix: Rethinking literacy programs in America's elementary schools.* New York: Teachers College Press.

Au, K. H. (2005). Negotiating the slippery slope: School change and literacy achievement. *Journal of Literacy Research, 37*(3), 267–288.

Au, K. H. (2013). Helping high schools meet higher standards. *Journal of Adolescent and Adult Literacy, 37*(3), 267–288.

Au, K. H., & Raphael, T. E. (2011). The staircase curriculum: Whole-school collaboration to improve literacy achievement. *New England Reading Association Journal, 46*(2), 1–8.

Bakhtin, M. M. (1986). *Speech genres and other essays* (V. McGee, Trans.; M. Holquist & C. Emerson, Eds.). Austin: University of Texas Press.

Ball, D. L., & Cohen, D. K. (1999). Developing practice, developing practitioners: Toward a practice-based theory of professional education. In G. Sykes & L. Darling-Hammond (Eds.), *Teaching as the learning profession: Handbook of policy and practice* (pp. 3–32). San Francisco: Jossey Bass.

Beck, I. L. (2010). Half-full or half-empty. *Journal of Literacy Research, 42*(1), 94.

Birman, B. F., Desimone, L., Porter, A. C., & Garet, M. S. (2000). Designing professional development that works. *Educational Leadership, 57*(8), 28.

Brown, J., Collins, A., & Duguid, P. (1989). Situated cognition and the culture of learning. *Educational Researcher, 18*(1), 32.

Bryk, A. S., Sebring, P. B., Allensworth, E., Luppescu, S., & Easton, J. Q. (2010). *Organizing schools for improvement: Lessons from Chicago.* Chicago: University of Chicago Press.

Burbules, N. C. (1993). *Dialogue in teaching: Theory and practice* (Vol. 10). New York: Teachers College Press.

Cambone, J. (1995). Time for teachers in school restructuring. *Teachers College Record, 96*(3), 1–32.

Chappuis, J., Stiggins, R. J., Chappuis, S., & Arter, J. A. (2011). *Classroom assessment for student learning: Doing it right—using it well* (2nd ed.). Upper Saddle River, NJ: Pearson.

Clancey, W. J. (1997). *Situated cognition: On human knowledge and computer representation.* Cambridge, UK: Cambridge University Press.

Coburn, C. E. (2003). Rethinking scale: Moving beyond numbers to deep and lasting change. *Educational Researcher, 32*(6), 3–12.

Collinson, V., & Cook, T. F. (2001). "I don't have enough time": Teachers' interpretations of time as a key to learning and school change. *Journal of Educational Administration, 39*(3), 266–281.

Common Core State Standards Initiative. (2010). Common Core State Standards for English language arts and literacy in history/social studies, science, and technical subjects. Retrieved from *www.corestandards.org/assets/CCSSI_ELA%20Standards.pdf.*

Correnti, R., & Rowan, B. (2007). Opening up the black box: Literacy instruction in schools participating in three comprehensive school reform programs. *American Educational Research Journal, 44*(2), 298–338.

Crocco, M. S., & Costigan, A. T. (2007). The narrowing of curriculum and pedagogy in the age of accountability: Urban educators speak out. *Urban Education, 42*(6), 512–535.

Curry, M. (2008). Critical friends groups: The possibilities and limitations embedded in teacher professional communities aimed at instructional improvement and school reform. *Teachers College Record, 110*(4), 733.

Darling-Hammond, L. (1993). Reframing the school reform agenda: Developing capacity for school transformation. *Phi Delta Kappan, 74*(10), 752–761.

Darling-Hammond, L., Wei, R. C., Andree, A., Richardson, N., & Orphanos, S. (2009). *Professional learning in the learning profession.* Washington, DC: National Staff Development Council.

Desimone, L. (2009). Improving impact studies of teachers' professional development: Toward better conceptualizations and measures. *Educational Researcher, 38*(3), 181–199.

Desimone, L., Smith, T. M., & Phillips, K. J. R. (2013). Linking student achievement growth to professional development participation and changes in instruction: A longitudinal study of elementary students and teachers in Title I schools. *Teachers College Record, 115*(5), 1–46.

Duffy, G. G., Roehler, L. R., Meloth, M. S., Vavrus, L. G., Book, C., Putnam, J., et al. (1986). The relationship between explicit verbal explanations during reading skill instruction and student awareness and achievement: A study of reading teacher effects. *Reading Research Quarterly, 21*(3), 237–252.

DuFour, R., DuFour, R. B., & Eaker, R. E. (2008). *Revisiting professional learning communities at work: New insights for improving schools.* Bloomington, IN: Solution Tree.

Dutro, E., Fisk, M. C., Koch, R., Roop, L. J., & Wixson, K. (2002). When state policies meet local district contexts: Standards-based professional development as a means to individual agency and collective ownership. *Teachers College Record, 104*(4), 787–811.

Fisher, D., & Frey, N. (2007). Implementing a schoolwide literacy framework: Improving achievement in an urban elementary school. *Reading Teacher, 61*(1), 32–43.

Florio-Ruane, S., Berne, J., & Raphael, T. E. (2001). Teaching literature and literacy in the eye of reform: A dilemma in three acts. *New Advocate, 14*(3), 197–210.

Florio-Ruane, S., & Raphael, T. E. (2004). Reconsidering our research: Collaboration, complexity, design, and the problem of "Scaling up what works." In J. Worthy, S. J. McCarthey, National Reading Conference, et al. (Eds.), *53rd yearbook of the National Reading Conference* (pp. 170–188). Oak Creek, WI: National Reading Conference.

Gallucci, C. (2008). Districtwide instructional reform: Using sociocultural theory to link professional learning to organizational support. *American Journal of Education, 114*(4), 541–581.

Garet, M. S., Porter, A. C., Desimone, L., Birman, B. F., & Yoon, K. S. (2001). What makes professional development effective?: Results from a national sample of teachers. *American Educational Research Journal, 38*(4), 915–945.

Gavelek, J. R., & Raphael, T. E. (1996). Changing talk about text: New roles for teachers and students. *Language Arts, 73*(3), 182–192.

Goatley, V., Highfield, K., Bentley, J., Pardo, L. S., Folkert, J., Scherer, P., et al. (1994). Empowering teachers to be researchers: A collaborative approach. *Teacher Research: Journal of Classroom Inquiry, 1*(2), 128–144.

Goldman, S. R., Lee, C. D., Britt, A., Greenleaf, C., & Brown, M. (2009). *Reading for understanding across grades 6–12: Evidence-based argumentation for disciplinary learning* (USDE Grant No. R305F100007). Washington, DC: U.S. Department of Education, Institute for Educational Sciences.

Harré, R. (1983). *Personal being: A theory for individual psychology*. Oxford, UK: Blackwell.

Horn, I. S., & Little, J. W. (2010). Attending to problems of practice: Routines and resources for professional learning in teachers' workplace interactions. *American Educational Research Journal, 47*(1), 181 –217.

Hubbard, L., Mehan, H., & Stein, M. K. (2006). *Reform as learning: School reform, organizational culture, and community politics in San Diego*. New York: Taylor & Francis.

Hurry, J., & Sylva, X. (2007). Long-term outcomes of early reading intervention. *Journal of Research in Reading, 30*(2), 227–248.

Johnston-Parsons, M. (2012). *Dialogue and difference in a teacher education program: A 16-year sociocultural study of a professional development school*. Charlotte, NC: Information Age Publishing.

Kelleher, J. (2003). A model for assessment-driven professional development. *Phi Delta Kappan, 84*(10), 751.

Kerr, K. A., Marsh, J. A., Ikemoto, G. S., Darilek, H., & Barney, H. (2006). Strategies to promote data use for instructional improvement: Actions, outcomes, and lessons from three urban districts. *American Journal of Education, 112*(4), 496–520.

Kruse, S. D., & Louis, K. S. (1997). Teacher teaming in middle schools: Dilemmas for a schoolwide community. *Educational Administration Quarterly, 33*(3), 261–289.

Lai, M. K., McNaughton, S., Amituanai-Toloa, M., Turner, R., & Hsiao, S. (2009). Sustained acceleration of achievement in reading comprehension: The New Zealand experience. *Reading Research Quarterly, 44*(1), 30–56.

Lasky, S. (2005). A sociocultural approach to understanding teacher identity, agency and professional vulnerability in a context of secondary school reform. *Teaching and Teacher Education, 21*(8), 899–916.

Lave, J., & Wenger, E. (1991). *Situated learning: Legitimate peripheral participation.* New York: Cambridge University Press.

Long, R. (2011). Professional development and education policy: Understanding the current disconnect. *Reading Today, 29*(3), 29–30.

Louis, K. S., Marks, H. M., & Kruse, S. (1996). Teachers' professional community in restructuring schools. *American Educational Research Journal, 33*(4), 757–798.

McLaughlin, M. W., & Mitra, D. (2001). Theory-based change and change-based theory: Going deeper, going broader. *Journal of Educational Change, 2*(4), 301–323.

McLaughlin, M. W., & Talbert, J. E. (2006). *Building school-based teacher learning communities: Professional strategies to improve student achievement.* New York: Teachers College Press.

McNaughton, S. (2002). *Meeting of minds.* Wellington, New Zealand: Learning Media.

McVee, M. B., Dunsmore, K., & Gavelek, J. R. (2005). Schema theory revisited. *Review of Educational Research, 75*(4), 531–566.

Meier, D., & Wood, G. H. (2004). *Many children left behind: How the No Child Left Behind Act is damaging our children and our schools.* Boston: Beacon Press.

Nelson, T., Slavit, D., Perkins, M., & Hathorn, T. (2008). A culture of collaborative inquiry: Learning to develop and support professional learning communities. *Teachers College Record, 110*(6), 1269.

Newmann, F. M., Smith, B., Allensworth, E., & Bryk, A. S. (2001). Instructional program coherence: What it is and why it should guide school improvement policy. *Educational Evaluation and Policy Analysis, 23*(4), 297–321.

Pearson, P. D. (1985). Changing the face of reading comprehension instruction. *Reading Teacher, 38*(8), 724–738.

Raphael, T. E. (2010). Defying gravity: Literacy reform in urban schools. *Literacy Research Association Yearbook, 59,* 22–42.

Raphael, T. E., Au, K. H., & Goldman, S. (2009). Whole-school instructional improvement through the standards-based change process: A developmental model. In J. V. Hoffman & Y. M. Goodman (Eds.), *Changing literacies for changing times: An historical perspective on the future of reading research, public policy, and classroom practices* (pp. 198–229). New York: Routledge/Taylor & Francis.

Raphael, T. E., Au, K. H., & Popp, J. S. (2013). Transformative practices for literacy teaching and learning: A complicated agenda for literacy researchers. In S. Szabo, L. Martin, T. Morrison, L. Haas, & L. Garza-Garcia (Eds.), *Yearbook of the Association of Literacy Educators and Researchers, 35,* 9–32.

Raphael, T. E., Gavelek, J. R., Hynd, C. R., Teale, W. H., & Shanahan, T. (2002). Christmas trees are great, but not as models for instructional coherence. *Illinois Reading Council Journal, 30*(2), 5–7.

Reinking, D., & Bradley, B. A. (2008). *On formative and design experiments: Approaches to language and literacy research.* New York: Teachers College Press.

Robbins, P., & Aydede, M. (2009). *The Cambridge handbook of situated cognition.* Cambridge, UK: Cambridge University Press.

Routman, R. (2012). *Literacy and learning lessons from a longtime teacher.* Newark, DE: International Reading Association.

Rowan, B., Camburn, E., & Barnes, C. (2004). Benefiting from comprehensive school reform: A review of research on CSR implementation. In C. T. Cross (Ed.), *Putting the pieces together: Lessons from comprehensive school reform research* (pp. 1–52). Washington, DC: National Clearinghouse for Comprehensive School Reform.

Schatzki, T. R., Cetina, K. K., & von Savigny, E. (2001). *The practice turn in contemporary theory.* London: Routledge.

Schoenbach, R., Braunger, J., Greenleaf, C., & Litman, C. (2004). Apprenticing adolescents to reading in subject-area classrooms. *Phi Delta Kappan, 85*(2), 133–138.

Scribner, J. P., Sawyer, R. K., Watson, S. T., & Myers, V. L. (2007). Teacher teams and distributed leadership: A study of group discourse and collaboration. *Educational Administration Quarterly, 43*(1), 67–100.

Seymour, J. R., & Osana, H. P. (2003). Reciprocal teaching procedures and principles: Two teachers' developing understanding. *Teaching and Teacher Education, 19*(3), 325–344.

Shanahan, T., & Barr, R. (1995). Reading Recovery: An independent evaluation of the effects of an early instructional intervention for at-risk learners. *Reading Research Quarterly, 30*(4), 958–996.

Slavin, R. E., & Madden, N. A. (2001). *Success for all: Research and reform in elementary education.* New York: Routledge.

Smith, J. B., Smith, B., & Bryk, A. S. (1998). *Setting the pace: Opportunities to learn in Chicago public elementary schools.* Chicago: University of Chicago, Consortium on Chicago School Research. Retrieved from *https://ccsr.uchicago.edu/publications/setting-pace-opportunities-learn-chicago-public-elementary-schools.*

Stiggins, R. (2007). Assessment through the student's eyes. *Educational Leadership, 64*(8), 22.

Stoll, L., Bolam, R., McMahon, A., Wallace, M., & Thomas, S. (2006). Professional learning communities: A review of the literature. *Journal of Educational Change, 7*(4), 221–258.

Talbert, J. E. (2009). Professional learning communities at the crossroads: How systems hinder or engender change. In A. Hargreaves, A. Lieberman, M. Fullan, & D. Hopkins (Eds.), *Second international handbook of educational change* (pp. 555–571). Dordrecht, The Netherlands: Springer.

Taylor, B. M., Pearson, P. D., Peterson, D. S., & Rodriguez, M. C. (2005). The CIERA School Change Framework: An evidence-based approach to professional development and school reading improvement. *Reading Research Quarterly, 40*(1), 40–69.

Taylor, B. M., Raphael, T. E., & Au, K. H. (2011). School reform in literacy. In M. L. Kamil, P. D. Pearson, E. B. Moje, & P. P. Afflerbach (Eds.), *Handbook of reading research* (Vol. 4, pp. 594–628). New York: Routledge/Taylor & Francis.

Timperley, H. S., & Parr, J. M. (2007). Closing the achievement gap through evidence-based inquiry at multiple levels of the education system. *Journal of Advanced Academics, 19*(1), 90–115.

Valli, L., & Buese, D. (2007). The changing roles of teachers in an era of high-stakes accountability. *American Educational Research Journal, 44*(3), 519–558.

Venezky, R. (1998). An alternative perspective on Success for All. In K. K. Wong (Ed.), *Long-term outcomes of early reading intervention* (Vol. 4, pp. 145–165). Stamford, CT: JAI Press.

Voloshinov, V. N. (1973). *Marxism and the philosophy of language* (L. Matejka & I. R. Titunik, Trans.). New York: Seminar Press.

Vygotsky, L. S. (1978). *Mind in society: The development of higher psychological processes* (V. John-Steiner, M. Cole, S. Scribner, & E. Souberman, Trans.). Cambridge, MA: Harvard University Press.

Weber, C. M., & Raphael, T. E. (2013). Constructing a collective identity: Professional development for twenty-first-century pedagogy. In K. Hall, T. Cremin, B. Comber, & L. C.

Moll (Eds.), *International handbook of research on children's literacy, learning, and culture* (pp. 469–484). New York: Wiley.

Webster-Wright, A. (2009). Reframing professional development through understanding authentic professional learning. *Review of Educational Research, 79*(2), 702–739.

Wertsch, J. V., & Toma, C. (1995). Discourse and learning in the classroom: A sociocultural approach. In L. P. Steffe & J. Gale (Eds.), *Constructivism in education* (pp. 159–174). Hillsdale, NJ: Erlbaum.

Wood, D. R. (2007a). Teachers' learning communities: Catalyst for change or a new infrastructure for the status quo? *Teachers College Record, 109*(3), 699–739.

Wood, D. R. (2007b). Professional learning communities: Teachers, knowledge, and knowing. *Theory into Practice, 46*(4), 281–290.

CHAPTER 9

Professional Development in Early Childhood Education
Models and Recommendations

MARYANN MRAZ
BRIAN KISSEL

- Research has established a clear link between teachers' professional development and children's learning progress.
- Teachers should be active participants in setting the agenda for professional development initiatives in which they participate.
- There are general strategies that school personnel can apply to foster effective professional development within their setting.
- Effective professional development can take many forms, such as (1) literacy coaching, (2) in-class mentoring, (3) professional learning communities, and (4) Web-based coaching.
- Professional learning communities are centered on the belief that knowledge must be collectively shared through ongoing interactions among all members of the community.

As curriculum standards and assessment mandates have changed in recent years, often moving to early childhood programs those expectations that used to be common in early elementary programs, those engaged in early childhood education are asked to support professional development that is responsive to new expectations and needs. Early childhood educators must, as Neuman and Cunningham (2008) explain, "bring a substantial knowledge base, reflecting an understanding of child development, and the knowledge, skills, and dispositions necessary to shape appropriate learning experiences that are engaging to young children" (p. 533). Teachers, literacy coaches, and administrators are more frequently asked to implement professional development practices designed to improve instruction and establish collaborative learning communities among early childhood educators.

The link between effective professional development and children's learning progress is clear: When schools support teachers' growth and their ability to make informed instructional decisions, increased opportunities arise for children to improve their learning (Knight, 2009; Neuman, 2010; Zaslow & Martinez-Beck, 2006). Research has shown that, in early childhood settings, the types of professional development and the qualifications of those delivering it make a difference in improving the quality of educational experiences for children (Neuman, 2010; Neuman & Dickinson, 2011; Zaslow, Tout, Halle, & Starr, 2011). Findings also suggest that effective professional development models have a positive effect on teachers' language and literacy instruction and on children's vocabulary growth (Wasik, 2010). This chapter discusses the link between professional development and teachers' effectiveness; describes the characteristics of effective professional development; offers general strategies for professional development; describes a specific professional development initiative for early literacy coaches; and discusses how in-class mentoring, professional learning communities, and digital or Web-based coaching can be used to support professional development for early childhood educators.

PROFESSIONAL DEVELOPMENT AND TEACHER EFFECTIVENESS

Professional development research suggests several characteristics common to effective professional development initiatives. These characteristics include consensus among the group participants on goals; continuous support from administrators; opportunities for participants to engage in active learning; activities that are integrated into the daily routine of the curriculum; sustained collaboration with opportunities for follow-up; and collegiality between teachers, coaches, and administrators on the professional development team (Bellanca, 2009; Darling-Hammond, Wei, Andree, Richardson, & Orphanos, 2009; Duncan, 2010; Mraz, Vintinner, & Vacca, in press).

Too often, traditional professional development programs require only passive involvement on the part of teachers. Teachers, for example, may listen to a presenter explain a concept or demonstrate a new strategy. Following such an inservice session, more often than not, teachers return to their classroom routines, applying little if any of the new information to their own instructional practice (Kissel, Mraz, Algozzine, & Stover, 2011). Professional development that supports effective teaching must be infused throughout teachers' professional lives as they develop and refine their capabilities as thoughtful, responsive practitioners (Renyi, 1998).

The U.S. Department of Education (2010) and the National Council on Teacher Quality (2011) acknowledge that an effective teacher is a key factor in student success. Effective teachers help narrow achievement gaps and create environments in which children approach learning with purpose and enthusiasm (Vacca, Vacca, &

Mraz, 2014). Whereas policy organizations define teacher effectiveness in terms of student achievement, researchers offer broader descriptions. Pearson and Hoffman (2011) describe effective teachers as thoughtful, effective, pragmatic, and reflective. Darling-Hammond (2009) describes traits and characteristics exemplified in the instructional practices of effective teachers. Those traits include a strong verbal ability, the ability to identify individual student needs and differentiate instruction based on those needs, strong knowledge of content, and knowledge of how to develop higher-order thinking skills.

A number of strategies can be useful in supporting teachers' professional development (Hall, 2005; Hirsh, 2005; Mraz et al., in press; Richardson, 2003):

- Time to visit one another's classrooms so that they can observe different methods in action and collaborate on solutions to instructional challenges.
- Mentoring programs for new teachers or for teachers new to early childhood instruction.
- Book clubs, either face-to-face or electronic, that provide a forum through which teachers can discuss a professional literature selection.
- Web-based forums that allow teachers to share resources, instructional strategies, information about professional conferences, and policy updates.

Whatever the strategy used, effective professional development needs to be both systematic and participatory. It needs to be guided by input from teachers, literacy coaches, and administrators so that it can be tailored to meet the needs of a particular school or early childhood center. Professional development should be based on the principles of adult education. As Girolametto, Weitzman, and Greenberg (2012) explain, "Adults are motivated to acquire new skills when instructional activities are clearly tied to their needs and reflect content they require in the practice setting" (p. 49). Often, it is helpful to begin professional development plans with a survey or needs assessment that gives the participants an opportunity for input. Next, by analyzing the feedback from the survey or needs assessment, professional development providers will be better able to identify interests, needs, and patterns in feedback, as well as resources that can support professional development plans. Finally, the implementation of professional development should be thoughtfully planned and should include appropriate follow-up that encourages participants to ask questions about implementation, to celebrate successes, and to brainstorm solutions to challenges (Mraz et al., in press). The next section describes several forms of effective professional development.

COACHING TEACHERS IN LITERACY STRATEGIES

Having specialists in schools providing guidance for classroom teachers and addressing children's literacy needs has been widely accepted for many years. The roles these educators fulfill have changed over the years. Traditionally, the role of the reading specialist as a teacher for students identified as at risk for school failure emerged under the Elementary and Secondary Education Act (ESEA) of 1965. Under Title I of the early ESEA legislation, reading specialists worked with struggling readers in "pullout" programs to supplement their general classroom instruction. The limited success of this model (Allington & Walmsley, 1995) led to ongoing concerns about reading proficiency levels. These concerns led educators and policymakers to seek ways to improve students' reading development and achievement. Recent policy initiatives, such as No Child Left Behind and Race to the Top, have prompted educators to shift the role of the reading specialist from teaching students to coaching teachers.

The literacy coaching initiative is designed to improve reading instruction by providing ongoing, consistent, and relevant professional development to teachers (Bean, 2004). The literacy coach has become a more common and integral part of a school's literacy team. According to Toll (2004), a coach helps teachers build on their strengths and supports them as they work to improve their teaching practice. The International Reading Association (IRA; 2010) has outlined standards for the role of the literacy coach across six areas: foundational knowledge, curriculum and instruction, assessment and evaluation, diversity, professional learning, and leadership.

Literacy coaches can support professional development and improved instructional practice in a variety of ways: They can help teachers plan for instruction, support teachers in developing manageable routines and organizing instructional materials, and offer suggestions for creating an engaging learning environment for children. Embedded professional development that is linked to a literacy coaching model has been found to be effective in improving developmental and learning outcomes (Algozzine et al., 2011; Neuman & Cunningham, 2008).

Professional development models, such as Exceptional Coaching for Early Language and Literacy (ExCELL), provide coaching interventions to early childhood teachers. Through this model, teachers receive intensive, ongoing staff development in the areas of interactive book reading, guiding conversations across the curriculum, phonological awareness, alphabet knowledge, and writing. They also receive individual support as they work to integrate these components into engaging instruction for children. Teachers' instructional practices through the use of this model were found to have positive impacts on children's vocabulary development (Wasik, 2010).

Research suggests that coaches can promote changes in classroom practice when they have a thorough understanding of adult learners, a mastery of successful coaching techniques, knowledge of effective literacy instructional practices, and clear roles and responsibilities (IRA, 2004; Toll, 2005). Teachers who work with coaches have improved their teaching practices by incorporating more high-level thinking questions, encouraging children's active engagement in learning, and increasing their ability to adapt and differentiate instructional materials and skills (Bean et al., 2008).

Even with broad guidance from major professional organizations, researchers have found some variation in the roles these literacy professionals are expected to fulfill. Some literacy coaches focus specifically on supporting classroom teachers in their daily implementation of the school's literacy program. Others support teachers by providing formal and informal professional development sessions. Still others report that administrative tasks and paperwork consume much of their time (Bean, Draper, Hall, Vandermolen, & Zigmond, 2010; Deussen, Coskie, Robinson, & Autio, 2007; Dole & Donaldson, 2006.) Additionally, role expectations of the coach have been found to vary among administrators, teachers, and coaches (Knight, 2009; Mraz, Algozzine, & Watson, 2008).

PROFESSIONAL DEVELOPMENT
FOR EARLY LITERACY COACHES

As literacy coaching evolves, it is important for teachers and administrators in early childhood programs to recognize that there is a need for professional development that will bring clarity and consistency to the coaching role while helping coaches to respond effectively to the needs of the teachers and children with whom they work. Professional development that is ongoing, supportive, and responsive to the needs of coaches, teachers, and administrators can serve to enhance educational experiences for children. Professional development is particularly important in schools and districts that are transitioning from a reading specialist model to a literacy coaching model.

As programs to support the work of literacy coaches are established, it is important to consider the roles of the literacy coach that have potential to affect instruction. Mraz, Algozzine, and Kissel (2009) suggest four broad coaching roles:

- The coach as content expert.
- The coach as a promoter of reflective instruction.
- The coach as a professional development facilitator.
- The coach as a builder of a schoolwide learning community.

In designing professional development initiatives, it is important to ensure that coaches have opportunities to grow as both content experts and as coaches. As content experts, coaches can expand their knowledge of early childhood education and early literacy development by participating in book study groups, exploring research-based and practitioner-oriented articles, and using that acquired knowledge to inform inservice programs for teachers. In developing their skills as literacy coaches, professional development for coaches can focus on topics such as establishing professional learning communities, building trust and rapport with teachers, conferring with teachers, and promoting self-reflection among members of the school learning community.

One example of an effective, ongoing professional development initiative for early literacy coaches involved collaboration between administrators, coaches, teachers, and university colleagues. Monthly meetings with all members of the initiative included formal presentations on early literacy content, informal question-and-answer sessions, collaboration on solutions to challenges faced by literacy coaches in their daily work, and recognition of points of achievement.

During a 4-year collaboration, the professional development program transitioned along a continuum of growth. At the beginning, university colleagues provided information to early childhood coaches regarding early literacy content and coaching techniques. As the program evolved, coaches played a more active role in setting the agenda for each meeting based on their needs, as well as on the needs of the teachers and children with whom they worked. Still further along in the program, coaches worked with one another to implement professional development plans appropriate for their individual schools. At the end of the program, coaches, administrators, and teachers moved closer to making collaborative professional development decisions. The extent to which early childhood educators who participated in the professional development activities increased and maintained language-rich instruction and environments was also encouraging: Data suggest that participating teachers made consistent efforts to improve and sustain the quality of their instruction in early childhood classrooms (Algozzine et al., 2011).

IN-CLASS MENTORING

As noted by Hindman and Wasik (2012), "We cannot assume that providing teachers with a curriculum and brief training will produce best practices in the classroom and rapid learning among children" (p. 132). Effective professional development depends on the quality of the professional development, the frequency of it, and how it contextually applies to the teacher participating within it. The literature suggests that in-classroom support can make a profound impact on the quality of teaching that takes place in early childhood settings.

Teachers' effectiveness may be bolstered by the amount of time they are supported by professional development within their own classroom environments. In-class mentoring is a method by which teachers can receive professional development support to enhance their knowledge and deepen their understanding of pedagogy (Domitrovich et al, 2009; Wasik, Bond, & Hindman, 2006). In-class mentoring involves weekly visits by mentors (local educational consultants, literacy coaches, or master teachers) who come into classrooms and implement a series of recursive loops to support teachers. The recursive loop is composed of the following: The mentor teacher provides modeling of effective instruction, followed by a debriefing session. Next, the teacher instructs and the mentor observes, followed by a debriefing session. The feedback that is shared between the mentor and teacher becomes part of the teacher's plan for instruction. The conversations become supportive, ongoing professional development sessions for the teacher.

Teachers who receive in-class mentoring enrich their professional development in a new setting: their own classrooms. This becomes an efficacious model when teachers are able to see teaching possibilities within the context of their own classrooms and among their own students. It becomes particularly important when the mentor working with teachers within their classrooms assumes the role of supporter and cheerleader, rather than evaluator.

Wasik and colleagues (2006) sought to determine whether in-class mentoring could influence how teachers talk to children, including asking questions that would elicit more than one-word responses, building vocabulary, and making connections. They conducted this study within 10 Head Start classrooms with a total of 16 teachers. In their study, teachers received 2-hour monthly workshops in specific book-reading and conversation strategies, followed by in-class mentoring to support what was learned during the workshop. In-class mentoring included observations in which the teacher received both written and verbal feedback regarding the demonstration of the strategy. The researchers found that this model of professional development had positive effects on children's language and literacy development. Teachers had ongoing opportunities to practice the strategies taught during the workshops and follow-up support through in-class mentoring. After this intervention, 70% of teachers significantly changed the way they talked to students, including increasing their use of open-ended questions to engage students in book talks and providing students with more opportunities to engage in conversations. Workshops, combined with in-class mentoring, made a real impact on the teachers and their students in the Head Start classrooms.

Besides literacy, in-class mentoring has shown promise in other areas of the preschool curriculum as well. Raver and colleagues (2008) conducted a study in 18 Head Start sites, including 35 classrooms with 94 teachers and 602 children. Rather than examining vocabulary outcomes, Raver and colleagues sought to understand how teachers could improve their behavior management practices by creating more emotionally supportive classroom practices. Teachers in the treatment group participated in five 6-hour trainings over the fall and winter of 1 year. Then, to support what they learned in these series of trainings, each teacher was matched with a professional who had a master's degree in social work who met weekly with teachers within their classroom environments to support them with different aspects of classroom management. The researchers found that teachers changed the ways they managed their classrooms based on the support they received through training and in-class mentoring and that their changes improved the climate of their classrooms.

In a randomized study of Head Start classrooms, in which in-class mentoring was employed as a professional development stance, researchers found improvements in multiple domains of teaching quality (Domitrovich et al., 2009). The researchers studied 84 teachers within 44 Head Start classrooms as the teachers implemented a REDI (research-based developmentally informed) intervention for the first time. During this intervention, the teachers experienced a 3-day workshop in which they learned the theoretical, developmental, and implementation model underlying REDI, the importance of language and literacy instruction within a preschool setting, and the role that social-emotional instructional designs play in the development of young children. This workshop was followed by weekly (3 hours a week) mentoring sessions by experienced master teachers who provided modeling, coaching, and ongoing feedback. The researchers found that this form of professional development produced improvements in multiple domains of teacher quality. When compared with the control classrooms, teachers in the intervention were able to provide better, more effective emotional, behavioral, and linguistic support for their students. The researchers attribute this to the ongoing support teachers received through in-class mentoring.

Professional development in teacher education has long been delivered using a 1-day workshop model; that is, teachers attended a day-long conference session at which they learned about new instructional approaches but had no follow-up sessions to support their newly acquired understandings of pedagogy (Mraz et al., 2009). Professional development in teacher education has moved from a 1-day workshop model to a model that includes both workshops and in-class mentoring. This combination allows the teacher to learn new models of instruction through seminars and direct application of that instruction in their classrooms with support from in-class mentors. As seen in the studies described earlier, the ongoing, in-class support for teachers led to significant improvements in vocabulary development, behavior management, and emotional support for their students.

PROFESSIONAL LEARNING COMMUNITIES

For the early childhood teacher, the classroom can be an isolating environment. Much of what happens in the classroom happens between the teacher and the students, with little opportunity for social or professional interaction with other adults. It is for this reason that professional learning communities, or PLCs, have gained in popularity in recent years as a viable professional development experience. In a PLC, teachers work collaboratively to build capacity to promote student learning.

PLCs are defined as "ongoing groups...who meet regularly for the purposes of increasing their own learning and that of their students" (Lieberman & Miller, 2008, p. 2). In this professional development model, teachers gather together to learn from one another. The concept is based on the belief that knowledge is not contained by the few; rather, is it shared by the collective. When this knowledge is shared by a community of educators, it "fosters collaboration, honest talk, and a commitment to the growth and development of individual members and to the group as a whole" (Lieberman & Miller, 2011, p. 16). The idea of *community* encompasses five major features, according to Westheimer (1999): (1) shared beliefs and understandings; (2) interaction and participation; (3) interdependence; (4) concern for individual and minority views; and (5) meaningful relationships. Successful learning communities, according to Galinsky (2012), have 10 more features that bear noting:

1. They have the power to bring new players together.
2. They do not shy away from reaching those most in need.
3. They focus on learning from and with each other—there is expertise among everyone.
4. They focus on active learning.

5. They use new media in creative ways.
6. They actively create new curricula based on child and adult development.
7. They focus on assessment tied to child development.
8. They reframe teaching as teaching and learning.
9. They connect policy to practice.
10. They have strategies to "pay it forward." That is, they carry their knowledge onward so other teachers can benefit from what they've learned.

When these features converge in schools, teachers are able to seek and provide supportive relationships that help bolster their professional knowledge while affecting student outcomes. Because of this, the use of PLCs in early childhood settings is showing promise as an effective mode of professional development.

In their qualitative study, Hipp, Huffman, Pankake, and Olivier (2008) followed two schools (PreK–8 and 6–8) in their journeys toward developing learning communities. In the elementary school, the researchers conducted numerous individual and group interviews within a 2-day site visit. They found that the teachers within the PLC functioned as a team, that their professional development focused on teachers working together to solve problems around critical issues, that leadership was shared and inclusive, and that the staff was united around a singular purpose—"an undeviating focus on student learning" (p. 179). As a result, there was little teacher turnover at the school, responsibility for student learning was shared among all constituents, and leadership broadened to include both teachers and administrators. The positive climate of the school showed that teachers felt respected and honored. It is in such environments that teachers thrive because they feel empowered, their knowledge is sought, and their professional growth is honed through meaningful conversations with peers.

In their collaborative work with early childhood teachers, Ladson-Billings and Gomez (2001) created a PLC in which they, university professors, partnered with teachers to understand the emergent literacy abilities of children who are noted as being at risk for school failure. They conducted monthly seminars with teachers in which the group engaged in a series of conversations centering on critical questions about student outcomes—many of which focused on the failure to achieve growth in students who were poor and minority. Their strategy was "to allow teachers to talk frankly about their students and to encourage them to think about what capabilities they might have" (p. 677). After 18 months of sustained learning community meetings and conversations, teachers began to see changes in student achievement. All students, including those from poor and minority backgrounds, met the target scores on standardized testing. By observing students, noting statistical trends, and engaging in conversations with one another, teachers were able to see the gaps that existed, address those gaps by altering instruction, and meet the needs of all students within their classrooms. Conversations, facilitated through focused learning communities, helped students thrive.

Maloney and Konza (2011), also university professors who sought to build partnerships with schools through PLCs, noted, "the development of professional learning communities relies on teachers having the desire to participate in practitioner research in order to extend their knowledge and skills, and to improve their practice" (p. 76). They examined teachers in one primary school as they engaged in a university-led PLC. Using a case study approach, the researchers studied 12 teachers and 8 educational assistants who took part in a professional learning project in which teachers would develop a whole-school approach to early childhood education, create a shared vision, and negotiate a shared understanding of effective early childhood education. Maloney and Konza found that there were obstacles to the teachers' willingness to engage in the PLC, to commit to thorough reflection, and to confront their differences in philosophical perspectives. There was some resistance from teachers whose philosophies did not always gel with those of their colleagues and who resented the time that engaging in a PLC took from other aspects of teaching. The researchers learned that the nature of the PLC is not always a calm, steady ride; rather, there are several instances of turbulence within the ebb and flow of coming together to create a shared vision within a school.

The research on the effects of PLCs in early childhood settings is still limited. However, there is an emergence of research suggesting that such communities are having an impact on student achievement. Teachers who work in environments in which they experience positive professional communities also have higher student achievement on standardized testing (Louis & Marks, 1998). When they gather for conversations, the teachers within the PLC bring forward their observations of students, collected data and analysis, and reflections on what is happening among learners in the classroom. Because so much of the conversation is driven by the data from their anecdotal records, teachers develop into mature researchers engaged in authentic conversations about the students within their classrooms (McLaughlin & Talbert, 2001).

DIGITAL AND WEB-BASED COACHING

Much of professional development in the past century has required face-to-face interactions: teachers gathering at conference centers, coaches coming into classrooms, and groups meeting in schools for their PLCs. The 21st century and advancements in technology have ushered in a whole new space in which professional development can occur.

The concept of Web coaching is not new in fields outside of education. Psychologists have used Web coaching (or live coaching) to train patients in parenting skills when time, distance, and the unavailability of skilled providers often cause roadblocks to seeking treatment (Wade, Oberjohn, Conaway, Osinska, & Bangert, 2011). Medical doctors use Web-based coaching to allow patients to communicate with nurses to get feedback, support, and recommendations for lifestyle and medical treatments (Goessens et al., 2008). It is not surprising, then, that many schools are finding ways to merge together coaching and the Internet to synchronize professional development with the 21st-century teacher.

One type of Web-based coaching is MyTeachingPartner (MTP), a system of professional development that includes video exemplars and Web-mediated consultations on specific dimensions of interactions with children for various PreK programs (Pianta, Mashburn, Downer, Hamre, & Justice, 2008). Targeting a population that serves children deemed "at risk" for school failure, the researchers studied teachers who received access to Web-based MTP lesson plans and other Web-based curricula. The teachers videotaped their implementation of an instructional activity and mailed the tape to their consultants. The consultants then edited the tapes, provided feedback, and asked participants specific probing questions, to which the teachers responded via the Web. Then the teachers and consultants met online in a video chat to discuss the feedback. This process of record, respond, ask, and share was a cyclical process that took place every 2 weeks for an entire year. The researchers found that the teachers who participated in the online coaching component of the intervention had more positive growth in each of the seven dimensions of teacher–child interactions than teachers who did not participate in the online coaching.

Powell, Diamond, and Koehler (2010) examined prekindergarten teachers' experiences using a hypermedia resource (HR) in a Web-based early literacy coaching intervention. In their study, they used Web usage logs, written records of coach feedback to teachers, and teacher questionnaires to describe how HRs were used to facilitate literacy coaching. The study examined teachers' views of the helpfulness of video exemplars. Teachers submitted videos of their teaching, and the coach reviewed the tapes and provided feedback using a split-screen arrangement in which the left side showed the teacher in action and the right side showed the coach's written feedback. The researchers found that teachers and coaches used the HR as it was intended—as a resource library of video exemplars they could use to learn more about how to best teach literacy and language to their students.

Although only a limited number of studies have examined Web-based coaching, it is easy to envision a time in our near future when popular e-tools such as Skype and Facetime will allow coaches to make virtual visits to early childhood classrooms to see teaching in real time and offer supportive feedback to the teacher. This is already beginning to happen in student teaching, as university personnel are able to supervise and support students' clinical experience from a distance (Rock et al., 2012). Web 2.0 technology allows literacy coaches to expand the possibilities of coaching beyond face-to-face interactions to include the vast array of tools available on the Internet.

The preceding approaches to coaching encompass an amalgam of possibilities for schools seeking to enrich the knowledge of teachers. Perhaps one of the strongest models of professional development is differentiated coaching (Stover, Kissel, Haag, & Shoniker, 2011). In this model of professional development, coaches foster reflection and promote a culture of ongoing professional learning by differentiating their professional development to meet the specific, individual needs of teachers and school administrators. Differentiated coaching incorporates a triad of exercises teachers and coaches conduct to reflect on their instruction. These exercises include maintaining daybooks, completing surveys, and analyzing videotapes. Based on an analysis of all three (daybooks, surveys, and videotapes), the coach and teacher work to analyze these data sources and use their analysis to differentiate coaching to address specific needs of the teacher and the students within the teacher's class. When differentiated methods of professional development and coaching are used to enrich teacher learning, students become the beneficiaries.

CONCLUSION

When early childhood teachers are supported within the school community through effective professional development opportunities, they can strengthen their own professional knowledge, problem-solve to meet the needs of individual children, build community, and enhance instruction. Professional development strategies, including literacy coaching, in-class mentoring, PLCs, and Web-based coaching, can all contribute to improved teacher effectiveness and, in turn, improved educational experiences for young children.

Continued research is needed to investigate the effectiveness of specific professional development initiatives, particularly those that use contemporary strategies such as Web-based coaching and PLCs, and to explore how these strategies can be refined and adapted to support the needs of teachers in early childhood communities. Early childhood educators need to be active participants in determining the direction of their own professional development so that they can better meet the diverse learning needs of the children they serve. Future research is needed to explore the degree to which this happens and how the participation of early childhood educators in professional development initiatives might be improved. Young children need intentional, appropriate instruction in order to establish a foundation on which future learning can be built. Effective professional development for early childhood educators supports this important goal.

QUESTIONS FOR DISCUSSION

1. This chapter supports the concept that professional development needs to be sustained and to reflect input from teachers in order to be successful. What initiatives could be instituted at your school or in your early childhood center to provide continued support for teachers?

2. How would you explain to a policymaker the links between professional development, teacher effectiveness, and learning benefits for young children? Why should they be encouraged to support such initiatives?

3. What steps might an administrator take to develop a PLC among early childhood educators? Consider the types of questions he or she might ask in a survey of teachers to determine their perceived interests and needs.

4. What is Web-based coaching? What are the benefits of Web-based coaching, compared with traditional face-to-face coaching models? What are some of the different ways in which Web-based coaching can be implemented?

REFERENCES

Algozzine, B., Babb, J, Algozzine, K., Mraz, M., Kissel, B., Spano, S., et al. (2011). Classroom effects of an early childhood educator professional development partnership. *NHSA Dialog: A Research-to-Practice Journal for the Early Childhood Field, 14*(4), 246–262.

Allington, R. I., & Walmsley, S. A. (1995). *No quick fix: Rethinking literacy programs in America's elementary schools.* New York: Teachers College Press.

Bean, R. M. (2004). Promoting effective literacy instruction: The challenge for literacy coaches. *California Reader, 37,* 58–63.

Bean, R. M., Belcastro, B., Hathaway, J., Risko, V., Rosemary, C., & Roskos, K. (2008, April). *A review of the research on instructional coaching.* Paper presented at the annual conference of the American Educational Research Association, New York.

Bean, R. M., Draper, J. A., Hall, V., Vandermolen, J., & Zigmond, N. (2010). Coaches and coaching in Reading First schools: A reality check. *Elementary School Journal, 111*(1), 87–114.

Bellanca, J. (2009). *Designing professional development for change* (2nd ed.). Thousand Oaks, CA: Corwin Press.

Darling-Hammond, L. (2009). Recognizing and enhancing teacher effectiveness. *International Journal of Education and Psychology Assessment, 3,* 1–24.

Darling-Hammond, L., Wei, R. C., Andree, A., Richardson, N., & Orphanos, S. (2009). *Professional learning in the learning profession: A status report on teacher development in the United States and abroad.* Washington, DC: National Staff Development Council.

Deussen, T., Coskie, T., Robinson, L., & Autio, E. (2007). *"Coach" can mean many things: Five categories of literacy coaches in Reading First* (Issues & Answers Report No. REL 2007-No. 005). Washington, DC: U. S. Department of Education, Institute of Education Sciences, National Center for Education Evaluation and Regional Assistance, Regional Educational Laboratory Northwest. Retrieved from *http://ies.ed.gov/ncee/edlabs/regions/northwesst/pdf/REL_2007005.pdf*

Dole, J. A., & Donaldson, R. (2006). "What am I supposed to do all day?": Three big ideas for the reading coach. *Reading Teacher, 59*(5), 486–488.

Domitrovich, C., Gest, S., Sukhdeep, G., Bierman, K., Welsh, J., & Jones, D. (2009). Fostering high-quality teaching with an enriched curriculum and professional development support: The Head Start REDI program. *American Educational Research Journal, 46*(2), 567–597.

Duncan, S. (2010). Intentional and embedded professional development: Four steps to success. *Exchange, 191,* 70–72.

Galinsky, E. (2012). Learning communities: An emerging phenomenon. *Young Children, 67*(1), 20–27.

Girolametto, L., Weltzman, E., & Greenberg, J. (2012). Facilitating emergent literacy: Efficacy of a model that partners speech–language pathologists and educators. *American Journal of Speech–Language Pathology, 21,* 47–63.

Goessens, B., Visseren, F., de Nooijer, J., van den Borne, H., Algra, A., Wierdsma, J., et al. (2008). A pilot study to identify the feasibility of an Internet-based coaching programme for changing the vascular risk profile of high-risk patients. *Patient Education and Counseling, 73*(1), 67–72.

Hall, P. (2005). A school reclaims itself. *Educational Leadership, 62*(5), 70–73.

Hindman, A., & Wasik, B. (2012). Unpacking an effective language and literacy coaching intervention in Head Start. *Elementary School Journal, 113*(1), 131–154.

Hipp, K., Huffman, J., Pankake, A., & Olivier, D. (2008). Sustaining professional learning communities: Case studies. *Journal of Educational Change, 9,* 173–195.

Hirsh, S. (2005). Professional development and closing the achievement gap. *Theory into Practice, 44,* 38–44.

International Reading Association. (2004). *The role and qualifications of the reading coach in the United States.* Newark, DE: Author.

International Reading Association. (2010). *Standards for reading professionals—revised 2010.* Newark, DE: Author.

Kissel, B., Mraz, M., Algozzine, R., & Stover, K. (2011). Early literacy coaches' role perceptions and recommendations for change. *Journal of Research in Childhood Education, 25,* 205–220.

Knight, J. (2009). Coaching. *Journal of Staff Development, 30*(1), 18–22.

Ladson-Billings, G., & Gomez, M. (2001). Just showing up: Supporting early literacy through teachers' professional communities. *Phi Delta Kappan, 82*(9), 675–680.

Lieberman, A., & Miller, L. (2008). *Teachers in professional communities: Improving teaching and learning.* New York: Teachers College Press.

Lieberman, A., & Miller, L. (2011). Learning communities: The starting point for professional learning is in schools and classrooms. *Journal of Staff Development, 32*(4), 16.

Louis, K., & Marks, H. (1998). Does professional community affect the classroom? Teachers' work and student experience in restructured schools. *American Journal of Education, 106*(4), 532–575.

Maloney, C., & Konza, D. (2011). A case study of teachers' professional learning: Becoming a community of professional learning or not? *Issues in Educational Research, 21*(1), 75–87.

McLaughlin, M., & Talbert, J. (2001). *Professional communities and the work of high school teaching.* Chicago: University of Chicago Press.

Mraz, M., Algozzine, B., & Kissel, B. (2009). *The literacy coach's companion: PreK–3.* Thousand Oaks, CA, and Newark, DE: Corwin Press and International Reading Association.

Mraz, M., Algozzine, B., & Watson, P. (2008). Perceptions and expectations of roles and responsibilities of literacy coaching. *Literacy Research and Instruction, 47*(3), 141–157.

Mraz, M., Vintinner, J., & Vacca, J. L. (in press). Professional development. In S. B. Wepner, D. S. Strickland, & D. Quatroche (Eds.). *The administration and supervision of reading programs* (5th ed.). New York: Teachers College Press.

National Council on Teacher Quality. (2011). Removing roadblocks: How federal policy can cultivate effective teachers. Retrieved from *www.nctq.org/p/publications/docs/nctq_eseaReauthorization.pdf.*

Neuman, S., & Cunningham, L. (2008). The impact of professional development and coaching on early language and literacy instruction. *American Educational Research Journal, 46,* 532–566.

Neuman, S. B. (Ed.). (2010). *Preparing teachers for the early childhood classroom: Proven models and key principles.* Baltimore: Brookes.

Neuman, S. B., & Dickinson, D. K. (Eds.). (2011). *Handbook of early literacy research* (Vol. 3). New York: Guilford Press.

Pearson, P. D., & Hoffman, J. V. (2011). Principles of practice for the teaching of reading. In T. V. Rasinski (Ed.), *Rebuilding the foundation: Effective reading instruction for 21st-century learning* (pp. 9–40). Bloomington, IN: Solution Tree Press.

Pianta, R., Mashburn, A., Downer, J., Hamre, B., & Justice, L. (2008). Effects of web-mediated professional development resources on teacher–child interactions in pre-kindergarten classrooms. *Early Childhood Research Quarterly, 23*(4), 431–451.

Powell, D., Diamond, K., & Koehler, M. (2010). Use of a case-based hypermedia resource in an early literacy coaching intervention with pre-kindergarten teachers. *Topics in Early Childhood Special Education, 29*(4), 239–249.

Raver, C., Jones, S., Li-Grining, C., Metzger, M., Champion, K., & Sardin, L. (2008). Improving preschool classroom processes: Preliminary findings from a randomized trail implemented in Head Start settings. *Early Childhood Research Quarterly, 23,* 10–26.

Renyi, J. (1998). Building learning into the teaching job. *Educational Leadership, 55*(5), 70–74.

Richardson, V. (2003). The dilemmas of professional development. *Phi Delta Kappan, 84,* 401–406.

Rock, M., Gregg, M., Gable, R., Zigmond, N., Blanks, B., Howard, P., et al. (2012). Time after time online: An extended study of virtual coaching during distant clinical practice. *Journal of Technology and Teacher Education, 20*(3), 277–304.

Stover, K., Kissel, B., Haag, K., & Shoniker, R. (2011). Differentiated coaching: Fostering reflection with teachers. *Reading Teacher, 64*(7), 498–509.

Toll, C. (2004). *The literacy coaches survival guide: Essential questions and practical answers.* Newark, DE: International Reading Association.

Toll, C. (2005). *The literacy coach's survival guide: Essential questions and practical answers.* Newark, DE: International Reading Association.

U.S. Department of Education Office of Planning, Evaluation and Policy Development. (2010). *ESEA Blueprint for Reform.* Washington, DC: Author.

Vacca, R. T., Vacca, J. L., & Mraz, M. (2014). *Content area reading: Literacy and learning across the curriculum* (11th ed.). Boston: Pearson.

Wade, S., Oberjohn, K., Conaway, K., Osinska, P., & Bangert, L. (2011). Live coaching of parenting skills using the Internet: Implications for clinical practice. *Professional Psychology: Research and Practice, 42*(6), 487–493.

Wasik, B. A. (2010). What teachers can do to promote preschooler's vocabulary development: Strategies from an effective language and literacy professional development coaching model. *Reading Teacher, 63*(8), 621–633. .

Wasik, B. A., Bond, M. A., & Hindman, A. (2006). The effects of a language and literacy intervention on Head Start children and teachers. *Journal of Educational Psychology, 98,* 63–74.

Westheimer, J. (1999). Communities and consequences: An inquiry into ideology and practice in teachers' professional work. *Educational Administration Quarterly, 35*(1), 71–105.

Zaslow, M., & Martinez-Beck, I. (Eds.). (2006). *Critical issues in early childhood professional development.* Baltimore: Brookes.

Zaslow, M., Tout, K., Halle, T., & Starr, R. (2011). Professional development for early childhood educators: Reviewing and revising conceptualizations. In S. B. Neuman & D. K. Dickinson (Eds.), *Handbook of early literacy research* (Vol. 3, pp. 425–434). New York: Guilford Press.

CHAPTER 10

The Design and Implementation of Effective Professional Development in Elementary and Early Childhood Settings

PRISCILLA L. GRIFFITH
JIENING RUAN
JENNIFER STEPP
SUSAN J. KIMMEL

- High-quality professional development can lead to increased teacher performance and improved student learning.
- Professional development needs to be job-embedded and related to the work of teachers in classrooms.
- Research has identified core features of high-quality professional development.
- Teachers need metacognitive understanding about their classroom work, including declarative, conditional, and procedural information.
- Actualizing design principles derived from research into practice in developing professional development programs is a complex task.
- Core features of effective professional development have been manifested in a delivery framework for professional development that includes the following components: research-based practices, standards-based content, reflection and metacognitive understanding, data-informed instruction, community of practice, and coaching and mentoring.
- Principals play a key role in establishing a community of practice and maintaining the sustainability of professional development.

Although educators are beginning to understand the difference that high-performing teachers can make in a classroom, this has not always been the case.

Beginning with the Coleman and colleagues report (1966) and through the mid-1990s, the belief was that schools contributed in minimal ways to student achievement, and teachers' contributions to student academic growth were considered secondary to the influence of parents. However, recent research points to a belief that teachers can be a powerful influence on student learning (Lasley, 2009). According to the National Commission on Teaching and America's Future (1996), "what teachers know and can do makes the crucial difference in what children learn" (p. 5). Fallon (cited in Payne & Wolfson, 2000) has stated that teacher quality is the most important variable in producing student achievement.

CHARACTERISTICS OF HIGH-QUALITY PROFESSIONAL DEVELOPMENT

Teacher professional development is seen as one way to increase teacher performance, leading to improved student outcomes and accelerated learning. For nearly two decades researchers (Darling-Hammond & McLaughlin, 1995; Guskey & Huberman, 1995; Hawley & Valli, 1999; Joyce & Showers, 2002) have discussed the need to reform professional development in education by moving away from brief workshops that do not affect practice to inservice that is context specific and related to classroom instruction.

However, our own experiences suggest that most professional development programs implemented in many school districts still follow the traditional one-shot, drive-through paradigm and that the quality of professional development varies significantly. "Better Teaching" (pseudonym) was a recent professional development event in one of the school districts in our state. This one-day conference was a collection of sessions on various topics presented by local teachers and university faculty members. Those attending the conference selected from a menu of presentations to earn their required professional development points. The attributes of this professional development included a "one-shot workshop model" with content that was fragmented and not directly related to the teachers' classroom contexts or curricula. The assumption was that teachers would be able to implement instructional changes introduced in the workshop into their classrooms with little or no support. This description of professional development, though no longer supported by research (Darling-Hammond & Richardson, 2009), is not uncommon. In fact, a recent report (Darling-Hammond, Wei, Richardson, & Orphanos, 2009) indicates that well-designed professional development is relatively rare and that few teachers in the United States have access to regular opportunities for intensive learning (p. 19). As one teacher told the authors, "I go to these workshops, and see something that I think would work with my students, but when I get back to my classroom, I really have no idea how to implement it." In sharp contrast to this scenario, current research suggests that teacher professional development should be job-embedded, ongoing, and directly related to the challenges teachers face in daily classroom instruction (Deussen, Coskie, Robinson, & Autio, 2007).

Core Features of Effective Professional Development

Desimone (2009) describes five core features of effective professional development. These core features include content focus, collective participation, active learning, duration, and coherence. *Content focus* refers to subject-matter content, as well as the understanding of how students learn that content. *Collective participation* of teachers, frequently from the same school, allows interaction and discourse around the content of the professional development. *Active learning* involves hands-on and minds-on activities that involve teachers in working with the content through vicarious and direct experiences. Vicarious experiences might include watching videos of expert teachers. Direct experiences incorporate discussion, classroom coaching, and reviewing student work embedded within and drawn from the classroom experience. Professional development that incorporates active learning is context specific and related to classroom instruction. *Duration* refers to time spent in professional development activities and includes both the way in which the span of time is structured and the number of hours of professional development. The concept of duration is in direct contrast to a one-shot workshop model with content that is fragmented and not directly related to teachers' classroom contexts or curricula. Although a critical amount of time is required for professional development to reach duration (at least 20 hours of contact time), according to Desimone the manner in which the time is allocated might vary. For example, professional development might be provided across a semester or in an intense summer institute with follow-up. *Coherence* refers to teachers' understandings that the content of the professional development is consistent with their own knowledge and beliefs and with school, district, and state reforms and policies.

Metacognition

Teaching is a cognitive process involving both awareness and judgment. Attention to teachers' metacognitive understandings is also important when designing effective professional development. Flavell (1976, 1979) provided an early definition of metacognitive knowledge as an individual's own knowledge about his or her cognitive processes and the products or outcomes of these cognitive processes. Garner (1994) described metacognitive knowledge as what we know about ourselves, the tasks we face, and the strategies we employ. Tasks and strategies are important understandings for teachers. Because not all strategies are appropriate for all situations, a teacher must develop knowledge of different conditions and tasks in which different strategies are used most appropriately (Pintrich, 2002, p. 221). That is, teachers must have a deep understanding of their subject areas, understand how students learn, and be able to use their knowledge to teach well (Hunt & Carroll, 2003.)

Paris, Lipson, and Wixson (1994) provide additional information in their discussion of the types of knowledge learners acquire as they change from novices to experts. According to Paris and colleagues, learners need to have declarative, procedural, and conditional knowledge. In terms of teacher professional development, teachers need declarative knowledge about instruction; that is, they need to know the task structure and task goals of the content—what they should teach. However, they also need information about how to accomplish their tasks, and they need to be strategic about when and why to deploy appropriate instructional strategies—the procedural and conditional knowledge of instruction.

An additional component of metacognitive knowledge is self-knowledge (Flavell, 1979; Pintrich, 2002), that is, knowledge of one's own strengths and weaknesses. One of the tenets of metacognitive theory as it applies to learning is the emphasis on helping learners become more knowledgeable about and responsible for their own cognition and thinking (Pintrich, 2002). The goal of effective professional development is the application of that tenet at both the teacher and the student levels.

Effective professional development needs to be designed to move teachers along a continuum from novice to expert in being able to integrate student assessment data into instructional planning. One of the characteristics of experts is that they know when they do not know something and have strategies for finding the appropriate information (Pintrich, 2002, p. 221). Self-knowledge also includes beliefs about ability to perform a task (efficacy). An additional goal of professional development should be increasing teachers' efficacy to make a difference in student achievement through the regular scrutiny of child assessment data and realization that students make progress in small, perhaps daily increments. Self-knowledge is linked to how students perform in the classroom. Teachers learn to create a discourse around metacognitive knowledge by asking students to assess how what they are learning is beneficial to them and by holding students accountable for their own progress. As part of the content component of professional development, teachers should grow in their ability to provide instruction that enables students to become aware of their own strengths and weaknesses and to make personal adjustments that will facilitate their learning.

FRAMEWORK FOR DELIVERING PROFESSIONAL DEVELOPMENT

The task in providing effective professional development is to design a program that is classroom-embedded and that combines characteristics of high-quality professional development with metacognitive theory. When one considers the application of these characteristics to a professional development project, the actual designing becomes complex. Bredeson and Johansson (2000) have stated:

> Developing lists of design principles is important, but identifying them is generally much easier than implementing them effectively. The hard work comes in putting the design principles into practice with real people in the dynamic and complex environments of schools. (p. 386)

Through our work with early childhood and elementary schoolteachers, we have developed a delivery framework for professional development that incorporates the characteristics of effective professional development discussed previously. The framework is presented in this section. We have assessed the impact of professional development designed with the components in this framework on teacher outcomes using concept maps, a teacher efficacy scale, and classroom observations. Concept maps developed as pre-, post-, and delayed posttest measures have indicated significant differences in teachers' knowledge from pre- to posttesting and maintenance of gains over the course of the professional development. The Teacher Sense of Efficacy for Literacy Instruction (TSELI) scale (Tschannen-Moran & Johnson, 2011), administered as a pre-, post-, and delayed posttest measure of teacher efficacy, has produced the same pattern of results. Classroom observations of teachers at the beginning and end of the school year have shown growth in the implementation of research-based instructional strategies presented in the professional development.

In the remainder of this chapter, we discuss how we have actualized these characteristics to provide effective professional development. We draw on examples from our various projects, including the one described in the vignette, "Successful Staff Development Transforms Writing Instruction in an Oklahoma School," which appears in the Appendix of this book, to illustrate how professional development was designed and implemented to give attention to these characteristics.

The outer circle of the delivery framework in Figure 10.1 contains Desimone's five core features of effective professional development. The inner circles depict

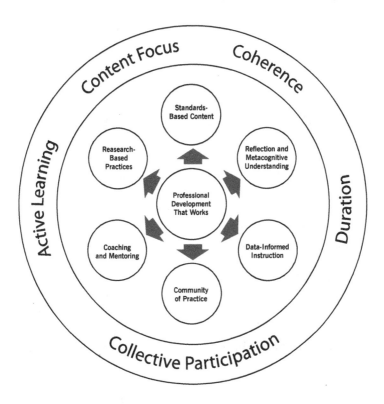

FIGURE 10.1. Framework for professional development.

the way in which these core features have been manifested in professional development projects implemented by us, including the project described in the vignette. Although the circles are presented as separate entities, in the actual delivery of professional development there is much interaction across circles; thus the arrows emanating from the center circle. In total, we have implemented seven professional development projects guided by the concepts depicted in the model. These projects have been funded through three different sources: Early Reading First (ERF), No Child Left Behind–Increasing Teacher Quality (NCLB-ITQ), and the National Writing Project (NWP). In each project, the professional development has focused on an aspect of literacy instruction in elementary and early childhood classrooms. Although funders have their unique requirements, all of these projects have been guided in some way by the concepts depicted in the model. Four of our projects have incorporated an intensive, week-long summer institute bringing teachers from different schools and districts together and focusing on development of teachers' declarative knowledge. Through ongoing support during the school year, procedural and conditional knowledge were supported. Other projects have been school-based, in which delivery of declarative, procedural, and conditional knowledge has been spread across a school year through workshops, inquiry groups, and coaching. Three inservice structures are prominent through all of the projects: workshops, inquiry groups, and coaching. Workshops are a time for the presentation of declarative information about teaching. In inquiry groups, teachers discuss student work, instructional strategies, and schoolwide goals or initiatives in a supportive and interactive environment. Coaching provides an opportunity for individual attention to the integration of declarative, procedural, and conditional knowledge in one teacher's classroom.

COMPONENTS OF THE FRAMEWORK

Standards-Based Content and Research-Based Practices

Content focus and *coherence* are among the most important features of effective professional development. Teachers want to know that what they are learning has application to their classroom in a way that will affect student achievement. Content focus incorporates both curriculum (what is taught) and instruction (how the curriculum is taught) and is depicted in this model as "standards-based content" and "research-based practices." An equal emphasis on both is needed to have balanced professional development. In the vignette, teachers are aided in understanding the structure of the Common Core State Standards with activities that involve them in a deep scrutiny of the grade-level standards. In addition, content focus and coherence draw upon notions of "coaching and mentoring" and "data-informed instruction" to be realized in any professional development project. In inquiry groups, teachers in the vignette reviewed student work samples in light of their grade-level focuses for student achievement. Teachers in both the vignette and those attending our NCLB-ITQ intensive summer institutes were introduced to research-based practices as they viewed and discussed videos in workshops and through coaching sessions in which they observed and deconstructed classroom-based lessons.

Coaching and Mentoring

Active learning and content focus cross boundaries in coaching situations. According to Elish-Piper and L'Allier (2010), coaching is a promising approach to helping teachers learn to provide high-quality classroom instruction. In professional development that we have designed, coaches frequently work directly in the classroom one-on-one with teachers, showing them how to implement instructional strategies, demonstrating good teaching, and providing feedback (Deussen et al., 2007). They do not, however, work in the role of instructional specialists to provide intervention to struggling students or as evaluators for the purposes of contract renewal, tenure, and merit pay. Among the coaching techniques refined and implemented in ERF and NCLN-ITQ grants are the following:

- Demonstrations in which the coach teaches the class, while the teacher observes and takes notes on content presentation, classroom organization, and management routines. A version of this technique is depicted in the vignette.
- Shadow coaching, in which the coach demonstrates a short and fairly simple procedure and the teacher immediately implements what the coach modeled.
- Side-by-side coaching across several lessons, in which (1) the coach demonstrates an instructional strategy with specific content while the teacher watches; (2) the teacher and the coach together implement the instructional strategy with new content; and (3) ultimately the teacher implements the instructional strategy as the coach watches (Casey, 2006; Griffith, Kimmel, & Biscoe, 2010).

In many cases, these coaching techniques are integrated into a three-stage approach fulfilling one cycle of coaching. A typical cycle of coaching begins with an observation of a classroom and teacher. This allows the coach to see how the teacher introduces a strategy and interacts with the students. The second stage of the coaching cycle occurs when the coach demonstrates a strategy or lesson that both the teacher and the coach have agreed upon. Each person (coach and teacher) has a very specific role in this stage of the coaching cycle. The coach teaches/demonstrates the lesson while the teacher engages in structured note taking. Focusing on lesson chunks, the teacher makes notes about what, how, and why the teacher implemented each portion of the lesson. During the third stage of the cycle, the teacher and coach coteach a lesson using either of the two coaching techniques, side-by-side or shadow coaching, to implement the strategy taught in the demonstration lesson. Included at each stage is a pre- and post-conference. During this time, the coach and teacher begin to discuss the pros and cons of the strategy and how it could have an impact on the learning process of the teacher's students. Possible questions the coach might ask during the conference are as follows:

- "What are your concerns as a teacher for your students in reading, math, science, and so forth?"
- "What are your strong lessons?"
- "What type of strategies would you like to work on?"
- "How do you think that went?"
- "Where did you notice the students struggled or succeeded with that strategy?"
- "How would you change the lesson to better fit your students?"
- "Is there flexibility to differentiate instruction with this strategy?"
- "How did you feel teaching the lesson?"

In one of our NCLB-ITQ professional development projects, a veteran fourth-grade teacher was resistant to use the new instructional strategies for developing vocabulary and comprehension that she had studied in the intensive summer institute. Using the questions listed above, she and the coach were able to come to the conclusion that they would first work on strategies to support vocabulary development in her classroom. The teacher chose a vocabulary strategy she wanted to work on through one coaching cycle. Together they looked at how students could use new vocabulary in their writing. Using the "said web" strategy introduced in the intensive summer institute, the students begin to write and illustrate stories, replacing overused words with vocabulary from the webs they developed. During conferences, the teacher expressed that she was surprised at the engagement of the students during the lessons, not only those taught by the coach but during those cotaught as well. The teacher indicated that the coaching cycle allowed her to feel confident in teaching new vocabulary through new strategies, and she believed the students benefited by her reaching "outside the box" to meet their needs in new ways.

Reflection and Metacognitive Understanding

Coaching and "reflection and metacognitive understanding" are closely related in this delivery model and promote active learning. We have begun to conceptualize effective instruction as the intersection of declarative, conditional, and procedural knowledge, with coaching as the catalyst allowing the three forms of metacognitive knowledge to converge (Griffith et al., 2010; Kimmel & Griffith, 2010). This relationship is depicted in Figure 10.2. Coaching ameliorates the problem reported earlier: "I have no idea how to actually implement it in my classroom." Taking a metacognitive view of coaching, we have been able to increase PreK children's growth in the mastery skills of phonological awareness, letter knowledge, and concepts about print (Griffith et al., 2010).

As a result of coaching, a preschool teacher in one of the ERF projects had a realization that there is a difference between giving children work to do and actual teaching. During an observation, the ERF coach observed a lesson in which the class was working with paint and stamps. Through the following dialogue with a

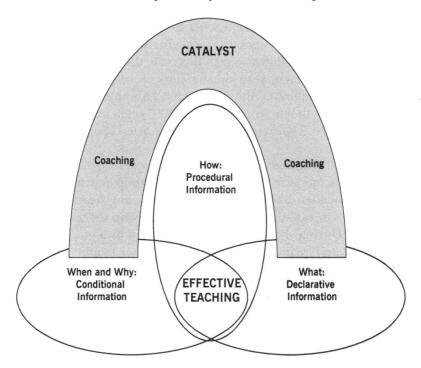

FIGURE 10.2. Instruction informed by professional development.

reflective question, the coach enabled the teacher to think about the quality of the oral communication that had occurred during the lesson.

> COACH: If you could think back to that lesson, how do you feel that you did when you were communicating with them?
>
> TEACHER: There was no oral communication much because I was so focused on trying to get them [to hurry] to get the stuff out of the way because I wanted them all to touch the paint.
>
> COACH: Right.
>
> TEACHER: They really weren't involved, except to make a mess. And, I was even cutting down on how much mess they were making. So, technically, no [focus on oral language].
>
> COACH: (*Nods in agreement.*)
>
> TEACHER: It was more like just get them some paint.

Steckel (2009) speaks of coaching as a process that empowers teachers "with reflective, problem-solving skills" (p. 22). Empowerment occurred in the discussion between this teacher and coach. As the teacher reflected on how the activity went, the coach tied her comments to literacy goals introduced in professional development classes. This enabled the teacher to delve deeper into her teaching and specifically into oral language. Steckel makes a further point: that effective coaching does not happen in a top-down way. In this case, the coach verifies whether the teacher would be in agreement with side-by-side coaching on how to incorporate oral language development into a similar activity. This engagement between coach and teacher is very much in line with Burkins's (2007) view about the importance of relationship competence. The coach positively supported learning while displaying communicative respect.

Subsequent to this conversation, with the teacher's permission, the coach returned to this teacher's classroom during a small-group activity in which the children were involved in a story follow-up activity by making steering wheels for dramatic play around a story about cars. The coach sat next to the teacher as she implemented the lesson. During the lesson, the coach acted as a guide for the teacher, making suggestions and giving reminders as the teacher taught the lesson. Following this side-by-side coaching session, the coach and teacher discussed the lesson.

> COACH: Think back to that [lesson] that you did. Let's think about components of early literacy. How many of those do you feel that you targeted throughout that whole activity?
>
> TEACHER: To be honest I wasn't thinking about [the components]. I was thinking more of the examples [suggestions] that you gave.... So I'm sure I hit some, but I can't say [inaudible].
>
> COACH: In that whole session you hit every component at least twice, and that's one thing I wanted to bring to your attention. Asking questions [and] drawing their attention to print all relate back to the [early literacy] components. What question did you ask that helped them with their comprehension?
>
> TEACHER: I was asking...where do you use a steering wheel, and I was trying to use [what happened] this morning with Mrs. Daniel's car. [Earlier children had looked at the steering wheel in one of the teachers' cars.] She walked outside and remember what she had inside of the car? (*Demonstrates steering with her hands.*)
>
> COACH: One of the things I wanted you to see is that connecting background knowledge [is the foundation of comprehension]. So you've covered oral language [and] comprehension. What do you think you did to do alphabet knowledge?
>
> TEACHER: Oh with the "s" I was trying to see if they could find steering wheel.
>
> COACH: (*Reiterates what the teacher did as she pointed out the letters in "steering wheel."*)
>
> TEACHER: That was subconscious.
>
> COACH: There you go. That's really, really good.... So we've talked about oral language, comprehension, alphabet knowledge. What do you think you did for concepts about print?

The coach and teacher continue the discussion about the lesson and review what the teacher did to develop concepts about print and phonological awareness. They conclude with two comments.

COACH: So overall how do you feel that whole experience was?

TEACHER: It was good because I learned a lot, and I never thought about that I had to think so much about...(*both laugh*). I just thought I was giving them the work, and they were doing it.

In this follow-up discussion, we see two examples of the power of coaching. First, change in teachers' beliefs comes after changes in their practices (Steckel, 2009). Through a side-by-side coaching session, the coach helps the teacher improve her practice. Subsequently the teacher expresses her understanding that teaching is more than giving children work to do. Likewise, the coach helps empower the teacher's thinking about her ability to incorporate effective practice, as she points out in this brief discussion the components of early literacy the teacher incorporated in her lesson.

Community of Practice and Data-Informed Instruction

In this delivery model, *collective participation* and *duration* are manifested through a "community of practice." According to Lave and Wenger (1991), a community of practice is a group of people who share a profession, learn from one another, and grow personally and professionally. The professional development in the vignette consisted of 45 hours extended over the school year. In other projects, duration has varied from 40 to 75 contact hours. In projects with an intensive summer institute, follow-up inquiry group meetings during the school year have involved teachers in an examination of student work samples and of the lessons they have taught.

The vignette illustrates how teachers working in a community of practice changed their thinking about writing. The teachers engaged in community work as they participated in workshop discussions in vertical and horizontal grade-level groups, examined student work samples in inquiry groups, and deconstructed instructional practices in a classroom setting. Their understanding of what defines quality of writing instruction expanded when they recognized student outcomes change when writing is authentically taught as compared with simply assigned.

In a school setting, the community of practice is enhanced in several ways. First, the professional development providers value the knowledge teachers bring to the work in their school. There are opportunities for them to be actively engaged during workshops. In addition, the administration participates in all of the professional development as a member of the community. Finally, the voices of both the professional community and the professional development providers are represented in the planning. This ensures that the goals and needs of the school are met. In the vignette, the planning team reflected the voices of both the school and the writing project. When the voices of both entities are represented, the planning can include attention to subtle details and enhance the environment within the professional development activities. These components contributed to the community of practice that developed in the school vignette.

SUSTAINING PROFESSIONAL DEVELOPMENT

The *power* of a community of practice to sustain momentum has to be underscored in any discussion of high-quality professional development. According to McLaughlin and Talbert (1993), "the path to change in the classroom core lies within and through teachers' professional communities: learning communities which generate knowledge, craft new norms of practice, and sustain participants in their efforts to reflect, examine, experiment, and change" (p. 18). And as emphasized by the National Writing Project and Nagin (2006), "instructional change is a long, multistage process" (p. 58), not something to be accomplished in a single afternoon workshop. Communities of practice provide a context for this process. Table 10.1 lists professional development structures that can be employed by a community of practice.

At the vignette school, professional development was coplanned by the school and the local writing project, a site of the National Writing Project. The National Writing Project involves teachers in a professional community beyond their classrooms, and this notion of community was interjected into the thinking of staff at the school. The National Writing Project premise of professional development is that "in-service programs must be conducted by the folks on the ground" (Gray, 2000,

TABLE 10.1. Professional Development Structures

- Participating in inquiry groups formed to solve a problem or study a question of mutual interest
- Responding to videos of master teachers at work
- Participating within and across grades in peer observations and discussing outcomes/insights
- Reading and responding to professional literature in book clubs
- Coplanning of lessons with follow-up critique
- Videotaping and deconstructing a lesson to identify what, how, and why content was taught
- Reviewing student work samples
- Sharing written reflections
- Participating in shadow and side-by-side coaching with a peer
- Working in curriculum alignment groups
- Sharing results of new teaching techniques tried in the classroom
- Attending conferences and sharing results

p. 103) and is manifested through a model of "teachers teaching teachers." In the vignette, teacher-consultants from the local writing project, who had attended an intensive summer institute on teaching writing, provided the professional development. This models not only good writing instruction but also a teacher-researcher mindset: that to remain engaged in focused and extended concentration on best practice by continued and in-depth examination of what is going on in their classrooms (National Writing Project & Nagin, 2006) is at the heart of sustainability.

The principal is important to the sustainability of any professional development project and to the creation of a school learning community (Bredeson & Johansson, 2000). In Table 10.2, we list terms that have been associated with the principal's role in professional development. In addition to making resources and funds available for professional development, the principal serves as a role model by establishing the school culture as a learning organization where ongoing professional development is the norm (Payne & Wolfson, 2000). Principals model what they espouse by willingly participating in staff development in their schools. Bredeson and Johansson (2000) stated:

> Principals who warmly welcome teachers to a staff development day and then quickly excuse themselves...undercut teacher development and the learning culture of their school in several ways.... Such cavalier administrator behavior suggests that other tasks in school are more important than the learning that will occur. . . . This negative modeling also underscores the traditional power differential between teachers and principals, especially in the area of professional autonomy. Teachers are required to attend, while principals can choose whether or not the activity meets their needs. (p. 392)

In our NCLB-ITQ grants, we have always built in a stipend for principals to attend the intensive summer institutes and follow-up activities and have observed principals participating as professional colleagues alongside the teachers in their schools. Sadly, in one of our other projects, we had the opposite situation. A principal did not attend any of the ongoing professional development in the school, and the resistance and resentment from several teachers was evidenced by their arriving late to and leaving early from scheduled inservice days.

TABLE 10.2. Roles of the Principal

- Role model
- Procurer of resources
- Motivator
- Instructional leader
- Critical friend
- Collaborator
- Professional colleague

CONCLUSION

High-performing teachers can make a difference in student outcomes. The impetus for increasing inservice teachers' performance is well-designed professional development. However, we emphasize that although there may be many designs for a professional development project, there are overarching characteristics, including a classroom-embedded context; core features of content focus, coherence, duration, collective participation, and active learning; and attention to metacognitive knowledge. These characteristics can be achieved through the delivery framework described in this chapter.

QUESTIONS FOR DISCUSSION

1. As a teacher or administrator, how would you describe professional development in your school or district?

2. Describe successful professional development projects you have been involved with. What made them successful?

3. Outline the components of an ideal professional development project for your grade level and subject area.

4. What do you see as the benefits of having a coach in your classroom? What hesitations do you have about having a coach work with you in your classroom?

5. As a principal, what can you do at your school to make professional development meaningful for teachers?

6. What types of activities would you benefit from within a community of practice?

REFERENCES

Bredeson, P. D., & Johansson, O. (2000). The school principal's role in teacher professional development. *Journal of In-Service Education, 26*(2), 385–401.

Burkins, J. M. (2007). *Coaching for balance: How to meet the challenges of literacy coaching.* Newark, DE: International Reading Association.

Casey, K. (2006). *Literacy coaching: The essentials.* Portsmouth, NH: Heinemann.

Coleman, J. S., Campbell, E. Q., Hobson, C. J., McPartland, J., Mood, A. M. Weinfeld, P. D., et al. (1966). *Equality of educational opportunity.* Washington, DC: National Center for Educational Statistics.

Darling-Hammond, L., & McLaughlin, M. W. (1995). Policies that support professional development in an era of reform. Retrieved from *www.middleweb.com/PDPolicy. html.*

Darling-Hammond, L., & Richardson, N. (2009). Teacher learning: What matters? *Educational Leadership, 66*(5), 46–53.

Darling-Hammond, L., Wei, R. C., Andree, A., Richardson, N., & Orphanos, S. (2009). *Professional learning in the learning profession: A status report on teacher development in the United States and abroad.* Dallas, TX: National Staff Development Council. Retrieved from *www.nsdc.org/news/NSDCstudy2009.pdf.*

Desimone, L. M. (2009). Improving impact studies of teachers' professional development: Toward better conceptualizations and measures. *Educational Researcher, 38*(3), 181–199.

Deussen, T., Coskie, T., Robinson, L., & Autio, E. (2007). *"Coach" can mean many things: Five categories of literacy coaches in Reading First.* Washington, DC: U.S. Department of Education, Institute of Education Sciences, National Center for Education Evaluation and Regional Assistance, Regional Educational Laboratory Northwest.

Elish-Piper, L., & L'Allier, S. K. (2010). Exploring the relationship between literacy coaching and student reading achievement in grades K–1. *Literacy Research and Institution, 49,* 162–174.

Flavell, J. H. (1976). Metacognitive aspects of problem solving. In L. B. Resnick (Ed.), *The nature of intelligence* (pp. 231–235). Hillsdale, NJ: Erlbaum.

Flavell, J. H. (1979). Metacognition and cognitive monitoring: A new area of cognitive-developmental inquiry. *American Psychologist, 34,* 906–911.

Garner, R. (1994). Metacognition and executive control. In R. B. Ruddell, J. R. Ruddell, & H. Singer (Eds.), *Theoretical models and processes of reading* (pp. 715–732). Newark, DE: International Reading Association.

Gray, J. (2000). *Teachers at the center: A memoir of the early years of the National Writing Project.* Berkeley, CA: National Writing Project.

Griffith, P. L., Kimmel, S. J., & Biscoe, B. (2010). Teacher professional development for at-risk preschoolers: Closing the achievement gap by closing the instruction gap. *Action in Teacher Education, 31*(4), 41–53.

Guskey, T. R., & Huberman, M. (Eds.). (1995). *Professional development in education: New paradigms and practices.* New York: Teachers College Press.

Hawley, W., & Valli, L. (1999). The essentials of effective professional development: A new consensus. In L. Darling-Hammond & G. Sykes (Eds.), *Teaching as the learning profession: Handbook of policy and practice* (pp. 127–150). San Francisco: Jossey-Bass.

Hunt, J. B., & Carroll, T. G. (2003). *No dream denied: A pledge to America's children.* Washington, DC: National Commission on Teaching and America's Future. Retrieved from *http://nctaf.org/wp-content/uploads/2012/01/no-dream-denied_summary_report.pdf.*

Joyce, B., & Showers, B. (2002). *Student achievement through staff development* (3rd ed.). Alexandria, VA: Association for Supervision and Curriculum Development.

Kimmel, S. J., & Griffith, P. L. (2010). Evaluation: Practical applications for closing achievement gaps. In M. C. McKenna, S. Walpole, & K. Conradi (Eds.), *Promoting early reading: Research, resources, and best practices* (pp. 142–163). New York: Guilford Press.

Lasley, T. J., II. (2009). Using data to make critical choices. In T. J. Kowalski & J. J. Lasley II (Eds.), *Handbook of data-based decision making in education* (pp. 243–258). New York: Routledge/Taylor & Francis.

Lave, J., & Wenger, E. (1991). *Situated learning: Legitimate peripheral participation.* Cambridge, UK: Cambridge University Press.

McLaughlin, M. W., & Talbert, J. E. (1993). *Contexts that matter for teaching and learning: Strategic opportunities for meeting the nation's educational goals* (Research report). Stanford, CA: Center for Research on the Context of Secondary School Teaching. Retrieved from *www.eric.ed.gov/PDFS/ED357023.pdf.*

National Commission on Teaching and America's Future. (1996). *What matters most:*

Teaching for America's future. Washington, DC: Author. Retrieved from *http://nctaf. org/wp-content/uploads/2012/01/WhatMattersMost.pdf.*

National Writing Process & Nagin, C. (2006). *Because writing matters: Improving student writing in our schools.* San Francisco: Jossey-Bass.

Paris, S. G., Lipson, M. Y., & Wixson, K. K. (1994). Becoming a strategic reader. In R. B. Ruddell, M. R. Ruddell, & H. Singer (Eds.), *Theoretical models and processes of reading* (pp. 788–810). Newark, DE: International Reading Association.

Payne, D., & Wolfson, T. (2000). Teacher professional development: The principal's critical role. *NASSP Bulletin, 84,* 13–21.

Pintrich, P. R. (2002). The role of metacognitive knowledge in learning, teaching and assessing. *Theory into Practice, 41*(4), 219–225.

Steckel, B. (2009). Fulfilling the promise of literacy coaches in urban schools: What does it take to make an impact? *Reading Teacher, 63,* 14–23.

Tschannen-Moran, M., & Johnson, D. (2011). Exploring literacy teachers' self-efficacy beliefs: Potential sources at play. *Teaching and Teacher Education, 27,* 751–761.

CHAPTER 11

Effective Professional Development in Secondary Schools

DOUGLAS FISHER
NANCY FREY

- What are the differences among content knowledge, pedagogical knowledge, and pedagogical content knowledge, and how might they help differentiate professional development for middle and high school teachers?
- What content do secondary school teachers need to learn as part of their professional development efforts?
- How can teachers develop habits that students can use to access information? Can these habits be used across content areas and across time?
- What professional development structures are effective in middle and high schools?
- What are the characteristics of effective professional development for middle and high school teachers?

Middle and high schools are exciting places where students begin to specialize in their studies. As they move from class to class, students encounter information that stretches their imagination and understanding. Teachers are often experts in their respective content areas and are very interested in their own subject areas. Just think about a student who knows she wants to become a physician and her ability to interact with teachers who have a deep level of understanding of biology, genetics, and anatomy, not to mention mathematics, literacy, art, and history.

Although there are many positive aspects of middle and high schools, there are also potential areas of concern. Sometimes teachers have a deep knowledge of their content area, but not how to teach it. Other times, teachers have superior pedagogical skills, but not the level of expertise required by their disciplines. And still other times, teachers know their content well, understand and can implement general teaching approaches, but cannot teach their specific content. As Shulman (1986) recognized, teachers need pedagogical content knowledge, or knowledge about the content they are expected to teach; understanding of general teaching approaches; and instructional routines specific to the content they are teaching. According to Shulman (1987), content-area teachers, such as those working in middle and high school classrooms, need knowledge of the subject matter (content knowledge), general pedagogical knowledge (or teaching strategies), and an understanding of the teaching and learning implications that are associated with the specific subject matter.

Effective models of professional development must consider the needs of each middle and high school teacher. Rather than simply focusing on general teaching strategies, for example, professional development must be responsive to the staff of a given school or district. This requires careful analyses of data, in the form of needs assessments and classroom observations, to determine which areas of pedagogical content knowledge must be addressed in a given school. In other words, one-size-fits-all professional development will likely fail.

To complicate things further, there is evidence that students experience middle and high school classrooms in fragmented and piecemeal ways. For example, Fisher and Frey (2007) compared student performance in middle schools that did or did not focus on instructional consistency. In their study, they found that developing student habits that could be used in different classes contributed to student achievement. In particular, the more successful schools assessed their teachers and determined that the majority of teachers needed general instructional skills that students could predictably use in the majority of their classrooms. In a study of a historically low-performing high school, Fisher, Frey, and Lapp (2009) found that providing teachers with professional development and coaching focused on a limited number of general pedagogical approaches, as well as targeting the content knowledge of specific teachers, resulted in success.

To ensure that professional development is effective for teachers in middle and high school classrooms, there must be an understanding of the need and an ability to meet that need (e.g., Dahlberg & Philippot, 2008). Professional development providers should ask themselves, Is the need for content knowledge, for general instructional approaches, or for disciplinary-specific instructional routines? In doing so, they can better differentiate the professional development offerings. As Tomlinson (2004) noted, there are a number of ways to differentiate, including a focus on the content, the process, and the products. We use these three categories to discuss effective professional development for middle and high school teachers. In the next section, we focus on aspects of professional development content. In the section that follows, we examine structures of professional development that have been effective in secondary schools. And finally, we focus on the products that are expected to emerge from effective professional development efforts.

PROFESSIONAL DEVELOPMENT CONTENT
FOR SECONDARY TEACHERS

As we have noted, effective professional development for teachers in secondary schools requires a careful analysis of pedagogical content knowledge. This can occur through a needs assessment in which teachers are asked directly about areas of growth or through classroom observations in which needs are identified by others. For example, the leadership team of Mountain View Middle School noted that student performance in science was poor. The students generally did well in history, English, and mathematics, but not as well in science. In sharing this finding with the school community, the leadership team asked for ideas about improving student performance. Some in the group recommended after-school tutoring for students, whereas others suggested that they try reading and writing across the curriculum. In discussing this issue with the teachers, the principal learned that the majority of the department staff members felt that they did not possess strong enough science backgrounds to ensure that students performed at the advanced levels. As one of the teachers commented, "I really liked science in school but I have a K–8 general teaching credential. I think that my knowledge is great for basic science information, but now our students are generally at grade level, and I'm not sure that I can push them to excellence." In discussing this further, the principal realized that this was a common concern in the department. As a result, the content of the professional development for the science teachers was science itself. The principal made connections with local museums, field study organizations, and the local university, creating a number of hands-on opportunities for teachers in the science department to develop deeper understanding of the contents. At one of the sessions, the teachers explored a local planetarium and were quizzed on the location of specific constellations. They also were able to experience a new exhibit on black holes and to participate in the lecture series on star death. As one of the teachers, a veteran of 18 years, noted, "This is the best professional development that I've ever been a part of. I really understand this content now and I'll be a much better teacher as a result. I know how to teach, but now I am more confident in what I'm teaching."

In other cases, there is evidence that teachers have the prerequisite content knowledge but that their instructional repertoires are rusty or inconsistent. In some schools, teachers use outdated approaches to instruction, such as round-robin reading, sit-and-get lectures, or having students answer the questions in the back of the book. In these cases, teachers need to be supported in integrating interactive learning approaches in their classrooms. For example, the entire school, a department, or select teachers may engage in a book study using *Classroom Strategies for Interactive Learning* (Buehl, 2008) to investigate approaches that they can support. As we discuss in greater detail later, simply scheduling a one-shot professional development event and expecting people to immediately implement the ideas from the session is foolhardy. Creating change requires much more support than this, which is probably why most professional development is ineffective, not to mention despised by many secondary school teachers (Joyce & Showers, 2002).

In other cases, the teachers are not consistent, and students spend more time focused on how they are being taught rather than on what they are being taught. This was the case at Hoover High School. When the instructional leadership team, a group of elected teachers, staff, parents, and the administrator, conducted a series of classroom observations, they noted that different teachers had different ways of providing the same basic instruction. For example, in some classrooms students were expected to take Cornell (or two-column) notes, in other classrooms students were expected to use outlines for their notes, in still other classrooms students were required to produce graphic and visual notes, and in other classrooms no notes were required. In discussing their observations, the team agreed that some instructional consistency might help students develop habits that they could take with them, from class to class and then to college. In creating their professional development plan, they engaged the entire faculty in discussions about instructional routines that could become constant. The instructional leadership team focused on approaches that were *transparent*, meaning that students would be able to develop a habit and thus not focus on the instructional approach, and transportable, meaning that students would be able to use the selected approaches across their school day. They agreed to seven specific instructional routines, as noted in Figure 11.1. Over the next couple of years, the professional development offerings focused on these instructional routines, going deeper into implementation at each session. In

---

Anticipatory activities. Such strategies as bellwork, anticipation guides, and KWL charts (i.e., what I know, what I want to know, what I learned) are designed to activate background knowledge and make connections between what students already know and what they are learning. These strategies also help students see the relevance of the curriculum.

Cornell note-taking. Students use split pages to take notes on the right side, identify key ideas on the left, and write a summary at the bottom. This strategy improves listening comprehension and provides students with a study tool.

Graphic organizers. Any number of tools are used to display information in visual form. Common graphic organizers include semantic webs, cause and effect charts, Venn diagrams, matrices, and flow charts.

Read alouds and shared reading. On a daily basis, the teacher reads aloud material connected with the content standards being taught. This short, 3- to 5-minute reading provides students with a context for learning, builds their background knowledge, improves vocabulary, and provides them with a fluent reading model.

Reciprocal teaching. In small groups, students read a piece of text and engage in a structured conversation in which they summarize, clarify, question, and predict. In doing so, they learn to use cognitive strategies appropriate for use while reading for information.

Vocabulary development. In addition to the incidental vocabulary learning that is done through read alouds and anticipatory activities, students are taught specific content vocabulary words required in various disciplines.

Writing to learn. These brief writing prompts provide students an opportunity to clarify their understanding of the content as well as provide the teacher a glimpse into the students' thinking. As a result, teachers know when reteaching or clarifications are necessary.

FIGURE 11.1. Schoolwide content-literacy instructional routines. From Fisher and Frey (2006). Copyright 2006 by the National Association of Secondary School Principals. Reprinted by permission.

addition, part of the structure that was used involved peer coaching and feedback such that there was accountability for implementation. The results were impressive. During the years of implementation and attention, Hoover had the greatest change in achievement for all high schools in the district: an impressive 136-point gain on California's Academic Performance Index, a composite measure of test scores across subject areas (Fisher & Frey, 2006). Unfortunately, when the professional development initiative changed, new priorities were established, and peer coaching was all but eliminated, student achievement stalled and eventually faltered.

At Health Sciences High, the needs assessment indicated that the teachers had significant content knowledge, as well as a deep understanding of pedagogy. What they needed was a systematic approach to instruction in which responsibility was intentionally shifted from teachers to students, with students given support to succeed. This is probably the most common situation in secondary schools today. There is evidence that the revision of the Elementary and Secondary Education Act, known as No Child Left Behind, has resulted in more teachers with more content knowledge (e.g., DeAngelis, White, & Presley, 2010). That's not to say that all teachers who are highly qualified are highly effective. To imply that would suggest a lack of understanding of pedagogical content knowledge. It does suggest that fewer middle and high schools will have to devote their limited resources to content knowledge. There is also evidence that teachers completing their professional preparation programs are fairly cognizant about instructional routines useful for targeted groups of students (e.g., Jones & Vesilind, 1996; Newman, Samimy, & Romstedt, 2010) and thus may require less attention in this area.

What remains is the need to ensure that teachers are intentional about their scaffolding and support such that students assume increasing responsibility for learning. Based on the work in reading comprehension by Pearson and Gallagher (1983), the gradual release of responsibility model provides a structure for the teacher to move from assuming "all the responsibility for performing a task...to a situation in which the students assume all of the responsibility" (Duke & Pearson, 2002, p. 211). Professional development that ensures that teachers internalize this instructional framework focuses on three areas:

1. *Task control*: decisions about the task, how students will be involved in the task, and how it will be assessed.
2. *Authenticity*: decisions about the choice of tasks as they relate to meaningful and relevant learning in students' lives.
3. *Teacher's role*: when, where, and to what extent the teacher will participate in each task (Pearson & Fielding, 1991, p. 847).

The gradual release of responsibility framework can be implemented in a number of ways. A needs assessment used at Health Sciences High contains the following aspects:

• *Establishing purpose*, in which the student knows what he or she is expected to learn and why the content is important or relevant. The purpose contains both content and language components because humans learn through language and because every lesson in a middle school or high school should require reading, writing, speaking, listening, or viewing—literacy.

• *Modeling*, in which teachers share their thinking aloud with students, including the metacognitive moves that demonstrate how teachers think, not just what they think. In addition, the modeling provides language support for students through multiple examples.

• *Guided instruction*, which ensures that errors and misconceptions are addressed. During guided instruction, students are not told the answer, but rather the teacher questions, prompts, and cues the learner to guide that learner's thinking.

• *Productive group work*, in which students interact with their peers, using academic language and argumentation skills, as they complete a project or solve a problem worthy of their efforts.

• *Checking for understanding*, in which teachers determine levels of understanding for all students and consider which students need additional instruction to master the content.

• *Independent practice*, in which students apply what they have learned in new situations.

At Health Sciences High, the leadership team used the needs assessment found in Figure 11.2 to determine professional development needs. Each teacher completed the needs assessment, and classroom observations were conducted to clarify the responses to the survey. In analyzing the findings, the leadership team noted that there was a group of teachers who needed additional practice with establishing the purpose of the lesson. This group was allowed time during professional development sessions to focus on this topic. Another group of teachers needed help with modeling, and they were allowed to focus on that aspect. The entire staff noted that they wanted to know more about small-group guided instruction, which is fairly uncommon in most high schools. As one of the teachers noted, "In my credential program, it was all whole class. We never had time to meet with small groups of students based on their needs. I think it's a great idea and I have my students working in groups, so I could meet with a small group, but I'm not sure what to do once I get them there." In collaboration with their peers, the teachers learned the answers to this question and were supported in implementing what they learned. The professional development focused on increasing student responsibility and holding students accountable for their learning, and the results were positive. Grade point averages, test scores, attendance, and morale increased (Fisher, Frey, & Pumpian, 2011).

Sometimes the needs assessment reveals that teachers understand the content well and regularly implement high-quality instruction. The needs assessments at these schools often reveal a need to focus on discipline-specific instruction. This might involve a group of math teachers learning about cognitively guided instruction

	Proficient—4	Skillful—3	Approaching—2	Minimal —1
Component 1: Establishing Purpose				
Lesson is established for both content and language objectives, along with application to students, and is based on formative assessments.	Lesson is explicitly presented through content and language objectives, which are based on content standards and language demands of the task, as well as students' needs.	Language and content objectives are stated but are not well connected to content standards or language demands of the task, but do address students' needs identified via formative assessments.	Only one objective is stated (i.e., either content or language is missing), or purpose is not well connected with objective or connected to real-life application.	No content or language objective is stated or implied. There is no evidence of formative assessments to plan.
Student understanding of lesson: Students can explain objectives/purpose in their own words: *What* they are learning *How* they show their learning *Why* they need to learn lesson	Randomly selected students can explain or demonstrate how the stated objectives relate to their own learning.	Students can accurately restate the objectives of the lesson but lack a clear understanding of why they are being taught content.	Students can restate portions of the objectives of the lesson but lack an understanding of why they are being taught the content.	Students are unable to correctly state the objectives of the lesson.
Routines are established for student interaction with both one another and teacher.	Students immediately move into multiple-response modes with their peers, using supports available (sentence frames, organizers, roles, etc.).	Students are aware of the procedures and transition easily. Teacher directs them to response mode.	Procedures are established with students. Students are able to share knowledge with each other and teacher.	Procedures for students' responses are not clear. Responses generated from few volunteers.

(continued)

FIGURE 11.2. Gradual release of responsibility (GRR) quality indicators (Health Sciences High, 2013).

	Proficient—4	Skillful—3	Approaching—2	Minimal —1
		Component 2: Modeling		
Visual supports are available for teaching and learning of concepts and skills.	Concept attributes and skills steps are modeled and students actively use and are encouraged to use them in guided instruction and productive group work.	Concept attributes and skills steps are modeled and students actively use them during practice with the teacher.	Concept attributes or skills steps are posted. Examples and nonexamples are provided. Usage is not. Skill steps too abbreviated.	Concept attributes or skill steps are not posted. Teacher verbally presents information.
Language support: Written, verbal, teacher, and peer supports are available to boost academic language usage.	Sentence frames are differentiated based on students' proficiency and need. Wide ranges of frames are available for students and students use the frames independently in academic language and writing. Teacher modeling includes the use of frames, as well as academic vocabulary and high expectations for language production.	Students use one or two sentence frames from the variety that are available in a structured setting. A set of target vocabulary is available and used. Teacher models the use of frames. Students are encouraged to use the language support in guided instruction and productive group work.	Academic language related to the concept/standard is present. A frame may be provided. The teacher models at least once using target vocabulary or language frame. Students are encouraged to attempt using target vocabulary without opportunities for guided practice.	Vocabulary is posted but its use is not modeled. Students are simply told to use words. Language frames are not provided.
Teacher provides an authentic model.	Modeling includes naming task or strategy, explaining when used, using analogies to link to new learning. Teacher demonstrates task or strategy, alerts of errors to	Modeling contains all the indicators (naming, explaining, analogies, demonstration, errors to avoid and checking), but the teacher only uses some "I" statements.	Modeling contains some indicators (naming, explaining), but the teacher directs students through the use of "you" statements.	Modeling contains few indicators. Teacher uses "you" statements that focus process, not modeling thinking.

avoid, shows how applied to check for accuracy. Modeling consistently contains "I" statements.			
Multiple examples are provided during instruction.	Engages in teacher-led practice that extends lesson beyond model example.	Multiple examples provided where students are required to participate.	Several examples provided. Students may be asked to participate.	Single example provided during teacher model/demonstration.

Component 3: Guided Instruction

Teacher scaffolds support for students.	Teacher poses question, asks for clarification, and, if answer incorrect, directs student to previous learning via prompt. If answer still incorrect, provides cues before moving to reinstruction.	Teacher poses question, asks for clarification and if answer incorrect, directs student to previous learning via prompt.	Teacher poses question and asks for clarification when response is correct (e.g. *How do you know? How did you figure that out?*).	Teacher poses question, student(s) respond, and teacher moves onto next question or next student.
Teacher differentiates instruction and practice based on formative assessment.	Group formation always based on formative assessments from daily lessons. Groups are heterogeneous, but with leveled skills. Students able to apply information based on the support provided by instruction. Tasks differ based on students' needs and/or students' selection.	Group formation usually based on formative assessments from weekly lessons. Students apply information based on initial instruction and teacher support.	Group formation is flexible and based on multiple formative assessments. Tasks are similar to those presented in lesson.	Group formation based on single formative assessment. Tasks are same as presented in lesson.

FIGURE 11.2. (*continued*)

(continued)

	Proficient—4	Skillful—3	Approaching—2	Minimal —1
Component 4: Productive Group Work				
Students use strategies and skills that were modeled.	After receiving adequate time in scaffolded instructional support, all students can complete tasks using the strategy or skill that was modeled.	After receiving limited time in scaffolded instructional support, students complete tasks using the strategy or skill that was modeled.	Students move directly from teacher modeling to independent work, with little to no scaffolded instructional support.	There is a mismatch between what was modeled and what students are asked to do.
Complexity of task: The task is a novel application of a grade-level appropriate concept and is designed so that the outcome is not guaranteed (a chance for productive failure exists).	Task reflects objective and what was modeled. Task allows students an opportunity to use a variety of resources to creatively apply their knowledge of what was modeled. Students have an opportunity to experiment with concepts.	Tasks provide multiple, clear opportunities for students to apply and extend what was modeled. Students have an opportunity to use a variety of resources to creatively apply their knowledge of what was modeled.	The task is somewhat reflective of the objective of the lesson, but there is little opportunity for student experimentation or innovation.	Task is an exact replication of what was modeled, with little or no opportunity for student experimentation with concepts.
Grouping for productive group work: Small groups of two to five students are purposefully constructed to maximize individual strengths without magnifying areas of need.	Groups are flexible and change based on students' proficiency, academic need, and/or content area. Productive group work occurs throughout the lesson.	Purposeful heterogeneous grouping occurs. Groups are fluid in response to students' proficiency.	Some heterogeneous grouping occurs, but homogeneous grouping practices dominate. Decisions based on assessments are not apparent.	Grouping practices are solely homogeneous and are done primarily for scheduling convenience.
Joint attention to tasks or materials: Students are interacting with one	Students ask critical questions of each other, developing and forming personal opinions and	Body language, visual gaze, and language interactions provide evidence of joint	Body language, visual gaze, and language interactions provide some evidence of	Students divide up the task so that they can work, then meet near end to assemble

214

another to build each other's knowledge. Outward indicators include body language and movement associated with meaningful conversations and shared visual gaze on materials.	conclusions. They evaluate and synthesize information, and independently use a variety of resources to acquire new or unknown information.	attention to the task or materials by all members of the group. Students can explain their contributions and the contributions of other group members.	mutual attention to the task or materials by most members. Students are not holding each other accountable for purposeful contributions.	components. Body language, visual gaze, and lack of language interaction provide evidence of independent work occurring within the group.
Argumentation, not arguing: Students use accountable talk to persuade, provide evidence, ask questions of one another, and disagree without being disagreeable.	Students reach a better understanding or consensus based on evidence and opinions provided by others. Students hold each member of the group accountable by using questioning strategies and evidence to persuade or disagree. The conversation is respectful and courteous.	Students ask for and offer evidence to support claims. However, members continue to maintain initial beliefs or positions about a topic without considering the arguments of others. The conversation is generally respectful but some members may not participate.	There is a process in place for accountable talk. However, student dialogue is limited, and there are minimal efforts to support the product. The conversation is generally respectful, but is often dominated by one member of the group or group or veers off topic.	No clear process is in place to facilitate accountable talk. Lack of structure is evidence as students are off task, in conflict, and/or are unable to complete product.
Component 5: Checking for Understanding (CFU) throughout the Lesson/Closure				
Ensures students are learning the components/elements of the new skill or concept; shows their ability to apply the skill or concept by asking appropriate questions to ascertain students' understanding.	Teacher asks carefully crafted questions about steps of skill or components of concepts based on the understanding of the students' skill levels and language proficiencies.	Teacher asks carefully crafted questions about steps of skill or components of concepts presented and based on students responses adjusts instruction from initial instructional plan.	Teacher asks questions and returns to students who answered incorrectly to ensure correct understanding.	Teacher asks questions and continues with initial instructional plan.

FIGURE 11.2. (continued)

(continued)

215

	Proficient—4	Skillful—3	Approaching—2	Minimal —1
Asks a variety of multileveled questions to help determine students' understanding and provides wait time for students' response.	Teacher moves expertly through a variety of questions, focusing on metacognition. Students are able to ask themselves questions as they share their answers. Consistently provides appropriate wait time (5–8 seconds).	Questions are generally open-ended. Teacher follows answer with metacognitive question (e.g., "How did you figure that out?" "What evidence do you have?" [prompts]). If student answers incorrectly, teacher moves into cues before moving onto reteaching. Consistently provides appropriate wait time (3–5 seconds).	Questions vary between closed and open ended. Teacher follows answer with metacognitive question (e.g., "How did you figure that out?" "What evidence do you have?" [prompts]). Provides wait time often.	Questions are generally closed (single answer). Generally no follow-up question. Occasionally provides wait time.
Engages students in variety of techniques throughout the lesson to ensure all students' understanding.	Teacher has variety of techniques, verbally and written, to demonstrate students' understanding. Teacher checks in with each student throughout the lesson.	Teacher has variety of techniques, verbally and written, to demonstrate students' understanding. Teacher checks in with each student at the end of each component of lesson.	Teacher has one to two techniques to check on understanding. Teacher checks on all students once or twice during the lesson.	Students volunteer response. Teacher may check on all students' understanding at the end of the lesson.
Provides explicit feedback in order to deepen or solidify students' understanding.	In addition to the teacher providing feedback, peers also support one another by asking follow-up questions or restating answer and how it assisted them with their understanding.	Teacher responds to students' answers by explicitly stating what was correct or moves into asking additional questions to move the student to the correct answer.	Teacher attempts to respond to students' answers by referring to the skill or concept taught. Additional supports may be referenced.	Students are praised for answering correctly or teacher moves on to another student if answer is incorrect.

During closure, students demonstrate their ability to use the skill/concept successfully and teacher notes those students who did not in order to provide future instructional support.	Teacher engages all students in the checking for understanding process to ascertain final level of understanding. Students are able to use skill or concept presented during lesson to a high degree of success (90%+) and can share their own thought processes. When students lack confidence or sufficient practice, teacher explicitly adjusts delivery or plans additional lessons as appropriate.	Teacher engages all students in the checking for understanding process to ascertain final level of understanding. Students are able to use skill or concept presented during lesson to a high degree of success (90%+). When students lack confidence or sufficient practice, teacher adjusts additional practice, delivery or plans additional lessons as appropriate.	Teacher engages some students in the checking for understanding process to ascertain final level of understanding. Students are able to use skill or concept presented during lesson with some success (80%).	Teacher does not check for final level of understanding. Students unsure about skill component or concept element.
Component 6: Independent Practice				
Practice is meaningful, relevant, and extension of learning.	Learning tasks provide opportunities to apply their learning in unique or different situations (e.g., Bloom's taxonomy).	Learning tasks provide students with opportunities to apply what they have learned.	Learning tasks are based on instruction.	Learning tasks are unconnected to instruction.
Students take responsibility for learning.	Students self-evaluate their own learning and develop next steps to increase their understanding of the learning.	Students routinely self-evaluate their own learning.	Students discuss their own learning with peers and/or teacher.	Teacher provides feedback on student learning.

FIGURE 11.2. (continued)

(Carpenter, Fennema, Franke, Levi, & Empson, 1999), a group of science teachers focused on inquiry-based education (Furtak, Seidel, Iverson, & Briggs, 2012), or a whole school focused on the difference between generic literacy instruction and disciplinary literacy (Shanahan & Shanahan, 2008).

This was the case at Monroe Clark Middle School. The teachers knew their subjects well and had a good understanding of generic instructional routines. In discussions with their peer coach, they realized that they were approaching writing in generic ways rather than focusing on the differences in writing history, science, and literature. Their professional development efforts provided teachers in different content areas time to focus on what it meant to write like an art critic, a historian, a mathematician, a literary critic, a sports reporter, a scientist, and so on. They read professional articles from their disciplines and discussed the moves of the writers. They also engaged outside consultants in conversations about these differences and started their own writing clubs. The student achievement 2 years later suggested that their disciplinary focus was on track. More students than ever scored at the advanced levels on the state writing assessment (Fisher, Frey, Farnan, Fearn, & Petersen, 2004).

Focusing on the content of professional development is important. Providing the wrong content to teachers will not change their practices or the achievement of students. But understanding the content that teachers need is not enough. The way in which the professional development is provided is also an important consideration. As we discuss in the next section, there are a number of different processes or structures that are useful in providing middle and high school teachers with excellent professional development.

PROCESSES OF PROFESSIONAL DEVELOPMENT IN SECONDARY SCHOOLS

As we have noted, there is not a single means of designing and delivering professional development. However, there seem to be infinite ways of doing them badly. As Sleeter (1990) noted, "many school districts are still hindered by ineffective or fragmented approaches to staff development" (p. 33). The situation is not much better more than two decades later, despite some promising schools and districts that have found ways to differentiate professional development and meet more teachers' needs (e.g., Kose, 2007). Assuming the content is the right content, the problem often lies in the processes used. There has to be a match between the processes or structures used and the intended outcomes. For example, there is a great deal of interest in teacher study groups, learning communities, communities of practice, or inquiry groups (e.g., Nelson, Slavit, Perkins, & Hathorn, 2008). Ideally, these professional development structures "foster teacher learning through a collaborative culture and the codification of group members' collective knowledge" (Stanley, 2011, p. 71). But sometimes they don't. Sometimes there is conflict and tension (Rousseau, 2004) or simply different desires and goals (Stanley, 2011). Effective professional development relies on an appropriate structure to get the job done.

We have organized the processes into five categories. Selecting one process over another requires careful consideration of the type of learning desired. As Tennant (1993) noted, there are three types of learning: attitudes, skills, and knowledge. The goal of any given professional development effort will likely be a combination of these three:

- **A** represents attitude. An example of this type of learning is a shift in attitude toward the academic abilities of English learners.
- **S** represents skills. Learning to ask text-dependent questions is a skill required in close reading instruction.
- **K** represents knowledge. An example is knowing how writing strategies are assessed on the state accountability measures.

In terms of the specific formats, the following structures can provide guidance for those responsible for delivering quality professional development. These include whole staff, groups of staff members, collaborative conversations, peer coaching, and blended learning.

Structure 1

Whole-faculty sessions are used to introduce initiatives, motivate and challenge faculty, and provide a sense of the larger community. The sessions set the tone for the year and remind teachers about the value of public education. They tend to be focused on attitudes and to serve as introductory events. In addition, these whole-faculty sessions provide the administration with an opportunity to clarify expectations and acknowledge individuals who make a difference. They can also be used to focus on schoolwide needs, such as improved vocabulary instruction or establishing routines and procedures with students. As a case in point, a whole-staff session at Health Sciences High focused on the school climate. The faculty discussed the look of the school and how to ensure that the facility matched the vision they all had for the school. At the end of the session, the faculty committed to maintaining the environment in such a way that communicated to students that they cared.

Structure 2

Smaller groups of teachers, approximately 20% of the staff at a time, can meet during their preparation periods, with substitutes to cover a period of class, or in groups after school. These sessions tend to focus on knowledge development. For example, Hoover High School focused on content literacy strategies. Teachers met monthly during the preparation periods to demonstrate general literacy instructional routines for their peers. This structure allows the faculty to go deeper while remaining focused on the same seven instructional approaches year after year. The drawback of this system is that the staff development committee has to organize several sessions on the same day; the benefit is that teachers attend the sessions in smaller groups.

Structure 3

During other scheduled times such as prep periods, teachers meet in groups of four. These "coaching corners" meetings focus mainly on skill development. These coaching sessions can be used for different content. At Monroe Clark, the coaching corners focused on writing instruction aligned with disciplinary thinking. At Hoover, the focus was on implementation of general content literacy instructional approaches. At Hoover, all of the teachers on prep for a specific period meet in an extra-large classroom. They meet in groups of four in each of the corners of the room. Before the meeting, the staff development committee identifies teachers who will serve as coaches. These teachers identify the specific instructional routine on which they will provide coaching. A sign-up sheet is posted a week in advance of the session, and teachers identify the coaching session they would like to attend. Many different topics are explored, such as creating anticipation guides and effective writing prompts. During the session, the coach provides a 10-minute overview of the instructional routine and how he or she uses it. Then each of the four participant teachers rehearses the approach in front of her or his peers. This rehearsal increases the likelihood that teachers will implement the routine back in their classrooms.

Structure 4

To ensure that professional development is implemented, coaching has been identified as a useful adjunct to information sessions (Bean & Eisenberg, 2009). There is evidence that coaching ensures implementation of the professional development, which then results in improved student achievement (Fisher, Frey, & Lapp, 2011). The 1:1 structure involves teachers coaching one another on an individual basis, serving to solidify knowledge and skills. Given funding limitations, schools can afford to have only limited numbers of coaches at a time. At Health Sciences, there are five coaches who have one period each for release to engage with their peers. At Hoover, there is enough money to support 60 teachers (30 pairs) every 6 weeks. Hoover operates three rounds per school year. Each pair submits its "collegial coaching" proposal, which identifies the specific instructional routines the pair would like to focus on. The 30 best papers are selected. Those 60 teachers receive compensation for attending two 2-hour sessions after school in which they focus on the role of the peer coach, how to conduct classroom observations, structuring the feedback, and so forth. The partners are also compensated for three buy-out periods, during which each observes his or her partner's classroom instruction. After each partner has observed three periods, the pair meets after school to debrief the entire experience.

Structure 5

There are a number of blended learning opportunities for teachers to engage in professional development. They can focus on attitudes, skills, or knowledge.

Typically, they involve an online learning management system (LMS) and either synchronous or asynchronous interactions with peers. For example, Mountain View Middle School focused on 21st-century learning as an entire school. They used the Pathways Professional Development LMS developed by the National Council of Teachers of English (NCTE; *www.ncte.org/pathways*). They interacted with the content and each other in an online environment, completing tasks to further their understanding of 21st-century skills. As part of this blended learning experience, teachers were asked to implement various technology tools with their students and then load evidence into the system so that their peers could comment. Interestingly, the comments were often made face-to-face as teachers saw each other during the day. For example, after reviewing a podcast that a seventh-grade history teacher posted, the eighth-grade teacher said, "I think that really worked for your students to have that information before their group task. I did a Glogster page (*edu.glogster.com*) for my project but I'd like to add a podcast. Can you show me how you did it?" At Health Sciences High, the faculty use Haiku LMS (*www.haikulearning.com*) to create blended learning opportunities for students. To maximize the time that they have in their classrooms preparing for the start of the school year, the state-mandated training content (including appropriate test preparation, accommodations and modifications for students with disabilities, mandatory reporting requirements for abuse and neglect, and universal precautions) was created in Haiku so that teachers could complete their learning on their own schedules. There was a combination of tasks that required teachers to consider their attitudes, skills, and knowledge. For example, the first section of the content, relating to accommodations and modifications for students with disabilities, required that teachers analyze their own attitudes about appropriate support. They then engaged in some online readings, wrote a reflection about their own support for students with disabilities, made recommendations for improving the support system at school, and then uploaded an example of an appropriate accommodation or modification. As one of the teachers noted:

> "This really helped me. I was able to get more done in my class during the school day and then do some PD when I had time after my kids went to bed. Every year before this, I had to stay late or come in the weekend before school started to finalize my room because my days were taken with mandatory PD. This year, I'm ready to go because I had my days free, and I still completed the professional development. And, the professional development was much more informative this year. I didn't just listen to someone tell me the same information again this year. I really engaged with the content and I really understand it a lot better this year. Thank you."

Using the right process combined with the right content has the potential for success. Stated another way, the wrong content isn't going to improve teacher practice or student performance. Neither will the wrong processes. Every person involved in schooling has experienced poor processes related to professional development. Perhaps it was a large-group session in which the presenter was trying to teach a new skill. Or perhaps it was a monthly event in which the content changed each month and it seemed that there was no connection with previous professional development events. Matching the need with the structure helps address these issues and contributes to a more successful experience, assuming that the individuals providing the professional development are knowledgeable and skilled themselves. Having said that, it's important to emphasize that the product of professional development should be improved teacher performance and increased student achievement. Unfortunately, too many professional development efforts culminate in a satisfaction survey. Happiness scales, on which participants simply rate their satisfaction with the professional development event, are insufficient products (Guskey, 2009). Instead, the product of professional development should be implementation. And there is probably no better way to assess implementation than to examine student work and students at work.

PRODUCTS OF PROFESSIONAL DEVELOPMENT
FOR SECONDARY TEACHERS

Schools spend upward of $20 billion annually on professional development (National Center for Educational Statistics, 2008). It seems reasonable to ask whether that investment is paying off, and even more reasonable to ask, How would the public ever know? Ultimately, professional development should result in improved student achievement. And there is evidence that effective professional development does produce increases in student performance (e.g., Magidin de Kramer, Masters, O'Dwyer, Dash, & Russell, 2012; Sample McMeeking, Orsi, & Cobb, 2012). But waiting until the summative assessment results arrive is not rewarding for most of the teachers participating in the professional development events. They want more immediate feedback. They want to know whether their efforts are worth it. To address this issue, professional development efforts in middle and high schools should include time for groups of teachers to analyze student work to determine for themselves whether their efforts are paying off. That's not to say that professional development efforts should not also be evaluated using outcome and accountability data, but rather that regularly examining student work can serve to refine the professional development and teachers' practices. It also reinforces newly acquired skills to ensure that teachers remain committed to implementation.

When groups of teachers meet to analyze student work, they will likely want to develop interventions for students who are not performing as expected. This is natural and appropriate. From a teaching and learning perspective, this is exactly what we'd like for teachers to do. But when thinking about professional development, looking at student work assumes another role. As teachers examine student work, they should consider the impact that their professional development has had, whether or not the efforts have been effective, and whether they need additional professional development to meet student needs. The general protocol that is commonly used in product-focused professional development follows (see Figure 11.3):

Grade Level: _____ **Date:** _____

Facilitator: _____ **Time Keeper:** _____ **Recorder:** _____

Other Members Present: _____

_____

Previous SMART Goal (leave blank if first meeting):
The % of _____ grade students scoring at _____ or higher in _____
will increase from _____ % to _____ % by the end of _____ as measured
by _____ given on _____ .

Collect Data

Groups (teacher, grade level, target group, etc.)	# of Students Taking Assessment	% and # of Students Scoring Proficient and Above		% and # of Students Scoring Nonproficient		#/% Basic	#/% of Below Basic	#/% Far Below Basic
1.								
2.								
3.								
4.								
5.								
6.								
7.								
8.								
Totals:								

We *did* / *did not* meet our goal.

Target Students:

Basic	Below Basic	Far Below Basic

(continued)

FIGURE 11.3. Data analysis tool.

Analyze Strengths and Obstacles

Looking at the performance bands, list students' strengths
Looking at the performance bands, list obstacles of targeted students

Look for trends and patterns that will identify the specific areas of need:

New and/or Revised SMART Goal:
The % of _____ grade students scoring at _____ or higher in _____
will increase from _____% to _____% by the end of _____ as
measured by _____ given on _____ .

Brainstorm Instructional Interventions for Targeted Students

Agree on one or two strategies that everyone will use.

Identify Results Indicators

Approach: _____

   Evidence that we are implementing the strategy:

   What evidence would show that the strategy *is / is not* working:

Approach: _____

   Evidence that we are implementing the strategy:

   What evidence would show that the strategy *is / is not* working:

FIGURE 11.3. *(continued)*

- *Introduction (5 minutes)*: Facilitator reviews the purpose/topic, norms, protocol steps including Parking Lot (a place to record items to discuss later), time frames, and focus of each step/time frame. Review the goal set at the last meeting. (If this is the first meeting, there will not be a previous SMART [specific, measurable, attainable, relevant, and time-bound] goal.)
- *Collect data (5–10 minutes)*: Using the available data, enter the assessment data for each classroom, grade level, or targeted group of students. Compute the totals. Also list the nonproficient students in the Basic, Below Basic, or Far Below Basic columns.
- *Analyze strengths and obstacles (10 minutes)*: Looking at the actual student work/assessments, list the strengths of proficient work and the obstacles of nonproficient work, and chart this information. Look for trends and patterns that will identify specific areas of need. Consider the impact of the professional development that has been provided.
- *New and/or revised SMART goal (10 minutes)*: Evaluate whether the goal was met. If met, discuss those students who did not reach proficiency. What do they need? Will each teacher work with his or her own students, or should these students be grouped within the team for short-term acceleration? Is it possible to reset the goal higher, and if so, is it achievable? If not met, determine whether to revise the goal and how to proceed with instruction: How will this affect our agreed-upon pacing guide? How will we differentiate for the students who reached proficiency? Discuss additional professional development that team members may need. After reviewing the data, write a new or revised SMART goal. If this is the first meeting, develop a SMART goal.
- *Brainstorm instructional interventions for targeted students (10 minutes)*: Brainstorm approaches that might be successful in meeting the needs of the nonproficient students. Agree on one or two things that all members of the team will use.
- *Identify results indicators (5 minutes)*: For each approach agreed upon by the team, record what evidence will show that every teacher is implementing the intervention and what observable evidence will show that it is working. The latter *may* involve short, formative assessments to monitor progress toward the goal.
- *Debriefing (5 minutes)*: The entire group reflects about how well the process worked, for example, adhering to team norms, staying on topic, following the protocol, and adhering to time frames.

For additional information about using student work in professional development, see Langer, Colton, and Goff (2003). These product conversations require facilitation and leadership but can yield valuable results. Of course, they cannot replace the content of professional development; there are still things for teachers to learn. The professional development time available should be used for developing teachers' attitudes, skills, and knowledge, and periodically the time should be used to examine the products of the effort. Some schools, such as Hoover High, engage in discussions about student work on a monthly basis. This is done in addition to their professional development content session. Other schools, such as Health Sciences High, engage in discussions about student work on a quarterly basis. It really depends on the time a given faculty has available.

CHARACTERISTICS OF EFFECTIVE PROFESSIONAL DEVELOPMENT

As noted elsewhere in this book, some things are more effective than others in creating change through professional development. As Garet, Porter, Desimone, Birman, and Yoon (2001) noted, professional development should: "(a) focus on content knowledge; (b) opportunities for active learning; and (c) coherence with other learning activities" (p. 915). In addition, as we have noted, structural factors have an impact on the effectiveness of professional development, including "(a) the form of the activity (e.g., workshop vs. study group); (b) collective participation of teachers from the same school, grade, or subject; and (c) the duration of the activity" (p. 915).

In sum, effective professional development for middle and high school teachers should be based on needs assessments and classroom observations. An analysis of these data should lead to differentiated content and processes. Sometimes teachers need content knowledge; other times they need general pedagogical strategies. Still other times they need disciplinary-specific support. In addition, there should be opportunities for teachers to determine the success of their efforts through analysis of products. Much like the students they teach, middle and high school teachers benefit from high-quality instruction that is aligned with clear learning goals and based on assessed needs.

Hopefully, future professional development efforts for secondary school teachers will look less like classrooms of the past and more like the learning environments that students in the 21st century expect. Now, and for the foreseeable future, learners expect to communicate and collaborate with each other. They want to experience learning, and not just be told things. And they expect to have opportunities to apply what they have learned in a variety of settings. Of course, this will involve new technology tools, but the purpose will remain the same. Professional development is about developing the attitude, skills, and knowledge necessary to ensure that all students learn at high levels.

QUESTIONS FOR DISCUSSION

1. What are the characteristics of effective professional development? When have you experienced this and what has it done for you as a professional educator?

2. Which teachers need which types of professional development? How can you differentiate the offerings for teachers?

3. Would the approach Hoover High took, namely focusing on transparent and transportable instructional routines, help your school?

4. What changes to the student work protocol would be necessary for its use at your school? How comfortable are people in discussing student performance?

5. How can district and state polices be revised and updated to reflect the professional development needs of teachers?

REFERENCES

Bean, R. M., & Eisenberg, E. (2009). Literacy coaching in middle and high schools. In K. D. Wood & W. E. Blanton (Eds.), *Literacy instruction for adolescents: Research-based practice* (pp. 107–124). New York: Guilford Press.

Buehl, D. (2008). *Classroom strategies for interactive learning* (2nd ed.). Newark, DE: International Reading Association.

Carpenter, T., Fennema, E., Franke, M., Levi, L., & Empson, S. (1999). *Children's mathematics*. Portsmouth, NH: Heinemann.

Dahlberg, K. R., & Philippot, R. A. (2008). The power of collaboration: A case for teachers helping to determine professional development agendas. *Planning and Changing, 39*(1/2), 21–41.

DeAngelis, K. J., White, B. R., & Presley, J. B. (2010). The changing distribution of teacher qualifications across schools: A statewide perspective post-NCLB. *Education Policy Analysis Archives, 18*(28), 1–31.

Duke, N. K., & Pearson, P. D. (2002). Effective practices for developing reading comprehension. In A. E. Farstrup & S. J. Samuels (Eds.), *What research has to say about reading instruction* (pp. 205–242). Newark, DE: International Reading Association.

Fisher, D., & Frey, N. (2006). Majority rules: A schoolwide literacy success. *Principal Leadership, 6*(7), 16–21.

Fisher, D., & Frey, N. (2007). A tale of two middle schools: The role of structure and instruction. *Journal of Adolescent and Adult Literacy, 51*, 204–211.

Fisher, D., Frey, N., Farnan, N., Fearn, L., & Petersen, F. (2004). Increasing achievement in an urban middle school. *Middle School Journal, 36*(2), 21–26.

Fisher, D., Frey, N., & Lapp, D. (2009). Meeting AYP in a high need school: A formative experiment. *Journal of Adolescent and Adult Literacy, 52*, 386–396.

Fisher, D., Frey, N., & Lapp, D. (2011). Coaching middle-level teachers to think aloud improves comprehension instruction and student reading achievement. *Teacher Educator, 46*, 231–243.

Fisher, D., Frey, N., & Pumpian, I. (2011). No penalties for practice. *Educational Leadership, 69*(3), 46–51.

Furtak, E., Seidel, T., Iverson, H., & Briggs, D. C. (2012). Experimental and quasi-experimental studies of inquiry-based science teaching: A meta-analysis. *Review of Educational Research, 82*(3), 300–329.

Garet, M. S., Porter, A. C., Desimone, L., Birman, B. F., & Yoon, K. S. (2001). What makes professional development effective? Results from a national sample of teachers. *American Educational Research Journal, 38*, 915–946.

Guskey, T. R. (2009). Closing the knowledge gap on effective professional development. *Educational Horizons, 87*(4), 224–233.

Jones, M., & Vesilind, E. (1996). Putting practice into theory: Changes in the organization of preservice teachers' pedagogical knowledge. *American Educational Research Journal, 33*, 91–117.

Joyce, B., & Showers, B. (2002). *Student achievement through staff development* (3rd ed.). Alexandria, VA: ASCD.

Kose, B. W. (2007). One principal's influence on sustained, systemic, and differentiated professional development for social justice. *Middle School Journal, 39*(2), 34–42.

Langer, G. M., Colton, A. B., & Goff, L. S. (2003). *Collaborative analysis of student work: Improving teaching and learning.* Alexandria, VA: ASCD.

Magidin de Kramer, R., Masters, J., O'Dwyer, L., Dash, S., & Russell, M. (2012). Relationship of online teacher professional development to seventh-grade teachers' and students' knowledge and practices in English language arts. *Teacher Educator, 47*(3), 236–259.

National Center for Educational Statistics. (2008). *Revenues and expenditures for public elementary and secondary education: School year 2005–06 (Fiscal Year 2006).* Washington, DC: U.S. Department of Education, Institute for Education Sciences. Retrieved from *http://nces.ed.gov/pubs2008/expenditures.*

Nelson, T. H., Slavit, D., Perkins, M., & Hathorn, T. (2008). A culture of collaborative inquiry: Learning to develop and support professional learning communities. *Teachers College Record, 110,* 1269–1303.

Newman, K. L., Samimy, K., & Romstedt, K. (2010). Developing a training program for secondary teachers of English language learners in Ohio. *Theory into Practice, 49*(2), 152–161.

Pearson, P. D., & Fielding, L. (1991). Comprehension instruction. In R. Barr, M. L. Kamil, P. Mosenthal, & P. D. Pearson (Eds.), *Handbook of reading research* (Vol. 2, pp. 815–860). Mahwah, NJ: Erlbaum.

Pearson, P. D., & Gallagher, G. (1983). The gradual release of responsibility model of instruction. *Contemporary Educational Psychology, 8,* 112–123.

Rousseau, C. K. (2004). Shared beliefs, conflict, and a retreat from reform: The story of a professional community of high school mathematics teachers. *Teaching and Teacher Education, 20,* 783–796.

Sample McMeeking, L., Orsi, R., & Cobb, R. B. (2012). Effects of a teacher professional development program on the mathematics achievement of middle school students. *Journal for Research in Mathematics Education, 43*(2), 159–181.

Shanahan, T., & Shanahan, C. (2008). Teaching disciplinary literacy to adolescents: Rethinking content-area literacy. *Harvard Education Review, 78,* 40–59.

Shulman, L. S. (1986). Those who understand: Knowledge growth in teaching. *Educational Researcher, 15*(2), 4–14.

Shulman, L. S. (1987). Knowledge and teaching: Foundations of the new reform. *Harvard Educational Review, 57,* 1–22.

Sleeter, C. (1990). Staff development for desegregated schooling. *Phi Delta Kappan, 72,* 33–40.

Stanley, A. M. (2011). Professional development within collaborative teacher study groups: Pitfalls and promises. *Arts Education Policy Review, 112,* 71–78.

Tennant, M. (1993). *Psychology and adult learning.* London: Routledge.

Tomlinson, C. A. (2004). *How to differentiate instruction in mixed ability classrooms* (2nd ed.). Alexandria, VA: ASCD.

PART III

DEVELOPING SOLUTIONS FOR EFFECTIVE PROFESSIONAL DEVELOPMENT

Professional development for teachers needs to be meaningful and relevant. Teachers always look for something they can use the next day in their classrooms, but they also look for ways to advance themselves professionally and as lifelong learners. I believe we do teachers a disservice when we don't connect our professional development, offered or mandated by our school districts, to those areas that excite teachers about their own learning. Just as we want our students to be engaged in the classroom, we need teachers engaged in professional development where they can take what they learn and apply it to their instruction.

—KURT SIEBOLD
Principal
Slavens K–8 School
Denver, Colorado

DEVELOPING SOLUTIONS FOR EFFECTIVE PROFESSIONAL DEVELOPMENT

CHAPTER 12

Characteristics of Adult Learning
Implications for the Design and Implementation of Professional Development Programs

RUTH L. ROHLWING
MAUREEN SPELMAN

- The work of Knowles and Mezirow laid the foundation for current models of adult learning.
- Adult learning can be either informational or transformational in nature.
- Four recurring themes spiral through the work of various adult learning theorists/models: experience, reflection, dialogue, and context.
- Adults' ways of knowing have implications for professional development designs.
- Sustainable change in professional practice is best viewed as a process.

UNDERSTANDING ADULT LEARNERS

Do adults learn in different ways than children do? In the early 1970s adult educators attempted to distinguish adult learning as a separate body of information from the psychologists' studies of learning in general. However, due to the complex nature of learning, no single theory or set of principles emerged as an explanation of how learning in adulthood might differ from learning in childhood. About that same time, Malcolm Knowles (1968) introduced the European concept of andragogy, a label to distinguish adult learning from that of children, or pre-adult learning. As a pioneer in the field of adult learning, Knowles advanced four assumptions about adult learners: adults maintain the concept of responsibility for their own decisions, moving from dependent to self-directing learners; adults enter the educational setting with a growing reservoir of experience and more varied learning experiences than children; adults have a readiness to learn those things that they need to know in order to cope effectively with real-life situations; and adults are life-centered in their orientation to learning (Knowles, 1980, pp. 44–45).

Knowles later expanded that list of four assumptions, adding two more: adults are more responsive to internal motivators than external motivators (Knowles & Associates, 1984, p. 12), and adults need to know why they need to know something (Knowles & Associates, 1984). Knowles saw these six assumptions as foundational to the design of adult programs and thought they could be used to strengthen the learning experience. He suggested these assumptions could guide the design, implementation, and evaluation of adult-focused learning activities. However, Knowles's assumptions have been criticized for their isolation of the learner from the learning context with little regard to how the individual is socially situated and the product of a cultural condition (Merriam, Caffarella, & Baumgartner, 2007).

INFORMATIONAL VERSUS TRANSFORMATIONAL LEARNING

The concept of andragogy is, perhaps, the best known of theories on adult learning, but a number of other theories have gained significant recognition in the field. Mezirow's (1978b) theory of transformational learning examines how adults make sense of their life experiences; he posits that inherent in all humans is the need to make sense of and understand life experiences so as to avoid the threat of chaos. This particular theory suggests a learning cycle initiated by a disorienting dilemma; this dilemma is followed by self-examination, with possible feelings of fear, anger, guilt, or shame. This critical assessment of previous assumptions may then result in an exploration of options that have the potential to transform long-held beliefs (Mezirow, 2000). However, if adults are unable to understand or reintegrate new perspectives, they often return to traditional ways of knowing (Mezirow, 2000).

Mezirow defined learning as "the process of using a prior interpretation to construe a new or a revised interpretation of the meaning of one's experience in order to guide future action" (2000, p. 5). *Informational learning* takes place when there is an increase in knowledge and skills; the learner elaborates upon existing frames of reference or adds new frames of reference. *Transformational learning*, in contrast, transforms individuals' points of view or habits of mind (Mezirow, 2000). Transformational learning will "place the form itself at risk for change and focuses on changes in how people know; it is essentially an *educational* model for personal change" (Kegan, 1994, pp. 163–164). Informational learning increases *what* a person knows, whereas transformational learning changes *how* a person knows (Kegan, 1994).

Mezirow's transformative learning theory includes four main components that inform the learning process: expanded awareness of the experience, critical reflection, validating discourse, and reflective action (Mezirow, 2000). Transformative learning takes place when experience changes the schema or perspective of the learner. Mezirow (1978a) originally suggested that perspective transformations occurred suddenly as the result of a disorienting dilemma or triggered by a significant personal event. However, Taylor (2000) notes that perspective transformation is a recursive journey and not always a stepwise process. Later studies suggest that the process of triggering a transformation is subtle and less profound, with opportunities for consideration of past experiences resulting in the gradual change of the learner's point of view (Taylor, 2000). In later publications, Mezirow (1995) concurs that the transformative process does not always follow the exact sequence of phases but includes some variations of the identified phases.

RECURRING THEMES IN ADULT LEARNING

Knowles's evolving body of work, combined with Mezirow's transformative learning theory, laid the foundation for a number of subsequent frameworks or models of adult learning. Although no one theory can offer a complete view of adult learning, there are a number of individuals who have contributed to the literature on this important topic. In reviewing that rich body of work, four recurring themes spiral through the work of various theorists: experience, reflection, dialogue, and context.

Experience

Educators have long agreed that students of all ages learn from experiences. John Dewey (1938) posited, "all genuine education comes about through experience" (p. 13). Dewey cautioned, however, that not all experiences are equally educative (p. 13). References to experience appear again and again in the work of various adult learning theorists. Even prior to Knowles's development of the andragogy framework, Lindeman (1961) emphasized the value of the learner's experience. He described the learner's life experiences as a "living textbook" (p. 7).

Knowles subsequently proposed his framework, noting that adults accumulate experiences, which then serve as a rich resource for learning (Knowles, 1980). Kolb (1984), a contemporary of Knowles, also described learning as grounded in the experience of the learner. Shortly thereafter, Brookfield (1986, 1987) investigated adult learning and critical thinking, but through a different lens. Even as he questioned the assumptions framing andragogy, Brookfield (1986) did agree with the value of the experience assumption; he concluded that this assumption was, indeed, well grounded. Well-known theorists Jarvis (1987) and Mezirow (1981) concur; both stated that the learning process begins with the experience of the adult learner. Mezirow, and later Daloz (1999), expanded upon that stance, noting that experience alone was not sufficient; they suggest that adult learners need to first make meaning of their experiences. Illeris (2002) also discussed the role of experience in learning; however, he defined experience as both perception and transmission. Illeris proposed that experience implies not only receiving but also acting upon the event.

More recently, Merriam and colleagues (2007) returned to Dewey's warnings as they argued that experiences accumulated by adults can serve as either a resource or a barrier. When it comes to the value of experience and adult learning, it appears that quantity does not necessarily equal quality; adults learn from their experiences in a variety of ways (Dewey, 1938; Merriam et al., 2007). The lens through which these various scholars have viewed the relationship between experience and learning appears to stem from their theoretical orientation. Whether those orientations were constructivist, situative, or some other theoretical underpinning, most scholars recognized the foundational value of experience (Merriam et al., 2007).

Reflection

Kolb's model of adult learning (1984) proposed that learning from experience requires a specific set of abilities; one of those abilities, he posited, was the need to develop reflective skills. Mezirow (1985) and Brookfield (1986, 1987) also referenced the importance of reflection in their discussions related to transformational learning. Mezirow's theory emphasized the need for what he termed critical reflection, and Brookfield (2000), in later writings, pointed to critical reflection as a cardinal function of adult education. Their contemporary, Jarvis (1987, 2001), expanded upon this discussion as he described two types of learning from experiences: nonreflective learning and reflective learning. He defined reflective learning as the practice of planning, monitoring, and reflecting upon experiences (Jarvis, 2001).

A number of other adult learning theorists placed an emphasis on reflection. The adult learning framework proposed by Hammond and Collins (1991) listed critical reflection as the second of seven essential components. And Criticos (1993) agreed that critical reflection was an essential requirement for effective learning. Freire (2000) also pointed to critical reflection as a key component of his theory. Mezirow (2000) later revisited the concept of reflection and differentiated among three types of reflection: content reflection, process reflection, and premise reflection. And in his later work, Brookfield (2000) expanded upon the importance of critical reflection; he eventually proposed a more narrow definition of critical reflection that focused on analyzing "hegemonic (taken for granted) assumptions" (Brookfield, 2000, p. 138).

Dialogue

Several theorists made the connection between reflecting upon experiences and subsequent collaborative conversations—or dialogue. Experts argued that through conversations, discussions, and/or dialogue, adult learners shared learning and began to develop common understandings (Mezirow, 2000). Mezirow (1996) cautioned that dialogue does not imply debate but more a collaborative effort to reach agreement and build new understandings (p. 170). In that same vein, Daloz (1999) referenced dialogue as an integral part of transformational learning. His view of adult learning took a slightly different path and examined conversations between the learner and the mentor. Writing at that same time, Boyd (1991) and Dirkx (1998) also considered dialogue to be an important component of the learning process. Later, Dirkx expanded upon that conversation to include the concept of inner dialogue in the transformational learning process. Freire (2000) also discussed this issue; he was more emphatic as he described dialogue as "indispensable to the act of cognition" (p. 64).

Taylor (2000) added to the ongoing conversation by pointing out the importance of the supportive environment necessary to ensure "rational discourse" (p. 306). Mezirow (2000) concurred as he discussed the importance of supportive conversations with like-minded peers. Mezirow described the importance of "ideal" conditions necessary to foster productive dialogue (p. 13). More recently, Johnson-Bailey and Alfred (2006) have continued to examine the importance of dialogue; they proposed the concept that adult learners effectively deconstruct assumptions through dialogue with others.

Context

A review of the literature reveals that many adult learning theorists recognized that context shapes the learner's experience in a variety of ways (Boud & Walker, 1991; Fenwick, 2001). Although in early writings the context or social situation for; learning is largely ignored by theorists such as Knowles (Clark & Wilson, 1991; Grace, 1996; Merriam et al., 2007), a significant number of theorists from various perspectives expressed the belief that adult learning needs to be set in the context of the learner's environment (Alfred, 2000; Jarvis, 1987; Lee, 2003; Sandlin, 2005). Although McCluskey's (1970) theory of margin did not directly address the act of learning, it examined how learning intersects with the context of the learner. His discussion of increasing margin by adjusting load and power probed the link between learning and social roles (Merriam et al., 2007).

Mezirow (1996, 2000) revisited the element of context in his later writings; he pointed to the importance of learning through the lens of "biographical, historical, and cultural contexts" (2000, p. 3). About that same time, Illeris's (2002) model of the learning process offered three dimensions: cognition, emotion, and environment. In fact, his model set these three dimensions within the backdrop of the social context. A number of more current adult learning frameworks examined the impact of various cultural contexts (Feinstein, 2004; Henderson, 2002; Sheared, 1994; Taylor, 2000; Tisdell, 2003); in fact, the work of Kappel and Daley (2004) targeted the specific context encountered in urban settings.

ADULT LEARNING IN PROFESSIONAL CONTEXTS

The change in language from "professional development" to "professional learning" in the newly revised *Standards for Professional Learning* (Learning Forward, 2011), formerly the *Standards of the National Staff Development Council,* reflects the emphasis on adults' learning in professional contexts and signals the importance of adults taking active roles in their learning. The standards emphasize the essential elements of professional learning that "function in **synergy** to enable educators to increase their effectiveness and student learning" (Learning Forward, 2011, p. 14, emphasis in original). Implicit in the standards are four prerequisites for professional learning that are fundamental to understanding the standards:

1. Educators' commitment to students—all students—is the foundation of effective professional learning.
2. Each educator involved in professional learning comes to the experience ready to learn.
3. Because there are disparate experience levels and use of practice among educators, professional learning can foster collaborative inquiry and learning that enhances individual and collective performance.
4. Like all learners, educators learn in different ways and at different rates. (Learning Forward, 2011)

The second and fourth prerequisites are of particular importance to understanding professional learning with direct applications to adult learning theory. Knowles (1980) recognized the importance of adults' readiness to learn those things that they need to know in order to cope effectively with real-life situations and that adults are life-centered in their orientation to learning; educators today want direct and immediate applications of their learning to their teaching contexts. Learning Forward's fourth prerequisite acknowledges that adults learn in different ways and at different rates; each learner must be engaged in a way that meets his or her learning needs. Not unlike PreK–12 students, some adult learners have more needs than others, requiring more time, more support, or different types of learning experiences.

Kegan's (1982, 1994) developmental theory of adult development recognizes that each learner is different. Building on Kegan's work, Drago-Severson (2009) emphasized three ways of knowing that reflect the developmental levels adults use to make sense, often resulting in different reactions within similar professional contexts. Drago-Severson's three ways of knowing can be described as:

1. *The instrumental way of knowing: "Rule-bound self."* Those who have a concrete orientation to the world and recognize that others' points of view are separate from theirs. They are able to understand observable events, processes, and situations through only their own personal lens.
2. *The socializing way of knowing: "Other-focused self."* Those who have enhanced capacity for reflection and are able to think abstractly. They often subordinate their own needs to the needs of others and adopt authorities' solutions and perspectives.
3. *The self-authoring way of knowing: "Reflective self."* Those who have the capacity for their own internal authority and can reflect on different perspectives and various relationships.

The three ways of knowing represent adult learners' development of increasing capacities for self-reflection and understanding others' perspectives as they engage in collaborative work. Although each way of knowing allows the adult learner to make meaning in a developmentally different way, the progression to higher levels occurs when the demands of the environment call for higher-level capacities (Drago-Severson, 2004, 2009).

FACILITATING CHANGE IN PROFESSIONAL PRACTICE

Facilitating sustainable changes in professional practice can be a daunting task; every professional can discuss wave after wave of professional development programs that have rolled by with few positive or long-lasting effects (Sirkin, Keenan, & Jackson, 2011). It is not surprising that leaders in education, business, government, and various professional practices cite change as their single greatest challenge (Reeves, 2009). And yet, professional development programs aimed at transformational learning are all about change—at the individual level.

Adult learning theorists generally agree that experience, reflection, and individual development are critical components of transformational learning (Merriam et al., 2007) and that these critical components must be viewed through the lens of the particular context of the learner. However, if the goal of any given professional development program is a long-lasting change in practice, then such programs need to be designed and implemented considering the conditions necessary for change. Culture is very often a deeply ingrained factor that can serve as a barrier to both individuals and organizations/schools (Reeves, 2009).

Kotter (1996, 2008; Kotter & Rathgeber, 2005) suggests an 8-step process for successful change in any organization. He notes that the first step, creating a sense of urgency, is the most critical and most challenging of this guiding sequence (Kotter, 1996; Kotter & Rathgeber, 2005). He cautions, however, that complacency can serve as a subtle barrier to any change effort. Complacency could even be considered the direct opposite of urgency (Kotter, 2008). Reeves (2009) agrees upon the importance of a sense of urgency but cautions that it needs to be framed within a thoughtful approach if we hope to move adult learners out of their entrenched positions. Resistance to change can be erroneously dismissed as institutional inertia when the real issue is clarity of purpose. Apprehensions can be lessened when the purpose is explained in concrete, practical terms: What do these changes mean for me? What are the reasons supporting the need for change? What are the expected benefits? How will these changes affect my current practices (Spelman, 2006)?

Even the best change insights fail to get translated into action in the absence of trust, shared aspirations, and clear mental models (Senge, 1990). It is important to keep in mind that change is a highly personal experience; every individual is different, and responses to change vary greatly. Individuals generally react to change by measuring it against their personal schemas. Thus some will adapt to a new practice more readily than others. One of the most persistent misconceptions regarding change is that change is an event. This false tenet fails to recognize that change is more appropriately defined as a process (Spelman, 2007).

Viewing change as a process can lead professional development designers to an appreciation of the complexities and human processes of change, particularly the demands that the change process imposes at every level of implementation. Those who design and implement professional development programs need to acknowledge that there are human limits to the number of change components that people or institutions can effectively implement. Change, of any variety, frequently creates conflict and division among the competing stakeholders (Bolman & Deal, 2003). Often the imposition of change spawns a tug-of-war between those in support of change and those determined to hold the status quo. The scenarios are practically predictable. Change where it counts most, the practical implementation level, is the hardest to achieve and the most important (Spelman, 2006).

IMPLICATIONS FOR PROFESSIONAL DEVELOPMENT DESIGNS

Understanding that professional development programs can focus on either informational or transformational learning, designers need to first identify the purpose. There are certainly instances in which the aim of a particular professional development program or workshop is primarily informational. New assessment systems, reporting systems, and even text adoptions present the need to increase participants' knowledge and/or skill levels. When, on the other hand, the intended goal is transformational learning, professional development program designers need to address not only the continuum of ways of knowing but also the need to lay the foundation for sustainable change in practice.

A majority of scholars seem to agree that allowing for differences in experience, engaging adult learners in self-reflection and/or critical reflection, facilitating dialogue, and considering the social context are elements that can and do influence adult learning. These four recurring and evolving themes can be traced throughout the mosaic of adult learning theories, models, and frameworks. Given that the majority of scholars cite these themes as critical to adult learning, applying these elements may strengthen professional development models.

The wide range of experiences that professional development participants bring with them, then, should be an important consideration in the design of effective programs. Kegan (2000) reminds us that every adult student comes to us with a personal learning history. Professional development participants bring with them a variety of experiences that can be drawn from and also have the potential to be valuable resources. Applying that information to professional development suggests that it may be important to solicit experiential information from participants prior to the design and implementation of professional development programs. Using that information, professional development designers can support adult learning by consciously linking explanations and illustrations to the prior and/or current experiences of the participants (Tennant, 1991).

Illeris (2002) suggested that the experiences of adult learners might also be framed around current activities. Rather than simply presenting information about a given topic, professional development designs may be more effective if participants are allowed to experience new information—learning by doing (Taylor, 2000). This suggests that professional development programs need to consider concrete activities that allow adult learners to experience new concepts; this type of active engagement provides the opportunity to incrementally deepen the understanding of the participants (Brookfield, 2000).

Kegan (2000) cautioned, however, that there are features of experience that can, indeed, serve as barriers in learning. He suggested that the personal relationship of the learner to the topic at hand has the potential to influence the level of learning that can take place. Not every participant approaches a given professional development program with the same enthusiasm for the subject featured. In addition, Kegan suggested that the adult learner's disposition toward learning in general could serve as a potential barrier in any professional development experience. He wisely cautioned designers, "We must be careful not to create learning designs that get too far ahead of the learner" (p. 66).

Understanding and respecting the prior experiences of the adult learner should, then, guide professional development designers in creating effective activities to guide participants toward new knowledge and deeper understandings (Kegan, 2000). However, we must also consider, as Criticos (1993, p. 162) pointed out, that "effective learning does not follow from a positive experience but from positive reflection." The model proposed by Jarvis (2001) supports Criticos, as it describes two main types of learning from experiences. When learners simply remember and repeat an experience, they are engaging in nonreflective learning. However, deeper learning is more likely to take place when the activities include opportunities for reflection and evaluation connected to the program experiences (Hammond & Collins, 1991; Jarvis, 2001).

Scholars in several areas have expressed agreement regarding the importance of including opportunities for reflection and reflective practice in professional development programs; engaging in reflective practices appears to improve not only instructional practice but also student achievement (Cochran-Smith 2006; Darling-Hammond, 2003; Elmore, 2000; Fullan, 2005). Professional development designs that are ongoing or continuous have the potential to support participant movement through the reflective cycle; this cycle of reflection is less likely to occur in the traditional "one-shot workshop" model. Professional development programs that are delivered over time allow participants to interpret, analyze, and experiment (Rodgers, 2002), as well as allowing time to reflect on the experience.

Reflection-on-action is an analytical exercise that allows the adult learner to revisit experiences, create plans, and take action (Merriam et al., 2007; Schön, 1987); it follows, then, that allowing for reflection-on-action activities can be an effective component in continuous professional development program designs. Cranton (2002), for instance, recommended the use of reflective journals as a means of supporting such critical reflection. Likewise, reflection on professional practice activities might include peer observations or reviews, classroom action research, or even data analysis to guide instructional planning (Curry, 2008; McTighe, 2008). Reflection-on-action activities might also include portfolio development, mapping, and/or critical reflection exercises (Merriam et al., 2007; Osterman & Kottkamp, 2004; York-Barr, Sommers, Ghere, & Montie, 2006).

Reflective activities can be even more effective when supported by reflective discourse or dialogue. Mezirow's (2000) model of adult learning suggests that the learner needs to reflect on his or her experience and talk with others to solidify new knowledge. Drago-Severson (2009) takes a similar stance as she proposes the concept of collaborative reflective practice; "collegial inquiry" is a dialogue that takes place between two or more participants (p. 154). Drago-Severson suggests that thinking and examining an issue together is an act of dialogue that moves the conversation to a level of collegial inquiry. Killon (2000) also advocates for professional development experiences that allow participants not only to analyze practice but also to engage in dialogue about their learning with colleagues.

Effective dialogue, then, is not a debate but an effort to find agreement, search for common ground, engage in evaluation, and use collective experiences to build new understandings (Mezirow, 2000). Creating an environment that is conducive to dialogue is an important factor to consider in professional development designs. "Feelings of trust, solidarity, security, and empathy are essential preconditions for free full participation in discourse" (Mezirow, 2000, p. 12). Several theorists have discussed the ideal conditions for collegial conversations; a common theme that emerges points to the importance of deep and empathetic listening (Wiesner & Mezirow, 2000).

Professional development designers can strengthen their programs by carefully including opportunities for dialogue. A number of conditions need to be considered when creating professional learning experiences that will include effective dialogue. Drago-Severson (2009) suggests a focus on providing resources and posing questions to encourage collaborative inquiry. Providing adult learners with data to analyze can scaffold effective dialogue (Boudett, City, & Murnane, 2005). It is also important to provide participants with the tools and protocols to facilitate collaborative dialogue (McTighe, 2008; Wiggins & McTighe, 2007). Finally, designers must also consider the composition of the participants, perhaps even assigning roles to facilitate dialogue activities (York-Barr et al., 2006).

Although professional development programs can be designed and delivered in a manner that honors experience, encourages reflection, and facilitates dialogue, all of those factors must be carefully framed with the specific context of the learning audience in mind. Adult learning does not take place in a vacuum; it is important to remember that the role of learner is but one of the roles and responsibilities juggled by adult participants in professional development programs. The social context in which adults work and live sets the stage for learning; this context can support, shape, or challenge the intended learning activities (Merriam et al., 2007).

The learning experience, reflective activities, and collaborative dialogues embedded in any given professional development program will take place within a particular local context. To complicate matters, each learner's context includes "the social relations and political cultural dimensions of the community...the nature of the task...the vocabulary and cultural beliefs through which the individual makes meaning of the whole situation, and the historical, temporal, and spatial location of the situation" (Fenwick, 2003, p. 79). And so, ideally, professional development programs should be designed to consider the unique context of each group—from the time of day to the physical room arrangements and, most important, to the local culture. Not unlike younger students, adults possess a variety of learning styles and a wide range of comfort levels when it comes to learning; these points should be carefully considered in the design and delivery of professional development programs. In addition, adult learners need to feel safe and respected as they participate in professional development experiences (Mezirow, 2009).

Engaging activities are an essential component if we are aiming at learning for transfer and application; however, cooperative environments supported with modeling and coaching may be more effective than a competitive model. Whole-group, small-group, and short presentations can be interspersed with the introduction of new concepts, vocabulary, and resources (Mezirow, 2009). Reflection-in-action on the part of the program presenters is another essential contextual factor. As Schön (1987) notes, reflection-in-action allows us to reshape "what we are doing while we are doing it" (p. 26). Gathering feedback from participants at various intervals throughout the program provides data to help the presenter adapt and adjust activities to better meet the needs of the audience (Merriam et al., 2007.)

Drago-Severson (2004, 2009) emphasizes that adult learners construct experiences as they move along a developmental continuum. Professional development designers need to recognize the need for a "good developmental match" (2009, p. 282) between the program activities and the capacities of the participants. Designers need to avoid the trap of designing programs from their own perspective; rather, the goal should be to understand and respect the experiences, capacities, feelings, and context of program participants.

CONCLUSION

The body of research related to adult learning provides a wealth of information to guide the development of effective professional development programs. Careful consideration of the purposes, the recurring themes, the ways of knowing, and the process of change can maximize the results of professional development efforts. Those who design and deliver programs aimed at either informational or transformational learning need to consider the unique perspectives and contexts of the participants. In addition, designers should be cautioned against anticipating how they personally are invested in the topic at hand and instead focus on understanding and honoring each participant's point of view and behavior patterns.

Kegan (2000) compares the journey of a lifelong learner to the traversing of a series of increasingly more elaborate bridges. His analogy suggests that professional development designers need to carefully assess the location of their adult learners on such a series of bridges. First, establish just which "bridge" the learners are currently traversing. Next, assess just how far along the learners are on that particular bridge and whether that bridge is well anchored on either side. Understanding who adult learners are and where they are in their journey as lifelong learners will enable those who design and deliver professional development programs to gradually move them to the far side of the bridge and continue their journey (Kegan, 2000).

QUESTIONS FOR DISCUSSION

For Teachers

1. In what ways does Mezirow's process (i.e., expanded awareness of experience, critical reflection, validating discourse, and reflective action) for learning transformation help you as an adult learner? Can you recall specific times at which this process has enhanced your learning?

2. In what ways have you assumed personal responsibility for your professional learning?

For Administrators

1. When you consider informational and transformational learning, in what ways are you promoting teachers' professional learning?

2. What are two or three practices that might be useful in countering resistance to change while still creating a sense of urgency in teachers' work?

For Policymakers

1. In what ways can you incorporate the tenets of adult learning theory into the policies that you design?

REFERENCES

Alfred, M. (2000). Philosophical foundations of andragogy and self-directed learning: A critical analysis from an Africentric feminist perspective. In M. Glowacki-Dudka (Ed,), *Proceedings of the 19th Annual Midwest Research to Practice Conference in Adult, Continuing, and Community Education* (pp. 21–26). Madison: University of Wisconsin.

Bolman, L., & Deal, T. (2003). *Reframing organizations: Artistry, choice, and leadership.* San Francisco: Jossey-Bass.

Boud, D., & Walker, D. (1991). *Experience and learning: Reflection at work.* Geelong, Victoria, Australia: Deakin University Press.

Boudett, K., City, E., & Murnane, R. (Eds.). (2005). *Data wise: A step-by-step guide to using assessment data results to improve teaching and learning.* Cambridge, MA: Harvard Education Press.

Boyd, R. (1991). *Personal transformations in small groups: A Jungian perspective.* New York: Routledge.

Brookfield, S. (1986). *Understanding and facilitating adult learning.* San Francisco: Jossey-Bass.

Brookfield, S. (1987). *Developing critical thinkers.* San Francisco: Jossey-Bass.

Brookfield, S. (2000). Transformative learning as ideology critique. In J. Mezirow & Associates (Eds.), *Learning as transformation: Critical perspectives on a theory in progress* (pp. 125–148). San Francisco: Jossey-Bass.

Clark, M., & Wilson, A. (1991). Context and rationality in Mezirow's theory of transformational learning. *Adult Education Quarterly, 41*(2), 75–91.

Cochran-Smith, M. (2006). The future of teacher education: Ten promising trends (and three big worries). *Educational Leadership, 63*(6), 20–25.

Cranton, P. (2002). Teaching for transformation. In J. M. Ross-Gordon (Ed.), *Contemporary viewpoints on teaching adults effectively* (pp. 111–117). New York: Palgrave Macmillan.

Criticos, C. (1993). Experiential learning and social transformation for a post-apartheid learning future. In D. Boud, R. Cohen, & D. Walker (Eds.), *Using experience for learning* (pp. 157–168). Buckingham, UK, and Bristol, PA: Society for Research into Higher Education and Open University Press.

Curry, M. (2008). Critical friends groups: The possibilities and limitations embedded in teacher professional communities aimed at instructional improvement and school reform. *Teachers College Record, 110*(4), 773–774.

Daloz, L. (1999). *Mentor: Guiding the journey of adult learners* (2nd ed.). San Francisco: Jossey-Bass.

Darling-Hammond, L. (2003). Enhancing teaching. In W. Owens & L. S. Kaplan (Eds.), *Best practices, best thinking, and emerging issues in leadership* (pp. 75–78). Thousand Oaks, CA: Corwin Press.

Dewey, J. (1938). *Experience and education.* New York: Collier Books.

Dirkx, J. (1998). Transformative learning theory in the practice of adult education: An overview. *PAACE Journal of Lifelong Learning, 7*, 1–14.

Drago-Severson, E. (2004). *Helping teachers learn: Principal leadership for adult growth and development.* Thousand Oaks, CA: Corwin Press.

Drago-Severson, E. (2009). *Leading adult learning: Supporting adult development in our schools.* Thousand Oaks, CA: Corwin Press.

Elmore, R. (2000). *Building a new structure for school leadership.* Washington, DC: Albert Shanker Institute.

Feinstein, B. (2004). Learning and transformation in the context of Hawaiian ecological knowledge. *Adult Education Quarterly, 11*(1), 57–70.

Fenwick, T. (2001). *Experiential learning: A theoretical critique from five perspectives* (Information Series No. 385). Columbus: Ohio State University, College of Education, ERIC Clearinghouse on Adult, Career, and Vocational Education, Center on Education and Training for Employment.

Fenwick, T. (2003). *Learning through experience: Troubling orthodoxies and intersecting questions.* Malabar, FL: Krieger.

Freire, P. (2000). *Pedagogy of the oppressed* (20th anniversary ed.). New York: Continuum.

Fullan, M. (2005). *Leadership and sustainability: Systems thinkers in action.* Thousand Oaks, CA, and Toronto, Canada: Corwin Press and the Ontario Principal's Council.

Grace, A. (1996). Taking a critical pose: Andragogy-missing links, missing values. *International Journal of Lifelong Education, 15*(5), 382–392.

Hammond, M., & Collins, R. (1991). *Self-directed learning: Critical practice.* London: Nichols/GP.

Henderson, J. (2002). Transformative learning in the executive suite: CEOs and the role of context in Mezirow's theory. *Dissertation Abstracts International, 62*(12), 4026A. (UMI No. 3037842)

Illeris, K. (2002). *Three dimensions of learning.* Roskilde, Denmark, and Leicester, UK: Roskilde University Press and National Institute of Adult Continuing Education.

Jarvis, P. (1987). *Adult learning in the social context.* London: Croom Helm.

Jarvis, P. (2001). *Learning in later life: An introduction for educators and carers.* London: Kogan Page.

Johnson-Bailey, J., & Alfred, M. (2006). Transformational teaching and the practice of black women adult educators. In E. W. Taylor (Ed.), *Fostering transformative learning in the classroom: Challenges and innovations* (pp. 49–58). San Francisco: Jossey-Bass.

Kappel, P., & Daley, B. (2004). Transformative learning and the urban context. In L. G. Martin & E. E. Rogers (Eds.), *Adult education in the urban context: Problems, practices, and programming for inner city communities* (pp. 69–81). San Francisco: Jossey-Bass.

Kegan, R. (1982). *The evolving self.* Cambridge, MA: Harvard University Press.

Kegan, R. (1994). *In over our heads.* Cambridge, MA: Harvard University Press.

Kegan, R. (2000). What "form" transforms? A constructive-developmental approach to transformative learning. In J. Mezirow & Associates (Eds.), *Learning as transformation: Critical perspectives on a theory in progress* (pp. 35–69). San Francisco: Jossey-Bass.

Killon, J. (2000, December/January). Exemplary schools model quality staff development. *Results,* p. 3.

Knowles, M. (1968). Andragogy, not pedagogy. *Adult Leadership, 16*(10), 350–352, 386.

Knowles, M. (1980). *The modern practice of adult education: From pedagogy to andragogy* (2nd ed.). New York: Cambridge Books.

Knowles, M., & Associates. (1984). *Andragogy in action: Applying modern principles of adult learning.* San Francisco: Jossey-Bass.

Kolb, D. (1984). *Experiential learning: Experience as the source of learning and development.* Englewood Cliffs, NJ: Prentice Hall.

Kotter, J. (1996). *Leading change.* Boston: Harvard Business School Press.

Kotter, J. (2008). *A sense of urgency.* Boston: Harvard Business School Press.

Kotter, J., & Rathgeber, H. (2005). *Our iceberg is melting.* New York: St. Martin's Press.

Learning Forward. (2011). *Standards for professional learning.* Oxford, OH: Author.

Lee, M. (2003). Andragogy and foreign-born learnings. In L. M. Baumgartner, M. Lee, S. Birden, & D. Flowers (Eds.), *Adult learning theory: A primer* (pp. 11–16). Columbus: Ohio State University, College of Education, Center on Education and Training for Employment.

Lindeman, E. (1961). *The meaning of adult education in the United States.* New York: Harvest House.

McCluskey, H. (1970). An approach to a differential psychology of the adult potential. In S. M. Grabowski (Ed.), *Adult learning and instruction* (pp. 80–95). Syracuse, NY: ERIC Clearinghouse on Adult Education.

McTighe, J. (2008). Making the most of professional learning communities. *Learning Principal, 3*(8), 1, 4–7.

Merriam, S., Caffarella, R., & Baumgartner, L. (2007). *Learning in adulthood: A comprehensive guide* (3rd ed.). San Francisco: Wiley.

Mezirow, J. (1978a). *Education for perspective transformation: Women re-entry programs in community college.* New York: Columbia University, Teachers College, Center for Adult Education.

Mezirow, J. (1978b). Perspective transformation. *Adult Education Quarterly, 28,* 100–110.

Mezirow, J. (1981). A critical theory of adult learning and education. *Adult Education, 32*(1), 3–27.

Mezirow, J. (1985). A critical theory of self-directed learning. In S. Brookfield (Ed.), *Self-directed learning: From theory to practice* (pp. 17–30). San Francisco: Jossey-Bass.

Mezirow. J. (1995). Transformation theory of adult learning. In M. Weldon (Ed.), *In defense of the lifeworld* (pp. 39–70). New York: State University of New York Press.

Mezirow, J. (1996). Contemporary paradigms of learning. *Adult Education Quarterly, 46*(3), 158–172.

Mezirow, J. (2000). Learning to think like an adult: Core concepts of transformation theory. In J. Mezirow & Associates (Eds.), *Learning as transformation: Critical perspectives on a theory in progress* (pp. 3–33). San Francisco: Jossey-Bass.

Mezirow, J. (2009). Transformative learning theory. In J. Mezirow, E. W. Taylor, & Associates (Eds.), *Transforming learning in practice: Insights from community, workplace, and higher education* (pp. 18–31). San Francisco: Jossey-Bass.

Osterman, K., & Kottkamp, R. (2004). *Reflective practice for educators: Professional development to improve student learning* (2nd ed.). Thousand Oaks, CA: Corwin Press.

Reeves, D. (2009). *Leading change in your school: How to conquer myths, build commitment, and get results.* Alexandria, VA: ASCD.

Rodgers, C. R. (2002). Seeing student learning: Teacher change and the role of reflection. *Harvard Educational Review, 72*(2), 230–253.

Sandlin, J. (2005). Andragogy and its discontents: An analysis of andragogy from three critical perspectives. *PAACE Journal of Lifelong Learning, 14,* 25–42.

Schön, D. (1987). *Educating the reflective practitioner.* New York: Basic Books.

Senge, P. M. (1990). *The fifth discipline: The art and practice of the learning organization.* New York: Currency Doubleday.

Sheared, V. (1994). Giving voice: An inclusive model of instruction: A womanist perspective. In E. Hayes & S. A. J. Collin III (Eds.), *Confronting racism and sexism in adult education* (pp. 27–37). San Francisco: Jossey-Bass.

Sirkin, H., Keenan, P., & Jackson, A. (2011). The hard side of change management. In *Harvard Business Review's 10 must reads on change management* (pp. 155–197). Boston: Harvard Business School Press.

Spelman, M. (2006). From policy to practice: A case study of initial certification reforms in schools of education. *Dissertation Abstracts International, 67*(02). (UMI No. 3202747)

Spelman, M. (2007). From policy to practice: A case study of initial certification reforms in three private university schools of education. *Journal of Ethnographic and Qualitative Research, 2*(1), 61–69.

Taylor, E. (2000). Analyzing research on transformative learning theory. In J. Mezirow & Associates (Eds.), *Learning as transformation: Critical perspectives on a theory in progress* (pp. 285–328). San Francisco: Jossey-Bass.

Tennant, M. (1991). The psychology of adult teaching and learning. In J. M. Peters, P. Jarvis, & Associates (Eds.), *Adult education: Evolution and achievements in a developing field of study* (pp. 191–216). San Francisco: Jossey-Bass.

Tisdell, E. (2003). *Exploring spirituality and culture in adult and higher education.* San Francisco: Jossey-Bass.

Wiesner, C., & Mezirow, J. (2000). Theory building and the search for common ground. In J. Mezirow & Associates (Eds.), *Learning as transformation: Critical perspectives on a theory in progress* (pp. 329–363). San Francisco: Jossey-Bass.

Wiggins, G., & McTighe, J. (2007). *Schooling by design.* Alexandria, VA: ASCD.

York-Barr, J., Sommers, W. A., Ghere, G. S., & Montie, J. (2006). *Reflective practice to improve schools* (2nd ed.). Thousand Oaks, CA: Corwin Press.

CHAPTER 13

Focusing Attention on Beliefs about Capability and Knowledge in Teachers' Professional Development

MEGAN TSCHANNEN-MORAN
JASON A. CHEN

- Efforts to support the ongoing professional learning of teachers will be hampered if we fail to attend to their efficacy beliefs because these beliefs drive their motivation to implement new instructional strategies.
- Teachers who are not confident in their capabilities are more likely to perceive innovations as a threat and to give up in the face of difficulties, even if they actually possess the necessary skills and knowledge to successfully instruct their students.
- Adopting a growth mindset regarding student capability, as well as one's own capability to teach, will foster greater motivation and persistence than a notion of capability as fixed.
- Attending to the sources of efficacy beliefs when planning professional development experiences will likely result not only in improved instruction but also in teachers who expend greater effort and persistence through even the most challenging circumstances.

Many efforts to improve students' learning outcomes over the past two decades have focused on improving the quality of teachers' instruction. As the stakes get higher for students to pass state and national tests of basic competence, teachers are increasingly seen as the primary facilitators of student success. With the onus of student success being placed squarely on teachers' shoulders, many policymakers and educators at the local, state, and national levels are therefore looking to high-quality professional development opportunities to equip teachers to improve their instructional practices in order to reform education (Corcoran, Shields, & Zucker, 1998). Although there are numerous studies exploring the content of effective professional development opportunities for teachers, we claim that efforts to support the ongoing professional learning of teachers will be hampered if we fail to attend to the cultivation of teachers' self-efficacy, as well as their collective efficacy, for successfully implementing high-quality instruction. Teachers' beliefs about the extent to which they can influence how well and how much students learn drive their motivation to put forth the effort required to implement new instructional strategies (Tschannen-Moran, Hoy, & Hoy, 1998). In this chapter, we outline social cognitive theory, which forms the framework upon which we base our claims. We explore the role of teachers' self-efficacy and collective efficacy beliefs, as well as their epistemological beliefs concerning student capabilities. We next present a model of teacher conceptual change that incorporates self-efficacy beliefs and explores the implications of this theory for supporting the ongoing professional learning of teachers. We provide recommendations for teachers, school administrators, and policymakers and end with future directions for research into teachers' professional learning.

BANDURA'S SOCIAL COGNITIVE THEORY

Social cognitive theory (SCT) is rooted in a view of human agency in which individuals are seen as proactively engaged in their own development. As Bandura (1997) argued, people are "partial architects of their own destinies" (p. 8). Bandura (1986) argued that agency operates via three modes of influence. First, when people's own influence is brought to bear on their surroundings, they are exercising their *individual agency*. People can also attain outcomes through *proxy agency*, whereby another person secures desired outcomes for an individual. Finally, because people do not live their lives in isolation, Bandura argued that people work together on common goals to improve their lot in life. In this sense, people exercise their *collective agency*.

Standing at the core of SCT are the efficacy beliefs of individuals, which can be defined as the beliefs that people possess about how capable they are as individuals or as teams in performing or learning to perform courses of action at particular levels of proficiency (Bandura, 1997). Bandura posited that these beliefs touch virtually every aspect of people's lives: whether they think productively or in a self-debilitating fashion, the choices they make, the extent to which they persist in the face of adversity, and how vulnerable they are to stress and depression. As a consequence, teachers who are not confident in their own or their team's capability to prepare and deliver instruction for their students are more likely to give up in the face of difficulties, even if they actually possess the necessary skills and knowledge to successfully instruct a particular group of students.

Teacher Self-Efficacy Beliefs

Over the past four decades, researchers have repeatedly found that the sense of efficacy of teachers is related to their motivation, to the level of challenge in the goals to which they aspire, and to the effort they invest in pursuit of those goals (Klassen, Tze, Betts, & Gordon, 2011; Tschannen-Moran et al., 1998). These, in turn, affect their instructional practices and their behavior in the classroom. Teachers with higher self-efficacy exhibit greater levels of planning, organization, and persistence in assisting struggling learners (Allinder, 1994; Ashton & Webb, 1986; Gibson & Dembo, 1984). Those with strong self-efficacy have been found to be more open to new ideas and more willing to experiment with new methods to better meet the needs of their students (Berman, McLaughlin, Bass, Pauly, & Zellman, 1977; Guskey, 1988; Stein & Wang, 1988). Teacher self-efficacy has been tied to the implementation of new instructional strategies, especially when the introduction of these strategies has been followed by work with an experienced coach or the provision of peer-coaching arrangements (Bruce & Ross, 2008; Tschannen-Moran & McMaster, 2009). Teachers' self-efficacy beliefs also have been found to be related to important student outcomes. What teachers believe about their own capabilities is related to their sense of self-efficacy and to their motivation of students (Midgley, Feldlaufer, & Eccles, 1989) and predicts student achievement outcomes (Anderson, Greene, & Loewen, 1988; Ashton & Webb, 1986; Moore & Esselman, 1992; Pajares, 1996; Ross, 1992). Efficacy beliefs are, therefore, central to student learning.

Teacher self-efficacy is context-specific; thus a teacher's sense of efficacy is not necessarily uniform across the different types of professional tasks that they perform, nor is it uniform across different subject matter (Bandura, 1997). Teachers who are self-efficacious in one context may feel inefficacious in another. In fact, teachers may report different levels of self-efficacy for the different courses and student groups they encounter during the course of a school day (Ross, Cousins, & Gadalla, 1996).

Collective Efficacy Beliefs

Reform efforts in schools have focused intensely on the individual teacher as the unit of analysis. For example, value-added modeling aims to improve factors of individual teachers, such as their amount of experience, subject knowledge, and pedagogical knowledge. However, focusing on the individual teacher may not be the best way to improve the educational outcomes of students. In addition to targeting individual teacher factors, educational reformers would do well to focus on teachers' collective resources that reside in the relationships between the staff and personnel of a school. In exploring why students at one school do better than students at other schools, policymakers may note that some schools have teachers with more advanced degrees and more years of experience than do teachers in other schools. But if the focus shifts to a collective level of analysis, the collective ability of a school staff to work together and the collective belief of a school staff that they are able to effectively teach students and effect change are found to be potent factors separating the outcomes of one school from those of another, even when the socio-economic status of students is held constant (Goddard, 2001; Goddard, Hoy, & Hoy, 2000; Goddard, Tschannen-Moran, & Hoy, 2001; Tschannen-Moran & Barr, 2004).

Collective efficacy is a group belief that relates to group performance. Teachers' collective efficacy, which means the beliefs of teachers within a school that the faculty as a whole can enact the necessary steps to produce positive student outcomes, plays an important role in whether or not teachers successfully adopt and implement instructional approaches derived from professional development opportunities. Collective efficacy beliefs may refer to the beliefs of an entire faculty or to smaller subcultures within the whole, such as departments or grade-level teams. As Bandura (1997) noted, "teachers operate collectively within an interactive social system rather than as isolates. Therefore, educational development through efficacy enhancement must address the social and organizational structure of educational systems" (p. 243). Collective efficacy may have a socialization effect shaped by the attitudes of other teachers about the task of teaching, the availability of resources, the challenges posed by the environment, and the prospects for student success (Goddard & Goddard, 2001). A teacher who is highly self-efficacious about implementing high-quality instructional practices will be severely hampered if she believes that her colleagues and administrators are ineffective and unable to provide the resources to aid in this endeavor. Individual teacher self-efficacy, teacher collective efficacy, and teacher goals are three factors that have been found to be related such that a change in one dimension affects the others (Kurz & Knight, 2004). Beliefs of competence, both at the individual and collective levels, have implications within the context of designing professional learning opportunities for teachers such that improvement efforts are actually implemented and result in lasting change. These implications are explored next.

PROFESSIONAL DEVELOPMENT

Given the powerful role of teachers' self-efficacy and collective efficacy beliefs, those charged with supporting the professional learning of teachers would do well to attend to these beliefs as they plan and structure professional development activities for teachers. In his model of teacher change, Guskey (1986) hypothesized that the majority of instructional improvement programs fail because they do not take into account what motivates teachers to engage in professional development and the process by which change in teachers typically takes place. Researchers examining teacher attitudes toward the implementation of new instructional practices have frequently found teachers' self-efficacy to be among the most powerful influences on receptivity to change (Guskey, 1988; Poole & Okeafor, 1989; Smylie, 1988). Scribner (1999) observed that teachers' levels of efficacy influenced their responses to professional development. He found that teachers with high self-efficacy were "opportunistic in their approach to professional learning and they sought knowledge through their involvement in activities that often were not overtly professional development opportunities" (p. 220). Conversely, teachers with a low sense of efficacy were unable or unwilling to engage in many reforms because of a "perceived disconnection between the purposes of the efforts and their own needs as professionals" (p. 221). Similarly, when McKinney, Sexton, and Meyerson (1999) used an efficacy-based change model with inservice teachers introduced to whole-language teaching strategies, they found that as these teachers moved through the three stages of initiation, implementation, and refinement, a relationship between their self-efficacy and the concerns they expressed was observed. Teachers with lower self-efficacy beliefs expressed concerns characteristic of those in an early stage of change, focusing on the impact it would have on them. Those teachers with higher self-efficacy turned their attention to how new strategies might affect their students and schools and how they might work to refine their practices and relationships to better fit within their respective contexts—concerns that are typical of later stages of change. Participants with the highest self-efficacy tended to view innovations as both important and possible.

There seems to be a complex interplay between teachers' self-efficacy beliefs and their knowledge and skills to implement new instructional strategies. In a study of the conditions required to achieve change in instructional practices in reading, Timperley and Phillips (2003) found generally low expectations and low levels of self-efficacy among the teachers of students from disadvantaged backgrounds. After participating in the intervention, in which they learned new and more powerful literacy teaching strategies and witnessed improved student outcomes as a result, teacher self-efficacy beliefs increased significantly. The teachers' expectations of both themselves and their students increased irrespective of student backgrounds. Timperley and Phillips (2003) found that change involved changes not only in teachers' beliefs about their capabilities but also in their conceptions of the nature of reading and how to teach it. When teachers implemented the new methods and witnessed unanticipated changes in their students' achievement, their self-efficacy beliefs were enhanced. Timperley and Phillips proposed that "the change process is likely to be an iterative rather than a sequential one, where changes in beliefs, actions or outcomes are both shaped by, and built on, each other" (p. 630). The findings of the interplay of new knowledge, changes in students' achievement, and teachers' self-efficacy led Timperley and Phillips to assert that teacher professional development needs to address teachers' beliefs, as well as the improvement in their practices. Similarly, Stein and Wang (1988) sought to identify factors related to teachers' commitments to acquire and consistently use the knowledge and skills necessary for the successful implementation of a new model of reading instruction. They found a "pattern consisting of improvement in teachers' actual expertise in program implementation, followed by increases in their perceptions of self-efficacy for implementing the program" (p. 181).

The cultivation of efficacy beliefs among teachers has not been found to be a straightforward process of incremental gains as teachers move through the change process. As teachers apply new learning, they may experience an "implementation dip" in efficacy beliefs as they begin to implement a change initiative (Hoy & Burke-Spero, 2005; Ross, 1994; Stein & Wang, 1988). These efficacy beliefs tend to rebound for teachers who are able to successfully implement the new instructional practices. In a quasi-experimental study, Tschannen-Moran and McMaster (2009) tested four professional development formats, presenting the same teaching strategy for beginning readers structured to provide increasing levels of efficacy-relevant input. Results indicated that the professional development format that supported mastery experiences through follow-up coaching had the strongest effect on self-efficacy beliefs for reading instruction, as well as for implementation of the new strategy. A substantial proportion of the teachers who participated in formats that included a demonstration with local students and a planning and practice session but no follow-up coaching experienced a decrease in their self-efficacy for reading instruction. This unexpected finding makes clear that professional development activities that are poorly structured and do not provide teachers with the resources needed to effectively implement the innovation can do real harm in terms of teacher motivation.

Follow-up coaching has been found to be a potent factor in supporting teachers' self-efficacy as reforms are introduced. In examining the effect of various components of professional development models, Joyce and Showers (1988) found a jump in effect sizes when practice feedback was added to information, theory, and demonstration components within professional development programs. There was a further increase in effect size when coaching to support the implementation was added. Professional development programs that aim to support teachers' ongoing utilization of new knowledge of effective practice need to develop a delivery system that includes the provision of continued support and follow-up coaching after initial training (Guskey, 1989; Stein & Wang, 1988).

Increased teacher self-efficacy, as well as willingness to innovate and collaborate with others, are causes as well as outcomes of witnessing improvements in student achievement in response to a reform initiative (Guskey, 1988, 1989). An intervention designed specifically to address teachers' self-efficacy beliefs as they encountered new instructional processes was found to raise teachers' self-efficacy and their implementation of problem-based instructional practices in science (Haney, Wang, Keil, & Zoffel, 2007). In addition, such interventions have been found to raise the self-efficacy for classroom management among mathematics teachers when compared with a control group (Ross & Bruce, 2007). The role of teachers' self-efficacy beliefs in the process of teachers' conceptual change when confronted with reform initiatives is a topic we turn to next.

THE COGNITIVE–AFFECTIVE MODEL OF CONCEPTUAL CHANGE

Understanding what it takes to change teachers' minds with regard to their teaching practice is essential for those who hope to change teachers' behaviors in their classrooms. Gregoire (2003) has proposed a model of teacher conceptual change, the cognitive–affective model of conceptual change (CAMCC), which explores how teachers process new information concerning their professional practice. When presented with an instructional reform initiative, this model proposes that teachers'

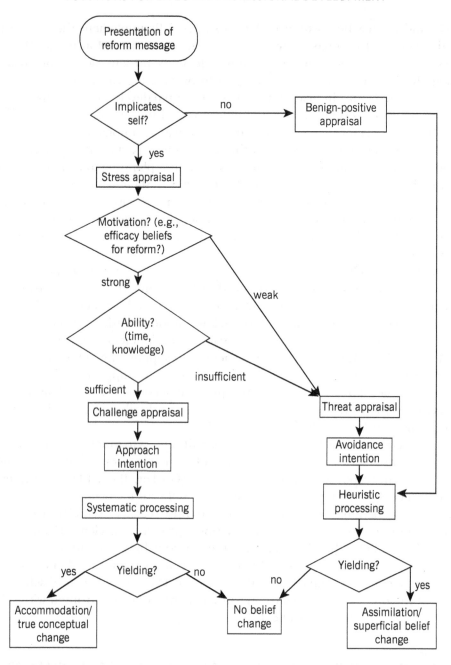

FIGURE 13.1. The cognitive–affective model of conceptual change. From Gregoire (2003). Copyright 2003 by Plenum Publishing Corporation. Reprinted with permission.

reactions and, consequently, their level of conceptual change will be influenced by whether they appraise the initiative as a threat or a challenge (see Figure 13.1). This model explicates the mechanisms through which teachers' self-efficacy mediates their responses to instructional change.

According to the model, teachers who are presented with a reform initiative begin by assessing whether or not they are implicated in the reform. Teachers who believe that they are already implementing the reform practices (whether they are, in fact, doing so with fidelity or not), or who believe that the practices are not relevant to them, will assess the changes being proposed as not applying to them and will respond to the reform messages with a "benign-positive appraisal." Such teachers will consequently process the new content heuristically, which is to say, through an already "taken-for-granted" set of beliefs and assumptions. They will then decide whether or not to yield to the reform, but even if they do, the level of belief change will be superficial.

Teachers who, on the other hand, do feel implicated by the reforms presented will experience stress and discomfort; they must then decide how to respond to that stress appraisal by determining their level of motivation to change. Those with low self-efficacy are predicted to have a weak motivation to change and thus to respond to the reform initiative as a threat. This will likely lead to an avoidance intention, which in turn produces heuristic processing and superficial belief change, if there is any belief change at all. Conversely, teachers with high self-efficacy are predicted to have a strong motivation to engage with the ideas presented in a deeper way. They will assess whether they perceive that they have the resources, time, and support necessary to engage deeply with the proposed changes. If they determine that they do, they would likely interpret the reform as a challenge and consequently engage in more systematic (and thus effortful) processing of the information presented. After this more in-depth processing, teachers would consider whether they had the resources available to be successful. Thus they would still come to a decision point as to whether to yield to the reform initiative. If teachers reject the reform message, they would choose not to yield, and there would be no belief change. If teachers are persuaded of the value of the challenging reform initiative, however, they would accommodate their prior beliefs, resulting in true conceptual change and likely robust changes in instructional practice.

One aspect of the CAMCC that is particularly relevant for the collective efficacy of a school in attaining desired outcomes involves the "meaning systems" that teachers and administrators of a school possess, which include a school staff's conceptions of ability (Dweck & Leggett, 1988). In particular, teachers who believe that their students' abilities are augmentable (i.e., "my students can become smarter if I motivate them to put forth more effort") are said to hold a *growth mindset* toward their students' abilities. On the other hand, teachers who believe that, no matter what, their students' abilities are static (i.e., "my students' level of achievement is basically determined by their ability") possess a *fixed mindset* about their students' abilities. Therefore, teachers and administrators who believe that their students' abilities can grow, regardless of the disadvantages and obstacles they face, are more likely to promote a positive sense of collective efficacy. In contrast, teachers and administrators who possess a fixed mindset about students' abilities are likely to undermine a school's sense of collective efficacy (Bandura, 1997).

In bringing this meaning system to the individual level, Gregoire (2003) posited that "teachers' epistemic beliefs may be a type of ability factor that can promote or constrain the process of conceptual change" (p. 172). These epistemic beliefs are defined as teachers' beliefs about the nature of knowledge and the process of knowing. Although epistemic beliefs are not traditionally labeled as "ability beliefs," some researchers have included conceptions of ability in their definition of epistemic beliefs (see Hofer & Pintrich, 1997). Chen (2012), however, has shown that epistemic beliefs and conceptions of ability, although they are likely different constructs (conceptions of ability reflect an ability belief and epistemic beliefs reflect a belief about what knowledge is and how one attains it), both may be considered *meaning systems* that substantively color the way we interpret information. Conceptions of ability, therefore, may play an important role not only in creating the collective efficacy of a school but also in setting the stage for an individual teacher's sense of efficacy.

For teachers who process the reform initiative in a superficial way, either because they do not feel implicated in the reform or because they perceive it as a threat, there will be no substantial conceptual change, and consequently there is not likely to be any lasting behavior change. And unless there is behavior change on the part of teachers, student outcomes are likely to remain unchanged. Only when teachers engage in systematic processing of the reform strategy and conclude that it has value will true conceptual change of the sort that leads to behavior change in instructional practices come about. Then, and only then, will the investment of resources in professional development efforts aimed at improving student outcomes as a result of improved instructional practices pay the intended dividends.

RECOMMENDATIONS FOR PRACTICE

If beliefs about capability, both at the individual and collective levels, are so powerfully related to teachers' reactions to the reform messages presented to them and to their motivation to engage in professional learning and adaptive practices, then it is important to understand the mechanisms by which these beliefs are developed and sustained over time. Because fostering a belief in one's own capacity, as well as the capacity of the collective unit of which one is a part, has been shown to be so important to teachers' motivation and persistence, attention should be paid to how these beliefs might be augmented. Fortunately, the tenets of Bandura's SCT (1997) outline helpful ways in which teachers can develop their sense of efficacy for adapting to new instructional and pedagogical approaches. Bandura has pointed to four sources of self-efficacy, and, by analogy, we can infer some sources of collective efficacy as well. In addition, it is useful to pay attention to teacher beliefs about the nature of ability in oneself and in one's students in creating more effective learning environments.

Beliefs about the Incremental Nature of Ability

Although educators may not openly admit it, many may indeed believe that, regardless of what they do in their positions, students will continue to achieve at whatever level they are currently achieving. This belief in the fixedness of students' capacities to achieve or improve through schooling can be a substantive roadblock to the effectiveness of the professional development experience. On a related note, some educators may espouse a firm belief that, regardless of any type of training they receive, their capacities to serve and educate students simply cannot be augmented. This belief in the fixedness of one's own capacities to educate or serve students appropriately can also thwart the effectiveness of a professional development experience.

Given the potential detrimental effect that holding a fixed worldview has on individual and collective change, professional development instructors would do well to encourage a more incremental view of capacity. Because the type of leadership that is provided within schools appears to have a substantial impact on the climate that schools develop, these institutional mindsets, or meaning systems, are particularly susceptible to change through school administrative leadership (Bandura, 1997). Principals who create a school climate focused on academic achievement therefore promote a growth mindset with respect to both teachers and students. Those who serve as strong advocates for teachers' instructional efforts are more likely to have a growth mindset regarding students, to positively influence the school's collective efficacy, and, in turn, to elevate student achievement (Bandura, 1997; Goddard, 2001). Schunk (1987) suggested that one way to demonstrate the expanding capacities of individuals is to document the improvements that people make in their capabilities. Keeping track of short-term goals, such as being able to successfully implement one or two new inquiry-oriented laboratory projects per month that result in student learning, could, for example, aid teachers to see the growth of their capacity to change their pedagogical approaches.

Change seldom occurs, of course, without running into significant barriers. Teachers do not decide to significantly change their pedagogical approaches one day and succeed on their first attempt. However, as Dweck and Leggett (1988) argued, individuals benefit when receiving "process" rather than "product" feedback. This means that it is beneficial for professional development instructors and those who support teachers in a change process to discuss the strategies being implemented, as well as the modifications to those strategies that they may want to experiment with to achieve desired results. As Bandura (1997) asserted:

> People often forsake realizable challenges because they believe they require extraordinary aptitude. People see the extraordinary feats of others but not the unwavering commitment and countless hours of perseverant effort that produced them. Such partial information generally leads people to overestimate inherited endowments and underestimate self-regulatory factors in human accomplishments. (p. 119)

Understanding the mechanisms through which others have achieved success can bolster one's own sense of capability to achieve similar successes. Bolstering self-efficacy and collective efficacy through attention to the four sources are also likely to yield stronger effort and persistence as teachers enact change initiatives.

Verbal Persuasion

One way that people sustain and develop efficacy beliefs occurs as the result of verbal persuasion, or the verbal assessments that others provide. Effective persuaders cultivate other people's beliefs in their own capabilities while simultaneously ensuring that the success they envision is attainable. Although positive verbal messages may encourage and empower people, negative messages can defeat and weaken efficacy beliefs. In fact, it is usually easier to weaken a sense of efficacy through criticism than to strengthen such beliefs through encouragement. Nevertheless, when the teachers and administrators of a school are convinced that they can effect both significant and meaningful change, their conviction, when verbalized, enhances the sense of efficacy of individuals, as well as of the school as a whole.

Persuasive verbal messages may be limited in their power to create enduring increases in self-efficacy, but they can bolster it significantly if the positive appraisal leads to greater effort in the development of skills that subsequently leads to more success. These messages can become self-fulfilling prophecies and self-reinforcing cycles. Too often, however, teachers receive verbal messages in the form of professional development workshops that provide knowledge of new strategies, as well as persuasive claims about their usefulness, with little in the way of specific feedback regarding their implementation attempts in the field after the workshops are complete (Stein & Wang, 1988). A much more useful and meaningful form of verbal persuasion is the specific feedback or encouragement received from a coach or colleague trained to observe and reflect on practice from a strengths-based stance. Such uplifting yet reflective coaching conversations bolster skills and evoke a sense of confidence that teachers can successfully implement new teaching strategies. Verbal persuasion alone may not foster a robust sense of efficacy, but in partnership with other sources of self-efficacy and collective efficacy it may provide teachers with the encouragement necessary to expend significant effort toward realistic goals aimed at strengthening their skills.

Vicarious Experiences

Bandura (1997) argued that, when individuals have little to no experience with a task or activity, the vicarious experiences of watching others perform a task may evoke a strong sense of efficacy. The motivational impact of watching others can be enhanced when the model is perceived to be similar to the observer in salient ways. Although very little research has been conducted about what characteristics constitute relevant similarities between models and observers, some research suggests that perceived relative ability, as well as ostensible characteristics such as race/ethnicity or gender, is an important variable (Schunk, 1987).

Teachers experiencing professional development on an approach that they are not familiar with are often ambivalent about changing their current approach; thus successful vicarious experiences with implementing that approach represent a powerful source of self-efficacy for such changes. In order to show doubting teachers that such changes can in fact happen and be beneficial, professional development instructors may want to incorporate opportunities to observe proficient models among their colleagues or videos of similar teachers embarking on such changes in their instructional approaches. Schunk and his colleagues have shown that *coping models*—those who struggle through problems until they reach a successful end—are more likely to boost the confidence of observers than *mastery models*—those who ignore mistakes or act as though they never make them (e.g., Schunk, 1987; Schunk & Hanson, 1985, 1989). For example, a teacher who struggles with classroom management may benefit from watching another teacher with similar classroom management challenges who struggles initially but eventually succeeds by using key strategies. These struggling teacher observers are likely to gain much more cognitively and motivationally than if they watched an accomplished veteran effortlessly work through these same issues. Watching such videos could send the message that the ability to effectively manage a classroom is an incremental attribute (i.e., an expandable ability that can develop with effort over time) rather than a fixed one and that the use of particular strategies can produce desired results.

Because a sense of efficacy operates at both individual and collective levels, using vicarious experiences can also build an entire school's sense of efficacy. Professional development instructors who aim for a school-level change can report on other, similar schools that have succeeded in implementing such an instructional approach. In showing the similarities between the model school and the school looking to make comparable changes, professional development instructors would do well to provide as much salient detail as possible about how the two schools are similar. Information on student and teacher demographics, the history of reforms attempted in the past, and the struggles that schools are facing are salient and representative details to include. A school's collective efficacy can be bolstered, for example, if a neighboring school that is perceived to be similar in context, population, or resources is able to implement successfully particular strategies to elevate the achievement of its population of English language learners (ELLs) on state achievement tests. Handled properly, such neighboring schools can become occasions for encouragement, learning, and respect rather than for competition, discouragement, or disdain.

Mastery Experiences

The most influential source of self-efficacy, as well as collective efficacy, is the interpreted results of previous successful performances, or "mastery experiences." People engage routinely in tasks and activities, interpret the results of their actions, and use those interpretations to develop beliefs about their own and their group's capability to engage in subsequent tasks or activities; as a result, they act in concert with the beliefs created. When the outcomes of such tasks and activities are interpreted as successful, they raise a sense of efficacy; that sense is lowered when those tasks and activities are interpreted as failures. In the context of teaching, when teachers or departments witness improvement in student performances as a result of their teaching or efforts, their sense of efficacy is likely to improve. Repeated student failures, however—especially failures attributed to individuals or specific groups of people—are likely to lower the efficacy of those individuals or groups (Guskey, 1988; Ross, 1998; Tschannen-Moran et al., 1998). Professional development experiences that result in quick wins, early successes, and relevant evidence of student learning, both for individual and collective units, are examples of ways that mastery experiences can be incorporated strategically in professional development planning. Such experiences build confidence and a sense of efficacy; however, it is also important for professional development instructors and school leaders to stretch teachers beyond their comfort zones by making sure they receive ample opportunities to practice new instructional approaches that become progressively more difficult and challenging over time. Successfully "going to the next level" in any game can be rewarding and fun; so, too, when it comes to structuring professional development experiences. Celebrating and learning from success, whether at the individual, team, department, or school level, increases both motivation and capacity. Elevating the achievement of underperforming students after implementing new instructional strategies represents a special achievement that bolsters both individual and collective efficacy, whereas repeated failures in this area serve to undermine it.

An area in which it is particularly important to create conditions for early success is in the induction of novice teachers. SCT proposes that self-efficacy beliefs, once established, will be fairly stable until and unless some kind of shock (either positive or negative) causes a reassessment of one's own or one's team's capabilities (Bandura, 1997). Tschannen-Moran and Hoy (2007) found evidence for this when they discovered that contextual factors such as administrator support and the resources they had available were far more salient in the self-efficacy beliefs of novice teachers than of veteran teachers whose self-efficacy beliefs had stabilized. This finding has significant implications for school leaders as they design induction programs and make class assignments for novice teachers. If self-efficacy beliefs stabilize at a high level, the result is likely to be higher goals, stronger effort, greater persistence, and more openness to innovation throughout the length of a teacher's career. Beginning teachers who are given the toughest teaching assignments and inadequate support, however, are likely to come away from their first years of teaching with low self-efficacy. As a result they will be less motivated throughout their careers and have an increasing likelihood of leaving the field of teaching altogether.

Physiological and Affective States

Finally, people can gauge their own self-efficacy by the physiological and affective states (e.g., anxiety, stress, and arousal) that they experience as they contemplate an action. This rings true for both solo efforts and the efforts of individuals in team context, such as schools. Strong emotional reactions to a task, such as excitement or fear, provide cues about the anticipated success or failure of the outcome. Therefore, when teachers experience positive energy and emotions toward a task, they have a higher and more robust sense of efficacy for that task. Teachers' passion for their subject matter or even for their students as people, although not studied as boosters of self-efficacy, may do just that. Positive emotional states generate more positive emotional states, which can, in turn, bolster a group's sense of collective efficacy for learning and success. The reverse is also true. A school in which morale is low or with a climate that conveys a "negative vibe" can have a detrimental effect on the school's academic outcomes. Other common feelings among teachers that work against success are "initiative fatigue" and a feeling of being overwhelmed at the sheer number of reform initiatives being implemented simultaneously. These feelings are compounded when teachers find they do not have the resources they need, either of time, materials or wherewithal, to implement all the new initiatives successfully. Recognizing the importance of teachers' affective responses to professional development initiatives should encourage professional developers to pay attention to and to facilitate positive feelings when implementing new instructional approaches. Using frequent strengths-based formative assessments of teacher practices within a safe and trusting environment may be a useful and informative tool in this regard, thereby reducing anxiety and facilitating growth as teachers implement new instructional approaches.

RECOMMENDATIONS FOR FUTURE RESEARCH

An area ripe for future research deals with conceptions of ability. Although a great deal of research has been conducted on *individuals'* beliefs about whether ability is static or augmentable, very little research has been conducted on *collective* levels. How do researchers assess the collective belief that a school's ability, for example, to serve even the most at-risk students is static or augmentable? What about departments in different subject areas? Just as there are sources for a sense of self-efficacy and collective efficacy, what are the sources of conceptions of ability for individuals and groups? Although Dweck and her colleagues have shown that process feedback, such as "you did really well on that assignment, you must have worked hard at it," helps to foster an incremental view of ability, there must be other sources of these beliefs (Dweck & Leggett, 1988). Might some of the sources of efficacy also serve as sources for conceptions of ability? For example, to what extent does observing other teachers successfully implement a particular instructional innovation increase the observer's self-efficacy, and also help teachers realize that their own capacity is augmentable? Research is needed to explore these and other similar questions.

Another area ripe for future research is investigating the characteristics of models that observers deem similar. This applies both at the individual and the collective levels. For example, for individual teachers, what are the most salient characteristics for which observers might look when finding similar models? Years of experience? Level of education attained? Subjects taught? Other variables? And for schools as a whole, what are the most salient characteristics to look for when deciding what types of reform to implement? Student and teacher demographics? Student achievement on standardized test scores? Instructional strategies implemented? What variables from the observation of individual teachers might be the most salient analogues to observe for the various collective levels of schools (teams, departments, buildings, etc.)? These and other similar questions would contribute important theoretical and practical insights for those hoping to make an impact in the professional development of teachers.

Finally, given the dramatic rise in technological capabilities and the continual accessibility of technology, researchers could explore the ways in which technology can be used to bolster the collective efficacy of a team, department, or school to realize a future of its own choosing. Providers of professional development have long used videos to provide vicarious experiences for those learning new strategies. Researchers might now vary the use of models with differing levels of skill and success to assess most effective types of modeling. Newer technologies also provide other avenues for research. For example, what are the effects of using social networking tools (e.g., Twitter, wikis, Edmodo) through which teachers share challenges and successes with each other to improve instruction? These technologies can leverage this capacity to bring together into one virtual space many different people who can collectively exercise their agency to solve difficult problems. Technologies may also be used in innovative ways to quickly assess teachers' beliefs, such as their anxiety levels throughout their implementation of new instructional strategies, and to intervene with just-in-time supports to aid in their belief that they can ultimately be successful in the implementation of the new strategy.

CONCLUSION

Those charged with fostering the ongoing professional learning of teachers would do well to take seriously the extent to which teachers perceive the reform initiatives being presented as a threat or a challenge and thus whether they are motivated to invest the effort required for true conceptual and behavioral change. Teacher sense of efficacy, the beliefs in one's own capabilities and the capabilities of the various collectives of which one is a part to accomplish desired outcomes, powerfully affects people's behavior, motivation, and, thereby, their success or failure (Bandura, 1997). Without strong efficacy beliefs, people do not expend effort in endeavors, as they may perceive their efforts will be futile. To counter the debilitating effects of a low sense of efficacy, providers of professional development should model a growth mindset in relation to the teachers with whom they work and attend to the sources of efficacy beliefs as identified in this chapter. They might consider incorporating demonstrations, for example, as well as processing feedback, coaching, monitoring of student progress, and ensuring that teachers have the resources of time and materials necessary to be able to successfully implement the requisite reforms, ideally relatively early in the learning process. In addition to improved instruction, the result is likely to be teachers who expend greater effort and persistence even in challenging circumstances. Bolstering the efficacy beliefs of teachers is likely to contribute to their motivation to engage in disciplined professional inquiry throughout their careers.

QUESTIONS FOR DISCUSSION

For Teachers

1. Looking back over your teaching career, what professional development experiences had the most significant impact on your teaching practice? To what extent did these experiences affect your sense of self-efficacy? Can you identify the sources of self-efficacy that were operative?

2. What resources would be important to you as you anticipate implementing a new instructional strategy or current initiative being enacted in your school? What might assist you to perceive this change as a challenge rather than a threat?

3. How might you carry a growth mindset in your work on a daily basis? How might you convey that mindset to both your students and your colleagues?

For Administrators

1. How might an awareness of the importance of self-efficacy and collective efficacy beliefs change the way you structure professional development in your school?

2. What changes are you willing to make for the teaching assignments and induction of novice teachers in your school to bolster their developing sense of efficacy during their first years in the profession?

3. How might you better foster a growth mindset in yourself as you work with both children and adults in your school? What implications might that have for the climate of your school?

For Policymakers

1. In your experience, what policies have you seen that promote teachers' growth? How could you invigorate teachers to take on the challenges of new instructional methods rather than to resist them?

2. How does the evidence regarding the role of collective efficacy beliefs challenge the current emphasis on a value-added model? How does it support that model? What model attracts you most? Why?

3. What might you do right now to equip building-level administrators with the resources they need to assist teachers to regard reform strategies as challenges rather than as threats? In the coming months? In the next school year?

REFERENCES

Allinder, R. M. (1994). The relationship between efficacy and the instructional practices of special education teachers and consultants. *Teacher Education and Special Education, 17*, 86–95.

Anderson, R., Greene, M., & Loewen, P. (1988). Relationships among teachers' and students' thinking skills, sense of efficacy, and student achievement. *Alberta Journal of Educational Research, 34*(2), 148–165.

Ashton, P. T., & Webb, R. B. (1986). *Making a difference: Teachers' sense of efficacy and student achievement.* New York: Longman.

Bandura, A. (1986). *Social foundations of thought and action: A social cognitive theory.* Englewood Cliffs, NJ: Prentice-Hall.

Bandura, A. (1997). *Self-efficacy: The exercise of control.* New York: Freeman.

Berman, P., McLaughlin, M., Bass, G., Pauly, E., & Zellman, G. (1977). *Federal programs supporting educational change: Vol. 7. Factors affecting implementation and continuation* (Report No. R-1589/7-HEW). Santa Monica, CA: RAND Corporation. (ERIC Document Reproduction Service No. 140 432)

Bruce, C. D., & Ross, J. A. (2008). A model for increasing reform implementation and teacher efficacy: Teacher peer coaching in grades 3 and 6 mathematics. *Canadian Journal of Education, 31*, 346–370.

Chen, J. A. (2012). Implicit theories of ability, epistemic beliefs, and science motivation: A person-centered approach. *Learning and Individual Differences, 22*, 724–735.

Corcoran, T. B., Shields, P. M., & Zucker, A. A. (1998, March). *Evaluation of NSF's State-wide Systemic Initiatives (SSI) program: The SSIs and professional development for teachers.* Menlo Park, CA: SRI International.

Dweck, C. S., & Leggett, E. L. (1988). A social cognitive approach to motivation and personality. *Psychological Review, 95*, 256–273.

Gibson, S., & Dembo, M. (1984). Teacher efficacy: A construct validation. *Journal of Educational Psychology, 76*, 569–582.

Goddard, R. D. (2001). Collective efficacy: A neglected construct in the study of schools and student achievement. *Journal of Educational Psychology, 93*(3), 467–476.

Goddard, R. D., & Goddard, Y. L. (2001). A multilevel analysis of the relationship between teacher and collective efficacy in urban schools. *Teaching and Teacher Education, 17*, 807–818.

Goddard, R. D., Hoy, W. K., & Hoy, A. W. (2000). Collective teacher efficacy: Its meaning, measure, and impact on student achievement. *American Research Journal, 37*, 479–508.

Goddard, R. D., Tschannen-Moran, M., & Hoy, W. K. (2001). Teacher trust in students and parents: A multilevel examination of the distribution and effects of teacher trust in urban elementary schools, *Elementary School Journal, 102*, 3–17.

Gregoire, M. (2003). Is it a challenge or a threat?: A dual process model of teacher's cognition and appraisal processes during conceptual change. *Educational Psychology Review, 15*, 147–179.

Guskey, T. (1986). Staff development and the process of teacher change. *Educational Researcher, 15*(5), 5–12.

Guskey, T. (1988). Teacher efficacy, self-concept, and attitudes toward the implementation of instructional innovation. *Teaching and Teacher Education, 4*(1), 63–69.

Guskey, T. (1989). Attitude and perceptual change in teachers. *International Journal of Educational Research, 13*, 439–454.

Haney, J. J., Wang, J., Keil, C., & Zoffel, J. (2007). Enhancing teachers' beliefs and practices through problem-based learning focuses on pertinent issues of environmental health science. *Journal of Environmental Education, 38*(4), 25–33.

Hofer, B. K., & Pintrich, P. R. (1997). The development of epistemological theories: Beliefs about knowledge and knowing and their relation to learning. *Review of Educational Research, 67*, 88–140.

Hoy, A. W., & Burke-Spero, R. (2005). Changes in teacher efficacy during the early years of teaching: A comparison of four measures. *Teaching and Teacher Education, 21,* 343–356.

Joyce, B., & Showers, B. (1988). *Student achievement through staff development.* White Plains, NY: Longman.

Klassen, R. M., Tze, V. M. C., Betts, S. M., & Gordon, K. A. (2011). Teacher efficacy research 1998–2009: Signs of progress or unfulfilled promise? *Educational Psychology Review, 23,* 21–43.

Kurz, T., & Knight, S. (2004). An exploration of the relationship among teacher efficacy, collective teacher efficacy, and goal consensus. *Learning Environments Research, 7,* 111–128.

McKinney, M., Sexton, T., & Meyerson, M. (1999). Validating the efficacy-based change model. *Teaching and Teacher Education, 15,* 471–485.

Midgley, D., Feldlaufer, H., & Eccles, J. (1989). Change in teacher efficacy and student self- and task-related beliefs in mathematics during the transition to junior high school. *Journal of Educational Psychology, 81,* 247–258.

Moore, W., & Esselman, M. (1992, April). *Teacher efficacy, power, school climate, and achievement: A desegregating district's experience.* Paper presented at the annual meeting of the American Educational Research Association, San Francisco.

Pajares, F. (1996). Self-efficacy beliefs in achievement settings. *Review of Educational Research, 66,* 543–579.

Poole, M., & Okeafor, K. (1989). The effects of teacher efficacy and interactions among educators on curriculum implementation. *Journal of Curriculum and Supervision, 4*(2), 146–161.

Ross, J. (1992). Teacher efficacy and the effects of coaching on student achievement. *Canadian Journal of Education, 17*(1), 51–65.

Ross, J. (1994). The impact of an inservice to promote cooperative learning on the stability of teacher efficacy. *Teaching and Teacher Education, 10,* 381–394.

Ross, J., & Bruce, C. (2007). Professional development effects on teacher efficacy: Results of randomized field trial. *Journal of Research in Education, 101,* 50–60.

Ross, J. A. (1998). The antecedents and consequences of teacher efficacy. In J. Brophy (Ed.), *Advances in research on teaching* (Vol. 7, pp. 49–74). Greenwich, CT: JAI Press.

Ross, J. A., Cousins, J. B., & Gadalla, T. (1996). Within-teacher predictors of teacher efficacy. *Teaching and Teacher Education, 12,* 385–400.

Scribner, J. (1999). Teacher efficacy and teacher professional learning: Implications for school leaders. *Journal of School Leadership, 9,* 209–234.

Schunk, D. H. (1987). Peer models and children's behavioral change. *Review of Educational Research, 57,* 149–174.

Schunk, D. H., & Hanson, A. R. (1985). Peer models: Influence on children's self-efficacy and achievement. *Journal of Educational Psychology, 77,* 313–322.

Schunk, D. H., & Hanson, A. R. (1989). Influence of peer-model attributes on children's beliefs and learning. *Journal of Educational Psychology, 81,* 431–434.

Smylie, M. A. (1988). The enhancement function of staff development: Organizational and psychological antecedents to individual teacher change. *American Educational Research Journal, 25,* 1–30.

Stein, M., & Wang, M. (1988). Teacher development and school improvement: The process of teacher change. *Teaching and Teacher Education, 4,* 171–187.

Timperley, H., & Phillips, G. (2003). Changing and sustaining teachers' expectations through professional development in literacy. *Teaching and Teacher Education, 19,* 627–641.

Tschannen-Moran, M., & Barr, M. (2004). Fostering student learning: The relationship of collective teacher efficacy and student achievement. *Leadership and Policy in Schools, 3,* 189–209.

Tschannen-Moran, M., & Hoy, A. W. (2007). The differential antecedents of self-efficacy beliefs of novice and experienced teachers, *Teaching and Teacher Education, 23,* 944–956.

Tschannen-Moran, M., Hoy, A. W., & Hoy, W. K. (1998). Teacher efficacy: Its meaning and measure. *Review of Educational Research, 68,* 202–248.

Tschannen-Moran, M., & McMaster, P. (2009). Sources of self-efficacy: Four professional development formats and their relationship to self-efficacy and implementation of a new teaching strategy. *Elementary School Journal, 110,* 228–248.

CHAPTER 14

Investing in Youth
by Investing in Teachers

Transforming Adolescent Literacy
through Responsive Professional Development

WILLIAM G. BROZO

- Secondary literacy professional development and reform initiatives should be responsive to the unique cultural and curricular conditions of secondary schools.

- Content-literacy reform at the secondary level should be guided by principles of responsive professional development.

- Six principles are described and exemplified using research evidence and personal experiences in adolescent literacy reform projects.

- Responsive secondary literacy reform involves evidence-based content literacy practices, workshop- and classroom-level coaching, and opportunities for teachers to contextualize and take ownership of the reforms.

Literacy reform at the secondary level has been shown to occur under a variety of conditions and through a range of broad school-level initiatives and specific day-to-day instructional practices (Brozo & Hargis, 2003; Sturtevant et al., 2006; Supovitz & Weinbaum, 2008). One element of adolescent literacy reform that is arguably the most essential to success, however, is to provide teachers—who more than any other factor have the greatest influence on student achievement (Flynt & Brozo, 2009; Hattie, 2003)—with ongoing support in the form of responsive professional development (Brozo & Fisher, 2010). In this chapter, I argue that investing in secondary teachers through quality professional development will lead to dividends in the form of greater student engagement and higher student achievement.

To expand middle and high school teachers' expertise in literacy, however, adolescent literacy reformers and professional developers must understand the unique challenges of this situation. One such challenge is the limited training these teachers receive in literacy practices for students at the middle and high school levels. After all, across the United States most secondary-level teacher certification programs require only one course in adolescent or content-area reading. It is not surprising, therefore, that Barry's (1997) survey of literacy practices in high schools revealed that over 40% of the teachers did not feel competent addressing reading problems or planning instruction to foster reading development and that another 30% were unsure of their competencies.

A related challenge in working with secondary teachers, particularly teachers of the disciplines, is their discomfort with and outright resistance to the idea that beyond content expertise they should also be skillful in developing the literacy abilities of students (Dillon, O'Brien, Sato, & Kelly, 2010; O'Brien & Stewart, 1992; O'Brien, Stewart, & Moje, 1995). Barry (1997) found that many secondary-level teachers perceived literacy instruction as low priority, unnecessary, the responsibility of an English or reading teacher, or a burdensome addition to an already full workload.

Further complicating literacy reform at the middle and high school levels is the fact that teachers in the content areas can be regarded as highly qualified according to No Child Left Behind (NCLB) standards while lacking any meaningful training in the reading and writing instruction needed to address the literacy challenges of a growing number of adolescents (Langer, 2004). When secondary teachers lack understanding of content literacy and effective practices to make disciplinary knowledge accessible to all, this may be especially detrimental to striving readers and learners (Brozo & Simpson, 2007; Greenleaf, Jimenez, & Roller, 2002).

No secondary teacher can truly be considered highly qualified if he or she is lacking fundamental knowledge about adolescent literacy and practices to meet the range of reading and writing needs these students present. As I have discovered in my own secondary literacy reform projects, without responsive and sustained professional development, secondary-level teachers may never gain the tools needed to enhance reading achievement and expand disciplinary knowledge for youth. Therefore, professional development must be at the heart of any reform effort intended to help all adolescents maximize their literacy and learning potential (Richardson & Anders, 2005).

In this chapter, I share my experiences and insights as a secondary literacy professional developer. I frame what I've learned around six guiding principles, or what I call the "six C's" of effective professional development. I consider these six C's essential to any quality professional development program for secondary teachers. Examples of how these principles guided secondary literacy reform come from the challenges and successes of work in schools from the mid-Atlantic region to the deep South of the United States.

CONTENT-LITERACY INSTRUCTIONAL ROUTINES

Secondary teachers need effective literacy strategies to help promote consistent, interactive content learning across the curriculum (Brozo & Simpson, 2007).

Teachers need to develop expertise and ownership of a manageable and appropriate number of literacy strategies and practices for readiness, interactive comprehension, and extending new learning phases of a lesson.

There are virtually hundreds of strategies available to secondary teachers for linking content from the disciplines to reading and writing (Brozo & Simpson, 2007; Fisher, Brozo, Frey, & Ivey, 2011). It is perhaps because of this enormous variety that teachers find it difficult to know which ones are most relevant to their content and for their students. Professional developers can play an essential role in (1) supporting teachers in gaining knowledge of and experience with effective instructional routines for content literacy and (2) helping teachers make principled decisions about which content literacy practices to adopt for and adapt to their instructional contexts.

In a large multicultural urban school system in the mid-Atlantic region, I was one of a team of consultants providing year-long professional development and technical assistance to teachers in a cluster of seven middle and high schools, all of which had failed to make adequate yearly progress (AYP) based on NCLB funding mandates.

Our team and several others from local universities were brought together by the school district's literacy leaders and central office professional development personnel, and it was decided that a 10-session series of content-literacy workshops would be delivered by subject area (math, science, social studies, English/language arts) to middle and high school teachers over the course of 6 months during the upcoming school year. In designing the workshop modules, a framework for organizing strategy instruction was created to guide teachers in connecting an instructional routine with the goal of each lesson phase (see Figure 14.1).[1]

The central planning office delegated our consultants to lead the summer writing of the curriculum, which involved university literacy consultants together with district teachers and literacy leaders. Late in the summer secondary school groups and universities were paired into clusters. Principals were brought on board, and logistical planning was to start for the coordination of twice-monthly half-day workshops. In the fall and winter of that school year a series of 10 workshops for each of the content-area groups within each of the university clusters were offered during the school day, and later as a Saturday option. These workshops utilized literacy and content-area resources, the instructor's subject-matter expertise, and a structure that was designed to routinely allow reflection, research-based strategy instruction, demonstration, discussion, and 1 hour of collaborative planning. Selected content-literacy texts, along with a curriculum notebook, were given to each participant and used throughout the series. At the end of the series and during the following summer months, each of the universities offered extension opportunities for the cluster schools in its partnership.

Throughout the workshops, I emphasized to the content teachers that although they were given exposure to and guided practice with nearly 20 instructional routines, they should focus first on adopting those that could more readily be incorporated into their subject matter and fit their teaching style. All the subject-area

---

[1] See the Glossary at the end of the chapter for explanations of abbreviations and definitions of terms.

Readiness	Interactive Comprehension	Extending New Learning
SQPR (Student Questioning for Purposeful Reading) Opinionnaire/Anticipation Guide Vocabulary Self-Awareness Text Impressions	Word Grid Process Guide Reciprocal Teaching GISTing Questioning the Author (QtA) Split-Page Note Taking DR-TA	Professor Know-It-All RAFT Story Chains Learning Logs Vocabulary Cards SPAWN

FIGURE 14.1. Framework for organizing strategy instruction.

teachers from one middle school in our cluster jointly agreed that they would select one strategy from each phase of a lesson and work to become skilled in applying it. In this way, they reasoned, students would receive experience with the same content-literacy strategies throughout the school day in each of their subject-area classes. This consistency would increase students' use of the strategies and encourage ownership (McDonald, Thornley, Staley, & Moore, 2009).

"The Barrett 3," as it came to be known, gave the school and the literacy strategies that its teachers and administrators adopted a special identity. SQPR (Brozo & Simpson, 2007), split-page note taking (Donahoo, 2010; Faber, Morris, & Lieberman, 2000), and RAFT (Santa, Havens, & Valdes, 2004) were even labeled on the school's marquee, so as to emphasize the buy-in from everyone—students, faculty, and the community alike. A commitment to a smaller but more manageable set of strategies at the middle school helped all teachers feel that they were putting a common shoulder to the wheel in advancing the literacy reforms while not being overwhelmed by them. Three is not a magic number; depending on experience with and knowledge of content-literacy strategies, other schools may find that they can launch adolescent literacy reform work employing several instructional routines. Barrett teachers found after the first year of the reform project that they had mastered flexible delivery of the three featured strategies. In the following years, they were able to expand their instructional repertoires by adopting additional strategies learned in the professional development workshops.

COACHING

Teachers need time to work with professional developers in workshops and in the classroom setting to plan, conduct, analyze, and refine new literacy instructional practices. This is a critical aspect of reform work because it must be recognized that teachers need scaffolding for change just as much as their students do (Hargreaves & Goodson, 2006; van Veen, Sleegers, & van de Ven, 2005). To tell teachers, particularly those in the disciplines of science and math, to increase the reading and writing achievement of their students without appropriate support is no different from telling students to read better without showing them how. Both need scaffolding for their respective challenges with teaching and texts (Broaddus & Bloodgood, 1999). Guided practice and gradual release approaches allow teachers time to reflect on and develop expertise with new instructional routines (Boling & Evans, 2008)

Cooter (2004) stresses that professional development workshops may provide teachers "first exposure" to particular approaches but that these are not sufficient for building capacity to apply them in actual instructional contexts. Cooter goes on to assert that one or two workshops alone rarely bring about "deep learning" needed for lasting change. Thus workshops and other means of providing initial exposure to literacy and learning reform practices need to be coupled with provisions for supporting teachers' sustained efforts to implement these innovations (Cantrell & Callaway, 2008). Most of us who provide professional development services to teachers and schools understand Cooter's points firsthand. Giving a large, 1-day workshop may be an efficient way to reach a broad audience, but its impact is rarely long term.

As an alternative, we exploited the coaching model in a statewide reform project focusing on literacy across the curriculum. This Gulf Coast state had no specific requirements or certificates for literacy coaches, so we decided to build the coaching capacity among promising project participants. These were subject-area teachers who were eagerly absorbing and applying the content-literacy practices from initial workshops. These were also individuals who were already recognized as leaders or potential leaders in their middle and high schools. They possessed excellent interpersonal skills and could relate well to colleagues, but they could also be "warm demanders" (Irvine & Fraser, 1998). Warm demanders send a consistent message to their colleagues that all students are capable of meeting the literacy and learning expectations of the content classroom (Ross, Bondy, Gallingane, & Hambacher, 2008). They engage their colleagues through insistence, using tact and support, and help them recognize that instructional practices that are ineffective in elevating students' literacy abilities and expanding their content knowledge are not acceptable (Flynt & Brozo, 2009).

For virtually the entire first year of the reform initiative in the state, those individuals identified as potential coaches continued to develop credibility by broadening their expertise in adolescent literacy. To be an authoritative and respected mentor and model for colleagues, the coaches needed deep knowledge of literacy principles and practices. This is especially critical at the secondary level and for teachers in math and science, who may be skeptical about the value of content literacy (Draper, Broomhead, Jensen, Nokes, & Siebert, 2010).

In the second year, with financial and philosophical commitments from the school administration, the teachers chosen to be coaches took on their formal roles as support staff to their colleagues to reinforce and extend systemic reforms in literacy across the curriculum. With our ever-present guidance, we collaborated with coaches and offered technical assistance for each role.

The coaches crafted and delivered whole-school staff development workshops. These were full-day sessions that occurred just before the start of each half of the school year. In these sessions, the coaches reviewed content-literacy instructional routines, gave additional input from experience, provided additional examples of how the strategies had been implemented by colleagues, and created opportunities for teachers to write strategies into their curricula. In addition, coaches were expected to provide leadership for whole-school literacy initiatives—such as, in one high school, a sustained silent reading (SSR) program called "Tigers Read." SSR has been shown to be a valuable facet of a comprehensive secondary reading program (Brozo & Hargis, 2003; Fisher, 2004).

In addition to whole-school staff development and helping to establish a literate culture at the school, the coaches were also expected to provide subject-area teams with focused strategy workshops. These typically occurred during team planning meetings during or right after school and would last 30–45 minutes. For instance, in one middle school, the math department wanted to know more about how to construct word grids that fit their content. The coach, who had a math background herself, demonstrated how words, equations, and symbols could be used by the math teachers and their students to reinforce understanding of important concepts and processes. The coach encouraged the teachers to brainstorm applications of the word grid while she offered reactions and suggestions.

The ultimate goal of coaching was to assist individual teachers in their efforts to employ content-literacy practices in their classrooms. The coaches first identified interested colleagues.

We encouraged them to begin by working with those who were most eager to be innovative, while creating opportunities for all to learn and grow together. As one coach reported to us, "I don't want to water the rocks," that is, put a great deal of effort into trying to help teachers who are opposed to the content-literacy reforms and are not ready to change their practices.

In a suburban high school in the state, the literacy coach, after providing large- and small-group workshops and observing several teachers, formed a close relationship with a colleague in biology, who was eager to expand his instructional repertoire but wasn't sure how to begin. The teacher had had a previous career in nuclear physics but had been teaching for only 3 years. The coach began by participating in joint lesson planning. The teacher told the coach that he was searching for ways to engage his students in more meaningful interactions with his course content. He was disappointed to discover that his students had difficulty understanding the textbook, did not complete homework assignments, and were trying to memorize information instead of learning to observe and think about scientific phenomena.

With the literacy coach's help, he decided to incorporate a variety of readiness strategies into his upcoming unit on genetics in the hope of gaining and sustaining student interest in the topic. The coach shared with the teacher a graphic novel called *The Stuff of Life: A Graphic Guide to Genetics and DNA* (Schultz, Cannon, & Cannon, 2009). In the book, an alien scientist from a race threatened by disease comes to Earth to research the fundamentals of DNA and evolution. He does so in clear and simple language so even his dull-witted leader gets it. The narrative is accompanied by fun and explanatory illustrations. In addition, they gathered examples of exciting experiments done by genetics researchers that his students would find interesting. For example, scientists were able to raise tobacco plants that glowed in the dark by inserting the gene that makes fireflies glow into the DNA of tobacco.

Together, the coach and teacher found articles on genetic engineering in news magazines and planned for students to summarize the key ideas on index cards. The students were to include in their summaries the advantages and disadvantages of this technology. Afterward, a discussion web strategy would be used in which students would be in pairs, then in groups of four to discuss and prepare what they would say to the whole class on the central question of whether genetic engineering is morally responsible. As a final activity, they planned for students to write to the Food and Drug Administration explaining their views on the subject of genetically engineered food. This would be an argumentative essay that fulfilled key content and literacy standards in science.

After joint lesson planning, the literacy coach continued to support the biology teacher. She conducted a demonstration lesson with his class, guiding students through an anticipation guide (Duffelmeyer & Baum, 1992) during the readiness phase, GISTing during the interactive comprehension phase, and Professor Know-It-All (Fisher et al., 2011) during the final, extending-new-learning phase of the lesson. The teacher observed and assisted individual students during the class. Later, the teacher and coach met to debrief on the lesson and strategies. Subsequent lessons were cotaught in which these and other content-literacy strategies were employed. Finally, the biology teacher conducted content-literacy lessons on his own while the coach observed and provided helpful feedback afterward.

COHERENCE

Teachers need new strategies and practices in professional development contexts that can be integrated coherently into their existing instructional repertoires and routines. When ideas do not fit together coherently from the reform effort to established practice, many teachers find it difficult to buy in, and professional developers may have a harder time establishing the reform effort's credibility (Swinnerton, 2007). In some underperforming districts and schools where there is urgency to find a "magic bullet" to turn around student achievement, teachers can feel "assaulted" by reform efforts. There have been occasions when I have found myself competing for attention with my content-literacy agenda because of several ongoing reform projects. One teacher even told me to "get in line" after I gave a presentation about literacy strategies across the curriculum, then she proceeded to tick off five different ongoing programs the school had adopted for raising test scores. Is it any wonder, under these conditions, that teachers may find it difficult to prioritize how much time and energy to give various reform activities, especially when there is a lack of articulation among the various reforms? Thus it is essential that professional developers are aware of all other reform initiatives to ensure as much coherence as possible.

In the project I spearheaded in a state in the Southern United States, teachers in pilot schools had already been exposed to and were familiar with the strategic instruction model (SIM; Deshler, Palincsar, Biancarosa, & Nair, 2007) training strategies, such as graphic organizers and vocabulary cards. We discussed how some of our project strategies resembled strategies with which they were familiar and encouraged and supported teachers in their efforts to blend them. For example, the teachers had been using SIM-type vocabulary cards with the LINCing strategy (a mnemonic approach to remembering word meanings) as part of their regular instruction. To make these cards, students include the target word along with other information and an illustration to reinforce understanding and recall. And, because the LINCing process entails self-testing, it served as a complement to two of the vocabulary strategies advocated in our project—vocabulary self-awareness and word grids. Teachers were shown how target words from their science, social studies, math, and English/language arts content could be put into vocabulary self-awareness charts or on word grids, and then, after working through the processes with those two strategies, students could put into LINCing vocabulary cards those words that continued to pose problems. This solution made it possible for teachers to add effective practices to their instructional toolkits once they were made aware of how strategies from different programs need not be in competition but could articulate to maximize student learning.

CONTEXTUALIZATION

Teachers need contextually relevant examples to understand how instructional routines and practices can be integrated with existing standards, classroom exigencies, and students' learning needs (Spencer & Logan, 2003). As I described in the previous section on coaching, when professional development includes demonstration teaching and coteaching in actual classrooms, teachers are able to witness and experience authentic integration of workshop strategies.

In my own experience I have come to recognize that resistance to content-literacy strategies and practices is directly related to how contextualized the work is around these instructional reforms. If they are forced on teachers blindly and uncritically, then resistance may be more likely. If they are offered with sensitivity to context, teacher agency, and purpose, then there is likely to be less resistance.

I have witnessed firsthand the benefits and transformative power of an approach that encourages teachers to explore feasible and relevant contextual applications of generic content-literacy strategies. For example, as a consultant on a curriculum reform project in a seriously struggling urban school system that was in receivership, I observed a highly skilled and knowledgeable science teacher in a charter middle school breathe new life into the RAFT (Role–Audience–Format–Topic; Santa et al., 2004) strategy by having her students create dioramas of the systems of the body, then assume the role of a docent guiding "museum goers" through lungs, intestines, and arteries. This science teacher, who had one of the strongest negative reactions to the content-literacy approach at the outset of the project, became one of its staunchest supporters after realizing she was free to adapt and personalize the strategies according to the nature of the content and needs of her students.

In another, very different setting—a rural high school in Appalachia—teachers were first provided two full-day workshops just before the start of the new school year. This was immediately followed by work in teachers' classrooms throughout the year to conduct lessons using the strategies demonstrated in the workshops, then by opportunities for teachers to team-teach the strategies with us or to try them on their own with our feedback.

For example, in the workshops, I demonstrated several content-literacy strategies, including lesson impressions. This instructional routine involves asking students to form a written impression of the topic to be discussed or the text to be read based on a list of words and short phrases from the target source. Once students create their impression texts, they become eager to discover how closely they match the actual content (Brozo, 2004). This approach has been found to keep students focused and engaged during a lesson (McGinley & Denner, 1987) and can increase motivation by heightening anticipation and providing a meaningful purpose for learning (Guthrie & Humenick, 2004)

I conducted a lesson impression in a 10th-grade history class as a prelude to an essay on the Civil War by Stephen Crane. Afterward, during the history teacher's planning period, we met to reflect on the effectiveness of the strategy and discuss ways he might begin to use it himself. In the following week, I worked with the teacher to develop his own lesson-impression activity for another Civil War topic and textbook chapter. After observing the strategy lesson, I met again with the teacher to offer feedback and respond to his questions concerning different possibilities for implementing lesson impressions with other content and making it even more engaging for his 10th graders. Within three or four attempts to employ the lesson-impression strategy, the teacher had reached a level of comfort and confidence enough to add it to his instructional repertoire. With in-class modeling and subsequent support of teachers' efforts to apply content-reading innovations within authentic learning environments, I observed many secondary-level teachers adopt new innovative instructional practices by adapting them to their content. To emphasize a point, teachers do not become effective simply by trying to reproduce strategies observed in professional development workshops in lockstep fashion. Instead, effectiveness will result when teachers reframe and expand existing strategies in ways that are more ideally suited to them, their instructional contexts, and the needs and interests of their students.

COLLABORATIVE COMMUNICATION TIME

Teachers need time within professional development and school settings to mentor or be mentored by their colleagues. Collaborative planning time, often missing in secondary contexts, can support the orchestration of standards, resources, assessment, and instruction to promote student learning (Moran, 2007). Many secondary teachers need not only to acquire knowledge of new adolescent literacy strategies but also to change beliefs about their role in literacy development. Transforming strategies and beliefs requires that forums be established so that teachers can have a genuine voice in planning, implementing, and evaluating reforms (Holcomb, 2001).

In a secondary literacy reform project in a large inner-city district in the mid-Atlantic region, we conducted bimonthly workshops in which teachers had structured time to discuss within- and across-school teams' challenges and successes with the workshop strategies. Teachers shared their input with us, and it was used to modify content and delivery to accommodate the needs and issues raised by teachers. Furthermore, school teams reflected on implementation of strategies and planned ways of supporting each other.

Emerging from these conversations were such initiatives as collegial consultations, in which teachers observed colleagues conducting content-literacy lessons and then debriefed them afterward to refine delivery of the lesson and increase its impact on student reading, writing, and learning.

In one case, we supported the teaming of English teachers to reinforce instruction in the split-page method of note taking. The beneficiaries of their collaboration were new first-year students grappling with the demands of high school textbook reading. This example of cooperative planning between teachers demonstrates the power of collaboration as an effective way to influence teachers' beliefs about reading, writing, and learning (Buckley, 2000).

Another way teachers can support each other to make the reading and learning strategies gained in professional development contexts more meaningful to them and ultimately more accessible and engaging for youth is by collaborating on thematic units (Gross, 1997; Moore & Hinchman, 2006; Murata, 2002). For example, in our project, we brought together an eighth-grade history teacher with a language arts teacher. With our guidance, they decided to coordinate their curriculum around a unit on World War I. In the language arts classroom, students listened to their teacher read aloud a young adult novel, *No Hero for the Kaiser* (Frank, 1986). In response to the book, they kept a log in which they wrote their reactions and how the fiction content related to what they were learning in the history class. Students used the Internet to research their own family histories to determine who fought in the war and built spreadsheets relating battles described in their history books to the effects of the battles on the characters in the novel. They engaged in many other literacy experiences designed to integrate the various texts.

This support of the history teacher's unit helped all students, especially striving readers, increase their understanding of information and concepts related to World War I, as well as their reading, writing, and research skills. Moreover, the collaboration elevated both the students' and the teachers' enthusiasm for the unit. In this way, the history teacher had time to cover the content he felt was important, while the language arts teacher engaged students in functional and meaningful literacy experiences. In the process, everyone benefited.

CREATIVE CONTROL OVER EXTENSION OPPORTUNITIES TO BUILD TEACHER OWNERSHIP

Teachers need opportunities to create programs that extend beyond ongoing staff development workshops and build teacher and school capacity. Supporting teachers as they expand on what professional developers provide and craft their own innovations and reform experiences goes a long way toward ensuring teacher ownership and sustainability of reform initiatives.

In the pilot schools of the secondary literacy statewide reform project in the Southern United States, I helped coaches, teacher leaders, and administrators establish a professional development committee and incorporate this structure into school improvement plans. The committee set the overall literacy agenda for the pilot school. One of its responsibilities was identifying particular literacy-across-the-curriculum strategies, acquired through professional development I provided, that all teachers were expected to incorporate into their lessons. The committee was also responsible for identifying appropriate inservice workshop topics and facilitators to present on these topics at the beginning of the year, using examples from a variety of content areas. The committee and school administrators provided additional monthly meetings to allow teachers to discuss their challenges and successes implementing the selected strategies. Teachers also demonstrated how they employed these strategies before their peers during their prep period professional development sessions.

To achieve broad-based support for literacy practices, secondary teachers need to work in purposeful groups. When teachers work together, they are far more likely to solve complex problems and bring about more responsive curricula for youth, particularly those in the greatest need of literacy development. A forum that has been shown to bring teachers together is a professional learning community (DuFour & Eaker, 1998; Stoll & Lewis, 2007).

Professional learning communities grew out of the realization that teachers make or break educational innovation. Policymakers can enact the laws, administrators can supply the pressure, staff developers can present the innovative strategies, but teachers make the decision to change or not to change the ways they teach. The growing realization among those seeking restructuring of the curriculum, modifications of school policies, or enhancement of faculty professionalism is that without teacher support and ownership of the processes involved in making these changes, success will always remain elusive.

Professional learning communities are composed primarily of teachers but can be expanded when appropriate to include as partners administrators, parents, and even students. Members are vested with the responsibility of setting curricular direction and, consequently, are more likely to bring about school improvements (Tichenor & Heins, 2000). Putnam and Borko (2000) assert, "For teachers to be successful in constructing new roles they need opportunities to participate in a professional community that discusses new teacher materials and strategies and that supports the risk taking and struggle entailed in transforming practice" (p. 8).

In the rural high school in Appalachia, I assisted teachers in forming professional learning communities to explore factors unique to their school that contributed to the lack of full participation by all faculty and staff in the secondary literacy reform initiative and to study potential solutions. Members created and responded to questionnaires about the reforms, such as the level of involvement teachers had in deciding on the literacy reform program, the extent to which teachers had used content-literacy instructional strategies, and suggestions that would make it easier for teachers to take up the new literacy strategies.

In addition to soliciting input from colleagues, members of the faculty learning communities also gathered input from students. Rhodes and Dudley-Marling (1988) put it well when they said, "We can teach but we can't force learning; learning is a student's prerogative" (p. 273). Students in the middle and upper grades are more likely to choose to learn when they are respected as curricular informants and allowed a hand in determining course topics, materials, learning experiences, projects, and evaluation (Cook-Sather, 2002). Involving students in course decisions will encourage commitment to, cooperation with, and investment in the learning process. Without students' active complicity in their own education, the chances of expanding their content knowledge, as well as their literacy skills, are greatly diminished (Brozo, 2006).

What was learned through this process was that several teachers, mostly in math and science areas, were not enthusiastic about the content-literacy strategies because they were not convinced that they would make a difference in terms of achievement with their students. They also felt inhibited by the number of new strategies presented and confused about which ones would fit best with their content. Furthermore, they expressed concern that they had not been provided enough practical and realistic examples of how to apply the strategies to their texts and other materials of instruction. Student input suggested overall that in the classes in which teachers were employing the innovative literacy strategies, they were more engaged and attentive.

With this information, learning community members created and executed a plan to provide extra scaffolding and coaching for teachers in math and science. Respected teachers in these disciplines who had tried out and experienced success with certain strategies were given release time to work closely with their colleagues in consultation, modeling, and team-teaching contexts. For instance, a science teacher who had discovered numerous applications of various strategies assisted her colleagues in developing word grids (Johnson & Pearson, 1984), SPAWN prompts (Martin, Martin, & O'Brien, 1984; see examples in Figure 14.2), and several others adapted for science content. This level of cooperation and teaming greatly increased the level of teacher participation across the disciplines in the content literacy program at the school.

What was learned in this rural high school was that, in addition to professional development concerning content-literacy strategies and practices, teacher agency was supported as well. In professional learning communities, the teachers themselves asked critical questions about their practices related to the literacy reforms

SIX KINGDOMS OF LIFE								
Kingdoms	Eukaryotic	Prokaryotic	Heterotrophic	Autotrophic	Cell Wall	Unicellular	Multicellular	Locomotion
Archaebacteria	0	2	1	1	2	2	0	2
Eubacteria	0	2	1	1	2	2	0	2
Protista	2	0	1	1	1	2	0	2
Fungi	2	0	2	0	2	1	1	0
Plantae	2	0	0	2	2	0	2	0
Animalia	2	0	2	0	0	0	2	2

Key: 2 = All organisms in this kingdom exhibit this characteristic

1 = Some organisms in this kingdom exhibit this characteristic

0 = No organisms in this kingdom exhibit this characteristic

PANDEMIC ALERT	
S = special powers	The Centers for Disease Control and Prevention and the World Health Organization have issued a pandemic alert. The influenza virus has now infected an alarming number of people. The state governments have been given unlimited power in order to contain outbreaks. How will they use this power?
P = problem solving	A vaccine must be created to halt this deadly viral infection. What stages of viral infection will the vaccine target in order to prevent infection or to stop its transmission? How will this vaccine work?
A = alternative viewpoints	The government has decided to limit access of the vaccine to children and the elderly. Write a letter from the government to those denied access to the vaccine explaining why they will not receive the vaccine.
W = what if	What if the influenza virus mutated and the available vaccines are no longer effective? How will state governments prevent transmission of this deadly virus?
N = next	There is news of a tribe genetically resistant to influenza infections in a remote Alaskan village. What do you think the CDC and the WHO will do next?

FIGURE 14.2. A science teacher's application of word grid and SPAWN content-literacy strategies.

in their school and built a collaborative framework for finding answers. In this way, teachers took control of their literacy reforms by actively participating in problem-centered discussions and activities (Robb, 2000) related to them. Learning communities helped the teachers to find new ways of meeting the literacy needs of students in all disciplines, to reflect on and analyze practices with these students, and to modify instruction as appropriate.

CONCLUSION

Studies of secondary reading programs with demonstrated effectiveness make clear the essential role of comprehensive staff development (Sturtevant et al., 2006). Indeed, successful secondary literacy programs are distinguished by an investment in quality teacher professional development (Richardson & Anders, 2005). This investment leads to dividends in the form of greater student engagement and higher student achievement. Responsive professional development can transform secondary teachers into highly qualified professionals with expertise in both subject matter and content literacy.

It is a sad fact that educational reforms are often abandoned if they fail to produce instant results; yet reforms may be viable. The professional knowledge base regarding secondary school reform makes it clear that change comes slowly (Darling-Hammond, Ancess, & Ort, 2002; Fullan, 2001; Sunderman, Amoa, & Meyers, 2001), and desired improvement on high-stakes tests may not occur immediately (Fisher, Frey, & Lapp, 2009). Most effective schoolwide reform initiatives take 1–3 years of consistent effort to produce results. Thus responsive professional development can play a vital role in bringing about sustained commitment and effort by teachers, teacher leaders, and other stakeholders to expand literacy and learning opportunities for youth.

The six C's are reminders that responsive secondary literacy professional development is multidimensional. It requires persistent effort, sensitivity to the daily exigencies of teachers and students, and has as its ultimate goal building capacity so the innovations and reforms are owned and enacted with fidelity and consistency by the members of the school culture. In the end, it must be the administrators, curriculum specialists, reading coaches, and classroom teachers who are the instigators and supporters of their own professional development (Sturtevant et al., 2006).

QUESTIONS FOR DISCUSSION

1. In your role as a teacher, administrator, or policymaker, which of the six C's do you think could be implemented and supported most readily? Why?

2. What barriers at the school, administrative, and policy levels exist that restrict implementation of the six C's? How could these barriers be overcome?

3. What other factors do teachers, administrators, and policymakers need to consider when attempting to reform secondary literacy through professional development?

4. What have you done to further adolescent literacy reform? How were/are your actions consistent with the six C's of responsive professional development?

REFERENCES

Barry, A. (1997). High school reading programs revisited. *Journal of Adolescent and Adult Literacy, 40,* 524–531.

Boling, C. J., & Evans, W. H. (2008). Reading success in the secondary classroom. *Preventing School Failure, 52*(2), 59–66.

Broaddus, K., & Bloodgood, J. (1999). "We're supposed to already know how to teach reading": Teacher change to support struggling readers. *Reading Research Quarterly, 34,* 426–451.

Brozo, W. G. (2004). Gaining and keeping students' attention. *Thinking Classroom, 5,* 38–39.

Brozo, W. G. (2006). Tales out of school: Accounting for adolescents in a literacy reform community. *Journal of Adolescent and Adult Literacy, 49,* 410–418.

Brozo, W. G., & Fisher, D. (2010). Literacy starts with the teachers. *Educational Leadership, 67*(6), 74–77.

Brozo, W. G., & Hargis, C. (2003). Taking seriously the idea of reform: One high school's efforts to make reading more responsive to all students. *Journal of Adolescent and Adult Literacy, 43,* 14–23.

Brozo, W. G., & Simpson, M. L. (2007). *Content literacy for today's adolescents: Honoring diversity and building competence* (5th ed.). Upper Saddle River, NJ: Pearson.

Buckley, F. (2000). *Team teaching: What, why and how?* Thousand Oaks, CA: Sage.

Cantrell, S. C., & Callaway, P. (2008). High and low implementers of content literacy: Portraits of teacher efficacy. *Teaching and Teacher Education, 24*(7), 1739–1750.

Cook-Sather, A. (2002). Authorizing students' perspectives: Toward trust, dialogue, and change in education. *Educational Researcher, 31,* 3–14.

Cooter, R. B. (2004). *Deep training + coaching: A capacity-building model for teacher development. Perspectives on rescuing urban literacy education: Spies, saboteurs, and saints.* Mahwah, NJ: Erlbaum.

Darling-Hammond, L., Ancess, J., & Ort, S. (2002). Reinventing high school: Outcomes of the Coalition Campus School Project. *American Educational Research Journal, 39*(3), 639–673.

Deshler, D., Palincsar, A. M., Biancarosa, G., & Nair, M. (2007). *Informed choices for struggling adolescent readers: A research-based guide to instructional programs and practices.* Newark, DE: International Reading Association.

Dillon, D. R., O'Brien, D. G., Sato, M., & Kelly, C. M. (2010). Professional development and teacher education for reading instruction. In M. L. Kamil, P. D. Pearson, E. B. Moje, & P. Afflerbach (Eds.), *Handbook of reading research* (Vol. 4, pp. 629–659). Mahwah, NJ: Erlbaum.

Donahoo, J. (2010). Learning how to learn: Cornell notes as an example. *Journal of Adolescent and Adult Literacy, 54*(3), 224–227.

Draper, R. J., Broomhead, P., Jensen, A. P., Nokes, J. D., & Siebert, D. (Eds.). (2010). *(Re)imagining content-area literacy instruction.* New York: Teachers College Press.

Duffelmeyer, R., & Baum, D. (1992). The extended anticipation guide revisited. *Journal of Reading, 35,* 654–656.

DuFour, R., & Eaker, R. (1998). *Professional learning communities at work: Best practices for enhancing student achievement.* Bloomington, IN: National Educational Service.

Faber, J. E., Morris, J. D., & Lieberman, M. G. (2000). The effect of note taking on ninth-grade students' comprehension. *Reading Psychology, 21,* 257–270.

Fisher, D. (2004). Setting the "opportunity to read" standard: Resuscitating the SSR program in an urban high school. *Journal of Adolescent and Adult Literacy, 48*(2), 138–150.

Fisher, D., Brozo, W. G., Frey, N., & Ivey, G. (2011). *50 instructional routines to develop content literacy.* Boston: Pearson.

Fisher, D., Frey, N., & Lapp, D. (2009). Meeting AYP in a high-need school: A formative experiment. *Journal of Adolescent and Adult Literacy, 52*(5), 386–396.

Flynt, S., & Brozo, W. G. (2009). It's all about the teacher. *Reading Teacher, 62*(6), 536–538.

Frank, R. (1986). *No hero for the kaiser.* New York: Lothrop, Lee, & Shepard Books

Fullan, M. (2001). *The new meaning of educational change* (3rd ed.). New York: Teachers College Press.

Greenleaf, C., Jimenez, R., & Roller, C. (2002). Reclaiming secondary reading interventions: From limited to rich conceptions, from narrow to broad conversations. *Reading Research Quarterly, 37,* 484–496.

Gross, P. A. (1997). *Joint curriculum design.* Mahwah, NJ: Erlbaum.

Guthrie, J. T., & Humenick, N. M. (2004). Motivating students to read: Evidence for classroom practices that increase reading motivation and achievement. In P. McCardle & V. Chhabra (Eds.), *The voice of evidence in reading research* (pp. 329–354). Baltimore: Brookes.

Hargreaves, A., & Goodson, I. (2006). Educational change over time: The sustainability and nonsustainability of three decades of secondary school change and continuity. *Educational Administration Quarterly, 42*(1), 3–41.

Hattie, J. (2003, October). *Teachers make a difference: What is the research evidence?* Paper presented at the annual conference of the Australian Council for Educational Research, Melbourne, Victoria, Australia. Retrieved August 22, 2012, from *www.acer. edu.au/documents/RC2003_Hattie_TeachersMakeADifference.pdf.*

Holcomb, E. L. (2001). *Asking the right questions: Techniques for collaboration and school change* (2nd ed.). Thousand Oaks, CA: Corwin Press.

Irvine, J. J., & Fraser, J. W. (1998). Warm demanders. *Education Week, 17,* 56–57.

Johnson, D., & Pearson, P. D. (1984). *Teaching reading vocabulary.* New York: Holt, Rinehart & Winston.

Langer, J. A. (2004). *Getting to excellent.* New York: Teachers College Press.

Martin, C., Martin, M., & O'Brien, D. (1984). Spawning ideas for writing in the content areas. *Reading World, 11,* 11–15.

McDonald, T., Thornley, C., Staley, R., & Moore, D. W. (2009). The San Diego striving readers' project: Building academic success for adolescent readers. *Journal of Adolescent and Adult Literacy, 52*(8), 720–722.

McGinley, W. J., & Denner, P. R. (1987). Story impressions: A prereading/writing activity. *Journal of Reading, 31,* 248–253.

Moore, D. W., & Hinchman, K. A. (2006). *Teaching adolescents who struggle with reading: Practical strategies.* Boston: Allyn & Bacon.

Moran, M. C. (2007). *Differentiated literacy coaching: Scaffolding for student and teacher success.* Alexandria, VA: ASCD.

Murata, R. (2002). What does team teaching mean?: A case study of interdisciplinary teaming. *Journal of Educational Research, 96*(2), 67–77.

O'Brien, D., Stewart, R., & Moje, E. (1995). Why content literacy is difficult to infuse into the secondary school: Complexities of curriculum, pedagogy, and school culture. *Reading Research Quarterly, 30,* 442–463.

O'Brien, D. G., & Stewart, R. A. (1992). Resistance to content area reading: Dimensions and solutions. In E. K. Dishner, T. W. Bean, J. E. Readence, & D. W. Moore (Eds.), *Reading in content areas: Improving classroom instruction* (3rd ed., pp. 30–40). Dubuque, IA: Kendall-Hunt.

Putnam, R., & Borko, H. (2000). What do new views of knowledge and thinking have to say about research on teacher learning? *Educational Researcher, 29,* 4–15.

Rhodes, L., & Dudley-Marling, C. (1988). *Readers and writers with a difference: A holistic approach to teaching learning disabled and remedial students.* Portsmouth, NH: Heinemann.

Richardson, V., & Anders, P. (2005). Professional preparation and development of teachers in literacy instruction for urban settings. In J. Flood & P. Anders (Eds.), *Literacy development of students in urban schools: Research and policy.* Newark, DE: International Reading Association.

Robb, L. (2000). *Redefining staff development: A collaborative model for teachers and administrators.* Portsmouth, NH: Heinemann.

Ross, D. D., Bondy, E., Gallingane, C., & Hambacher, E. (2008). Promoting academic engagement through insistence: Being a warm demander. *Childhood Education, 84*(3), 142–145.

Santa, C. M., Havens, L. T., & Valdes, B. J. (2004). *Project CRISS: Creating independence through student-owned strategies.* Dubuque, IA: Kendall-Hunt.

Schultz, M., Cannon, Z., & Cannon, K. (2009). *The stuff of life: A graphic guide to genetics and DNA.* New York: Hill & Wang.

Spencer, S. S., & Logan, K. R. (2003). Bridging the gap: A school-based staff development model that bridges the gap from research to practice. *Teacher Education and Special Education, 26*(1), 51–62.

Stoll, L., & Lewis, K. S. (2007). *Professional learning communities: Divergence, depth, and dilemmas.* Berkshire, UK: Open University Press.

Sturtevant, E., Boyd, F., Brozo, W. G., Hinchman, K., Alvermann, D., & Moore, D. (2006). *Principled practices for adolescent literacy: A framework for instruction and policy.* Mahwah, NJ: Erlbaum.

Sunderman, G., Amoa, M., & Meyers, T. (2001). California's reading initiative: Constraints on implementation in middle and high schools. *Educational Policy, 15,* 674–698.

Supovitz, J. A., & Weinbaum, E. H. (2008). *The implementation gap: Understanding reform in high schools.* New York: Teachers College Press.

Swinnerton, J. (2007). Brokers and boundary crossers in an urban school district: Understanding central-office coaches as instructional leaders. *Journal of School Leadership, 17*(2), 195–221.

Tichenor, M., & Heins, E. (2000). Study groups: An inquiry-based approach to improving schools. *Clearing House, 73,* 316–319.

van Veen, K., Sleegers, P., & van de Ven, P.-H. (2005). One teacher's identity, emotions, and commitment to change: A case study into the cognitive-affective processes of a secondary school teacher in the context of reforms. *Teaching and Teacher Education, 21*(8), 917–934.

GLOSSARY OF TERMS

DR-TA (Directed Reading–Thinking Activity)—The teacher models making and checking predictions while reading, then eliciting this process from students.

GISTing—Students learn to compose summaries of text, first at the paragraph level, then from the entire passage, by limiting the number of words they can use to craft a summary.

Learning Logs—Students use a notebook, binder, or some other repository to record ideas, questions, reactions, and reflections and to summarize newly learned content.

Opinionnaire/Anticipation Guide—Students are presented with and respond to statements about a topic before reading and then, while reading, defend or revise their initial responses based on textual information.

Process Guide—Students are given a guide to processing content as they read a required text. The guide helps students focus on important information and ideas and use study reading strategies.

Professor Know-It-All—In small groups, students assume the role of expert and answer questions from their classmates about material just read or content covered.

Questioning the Author (QtA)—Students follow a protocol of questions about various aspects of a text in order to maximize comprehension.

RAFT—Students write in response to what they have just read or learned using each letter of RAFT, as in Role, Audience, Format, and Topic.

Reciprocal Teaching—The teacher models predicting, questioning, summarizing, and clarifying as a text is read, then elicits these same reading processes from students.

SPAWN—Stands for five categories of writing prompts (*Special Powers, Problem Solving, Alternative Viewpoints, What If?*, and *Next*), which can be crafted in numerous ways to stimulate students' predictive, reflective, and critical thinking about content-area topics.

Split-Page Note Taking—A note-taking process from lecture or text in which big ideas and key concepts are written in the left column and supporting information in the right column.

SQPR (Student Questions for Purposeful Reading)—Students are prompted with a thought-provoking statement to ask questions in advance of the material to be read and to answer their questions as they read.

Story Chains—In small groups, students take turns writing a sentence about a topic or process just read or learned until a coherent and accurate paragraph is completed.

Text Impressions—Students are presented with a list of words and phrases from the upcoming reading and write a short passage or essay using the words. After the text is read, students return to their impression text and compare and contrast it with the actual reading.

Vocabulary Cards—On an index card, students write a key term in the center and, in the corners, write a definition, characteristics, examples, and an illustration. Cards are used for review and test preparation.

Vocabulary Self-Awareness—Students are given a list of key vocabulary terms from the upcoming reading and rate their knowledge of them. As the content is read and studied, they return to the list to revise and add fuller definitions and examples of each term.

Word Grid—As students read and learn about topics, they are presented with important words and relevant features in a grid. Students indicate which features are possessed by each term and use the completed grid as a study aid.

CHAPTER 15

Involving Teachers in Their Own Professional Development

PETER YOUNGS
JOHN LANE

- The Common Core State Standards and other recent curricular reforms call for teachers to enact ambitious instruction and engage all students in high-level learning.
- In order to accomplish these goals, teachers must have opportunities to participate in professional development activities that meaningfully involve them in sustained inquiry.
- For teachers, adopting an inquiry stance entails, for example, examining students' thinking and learning, utilizing preassessments and formative assessments to gauge student understanding, learning to teach experimentally based on particular situations, and drawing on knowledge of students to make changes in teaching practice.
- Lesson study, teacher action research, cognitively guided instruction, and instructional coaching represent four efforts to conceptualize professional development differently and to engage teachers in analyzing and learning from their own practice on an ongoing basis.
- To enact these approaches to professional development effectively and sustain them over time, principals and district administrators must help teachers develop research skills, promote teacher ownership over the approaches, enable teachers to learn from their peers, promote inquiry and collaboration across school faculties, and draw on outside experts.

The Common Core State Standards (CCSS) and other recent reforms in the United States call for teachers to enact ambitious instruction and engage all students in critical thinking, analytical writing, mathematical problem solving, and other forms of high-level learning. These reforms have been accompanied by an increased emphasis on accountability, first with the federal No Child Left Behind (NCLB) legislation in 2002 and more recently with a sharp focus on teacher evaluation spurred by the federal Race to the Top initiative and the effort to develop student assessments in mathematics and English/language arts aligned with the CCSS. Along with the press for rigorous curricular standards and accountability, there has also been widespread recognition that in order to engage all students in high-level learning, teachers need meaningful opportunities to acquire new knowledge and to learn to teach in new ways.

Through the 1990s, though, most teacher professional development activities in the United States were widely criticized for being short term and intellectually superficial, neglecting substantive issues of curriculum and subject matter, and failing to take account of teachers' school contexts. In addition, most professional development activities placed teachers in a passive role with regard to their own learning. But over the past 10–15 years, school districts, schools, administrators, and teachers have made numerous efforts to conceptualize professional development differently and to place teachers in active roles in their own learning.

In this chapter, we focus on four efforts to conceptualize professional development differently: lesson study, teacher action research, cognitively guided instruction (CGI), and instructional coaching. In contrast to traditional approaches, all four efforts focus on helping teachers learn in and from their teaching practice. We first draw on Ball and Cohen (1999) to describe the type of teacher development, necessitated by recent curricular reforms, that involves learning in and from practice. Then we describe each of the four approaches, provide a hypothetical example of how each approach would be implemented in a school or district, draw on the research literature to highlight instances in which each approach has been successfully implemented, and consider the conditions that support their effective implementation.

At the same time, despite making significant advances in the United States, each of these approaches continues to face a myriad of challenges. Some of these challenges are inherent in professional development activities that put teachers in a more active role with regard to their own learning. In addition, there are other challenges that pertain to the relation between lesson study, teacher research, CGI, and instructional coaching and other aspects of the current policy context, especially the emphasis on curricular standards, high-stakes testing, and teacher evaluation. After describing each approach and providing examples of what they look like in practice, we consider conditions that support their enactment and sustained implementation. Although all four approaches have much potential to support teacher learning in and from practice, we caution teachers, administrators, and policymakers that sustaining them over time is likely to be an arduous endeavor.

THE ROLE OF INQUIRY IN TEACHER LEARNING

In an influential chapter, Ball and Cohen (1999) articulated the knowledge, skills, and dispositions (i.e., habits of mind) that teachers need in order to enact ambitious instruction and engage all students in high-level learning. Along with knowledge of subject matter, pedagogy, students, and cultural differences, they argue that teachers should adopt a stance of inquiry. This involves, for example, examining the thinking and learning of their students, utilizing preassessments and formative assessments to gauge student understanding, learning to teach experimentally based on particular situations, and drawing on knowledge of students to make changes in teaching practice (Ball & Cohen, 1999). For the purposes of this chapter, we adopt Ball and Cohen's notion that "a stance of inquiry should be central to the role of teacher" (1999, p. 11). Furthermore, we argue that professional development activities that meaningfully engage teachers in sustained inquiry with colleagues are likely to support continued teacher learning in and from practice over time, implementation of ambitious instruction, and engagement of students in high-level learning.

 ## Lesson Study

Over the past decade, several schools and school districts in the United States have enacted lesson study, an approach to teacher development that has been widely used in Japanese elementary schools for many years. In this section, we first describe lesson study and provide a hypothetical example of how it would be implemented in a school. Then we draw on research on the implementation of lesson study in a California district to identify conditions that support effective enactment of this approach.

In lesson study, teachers from the same or different schools collaboratively plan a lesson that addresses identified student-learning goals; one teacher then teaches the lesson while his or her colleagues observe the instruction, take extensive notes on student learning, and assess what worked well in the lesson and what did not. As a group, the teachers then "reflect on and discuss the evidence gathered during the lesson, using it to improve the lesson, the unit, and instruction more generally" (Perry & Lewis, 2009, p. 366). These lessons are often referred to as "research lessons." The changes that a lesson study group makes to a given research lesson are usually based on instances in which student misunderstandings were observed during the lesson. For example, the teachers "might change the wording of the opening problem, or the kinds of follow-up questions they ask" (Hiebert & Stigler, 2000, p. 10). The entire process can last from 1–2 weeks to as long as 1–2 years, and it results in a revised lesson featuring descriptions of the learning goals and instructional activities; a rationale for the lesson design; anticipated student responses for various teacher-initiated questions, tasks, problems, or assessments; and suggested responses by teachers. The revised lesson can be shared with teachers at other schools or districts.

Let's assume that four third-grade teachers from the same elementary school are participating in a mathematics lesson study group together for an entire school year. Early in the year, the group decides to focus on strategies for teaching fractions based on the Common Core mathematics standards. As a group, they read and discuss the Common Core mathematics standards and several research articles on the teaching of fractions. Then they collaboratively plan a 30-minute lesson on the teaching of unit fractions (i.e., fractions with the numerator 1). One of the third-grade teachers then videotapes her class while she teaches this lesson to her students. Within a week, all of the group members view the video clip of the lesson, take notes on student and teacher behavior during the lesson, and evaluate the lesson. Then the group meets for 90 minutes to discuss the evidence from the video clip to determine what worked well in the lesson and to make changes to the lesson that promote student understanding and result in revisions to the original lesson.

In terms of research on lesson study, in a series of journal articles, Catherine Lewis, Rebecca Perry, and colleagues have documented the efforts of the San Mateo–Foster City (SMFC) K–8 school district in California to implement lesson study. In the first 5 years of this initiative (2000–2001 to 2004–2005), "(t)he most common form of participation was for teachers to work in a lesson study group during the school year" (Perry & Lewis, 2009, p. 370). This involved being part of a group of three to five teachers that committed to spending at least 20 hours on lesson study work during a given school year. Each participating teacher's classroom was covered by substitutes for 2 full days per year to give them time to observe and discuss their research lessons.

A second way in which SMFC teachers engaged in lesson study was through intensive summer workshops that the district offered each year from 2001 through 2004. Although teachers were also organized into small groups during the summer workshops, these activities differed from the school-year groups in a few ways: Participants worked closely together for several days, they were able to interact with teachers across groups, and the workshops "included in-depth mathematics activities designed to enhance teachers' knowledge for teaching" (Perry & Lewis, 2009, p. 371). Finally, a third learning structure for lesson study employed in the district was the public research lesson. This involved an experienced teacher teaching a lesson in front of 50 to 100 or more observers; afterward, a few knowledgeable educators would comment on the lesson, and then the larger group would have opportunities to comment and ask questions.

Perry and Lewis (2009) document how most lesson study participants in this district initially viewed the research lesson as a teaching product and over time shifted their perspective to view it more as a process for improving their teaching. They argue that a few factors in SMFC brought about this change in perspective; these included increased use of lesson study models and guidelines that prompted teachers to focus on student thinking during the lesson study process and greater use of reflection and feedback loops in revising lessons (Perry & Lewis, 2009). In addition, Perry and Lewis identify several conditions that led to the successful enactment of lesson study in this district: strong administrative leadership that supported this approach to professional development; multiple, diverse opportunities for teachers to learn about and engage in lesson study; and access to expertise provided by individuals from outside the school district (i.e., mathematics professional development specialists and instructional coaches from other districts, educational researchers, and Japanese educators).

In terms of the effects of lesson study on a single-lesson study group, Lewis, Perry, and Hurd (2009) describe a group of six teachers from five different schools in SMFC who participated in an intensive 2-week workshop in August 2002. As part of the workshop, this group of teachers examined state mathematics standards, worked on and discussed mathematical problems, and collaboratively planned a research lesson designed to help students identify patterns and express them mathematically. After one teacher taught the lesson to a classroom of fourth graders, the group revised the lesson, and then a second group member taught it to a different group of fourth graders at the same school. In order to assess the possible effects of workshop participation on teacher knowledge and dispositions, the researchers focused on data that naturally occurred as part of the lesson study process, as opposed to collecting additional data from the focal teachers through interviews or surveys.

Lewis and colleagues (2009) reported that participating in this lesson study workshop seemed to affect the focal teachers' knowledge in several ways. These included apparent changes in teachers' mathematical knowledge, their knowledge of student thinking, and their knowledge of pedagogy. In addition, the researchers note that involvement in this workshop seemed to increase participants' commitment to instructional improvement and led them to develop an inquiry stance toward their own teaching. For example, in the first postlesson discussion, teachers drew on evidence of student thinking during the research lesson to suggest ways to revise the lesson and to question the group's strong reliance on the *Navigating through Algebra in Grades 3–5* textbook they were using.

With regard to effects of lesson study at an individual school in SMFC, Lewis, Perry, Hurd, and O'Connell (2006) document the experiences of Highlands Elementary School. In 2000–2001, one lesson study group at the school conducted two lesson study cycles. Over the next 2 years, the rest of the teachers at Highlands began participating in lesson study. As of 2005–2006, lesson study groups at the school usually consisted of three to five teachers from the same or adjacent grade levels. Each group "conduct[ed] two cycles of lesson study per year and share[d] what they learn[ed] with the entire faculty at regular intervals" (Lewis et al., 2006, p. 274). The researchers reported that for tenured teachers, teacher evaluation focused on their lesson study work as opposed to more traditional classroom observations. In addition, formal mentoring of beginning teachers took place in lesson study groups. Finally, the researchers reported evidence of an ongoing expectation at the school "that teachers will learn about subject matter and its teaching and learning through lesson study" (Lewis et al., 2006, p. 277).

As noted, several conditions seemed to be associated with the successful sustained enactment of lesson study in SMFC. One key factor was strong initial leadership from the district's instructional improvement coordinator, Mary Pat O'Connell, and a district mathematics instructional coach, Jacqueline Hurd. O'Connell became principal of Highlands in 2001 and continued to demonstrate strong support for lesson study in that role. A second condition was the provision of multiple, diverse opportunities for teachers from across SMFC to learn about and participate in lesson study (i.e., through school-based lesson study groups, summer workshops, and observation of public research lessons). A third factor was the district's extensive use of outside experts to support lesson study activities in an ongoing way. When these factors are present, they are likely to help teachers adopt an inquiry stance toward their work and engage in sustained analysis of their teaching practices over time.

Teacher Action Research

In the United States, there have been several efforts by schools and school districts over the past 20 years to support efforts by teachers to participate in action research. In this section, we first define teacher action research and provide a hypothetical example of how it would be implemented in a school. Then we draw on scholarship on teacher action research groups to consider conditions that support effective implementation of this approach.

For the purposes of this chapter, we draw on Zeichner (1993) to define teacher action research broadly as "a systematic inquiry by practitioners about their own practices" (p. 200). As Noffke (1997) notes, there are at least three possible reasons that teachers would elect to conduct research on their own practices. First, some teachers seek to better understand and improve their own practices and/or the contexts in which they are working. Second, some engage in action research in order to generate knowledge that will be helpful to other teachers. Third, some are attempting to promote greater equity and fairness in schooling through action research. In many cases, teachers are motivated by more than one of the above reasons to engage in research on their practice.

Zeichner (2003) describes several additional ways in which teacher action research can vary. One source of variation has to do with the context in which the research is carried out. Some teachers engage in research individually, in small groups, or as part of larger or even schoolwide groups. Another source of variation has to do with who coordinates or sponsors the research. Teacher research can be coordinated by teachers themselves, by school districts, teacher unions, universities, professional associations, and state agencies, and by other bodies. The form and content of individual action research studies are another source of variation; such studies can include conference presentations, journal articles, personal journals, and oral inquiries. Finally, in the context of action research programs, school administrators can differ with regard to the extent to which they value teachers and their knowledge, intellectually challenge them, and support them (Zeichner, 2003).

Let's consider a middle school in which the principal requires all of the teachers to engage in action research independently or in collaboration with one or more colleagues. Each year, the principal arranges for teachers to participate in two half-day professional development activities on research methods. In addition, the school leader conducts a research project herself on an annual basis. At this school, the seventh-grade teachers are concerned about the academic performance of boys, especially in English/language arts and history/social studies. They decide to investigate how seventh-grade students (male and female) spend their out-of-school time during the school year. They develop a short survey about out-of-school time use and ask each seventh grader to complete it daily for a week in the fall and again for a week in the spring. Both surveys indicate that seventh-grade boys spend much more time playing video games outside of school than seventh-grade girls do. Using the results of their study, the teachers work with the principal to initiate after-school activities for boys and girls that focus on academics.

With regard to research on teacher research groups, Vivian Troen, Katherine Boles, and Mieko Kamii examined the inquiry seminars that were part of a larger teacher-led professional development project, the Learning/Teaching Collaborative, in Boston and Brookline, Massachusetts (Boles, Kamii, & Troen, 1999; Troen, Kamii, & Boles, 1997). These seminars were held at a school in Boston and a school in Brookline. Participants included classroom teachers from across both school districts and faculty members from nearby universities. They met every 3 weeks for 3 hours during the school day; at these meetings, members of the groups presented their action research projects. During group meetings, members employed a protocol that focused on posing clarifying questions and providing supportive feedback, and they avoided offering direct answers to the teacher researchers' questions (Boles et al., 1999).

In their 3-year study, Troen and colleagues (1997) found that many teacher participants in the inquiry seminars reported making changes in their curricula, instructional practices, assessment practices, and teaching philosophies, in part as a result of the seminars. In addition, through their involvement in the seminars, several participants become more skilled at and disposed toward collaborating with teacher colleagues on issues related to instruction and student learning. Boles and colleagues (1999) identified a number of factors that seemed to explain teachers' active participation in the seminars. These included the fact that teachers chose research topics that were relevant to their own classrooms and schools, the intellectually engaging nature of the seminar conversations, and the ways in which teachers learned from and were influenced by their colleagues' research projects.

In a 2-year study, Zeichner and colleagues examined the district-sponsored action research program in Madison, Wisconsin (Brodhagen, Caro-Bruce, & Klais, 1999; Marion, 1998; Zeichner & Klehr, 1999; Zeichner, Marion, & Caro-Bruce, 1998). As part of their study, the university researchers documented the work of two action research groups, interviewed 74 teachers who had participated in the program, interviewed 10 action research group facilitators, and analyzed all of the research products that participants had produced. Like Boles and colleagues, Zeichner (2003) found that participants in action research groups in Madison reported being more likely to collaborate with school-based colleagues on issues related to teaching and to value such collaboration. Many teachers also indicated that participating in action research groups "caused them to look at their teaching in a more analytic, focused way" and made them "more concerned with the need to gather data and to understand the impact of their teaching" (Zeichner, 2003, p. 308).

In addition, several Madison participants reported that engaging in action research made them feel more able to influence the working conditions in their schools and increased their expectations for how others would treat them professionally. Furthermore, many participants developed higher expectations for other professional development activities, believing that such activities should demonstrate the same level of respect for teachers and their abilities as the action research groups had shown. Finally, Zeichner and colleagues found that many participants in the action research groups "claimed that they were now much more convinced of the importance of talking to their students and listening carefully to them, that they now listened much more closely and effectively to their students than before, and that they had developed higher expectations for what their students know and can do" (Zeichner, 2003, p. 308).

In a study of three elementary schools in different parts of the United States, Berger, Boles, and Troen (2005) investigated factors that shaped the schools' ability to implement teacher action research on a schoolwide basis. At Eastern Elementary (a pseudonym), the principal mandated that all teachers participate in action research, and each teacher at the school (including specialist teachers) actively worked on his or her own research project. In addition, the principal and assistant principal carried out their own research projects and actively served as models for the teachers. The school placed a strong emphasis on data-driven inquiry; as a result, the teachers' research projects were focused on quantifiably measurable aspects of their teaching, especially student test scores. At the same time, while teachers were required to engage in research, they were also learning to use quantitative data. As a result, they reported feeling a strong sense of ownership over their research projects (Berger et al., 2005).

Professional development time at Eastern Elementary was used by the principal to familiarize the teachers with research methods, which provided teachers with numerous opportunities to share and discuss their research projects in different types of groups. These included full faculty meetings, grade-level meetings, cross-grade teams, and content-specific teams. The researchers noted that very few teachers at the school struggled with formulating research questions or carrying out research. Rather, many of the teachers "clearly felt more empowered about their teaching, felt more expert and certain about their craft and they connected their research directly to curricular changes and/or student achievement" (Berger et al., 2005, p. 100).

In contrast to Eastern Elementary, the other two schools in the study struggled to enact action research on a schoolwide basis. At Southwest Intermediate Elementary (a pseudonym), one group of teachers engaged in action research for several years. They were supported by their principal, who secured grant funding to pay for their time, helped them schedule research team meetings, and encouraged some of the other teachers at the school to participate in similar research activities. But the effort never spread throughout the entire school. After the principal left, the grant funding continued for one additional year, during which time the original action research group continued to meet. After that, the group stopped meeting, and the research came to an end (Berger et al., 2005).

At Mountain Elementary (a pseudonym), the principal made an initial decision to require all teachers to participate in action research as a form of professional development and then reversed her decision. As a result, less than half of the teachers at the school elected to engage in action research. These teachers received release time to attend seminars and classes on action research as part of a partnership between a local university and the district in which Mountain Elementary was located. But Berger and colleagues (2005) found that most of the teachers involved in this effort carried out small-scale projects that failed to address substantive educational issues. The researchers added that the participating teachers "rarely talked about the connection between the research they were doing and students' learning" (Berger et al., 2005, p. 98).

Berger and colleagues (2005) described several factors that seemed to affect whether action research was sustained on a schoolwide basis at these schools. First, along with mandating that all teachers participate in action research, it was important for principals to enable teachers to feel a sense of initiative, ownership, and control over the research process. Second, school leaders needed to provide structures in which research could take place; at Eastern Elementary, these included faculty meetings, various group meetings (i.e., grade-level, cross-grade, and content-specific), and support and modeling from school administrators.

Third, teachers needed opportunities to learn about research and to develop their own research skills. At Eastern Elementary, the focus on basic quantitative methods meant that "teachers had little trouble formulating questions or finding out the answers to their questions and were able to begin their teacher research efforts more quickly and sustain them more easily" than teachers at the other schools (Berger et al., 2005, p. 102). Finally, it was important for the schools to develop an emphasis throughout their faculties on both inquiry and collaboration in order to sustain action research groups over time (Berger et al., 2005). When these factors are evident, they can support teachers' efforts to engage in meaningful inquiry into their own practices.

Cognitively Guided Instruction

Fennema and colleagues (1996) created and refined an approach to professional development for elementary mathematics teachers known as cognitively guided instruction (CGI). In this section, we first describe CGI and provide a hypothetical example of how it would be implemented in a school. Then we draw on research on the implementation of CGI to identify conditions that support effective enactment of this approach.

CGI features initial workshops that last from 2 days to 4 weeks, follow-up workshops during the school year, and school-based support. As part of the initial workshops, teachers learn about a research-based model of children's mathematical thinking. The CGI model features "an integrated perspective of basic number concepts and operations and how children usually think about them" (Fennema et al., 1996, p. 406). Basic problems of addition, subtraction, multiplication, and division are divided into various groups, and each group is characterized by distinct types of action or relationships. The model also offers "a way to identify the relative difficulty of the basic problems that is consistent with the way children develop their thinking and solutions to the problems" (Fennema et al., 1996, p. 406). As part of learning about the model, teachers view videotapes of children solving word problems and analyze children's solutions to the problems.

In addition to learning about the CGI model, teachers in the initial workshops discuss "principles of instruction that might be derived from the research and (design) their own programs of instruction on the basis of those principles" (Carpenter, Fennema, Peterson, Chiang, & Loef, 1989, p. 505). The principles include: (1) that "instruction should be organized to facilitate students' active construction of their own knowledge with understanding"; (2) that teachers should examine children's thinking by "asking appropriate questions and listening to children's responses"; and (3) that "instructional decisions should be based on teachers' knowledge of what children know and understand" (p. 505). The follow-up workshops and school-based support are designed to help teachers to reflect on the workshop "content and their students' thinking" and on "using knowledge of their students' thinking in making instructional decisions" (Fennema et al., 1996, p. 409).

Let's assume that four fourth-grade teachers from the same elementary school participate in an initial CGI workshop over the summer. As part of their district's fourth-grade mathematics curriculum, they are expected to focus extensively on multidigit multiplication with their students. Based on their experiences in the CGI workshop, all four teachers alter their approach to teaching this topic in order to engage students more frequently in problem solving, sharing solutions, and justifying solutions. In follow-up workshops during the school year, they meet with other teachers from across the district and discuss strategies for assessing students' prior knowledge of different aspects of multidigit multiplication and incorporating it into their mathematics instruction. Over the course of the year, three of the fourth-grade teachers stop using direct instruction altogether in their mathematics teaching and instead engage students regularly in solving mathematical problems, sharing their solutions to such problems, and providing justifications for their solutions. However, the fourth teacher continues to provide some direct instruction in mathematics while also engaging students in problem solving on an occasional basis.

In a series of studies, Carpenter and colleagues investigated the effects of participating in CGI professional development on outcomes for different cohorts of elementary mathematics teachers and their students. In one study, Carpenter and colleagues (1989) compared 20 first-grade teachers who participated in a 4-week CGI summer workshop with 20 first-grade teachers who worked in the same schools as the treatment teachers. The control-group teachers participated in two 2-hour workshops during the school year that focused on mathematical problems but did not address the CGI model. The researchers collected survey data on teacher and student outcomes in May 1987, which was almost a year after the CGI summer workshop had taken place.

Carpenter and colleagues (1989) reported that "CGI teachers spent significantly more time on word problems than did control teachers," whereas "control teachers spent significantly more time on number facts problems than did CGI teachers" (p. 520). They also reported that CGI teachers presented mathematical problems to students more frequently and listened to how students solved problems more often than did the control teachers. In terms of teacher knowledge, Carpenter and colleagues found that CGI teachers had significantly more knowledge of student strategies for both problem solving and number facts than control teachers did. With regard to beliefs, they reported that "CGI teachers were significantly more cognitively guided in their beliefs than were control teachers" (p. 523). Finally, in terms of effects on students, they found that students in CGI teachers' classrooms demonstrated greater confidence in their ability to solve mathematical problems than control students and "reported significantly greater understanding of mathematics than did control students" (p. 525).

In a second study, Fennema and colleagues (1996) collected baseline data on 21 teachers in grades 1–3 before they participated in an initial 2½-day CGI workshop and then collected additional data on them over a 3-year period. Prior to this study, seven of the teachers had participated in either a 4-week summer CGI workshop or a 10- to 20-hour CGI workshop during the school year, whereas 14 of the teachers had not had any exposure to CGI. Fennema and colleagues reported that the mathematics instructional practices of 18 of the 21 teachers became more cognitively guided over the 3-year period. In particular, for each of the 18 teachers, "there was increased emphasis on problem solving, more communication by the children about their problem-solving strategies, and clear evidence that the teacher was more apt to attend to her own students' thinking when she made instructional decisions" (p. 415).

In terms of associations between changes in instruction and student outcomes, the researchers concentrated on the 11 teachers for whom they had complete student and teacher data for each of the 4 years of the study. Of these 11 teachers, there were 8 teachers whose instruction became more cognitively guided from the baseline year to the end of Year 1. Of these 8 teachers, 7 experienced improvements in mean student achievement (on the tests of concepts and problem solving) of at least half a standard deviation during that year or the following year. In addition, in all 8 cases in which student achievement increased by at least half a standard deviation from Year 1 to Year 2 or from Year 2 to Year 3, the teacher's mathematics instructional practices became more cognitively guided (Fennema et al., 1996).

In a third study, Franke, Carpenter, Levi, and Fennema (2001) examined the instructional practices of 22 elementary teachers during the 1996–1997 school year; these teachers had all participated in CGI professional development from spring 1990 through spring 1993. Whereas all of the teachers had been teaching in grades 1–3 in 1992–1993, 19 were teaching in these grades in 1996–1997, one was teaching fourth grade, and two were teaching combined fourth- and fifth-grade classes. The data collection involved interviewing each teacher and observing his or her mathematics instruction during 1996–1997. In addition, the authors used a four-level classification scheme to characterize each teacher in terms of the degree to which their beliefs and instructional practices emphasized engagement with children's mathematical thinking.

Franke and colleagues (2001) reported that all 11 teachers who were at the highest levels of the classification scheme (i.e., Levels 4A and 4B) at the end of the CGI professional development in spring 1993 remained at those levels in 1996–1997.

These teachers, for example, were knowledgeable about individual children's mathematical thinking and viewed the development of children's thinking in terms of a framework that they used to guide their instructional decisions. In addition, of the 9 teachers who were at Level 3 in spring 1993, 4 remained at Level 3 and 1 moved to Level 4B. Like Level 4A and 4B teachers, Level 3 teachers used their knowledge of the mathematical thinking of individual students to plan instruction.

Franke and colleagues (2001) reported that the level of support from one's teacher colleagues was very important in helping these teachers to maintain CGI practices over time. Each teacher first became involved with CGI while working "in a school where the majority of teachers were participating in the professional development program" (p. 679). In addition, teachers indicated that their long-term relationships with members of the CGI research team were critical to their continued enactment of CGI principles in their teaching. Finally, the authors noted that the 10 teachers who were at the highest level according to their classification scheme (i.e., level 4B) "shaped both the form and content of their collaborative relationships to permit practical inquiry about children's mathematical thinking" (p. 684). In other words, these teachers modified existing structures for collaboration to help them maintain a strong focus on children's thinking.

To summarize the effects of CGI professional development on mathematics instruction, Carpenter and colleagues (1989) reported that CGI teachers spent more time on word problems than control teachers, presented mathematics problems to students more often, and listened to how students solved problems more frequently than control teachers. Fennema and colleagues (1996) found that 18 out of 21 teachers who participated in a 2½-day CGI workshop became more cognitively guided in their mathematics instruction over a 3-year period. Franke and colleagues (2001) reported that 16 out of 22 teachers who participated in CGI professional development over a 4-year period were using knowledge of students' mathematical thinking 4 years later to plan mathematics instruction, and 12 of the 22 viewed the development of children's thinking as a framework that they used to shape their decisions about instruction.

Finally, research on CGI indicates that this approach to professional development can help teachers learn to examine the thinking and learning of their students and to utilize knowledge of students to make changes in teaching practice (Ball & Cohen, 1999). In addition, CGI can enable teachers to promote greater understanding of mathematics among students.

Instructional Coaching

Instructional coaching has become an increasingly popular strategy that districts and schools use to attempt to improve teaching practice. If teacher learning and instructional improvement require learning from practice, as Ball and Cohen (1999) asserted, employing experts to guide teachers in meaningful inquiry into their own practice seems like a sensible place to start. Research suggests that effective instructional coaches can play an important role in connecting teachers to valuable resources and creating opportunities for them to engage in the types of professional discourse that help them better understand their practice (Coburn & Russell, 2008). However, although instructional coaches are now widely used in districts throughout the United States, questions remain concerning how instructional coaches should be integrated into existing school organizations and practices and who should serve as coaches.

In this section, we first describe instructional coaching and provide a hypothetical example of how it would be implemented in a school. Then we draw on research on instructional coaching to identify conditions that support effective implementation of this approach.

Establishing the role of the instructional coach has proven easier than defining it. For example, Taylor (2008) argued, "One of the largest obstacles to understanding instructional coaching is the lack of a clear definition of the phenomenon or agreement on what counts as coaching" (p. 11). Ostensibly, the instructional coach is charged with the daunting task of intervening in the instructional triangle (i.e., teachers, learners, and academic content) in effective ways and, in the process, trying to improve teaching practice and student learning. With this task in mind, it is helpful to consider the definition that Taylor ultimately provided; he described coaching as an endeavor characterized by "non-supervisory/non-evaluative individualized guidance and support that takes place directly within the instructional setting" (p. 12). This definition is consistent with principles for effective reform recommended by several researchers. For example, Elmore (2004) insisted that quality reform makes teaching more public and transparent and that professional development should occur close to practice. Furthermore, tasking instructional coaches with helping teachers to improve their practice can distribute school leadership among several educators in a school and can thus provide a powerful condition for school improvement (Spillane, Halverson, & Diamond, 2001).

Imagine that an instructional coach is tasked with the responsibility of helping elementary teachers improve their practice in ways consistent with the Common Core English/language arts standards. First, coaches can offer sustained, in-class assistance to teachers in which they provide descriptive and actionable feedback to them. Additionally, coaches can plan and teach with teachers, teach demonstration lessons with their students, and/or lead teachers through model lessons at faculty meetings. Although the coach should be a skilled and effective teacher, she or he does not need to be perfect. Rather, the coach would be wise to adopt the disposition of one who actively learns from her or his own practice, is eager to improve, and is open to feedback.

Direct, in-class assistance is not the only way for a coach to help improve teaching and learning. Coaches can also help develop a school climate in which teaching is a public act and subject to constant critique and improvement. First, coaches can relieve teachers so that they are able to observe their peers' instructional practices. Coaches and teachers can also visit several classrooms and meet at the conclusion of these rounds to discuss what they have observed. In the same vein, coaches can arrange meetings that focus on the challenges of instruction and ways of addressing them. In sum, the goal of instructional coaching is to help teachers grow accustomed to the constant critique and improvement of their instructional practice, open to the exposure of their practice, and receptive to feedback that such improvement requires. There are many strategies that a coach can use to realize these goals.

Defining instructional coaching and aligning it with well-established reform ideals, however, does not move us closer to deciding who should fill the role of instructional coach, how the coach should behave, or how teachers should best be included in the coaching process. And, unfortunately, empirical research that might help resolve these issues is sparse (Coburn & Russell, 2008; Mangin & Stoelinga, 2008). Nevertheless, the research that is available can suggest best practices for current practitioners and provide guidance to scholars in addressing the considerable research gap.

In one study, Coburn and Russell (2008) investigated the importance of teachers' social networks in the implementation of new mathematics curricula in two school districts, Greene and Region Z. Both of the districts under study provided teachers with initial professional development training related to the mathematics curricula and follow-up support from instructional coaches. In their study, the authors used a traditional conception of social capital, which posits that resources are embedded in one's social networks and that, in turn, the strength of these networks has "important consequences for knowledge development and diffusion of innovations" (p. 206). Furthermore, the authors argued that social capital has four sources: structure (including tie span and strength), access to expertise, trust, and content of interactions (including depth and congruence with reform ideals).

Coburn and Russell (2008) concluded that instructional coaches played a pivotal role in developing teachers' social capital, implementing the new mathematics curricula, and diffusing innovative ideas. However, the effectiveness of the coaches varied by district and, to a lesser extent, by school. In part, these variations can be attributed to differences in the ways the two districts selected coaches. In Greene, only candidates with a track record for strong instructional leadership in mathematics were considered to fill coaching vacancies. Once selected, the district provided coaches with extensive professional development that included an introduction to district reform initiatives in mathematics, a thorough training in the new curriculum, and ongoing, on-site support for coaches.

In contrast, in Region Z, the hiring of coaches was highly idiosyncratic and unstructured. Consequently, coaches in this district tended to have little experience in teaching mathematics or serving as instructional leaders. Once hired, Region Z coaches were offered very little professional development. As a result of these differences in selection and development, the Greene coaches were more skilled than their counterparts in Region Z and had much better and more frequent interactions with teachers. This meant that Greene teachers had greater access to expertise and improved network structures (in terms of tie span and tie strength).

The practices of the instructional coaches also affected the depth of teachers' professional interactions. Coburn and Russell (2008) found that teachers active in the coaching process participated in the types of discourse that Ball and Cohen (1999) described as essential to instructional improvement, concluding that "those teachers who were actively coached had much deeper conversations with other teachers in their network" (Coburn & Russell, 2008, p. 220). In particular, coaching had a clear impact on the structure of teachers' social networks (tie span and tie strength), the content of their interactions (depth and congruence), and their access to expertise. Coburn and Russell's work suggests that coaches should be carefully selected based on their expertise and experience and thoroughly prepared in district curricular and reform initiatives and that they should receive ongoing guidance that supports their work. Coaches, in turn, should be committed to interacting with teachers and engaging them in inquiry into their practices, as well as expanding teachers' social ties and connectedness to other teachers.

In the second work to be considered here, Gallucci, Lare, Yoon, and Boatright (2010) set out to study the learning and development of a single instructional coach. In their study, they drew on sociocultural theories that postulate that learning is deeply embedded in social contexts and can, therefore, be supported by improved organizational and environmental supports. Unlike the instructional coaches in Coburn and Russell's (2008) study, the focal coach for their work continued teaching, albeit in a reduced role, when he assumed instructional coaching duties.

Not surprisingly, Gallucci and colleagues (2010) found the role of instructional coach to be complex and challenging. First, the authors reported that instructional coaching requires extensive on-the-job learning; rather than being a "mediator and conduit" of reform ideas, the instructional coach lacked knowledge of reform initiatives and often learned about them shortly before he was to promote them among teachers. Second, the authors determined that the focal instructional coach's experiences both informed and were informed by his ongoing experiences as a teacher. This reciprocal relationship complicated the link between policy messages and classroom implementation, as the focal coach "had to appropriate these (reform) ideas, transform them in the context of his own work, and then share his new practices with others" (Gallucci et al., 2010, p. 953).

Because instructional coaching requires learning on the job, Gallucci and colleagues (2010) contended that districts would be wise to give special consideration to coaches' opportunities to learn and organizational supports that promote learning. However, the research base that describes best practices for ongoing professional development for instructional coaches remains underdeveloped (Mangin & Stoelinga, 2008). Whereas researchers have examined efforts to enact instructional coaching across entire districts (Camburn, Kimball, & Lowenhaupt, 2008; Coburn & Russell, 2008) and factors associated with effective coaching relationships (Coburn & Russell, 2008; Gallucci et al., 2010), there has been less research on (1) the types of professional development activities for coaches that foster effective coaching practices and (2) how coaching affects changes in teachers' instructional practices or student achievement gains.

With regard to factors that support implementation of instructional coaching, we can rely on the research cited above. First, as Coburn and Russell (2008) concluded, site administrators should select coaches carefully based on their content and pedagogical knowledge and, wherever possible, on the respect and trust they have earned with teachers in their school. Furthermore, as Gallucci and colleagues (2010) suggested, once on the job, coaches should be provided with extensive professional development. This should include not only training but also the opportunity to connect with other coaches and to discuss the challenges and successes they experience. Third, the coach's job is not to evaluate teachers but rather to provide them with sustained feedback on their instruction in the context of pedagogical goals and connect them with other resources for their improvement (Taylor, 2008). Site administrators must honor this arrangement and remember that opening up one's teaching practice to public scrutiny can be an intimidating proposition and that trust between the coach and teacher is critical to success in the position and to instructional improvement.

In sum, research on instructional coaching suggests that teachers benefit from the instructional leadership of others, from active participation in the coaching process, and from serving as instructional coaches themselves. Coaching can be a key strategy for engaging teachers in the cycle of inquiry necessary for instructional improvement. Coaching can help teachers learn from practice, another of Ball and Cohen's (1999) requirements for instructional improvement, and can lead to ongoing experiences that help teachers develop the kind of instruction that reformers propose.

CONDITIONS THAT SUPPORT IMPLEMENTATION

The approaches to professional development described in this chapter are all designed to involve teachers in analyzing and learning from their own practice. In order to enact these approaches effectively and sustain them over time, principals and district administrators must ensure that several conditions are present. These include providing opportunities for teachers to learn about these approaches and develop research skills, promoting teacher ownership over the approaches, enabling teachers to learn from their peers, promoting inquiry and collaboration across school faculties, and drawing on outside experts. In this section, we describe several ways in which principals and district administrators can influence whether these approaches to professional development are successfully implemented and sustained over time.

Research on lesson study and CGI is consistent with other research that has demonstrated the importance of school and district administrators' providing teachers with time, structures, and other opportunities to learn about and participate in professional development (Coburn, 2005; Kardos, Johnson, Peske, Kauffman, & Liu, 2001; Youngs & King, 2002). With regard to action research, Berger and colleagues (2005) showed that teachers need opportunities to learn about research and to develop research skills in order to carry out investigations of their own practices. For many teachers, collecting data on their own practices or their schools is an unfamiliar activity. Furthermore, some teachers will be inclined to focus in lesson study or action research on relatively trivial or mundane topics. District administrators and principals will need to provide opportunities for teachers to acquire research skills and to ensure that they address meaningful issues as they inquire into their own practice (Berger et al., 2005; Fennema et al., 1996; Perry & Lewis, 2009).

A second key condition is whether administrators promote a sense of ownership among teachers. In the SMFC district, teachers chose the focal topics on which their lesson study groups worked (Perry & Lewis, 2009). Similarly, in the CGI workshops, teachers developed their own programs of mathematics instruction based on their knowledge of CGI principles (Carpenter et al., 1989). Finally, teachers in the action research groups in Boston/Brookline, Madison, and Eastern Elementary all chose their own research topics (Berger et al., 2005; Zeichner, 2003). By having teachers choose their own research topics and design instructional strategies, administrators can promote a strong sense of ownership among teachers over their professional growth (Coburn, 2005; Newmann, King, & Youngs, 2000; Printy, Marks, & Bowers, 2009).

Another factor that supports successful enactment is whether principals promote inquiry and collaboration (associated with these approaches) across their faculties. Lewis and colleagues (2006) described the role of strong leadership at Highlands Elementary in supporting lesson study, while Berger and colleagues (2005) and Franke and colleagues (2001) documented the value of developing an emphasis on both inquiry and collaboration among the majority of teachers at a given school. In research on mathematics instructional coaches, Coburn and Russell (2008) found that effective coaches were able to connect teachers to other teachers at their schools. These findings are consistent with other research on the crucial role of school leaders in supporting teacher inquiry and collaboration (Kardos et al., 2001; Printy et al., 2009; Youngs & King, 2002).

Finally, access to outside expertise is a key ingredient in professional development that supports teacher inquiry (Coburn, 2005; Newmann et al., 2000). In order to enact lesson study, action research, and CGI and to sustain these approaches over time, teachers strongly benefited when administrators helped them secure access to outside expertise (Franke et al., 2001; Perry & Lewis, 2009; Zeichner, 2003). With regard to instructional coaching, Coburn and Russell (2008) reported that the selection and training of coaches had a significant influence on their effectiveness, that is, the extent to which they offered useful outside expertise to teachers.

When these conditions are present, research indicates that these approaches to professional development can have far-reaching effects. Perry and Lewis (2009) reported that participation in lesson study can lead to changes in teacher knowledge and the development of an inquiry stance among teachers. Zeichner (2003) showed that engagement in action research can lead to changes in teachers' instructional practices and collaborative skills, including a greater focus on student learning. For their part, Carpenter, Fennema, Franke, and colleagues demonstrated that participation in CGI can lead to changes in teachers' knowledge, beliefs, and mathematics instructional practices and to improved student learning in mathematics. Finally, Coburn and Russell (2008) found that effective mathematics instructional coaches can help teachers implement new mathematics curricula and connect with other teachers in their schools.

Despite the promise of these approaches to professional development, principals and district administrators face some challenges due to the current policy context in the United States in trying to enact them in meaningful ways and to sustain implementation of them over time. On the one hand, the CCSS can potentially provide a shared language about instruction (that can support teacher inquiry and collaboration), and these standards call for teachers to engage students in higher-order thinking and understanding. On the other hand, the CCSS will potentially lead schools and districts to focus on curricular breadth over depth; concentrating on the latter seems more consistent with the approaches to professional development described in this chapter (Porter, McMaken, Hwang, & Yang, 2011).

High-stakes testing, a second aspect of the current policy context, has the potential to undermine these approaches in two ways. First, pressure associated with high-stakes testing can lead teachers and principals to allocate less time for inquiry-oriented professional development. Second, most current state tests put more emphasis on basic literacy and numeracy skills than on high-level thinking. Although the inchoate CCSS assessments may eventually place greater priority on student understanding, a continued focus in state assessments on basic skills can undermine efforts in lesson study, action research, CGI, and instructional coaching to encourage teachers to address student understanding in their own instruction (Mintrop & Trujillo, 2007).

Finally, changes in teacher evaluation pose a challenge to these approaches to professional development. It should be acknowledged that more rigorous classroom observations can promote teacher inquiry and greater attention to student understanding. On the other hand, the emphasis in many states on using value-added scores to evaluate teachers may work against efforts to establish lesson study, action research, and CGI groups, to deprivatize teachers' instructional practices, and to promote teacher collaboration (Youngs, 2013). In particular, this approach to teacher evaluation may weaken attempts to build the teacher–teacher trust that is necessary to support inquiry-oriented professional development.

QUESTIONS FOR DISCUSSION

1. Why might teacher inquiry into their own instructional practices be associated with the enactment of ambitious instruction?

2. How do lesson study, teacher action research, CGI, and instructional coaching promote teacher inquiry and ambitious instruction?

3. What factors support sustained implementation of these approaches to professional development?

4. What are some outcomes of teacher participation in these approaches?

5. What are some challenges to enactment of these approaches to professional development?

REFERENCES

Ball, D. L., & Cohen, D. K. (1999). Developing practice, developing practitioners: Toward a practice-based theory of professional education. In L. Darling-Hammond & G. Sykes (Eds.), *Teaching as the learning profession: Handbook of policy and practice* (pp. 3–32). San Francisco: Jossey-Bass.

Berger, J. G., Boles, K. C., & Troen, V. (2005). Teacher research and school change: Paradoxes, problems, and possibilities. *Teaching and Teacher Education, 21*(1), 93–105.

Boles, K., Kamii, M., & Troen, V. (1999, April). *Transformative professional development: Teacher research, inquiry, and the culture of schools.* Paper presented at the annual meeting of the American Educational Research Association, Montreal, Canada.

Brodhagen, B., Caro-Bruce, C., & Klais, M. (1999). *The nature and impact of action research in one urban school district.* Paper presented at a Spencer Foundation–sponsored invitational conference on Collaborative Research for Practice, Chicago.

Camburn, E., Kimball, S., & Lowenhaupt, R. (2008). Going to scale with teacher leadership: Lessons learned from a district-wide literacy coach initiative. In M. M. Mangin & S. R. Stoelinga (Eds.), *Effective teacher leadership: Using research to inform and reform* (pp. 120–143). New York: Teachers College Press.

Carpenter, T. P., Fennema, E., Peterson, P. L., Chiang, C. P., & Loef, M. (1989). Using knowledge of children's mathematics thinking in classroom teaching: An experimental study. *American Educational Research Journal, 26*(4), 499–531.

Coburn, C. E. (2005). Shaping teacher sensemaking: School leaders and the enactment of reading policy. *Educational Policy, 19*(3), 476–509.

Coburn, C. E., & Russell, J. L. (2008). District policy and teachers' social networks. *Educational Evaluation and Policy Analysis, 30*(3), 203–235.

Elmore, R. F. (2004). *School reform from the inside out: Policy, practice, and performance.* Cambridge, MA: Harvard Education Press.

Fennema, E., Carpenter, T. P., Franke, M. L., Levi, L., Jacobs, V., & Empson, S. B. (1996). A longitudinal study of learning to use children's thinking in mathematics instruction. *Journal for Research in Mathematics Education, 27*(4), 403–434.

Franke, M. L., Carpenter, T. P., Levi, L., & Fennema, E. (2001). Capturing teachers' generative change: A follow-up study of professional development in mathematics. *American Educational Research Journal, 38*(3), 653–689.

Gallucci, C., Lare, M. D. V., Yoon, I. H., & Boatright, B. (2010). Instructional coaching: Building theory about the role and organizational support for professional learning. *American Educational Research Journal, 47*(4), 919–963.

Hiebert, J., & Stigler, J. W. (2000). A proposal for improving classroom teaching: Lessons from the TIMSS Video Study. *Elementary School Journal, 101*(1), 3–20.

Kardos, S. M., Johnson, S. M., Peske, H. G., Kauffman, D., & Liu, E. (2001). Counting on colleagues: New teachers encounter the professional cultures of their schools. *Educational Administration Quarterly, 37*(2), 250–290.

Lewis, C., Perry, R., Hurd, J., & O'Connell, M. P. (2006). Lesson study comes of age in North America. *Phi Delta Kappan, 88*(4), 273–281.

Lewis, C. C., Perry, R. R., & Hurd, J. (2009). Improving mathematics instruction through lesson study: A theoretical model and North American case. *Journal of Mathematics Teacher Education, 12*(4), 285–304.

Mangin, M. M., & Stoelinga, S. R. (Eds.). (2008). *Effective teacher leadership: Using research to inform and reform.* New York: Teachers College Press.

Marion, R. (1998). *Practitioner research as a vehicle for teacher learning: A case study of one urban school district.* Unpublished doctoral dissertation, University of Wisconsin-Madison.

Mintrop, H., & Trujillo, T. (2007). The practical relevance of accountability systems for school improvement: A descriptive analysis of California schools. *Educational Evaluation and Policy Analysis, 29*(4), 319–352.

Newmann, F. M., King, M. B., & Youngs, P. (2000). Professional development that addresses school capacity: Lessons from urban elementary schools. *American Journal of Education, 108*(4), 259–299.

Noffke, S. (1997). Professional, personal, and political dimensions of action research. *Review of Research in Education, 22*, 305–343.

Perry, R. R., & Lewis, C. C. (2009). What is successful adaptation of lesson study in the U.S.? *Journal of Educational Change, 10*(4), 365–391.

Porter, A., McMaken, J., Hwang, J., & Yang, R. (2011). Common Core standards: The new U.S. intended curriculum. *Educational Researcher, 40*(3), 103–116.

Printy, S. M., Marks, H. M., & Bowers, A. J. (2009). Integrated leadership: How principals and teachers share instructional influence. *Journal of School Leadership, 19*(5), 504–532.

Spillane, J., Halverson, R., & Diamond, J. B. (2001). Investigating school leadership practice: A distributed perspective. *Educational Researcher, 30*(3), 23–28.

Taylor, J. E. (2008). Instructional coaching: The state of the art. In M. M. Mangin & S. R. Stoelinga (Eds.), *Effective teacher leadership: Using research to inform and reform* (pp. 10–35). New York: Teachers College Press.

Troen, V., Kamii, M., & Boles, K. (1997, March). *From carriers of culture to agents of change: Teacher-initiated professional development in the learning/teaching collaborative inquiry seminars.* Paper presented at the annual meeting of the American Educational Research Association, Chicago.

Youngs, P. (2013). *How teacher evaluation reform coupled with comprehensive teacher and principal professional development can support implementation of the Common Core assessments.* Washington, DC: Center for American Progress.

Youngs, P., & King, M. B. (2002). Principal leadership for professional development to build school capacity. *Educational Administration Quarterly, 38*(5), 643–670.

Zeichner, K., & Klehr, M. (1999, April). *Teacher research as professional development in one urban school district.* Paper presented at the annual meeting of the American Educational Research Association, Montreal, Canada.

Zeichner, K., Marion, R., & Caro-Bruce, C. (1998). *The nature and impact of action research in one urban school district.* Chicago: Spencer and MacArthur Foundations.

Zeichner, K. M. (1993). Action research: Personal renewal and social reconstruction. *Educational Action Research, 1*(2), 199–219.

Zeichner, K. M. (2003). Teacher research as professional development for P–12 educators in the USA. *Educational Action Research, 11*(2), 301–325.

CHAPTER 16

Using Action Research to Target and Generate Professional Learning

JENNIFER JACOBS
DIANE YENDOL-HOPPEY

- Action research focuses on the concerns of teachers, rather than outside researchers, and provides a vehicle that teachers can use to untangle the complexities of their daily work.
- Teachers can use action research to target their own professional development needs, generate their own professional learning, and encourage schoolwide professional learning.
- When teachers use action research as a professional development tool, they have the opportunity to cultivate an inquiry stance.
- Action research and professional learning are intertwined, as action research serves as a vehicle for professional learning.

Teaching is a highly complex profession that requires sophisticated tools for stimulating, targeting, designing, producing, and capturing teacher learning by those closest to the students. One such tool that recognizes the complexity of teacher learning is action research. Also known as teacher research, teacher inquiry, classroom research, practitioner research, and practitioner inquiry, action research focuses on the concerns of teachers, rather than outside researchers, and provides a vehicle that teachers can use to untangle the complexities of their daily work.

Early in the 20th century, John Dewey (1933) suggested that resolving teaching complexities requires teachers who engage in "reflective action" that transforms teachers into inquiry-oriented practitioners. Extending Dewey's work, Schön (1983, 1987) later depicted teacher professional practice as a cognitive process of posing and exploring problems or dilemmas identified by the teachers themselves. In doing so, teachers ask questions that other researchers may not perceive as relevant and often discern patterns that "outsiders" may not be able to detect. As a part of a 30-year literature review, Zeichner and Liston (1996) advocated that, through the process of action research, teachers cultivate a more informed practice by assuming a variety of roles, including teachers as researchers, scholars, innovators, and participant observers. Given today's political context, in which much of the decision making and discussion regarding teachers occurs outside the walls of the classroom (Cochran-Smith & Lytle, 2009; Darling-Hammond, 1994), the time is ripe to prepare, position, and empower teachers to identify the type and focus of professional learning they need to enhance student learning.

WHAT IS ACTION RESEARCH?

Action research by teachers moves beyond the idea of reflection articulated by Schön (1983, 1987) and differs from teacher professional development opportunities that are typically facilitated by others. Action research for the purpose of professional learning consists of systematic and intentional study of one's own professional teaching practice that relies on the collection and analysis of purposefully designed, naturally occurring data within one's classroom (see, e.g., Cochran-Smith & Lytle, 1993; Dana, Gimbert, & Silva, 1999; Dana & Yendol-Hoppey, 2009; Hubbard & Power, 1993). The action research process specifically engages teachers in identifying a dilemma of practice, creating a research question that guides their study, designing a data collection plan, interpreting data related to their teaching practice, and identifying the next dilemma and question that often emerges from the action research study. Elliott (1988) describes the action research cycle as a continual set of spirals consisting of (1) clarifying and diagnosing a practical situation that needs to be improved or a practical problem that needs to be resolved, (2) formulating action strategies to improve the situation or resolve the problem, (3) implementing the action strategies, (4) evaluating their effectiveness, and (5) clarifying the situation. As a result of engaging in this process, new definitions of problems or target areas for improvement emerge. The cycle of inquiry becomes a vehicle for inciting and sustaining ongoing professional learning.

Although action research is a process that acknowledges the role classroom teachers can play as knowledge generators for the profession, action research often begins as a tool that facilitates teachers' own professional learning in the form of tacit and craft knowledge. Introduced by Polanyi (1958), tacit knowing and tacit knowledge refer to a type of knowledge that is revealed through practice in a particular context, difficult to verbally articulate, and typically informally shared. This knowledge is often local knowledge, knowledge that is specific to the particular teacher, classroom, and instruction. Carr and Kemmis (1986) indicate that action research generates tacit knowledge in the form of practitioner theories grounded in the realities of teaching practice. When teachers are engaged in this type of research process, they are more likely to facilitate change based on the knowledge they create.

WHAT TYPES OF KNOWLEDGE ARE CONSTRUCTED BY TEACHERS WHEN USING ACTION RESEARCH FOR PROFESSIONAL DEVELOPMENT?

Cochran-Smith and Lytle (1999) identify three types of knowledge that practitioners build when engaged in the action research cycle. Together, these knowledge types inform practitioner theories grounded in the reality of teaching. These three types of teacher knowledge include knowledge *for* practice, knowledge *in* practice, and knowledge *of* practice. Knowledge *for* practice is generally thought of as knowledge gained from formal domains. Specifically:

> These domains generally include content or subject matter knowledge as well as knowledge about the disciplinary foundations of education, human development and learners, classroom organization, pedagogy, assessment, the social and cultural contexts of teaching and schooling, and knowledge of teaching as a profession. (pp. 254–255)

This knowledge includes the theory and research that is typically developed by outside sources and shared through publications, taught as a part of traditional postsecondary teacher preparation, or provided through presentations by an outside expert.

The second type of knowledge is referred to as knowledge *in* practice. Knowledge in practice is considered to be the creation of tacit knowledge. This knowledge is generally constructed through practice and experience in the field. Action research provides teachers the opportunity to capture, critique, and evaluate practice. This process leads to authentic, context-specific knowledge construction. Action research as a professional learning tool allows teachers to learn both from external avenues and through personal experience.

The third type of knowledge that must be generated by teachers is referred to as knowledge *of* practice:

> Teachers across the professional life span—from very new to very experienced—make problematic their own knowledge and practice as well as the knowledge and practice of others and thus stand in a different relationship to knowledge. The third conception of teacher learning is not to be taken as a synthesis of the first and second conceptions. Rather, it is based on fundamentally different ideas: that practice is more than practical, that inquiry is more than an artful rendering of teachers' practical knowledge, and that understanding the knowledge needs of teaching means transcending the idea that the formal–practical distinction captures the universe of knowledge types. (Cochran-Smith & Lytle, 1999, pp. 273–274)

This added view highlights the teacher not just as a consumer or observer of teaching knowledge but also as a leader of his or her own professional learning. Knowledge *of* practice necessitates teachers' analyzing, critiquing, and understanding their practices and beliefs.

Engaging in action research provides a vehicle for creating new professional knowledge through job-embedded professional learning (Yendol-Hoppey & Dana, 2010). Action research is the type of activity that allows teachers to direct their own professional learning and identify the focus for such learning. In this way, a teacher's professional development needs to be targeted and guide the focus of action research, and the new knowledge generated as a result of the action research process informs their professional learning. Given that traditional professional development has focused on providing knowledge *for* practice (Cochran-Smith & Lytle, 1999) as a way of bringing external knowledge to the classroom teacher, providing opportunities to construct knowledge *in* and *of* practice has received less attention. Action research serves as a professional development tool by helping teachers develop all three types of professional knowledge.

HOW DOES ACTION RESEARCH FACILITATE THE DEVELOPMENT OF AN INQUIRY STANCE?

When teachers use action research as a professional development tool, teachers also have the opportunity to cultivate an inquiry stance. *Stance development* is the process of creating a disposition, norm, or habit of identifying problems or dilemmas of practice and systematically studying those problems using data collection and analysis procedures. Cochran-Smith and Lytle (1993) identify teachers who make a habit of systematically studying their practice, contributing to their own learning and the learning of others, and addressing inequities faced by children as having an *inquiry stance*. Cochran-Smith and Lytle originally defined an inquiry stance "as a grounded theory of action that positions the role of practitioners and practitioner knowledge as central to the goal of transforming teaching, learning, leading and schooling" (p. 119). They later added that an inquiry stance is:

> A worldview and a habit of mind—a way of knowing and being in the world of educational practice that carries across educational contexts and various points in one's professional career and that links individuals to larger groups and social movements intended to challenge the inequities perpetuated by the educational status quo. (2009, p. 5)

By developing an inquiry stance, teachers develop tacit knowledge and begin to understand that their role as teachers includes problematizing and improving their own practice to advance student learning. Teachers who possess an inquiry stance are better positioned to identify areas that are important to their own professional learning and improved teaching practice.

The purpose of this chapter is to provide educators with an exemplar of how action research can serve as both a professional development tool and a tool that can inform teachers of their professional learning needs. In order to make explicit how action research can serve as a professional development tool and as a vehicle for identifying professional development needs, we provide an illustration of an action researcher, named Amy, who engaged in a professional journey to create an inclusive classroom for culturally and linguistically diverse students. In this illustration, Amy demonstrates how teachers can use action research to target their own professional development needs, generate their own professional learning, and encourage schoolwide professional learning.

HOW CAN TEACHERS USE ACTION RESEARCH IN THEIR CLASSROOMS TO INFORM PROFESSIONAL DEVELOPMENT NEEDS?

Amy is a passionate teacher who has taught third grade at the same school in Central Texas for the past 7 years. One of Amy's core beliefs relates to developing a welcoming classroom environment for all students. She believes in differentiating instruction to meet the needs of all students. *Amy's focus for action research developed out of feeling that perhaps she really was not meeting the needs of all her students, specifically those from culturally and linguistically diverse backgrounds.*

How Did Amy Find a Focus for Action Research?

Over the previous 2 years, the demographics of Amy's school had slowly begun to change. Historically, her elementary school had a large white, upper-middle-class population of students. In the preceding 4 years this population began to diversify as more Latino families moved into the area and school boundaries changed. Currently, her school includes approximately 30% Latino, 10% Asian, and 60% white students. There are also increasing numbers of students who receive free and reduced lunches. Along with these changes, Amy began to notice an increasing number of behavioral issues in the classroom. In terms of academics, Amy observed that many students were not completing their homework and seemed to be struggling with understanding many of the concepts she presented. Amy also began to observe that there was less parent involvement with volunteers in the classroom. Particularly, she noticed these issues with the Latino students in her classroom. This began to nag at Amy, who had always been so successful with students in the past. She wondered what was so different. Therefore, she posed the question guiding her action research: In what ways do students' cultures influence their experience in the classroom? And how might I develop a classroom that is more inclusive to culturally and linguistically diverse students?

How Did Amy Collect and Analyze Data to Target and Refine Her Professional Learning?

Amy developed a data collection plan that involved hearing from multiple stakeholders, or those people with knowledge and experience connected with the focus of her action research. Talking to multiple stakeholders allowed Amy to hear multiple points of view. For example, talking to teachers might lead her to certain themes, but then by collecting data from parents, she might get a very different perspective.

She began by disaggregating her state achievement data by ethnicity over the past 2 years. She also developed a survey for parents and students focused on their beliefs about school. Furthermore, Amy developed an observation tool to use within the classroom as she observed students during different activities within the day (e.g., independent work, collaborative groups, lunch, and specials [art, music, etc.]).

After looking over her achievement data, Amy found that there were definite gaps in achievement between the white and Latino students in her classroom. She noticed an obvious difference in the areas of reading, writing, and science. Amy was surprised that she had not noticed this difference 2 years before. Perhaps due to the smaller numbers of Latino students, this trend was not highlighted by the administration.

Amy then gave a survey to all of her third graders about their feelings in regard to school. Several findings began to emerge from this survey. One finding was connected to relationships. When asked about how well Amy knew the students, many of the Latino students answered that they did not feel that she really knew them. When Amy asked if she included students' cultures in the classroom, most students replied no. When asked about what students disliked about school, several answered that they did not enjoy always having to sit quietly and rarely getting a chance to work with others on assignments and activities. During classroom observations, Amy noticed that most students, but particularly the Latino students, seemed to be very engaged when collaborative learning was a part of a lesson. Results regarding homework included comments about having to watch younger siblings after school or having to go to the family's business and help out. Students shared that they often did not have time to get their homework done because of this. One student wrote about being afraid to speak Spanish because the previous year's teacher had often scolded him when he conversed in Spanish with friends.

Parent surveys revealed that many families were appreciative of Amy and the school in general. There were some comments related to not always feeling welcome. These surfaced particularly in reference to a lack of materials translated into Spanish. They discussed often going to the school's parent support specialist with questions, especially about homework.

Based on the data she collected from parents, Amy went to talk with the parent support specialist. The parent support specialist said that Latino parents truly value education and hope for a better life for their children. She also explained that many parents feel like outsiders in the school. Parents often talk to her about the lack of connections to Latino culture within school festivals, holidays, and curriculum. Finally, she brought up the fact that the school had not done much to really learn about the Latino culture and how culture can influence students' experiences in the classroom.

How Did Action Research Serve as a Vehicle for Continued Professional Learning?

As Amy looked through all of the data she had collected from the different groups, larger themes emerged that provoked deep reflection. These themes included relationships, role of culture, and learning styles. According to the students, parents, and parent support specialist, these were areas in which both Amy and the school were falling short. However, now that she had uncovered this information, Amy felt that she was somewhat unprepared to make changes in her classroom without additional professional knowledge. Amy did not feel that she had a good understanding of the Latino culture. She needed to learn in this area to help her address the needs within her classroom.

Amy began by going back to the parent support specialist, as well as to the teacher of English language learners on her campus, for resources. They provided her with several books and articles to read. She also worked with the parent support specialist to organize an ongoing luncheon with several parents. Amy had given the survey, but now she really wanted to talk with parents face-to-face to hear their stories and learn from their perspectives.

Amy started to learn a great deal of information that she could use to make changes in her classroom. First, she read that she needed to begin by looking at herself and engaging in critical reflection about her own culture, as well as her experiences with diverse cultures. What types of prejudices and deficit thoughts did she hold? Amy learned that when teachers blame students, it results in a lack of reflection on the curriculum, pedagogy, and classroom environment. One resource suggested that she create a collage representing different aspects of her identity and culture. She went on to do this same activity with the students in her classroom. Although she had done a similar activity in previous years, this time she explicitly talked about issues connected to culture, values, and language with her students. The idea of building relationships became central to her vision for the year. She tried to purposefully allow time during the day for students to talk about their experiences.

Amy also began to analyze the curriculum and her instruction for possible connections to culture. In her readings as well as district trainings, Amy learned about the concept of culturally responsive pedagogy. Gay (2010, p. 29) described this as "using the cultural knowledge, prior experiences, frames of reference, and performance styles of ethnically diverse students to make learning encounters more relevant and effective for them." She searched for children's literature that connected to Latino culture. Amy talked openly with her students about language. She encouraged the Latino students to teach the other students Spanish words and phrases. The students began to create labels in Spanish for various items around the room. On certain assignments she encouraged students to write in whatever language they wished.

As part of Amy's inquiry she began to learn about how culture influences the way people view the world and what they value. She also read about how cultures differ from one another in regard to various dimensions, including communication styles, power distribution, and identity development (Hofstede, 1997). Specifically, she learned that Latino families tend to be more collectivistic than individualistic. Collectivists often value the well-being of the group, cooperation, interdependence, and family/group success. Latino students may experience a cultural mismatch as they enter U.S. schools that promote a more individualistic culture that values responsibility for oneself, the well-being of the individual, independence, self-reliance, and individual achievement (Hofstede, 1997; Trumbull, Rothstein-Fisch, Greenfield, & Quiroz, 2001). Amy saw how these differences played out in the school. For example, there was a definite emphasis on individual rather than collaborative work. Students were told to complete their own work and not help each other. Amy started to make changes in her classroom toward a more collectivistic orientation, such as in relation to how supplies were organized, giving students opportunities to work alone or with others, using collaborative assessment, and so forth.

During monthly luncheons, the parents provided a great deal of information that helped Amy reflect on the cultural values that were present in her classroom. Amy worked to build trust with the parents. This was facilitated by the fact that the parent support specialist was trusted and respected by the families. She vouched for Amy and explained that Amy truly wanted to learn in order to support greater success for students. The parent support specialist often framed her discussions with parents in terms of *What do you wish teachers knew about your child?* The parents talked to Amy about the importance of family and how this often was a priority. Parents viewed issues connected to academics as the role of the school. Parents also commented that they experienced difficulties trying to help students with homework. Amy began to analyze her use of homework to see whether certain students had an advantage over others because their parents could help them. The parents also discussed wanting to be a part of the classroom, but issues connected to language made this difficult. Amy found opportunities for families to come in and share cultural knowledge and used the parent support specialist and students as translators.

Amy's action research did not stay within the four walls of her classroom, but began to permeate into the rest of the school to influence the professional learning of her colleagues.

How Did Amy Move Outside of Her Classroom to Support Schoolwide Professional Learning?

Amy began to engage her principal in conversations about her action research and professional learning. They discussed including this action research as an alternative evaluation plan for the year. Amy's principal said that the overall school was struggling with Latino student achievement as well. He asked if Amy could share her findings at a faculty meeting. After Amy shared her data, the principal wanted her to facilitate a professional learning committee focused on cultural diversity that could continue this action research, but on a larger scale.

Six teachers volunteered to become a part of the cultural diversity committee. The group began their work by asking the question, "How can we support greater success for Latino students on our campus?" Their first action involved analyzing the overall standardized testing data from the school. After engaging in data analysis and disaggregating the data, they began to see noticeable achievement gaps between Latino students and white students, especially in the areas of language arts and science. The teachers adapted Amy's survey for parents and students to be given out schoolwide. Amy began to pull many of the articles and books she had read to share with the teachers in her learning community. After analyzing the data, many themes emerged that were similar to those that Amy had found within her original classroom action research.

This prompted the learning community to petition the principal for professional development at the school specifically connected to diversity. They felt that, because the topic might be contentious, they needed a skilled facilitator. In addition to this, the learning community also began to develop a database of multicultural literature that teachers could access and brought in the library to help purchase some of these books. Finally, the learning community decided to engage in their own professional learning through a book club focused on Latino culture. They began with a text that shared the personal stories of people who were second-language learners from a variety of cultures. The learning community hoped to build their own professional knowledge as they began to think about how to then promote this professional learning within the larger school community.

Although action research originated with Amy's wondering about data she collected within her own classroom, she soon found out from the principal that this was a topic that related to the whole school. Amy's professional learning became a springboard for professional learning within the school.

Amy's action research process, illustrated in Figure 16.1, outlines how Amy was able to improve her own teaching and influence the teaching of others within her school. Amy's action research began when she developed a question related to an area in which she struggled with her teaching. Amy felt that she needed to better understand the influence of students' culture on their experience in the classroom and how she could work to create a more inclusive classroom environment. In order to pursue this question, Amy needed to learn from others both inside and outside of her school to create knowledge *for* practice. After collecting and analyzing data within her classroom, Amy was able to target and refine the focus of her professional learning related to culturally and linguistically diverse students. This stage of the action research process required that she implement change to create knowledge *in* practice, collecting and analyzing data. She then continued with action research as she engaged in professional learning to make changes in her beliefs and practices related to areas such as classroom environment, curriculum, pedagogy, relationships with families, and so forth. She did this by collecting and analyzing data from her own context, as well as looking to outside research to inform her learning. Then Amy was able to move outside of her classroom to support schoolwide professional learning connected to this topic as well.

DISCUSSION

By witnessing this account of Amy's journey to improve her teaching, educators can better understand the mechanisms that are embedded throughout the action research cycle that lead to authentic professional learning. In the illustration, Amy

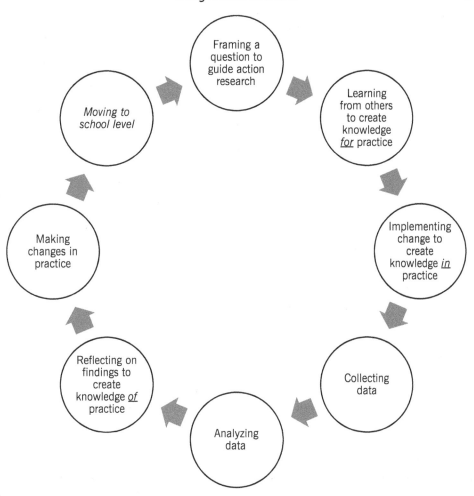

FIGURE 16.1. The action research cycle and professional knowledge generation.

provides an example of how teachers can use action research to target their own professional development needs, generate their own professional learning, and encourage schoolwide professional learning. Amy's initial wondering about the influence of culture and what she could do to make her classroom more inclusive resulted in ongoing professional learning. There was not a moment when action research ended and professional learning began, as these two concepts were intertwined. Action research was the vehicle for professional learning.

By engaging in action research, Amy generated knowledge *for, in,* and *of* practice (Cochran-Smith & Lytle, 1999). Amy began her learning by developing a question based on informal data that suggested that she was not meeting the needs of a group of children within her classroom. During this stage, she developed knowledge *for* practice by targeting professional learning from formal and informal external sources. For example, she listened to students, parents, and the parent support specialist to learn about how she supported the success of Latino students. Amy also utilized resources outside of her school to promote her learning. She attended district trainings and read a variety of books. As Amy learned from all of these sources, she began to engage in developing knowledge *in* practice by making systematic changes in her classroom and then continuing to study the effectiveness of these changes. She collected data throughout the cycle to improve her instruction for this group of children. Importantly, as a result of being systematic and intentional, Amy was able to create knowledge *of* practice as well. Specifically, she reflected on her work to identify underlying assumptions that she held about teaching practice and student learning that were interfering with her effectiveness in meeting the needs of this group of students. Amy's work truly shows a continual cycle of action and reflection, with professional learning occurring throughout the entire process. The product of this professional learning was the construction of knowledge *for, in,* and *of* practice that positioned Amy to enhance student learning within her classroom and school. When all three types of knowledge can be constructed through the action research process, teachers are able to implement deep and authentic changes in practice.

Amy's action research also illustrates the central role of stance within the process. Amy began questioning and wondering about how successful she was working with Latino students. Around the school campus, Amy often heard other teachers bringing up a similar issue. However, the other teachers framed the issue as Latino parents' and students' lack of motivation and care about education. Although Amy experienced struggles as well, she did not want to respond with such a negative way of thinking. Instead, Amy came to this issue with an inquiry stance and began to study this issue within in her own classroom. If this stance were not present, Amy might have responded to the original data using deficit thinking by blaming the students and parents for their lack of motivation and success. Instead, Amy asked questions and was open to learning. She looked closely at her beliefs, her practice, and the voices of those closely involved. Because of this stance, continued professional learning became a natural part of her action research.

Another area of focus related to Amy's professional learning includes the role of the leadership within her school and district. The culture and climate promoted by leadership helps to foster the conditions for teachers to feel empowered to inquire into their practice using action research. Often teachers feel that they do not have the space or ability to change their practice due to district mandates and the pressures of high-stakes testing. Amy's school was in Texas, a state that puts a high priority and stress on high-stakes testing. However, even within this context, action research served as a tool to promote teacher empowerment and learning (Jacobs, 2012). Amy's principal was key in supporting Amy's work within the classroom and finding a way to expand Amy's action research into a schoolwide effort involving a professional learning community of teachers. Principals play a key role in creating the conditions and support necessary to enhance the development of teacher leaders who are able to use action research to improve teaching and learning (Muijs & Harris, 2006; Taylor, Goeke, Klein, Onore, & Geist, 2011; York-Barr & Duke, 2004). Principals who trust teachers, empower teachers, share responsibility with teachers, and give teacher leaders credit for success (Barth, 2001) shift the nature of professional learning to become authentic and empowering. As Barth (2001) says, "If teacher leadership is crucial to the health and performance of a school, principals are crucial to the health and performance of teacher leaders" (p. 448). Jacobs, Beck, and Crowell (2012) found that schools that teacher leaders characterized as open to change and collegial possessed their principals' support for professional learning. Additionally, in these schools, not only were the principals more supportive of action research as a professional learning tool but also, when the teachers' action research focused on issues of equity, greater change for equity occurred.

RECOMMENDATIONS AND FUTURE DIRECTIONS

Action research can become a tool that supports both an individual teacher's professional learning needs and schoolwide professional development. Currently, in many school districts, teachers are describing professional development as *mandated* and *forced* (Jacobs, Burns, & Yendol-Hoppey, 2012). These conceptions of professional development reflect a lack of teacher voice and feelings of disempowerment. However, Amy's example illustrates that, although murky and possibly unpredictable, action research is a process that can not only highlight professional learning needs but also serve as a process for professional learning that does not feel mandated and forced but rather owned and empowering. This more positive orientation enhances the possibility for authentic instructional changes. Future research and practice efforts should include increasing opportunities for teachers to engage in action research within their classrooms and schools.

One area for future inquiry is studying specifically how principals, such as Amy's, are able to negotiate this tumultuous climate of high-stakes testing and teacher evaluation tied to student test scores while still creating a space within schools that values teacher-driven development of knowledge *for, in,* and *of* practice. Studying schools that are able to negotiate this accountability context and at the same time provide tools resulting in empowering professional learning will be key to changing the current context of professional development. It would also be important to look at outcomes connected to curriculum and instruction, as well as student learning, in contexts in which action research becomes a tool for professional development.

When we think about promoting schoolwide professional learning and change, action research is a process with a great deal of potential. Amy's principal was able to move an individual teacher's change within one classroom to the school level, where a community of teachers began reflecting and enacting change. This movement began to cultivate teacher leadership. In the future, this principal could promote the development of several more action research learning communities focused on other school needs identified by teacher feedback, parent feedback, assessment data (test scores, as well as additional assessments), and school improvement goals. This would be a way to expand professional development and promote teacher learning, teacher voice, and teacher leadership. Nieto (2007) writes that principals can be instrumental in creating the conditions for teacher leadership:

> It is up to those who administer schools and make policy to change the conditions in schools and in the broader societal context so that teachers can take their rightful place as intellectuals, as guides for our youth, and as the inspiration for new teachers joining the profession. Until school administrators and policymakers begin to make these changes, we are bound to lose some of the best leadership that is right in front of us. (p. 308)

Future research might include studies of how the use of action research becomes embedded and a part of the school's culture and the role that teacher leaders can play in that process.

The illustration offered by Amy focuses specifically on the use of action research to explore equity issues. Given the importance of creating an equity lens in order to meet the needs of diverse students, future research is needed in this area. Amy was able to frame her action research in connection to culture and equity from the onset. However, another teacher may have framed the action research in terms of: How do I get students to complete their homework? What type of support and additional knowledge would teachers need to be able view this question in connection to equity and culture? Can engaging in action research as professional development help support learning in relation to equity issues, when an equity lens is not already present within the teacher? How can school leaders provide professional development to help teachers build this lens? What is the role of graduate education in supporting the developing of this equity lens? These questions point to the importance of understanding the dynamics and support needed to facilitate professional development related to equity.

This chapter shows the potential of individual teacher inquiry within a classroom to target an individual teacher's professional learning needs based on her or his teaching practice and context. Second, the chapter provides evidence of how that inquiry can cultivate an inquiry stance, as well as generating three types of knowledge necessary for teacher professional development. Finally, the chapter illustrates how the findings generated from inquiry can move outward and influence the larger school environment. What started as the professional learning and growth of one teacher moved to professional learning of other teachers and greater change for students throughout the school.

QUESTIONS FOR DISCUSSION

For Teachers

1. Thinking about your specific context, what would be some wonderings or questions that might guide your action research? Consider both classroom- and school-level questions.

2. What kinds of equity issues inhibit all students from learning within your current context? What questions emerge as a result of identifying these issues?

For Administrators

1. Analyze your current school/district professional development plan. How are teachers able to generate knowledge *for*, *in*, and *of* practice? Is there a balance?

2. What types of structures would need to be put in place within your school to support action research as professional development?

3. How do principals help teachers identify issues of equity that could be explored within the school?

For Policymakers

1. How might districts and state policy related to teacher professional learning support action research as job-embedded teacher learning?

2. How might teacher evaluation be reconceptualized to include this type of evidence of teacher learning focused on student learning gains?

REFERENCES

Barth, R. S. (2001). Teacher leader. *Phi Delta Kappan, 82*(6), 443–449.

Carr, W., & Kemmis, S. (1986) *Becoming critical: Education, knowledge, and action research.* London: Falmer.

Cochran-Smith, M., & Lytle, S. L. (1993). *Inside/outside: Teacher research and knowledge.* New York: Teachers College Press.

Cochran-Smith, M., & Lytle, S. L. (1999). Relationships of knowledge and practice: Teacher learning in communities. *Review of Research in Education, 24,* 249–305.

Cochran-Smith, M. & Lytle, S. L. (2009). *Inquiry as stance: Practitioner research for the next generation.* New York: Teachers College Press.

Dana, N. F., Gimbert, B. G., & Silva, D. Y. (1999). Teacher inquiry: Staff development for the 21st century. *Pennsylvania Educational Leadership, 18*(2), 6–12.

Dana, N. F., & Yendol-Hoppey, D. (2009). *The reflective educator's guide to classroom research* (2nd ed.). Thousand Oaks, CA: Corwin Press.

Darling-Hammond, L. (1994). Performance-based assessment and educational equity. *Harvard Educational Review, 64*(1), 5–30.

Dewey, J. (1933). *How we think.* Boston: Heath.

Elliott, J. (1988, April). *Teachers as researchers: Implications for supervision and teacher education.* Paper presented at the annual convention of the American Educational Research Association, New Orleans.

Gay, G. (2010). *Culturally responsive teaching: Theory, research, and practice.* New York: Teachers College Press.

Hofstede, G. (1997). *Cultures and organizations: Software of the mind.* New York: McGraw-Hill.

Hubbard, R., & Power, B. M. (1993). *The art of classroom inquiry.* Portsmouth NH: Heinemann.

Jacobs, J. (2012, February). *Equity-centered teacher leadership: Promoting change through action research.* Paper presented at the meeting of the Association of Teacher Educators, San Antonio, TX.

Jacobs, J., Beck, J., & Crowell, L. (2012, April). *School improvement through action research: Conditions influencing equity-centered teacher leaders.* Paper presented at the American Educational Research Association, Vancouver, BC, Canada.

Jacobs, J., Burns, R. W., & Yendol-Hoppey, D. (2012, October). *Supervision in a climate of accountability: Understanding educators' experiences with professional learning.* Paper presented at the annual meeting of the Council of Professors of Instructional Supervision, Asheville, NC.

Muijs, D., & Harris, A. (2006). Teacher-led school improvement: Teacher leadership in the UK. *Teaching and Teacher Education, 22,* 961–972.

Nieto, S. (2007). The color of innovative and sustainable leadership: Learning from teacher leaders. *Journal of Educational Change, 8,* 299–309.

Polanyi, M. (1958). *Personal knowledge: Towards a post-critical philosophy.* Chicago: University of Chicago Press.

Schön, D. A. (1983). *The reflective practitioner: How professionals think in action.* New York: Basic Books.

Schön, D. A. (1987). *Educating the reflective practitioner.* San Francisco: Jossey-Bass.

Taylor, M., Goeke, J., Klein, E., Onore, C., & Geist, K. (2011). Changing leadership: Teachers lead the way for schools that learn. *Teaching and Teacher Education, 27,* 920–929.

Trumbull, E., Rothstein-Fisch, C., Greenfield, P., & Quiroz, B. (2001). *Bridging cultures between home and school.* Mahwah, NJ: Erlbaum.

Yendol-Hoppey, D., & Dana, N. (2010). *Powerful professional development: Building expertise within the four walls of your school.* Thousand Oaks, CA: Corwin Press.

York-Barr, J., & Duke, K. (2004). What do we know about teacher leadership?: Findings from two decades of scholarship. *Review of Educational Research, 74*(3), 255–316.

Zeichner, K. M., & Liston, D. P. (1996). *Reflective teaching: An introduction.* Mahwah, NJ: Erlbaum.

CHAPTER 17

Leading Professional Learning in Districts with a Student Learning Culture

WILLIAM A. FIRESTONE
MELINDA M. MANGIN

- Professional learning is more than formal professional development as workshops.
- Demographic changes that increase the need for a highly educated populace and that make it harder for students to get that education have generated a demand for increased professional learning opportunities. However, policy responses to those same changes create an accountability culture that can actually inhibit professional learning.
- District and school leaders can avoid the problems of an accountability culture by developing a student learning culture that (1) assumes that all children can learn while developing its own vision of improvement, (2) understands that teaching is complex, sensitive to student needs, and requires teachers to solve difficult problems, and (3) provides extensive, diverse professional learning opportunities coordinated around local problems.
- Leaders can generate such a culture when it starts at the very top. Leaders use a variety of symbolic and educational strategies, as well as their formal authority to cultivate the necessary assumptions internally, and focus on building external support for the district's approach.
- Leaders contribute further to professional learning when they treat professional learning as an interactive process, organize resources to support interactive learning, ensure that school and district improvement programs are coherent around student learning goals, engage teachers in decision making and treat them as professionals while expecting them to be active learners, and support the use of data in planning learning opportunities.

Increasingly, research is confirming the conventional wisdom that leadership is important in creating the context for effective schooling. Constructive leadership is second only to good teaching among within-school factors that contribute to student learning (Leithwood & Riehl, 2005). School improvement also depends on good leadership (Fullan, 2007). Leaders contribute to both school improvement and student learning by creating learning opportunities for teachers. Leithwood and Jantzi's (2005) formulation of transformational leadership, with its emphasis on helping people by providing intellectual stimulation and modeling key values and practices, points out the importance of leaders' support for professional learning. Robinson, Lloyd, and Rowe's (2008) meta-analysis of the principal leadership literature identifies promoting and participating in teacher learning as an explicit factor contributing to student learning. Thus we would expect strong leaders to facilitate professional learning in schools and districts as well. At the same time, we are learning increasingly about how leadership is distributed. Not all leadership work is done by principals and superintendents; it is often shared with teachers and others (Spillane, 2006).

To promote effective professional learning, formal leaders must respond to several challenges. These stem from the increasing accountability requirements facing schools, the growing barrage of information educators must sort through to determine when and how to improve, and changing student demographics that make the need for professional learning increasingly acute. Professional learning happens best in schools and districts with cultures committed to student learning as their ultimate goal. Although accountability creates the need for professional learning to contribute to schools' expected increases in educational effectiveness, it can also impede that professional learning. Without leadership intervention, schools and districts respond to accountability pressures by developing a culture that is inimical to professional learning. However, with appropriate leadership, schools can become places that support professional learning even in the face of accountability demands. In the pages that follow, we first describe three key challenges facing educators. Then we describe the characteristics of a student learning culture, drawing comparisons with the accountability culture that predominates in schools and districts. Next we address three issues that formal leaders face in developing a learning culture: creating a context in which professional learning can happen, performing the tasks of leading professional learning, and distributing the tasks of leading professional learning.

Throughout this chapter, we use the term "professional learning" intentionally where others might use "professional development." Although we are firm supporters of professional development for teachers, the term typically refers to the one-way transmission of knowledge with teachers as the passive recipients. These include the centrally planned, one-shot district workshops and other events that tie teachers to a narrow curriculum that may not meet the needs of specific teachers or their diverse students (Lieberman & Pointer Mace, 2008). The recent interest in professional learning communities encourages broadening teachers' learning environments to include opportunities where peer support is more possible (DuFour,

2004). Professional learning denotes the range of modes through which teachers learn to improve their practice, whether they involve learning from "experts," peers, materials, or practice.

CHALLENGES THAT REQUIRE PROFESSIONAL LEARNING

American educators face three recurring challenges: changing student demographics, a barrage of information (potentially helpful, but too much to absorb), and rising pressures from increasing state and federal accountability requirements to demonstrate high levels of performance. These challenges necessitate more and better professional learning for teachers.

Increasingly, American students must be prepared for the modern high-technology workplace where priority is given to conceptual and symbolic work using skills in writing, calculating, and other complex symbol systems. This is true in fields as diverse as medicine, technology, and starting a business. Yet students come to school with more challenges that make developing these skills more difficult. For instance, it is known that family background has substantial impacts on students' ability to do well in school, whether through its effects on a child's health and nutrition or on study habits, but the number of children in the United States living in poverty has increased over the last decade. Between 2000 and 2010, the percentage of children living in poverty rose from 17 to 23%. This trend occurred throughout the country. In New Jersey, the percentage rose from 10 to 14%. In Mississippi, it rose from 26 to 33%, and in California, from 20 to 22% (data provided by the Annie E. Casey Foundation Kids Count Data Center; *http://datacenter.kidscount. org/data/acrossstates/Trend.aspx?ind=43&dtm=322#*). Moreover, it is a trend that precedes and reflects economic changes more permanent than the downturn of 2007.

Other changes are also exacerbating stresses on American schools. The shift in the American population from one that is predominantly white to one that is increasingly Latino and Asian has been well documented. One effect of this change is a growing number of English language learners (ELLs) in schools. Between 2001 and 2010, the proportion of ELLs increased nationally from 8 to 9.7%, including over 4 million students. In eight states in the West and Southwest, more than one-tenth of students are ELLs (Aud et al., 2013). The proportion of children with disabilities has increased from 10 to 13% over the same time span (Aud et al., 2013).

As the challenges children bring to the system are increasing, so are the intellectual resources to address them; but these resources are proving a mixed blessing for American educators. As Rowan (2002) noted over a decade ago, the school improvement industry in the United States is alive, well, and growing. It consists of a myriad of textbook publishers, testing companies, research and development companies doing development and evaluation work, universities engaging in similar activities, and—to the point of this book—a wide variety of trainers and professional developers. One need only examine the pages, and especially the ads, in a publication such as *Education Week* to see how diverse this array of services is. Schools and districts have access to a wide variety of textbooks, curricula, and technology that promises to improve student learning or support effective educational management, from data for monitoring student progress, to trainers to help anyone in a school or district learn how to do some aspect of his or her job better. This variety can be helpful, but it creates three problems. One is knowing which products and services are generally high quality. Another is selecting products that fit the local context. The risk in this day and age is the creation of "Christmas tree" schools that adopt so many new, helpful innovations that they lose all programmatic coherence (Hatch, 2001). The third problem is implementing the chosen innovations so that they both do what they are supposed to do and support the direction a school or district chooses.

The final challenge facing educators is the mounting accountability pressures put on schools. These pressures come primarily through the expansion of state tests to publicize the productivity of schools and the increasing tendency to link sanctions, or what are perceived as sanctions, to test scores. These increase bureaucratic accountability while the rise of charter schools and other choice mechanisms increase economic accountability (Firestone & Shipps, 2005). The spread of accountability testing has been largely the work of the states, beginning with the minimum testing movement in the 1970s (Resnick, 1980). By now, all states test students in grades 3–5 and high school as a result of No Child Left Behind (NCLB). We know much more about two contradictory demands on these testing systems: first, the need for highly reliable, inexpensive assessments to support valid conclusions about when students and schools are reaching proficiency and when sanctions should be applied and, second, the need for assessments modeling the complex, cognitively challenging—but expensive to use—tasks to guide educators toward more intellectually stimulating instruction. In the past 20 years, state and federal policies have increased the sanctions linked to poor test performance. These began with sanctions for students, such as failure to advance to the next grade or to graduate from high school, which were used in only a few states. The policy-endorsed sanctions expanded to various forms of interventions to improve school functioning, leading more recently to district or school takeover and restaffing of poorly performing schools (Firestone, 2012). In the past decade, several states and the federal government began experimenting with performance incentives (usually for teachers, but sometimes for principals or for entire schools) linked to test scores, as well as observational data (Podgursky & Springer, 2007).

Although the biggest increase in accountability came through testing, choice and economic accountability have also expanded, especially through charter schools (Henig, 2008). By 2012, the country had more than 5,700 charter schools serving almost 2 million students (Center for Educational Reform, 2011). Choice creates accountability through competition. The idea is that if families have an alternative to public schools, then those schools must become more responsive and effective to maintain large enough enrollments to stay in business (Henig, 2008). Testing accountability and choice began to merge when reconstituting failing schools as charter schools—often with new staffs—became a sanction for low test scores.

PROFESSIONAL LEARNING AND SCHOOL AND DISTRICT CULTURES

The changing political context has affected the internal culture of schools and districts in ways that influence opportunities for professional learning. External pressures generate an internal "accountability culture" that impede opportunities for professional learning. Strong leadership, however, can create a student learning culture more supportive of professional learning. What is important about a culture for this purpose is its pattern of shared assumptions about teaching and learning and about how people work together (Lee, Bryk, & Smith, 1993). Here we briefly contrast the accountability and student learning cultures in terms of their assumptions about students, about how conceptions of teaching influence social relations, and about professional development.

Educators in districts with both cultures assume that increasing student achievement is important. However, in the accountability culture, the challenges of raising achievement become defined externally as the requirement to comply with external authorities rather than internally as the need to attend to the welfare of students. In an accountability culture, district leaders focus on raising test scores because they are made public. Although they may talk about student learning, their real concern is with raising test scores. This can be true of both urban and suburban districts (Bulkley, Fairman, Martinez, & Hicks, 2004). Educators in districts with a student learning culture also assume that increasing achievement is paramount, but this belief is grounded in the difficult-to-develop shared assumption that all children, including those from minority groups and low-income homes, can learn and achieve at high levels. In these districts, boards and superintendents develop concrete visions focusing on improving student achievement and on developing buy-in throughout (Snipes, Doolittle, & Herlihy, 2002; Togneri & Anderson, 2003). Although districts with a student learning culture are sensitive to external accountability demands, they are not driven by those expectations. They hold themselves accountable for their own vision for improvement (Newmann, King, & Rigdon, 1997).

These two cultures encompass different assumptions about how teaching influences social relations among adults. The accountability culture defines teaching as a routine technology with a well-defined knowledge base that is best understood by experts (Firestone & Bader, 1992). Therefore, relations are authority driven with the idea that expertise can be centralized at the top and that teachers do not need to be highly trained. Central administrators with a deeper understanding of the knowledge base about good teaching can monitor and supervise teachers. This approach lends itself to the centralized evaluations based on test scores and administrator ratings that have become popular recently, as well as to differential incentive systems (Podgursky & Springer, 2007). Teachers are often excluded from policy development, and deviation from centrally developed plans is unacceptable (Snipes et al., 2002). Central administrators expect quick results by requiring conformity to external directives; they prefer quick to optimal solutions. This orientation leads to several problems. One is latching on to functional but suboptimal solutions and staying with them too long (March, 1996). Another is to move so quickly among alternatives that none is developed sufficiently to be done well. A third is the "Christmas tree" pattern of aggregating programs without coordinating them.

In contrast, districts with a student learning culture assume that teaching is complex. At its best, it is sensitive to student needs and classroom settings and requires problem solving in the classroom as well as in the district office. The relevant knowledge is contextual, fluid, and developing. As a result, social relations between educators are more complex because expertise is more broadly distributed. Central office leaders and principals value teachers' knowledge more positively. Principals and teachers are held to high expectations for improving student performance (Cawelti & Protheroe, 2001), but leadership is often shared. District leaders in the student learning district rely greatly on effective, creative building and teacher leadership (Marsh et al., 2005). In keeping with the greater complexity of social relations and greater recognition of teacher expertise, student learning districts build trust among staff members through a mix of standardization and flexibility (Bryk & Schneider, 2002). To set clear standards, the district will develop firm program guidelines; but over time, it will adjust those guidelines to reflect developments in the field. The needs of all constituencies are not addressed equally, but central leaders listen to concerns more than they do in the accountability district. Trust facilitates sharing tacit knowledge (Cook & Yanow, 1996). There is also more emphasis on central administrators providing reciprocity, service, and support while demanding accountability (Supovitz, 2006).

Accountability districts use professional development to support their accountability systems. Often professional development helps teachers understand what is on state assessments and how to teach to tests (Bulkley et al., 2004). These districts still stress one-shot workshops because of their view of teaching as routine. Resources are not coordinated across events nor with curriculum implementation or change efforts (Desimone, Porter, Birman, Garet, & Yoon, 2002).

Districts with a student learning culture have more extensive, diverse, and coordinated professional learning opportunities. A substantial portion of these tend to be coherent, job-embedded, focused, synchronized with the curriculum, and guided by data (Desimone et al., 2002). Principals attend to teachers' professional learning as part of day-to-day interaction with teachers, which requires that they know a great deal about instruction (Hubbard, Mehan, & Stein, 2006). This requires considerable professional learning by principals before they can actually support teachers' learning. In addition, districts with student learning cultures develop teacher leaders and other roles to support teacher learning (Marsh, 2002; Togneri & Anderson, 2003). A substantial portion of district-provided professional learning opportunities are linked to implementation of established priorities to avoid the Christmas-tree effect (Snipes et al., 2002).

The accountability culture developed as a response to external pressures. Since the 1970s the American educational system has undergone a substantial reorganization that is still under way. That decade was the end of what David Tyack called "the one best system" (1974), in which superintendents dominated district policymaking and state and federal interventions were limited. During the 1970s, teachers had great autonomy in how they taught (Lortie, 1975). Since then, the rise of state testing, the publication of testing results in newspapers, and linking of poor test scores to such diverse consequences as the denial of high school graduation, school takeover and restaffing, and negative teacher evaluations with potential consequences for tenure and salary increases have created considerable pressure on educators to respond (McDermott, 2009). Districts with student learning cultures are found much less often. The policy context is not conducive to its development, so it occurs only when it is initiated and supported by appropriate leadership.

LEADERSHIP TO PROMOTE A STUDENT LEARNING CULTURE

Leaders contribute to a student learning culture internally by building a belief that all children can learn and externally by building support among a variety of constituencies. Internally, it is up to leaders to help everyone share and act on the belief that all students can learn and should be expected to do so. That this belief contributes to student learning is a consistent finding at both the school (Reynolds & Teddlie, 2000) and the district (Firestone, 2009) levels. Leaders are crucial to developing that consensus. At the district level, leadership starts at the very top. Sometimes the school board hires a superintendent to start the process. Sometimes it starts with the superintendent, but agreement between the board and superintendent is necessary, if only to support leadership continuity and to allow the superintendent and team to make the hard decisions that creating a student learning culture requires (Snipes et al., 2002; Supovitz, 2006). The contribution of principals to promoting shared assumptions about students' potential to learn and the importance of their doing so has been frequently documented (Reynolds & Teddlie, 2000).

The leadership activities that contribute to this belief are harder to describe; collectively, they often go under the heading of symbolic, cultural (Firestone & Wilson, 1985), or cognitive (Spillane, 2006) leadership. Good cultural leaders use several approaches. One is to examine existence proofs, that is, real examples that show how all children can learn. This can be done by having teachers and principals visit programs in other districts or cross-visit different schools in their own (Cawelti & Protheroe, 2001; Supovitz, 2006). Jointly developing a vision statement or strategic plan can also be a teachable moment.

Another approach to building shared assumptions that all children can learn is to use formal authority, which can be applied in several ways. The much discussed "walk through"—when led by top officials—is one way to illustrate the importance of examining practice, for instance, while giving people the opportunity to examine a variety of existence proofs (Hubbard et al., 2006). Mandates can also be crucial, and sometimes it is important to know when not to use that option. In one well-documented case, a superintendent allowed schools to choose between two whole-school reform programs. He clearly preferred one that he thought used a stronger approach to teaching and provided more resources for its implementation. However, he would not require schools to choose the program he favored because he believed school teams had to buy into the program they chose, which would not happen if he mandated that program. So he limited himself to providing additional resources and teaching. Ultimately, this approach generated substantial, but not universal, adoption of his preferred program (Supovitz, 2006).

Sometimes, however, these approaches do not work, either because teachers have alternative values too deeply ingrained to change or because they lack the skills and knowledge to carry out the practices demonstrated. In such cases, building a culture of student learning may require a change in personnel. In some instances, such changes are crucial. Recent research on the contribution of specific effective teachers to student learning (and the negative contributions of ineffective teachers) suggests that removing teachers who do not contribute and hiring more who do is an important step in improving student learning (Hanushek, 2011). Case studies of improving school districts suggest the importance of removing staff in order to change assumptions about what students can learn and how important prioritizing learning can be (Elmore & Burney, 1999). Removing principals can also build consensus about student learning (Cawelti & Protheroe, 2001).

A second way that leaders facilitate a culture of student learning is to work with a variety of external constituencies. Sometimes this work is closely linked to professional learning, as when leaders identify external resources to provide knowledge for teachers, principals, and others. Leaders' connections with universities, professional associations, and other sources of expertise help them find individuals and materials that both provide content to be learned and help create the settings for the learning.

Leaders can also use a variety of state and federal policies and external grant programs to create opportunities for both adult and student learning. However, if these are not defined appropriately by district leaders, what could be a good learning opportunity can turn into a source of external coercion and pressure to work harder without working smarter. Thus how district leaders interpret these opportunities is very important (Bulkley et al., 2004). Moreover, when a district has too many such programs operating simultaneously without coordinating them, they get in the way of learning (Hatch, 2001). Leaders are the gatekeepers who decide which programs a district adopts, how they are coordinated, and how they are interpreted, including whether or not they are seen as learning opportunities.

A crucial constituency for the superintendent is the school board. Earlier, we spoke of how the school board may promote a student learning culture by setting a direction and hiring the right superintendent. At other times, the superintendent may need to communicate to the school board the importance of supporting or continuing to support a student learning culture. One district that failed to develop a student learning culture was San Diego between 1998 and 2002. Although the school board brought in two strong external leaders who understood what needed to be done, those leaders were not able to convince that same board to continue to defend a student learning agenda. That lack of board consensus encouraged them to accelerate the pace of change so much that the speed of change reduced staff understanding of and support for the changes they tried to enact (Hubbard et al., 2006).

LEADING PROFESSIONAL LEARNING

The work of leading professional learning includes a range of tasks that cohere around the need to create interactive, instructionally focused, school-situated learning opportunities for teachers. Traditional professional development programs treat learning as a didactic process and as a fixed property of individuals. From this perspective, teachers are regarded as the recipients of training. Moreover, this training is likely disconnected from teachers' actual work and does little to connect teachers to one another (Feiman-Nemser, 2001). In contrast, sociocultural learning theorists understand learning as an interactive process, whereby people learn *with*, *through*, and *because of* their interaction with others in their contexts (Bransford, Brown, & Cocking, 2000). This view of learning is at the heart of efforts to lead professional learning for teachers. It requires that school and district leaders create increased opportunities for teachers to interact within the context of their schools. This interaction helps teachers build their understanding of school-specific instructional practices, facilitates the construction of new knowledge about how to best meet students' learning needs, helps teachers develop shared agreements about practice, and creates informal peer accountability mechanisms for meeting shared agreements (Putnam & Borko, 2000).

School and district leaders in a student learning culture dedicate existing resources and garner new resources to support increased professional learning. Educational leaders commonly voice concerns about being tasked with unfunded mandates; however, there is some evidence to suggest that schools can reallocate resources to better target professional learning needs (Odden & Archibald, 2010). For example, faculty meetings that are typically used to communicate administrative information can be restructured to include time for teachers to engage in conversation about teaching and learning. Similarly, leaders can reduce or eliminate traditional professional development activities such as offsite workshops or invited guest speakers and use those financial resources to create structures for school-embedded professional learning, such as common planning periods. Other ways that leaders can facilitate professional learning include the development of so-called professional learning communities, literature circles for teachers, creative use of substitute teachers so that teachers can work together, model classrooms for teachers to visit, educative mentoring, inquiry cycles, critical friends groups, lesson study, or the integration of summer professional development activities (such as curriculum development) into the regular professional work that teachers do collectively during the school year.

As leaders work to cultivate teachers' professional learning opportunities, they do so in line with strategic school and district student learning goals. Much has been made of the need to build greater standardization into school systems, including coherence of educational aims, materials, initiatives, and instructional programs (Smith & O'Day, 1990). These efforts build on the logic that coherence creates greater stability for increased student learning. As such, leaders in a student learning culture strive to align the content of their professional learning initiatives with systemwide goals. This, of course, presumes that districts set clear, non-negotiable goals for student learning (Marzano & Waters, 2009). When such goals are set, and when teachers hear a common message about the expectations for meeting those goals, they are more likely to demonstrate support and commitment to new professional learning initiatives. Moreover, systemwide coherence of teachers' professional learning can lead to deeper, more meaningful learning opportunities, as opposed to scattershot initiatives that add another "ornament" on the "Christmas tree."

Creating coherence is more than technical maneuvering of discrete organizational components to achieve an aligned outcome. Coherence is crafted through continual negotiation of external demands and internal goals (Honig & Hatch, 2004). As such, school and district leaders must work to negotiate and fit the internal aims they have for teachers' professional learning with external pressures coming from the larger policy context, in which demands for evaluation and external accountability predominate. This is done through the development and maintenance of collective decision-making structures and through information management (Honig & Hatch, 2004, p. 21). Foremost, decision-making procedures that involve a broad base of participants facilitate collective sense making and the social construction of common understandings. Conversely, lack of common understandings about new instructional content and pedagogy can inhibit faithful implementation of new initiatives, as evidenced in research on reading instruction in which teachers' misinterpretation of policy led to unintentionally erroneous implementation (Coburn, 2001). Moreover, when leaders manage the information that flows into schools, buffering staff from excessive or weak information streams, schools can more easily focus on crafting coherence in line with high-priority needs.

When leaders include teachers in the decision making related to professional learning, they not only facilitate the process of crafting coherence but they also treat teachers as professionals and facilitate the development of professional communities. The need to professionalize teaching has been a long-standing concern of educators (Darling-Hammond & Sykes, 1999). Professionalization reflects the belief, inherent in student learning cultures, that teachers have vital knowledge about students' learning needs due to their close connections to the classroom. Professional communities are understood as those in which teaching practice is deprivatized and teachers assume joint responsibility for student learning (Kruse, Louis, & Bryk, 1995). Contemporary views of teacher professionalization differ from past notions that focused on increasing teacher autonomy. Instead, professionalization is currently understood as intentionally building upon teachers' capacity to contribute to all facets of school functioning, including the development of interdependence and commitment to shared professional goals (Hargreaves & Fullan, 2012). When teacher professionalization is cultivated in schools, teachers are more willing and motivated to participate in new initiatives. Moreover, increased opportunities to participate as professionals can deepen reform efforts and increase its sustainability (Coburn, 2003).

In addition to treating teachers as professionals and honoring their contributions, school and district leaders must also communicate an expectation that teachers are learners. This increases the likelihood that teachers will engage in ongoing inquiry aimed at discerning not only students' learning needs but also teachers' learning needs. In a culture of accountability, in which high-stakes evaluations create a context of fear and anxiety, teachers feel pressure to demonstrate a high level of performance, making teachers less likely to acknowledge uncertainties or shortcomings in their teaching practice. As such, the accountability culture may perpetuate a "fix the kids" mentality, whereby inadequacies in student learning are perceived as a student deficit rather than an area for instructional improvement (Valencia, 1997). A student-deficit mentality is even more pronounced in hetero-geneous classrooms where diverse learners create a challenging context for teach-ing. Leaders in a student learning culture mitigate this student-deficit mentality by communicating that teachers are learners, making it acceptable and desirable for teachers to identify their own learning needs (see works by Blackwell, Trzesniewski, & Dweck, 2007, and Dweck, 2010, for a discussion of the "growth mindset" and its importance for learning). In this context, leaders encourage teachers to make con-nections between students' improvement areas and areas for instructional improve-ment. In such a school, metacognition—awareness of one's own knowledge and thinking—is valued for teachers as much as for students. As such, leaders cultivate the notion of teachers as learners and the belief that teachers' professional exper-tise includes being able to identify personal areas for growth and development.

Leaders can facilitate teachers' ability to identify their own learning needs by supporting teachers' use of data. Data can provide information about strengths and weaknesses of both students and teachers. When teachers examine data together, they develop shared understandings about what learning needs should be priori-tized and how to address those needs (Young, 2006). In the current accountability culture, data have commonly been used as a tool for evaluative supervision and, sometimes, for delivering punitive sanctions. This perspective posits teachers as the object of data use rather than active agents in collecting, interpreting, and responding to data. In a culture of student learning, leaders reposition data as an inquiry tool for teachers to use in the diagnostic process of discerning student learning needs and in the interpretive process of discerning linkages between stu-dents' needs, instructional practice, and teachers' learning needs (Kerr, Marsh, Ike-moto, Darilek, & Barney, 2006). Then analyzing data both constitutes and informs professional learning. Leaders confer value on this work by making time for it, by supporting teachers' learning related to data analysis, and by affording teachers ownership over the process. Moreover, leaders facilitate examination of a broad range of data, including summative assessments but also formative sources of data such as students' daily work. In particular, the use of formative data can reinforce the notion that data contribute to teachers' learning by providing a mechanism for inquiry, dialogue, experimentation, and reform.

Although leaders in a student learning culture recognize teachers as profession-als, leading professional learning is not synonymous with hands-off, laissez-faire leadership. Rather, leaders must monitor the professional learning process. The task of monitoring is often viewed as part of enforcing compliance and accountability; however, it is also a vital part of assessing and facilitating high-quality professional learning. Through monitoring, school and district leaders can gauge the quality of teachers' interactions, discern possible obstacles to learning, identify additional necessary supports, and examine evidence of teachers' learning. Without monitoring procedures in place, leaders are unable to determine the value of professional learning activities for improvement efforts or to identify steps that could be taken to improve the quality of professional learning. Leaders' roles in monitoring professional learning necessitate that leaders are knowledgeable about the content, procedures, and outcomes of high-quality professional learning. Developing leaders' capacity to adequately monitor, assess, and support professional learning constitutes one of the foremost needs in leadership development (Leithwood & Jantzi, 2005).

DISTRIBUTING LEADERSHIP FOR PROFESSIONAL LEARNING

As we consider the range of tasks that contribute to professional learning, it is equally important to ask who should do this work. That is, who should be responsible for these tasks, and who is best situated to accomplish them? One might argue that all the educators in a school system have responsibility to facilitate professional learning, either as supporters, leaders, or participants. And although this may be generally true, it is also important to delineate where responsibility resides and who can leverage the skills, knowledge, and authority to facilitate high-quality professional learning. Professional learning is too important to leave up to chance. Just as strategic school improvement plans identify human resources necessary for accomplishing their goals, schools and districts should identify the people involved in professional learning and the tasks they perform.

Rather than presenting a formulaic or absolute delineation of leadership responsibilities, we offer a discussion of how some educators may be better positioned to lead particular aspects of professional learning, based on their vantage points, knowledge, or skills. To facilitate this discussion we offer Figure 17.1, which outlines the tasks described above and four broad leadership designations: district level (superintendent and deputy superintendents), school level (most likely the principal), formal and informal teacher leaders (e.g., mentor teacher, literacy coach), and external sources of leadership (e.g., consultants, university partnerships). This figure can help the reader engage the content in this chapter or guide educators' conversations about how to strategically support leadership for professional learning.

Given the many tasks involved in leading professional learning, it seems logical that a broad base of leaders is necessary to accomplish this work. Traditional views of school leadership place primary responsibility in the hands of a single, charismatic leader—typically the principal—whose duties focus primarily on administrative tasks related to facilities and personnel management. Certainly, many of the tasks outlined here can be understood as being within the principal's purview. However, as teaching and learning have become more complex and the context for education becomes ever more turbulent, leadership is increasingly conceptualized as a set of functions carried out by a range of actors (Heller & Firestone,

	District level (superintendent)	School level (principal)	Classroom level (teachers)	External sources
Create interactive, situated learning opportunities.				
Allocate resources to professional learning.				
Align content with district goals and craft coherence.				
Grow teacher professionalism and professional communities.				
Cultivate a culture of inquiry with teachers as learners.				
Support teachers data use.				
Monitor professional learning.				

FIGURE 17.1. Sources of leadership for professional learning.

1995; Ogawa & Bossert, 1995). Most recently, this perspective has been described as distributed leadership. This social cognitive view posits that leadership occurs through interaction with people and artifacts in social context (Spillane, Halverson, & Diamond, 2004). Rather than being conferred through formal titles, leadership is understood as a process of influence, whereby any number of people, regardless of formal status, can act as leaders. There appear to be significant organizational benefits to distributed leadership. Foremost, distributed leadership builds overall capacity by expanding sources of knowledge and expertise necessary for meeting educational needs in schools (Harris, 2010). Following this logic, people in different locations of the organization—in the central office, in schools, in classrooms—are differentially positioned to be able to complete different leadership tasks.

District-level leaders working in the central office—primarily the superintendent and deputy superintendents—oversee the schools and their educational practices. Districts also look outward toward the environment, affording them a perspective on external demands and pressures. This elevated vantage point positions district leaders to set the vision and goals for districtwide improvement efforts and, more specifically, the vision and goals for professional learning. In their meta-analysis of district-level leadership, Marzano and Waters (2009) identify six key responsibilities of district-level leaders who positively influence student achievement. These responsibilities revolve around the need to collaboratively set non-negotiable goals for student achievement and instruction and then to align, support, and monitor these goals. Within this framework, superintendents have responsibility for allocating resources to professional learning that aligns with the district vision and goals. To facilitate alignment, districts must work to craft coherence of understanding about the districts' vision and goals for professional learning. Research indicates that central office staff must conceptualize their roles as being teachers of principals, developing principals' instructional leadership and their capacity to lead and support teachers' professional learning that coheres with the district's vision (Honig, 2012). Thus districts are positioned to set the vision and goals for professional learning, to allocate resources for professional learning that aligns with the vision and goals, and to facilitate alignment through the development of principals' understanding.

Whereas district-level leaders have an elevated view of schools and the external environment, school-level leaders—specifically the principal—have a concentrated view of school operations. This vantage point can provide them with in-depth knowledge of school-level instructional practices, as well as the authority to demand change in instructional practice, in line with the district vision and goals. Research indicates that principals have significant, albeit indirect, influence on student achievement through their ability to influence what and how teachers teach (Hallinger & Heck, 1998). However, changing teaching practice is not achieved through mere mandate; rather, it requires support for change in the form of capacity building (Cohen & Hill, 2001). Principals are positioned to provide support for this change through professional learning, which can help teachers build the necessary knowledge and skills for teaching new content in new ways. As such, principals are directly responsible for allocating school-level resources for professional learning that optimizes teachers' opportunities to learn through interaction with their colleagues in the context of their classrooms and schools (Knapp et al., 2003). To support this learning, principals must also create a positive instructional climate. Specifically, principals must cultivate a professional culture marked by inquiry in which teachers have the skills to access and interpret data that can inform their practice. Principals, as school-level leaders with a direct perspective on instructional practice, are positioned to lead teachers in the work of professional learning.

Teachers have an insider's perspective of school- and classroom-level practices, affording them the closest view of teaching and learning. This vantage point affords teachers a unique responsibility, as teachers are both the object and the leaders of professional learning. As the object of professional learning initiatives, teachers are responsible for positioning themselves as learners, being open to new knowledge and information and acting as agents in their own learning experiences. This demands the highest level of professionalism, whereby teachers value and work to develop a shared knowledge base, agreements about high-quality teaching, and collegial interdependencies (Little, Gearhart, Curry, & Kafka, 2003). Paradoxically, as teachers open themselves up to learning, they also position themselves as leaders of professional learning. Because learning is an interactive practice, when teachers engage with one another as learners they also influence one another, acting as leaders in professional learning. This mutual give-and-take of leading and learning is at the core of building a professional community. As teachers take responsibility for creating professional communities in schools, they may also accept or create new roles as teacher leaders. In some cases these roles will be informal, developed by individual teachers in response to their understanding of school needs. Teacher leader roles may also be formally assigned or created by the school organization in response to strategic efforts to build structures and procedures necessary to address needs and goals (see Mangin, Carver, & Berg, 2012, for a discussion of "individual" vs. "organizational" teacher leadership).

Teachers, as leaders and learners, are also responsible for monitoring professional learning, looking to data as a means to assess both student and teacher learning needs. Teachers have highly developed knowledge about content and pedagogy; however, as learning demands increase and student demographics shift, the knowledge base for teaching becomes a moving target, in need of continual assessment and response. In a student learning culture, the need to assess teaching and learning practice is understood as an inherent part of being a professional, rather than as a means of punitive evaluation. Thus teachers in a culture of student learning contribute to the process of leading professional learning when they engage in a cycle of inquiry–assessment–response, aimed at identifying and meeting learning needs. As a process of self-monitoring, this might be described as metacognition, whereby teachers seek personal awareness of their knowledge as a means to identify what they don't know and need to learn to better meet students' learning needs. When teachers engage in this process with their peers, they take stock of teachers' collective knowledge, identify areas of knowledge deficiency, and support one another in building collective instructional capacity. Knowing how to access and interpret multiple, formative sources of data is a fundamental part of this process and a key component of teachers' ability to lead professional learning (Coburn & Talbert, 2006).

Increasingly, districts and schools look to external sources of leadership to guide them in the process of professional learning. This may include contracted consultants, university-affiliated professionals, and various kinds of reformers whose work focuses on improving schools. Historically, schools have been slow to look outside themselves for solutions to educational challenges, owing to the unique properties of educational organizations as inclusive, compulsory, and comprehensive service providers. However, growing societal pressure to adapt business-oriented responses to market-based theories to enduring educational challenges has prompted many school organizations to look outside themselves for assistance. These external sources of leadership can contribute to professional learning in multiple ways. They may guide school and district leaders in the process of setting learning goals, assist with design and development of professional learning initiatives, or facilitate the delivery of interactive learning. This vantage point—looking from outside the schools inward—may provide new perspectives on how to respond to the challenge of student achievement (Rowan, 2002). Whereas external sources of leadership may not have line authority necessary to mandate change, they may be able to leverage knowledge gained from working in other districts with similar challenges.

SUMMARY AND CONCLUSION

High-quality professional learning for teachers is largely dependent on the efforts of educational leaders. Foremost, leaders must create a student learning culture in which students' needs are addressed for internal reasons rather than to comply with external accountability demands. Moreover, developing a student learning culture is consequential for educators' ability to meet student achievement goals in ways that are long term and sustainable and that transcend shifts in leadership. Leaders contribute to the creation of a student learning culture by building shared positive assumptions about all children's ability to learn and mobilizing external resources for learning.

A student learning culture creates the context for professional learning. Leaders contribute to teachers' opportunities to engage in professional learning by creating interactive and situated learning opportunities, allocating resources to professional learning, aligning the content with district learning goals, growing teacher professionalism and professional communities, cultivating a culture of inquiry and teacher learning, supporting data use, and monitoring professional learning. The leaders who take up these tasks are located at various vantage points within and outside schools and districts, situated in ways that enable them to contribute both collectively and differentially to the work of leading professional learning.

In this chapter we have described leadership practices that contribute to a culture of student learning and, subsequently, professional learning for teachers and the rationale for them. Although we know a great deal about the value of professional learning for student achievement, districts and schools continue to struggle to put in place the practices necessary to transform theory and research on professional learning into widespread daily practice. Ironically, the same pressures and demands that make learning for students and teachers invaluable are the same forces that overwhelm leaders and inhibit them from making long-term, strategic choices that support authentic learning. The accountability culture threatens to distract leaders from the real aims of education—deep and equitable learning aimed at cultivating excellence as opposed to achievement for the purpose of compliance and as a means to alleviate public scrutiny.

Leading high-quality professional learning, as opposed to leading mere professional development, requires continued attention to learning as an intrinsic component of all educators' work. We cannot position students as the only learners in school systems; rather, effective teachers, principals, and central office administrators are perpetual learners in the context of shifting educational needs, demands, and environments. With this understanding, we must envision the work of leading professional learning as a complex interplay of leaders and learners, whereby the lines that distinguish each are blurred and both are viewed as valuable.

QUESTIONS FOR DISCUSSION

1. What is a student learning culture, and why is it important for a district to have such a culture?

2. What can school and district leaders do to promote a student learning culture?

3. What else can school and district leaders do to support professional learning in their areas of responsibility?

4. What are some good ways to orchestrate the contributions of leaders in different locations (district, school, classroom, external) to teachers' professional learning?

REFERENCES

Aud, S., Wilkinson-Flicker, S., Kristapovich, P., Rathbun, A., Want, X., & Zhang, J. (2013). *The Condition of Education 2013* (NCES 2013-037). Washington, DC: U.S. Department of Education, National Center for Education Statistics.

Blackwell, L. S., Trzesniewski, K. H., & Dweck, C. S. (2007). Implicit theories of intelligence predict achievement across an adolescent transition: A longitudinal study and intervention. *Child Development, 78*(1), 246–263.

Bransford, J. D., Brown, A. L., & Cocking, R. R. (Eds.). (2000). *How people learn: Brain, mind, experience, and school* (Expanded ed.). Washington, DC: National Academy Press.

Bryk, A. S., & Schneider, B. (2002). *Trust in schools: A core resource for improvement.* New York: Russell Sage Foundation.

Bulkley, K., Fairman, J., Martinez, C., & Hicks, J. (2004). The district and test preparation. In W. A. Firestone & R. Y. Schorr (Eds.), *The ambiguity of test preparation* (pp. 113–141). Mahwah, NJ: Erlbaum.

Cawelti, G., & Protheroe, N. (2001). *High student achievement: How six school districts changed into high-performance systems.* Philadelphia: Laboratory for Student Success.

Center for Educational Reform. (2011, December). 2011–12 national charter school and enrollment statistics. Retrieved September 20, 2012, from *www.edreform.com/wp-content/uploads/2012/03/National-Charter-School-Enrollment-Statistics-2011-12.pdf.*

Coburn, C. E. (2001). Collective sensemaking about reading: How teachers mediate reading policy in their professional communities. *Educational Evaluation and Policy Analysis, 23*(2), 145–170.

Coburn, C. E. (2003). Rethinking scale: Moving beyond numbers to deep and lasting change. *Educational Researcher, 32*(6), 3–12.

Coburn, C. E., & Talbert, J. E. (2006). Conceptions of evidence use in school districts: Mapping the terrain. *American Journal of Education, 112*, 469–495.

Cohen, D. K., & Hill, H. C. (2001). *Learning policy: When state education reform works.* New Haven, CT: Yale University Press.

Cook, S. D. N., & Yanow, D. (1996). Culture and organizational learning. In M. D. Cohen & L. S. Sproull (Eds.), *Organizational learning* (pp. 430–459). Thousand Oaks, CA: Sage.

Darling-Hammond, L., & Sykes, G. (1999). *Teaching as the learning profession: Handbook of policy and practice.* San Francisco: Jossey-Bass.

Desimone, L., Porter, A. C., Birman, B. F., Garet, M. S., & Yoon, K. S. (2002). How do district management and implementation strategies relate to the quality of professional development that districts provide to teachers? *Teachers College Record, 104*(7), 1265–1312.

DuFour, R. (2004). What is a "professional learning community"? *Educational Leadership, 61*(8), 6–11.

Dweck, C. S. (2010). Mind-sets and equitable education. *Principal Leadership, 10*(5), 26–29.

Elmore, R. F., & Burney, D. (1999). Investing in teacher learning: Staff development and instructional improvement. In L. Darling-Hammond & G. Sykes (Eds.), *Teaching as the learning profession: Handbook of policy and practice* (pp. 263–291). San Francisco: Jossey-Bass.

Feiman-Nemser, S. (2001). From preparation to practice: Designing a continuum to strengthen and sustain teaching. *Teachers College Record, 103*(6), 1013–1055.

Firestone, W. A. (2009). Culture and process in effective school districts. In W. Hoy & M. DiPaola (Eds.), *Studies in school improvement* (pp. 177–204). Charlotte, NC: Information Age.

Firestone, W. A. (2012, October). *The irony of control in educational accountability*. Paper presented at the annual meeting of the Pennsylvania Educational Research Association, Philadelphia.

Firestone, W. A., & Bader, B. D. (1992). *Redesigning teaching: Professionalism or bureaucracy?* Albany: State University of New York Press.

Firestone, W. A., & Shipps, D. (2005). How do leaders interpret conflicting accountabilities to improve student learning? In W. A. Firestone & C. J. Riehl (Eds.), *A new agenda: Directions for research on educational leadership* (pp. 81–100). New York: Teachers College Press.

Firestone, W. A., & Wilson, B. (1985). Using bureaucratic and cultural linkages to improve instruction: The principal's role. *Educational Administration Quarterly, 21*(2), 7–30.

Fullan, M. (2007). *The new meaning of educational change* (4th ed.). New York: Teachers College Press.

Hallinger, P., & Heck, R. H. (1998). Exploring the principal's contribution to school effectiveness: 1980–1995. *School Effectiveness and School Improvement, 9*(2), 157–191.

Hanushek, E. A. (2011). The economic value of higher teacher quality. *Economics of Education Review, 30*, 466–479.

Hargreaves, A., & Fullan, M. (2012). *Professional capital: Transforming teaching in every school*. New York: Teachers College Press.

Harris, A. (2010). Distributed leadership: Evidence and implications. In T. Bush, L. Bell, & D. Middlewood (Eds.), *The principles of educational leadership and management* (pp. 55–69). Thousand Oaks, CA: Sage.

Hatch, T. (2001). Incoherence in the system: Three perspectives on the implementation of multiple initiatives in one district. *American Journal of Education, 109*(4), 407–437.

Heller, M. J., & Firestone, W. A. (1995). Who's in charge here?: Sources of leadership for change in eight schools. *Elementary School Journal, 96*(1), 65–86.

Henig, J. R. (2008). *Spin cycle: How research is used in policy debates: The case of charter schools*. New York: Russell Sage Foundation.

Honig, M. I. (2012). District central office leadership as teaching: How central office administrators support principals' development as instructional leaders. *Educational Administration Quarterly, 48*(4), 733–774.

Honig, M. I., & Hatch, T. C. (2004). Crafting coherence: How schools strategically manage multiple, external demands. *Educational Researcher, 33*(8), 16–30.

Hubbard, L., Mehan, H., & Stein, M. K. (2006). *Reform as learning: School reform, organizational culture, and community politics in San Diego*. New York: Routledge.

Kerr, K. A., Marsh, J. A., Ikemoto, G. S., Darilek, H., & Barney, H. (2006). Strategies to support data use for instructional improvement: Actions, outcomes, and lessons from three urban districts. *American Journal of Education, 112*, 496–520.

Knapp, M. S., Copland, M. A., Ford, B., Markholt, A., McLaughlin, M. W., Milliken, M., et al. (2003). *Leading for learning sourcebook*. Seattle: University of Washington, Center for the Study of Teaching and Policy.

Kruse, S. D., Louis, K. S., & Bryk, A. S. (1995). An emerging framework for analyzing school-based professional community. In K. S. Louis, S. D. Kruse, & Associates, *Professionalism and community: Perspectives on reforming urban schools*, (pp. 23–44). Thousand Oaks, CA: Corwin Press.

Lee, V. E., Bryk, A. S., & Smith, J. B. (1993). The organization of effective secondary schools. In L. Darling-Hammond (Ed.), *Review of research in education* (pp. 135–169). Washington, DC: American Educational Research Association.

Leithwood, K., & Jantzi, D. (2005). A review of transformational school leadership research 1996–2005. *Leadership and Policy in Schools, 4*(3), 177–199.

Leithwood, K., & Riehl, C. J. (2005). What do we already know about school leadership? In W. A. Firestone & C. J. Riehl (Eds.), *A new agenda: Directions for research on educational leadership* (pp. 12–27). New York: Teachers College Press.

Lieberman, A., & Pointer Mace, D. H. (2008). Teacher learning: The key to educational reform. *Journal of Teacher Education, 59*(3), 226–234.

Little, J. W., Gearhart, M., Curry, M., & Kafka, J. (2003). Looking at student work for teacher learning, teacher community, and school reform. *Phi Delta Kappan, 85*(3), 184–192.

Lortie, D. C. (1975). *Schoolteacher: A sociological analysis*. Chicago: University of Chicago Press.

Mangin, M. M., Carver, C. L., & Berg, J. H. (2012, November). *Conceptualizing teacher leadership: Implications for practice, preparation, policy, and research*. Paper presented at the annual conference of the University Council for Educational Administration, Denver, CO.

March, J. G. (1996). Exploration and exploitation in organizational learning. In M. D. Cohen & L. S. Sproull (Eds.), *Organizational learning* (pp. 101–123). Thousand Oaks, CA: Sage.

Marsh, J. A. (2002). How districts relate to states, schools, and communities. In A. Hightower, M. S. Knapp, J. A. Marsh, & M. W. McLaughlin (Eds.), *School districts and instructional renewal* (pp. 25–40). New York: Teachers College Press.

Marsh, J. A., Kerr, K. A., Ikemoto, G. S., Darilek, H., Suttrop, M., Zimmer, R. W., et al. (2005). *The role of districts in fostering instructional improvement*. Santa Monica, CA: RAND Corporation.

Marzano, R., & Waters, T. (2009). *District leadership that works: Striking the right balance*. Bloomington, IN: Solution Tree.

McDermott, K. A. (2009). The expansion of state policy research. In G. Sykes, B. Schneider, & D. N. Plank (Eds.), *Handbook of education policy research* (pp. 749–766). New York: Routledge.

Newmann, F. M., King, M. B., & Rigdon, M. (1997). Accountability and school performance: Implications from restructuring schools. *Harvard Education Review, 61*(1), 41–69.

Odden, A. R., & Archibald, S. J. (2010). *Doubling student performance...and finding the resources to do it*. Thousand Oaks, CA: Corwin Press.

Ogawa, R. T., & Bossert, S. T. (1995). Leadership as an organizational quality. *Educational Administration Quarterly, 31*(2), 224–243.

Podgursky, M., & Springer, M. G. (2007). Credentials versus performance: Review of the teacher performance pay research. *Peabody Journal of Education, 82*(4), 551–573.

Putnam, R., & Borko, H. (2000). What do new views of knowledge and thinking have to say about research on teacher learning? *Educational Researcher, 29*(1), 4–15.

Resnick, D. P. (1980). Minimum competency testing historically considered. In D. C. Berliner (Ed.), *Review of research in education* (Vol. 8, pp. 3–29). Washington, DC: American Educational Research Association.

Reynolds, D., & Teddlie, C. (2000). The processes of school effectiveness. In C. Teddlie & D. Reynolds (Eds.), *The international handbook of school effectiveness research* (pp. 124–159). London: Falmer Press.

Robinson, V. M. J., Lloyd, C., & Rowe, K. (2008). The impact of leadership on student outcomes: An analysis of the differential effects of leadership types. *Educational Administration Quarterly, 44*(5), 635–674.

Rowan, B. (2002). The ecology of school improvement: Notes on the school improvement industry in the United States. *Journal of Educational Change, 3*, 283–314.

Smith, M. S., & O'Day, J. (1990). Systemic school reform. In S. H. Fuhrman & B. Malen (Eds.), *The politics of curriculum and testing: Yearbook of the Politics of Education Association* (pp. 233–267). Bristol, PA: Falmer Press.

Snipes, J., Doolittle, F., & Herlihy, C. (2002). *Foundations for success: Case studies of how urban school systems improve student achievement.* New York: MDRC.

Spillane, J. P. (2006). *Distributed leadership.* San Francisco: Jossey-Bass.

Spillane, J. P., Halverson, R., & Diamond, J. B. (2004). Towards a theory of leadership practice: A distributed perspective. *Journal of Curriculum Studies, 36*(1), 3–34.

Supovitz, J. A. (2006). *The case for district-based reform.* Cambridge, MA: Harvard Education Press.

Togneri, W., & Anderson, S. E. (2003). *Beyond islands of excellence: What districts can do to improve instruction and achievement in all schools.* Baltimore: ASCD and the Learning First Alliance.

Tyack, D. B. (1974). *The one best system.* Cambridge, MA: Harvard University Press.

Valencia, R. (1997). *The evolution of deficit thinking: Educational thought and practice.* London: Falmer Press.

Young, V. M. (2006). Teachers' use of data: Loose coupling, agenda setting, and team norms. *American Journal of Education, 112*, 521–548.

CHAPTER 18

Developing Partnerships through Collaboration to Promote Professional Development

SHELLEY B. WEPNER

- School–university partnerships provide an important source of professional development for teachers and administrators.
- School–university and other partnerships are like marriages that require communication, compromise, and mutual respect.
- K–12 teachers and administrators can use school–university and other partnerships to enrich the way that they live their daily lives.
- University students and faculty can provide K–12 teachers and administrators with cutting-edge research about new ideas and methodologies for instruction and assessment.
- Partnerships work best when resources are available, two-way communication exists, and professional development strategies and activities fit teachers' needs.

Mr. Krament, a fifth-grade teacher, thought:

"Doesn't the principal understand that if I'm going to get my students' math test scores up, I can't have a slew of university students coming into my classroom to interfere with what I'm supposed to be teaching? I know that I said that I would support the principal's latest outreach efforts, but it's just not the right time to have to put aside what I'm doing once a week during my math period. On top of having university student visitors from a math methods class, I'm supposed to coteach math with the math methods instructor. I just see this as more busy work and more time without any benefit to my students or me. How do I get out of this?"

Mr. Krament's response is typical of those who find themselves pushed to work with a local university on some type of partnership arrangement. They agree to do something, yet resent the intrusion on their instructional time when they actually have to do what they said they would do. These teachers have not yet experienced the benefits of having extra help in their classrooms. Think about Mr. Krament's thoughts a year later after working with a university faculty partner and her students:

"Who would have thought that this experience could be a win–win? Dr. Grabo actually knows *Math in Focus* [Cavendish, 2013], the mathematics series that our district is using. Having taught elementary school before, with a special love for mathematics, she was determined to figure out how to teach the lessons with me. Dr. Grabo worked with me to scope out the topics that we would coteach, for example, understanding place value concepts through millions, multiplying multidigit numbers, converting decimals to fractions, and identifying cylinders, spheres, and cones. We then planned what each of us would teach and how we would differentiate instruction to meet the various needs of my students. She used her own class time to teach her students how to develop the same lessons and prepare them to work with individual and small groups of students. There was true differentiation. My students' scores went up! And I learned a few new tricks on how to present concepts and work with my struggling learners. I want Dr. Grabo and her class back because I was energized and excited once again about teaching math."

This experience worked for Mr. Krament because something was not *done to* him the way that he initially thought. Rather, there was real professional learning going on that acknowledged and honored his rich and diverse experiences, his knowledge and interests, and his teaching abilities. In other words, the principles of adult learning theory were applied to Mr. Krament (Kegan, 2000; Speck, 1996; Wepner et al., 2012). Although not obvious from the vignette, the university faculty member had done her homework before agreeing to work with Mr. Krament. She had learned that teaching math in general was not his problem, but that he was having difficulty getting his struggling learners to pass the statewide math test. She knew that this was a common problem for many new and experienced teachers and wanted to use this opportunity to help him target instruction. This experience would enable her to learn from him about the real challenges that teachers face with differentiation so that she could begin to help her teacher candidates understand how to work effectively with different types of learners.

THE IMPORTANCE OF COLLABORATION
FOR PROFESSIONAL DEVELOPMENT

Central to our efforts in fostering dignity in the teaching profession is professional development. Our usual image of professional development is something that occurs outside the school context. Teachers leave their classrooms and schools to engage in presentations and workshops provided by different experts. These sessions usually do not have an impact on classroom practices or on student learning because of the didactic nature of the information presented and the lack of relevance of such information to individual teachers' everyday realities. Follow-up and collaboration, two critical components of professional development, are not evident. As a result, teachers do not incorporate the information or practices into their instruction (Sykes, 1996; Wepner et al., 2012; Willis, 2002).

Additionally, a silo mentality exists in our field by which professional development programs are separated by institution and by role (Clift, 2008). K–12 and higher education faculty and administrators have not seen themselves as sharing joint custody in the education of K–12 students. Rather, teachers alone are considered responsible for student achievement, with everyone else having peripheral involvement or sporadic visitation rights.

Collaboration across the varied institutions (universities and colleges, districts, and agencies) can support teachers with their professional development across a developmental continuum (Borko, Whitcomb, & Liston, 2008; Clift, 2008). Cross-institutional cultures can be established so that K–12 and university faculty and administrators partner to contribute to the knowledge base about teaching and learning. K–12 education needs higher education to understand current instructional methodologies, provide instructional assistance to students, and learn how to best prepare a diverse student population for college, vocational, and societal success. Higher education needs K–12 education in order to be seen as credible and viable. Both K–12 education and higher education also benefit from third-party agencies to provide ideas and resources.

WHAT IS MEANT BY PARTNERSHIPS AND COLLABORATION?

Partnerships are relationships. They are two or more people or organizations involved in the same activity, two or more people or groups working together for a common cause, or an organization formed by two or more people or groups working together for some purpose. They often involve a formal, written agreement that describes the purpose of the partnership and responsibilities of each of the parties involved. Collaboration is the act of two or more people working together in order to achieve something. The terms are often used interchangeably (Hopkins, 2011).

Partnerships exist in fields outside of education to strengthen the capacity of individuals to do their jobs. Law and medical practices have partners to complement skill sets and to be able to serve more clients and patients, respectively. Police have partners to help with the safety of themselves and others. Television's crime-solving series on network and cable channels (e.g., *CSI, Law & Order, Blue Bloods, Rizzoli & Isles*) highlight how partners work together for a common cause. Each partner brings unique skills to the situation to accomplish something that probably could not have been accomplished alone. The old adage that two heads are better than one highlights the importance of such partnerships.

Partnerships in education usually involve school districts with universities, foundations, businesses, and other organizations to help with student achievement, professional development, and administrative needs. This chapter focuses primarily on the many ways in which school district–university partnerships can help with professional development through the collaborative efforts of K–12 and higher education faculty and administrators.

REASONS TO PURSUE SCHOOL–UNIVERSITY PARTNERSHIPS FOR PROFESSIONAL DEVELOPMENT

Universities provide to school districts students and faculty to help with cutting-edge research about new and improved curriculum ideas, instructional methods, and assessment trends. One of the best-kept secrets is the availability of student assistants, often free, who need and want to be involved in schools for fieldwork and community outreach activities. Teacher candidates need to clock hours to fulfill course and program requirements. Other university students are required or encouraged to engage in service learning and other community service initiatives (Wepner et al., 2012).

Although there is a general belief that having student teachers in the classroom means that there is too much work with very little reward, we discovered otherwise in our partnership network at Manhattanville College. When we conducted a formal survey of cooperating teachers who had student teachers in their classrooms, most of the cooperating teachers indicated that it was a very positive experience for their own professional development. The cooperating teachers commented on how they became more reflective about their teaching, more organized, and more flexible. They found themselves developing more engaging activities and striving to become better teachers because they wanted to serve as good role models for their student teachers. They also believed that their student teachers' field supervisors were an important source of professional development for themselves because the field supervisors provided them with frequent and consistent guidance and support on ways to help their student teachers and themselves work effectively with their students (Changing Suburbs Institute, 2012).

Teacher candidates also can be hired as interns, who spend half a year or an entire year serving as substitutes when needed and spend the remainder of their time assisting teachers with one-on-one, small-group, and whole-class instruction. Different configurations can be created to fit the needs of the schools. For example, interns can be hired to provide time for teachers to have a day a week away from teaching duties to assume an alternative role, such as researcher, student teacher supervisor, or administrative intern (Boles, 1992).

School districts provide real-world settings for university students and faculty to test new ideas amid the daily challenges of classroom instruction. University students see firsthand how teachers subscribe to curriculum and testing requirements as they grapple with student differences in ability, learning styles, language, culture, motivation, and home life. Such settings also help to remind university faculty about the differences between the idealized 21st-century classroom and the diverse classroom needs of neighboring schools.

THE SCHOOL–UNIVERSITY PARTNERSHIP CONTINUUM

There is a continuum of school–university partnerships, from those that exist for a short time period to accomplish a specific task, such as implementing a new literacy program, to those that exist for long periods of time to address multiple pursuits in the form of a professional development school (PDS). A PDS is a real school that partners with a college or university to provide professional development for teachers, prepare teacher candidates, improve student achievement, and encourage practitioner inquiry. PDS partners share responsibilities for professional development and blend their expertise and resources to meet shared goals.

The depth and breadth of such school–university partnerships depends on factors such as accessibility to and availability of partners, leadership interest and capability, teacher buy-in, funding opportunities, and community support. There needs to be a shared commitment among partners and a willingness to work across institutional settings and cultures (Byrd & McIntyre, 2011; Duffield & Cates, 2008).

Any type of school–university partnership, and especially PDS, can raise the level of teacher expectation and student work; increase the student–teacher ratio; expose teachers to new and enhanced methodology; increase teacher leadership; offer innovative and cutting-edge ideas that teachers can use and apply; stimulate collaborative inquiry about practice; cultivate students' improved attitudes toward learning; offer new and exciting dialogues about teaching and learning; infuse new blood into the building; and help with teacher renewal (Wepner et al., 2012).

IDEAS FOR USING SCHOOL–UNIVERSITY PARTNERSHIPS TO HELP WITH PROFESSIONAL DEVELOPMENT

Nine ideas are presented in this section on ways that school–university partnerships can help with professional development: (1) coteaching with university faculty members in the K–12 classroom; (2) teaching and coteaching onsite by university faculty members; (3) teaching onsite by K–12 faculty members and administrators; (4) conducting action research; (5) writing and publishing; (6) applying for grants; (7) teaching at a university; (8) conducting and attending presentations and workshops at a university; and (9) presenting at peer-reviewed conferences with university faculty members.

Coteaching with University Faculty Members in the K–12 Classroom

As Mr. Krament from our opening vignette discovered, coteaching with a university faculty member helped him to understand how to reach his struggling learners in math. As much as he thought that he understood how to differentiate instruction, he did not understand how to make math concepts concrete enough for his struggling fifth graders to grasp. His students' newfound success on the statewide test certainly changed his outlook about having university faculty members and students in his classroom as a source of professional development.

From elementary school through high school, coteaching with university faculty members has become an important source of professional development for both classroom teachers and university faculty members because of the give-and-take exchange of both theoretical and practical ideas. A secondary social studies teacher educator, intent on having his students spend most of their time in the schools for his course, reached out to a middle school social studies teacher to invite himself and his students to the social studies classroom. In exchange for this privilege, he agreed to coteach a few lessons to demonstrate how to use his newly published theory of instruction to motivate middle school students to learn. In return, the social studies teacher helped this social studies teacher educator and his students to learn firsthand about the many challenges of working with diverse student needs (Wepner et al., 2012).

An elementary science teacher educator wanted her teacher candidates to spend most of the semester in an elementary classroom to help them discover that the teaching of science does not have to be feared or ignored. She approached a second-grade teacher from a partnership school who agreed to host the teacher candidates. The university faculty member worked with the second-grade teacher and her teacher candidates to plan units of instruction, purchase science materials, and develop a schedule that allowed for classroom teacher–faculty member, classroom teacher–teacher candidate, and university faculty member–teacher candidate instruction. When the teacher candidates were not teaching, they were observing or working with small student groups to ensure that the second graders were successful with the hands-on experiences. The second-grade students had every possible opportunity to experiment with the science concepts as the adults in the room took turns providing direct instruction. The second-grade teacher has since become a spokesperson for this method of instruction and wants to help other classroom teachers branch out to work with university faculty members and students (Wepner et al., 2012).

Teaching and Coteaching Onsite by University Faculty Members

University faculty members are willing to come to a school or district to offer courses. A former assistant superintendent of a large, diverse suburban school district no longer wanted her teachers to submit for reimbursement courses offered by for-profit companies that had very little to do with their primary areas of responsibility. She wanted her teachers to engage in substantive coursework that could be applied to what they were actually doing. She specifically wanted her teachers to take courses in literacy and special education. She and the dean of an education program at her local university agreed on a specific tuition discount because of their preexisting partnership agreement and scheduled the appropriate courses on convenient days and times at the local school. Teachers who successfully completed the sequence of courses became eligible for an additional certification.

Coteaching with university faculty at a school site also becomes possible. A high school principal wanted his teachers to integrate technology into their teaching on a more regular basis. Although his instructional technology coordinator was showing incremental signs of success, he just was not working fast enough and was still facing too much resistance from a majority of the teachers. The principal reached out to his local university to see whether a faculty member would be willing and available to coteach a course with his technology educator. The principal would find the funds from the district's professional development budget to pay for each teacher's three-credit graduate course if they would be willing to use technology at least once for every unit they taught. The university faculty member found this idea intriguing because she would see firsthand what these high school teachers, with varying levels of technology expertise, could and would do in their classrooms. Once an agreement was reached by the high school and the university, the university faculty member and the technology coordinator used the university's syllabus as a framework for developing lessons to be cotaught and individual course assignments related to the high school subjects represented. In between class sessions, the technology coordinator worked with the teachers to help them with their assignments. By the end of the semester, the high school teachers actually were doing what they promised they would do as a result of the fresh ideas brought by the university faculty member and the coordinated efforts of the university faculty member and technology coordinator.

Teaching Onsite by K–12 Faculty and Administrators

With the incentive of not having to travel, teachers and administrators can work with colleges and universities to arrange to teach credit-bearing courses. A principal of a PDS, with a background in special education, knew that her teachers needed to better understand how to work with parents of the school's special needs students. She worked with the chair of the university's special education department to arrange to become an adjunct faculty member so that she could teach the course at her school to her own teachers and interested teachers across the district.

A teacher from the same building who had taken the principal's course offered to teach a course on children's literature because she had accumulated through the years an amazing collection of books and had become, according to her colleagues, a true expert in the area. Her colleague teachers pushed her to volunteer to teach such a course because they needed to learn more about finding and appropriately using fiction and nonfiction books. The principal again worked with the local university and arranged to have the course offered. The school's status as a PDS enabled the teachers to receive a one-third discount on tuition.

Conducting Action Research

An elementary teacher learned about the effects of playing slow-tempo music during poetry writing. One middle school teacher learned how to strengthen participation in class discussions among English language learners (ELLs), and a second middle school teacher learned about different modes of grouping students for science lab work. A high school teacher learned about the impact of an after-school tutoring program for developing literacy skills through history projects (Changing Suburbs Institute, 2012).

Action research is a powerful mechanism for testing hypotheses about learning and leading in classrooms and schools. It helps teachers to systematically investigate a question, problem, or issue that has arisen in their practice, with the goal of improving teaching and learning in classrooms and schools (Wepner et al., 2012). Action research does take time and expertise. University partners can provide faculty and students to assist classroom teachers to conduct or co-conduct action research.

As a result of a school–university partnership, one university faculty member already has worked with about a dozen middle school teacher volunteers on action research projects that they have designed to answer questions about their own classroom practices. These teachers have studied, for example, gender-based differences in student leadership, approaches to teaching mathematics to students with learning disabilities, and how to use e-pals and storytelling to improve foreign language learning (Collin, 2012).

Writing and Publishing

Two teachers from a PDS wrote a newsletter article and a blog with a university faculty member about the unique features of their PDS (Ferrara, Terracciano, & Simmons, 2011, 2012a, 2012b). The principal of the same school coauthored a book chapter with the same university faculty member about using her PDS to help teacher candidates work with her teachers to develop the whole child (Ferrara & Santiago, 2011). That same principal and university faculty member collaborated with the PDS community liaison, another principal, and the district's assistant superintendent to write a different chapter about working with universities to develop full-service community schools (Gómez, Ferrara, Santiago, Fanelli, & Taylor, 2012).

In a second PDS school, a primary school administrator for the district coauthored an article and a chapter with two faculty members on the influence of parent education on kindergarten children's achievement (Gómez, Lang, & Lasser, 2010; Lang, Gómez, & Lasser, 2009). The elementary principal of that school coauthored an article about a special project to implement a science-based literacy project with fifth-grade students (Wepner, Bettica, Gangi, Reilly, & Klemm, 2008).

Conducting research, often reserved for those in higher education because of job expectations, is a form of professional development that expands one's understandings of how to test new ideas and answer questions about instructional and leadership practices (Wepner et al., 2012).

Applying for Grants

School–university partnerships make it easier for both institutions to apply for grants, especially today, because of the national recognition from legislators, policymakers, politicians, and corporate leaders that K–12 and higher education must be interconnected to make inroads with student achievement.

An elementary principal was having a hard time convincing her primary teachers to use technology. They simply did not see how technology would help with literacy development. At the same time, the director of a center for education at a local university was feeling pressure to do something more substantial to ensure that teacher candidates left the program with the ability to integrate technology into teaching. This director and principal recently had signed a formal agreement to have the principal's school serve as a PDS.

Together, they decided that they would create a plan that would require teacher candidates, university supervisors, and primary teachers to work together to teach technology-based lessons. Coincidentally, their state had just issued a request for proposals (RFP) for schools and colleges to work together to develop, implement, and assess technology initiatives to improve K–12 students' learning. The principal, director, and other team members quickly wrote a proposal that required their primary teachers and teacher candidates to coteach eight technology-based lessons within a student teaching semester. University supervisors would be required to work closely with the teacher candidates and cooperating teachers to assist and ensure that the lessons were taught.

The grant application was funded for $250,000, enabling the director and principal to provide portable computer labs for their primary teachers, portable computers for their teacher candidates, instructional materials, and a series of workshops to prepare the teachers, teacher candidates, and university supervisors to use the technology. Within a year, the primary teachers were using computers on their own, the teacher candidates understood how and when to use technology to enrich students' learning, and the primary children were showing positive changes in their literacy development because of the multiple ways in which they were practicing skill development. The principal and director attributed their success to their partnership, in which they listened to each other, planned accordingly, and then went after the necessary resources to implement their plan. Neither could have done it without the other, and they knew it (Wepner, Bowes, & Serotkin, 2007). The principal believes that this grant transformed her primary teachers, and one in particular who had hated technology then became an avid user (Wepner, in press).

Teaching at a University

After hosting two different field-based courses for social studies and science, a fifth-grade teacher realized that he had something to offer teacher candidates at the university. He arranged with the department chair of curriculum and instruction to teach elementary education students courses in curriculum management. Two other teachers in this same school who had spent many years collecting and using multicultural literature in their classrooms worked with the department chair of literacy to arrange to coteach a course in multicultural children's literature. They worked closely with the department chair to make sure that they understood how to combine theory with practice and how to appeal to the wider graduate student population. These three teachers have found that this teaching experience is an intense and rewarding form of professional development.

Teaching at a university can be an important source of professional development for both teachers and administrators. It also helps to develop those preparing to become teachers and administrators because they learn about the feasibility of implementing research-based practices and theories in real-world classrooms.

Conducting and Attending Presentations and Workshops at a University

Another important source of professional development is making presentations and attending workshops, seminars, and conferences at a university. For teachers involved in a school–university partnership, any type of presentation showcases the work of the partnership, brings together key players to plan and present, reinforces the efforts of those involved, and communicates to others in the community just how fruitful the partnership is. Some examples include K–12 teachers and university faculty talking about their experiences with implementing projects in social studies, science, and math; a panel of principals speaking about the promises and challenges of forming a PDS; an elementary principal speaking about how a partnership can transform a school; a middle school principal speaking about the value of doing fieldwork at the middle school level; a high school teacher speaking about the benefits of an after-school math club begun by a university professor and his students; a panel of assistant superintendents speaking about ways in which university interns have found jobs in their districts; and a group of K–12 teachers speaking about their experience working with university faculty and its impact on their students. Such presentations reflect well on the school district and promote yet another level of professional development.

Attending presentations, seminars, and workshops helps set the stage for further inquiry and practice and reinforces current practices. For example, a sixth-grade teacher from a newly developed PDS was struggling with ways to help her ELL population. She tried to adapt the way she taught through her lesson plans, grouping patterns, and nonverbal cues, but she still did not really know what to do. Her status as a teacher in a PDS entitled her to attend an overview workshop on sheltered instruction observation protocol (SIOP), a research-based model of lesson planning for delivering sheltered instruction to ELLs (Echevarría, Vogt, & Short, 2008). The SIOP presenter helped this teacher to understand SIOP's components. She just could not figure out how she needed to adjust her current instructional methods to fit this new schema.

A few weeks later, she learned that the university was sponsoring an annual educational conference focused on ELLs with workshop presentations by classroom teachers who were using the SIOP model. She received permission to attend the conference so that she could attend these workshops. The workshops were very helpful because she could now envision exactly what these teachers were doing. She realized, though, that she needed help if she were ever going to implement SIOP properly. She again received permission to leave her building and arranged to visit these teachers' classrooms. She then worked with her PDS liaison to arrange to have a university faculty member coach her for a month on implementing SIOP in her classroom. She now is using SIOP quite successfully and credits her attendance at the original overview workshop as a springboard for her ability to instruct her ELLs with much more success.

Presenting at Peer-Reviewed Conferences with University Faculty

Presenting at peer-reviewed conferences is an important opportunity for professional development. Conference attendance, usually supported by school districts and universities, enables representatives from both types of institutions to have critical dialogues about ways to improve schooling. Each year, PDS liaisons from our network submit proposals to state and national organizations to present with their K–12 colleagues about classroom and schoolwide collaborative projects. Invariably, K–12 teachers and administrators comment on the value of this experience.

Final Thoughts about Ideas

The professional development opportunities described in this section contribute to teachers' and principals' development. Research on teacher development (Bullough & Baughman, 1997) in school–university partnerships, especially in PDS, indicates that teachers receive a sense of renewal and rejuvenation by learning from teacher education candidates and university faculty over an extended period of time. They become increasingly more reflective about teaching and, as a result, change their classroom practice. Teachers become part of a learning community that dialogues, asks questions, works together to achieve something for themselves and their students, and probes about their own practices (Wepner et al., 2012).

WORKING WITH OTHER ORGANIZATIONS

In addition to using school–university partnerships as an important source of professional development, foundations, businesses, and other organizations can be particularly helpful in providing assistance with specific professional development needs.

Foundations and Businesses

Foundations and businesses are interested in helping to improve schools to help with workforce competitiveness and build their own goodwill in the community. Partnerships can range from those that attempt to reform education at the national level to those with a local focus of helping children with specific learning needs (Byrd & McIntyre, 2011).

Reading Reform Foundation of New York

An excellent example of partnership work with schools that has been in operation for over 30 years to provide professional development for teachers is the Reading Reform Foundation of New York (RRF). RRF was developed to help K–3 teachers learn how to use a phonics-based, multisensory, Orton-based approach to teaching reading, writing, spelling, and comprehension to students. Mentor-consultants (usually retired schoolteachers) meet with classroom teachers in their schools twice a week for 30 weeks. They meet with them for two 1-hour preparation periods and two 1-hour classroom working visits per week (120 hours) "to help develop lesson plans, to practice the material concept by concept, and enhance the teacher's technique and delivery through repetition and steady monitoring" (Rose & Nelson, 2012, p. 26). The RRF mentor-consultant actually remains in the classroom while the teacher delivers the material to provide additional support and guidance. This foundation also provides training courses, workshops, and an annual conference. The schools are charged a small percentage of the expense of running the program because of RRF funding from outside sources. Teachers become so well trained that there is both quantitative and qualitative evidence of students' improved reading scores. To participate, principals must invite RRF into their schools because this foundation believes that a partnership can be successful only if the principal is on board wholeheartedly in allowing this intensive training to take place (Rose & Nelson, 2012).

Regionally Based Statewide Organizations

State-subsidized, regionally based organizations often have as one of their primary goals the professional development of educators. They provide workshops, training institutes, statewide conferences, consultations, and technical assistance on new requirements and current trends to help teachers and leaders know how to respond to instructional and assessment expectations. For instance, New York State has 37 Boards of Cooperative Educational Services (BOCES) throughout the state that work with schools and school districts to respond to the individualized professional development needs of teachers and leaders. Putnam/Northern Westchester BOCES, as one example, offers professional development services to thousands of teachers and administrators from 18 local school districts on the integration of state standards, test administration, innovative curricula, mentorship, crisis management, and data analysis. This BOCES also partners with universities to provide graduate-level coursework and programs for practicing teachers and administrators (Langlois, 2012).

GUIDELINES FOR DEVELOPING PARTNERSHIPS

Partnerships, like marriages, require communication, compromise, and respect. They also must have leadership and resources and maintain constant vigilance about their viability. The following guidelines are offered to help ensure that partnerships are developed with a solid foundation.

Assess Teachers' Current Interest and Participation with a University

Before embarking on any type of partnership arrangement, it helps to know ways in which teachers have been and currently are involved with a university for their own professional development. The survey in Figure 18.1 can help to reveal the level at which teachers are engaged with a university. Some teachers might be teaching as adjuncts and using the university's library; others might be serving as cooperating teachers and hosting university students for fieldwork; and still others might be working with university faculty to get help with their classrooms. Results from the survey reveal different levels of involvement and help to determine which teachers can help other teachers get involved and the type of involvement that should be encouraged. For example, before one school formed a partnership, one of the teachers from that school already was involved with her neighboring university in eight different survey items and ended up serving as a spokesperson for the partnership (Wepner et al., 2012).

Put Liaisons in Place

When school–university partnerships exist, a university liaison is usually assigned to be at the school a minimum number of days or hours per week. Such liaisons can assist principals, vice principals, and department chairs with a variety of instructional and administrative tasks. Liaisons, who essentially become members of the school staff (Rothstein, 2001), can weave in and out of classrooms to help school administrators identify classroom needs. They can help with scheduling events, acquiring resources, developing projects, and coordinating professional development initiatives for teachers. They can become principals' unofficial assistants in identifying needs and proposing solutions for the school. When used well, liaisons are a great asset to principals in helping with administrative needs.

School-based liaisons also are very useful for forging partnerships because they can work with the university liaison to shepherd personnel and professional development projects. School-based liaisons should be given release time from teaching or other administrative tasks, free college coursework, or administrative stipends as compensation for this additional work.

Professional development activities	Yes	No	Not sure
Serve as a cooperating teacher			
Work with university students for fieldwork			
Work with university students for literacy practicum			
Work with university faculty and students on field-based courses			
Use university students to tutor students			
Use university students as pen pals or electronic pals			
Use university students for small-group work			
Coteach with university faculty in K–12 classroom or university classroom			
Teach at a university			
Attend university events (conferences, workshops, symposia, lectures, etc.)			
Work on a committee or advisory board at a university			
Work with university faculty and/or administration on special projects (if so, please describe)			
Work with university faculty or administration on research (if so, please describe)			
Involved in a partnership or professional development school with a university			
Use university resources (library, fitness facilities, conference rooms, etc.)			
Serve on leadership team in your school and/or school district that involves university faculty			
Bring or send students to a university for visitations and/or university forums			
Attend professional development sessions with university faculty to help with instruction, content knowledge, or other areas of interest			
Communicate with university faculty through e-mail about something related to your job			
Work with university faculty and/or administration to get help with your classroom, school, or district			

FIGURE 18.1. Survey for K–12 educators' professional development activities with a university. From Wepner et al. (2012). Copyright 2012 by Corwin Press. Reprinted by permission.

Helping Individual Teachers

Ms. Franz was moved from second grade, where she taught all subjects, to fifth grade, where she was responsible for teaching social studies and English/language arts (ELA) only. She had to learn two new curriculum areas and was especially panicked about ELA because her students were going to be tested in that area. Although she did not have the lowest performing group of students in her classroom, they were simply not motivated to learn. She needed to learn the curriculum really fast so that she could teach in a way that would capture and sustain her students' attention. She knew that she needed help. She also knew that she had one thing on her side. Her school was a PDS, and she knew that she could go to the PDS liaison for advice and assistance.

The PDS liaison began by arranging for Ms. Franz to visit another fifth-grade classroom in the district so that she could see what another teacher was doing. The PDS liaison then set aside two periods each week to work directly with Ms. Franz. The PDS liaison also arranged for Ms. Franz to have a student teacher/intern in her classroom for the entire year to give her additional help and work with her on developing the curriculum. These three professional development opportunities helped Ms. Franz make it through the year with surprising student success.

Helping Teacher Teams

A PDS liaison worked with a team of fourth-grade teachers for an entire year to help them implement a writing workshop framework in their classrooms. They began by designing their own writing assessment and scoring rubric so that they could assess students' writing capabilities and monitor students' progress. The teachers actually read and discussed all fourth-grade students' writing so that they could determine writing patterns and trends that needed to be addressed across the grade level.

They then worked individually and in pairs to develop units of study related to specific genres and minilessons connected to students' needs. Teachers met together on a weekly basis to reflect on their teaching, discuss students' work, and discuss new ideas for working with students. At the end of each unit, and at the end of the year, teachers used the writing assessment rubric that they had developed to determine students' growth in writing. With the help of the PDS liaison, these teachers collaborated to develop ways to better understand their students' strengths and needs and to refine their teaching to meet the needs of their diverse learners (Wepner et al., 2012).

Ensure Communication among Stakeholders

A partnership requires frequent and productive communication among stakeholders so that participants have the same clear understanding of the partnership's purpose and function (Clark, 1999). Too often a university initiates and controls the types of partnership activities that take place. It is imperative that teachers are involved in working with the university to determine professional development initiatives so that there is mutual agreement on what will occur. For example, a third-grade teacher in a partnership school expressed concern to her PDS leadership team that she and her other third-grade colleagues needed help in implementing the new science program. The leadership team quickly figured out a way to bring a science education faculty member and her students to the third-grade classrooms to help them implement the program. The science education faculty member worked with the teachers on deciphering the new program's expectations, conducted demonstration lessons of some of the newer instructional methodologies, and cotaught lessons with the teachers. The university students worked with the students in small groups and individually on some of the more challenging science experiments. The third-grade teachers were motivated to receive the university faculty and students in their classrooms because they could observe and critique the use of new strategies with their students and have more time to observe their own students' responses to different strategies. Dyson (1999) explains that the most important outcome for a partnership is that it meets teachers' needs for their own development.

Have Written Agreements

Written agreements are very useful because they lay out the purpose of the partnership, roles and responsibilities of partners, any financial arrangements, and intended duration. A written agreement can help alleviate the impact of leadership turnover, a problem that is not uncommon in any kind of partnership, because the agreement serves as a formal document of what the partners agreed to accomplish for and contribute to the partnership. Signatures of the chief executive officers from each institution need to be part of the agreement to ensure official approval of the partnership (Byrd & McIntyre, 2011; Clark, 1999). Legal review and development of the written agreement helps the chief executive officers and their boards to more readily endorse the language used in the agreement (Wepner et al., 2012).

Make Sure Funding Is Available

Funding for partnership work needs to be adequate to support the partnership's mission. Everyone has limited funds. Grants can help, but they usually are temporary. Partnerships need long-term funding sources. Those who initiate partnerships need to figure out ways to reallocate funds, including the use of a barter system. For example, a principal in need of resources from the university offers her own services as a speaker for different university-based symposia as a way of saying thank you. A university faculty member provides workshops for students' parents at a school in exchange for using space in a building for her class.

Assess Partnership Viability

Accountability is at the forefront of many of today's educational innovations; therefore, it is important to produce the evidence that partnerships are improving teachers' and teacher candidates' knowledge and skills. This evidence must include data that can be shared with the larger educational community, school boards, media, and policymakers if school–university partnerships expect to receive the needed support (Byrd & McIntyre, 2011). Qualitative and quantitative assessments of both specific initiatives and the overall partnership should be conducted. Both school leaders and partnership participants should decide what, how, and who is assessed (Willis, 2011), remembering that partnerships usually take two steps forward and one step backward.

SUMMARY OF MAJOR POINTS

Professional development is critical for our vibrancy, vitality, and viability. Collaboration with those who offer consistent, useful, and engaging opportunities to help keep up with new demands contributes to our professional and personal growth. School–university and other partnerships offer new and intriguing ways to stretch our minds, challenge our habits, and improve our practices. From bringing students and faculty into our classrooms to conducting action research about lingering instructional and assessment questions, such collaborative initiatives prompt us to reach new levels of performance. Partnerships work when leaders from the partnering institutions are sincerely willing and administratively able to bring together their respective constituencies to engage in new and different opportunities. Partnerships are most effective for professional development when such collaborative relationships honor and respect individual and collective voices and views through communication and compromise.

RECOMMENDATIONS AND FUTURE DIRECTIONS

With our individual and collective worth being determined by student achievement on standardized tests, we really do need to work together to figure out how to best help students perform on such tests. School–university partnerships, in particular, can be used to help with the teacher preparation–teacher accountability continuum for K–12 students' performance. Research already has shown that when teacher candidates are involved in school–university partnerships, they not only do better on their own certification tests but also contribute to K–12 students' score increases on state-mandated achievement tests (Houston, Hollis, Clay, Ligons, & Roff, 1999). Additional research needs to be gathered to demonstrate how school–university and other partnerships affect teachers' professional development and, ultimately, student achievement. As partnerships are developed, keep in mind the following recommendations:

- Identify persons who excel at collaboration and outreach to serve as partnership leaders for your institutions.
- Identify and honor teachers' professional development needs.

- Start small, stay focused, and grow projects incrementally.
- Form leadership teams from the outset that represent a cross-section of critical stakeholders.
- Monitor and celebrate accomplishments frequently and broadly.

QUESTIONS FOR DISCUSSION

1. What should teachers' roles be in forming and supporting school–university partnerships for professional development?

2. Describe the roles and responsibilities of superintendents, assistant superintendents, and principals in forming school–university partnerships for professional development.

3. What do principals need to do to convince teachers about the value of school–university partnerships?

4. What can and should be done to convince legislators and policymakers to set aside funds for teachers' professional development through school–university partnerships?

REFERENCES

Boles, K. C. (1992, April). *School restructuring by teachers: A study of the teaching project at the Edward Devotion School.* Paper presented at the annual meeting of the American Educational Research Association, San Francisco.

Borko, H., Whitcomb, J., & Liston, D. (2008). An education president for the 21st century: Introducing eight letters to the 44th president of the United States. *Journal of Teacher Education, 59,* 207–211.

Bullough, R. V., & Baughman, K. (1997). *"First year teacher" eight years later: An inquiry into teacher development.* New York: Teachers College Press.

Byrd, D. M., & McIntyre, D. J. (2011). Types of partnerships. In S. B. Wepner & D. Hopkins (Eds.), *Collaborative leadership in action: Partnering for success in schools* (pp. 27–48). New York: Teachers College Press.

Cavendish, M. (2013). *Math in focus: Singapore math.* Boston: Houghton Mifflin Harcourt.

Changing Suburbs Institute. (2012). *Professional development school (PDS) liaison working group report: Summary of findings for 2011–2012.* Unpublished report.

Clark, R. W. (1999). *Effective professional development schools.* San Francisco: Jossey-Bass.

Clift, R. T. (2008). A letter to the 44th president of the United States. *Journal of Teacher Education, 59,* 220–225.

Collin, R. (2012). *Professional development year end report, 2011–2012.* Unpublished report.

Duffield, J. A., & Cates, W. M. (2008). Establishing and maintaining professional development schools: A Delphi study. *School–University Partnerships: Journal of the National Association for Professional Development Schools, 2*(2), 27–50.

Dyson, L. L. (1999). Developing a university–school district partnership: Researcher–district administrator collaboration for a special education initiative. *Canadian Journal of Education, 24*(4), 411–425.

Echevarría, J., Vogt, M., & Short, D. J. (2008). *Making content comprehensible for English learners: The SIOP model.* Boston: Pearson Allyn & Bacon.

Ferrara, J., & Santiago, E. (2011). Helping preservice teachers support the needs of the "whole child" in a PDS. In I. Guadarrama, J. Ramsey, & J. Nath (Eds.), *Investigating university-school partnerships* (pp. 373–378). Charlotte, NC: Information Age.

Ferrara, J., Terracciano, B., & Simmons, A. (2011). PDS with a unique focus. *PDS Partners Newsletter, 7*(1), 2–3.

Ferrara, J., Terracciano, B., & Simmons, A., (2012a). A new tradition evolves in our community school/PDS. *PDS Partners Newsletter, 7*(3), 5–6.

Ferrara, J., Terracciano, B., & Simmons, A. (2012b). Beyond university-assisted partnership: The professional development school within a community school. Retrieved from *http://Coalitionforcommunityschools.blogspot.com/2012/04/beyond-university-assisted Partnership.html.*

Gómez, D. W., Ferrara, J., Santiago, E., Fanelli, F., & Taylor, R. (2012). Full service community schools: A district's commitment to educating the whole child. In A. Honigsfeld & A. Cohan (Eds.), *Breaking the mold of education for culturally and linguistically diverse students: Innovative and successful practices for the 21st century* (pp. 65–73). Lanham, MD: Rowman & Littlefield.

Gómez, D. W., Lang, D. E., & Lasser, S. M. (2010). Nuevas avenidas: Pathways for modeling and supporting home-based literacy strategies with Hispanic parents. In A. Honigsfeld & A. Cohan (Eds.), *Breaking the mold of school instruction and organization: Innovative and successful practices for the 21st century* (pp. 123–128). Lanham, MD: Rowan & Littlefield.

Hopkins, D. (2011). The value of partnerships. In S. B. Wepner & D. Hopkins (Eds.), *Collaborative leadership in action: Partnering for success in schools* (pp. 7–26). New York: Teachers College Press.

Houston, W. R., Hollis, L. Y., Clay, D., Ligons, C. M., & Roff, L. (1999). Effects of collaboration on urban teacher education programs and professional development schools. In D. M. Byrd & D. J. McIntyre (Eds.), *Research on professional development schools: Teacher Education Yearbook VII* (pp. 6–28). Thousand Oaks, CA: Corwin Press.

Kegan, R. (2000). What "form" transforms?: A constructive-developmental approach to transformative learning. In J. Mezirow & Associates (Eds.), *Learning as transformation* (pp. 35–70). San Francisco: Jossey-Bass.

Lang, D. E., Gómez, D. W., & Lasser, S. M. (2009). Preparados, listos, ya!: An interpretative case study centered on teaching Hispanic parents to support early bilingual literacy development prior to kindergarten. *GiST (Revista Colombiana de Educación Bilingüe/ Colombian Journal of Bilingual Education) 3*, 90–106.

Langlois, J. (2012). From the superintendent's desk. Retrieved from *www.pnwboces.org/ superintendentDesk.htm.*

Rose, S. P., & Nelson, G. (2012). *Sunday is for the sun, Monday is for the moon: Teaching reading, one teacher and thirty children at a time.* New York: Reading Reform Foundation of New York.

Rothstein, A. L. (2001). A college goes to school: The history of an urban collaboration. *Education, 122*(2), 231–239.

Speck, M. (1996, Spring). Best practice in professional development for sustained educational change. *ERS Spectrum*, 33–41.

Sykes, G. (1996). Reform of and as professional development. *Phi Delta Kappan, 77*(7), 465–467.

Wepner, S. B., Bettica, A., Gangi, J., Reilly, M. A., & Klemm, T. (2008). Using a cross-curricular learning experience to promote student engagement through a school-college collaboration. *Excelsior, 3*(1), 27–45.

Wepner, S. B., Bowes, K. A., & Serotkin, R. (2007). Technology in teacher education: Creating a climate of change and collaboration. *Action in Teacher Education, 29*(1), 81–93.

Wepner, S. B., Ferrara, J., Rainville, K. N., Gómez, D. W., Lang, D. E., & Bigaouette, L. (2012). *Changing suburbs, changing students: Helping school leaders face the challenges.* Thousand Oaks, CA: Corwin Press.

Willis, J. (2011). Making evaluation useful: Improving partnerships through ongoing collaborative assessment. In S. B. Wepner & D. Hopkins (Eds.), *Collaborative leadership in action: Partnering for success in schools* (pp. 97–118). New York: Teachers College Press.

Willis, S. (2002). Creating a knowledge base for teaching: A conversation with James Stigler. *Educational Leadership, 59*(6), 6–11.

CHAPTER 19

Content Knowledge for Teaching
Framing Effective Professional Development

JENNIFER MERRIMAN

One major problem with the studies of teacher effectiveness was an almost total lack of concern for what actually occurred in the classroom.
—SHUELL (1993, p. 298)

- Converging lines of evidence suggest that neither proxy measures of teacher effectiveness based on observable data nor value-added models validly and completely capture teachers' knowledge and instructional practices.
- Direct attention to instruction in the classroom is needed to ensure that the Common Core State Standards have the desired effect on student knowledge and skills.
- Expert–novice research born out of the cognitive science literature yields important insights about what rigorous understanding of the content looks like; how it differs by domain-specific structures, associated evidence claims, and representations; how expertise develops; and what expert pedagogy looks like.
- Content knowledge for teaching is a strong predictor of student achievement, yet professional development on subject-matter content and how students learn that content is not typically sought out by teachers, especially those with weak content knowledge.
- Recent efforts to construct large-scale measures of teachers' mathematical knowledge for teaching indicate that such instruments can provide valid measures of teacher quality that are related to the actual tasks of teaching that occur in the classroom and are also related to student achievement.
- More work is needed to empirically define and measure teachers' content

knowledge for teaching, to identify teachers' current content knowledge for teaching, and to develop scalable models of professional development focused on increasing teachers' content knowledge for teaching to ensure that all students have equitable access to high-quality instruction focused on the Common Core State Standards.

In this chapter, I make a case for a renewed focus on the work of teaching, within the classroom environment, when thinking about issues of teacher quality and how to improve that quality through professional development. In the first part of the chapter, I present evidence that increasing students' rigorous coursework improves high school and college outcomes, most likely because it increases their deep understanding of the content; yet efforts to improve national achievement have been relatively ineffective. Increasing standards, such as through the Common Core State Standards (CCSS), may be a necessary but insufficient mechanism to increase students' knowledge and skills in that standards alone do not attend to what happens in the classroom. Process–product research focused on observable proxy measures of teacher effectiveness—such as certification, degrees, and experience—have not proved useful in identifying factors associated with improved student learning. More recent value-added models of teacher effectiveness suffer from various validity issues, both from a measurement perspective and also in that they cannot determine whether quality instruction is occurring.

The second part of the chapter builds on years of cognitive science research into differences between experts and novices to present the concept of teaching expertise. Characterized by knowledge and skills specific to the work of teaching, content knowledge for teaching includes both knowledge of the content being taught and knowledge of how students learn that content. Empirical evidence is beginning to converge to support the argument that content knowledge for teaching is related to both quality instruction and student achievement. Nationally, representative data indicate that low-income minority students disproportionately are assigned to teachers with low content knowledge for teaching, thus perpetuating achievement gaps. Professional development for teachers that focuses on content and content knowledge for teaching is shown to be more effective than professional development that does not. I conclude the chapter by arguing that more work is needed to empirically define and measure teachers' content knowledge for teaching, to identify teachers' current content knowledge for teaching, and to develop scalable models of professional development focused on increasing teachers' content knowledge for teaching to ensure that all students have equitable access to high-quality instruction.

THE NEED FOR GREATER STUDENT LEARNING

There is limited evidence that efforts to improve student achievement in the United States have had success (Braun, 2004; Nichols, Glass, & Berliner, 2006). For example, U.S. students' performance on the Trends in International Mathematics and Science Study (TIMSS) indicate that whereas average fourth- and eighth-grade performance in mathematics increased from 1995 to 2007, there was no change in the percentage of students at or above the advanced proficiency level in mathematics, no change in the average performance of fourth- and eighth-grade students in science, and a decline in the percentage of students at or above the advanced proficiency level in science (Gonzales et al., 2008). And although U.S. performance was higher than the average score across all countries in 2007, many countries continue to outperform U.S. students (Gonzales et al., 2008).

Moreover, national high school graduation rates for public schools have been steadily low, at 71%, since 1991, and graduation rates for minorities are even lower, at 56% for African Americans and 52% for Hispanic students (Green & Winters, 2005). Among those who graduate from high school, only 34% are college ready; that is, they can demonstrate "basic" proficiency on the National Assessment of Educational Progress (NAEP) reading exam and have taken a minimum number of courses in critical content areas (Green & Winters, 2005).

Improving aggregate national performance levels is crucial to our nation's success, as baby boomers currently make up the largest proportion of these technically skilled workers, and, as those workers retire, highly educated citizens will be needed to move into the workplace with the technological skills needed to become scientists, engineers, and physicians (Barton, 2002). Over the next 10 years, the bulk of job opportunities will be in professional, scientific, and technical services (Bureau of Labor Statistics, 2010).

Over the past three decades, dramatic changes in economic and technological forces have affected the structure and composition of the U.S. labor market, which in turn affected the demand for workers across industries and occupations (Sum, Kirsch, & Yamamoto, 2004). "Workers in professional, managerial, high-level sales, and service occupations gained the most from these labor market developments throughout the 1980s and 1990s, while many workers in entry-level office and blue-collar occupations, except construction-related craft workers, have lost ground" (Sum et al., 2004, p. 6).

The recent global recession demonstrates the continued vulnerability of those with low educational attainment. Demographic analyses of unemployment rates and the incidence of long-term unemployment (i.e., those out of work for at least 27 weeks) reveal disproportionate impacts of the 2007–2009 recession across demographic groups (Allegretto & Lynch, 2010). Unemployment has been more than 3.5 times higher for individuals without high school diplomas than for individuals with bachelor's degrees. Additionally, men, African Americans, Hispanics, teenagers, and workers in construction and manufacturing have experienced the highest rates of unemployment. In contrast, workers with at least a bachelor's degree and workers in management, business, financial, and professional occupations had the lowest unemployment rates.

No Child Left Behind (NCLB; 2001) was designed to increase achievement levels for all students, as well as to address achievement disparities among student subgroups by requiring states to set high standards and to develop tests to measure student progress toward those standards. However, the developed state standards varied substantially in their rigorousness, with many states' proficiency levels set at or below (NAEP) basic levels (Bandeira de Mello, 2011), resulting in uneven expectations for student learning. Indeed, in some states, the percentage of students scoring proficient on their state assessment is much higher than the percentage of students scoring proficient on the NAEP assessment because the state assessments hold less rigorous standards (Linn, Baker, & Betebenner, 2002). Recent analyses of the impact of NCLB on achievement using NAEP data revealed that for reading, national average achievement remained flat after NCLB and that achievement gaps were not significantly narrowed; while in mathematics, rate of achievement growth remained the same after NCLB implementation as before (Dee & Jacob, 2009; Lee, 2006; Lee & Reeves, 2012).

The CCSS were developed by states to ameliorate cross-state variation in expectations for students and were designed to provide a framework that makes clear what students need to know and be able to do to succeed in entry-level, credit-bearing academic college courses and in workforce training programs (*www.corestandards.org*). These standards were also designed to include rigorous content and application of knowledge through high-order skills so that all students are prepared to succeed in the global economy and society.

We expect that implementation of these standards will support student learning because a strong predictor of success in college is the quality and intensity, or rigor, of a student's high school curriculum. A rigorous high school curriculum is highly correlated with bachelor's degree attainment (.54), more so than test scores (.48) or class rank/GPA (.44; Adelman, 1999). A high level of academic rigor in high school courses has also consistently been shown to be related to postsecondary success (e.g., Adelman, 1999, 2006; Adelman, Daniel, & Berkovits, 2003; Riegle-Crumb, 2006; Wyatt, Wiley, Camara, & Proestler, 2011) and is inversely related to remediation in college (Hoyt & Sorenson, 2001).

Given that there are approximately 3 million elementary and secondary school teachers in the country (Bureau of Labor Statistics, 2011) and that for most of these teachers the standards to which they have been teaching are well below the expectations of the CCSS, significant professional development supports will be needed nationally if the new standards are to be successful. In the next section, I present an overview of the process–product research on teacher effectiveness and make an argument as to why this methodological approach is unlikely to solve the problems identified above.

TEACHER EFFECTIVENESS

Much has been made in academic and policy circles about the impact of effective teachers on students' learning. As labor market opportunities for women improved over the past few decades, talented college graduates who previously viewed teaching as a high-status profession have since turned to other occupations, resulting in a decline in the number of top achievers going into the teaching profession (Corcoran, Evans, & Schwab, 2004; Murnane & Steele, 2007). Despite these declines in the academic abilities of teachers, current teacher evaluation systems indicate that 94–99% of teachers are rated in the highest categories, which suggests that these evaluation systems fail to distinguish between effective and ineffective teachers (Weisberg, Sexton, Mulhern, & Keeling, 2009).

Of the qualified teachers in the workforce, there is not equitable distribution across schools, with low-income and minority students and schools being much less likely to be assigned teachers with more experience, who graduated from competitive colleges, or who passed the certification exam (Jacob, 2007; Lankford, Loeb, & Wyckoff, 2002; Murnane & Steele, 2007; Rivkin, Hanushek, & Kain, 2005). This inequity has impacts on students' achievement, with estimated increases in teacher quality by 1 standard deviation producing larger student gains than reducing class size by 10 students (Rivkin et al., 2005) and raising earnings at age 28 by 1% (Chetty, Friedman, & Rockoff, 2011).

When urban districts face more challenges than suburban districts in recruiting qualified teachers, particularly in math, they often respond to such shortages by hiring less qualified teachers, by using less qualified substitutes (or substitutes of unknown quality), or by increasing class size (Jacob, 2007; Lankford et al., 2002). "Historically, the demand for teachers has been driven by local preferences, and hiring decisions have not always been made based on estimates of teachers' instructional effectiveness" (Murnane & Steele, 2007, p. 23). Retention of qualified teachers also tends to be more problematic in high-poverty urban schools than in other public schools, and those who leave the profession tend to be more highly qualified than those who stay (Ingersoll, 2004).

While NCLB required that all teachers be highly qualified, process–product research found that these teacher characteristics (experience beyond 3–5 years, graduate degrees except perhaps in mathematics, and certifications) are generally unrelated to student learning (Boyd, Goldhaber, Lankford, & Wyckoff, 2007; Rockoff, 2004). In other words, the features that make teachers effective are often not readily observable. Although it may make sense not to eliminate these metrics altogether because they represent minimum expectations for classroom teachers, they clearly cannot be used alone to make teacher effectiveness judgments (Corcoran, 2010).

These findings pushed researchers to move away from a focus on education inputs (education production functions) and toward student achievement outcomes. The use of value-added models (VAMs) has grown in prominence as states' longitudinal data systems allowed linkages between students' and teachers' records. These models attempt to isolate the effects of teachers on students' achievement from year to year. Indeed, recent analyses indicate that students who have teachers identified as highly effective—defined as higher value-added teachers based on student achievement growth—enjoy both short-term academic benefits and long-term economic benefits in adulthood, such as likelihood of attending college, higher salaries, and lower teenage pregnancy rates (Chetty et al, 2011; Glazerman et al., 2010; Hanushek, 2011; Sanders & Rivers, 1996).

However, there are many statistical and measurement challenges associated with the use of VAMs to identify effective teachers. These challenges include uncertainty that a teacher's effect on achievement would be the same with different students; the fact that missing data (especially as it relates to student mobility) may produce biased estimates of teachers' effectiveness; and the suitability of standardized tests for use in accountability given the standards measured, the scale utilized, and the limited number of grades and subjects covered on the assessment (Murnane & Steele, 2007). In addition, the use of different tests—but with the same students and teachers—can produce different value-added results (Corcoran, 2010).[1] In fact, the Board on Testing and Assessment of the National Research Council of the National Academy of Sciences stated that "VAM estimates of teacher effectiveness should not be used to make operational decisions because such estimates are far too unstable to be considered fair or reliable" (cited in Baker et al., 2010).

Taken together, process–product research largely ignores student learning and focuses instead on student outcomes. However, a "student's prior knowledge, perception of the teacher's expectations, learning strategies, self-efficacy, interpersonal relationships, and so forth must all be taken into account for an adequate understanding of learning from instruction" (Shuell, 1993, p. 298). To this end, Hill, Kapitula, and Umland (2011) recommend the use of VAMs as only one component of teacher evaluation that also includes discriminating observation systems, especially in light of evidence that teachers' value-added scores may not be an accurate reflection of their instructional abilities. Indeed, case studies examining the instructional strength of teachers showed that teachers with high value-added scores are not necessarily strong in instruction and that scores may, in fact, be due to student sorting among classrooms (Hill et al., 2011).

> For an economist doing research, good teaching can be simplified into an estimate of the regressed gain scores of pupils who have studied with a teacher during some specified time period. That estimate of impact is often further corrected by estimating the cost of the teaching during that period. But I have yet to read of an economist who defined good teaching that way for her own kids or for a university professor of economics. (Lee Shulman, as cited in Loeb, Rouse, & Shorris, 2007, p. 6)

Seidel and Shavelson (2007) "recognize that the effects of teaching on student learning can be diverse," in that some teaching may affect cognition; some, motivation; some, learning process; and some, short- versus long-term effects. They examined two models—process–product and cognitive learning—to look at whether the research design systematically affects the effect size of the outcomes. Most effectiveness research reviewed followed process–product models, but when looking at the cognitive model meta-analyses, the effect of "domain-specific processing" had the highest effect on all outcomes, most notably on cognitive outcomes (.22), whereas

---

[1]Indeed, using different growth models for school-level accountability (such as student growth percentile, fixed effects gain, simple panel model, etc.) result in different classification of schools, are not consistent across states, vary across elementary and middle schools, are not consistent across years, and are influenced by immutable school intake variables, such as percentage of students who receive free or reduced-price lunches (Goldschmidt, Choi, & Beaudoin, 2012).

other teacher effects on cognitive outcomes were much smaller (.02). There were also large effects of domain-specific processing on reading, math, and science cognitive outcomes for both elementary and secondary grades. Domain-specific processes also showed positive impacts on motivations and affective outcomes. Indeed, "domain-specific activities consistently represented the most important influence of teaching on student learning and stood out from the other components" (Seidel & Shavelson, 2007, p. 483).

How, then, can we effectively measure and thus identify quality teachers and instruction while considering what actually occurs in the classroom and also domain-specific processing? To answer this question, I turn to some often overlooked research from cognitive psychology on differences between experts and novices. This broad literature can help inform us about how students learn and what skilled teaching looks like.

THE DEVELOPMENT OF KNOWLEDGE

In the late 1950s, the cognitive science revolution created a new science of learning that emphasized learning with understanding over memory of facts alone (Bransford, Brown, & Cocking, 2000). Bransford and colleagues (2000) summarize some key findings from the cognitive research on teaching and learning that undergird our understanding of effective instruction:

- Students come to the classroom with preconceptions about how the world works. If their initial understanding is not engaged, they may fail to grasp the new concepts and information that are taught, or they may learn them for purposes of a test but revert to their preconceptions outside the classroom.
- A "metacognitive" approach to instruction can help students learn to take control of their own learning by defining learning goals and monitoring their progress in achieving them.
- To develop competence in an area of inquiry, students must:
  - Have a deep foundation of factual knowledge.
  - Understand facts and ideas in the context of a conceptual framework.
  - Organize knowledge in ways that facilitate retrieval and application.
- Knowledge is organized in a framework, or schema, that allows people to create expectations based on existing knowledge and integrate new information within the framework (Anderson, 1977; Anderson, Spiro, & Anderson, 1978).

Experts versus Novices

The emphasis on knowledge and how it is structured turns out to be critical in understanding differences in expert and novice problem solving, which involve solution speed, errors, and patterns. The coemergence of interest in cognitive psychology and artificial intelligence generated extensive interest in the differences between experts and novices (Berliner, 1994). This body of work—drawing from studies in such varied domains as chess, radiology, taxi driving, and physics—yielded much insight into how experts' knowledge is structured and how they solve problems using sophisticated representations of the problem (e.g., Chi, Feltovich, & Glaser, 1981; Chi & Koeske, 1983). Chi, Glaser, and Rees (1982) argued "that the problem-solving difficulties of novices can be attributed mainly to inadequacies of their knowledge bases and not to limitations in either the architecture of their cognitive systems or processing capabilities" (p. 71). They also argued for a knowledge-based conceptualization of intelligence that would deemphasize general problem-solving skills and instead focus on the development of well-structured domain knowledge.

Estimates of the time it takes to become an expert—on the order of 10,000 hours (Newell & Simon, 1972)—provide support for the evidence that individuals generally become experts in only one domain. It is important to note that although experience is necessary to become an expert, it is not sufficient—not all people with experience will become experts.

Glaser (1985) developed a set of 24 propositions regarding expertise, of which several are paraphrased here:

- Experts and novices do not differ in their processing of information; rather, expert performance is based on their superior knowledge structures in a specific domain.
- Experts' representations of problems are based on knowledge of domain principles, whereas novices' are based on surface features.
- Experts recognize meaningful patterns faster than novices.
- Experts develop automaticity of performance, in part driven by routines.
- Experts develop skilled self-regulatory processes, such as allocation of attention and solution monitoring.
- Development of expertise is not linear. Non-monotonicities and plateaus occur, indicating shifts in understanding and stabilization of automaticity.

"Now, we must ask, how can this knowledge of human competence guide the development of learning theories and the design of conditions that foster learning?" (Glaser, 1989, p. 274). In other words, given what we know about how humans learn and develop expertise, what can we say about the development of teacher expertise as it applies to student learning?

Pedagogical Content Knowledge

Shulman (1986) argued that the prior century's focus on pedagogical approaches to the exclusion of content in the teaching profession resulted in a negative perception that teachers are ignorant and inept. He contrasted this view with Aristotle's view of the academy, in which the highest degrees available (master and doctor) quite literally meant "teacher," and individuals who attained these degrees were viewed as superior. Shulman argued for a balanced view of teaching that encompasses both content and pedagogical knowledge and coined the term "pedagogical content knowledge" (PCK). PCK, he argued, is subject-matter knowledge for teaching that includes the most useful forms of representation of the domain, along with analogies, illustrations, examples, explanations, and demonstrations. PCK also includes an understanding of what makes learning a particular domain easy or difficult, including students' preconceptions and misconceptions.

Shulman's (1987) model of pedagogical reasoning and action involves six mechanisms, as described next, though not necessarily in a linear trajectory. First is *comprehension*, whereby teachers must critically comprehend a set of ideas to be taught. Next comes *transformation*, whereby subject matter comprehended by a teacher is transformed (through preparation, representation, instructional selections, adaptation, and tailoring) to accommodate the minds of the students. *Instruction* involves the observable performance of teaching acts and includes many crucial aspects of pedagogy. *Evaluation* entails both formal and informal ongoing determination of student understandings. Teachers learn from experience through *reflection*, looking back on the teaching and learning that has occurred. Finally, *new comprehension* represents a new beginning, by which some teachers arrive at a new understanding of the purposes, the subjects taught, the students, and the processes of pedagogy.

Shulman's ideas on PCK were central to the development of the National Board for Professional Teaching Standards (NBPTS), which developed following the recommendations of the Carnegie Forum on Education and the Economy's Task Force on Teaching as a Profession. The task force's final report—*A Nation Prepared: Teachers for the 21st Century*—was released on May 15, 1986. Commissioned by the Carnegie Forum, the goal of the report was to raise the standards for teaching in America through an advanced certification system for highly accomplished teachers.

Although empirical evidence on the effectiveness of the certification program to identify expert teachers is slim, there is evidence to indicate that the features of expert teachers can be used to distinguish teachers who pass the NBPTS examination from those who do not (Bond, Smith, Baker, & Hattie, 2000) and that the academic achievement of the students of NBPTS-certified teachers is higher than that of noncertified teachers (Vandevoort, Amrein-Beardsley, & Berliner, 2004).

Focusing on the development of teacher expertise, Berliner (1994) outlines five stages of expert performance acquisition. These stages can apply both to students learning in a classroom and to teachers as they develop their craft. First is the novice stage, at which many errors are made, the common elements of the tasks must be learned, and context-free rules are provided. Only minimal skill at the tasks should be expected of novice teachers, such as student and first-year teachers. The second stage is the advanced beginner, where many second- and third-year teachers are likely to be. Here, experience merges with verbal knowledge and episodic and case knowledge are developed, but the teachers may still not know what is important. The third stage is the competence level, at which personal agency—willfully choosing what to do—is developed. Not all advanced beginners reach this level (i.e., teachers may be experienced but not competent). At this level, at about the third or fourth year of teaching, teachers make conscious choices about what to do based on determining what is important, set priorities and decide on plans, have rational goals, and choose sensible means for reaching those goals.

Proficiency is the fourth level, which a modest number of teachers reach at about the fifth year of experience. At this stage, intuition plays a larger role in practice based on the individual's wealth of experience. A more holistic recognition of patterns is possible based on their experience, which allows them to bring rich case knowledge to bear. The final stage is expertise, whereby individuals show fluid performance; they know where to be or what to do at just the right time. Experts are not consciously choosing what to attend to and what to do because choices are made automatically.

Berliner (1994), argues that because pedagogy is highly contextualized to a teacher's students and to the school at which he or she teaches, "it may only be possible to obtain valid judgments about the degree of expertise a teacher possesses from observing them in their own classrooms, an expensive form of assessment" (p. 22). He further argues that studying the performance of expert teachers might guide us in the design of training programs for beginning teachers or provide exemplary pedagogical performances that novices could study in a teacher education laboratory (Berliner, 1986). However, identifying expert teachers—unlike identifying expert chess players, as winning games is explicit—has proved challenging. Berliner (1986) has relied on teacher's reputations, classroom observations by three independent observers, and performance on laboratory tasks to identify experts but notes that such criteria as being named "Teacher of the Year" are fraught with problems.

Sabers, Cushing, and Berliner (1991), in an in-depth study of expert, advanced beginner, and novice middle and high school science teachers, examined differences in their ability to understand what was happening in videos of classroom instruction. Results indicated that experts are able to monitor, understand, and interpret events in more detail and with greater insight than novices, are better able to attend to the multidimensional nature of the class than are novices, but are similar to novices in their ability to select content and recall nonmeaningful events.

Research on expert pedagogy yielded the following propositions (Berliner, 1994) for expert teachers:

- They excel in specific domains and contexts. They develop automaticity for routines needed to accomplish their goals, allowing cognitive resources to be allocated toward higher-order activities.
- They are more opportunistic and flexible in their teaching.
- They are more sensitive to task demands and social situations when solving problems.
- They represent problems in qualitatively different ways.
- They have faster and more accurate pattern recognition capabilities.
- They perceive more meaningful patterns in their specified domains.
- They at first solve problems more slowly but bring richer and more personal sources of information to bear on the problems they are trying to solve.

Pedagogy in the Content Areas

Because different domains have different structures, evidence arguments, and reasoning processes, we need to dispute the "popular but dangerous" myth that teaching is a generic skill and that good teachers can teach any subject (Bransford et al., 2000). Therefore, in this section I present research on teaching and learning in the content areas through the lens of cognitive science expert–novice research. I focus on work examining science, history, and mathematics domains, as these areas are well developed, though similar research streams in other domains have been similarly developed and can inform teaching and learning. These sections are not meant to be fully inclusive of the research in each domain; rather, they are intended to provide exemplars of domain-specific structures, evidence arguments, and reasoning processes among content experts and novices, as well as among expert and novice teachers, and what those differences suggest for high-quality content instruction.

Science

Research on teaching and learning in science looks to understand the development of scientific thinking and how best to design instruction to support that development. Central to scientific thinking are processes such as conceptual change, understanding of experimental controls, and development and testing of scientific models.

Conceptual change is argued to be central to developing accurate representations of scientific phenomena, particularly for understanding the physical world. Because children naturally develop representations of the world around them that are often inaccurate, fundamental reorganization of knowledge structures (i.e., conceptual change) must occur before they can understand the implicit meanings of such scientific concepts as force, evolution, and day–night cycles (Chi, Slotta, & de Leeuw, 1994; Vosniadou, Ioannides, Dimitrakopoulou, & Papademetriou, 2001).

Classroom design studies in science work to change educational practice in ways that foster scientific thinking and to study the cognitive and other forms of development among participating students (Lehrer & Schauble, 2006). These design studies are developmental in focus, concerned with what can be learned over years of instruction, and yield much insight into students' developing knowledge of science.

For example, generating and testing models—representations that serve as analogues to scientific systems in the real world—is a central activity of science. "Lehrer and Schauble (2000c, 2003, 2005) reported observing characteristic shifts in understanding of modeling over the span of the elementary school grades, from an early emphasis on literal depictional forms to representations that were progressively more symbolic and mathematically powerful" (Lehrer & Schauble, 2006, p. 183). It is widely accepted that teachers need to be explicit and clear about the forms of evidence and argument valued in science (Lehrer & Schauble, 2006). Lehrer and Schauble (2006) argued that science instruction needs to focus on the overlapping efforts of building knowledge and theories, conducting experiments, and generating and testing models—these efforts are not mutually exclusive.

Schauble, Glaser, Raghavan, and Reiner (1991) examined the "reciprocal influences of strategy on knowledge and knowledge on strategy by focusing on a topic in which individuals have some beginning conceptions but then engage in self-directed experimentation to confirm, extend, or change those beginning theories" (p. 203)—related to the topic of electrical circuits. Results indicated that good and poor learners could be differentiated by strategic differences in goal-directed planning, generating and interpreting evidence, and managing data, whereby sophisticated initial representations of the problem were related to sophisticated reasoning and strategy. Thus initial conceptions and prior knowledge of the problem space can play a role in the strategies utilized in an experimental process, which in turn can influence the inferences drawn.

Chen and Klahr (1999) argue that mastery of the logic of control variables in scientific experimentation is critical for scientific literacy. They taught children to focus not on science content per se but rather on the structural relationships behind the content to identify causes of observed outcomes, such as determining what factors influence how far a ball will roll down a ramp. Among the trials observed were various forms of invalid tests, namely ones in which dependent variables were confounded such that it was impossible to tell whether one of the variables was the causal one. After training with explicit feedback, 7- and 10-year-olds improved their ability to judge the informativeness of the trials and to make inferences based on them, and older children were able to transfer these skills to other tasks 7 months later.

Schauble (1996) argues that previously dichotomized approaches to the study of scientific reasoning—experimentation and conceptual change—are actually closely interrelated and ought to be considered conjointly. Schauble investigated scientific reasoning in a complex, knowledge-rich domain by having participants (both fifth- and sixth-grade children, as well as adults) conduct experiments over time to discover the causal relations between variables and outcomes in multivariable contexts involving fluids and immersed objects. This work differs from typical studies of scientific reasoning using experimental methods, which often employed well-structured, knowledge-lean problems in a laboratory setting. Results showed that although all participants improved at generating systematic data about the experiment and in basing inferences on valid evidence, adults in general outperformed children and were more systematic in their approach. Schauble argues that both "strategic and knowledge-specific changes play a role in the development of scientific reasoning. These changes appear to bootstrap each other, so that appropriate knowledge supports the selection of appropriate experimentation strategies, and systematic and valid experimentation strategies support the development of more accurate and complete knowledge" (p. 118).

The Fostering Communities of Learners (FCL) project, directed by Ann Brown and Joseph Campione (1994, 1996), considered science learning to be socially constructed, whereby theories were developed and subjected to testing according to criteria developed within a community. Metacognition and self-regulation played a large role in FCL classrooms in which the goal was to progressively turn over to the students the responsibility for the progress of their own learning, particularly through reciprocal teaching. Reciprocal teaching (Palincsar & Brown, 1984), developed to improve students' reading comprehension strategies, involved students gradually taking over key teaching activities themselves, which resulted in significant and lasting improvements in reading comprehension, even for struggling students.

History

Historical thinking requires an orientation to the past informed
by disciplinary canons of evidence and rules of argument.
                              —WINEBURG (2007, p. 6)

Sam Wineburg (1999) cogently argued that there is a tension in historical thinking between the personal and the evidentiary whereby there is a "seduction of coming to know people in the past by relying on the dimensions of our 'lived experiences.'" Historical thinking differs from everyday thinking in that everyday thinking privileges information that is easily available and salient over information requiring evidence or proof when forming judgments and making decisions (Wineburg, 2007). "For example, presented with statistical data on the morbidity rates for smokers, a person will often appeal to more 'available' data, such as a grandfather who smoked three packs of cigarettes a day but lived to the ripe old age of 95" (Wineburg, 2007, p. 7).

To understand the nature of historical thinking, we can look to comparisons of expert and novice historians. Wineburg (1994) asked expert historians to review eight historical documents and to think aloud about what happened at the battle of Lexington on April 19, 1775. Constant across groups, the historians viewed the documents as a collective body of evidence from which they built a cognitive model of the event. These event models were joined with models of the document authors, which in turn were queried about their intentions. In other words, the historians engaged in a kind of dialogue with the document authors:

> Faced with an unfamiliar document, the historian's goal is not merely to issue a judgment about it, but to use it to stimulate new questions, to identify gaps in knowledge that prevent them from understanding the fullness of the historical moment. Students typically encountered this document and issued judgments. By painstakingly specifying what they did not know, historians positioned themselves not only to judge. They positioned themselves to learn. (Wineburg, 2007, p. 11)

Similarly, Wineburg (1991) compared gifted high school seniors with historians on two tasks: recall of information from a U.S. history textbook and interpreting competing claims in historical documents. Historians with backgrounds in U.S. history recalled most of the items, historians without that background knew less, and some students recalled more facts than some historians. However, historians excelled at document interpretations, whereas students were stymied at the task.

To this end, good history teaching needs to move beyond rote memorization of facts and dates and more toward the way historians approach the study of history: by following rules of evidence and the utilization of specific analytical skills. Leinhardt (1994, 1997) spent 2 years studying an Advanced Placement history teacher, Ms. Sterling, who encouraged her students to do just that. Her goal was to help students understand history as an evidentiary form of knowledge, not as clusters of fixed dates and names, to develop deep mindfulness of the subject matter. For example, "there is the difference between simple stories and the intricate, ambiguous ones of history. A simple story about the Civil War might hold that differences over slavery and the firing on Fort Sumter started the civil war; a more complex story includes social, political, and economic tensions that can be traced back to the Revolutionary Period" (Leinhardt, 1994, p. 253).

Not only does instruction need to reflect the rules of historical evidence, but history textbooks also need to be rewritten to make them more coherent and connected and to give them voice (McKeown & Beck, 1994). Although the resulting texts will be longer, McKeown and Beck (1994) found in their research that they serve to promote greater student recall and depth of comprehension, whereas original texts resulted in disconnected and surface-level representations of the information. To this end, they argued for textbooks that emphasize depth over breadth of history coverage.

Math

Learning mathematics is empowering. Mathematically powerful students are quantitatively literate. They are capable of interpreting the vast amounts of quantitative data they encounter on a daily basis and of making balanced judgments on the basis of those interpretations. They use mathematics in practical ways, from simple applications such as using proportional reasoning for recipes or scale models, to complex budget projections, statistical analyses, and computer modeling. They are flexible thinkers with a broad repertoire of techniques and perspectives for dealing with novel problems and situations. They are analytical, both in thinking issues through themselves and in examining the arguments put forth by others.

—SCHOENFELD (1992, pp. 4–5)

Comparing expert and novice elementary mathematics teachers, as defined by their students' achievement growth, Leinhardt (1989) found that experts gave better explanations than novices, had fewer and less serious errors, and were more likely to complete the explanation. Moreover, the experts' lessons were more integrated, used multiple representations to explain the same concept of subtraction with regrouping, and were denser and richer than the novices' lessons. "Experts also construct lessons that display a highly efficient internal structure, one that is characterized by fluid movement from one type of activity to another, by minimal student confusion during instruction, and by a transparent system of goals" (Leinhardt, 1989, p. 73).

In an analysis of expert teachers' lessons on fractions, Leinhardt and Smith (1985) examined the relationship between teachers' subject-matter knowledge and their classroom behavior. Fractions were selected because of their importance in elementary mathematics for operations such as equivalent fractions, raising fractions to a specific denominator, reducing fractions, adding and subtracting with like and unlike denominators, and mixed numbers and their conversions to fractions and back again. Among experts, there were "substantial differences in the details of their presentations to students" (Leinhardt & Smith, 1985, p. 269), which in turn can influence the completeness of students' knowledge base.

Particularly noteworthy in the area of mathematics content teaching is the work started with Deborah Ball at the University of Michigan on the Learning Mathematics for Teaching Project and which is being extended by various researchers, most notably Heather Hill, now at Harvard. This extensive line of research is a model for examining the intersection of PCK, high-quality instruction, and student achievement. Here I provide an overview of their ongoing work and highlight important findings from their research that have implications for measuring mathematical knowledge for teaching.

Ball, Hill, and Bass (2005) argue that "although the typical methods of improving U.S. instructional quality have been to develop curricula, and—especially in the last decade—to articulate standards for what students should learn, little improvement is possible without direct attention to the practice of teaching" (p. 14). Thus the quality of teaching depends on the teacher's knowledge of the content. They argue that, in addition to all the obvious aspects such as lesson planning, grading, and evaluating students' work, teachers also must do analysis of math errors and effectively use representations to express meaning. In other words, teaching involves mathematical reasoning as much as it does pedagogical thinking.

Thus an "emergent theme in [their] research is the centrality of mathematical language and the need for a special kind of fluency with mathematical terms" (Ball et al., 2005, p. 21). To answer the questions, Is there a body of mathematical knowledge for teaching that is specialized for the work teachers do? and Does it have a demonstrable effect on student achievement?, they developed a large-scale survey-based (multiple choice) instrument. Topics included numbers and operations; patterns, functions, and algebra; and geometry for elementary and middle school content.

They had content experts (math educators, mathematicians, professional development providers, project staff, and classroom teachers) write items that were ideologically neutral (e.g., neither traditional nor reform math oriented) and that were composed of two elements: (1) common knowledge of math that any well-educated adult should know and (2) math knowledge specialized to teaching that only teachers need to know.

Questions were scenarios, and the ones measuring specialized knowledge in mathematics asked teachers to represent numbers or operations using pictures or manipulatives and to provide explanations for common math rules (e.g., 35 times 25). Adults should know how to multiply, but teachers need to evaluate "unconventional student methods that produce correct answers, but whose generalizability or mathematical validity are not immediately clear. For teachers to be effective, they must be able to size up mathematical issues that come up in class—often fluently and with little time" (Ball et al., 2005, p. 43).

Items do not measure teachers' knowledge of students or how to teach multiplication (for example). "Unless we, as educators, are willing to claim that there is professional knowledge that matters for the quality of instruction and can back that claim with evidence, we will continue to be no more than one voice among many competing to assert what teachers should know" (Ball et al., 2005, p. 45).

Hill, Rowan, and Ball (2005) suggest that examples of work for teaching "include explaining terms and concepts to students, interpreting students' statements and solutions, judging and correcting textbook treatments of particular topics, using representations accurately in the classroom, and providing students with examples of mathematical concepts, algorithms, or proofs" (p. 373). They conducted a 2-year longitudinal study of the effects of three reform efforts (America's Choice, Success For All, and Accelerated Schools) on teachers' content knowledge and specialized content knowledge in reading and mathematics and on students' gain scores on the TerraNova test from first to third grade and from third to fifth grade in 115 schools. Results showed that most of the variance in gain scores resulted from students within classrooms; thus only a small amount of variance could be attributed to teacher effects (8% for first grade and 2% for third grade), though this may be artificially low.

In addition, teachers' content knowledge was a significant predictor of students' gain in both grades. Content knowledge for teaching mathematics (CKT-M) was the strongest predictor of student gains in the models (more than teacher background variables and average time spent on math instruction per day) and was on par with the effect size of students' socioeconomic status (SES). An increase of 1 standard deviation in mathematical knowledge for teaching (MKT) translates into an increase of 1/10th standard deviation in student performance over the course of a year. When looking at the effects by decile of teacher CKT-M, first-grade teachers in the two lowest deciles (0–20%) taught students who gained on average 10 points fewer than students in the highest category (the referent). But having teachers above the bottom two deciles does not linearly improve students' gains (e.g., having a teacher in the eighth decile does not produce bigger gains on average than having a teacher in the fourth decile). Similar trends were seen for third-grade teachers, with teachers in the bottom three deciles (0–30%) having students who made lower gains.

The content knowledge for teaching reading (CKT-R) measure, although positively related to student gains in first and third grades, was not significant and had only a small effect on the CKT-M variable. This suggests that the effect of teachers' knowledge on students' achievement is not simply general knowledge of teaching but, rather, is content specific. Moreover, teachers' content knowledge for teaching is not equitably distributed across students, further perpetuating achievement gaps. For first graders, teachers' math knowledge was evenly distributed across SES levels, but not by race, such that minority students had teachers with lower knowledge. For third graders, there was a significant relationship between teacher knowledge and both SES and minority status.

Using a validated measure of mathematical knowledge for teaching to assess a nationally representative sample of teachers, Hill (2007b) found that teachers with higher levels of MKT were unevenly distributed across students, whereby minority students and those receiving free or reduced-price lunches had less access to high-knowledge teachers.

In a study of 10 teachers' MKT and mathematics quality of instruction (MQI), teachers took a paper-and-pencil test of MKT, and nine of their lessons were videotaped for MQI so that the relationship between teacher knowledge and quality of instruction could be examined quantitatively (Hill, Blunk, et al., 2008). Elements of MQI, developed based on the literature on deficits and affordances of teaching, include mathematical errors, responding to students appropriately, responding to students inappropriately, connecting classroom practice to mathematics, richness of the mathematics, and mathematical language.

Results show "that there is a powerful relationship between what a teacher knows, how she knows it, and what she can do in the context of instruction" (Hill, Blunk, et al., 2008, p. 496). Of the elements of MQI, errors were negatively correlated with MKT scores (errors total = -.83, errors language subscale = -.80). Thus errors may help explain the relationship between MKT and student achievement. High-knowledge teachers both avoid errors and provide denser, more rigorous mathematics instruction (affordances). Other general teaching skills/knowledge seem not to affect MQI in that there was little variation in classroom management or motivation skills across teachers. Although not the focus of the study, the impact of the professional development on improving teachers' MKT was mixed at best. Sometimes the professional development served to improve teachers' knowledge and quality of instruction, but often new concepts were implemented without meaning, purpose, or even any mathematical connection.

PROFESSIONAL DEVELOPMENT TO DEVELOP EXPERT TEACHERS

What kinds of professional development will support teachers becoming experts, then? The last two decades of research brought a consensus about the following features that constitute effective professional development: a focus on content, active learning, coherence, duration, and collective participation (Desimone, 2009). Drawn from studies with varied methodologies (e.g., Borko, 2004; Desimone, Porter, Garet, Yoon, & Birman, 2002; Garet, Porter, Desimone, Birman, & Yoon, 2001; Guskey, 1994; Little, 1982; Penuel, Fishman, Yamaguchi, & Gallagher, 2007), these features address effectiveness in terms of improving teacher practices.

There is mounting evidence that certain features of professional development can also have an impact on student achievement. These features include training over an extended time period (Yoon, Duncan, Lee, Scarloss, & Shapley, 2007), a focus on the subject-matter content and how students learn that content (Dopplet et al., 2009; Kennedy, 1998), and opportunities for teacher teams to work collaboratively together on student learning (Saunders, Goldenberg, & Gallimore, 2009). However, teachers with weak content knowledge are less likely to participate in professional development that has a sustained content focus than teachers who already have strong content knowledge (Desimone, Smith, & Ueno, 2006).

Several of the features of professional development shown to be related to effective professional development (i.e., active learning, duration, training over extended time periods, and teacher collaboration) have been embraced widely by practitioners and are often the focus of much of the professional development sales industry. However, the research on subject-matter content and how students learn that content is not typically sought out by teachers (Hiebert, Gallimore, & Stigler, 2002), nor is it regularly addressed in the industry books and guides available to practitioners.

Some efforts have been made to translate this extensive cognitive science research base into professional development methods (cf. Arcavi & Schoenfeld, 2008; Ball & Bass, 2000; Brown, 1992; Carpenter, Fennema, Peterson, Chiang, & Loef, 1989; Cobb et al., 1991; Franke, Carpenter, & Levi, 2001; Gersten, Dimino, Jayanthi, Kim, & Santoro, 2009; Grossman, Wineburg, & Woolworth, 2001; Saxe, Gearhardt, & Nasir, 2001; Swafford, Jones, & Thornton, 1997). In these efforts, teachers received substantial instruction over extended periods of time on content that was very deep and challenging, typically from university-based educational researchers who had studied how to teach that content for years.

However, it is precisely because these concepts are complex and take time to comprehend that broad scale-up of teachers' professional development of this kind nationally is a challenge. Moreover, Hill (2009) argues that we must fix the economic marketplace considerations that promote the big business of teacher professional learning—supply, demand, information, and efficiency—to move away from that which only fulfills state licensure requirements toward more of a focus on content knowledge for teaching. The research on teacher expertise has potential as a framework for designing professional development that improves not only school climate and teacher learning opportunities but also student outcomes.

> To use a shopping metaphor, these research proven programs, which are often offered by university faculty or nationally recognized providers, are "boutiques" serving a handful of fortunate teachers while leaving many more to shop at the Wal-Marts of the professional development world. There, most teachers receive uninspired and often poor-quality professional development and related learning opportunities. (Hill, 2009, p. 470)

CONCLUSIONS

To conclude, I argue that we need to shift our focus from teacher effectiveness to teacher expertise, with specific attention to content knowledge for teaching and instructional quality within the classroom. Converging lines of evidence suggest that neither proxy measures of teacher effectiveness based on observable data nor VAMs validly capture teachers' knowledge and related instructional practices. Expert–novice research born out of the cognitive science literature yields important insights about what deep understanding of the content looks like; how it differs by domain-specific structures, associated evidence claims, and representations; how expertise develops; and what expert pedagogy looks like in the classroom. Recent efforts to construct large-scale measures of teachers' MKT indicate that such instruments can provide valid measures of teacher quality that are related to the actual tasks of teaching that occur in the classroom and that are also related to student achievement.

To shift the focus to content knowledge for teaching, several streams of related work are needed. First, continued development and validation of content knowledge for teaching measures are needed. Although great strides have been made in mathematics and some new work is beginning in other domains (cf. Carlisle, Kelcey, Rowan, & Phelps, 2011; Hill, 2005, 2007a; Hill, Ball, Blunk, Goffney, & Rowan, 2007; Hill, Ball, & Schilling, 2008; Hill, Dean, & Goffney, 2007; Hill, Schilling, & Ball, 2004; Kersting, 2008; McCray & Chen, 2012; Schilling, Blunk, & Hill, 2007), much more work can be done to empirically validate the argument that content knowledge for teaching is related to instructional quality and student learning across domains.

Second, to support the development of such measures, cognitive labs can serve to more clearly map out student misconceptions and learning progressions in the domains, as well as to conduct cognitive interviews of teachers to validate content knowledge for teaching instruments. These labs should be organized to include multidisciplinary research teams including educational psychologists, psychometricians, content experts, and teacher practitioners to ensure that the items developed are valid from all angles.

Once instruments are developed, policymakers should be careful to adhere to appropriate uses and inferences that can be drawn related to accountability for student achievement. For example, after examining the reliability of the MQI instrument, Hill, Charalambous, and Kraft (2012) recommended that the observation instrument be used only for relative decisions, not for absolute high-stakes decisions, given the low reliability of the instrument, especially if just one principal is doing the classroom observations.

The cognitive labs can also be utilized to create professional development based on cognitive science and content knowledge for teaching. For given domains, the careful analysis of students' learning progressions and students' common errors and misconceptions, effective problem representations and explanations, and appropriate forms of evidence can be identified and explicated, and more effective and content-focused professional development can be designed.

Because one limitation of similar professional development efforts was scalability, it may be possible to scale up professional development in which content knowledge for teaching is a primary focus through online videos of lessons that are indexed to the CCSS (Merriman Bausmith & Barry, 2011). Such an approach might reduce the likelihood that locally developed expectations are too low while also ensuring a deep focus on domain-specific instruction. By focusing on content knowledge for teaching and related instructional quality, we can get closest to the core of student learning (National Research Council, 2013).

QUESTIONS FOR DISCUSSION

1. What kinds of state and local policies might support the use of measures of content knowledge for teaching? How would these policies work with, or supplant, existing policies?

2. What role do universities play in developing teachers' content knowledge for teaching?

3. How can school administrators provide the "transformative leadership" needed to ensure that meaningful teacher evaluation occurs?

4. What recommendations would you make for administrators and coaches seeking to create a culture of professional learning based on content knowledge for teaching?

5. What role can professional learning communities play in building content knowledge for teaching? How can teachers be sure that the knowledge and expectations they have are accurately representing the Common Core Standards?

REFERENCES

Adelman, C. (1999). *Answers in the toolbox: Academic intensity, attendance patterns, and bachelor's degree attainment.* Washington, DC: U.S. Department of Education, Office of Education Research and Improvement.

Adelman, C. (2006). *The toolbox revisited: Paths to degree completion from high school through college.* Washington, DC: U.S. Department of Education.

Adelman, C., Daniel, B., & Berkovits, I. (2003). *Postsecondary attainment, attendance, curriculum, and performance: Selected results from the NELS: 88/2000 postsecondary education transcript study (PETS), 2000.* Washington, DC: U.S. Department of Education, Institute of Education Sciences, National Center for Education Statistics..

Allegretto, S., & Lynch, D. (2010, October). The composition of the unemployed and long-term unemployed in tough labor markets. *Monthly Labor Review,* 3–18.

Anderson, R. (1977). *Schema-directed processes in language comprehension* (Tech. Rep. No. 50). Urbana: University of Illinois, Center for the Study of Reading.

Anderson, R., Spiro, R., & Anderson, M. (1978). Schemata as scaffolding for the representation of information in connected discourse. *American Educational Research Journal, 15,* 433–440.

Arcavi, A., & Schoenfeld, A. (2008). Using the unfamiliar to problematize the familiar: The case of mathematics teacher in-service education. *Canadian Journal of Science, Mathematics, and Technology Education, 8*(3), 280–295.

Baker, E., Barton, P., Darling-Hammond, L., Haertel, E., Ladd, H., Linn, R., et al. (2010). *Problems with the use of student test scores to evaluate teachers* (EPI Briefing Paper No. 278). Washington, DC: Economic Policy Institute.

Ball, D. L., & Bass, H. (2000). Interweaving content and pedagogy in teaching and learning to teach: Knowing and using mathematics. In J. Boaler (Ed.), *Multiple perspectives on the teaching and learning of mathematics* (pp. 83–104). Westport, CT: Ablex.

Ball, D. L., Hill, H., & Bass, H. (2005). Knowing mathematics for teaching: Who knows mathematics well enough to teach third grade, and how can we decide? *American Educator, 29*(1), 14–17, 20–22, 43–46.

Bandeira de Mello, V. (2011), *Mapping state proficiency standards onto the NAEP scales:*

Variation and change in state standards for reading and mathematics, 2005–2009 (NCES No. 2011-458). Washington, DC: U.S. Government Printing Office. Retrieved from *http://nces.ed.gov/nationsreportcard/pdf/studies/2011458.pdf* .

Barton, P. E. (2002). *Meeting the need for scientists, engineers, and an educated citizenry in a technological society.* Princeton, NJ: Educational Testing Service, Policy Information Center Report. Retrieved from *www.ets.org/Media/Research/pdf/PICMEETING-NEED.pdf.*

Berliner, D. (1986). In pursuit of the expert pedagogue. *Educational Researcher, 15*(7), 5–13.

Berliner, D. (1994). Expertise: The wonders of exemplary performance. In J. N. Mangieri & C. C. Block (Eds.), *Creating powerful thinking in teachers and students* (pp. 141–186). Fort Worth, TX: Holt, Rinehart & Winston.

Bond, L., Smith, T., Baker, W. K., & Hattie, J. A. (2000, September). *The certification system of the National Board for Professional Teaching Standards: A construct and consequential validity study.* Greensboro: University of North Carolina, Center for Educational Research and Evaluation.

Borko, H. (2004). Professional development and teacher learning: Mapping the terrain. *Educational Researcher, 33*(8), 3–15.

Boyd, D., Goldhaber, D., Lankford, H., & Wyckoff, J. (2007). The effect of certification and preparation on teacher quality. *The Future of Children, 17*(1), 45–68.

Bransford, J., Brown, A., & Cocking, R. (2000). *How people learn: Brain, mind, experience, and school.* Washington, DC: National Academy Press.

Braun, H. (2004). Reconsidering the impact of high-stakes testing. *Education Policy Analysis Archives, 12,* 1.

Brown, A., & Campione, J. C. (1994). *Guided discovery in a community of learners.* Cambridge, MA: MIT Press.

Brown, A., & Campione, J. (1996). Psychological theory and design of innovative learning environments: On procedures, principles, and systems. In L. Schauble & R. Glaser (Eds.), *Innovations in learning: New environments for education* (pp. 289–325). Mahwah, NJ: Erlbaum.

Brown, A. L. (1992). Design experiments: Theoretical and methodological challenges in creating complex interventions in classroom settings. *Journal of the Learning Sciences, 2*(2), 141–178.

Bureau of Labor Statistics. (2010). Occupational outlook handbook, 2010–11 edition. Retrieved from *www.bls.gov/oco/oco2003.htm#industry.*

Bureau of Labor Statistics. (2011). Statistical abstract of the United States: 2011, Table 615. Retrieved from *www.census.gov/compendia/statab/.*

Carlisle, J., Kelcey, B., Rowan, B., & Phelps, G. (2011). Teachers' knowledge about early reading: Effects of students' gains in reading achievement. *Journal of Research on Educational Effectiveness, 4,* 289–321.

Carpenter, T., Fennema, E., Peterson, P., Chiang, C., & Loef, M. (1989). Using knowledge of children's mathematics thinking in classroom teaching: An experimental study. *American Educational Research Journal, 26*(4), 499–531.

Chen, Z., & Klahr, D. (1999). All other things being equal: Acquisition and transfer of the control of variables strategy. *Child Development, 70*(5), 1098–1120.

Chetty, R., Friedman, J. N., & Rockoff, J. E. (2011). *The long-term impacts of teachers: Teacher value-added and student outcomes in adulthood* (NBER Working Paper No. 17699). Cambridge, MA: National Bureau of Economic Research.

Chi, M., Feltovich, P., & Glaser, R. (1981). Categorization and representation of physics problems by experts and novices. *Cognitive Science, 5,* 121–152.

Chi, M., Glaser, R., & Rees, E. (1982). Expertise in problem solving. In R. J. Sternberg (Ed.), *Advances in the psychology of human intelligence* (Vol. 1, pp. 7–75). Hillsdale, NJ: Erlbaum.

Chi, M., & Koeske, R. (1983). Network representation of a child's dinosaur knowledge. *Developmental Psychology, 19*(1), 29–39.

Chi, M., Slotta, J. D., & de Leeuw, N. (1994). From things to processes: A theory of conceptual change for learning science concepts. *Learning and Instruction, 4*(1), 27–43.

Cobb, P., Wood, T., Yackel, E., Nicholls, J., Wheatley, G., Trigatti, B., et al. (1991). Assessment of a problem-centered second-grade mathematics project. *Journal for Research in Mathematics Education, 22,* 3–29.

Corcoran, S. (2010). *Can teachers be evaluated by their test scores? Should they be? The use of value-added measures of teacher effectiveness in policy and practice.* Providence, RI: Brown University, Annenberg Institute for School Reform.

Corcoran, S., Evans, W., & Schwab, R. (2004), Women, the labor market, and the declining relative quality of teachers. *Journal of Policy Analysis and Management, 23*(3), 449–470.

Dee, T. S., & Jacob, B. (2009). *The impact of No Child Left Behind on student achievement* (NBER Working Paper No. 15531). Cambridge, MA: National Bureau of Economic Research. Retrieved from *www.nber.org/papers/w15531.*

Desimone, L. M. (2009). Improving impact studies of teachers' professional development: Toward better conceptualizations and measures. *Educational Researcher, 38*(3), 181–199.

Desimone, L. M., Porter, A. C., Garet, M., Yoon, K. S., & Birman, B. (2002). Does professional development change teachers' instruction? Results from a three-year study. *Educational Evaluation and Policy Analysis, 24*(2), 81–112.

Desimone, L. M., Smith, T. M., & Ueno, K. (2006). Are teachers who need sustained, content-focused professional development getting it? An administrator's dilemma. *Educational Administration Quarterly, 42*(2), 179–215.

Dopplet, Y., Schunn, C., Silk, E., Mehalik, M., Reynolds, B., & Ward, E. (2009). Evaluating the impact of a facilitated learning community approach to professional development on teacher practice and student achievement. *Research in Science and Technology Education, 27*(3), 339–354.

Franke, M. L., Carpenter, T. P., & Levi, L. (2001). Capturing teachers' generative change: A follow-up study of professional development in mathematics. *American Educational Research Journal, 38,* 653–689.

Garet, M., Porter, A., Desimone, L., Birman, B., & Yoon, K. (2001). What makes professional development effective? Analysis of a national sample of teachers. *American Education Research Journal, 38*(3), 915–945.

Gersten, R., Dimino, J., Jayanthi, M., Kim, J., & Santoro, L. (2009). *An investigation of the impact of the Teacher Study Group as a means to enhance the quality of reading comprehension and vocabulary instruction for first graders in Reading First schools: Technical report.* Los Alamitos, CA: Instructional Research Group.

Glaser, R. (1985). *Thoughts on expertise* (Tech. Rep. No. 8). Pittsburgh, PA: University of Pittsburgh, Learning Research and Development Center.

Glaser, R. (1989). Expertise and learning: How do we think about instructional processes now that we have discovered knowledge structures? In D. Klahr & K. Kotovsky (Eds.),

Complex information processing: The impact of Herbert A. Simon (pp. 269–282). Hillsdale, NJ: Erlbaum.

Glazerman, S., Loeb, S., Goldhaber, D., Staiger, D., Raudenbush, S., & Whitehurst, G. (2010). *Evaluating teachers: The important role of value-added*. Washington, DC: Brookings Brown Center on Education Policy.

Goldschmidt, P., Choi, K., & Beaudoin, J. P. (2012). *Growth model comparison study: Practical implications of alternative models for evaluating school performance*. Washington, DC: Council of the Chief State School Officers, Technical Issues in Large-Scale Assessment and Student Standards.

Gonzales, P., Williams, T., Jocelyn, L., Roey, S., Kastberg, D., & Brenwald, S. (2008). *Highlights from TIMSS 2007: Mathematics and Science Achievement of U.S. Fourth- and Eighth-Grade Students in an International Context* (NCES No. 2009–001, Revised). Washington, DC: U.S. Department of Education, Institute of Education Sciences, National Center for Education Statistics.

Green, J., & Winters, M. (2005). *Public high school graduation and college-readiness rates: 1991–2002* (Education Working Paper No. 8). New York: Manhattan Institute for Policy Research.

Grossman, P., Wineburg, S., & Woolworth, S. (2001). Toward a theory of teacher community. *Teachers College Record, 103*(6), 942–1012.

Guskey, T. R. (1994). Results-oriented professional development: In search of an optimal mix of effective practices. *Journal of Staff Development, 15*(4), 42–50.

Hanushek, E. (2011). The economic value of higher teacher quality. *Economics of Education Review, 30*, 466–479.

Hiebert, J., Gallimore, R., & Stigler, J. (2002). A knowledge base for the teaching profession: What would it look like and how can we get one? *Educational Researcher, 31*(5), 3–15.

Hill, H. (2005). Content across communities: Validating measures of elementary mathematics instruction. *Educational Policy, 19*(3), 474–475.

Hill, H. (2007a). Learning in the teaching workforce. *The Future of Children, 17*(1), 111–127.

Hill, H. (2007b). Mathematical knowledge of middle school teachers: Implications for the No Child Left Behind policy initiative. *Educational Evaluation and Policy Analysis, 29*(2), 95–114.

Hill, H. (2009). Fixing teacher professional development. *Phi Delta Kappan, 90*(7), 470–477.

Hill, H. C., Ball, D. L., Blunk, M., Goffney, I. M., & Rowan, B. (2007). Validating the ecological assumption: The relationship of measure scores to classroom teaching and student learning. *Measurement, 5*(2–3), 107–118.

Hill, H. C., Ball, D. L., & Schilling, S. G. (2008). Unpacking pedagogical content knowledge: Conceptualizing and measuring teachers' topic-specific knowledge of students. *Journal for Research in Mathematics Education, 39*(4), 372–400.

Hill, H., Blunk, M., Charalambous, C., Lewis, J., Phelps, G., Sleep, L., et al. (2008). Mathematical knowledge for teaching and the mathematical quality of instruction: An exploratory study. *Cognition and Instruction, 26*, 430–511.

Hill, H., Charalambous, C., & Kraft, M. (2012). When rater reliability is not enough: Teacher observation systems and a case for the generalizability study. *Educational Researcher, 41*(2), 56–64.

Hill, H., Dean, C., & Goffney, I. (2007). Assessing elemental and structural validity: Data from teachers, non-teachers, and mathematicians. *Measurement, 5*(2–3), 81–92.

Hill, H., Kapitula, L., & Umland, K. (2011). A validity argument approach to evaluating teacher value-added scores. *American Educational Research Journal, 48*(3), 792–831.

Hill, H., Rowan, B., & Ball, D. (2005). Effects of teachers' mathematical knowledge for teaching on student achievement. *American Educational Research Journal, 42*(2), 371–406.

Hill, H. C., Schilling, S. G., & Ball, D. L. (2004). Developing measures of teachers' mathematics knowledge for teaching. *Elementary School Journal, 105*(1), 11–30.

Hoyt, J. E., & Sorenson, C. T. (2001). High school preparation, placement, testing and college remediation. *Journal of Developmental Education, 25*(2), 26–33.

Ingersoll, R. M. (2004). *Why do high-poverty schools have difficulty staffing their classrooms with qualified teachers?* Washington, DC: Center for American Progress.

Jacob, B. (2007). The challenges of staffing urban schools with effective teachers. *The Future of Children, 17*(1), 129–154.

Kennedy, M. (1998). *Form and substance in in-service teacher education* (Research Monograph No. 13). Madison: University of Wisconsin–Madison, National Institute for Science Education. Retrieved from *www.msu.edu/~mkennedy/publications/docs/ Teacher%20Learning/NISE/Kennedy%20effects%20of%20PD.pdf.*

Kersting, N. (2008). Using video clips of mathematics classroom instruction as item prompts to measure teachers' knowledge of teaching mathematics. *Educational and Psychological Measurement, 68*(5), 845–861.

Lankford, H., Loeb, S., & Wyckoff, J. (2002). Teacher sorting and the plight of urban schools: A descriptive analysis. *Educational Evaluation and Policy Analysis, 24*(1), 37–62.

Lee, J. (2006). *Tracking achievement gaps and assessing the impact of NCLB on the gaps: An in-depth look into national and state reading and math outcome trends.* Cambridge, MA: Civil Rights Project at Harvard University.

Lee, J., & Reeves, T. (2012). Revisiting the impact of NCLB high stakes school accountability, capacity, and resources: State NAEP 1990–2009 reading and math achievement gaps and trends. *Educational Evaluation and Policy Analysis, 34*(2), 209–231.

Lehrer, R., & Schauble, L. (2006). Scientific thinking and science literacy: Supporting development in learning in contexts. In W. Damon, R. M. Lerner, K. A. Renninger, & I. E. Sigel (Eds.), *Handbook of child psychology* (6th ed., Vol. 4). Hoboken, NJ: Wiley.

Leinhardt, G. (1989). Math lessons: A contrast of novice and expert competence. *Journal for Research in Mathematics Education, 20*(1), 52–75.

Leinhardt, G. (1994). History: A time to be mindful. In G. Leinhardt, I. Beck, & C. Stainton (Eds.) *Teaching and learning in history* (pp. 209–255). Hillsdale, NJ: Erlbaum.

Leinhardt, G. (1997). Instructional explanations in history. *International Journal of Educational Research, 27*(3), 221–232.

Leinhardt, G., & Smith, D. A. (1985). Expertise in mathematics instruction: Subject matter knowledge. *Journal of Educational Psychology, 77*(3), 247.

Linn, R. L., Baker, E. L., & Betebenner, D. W. (2002). Accountability systems: Implications of requirements of the No Child Left Behind Act of 2001. *Educational Researcher, 31*(6) , 3–16.

Little, J. W. (1982). Norms of collegiality and experimentation: Workplace conditions of school success. *American Educational Research Journal, 19*(3), 325–340.

Loeb, S., Rouse, C. E., & Shorris, A. (2007). Introducing the issue. *The Future of Children, 17*(1), 3–14.

McCray, J. S., & Chen, J. Q. (2012). Pedagogical content knowledge for preschool mathematics: Construct validity of a new teacher interview. *Journal of Research in Childhood Education, 26*(3), 291–307.

McKeown, M., & Beck, I. (1994). Making sense of accounts of history: Why young students don't and how they might. In G. Leinhardt, I. Beck, & C. Stainton (Eds.), *Teaching and learning in history* (pp. 1–26). Hillsdale, NJ: Erlbaum.

Merriman Bausmith, J., & Barry, C. (2011). Revisiting professional learning communities to increase college readiness: The importance of pedagogical content knowledge. *Educational Researcher, 40*(4), 175–178.

Murnane, R., & Steele, J. (2007). What is the problem? The challenge of providing effective teachers for all children. *The Future of Children, 17*(1), 15–42.

National Research Council. (2013). *Monitoring progress towards successful K–12 STEM education: A nation advancing?* Washington, DC: National Academies Press.

Newell, A., & Simon, H. A. (1972). *Human problem solving* (Vol. 14). Englewood Cliffs, NJ: Prentice-Hall.

Nichols, S., Glass, G., & Berliner, D. (2006). High-stakes testing and student achievement: Does accountability pressure increase student learning? *Educational Policy Analysis Archives, 14*(1), 1–56.

No Child Left Behind Act of 2001, Public Law No. 107-110, 115 Stat. 1425 (2002).

Palincsar, A., & Brown, A. (1984). Reciprocal teaching of comprehension-fostering and comprehension monitoring activities. *Cognition and Instruction, 1*, 117–175.

Penuel, W. R., Fishman, B., Yamaguchi, R., & Gallagher, L. P. (2007). What makes professional development effective? Strategies that foster curriculum implementation. *American Educational Research Journal, 44*(4), 921–958.

Riegle-Crumb, C. (2006). The path through math: Course sequences and academic performance at the intersection of race-ethnicity and gender. *American Journal of Education, 113*(1), 101.

Rivkin, S., Hanushek, E., & Kain, J. (2005). Teachers, school, and academic achievement. *Econometrica, 73*(2), 417–458.

Rockoff, J. (2004). The impact of individual teachers on student achievement: Evidence from panel data. *American Economic Review, 94*, 247–252.

Sabers, D., Cushing, K., & Berliner, D. (1991). Differences among teachers in a task characterized by simultaneity, multidimensionality, and immediacy. *American Educational Research Journal, 28*(1), 63–88.

Sanders, W., & Rivers, J. (1996). *Cumulative and residual effects of teachers on future student academic achievement.* Knoxville: University of Tennessee, Value-Added Research and Assessment Center.

Saunders, W., Goldenberg, C., & Gallimore, R. (2009). Increasing achievement by focusing grade-level teams on improving classroom learning: A prospective, quasi-experimental study of Title I schools. *American Educational Research Journal, 46*(4), 1006–1033.

Saxe, G. B., Gearhardt, M., & Nasir, N. S. (2001). Enhancing students' understanding of mathematics: A study of three contrasting approaches to professional support. *Journal of Mathematics Teachers Education, 4*, 55–79.

Schauble, L. (1996). The development of scientific reasoning in knowledge-rich contexts. *Developmental Psychology, 32*(1), 102–119.

Schauble, L., Glaser, R., Raghavan, K., & Reiner, M. (1991). Causal models and experimentation strategies in scientific reasoning. *Journal of the Learning Sciences, 1*(2), 201–238.

Schilling, S. G., Blunk, M., & Hill, H. C. (2007). Test validation and the MKT measures: Generalizations and conclusions. *Measurement, 5*(2–3), 118–128.

Schoenfeld, A. (1992). Learning to think mathematically: Problem solving, metacognition, and sense-making in mathematics. In D. Grouws (Ed.), *Handbook for research on mathematics teaching and learning* (pp. 334–370). New York: Macmillan.

Seidel, T., & Shavelson, R. (2007). Teaching effectiveness research in the past decade: The role of theory and research design in disentangling meta-analysis results. *Review of Educational Research, 77*(4), 454–499.

Shuell, T. J. (1993). Toward an integrated theory of teaching and learning. *Educational Psychologist, 28*(4), 291–311.

Shulman, L. S. (1986). Those who understand: Knowledge growth in teaching. *Educational Researcher, 15*(2), 4–14.

Shulman, L. S. (1987). Knowledge and teaching: Foundations of the new reform. *Harvard Educational Review, 57*(1), 1–22.

Sum, A., Kirsch, I., & Yamamoto, K. (2004). *Pathways to labor market success: The literacy proficiency of U.S. adults* (ETS Policy Information Report). Princeton, NJ: Educational Testing Service.

Swafford, J., Jones, G., & Thornton, C. (1997). Increased knowledge in geometry and instructional practice. *Journal for Research in Mathematics Education, 28*(4), 467–483.

Vandevoort, L. G., Amrein-Beardsley, A., & Berliner, D. C. (2004, September 8). National board certified teachers and their students' achievement. *Education Policy Analysis Archives, 12*. Retrieved from *http://epaa.asu.edu/ojs/article/view/201/327.*

Vosniadou, S., Ioannides, C., Dimitrakopoulou, A., & Papademetriou, E. (2001). Designing learning environments to promote conceptual change in science. *Learning and Instruction, 11*(4), 381-419.

Weisberg, D., Sexton, S., Mulhern, J., & Keeling, D. (2009). *The widget effect: Our national failure to acknowledge and act on difference in teacher effectiveness.* New York: New Teacher Project.

Wineburg, S. (1991). On the reading of historical texts: Notes on the breach between school and academy. *American Educational Research Journal, 28*(3), 495-519.

Wineburg, S. (1994). The cognitive representation of historical texts. In G. Leinhardt, I. Beck, & C. Stainton (Eds.), *Teaching and learning in history* (pp. 85–136). Hillsdale, NJ: Erlbaum.

Wineburg, S. (1999). Historical thinking and other unnatural acts. *Phi Delta Kappan, 80*(7), 488–499.

Wineburg, S. (2007). Unnatural and essential: The nature of historical thinking. *Teaching History, 129*, 6–11.

Wyatt, J., Wiley, A., Camara, W., & Proestler, N. (2011). *The development of an index of academic rigor for college readiness* (College Board Research Report 2011-11). New York: College Board.

Yoon, K. S., Duncan, T., Lee, S. W.-Y., Scarloss, B., & Shapley, K. (2007). Reviewing the evidence on how teacher professional development affects student achievement (Issues & Answers Report No. REL 2007-No. 033). Washington, DC: U.S. Department of Education, Institute of Education Sciences, National Center for Education Evaluation and Regional Assistance. Retrieved from *http://ies.ed.gov/ncees/edlabs.*

CHAPTER 20

Standards-Based Professional Learning and Certification

By the Profession, for the Profession

LAWRENCE INGVARSON

- Professional certification is an endorsement by a professional board that a member of that profession has attained a designated standard of accomplished practice.
- There are many accomplished teachers, but, unlike many other professions, teaching has been slow in developing its own system for recognizing their expertise and providing professional certification.
- Teaching standards provide a means by which the profession can take responsibility for building its own professional learning system linked to professional certification.
- The National Board for Professional Teaching Standards in the United States provides a viable and rigorous model for a national certification system for teachers.
- Professional certification provides a sounder basis on which to link teacher salaries to performance than annual bonus pay or merit pay schemes.
- A professional certification system with well-designed rewards provides incentives for all teachers to collaborate in attaining high standards, without divisive effects on staff relationships.

This chapter has its origins in a sabbatical I was fortunate enough to enjoy at Stanford University in 1989 on leave from Australia. Lee Shulman was leading an enthusiastic team exploring new methods by which accomplished teachers could demonstrate their expertise—the Teacher Assessment Project (TAP; Shulman, 1991). The main purpose of the project was to provide a foundation for the advanced certification system being developed by the recently formed National Board for Professional Teaching Standards (NBPTS, 1989).

The NBPTS had emerged after a decade of controversy about education in the United States that included the government report *A Nation at Risk* (National Commission on Excellence in Education, 1983), released by President Ronald Reagan. The deprofessionalizing effects of the report provoked a response among many educators, researchers, and policymakers that found its voice in the 1986 report *A Nation Prepared: Teachers for the 21st Century*, commissioned by the Carnegie Foundation, which included a recommendation that a national board for teachers be established with a three-part mission:

1. To establish high and rigorous standards for what accomplished teachers should know and be able to do.
2. To board-certify teachers who meet the standards.
3. To advance related educational practices and reforms.

The NBPTS was established in 1987 as a national but nongovernmental organization. It is the most ambitious attempt by any country to establish a certification system for teachers who reach high professional standards. It also stands alone as a genuinely independent professional body that has assiduously ensured that practicing teachers play a leading role in all phases of its operation, from developing the standards to conducting the processes for certifying those who meet the standards. The assessment methods being developed by the TAP were driven by a deep respect for the knowledge, skill, and wisdom that expert teachers had developed over many years of teaching experience (Collins, 1991). Unlike many methods for evaluating teachers at the time, the methods being tested by the TAP team aimed to reveal the reasoning behind what expert teachers thought and did. They also aimed to provide a vehicle by means of which teachers could demonstrate the quality of opportunities they provided for students to learn and develop.

Although the assessment methods developed by the TAP have been refined over time, they still form the foundation for the NBPTS's certification process (Ingvarson & Hattie, 2008). Relevant to this chapter, the process of preparing for certification was also conceived of as a powerful vehicle for engaging teachers in effective modes of professional learning (Baratz-Snowden, 1993; Darling-Hammond, 1992; Ingvarson, 1998; Snowden, 1993; Wolf & Taylor, 2008). Unlike so many traditional professional development activities that place teachers in a passive role, preparation for certification places teachers in the active role of documenting, analyzing, and evaluating their teaching in relation to challenging standards for accomplished teaching. These processes were entirely consistent with research on the characteristics of effective professional learning (Hawley & Valli, 1999).

This chapter presents a model for a standards-based professional learning and certification system, a system controlled and provided by the teaching profession itself. It is a model of a highly educated profession, capable of defining research-based standards for effective teaching, promoting the development of its members toward those standards, and providing a rigorous and respected process for recognizing and certifying those who reach them. It is a model that calls for the teaching profession to be entrusted with the responsibilities of a profession; one of these is the responsibility and resources to establish its own standards-based professional learning and certification system—a system that is elaborated later in this chapter.

A rigorous professional certification system has the potential to reform career paths and salary schedules for teachers' pay systems. Debate has long raged about how to strengthen links between pay and performance for teachers. Although most agree that the current pay system needs to become a more effective instrument for ensuring quality opportunities for students to learn, there is distinct disagreement about how this should be done.

A recent Organisation for Economic Cooperation and Development (OECD) report (2010) points out that if education systems are to provide high-quality education to the broader population, they need policies that will enable them to recruit their teachers from the top of the higher education pool. Getting serious about quality certainly means lifting salaries to levels whereby teaching can compete with other professions for the best high school and university graduates. *However, this will not be enough.* Attracting good teachers is one thing; retaining them and ensuring their development to higher standards of teaching is another. The latter calls for much more fundamental reforms—the evolution of a new conception of teaching as a strong and accountable profession—with career stages closely linked to evidence of increasing expertise in the classroom and in supporting colleagues. If teachers want employing authorities to create a stronger market for successful teachers, the profession has to show that it can identify those teachers in ways that are valid, reliable, and fair.

CERTIFICATION

Certification refers to an endorsement by a professional agency that a member of that profession has attained a designated standard of practice. Australian examples include "Chartered Engineer" and "Fellow of the Royal College of Surgeons." American examples include the national medical boards. A professional certification is portable. It is not a job or position with a particular school, though it may be a criterion for eligibility for promotion to one of these.

Certification is the way most professions drive continual improvement in their member's practice, in their own, and in the public interest. Professions provide novices with high performance standards to aim for over several years. They provide a rigorous and independent system for assessing when they have attained those standards. Successful applicants gain a respected certification that employers are willing to pay for, thus creating a strong market for their knowledge and expertise. They gain the esteem of having "made it" in their profession.

A certification system is a system for defining high-quality teaching standards, promoting development toward those standards, and identifying those who reach them. Professions are normally trusted to run their own certification systems. If convinced about the rigor of the process, employing authorities usually encourage members of the profession to seek certification and reward its attainment through access to higher salary scales and eligibility for promotional positions.

Certification systems for teachers aim to build a closer alignment between increasing expertise and career progression. The assumptions underlying such systems—about how to link teacher pay to performance and "incentivize" teachers—stand in stark contrast to those underlying quota-based merit pay schemes, typically limited to annual one-off bonus payments (Goe, Bell, & Little, 2008; Johnson, 1984, 1986; Murnane & Cohen, 1986). Reformed career structures based on professional certification aim to enhance student learning by driving higher-quality teaching. A rigorous certification system creates a basis for significantly increasing salaries for accomplished teachers, thereby making teaching a more attractive career option for abler graduates and allowing it to be better able to retain its best practitioners.

GETTING TO SCALE WITH SUCCESSFUL TEACHING PRACTICES

The kinds of change that matter in education, in terms of both quality and equity, are those that lead to the *widespread* implementation of successful teaching practices—practices consistent with research and high standards of teaching. Elmore (1996) estimated that in the United States during the 20th century there were many well-proven examples of good practice, but even the best of them were rarely adopted by more than 20% of teachers. Elmore asks why it is so hard to "get to scale"; that is, to ensure widespread implementation of proven educational practices and curriculum materials. One of the main reasons, he argues, is that the teaching profession does not have well-established institutions or procedures for using research to identify and define standards for what its members should know and be able to do; normative structures related to good practice are weak. The culture of teaching tends to encourage a view of teaching in which "everyone does their own thing" behind closed doors, practices that may only be loosely connected to research on teaching or profession-defined standards. Elmore attributes the problem of getting to scale with educational reforms to a belief common among teachers that good teaching is more a "bundle" of personality traits than something that most people can learn to get better at and that is informed by research. Getting to scale with educational reforms, Elmore argues, will depend on building new structures for defining and applying teaching standards in the teaching profession:

> The existence of external norms is important because it institutionalizes the idea that professionals are responsible for looking outward at challenging conceptions of practice in addition to looking inward at their values and competencies. (p. 319)

Thus the major challenge in improving teaching lies not so much in identifying and describing quality teaching as in developing structures and incentives that ensure *widespread use of successful teaching practices*: to make best practice common practice (Darling-Hammond & Baratz-Snowden, 2005; Elmore, 1996; OECD, 2005). This is a core function of a profession. This challenge calls for new institutions that will enable the teaching profession to build its own infrastructure for defining high-quality teaching standards, promoting development toward them, and providing recognition to those who reach them. For Elmore (1996), the key to effective professional learning is to build a new professional culture based on professional norms and characterized by collective responsibility for teaching practice and student learning. Central to this is the responsibility to establish its own standards-based professional learning and certification system.

EFFECTIVE MODES OF PROFESSIONAL LEARNING

The professional development "problem" is not a lack of knowledge about the characteristics of effective professional learning activities, activities that link professional learning to improved student learning outcomes. Numerous research reviews reveal a consensus on the matter (e.g., Cohen & Hill, 2000; Kennedy, 1998; Sykes, 1999; Wilson & Berne, 1999). The problem is how to ensure that all teachers have the opportunities and the incentives to engage in such activities.

Although the importance of professional development is widely recognized, current provision falls far short of what the research says is necessary to improve learning outcomes for all students. There are many individually effective professional development programs and activities operating at school and system levels, but the overall pattern of provision is brief, fragmentary, and rarely sequential. The capacity of the profession to engage most of its members in effective modes of professional learning over the long term is weak.

There is clear evidence from recent research that the content of professional learning matters as much as, if not more than, the process. Hawley and Valli (1999, p. 138) condense this research into a set of nine design principles for effective professional learning, the initial three of which are:

1. The content of professional development focuses on what students are to learn and how to address the different problems students may have in learning the material.
2. Professional development should be based on analyses of the differences between (a) actual student performance and (b) goals and standards for student learning.
3. Professional development should involve teachers in the identification of what they need to learn and in the development of the learning experiences in which they will be involved.

These principles clearly call for teachers to play an active role their own professional learning. They call for professional learning based on analyses of and feedback about current practice. And, as Elmore (1996) puts it, they embody the idea that professionals "are responsible for looking outward at challenging conceptions of practice in addition to looking inward at their values and competencies" (p. 319).

The time has come to build capacity for learning, not only at teacher, school, and district levels, but also at the level of the profession (Dinham, Ingvarson, & Kleinhenz, 2008). Policies are needed that will support the profession in building a national framework for continuing learning, from registration to advanced certification, guided by professional standards and assessments, and supported by career paths that recognize the central importance of teachers' knowledge and skill to successful learning outcomes for students.

What characteristics would a country's professional learning system need to have if its aim was to ensure that all teachers engaged in effective modes of professional learning and widespread use of successful practices? There would certainly be a need for greater clarity about the areas teachers need to improve with experience, that is, teaching standards, and a need for stronger incentives for teachers to engage in modes of professional learning that helped them attain those standards, that is, recognition for increasing expertise. Teachers would need a stronger sense of professional ownership and responsibility for the quality of that system, that is, greater control over their own professional learning system, as is common in most established professions.

A recent OECD (2011) report points out that:

> there may be a relationship between the degree to which the work of teaching has been professionalised and student performance. Indeed, the higher a country is on the world's education league tables, the more likely that country is working constructively with its unions and treating its teachers as trusted professional partners. (p. 240)

This sounds good, but the report does not provide details of what it might actually mean for teaching to be "professionalized." One thing it could mean is that teachers develop their own independent professionwide certification system (Ingvarson & Kleinhenz, 2006b).

A STANDARDS-BASED PROFESSIONAL LEARNING AND CERTIFICATION SYSTEM

The main components of a standards-based professional learning and certification system are:

1. High teaching *standards* that articulate what teachers and school leaders should get better at and that provide direction for professional development over the long term.
2. A rigorous, voluntary system of advanced professional *certification* based on valid methods for assessing teacher and school leader performance against the standards.

3. Staged career paths that provide *recognition* for good teaching and provide substantial incentives for teachers and school leaders to attain the standards for certification.
4. An infrastructure for *professional learning* that enables teachers and school leaders to gain the knowledge and skill embodied in the standards.

These components can be conceptualized as four pieces of a jigsaw, whose interlocking character is captured in Figure 20.1. Taken together, the four components form a "system" of interdependent and mutually supportive parts. Each component has its own functions and characteristics, but each is less effective without the others. If one is taken away, the system loses its capacity to function effectively as an instrument for encouraging and recognizing evidence of professional learning. For example, the standards define what accomplished teachers and school leaders know and do, but the certification procedures for assessing professional knowledge and performance define what counts as meeting the standards. Preparation for certification calls for schools and other providers of professional learning to use the standards to give long-term direction to their planning. Several universities in the United States now design their master's programs as preparation to meet NBPTS standards and certification requirements (Browne, Auton, Freund, & Futrell, 1999; Unrau, 2002). Recognition of certification is, of course, critical in providing incentives. Few teachers will undertake the certification process unless employing authorities are willing to reward teachers who have proven they have reached high professional standards. Career paths for teachers need to be reformed so that those salary structures value evidence of professional learning and give recognition to attaining high teaching standards.

A *professional* learning and certification system needs to be a stable system driven by research about what effective teachers know and do in their specialist fields of teaching, not by fluctuating political objectives. It is complementary to systems for implementing current government policy priorities. A professional learning system also calls for a radically revised model for how teachers should be paid—a model of a highly educated profession, capable of defining standards for effective

FIGURE 20.1. A standards-guided professional learning system.

teaching, promoting development toward those standards, and providing recognition for those who reach them.

A professional certification system should lead to a substantially higher salary scale that aims to provide strong incentives for *all* teachers to develop their practice to the level at which they can demonstrate that they have attained high professional standards and earned professional certification. This means that, to be effective, certification should be a career step that most teachers desire and aspire to—something achievable by most teachers given opportunities for effective professional learning, not just an elite few. Certification should be open to all teachers and be based on demonstrated attainment of the standards. I now discuss each of the components of a certification system in more detail.

STANDARDS: DEFINING ACCOMPLISHED TEACHING FOR CERTIFICATION PURPOSES

The current literature reveals two contrasting conceptualizations of effective teaching. They are:

1. *Outcomes*: The ability to produce higher than expected gains for their students on standardized test scores, for example, by using value-added models.
2. *Processes*: The quality of opportunities a teacher provides for students to learn, as defined by teaching standards.

Fenstermacher and Richardson (2005) make a distinction between *good* teaching and *successful* teaching that is useful here:

> By good teaching we mean that the content taught accords with disciplinary standards of adequacy and completeness, and that the methods employed are age appropriate, morally defensible, and undertaken with the intention of enhancing the learner's competence with respect to the content studied.
>
> By successful teaching we mean that the learner actually acquires, to some reasonable and acceptable level of proficiency, what the teacher is engaged in teaching. (p. 189)

Fenstermacher and Richardson (2005) point out that successful teaching, as they defined it, depends not only on good teaching but also on at least three other conditions: (1) willingness and effort on the part of the learner, (2) a social surround supportive of teaching and learning, and (3) opportunity to teach and learn. The distinction between good teaching and successful teaching points to two different approaches to conceptualizing and measuring *teacher quality* and two different views on what teachers should be held accountable for: one in terms of student achievement on standardized tests, the other in terms of the quality of opportunities for learning that teachers establish in their classrooms (Ingvarson & Rowe,

2008). Most certification systems for professions emphasize professional knowledge and ability to practice in ways consistent with current research and best practice, not outcomes.

Outcome measures or gain scores do not define good teaching. Goe and colleagues (2008) argue that the recent emphasis on outcomes-based definitions of teacher effectiveness is driven more by greater availability of student test data and technical developments in psychometrics, such as value-added models, than definitions of what effective teachers actually know and do. In contrast, the process view says we should first define what effective teachers know and do—and only then determine a technology for measuring it.

Recent research indicates that value-added approaches face increasing concern about their reliability and validity and rarely last (Baker et al., 2010; McCaffrey, Lockwood, Koretz, & Hamilton, 2003; Rothstein, 2009). This is especially the case when they are used to distribute annual bonus payments to teachers (as with the Teacher Incentive Fund in the United States). These concerns include the nonrandom assignment of students, the effects of other teachers, the effects of student characteristics (even when controlled), the effects of school policies, the nonrandom assignment of teachers, and the appropriateness of outcome measures for the students and curriculum taught. Recent research also indicates that estimates of a teacher's effectiveness vary significantly from year to year, also throwing doubt on the accuracy of value-added schemes (e.g., Schochet & Chiang, 2010).

Certification systems are based on the view that it makes more sense to evaluate teachers in terms of direct evidence of the skills they can demonstrate and the quality of opportunities for learning they provide in their own classrooms. Although some mystery about good teaching may remain, standards have the more prosaic aim of describing what good teachers know and do to promote quality learning. Standards draw attention to what an observer would expect to see students doing and learning as a result of good teaching. And, therefore, the argument is, standards provide a more valid basis on which to assess a teacher's knowledge and skill. They also provide a more useful basis for feedback about how a teacher might need to improve. Finally, standards clarify the nature of the expertise that the profession expects its members to gain with experience.

DEVELOPING STANDARDS FOR ACCOMPLISHED TEACHING

Dictionaries give two interrelated uses of the term "standard": to *rally*, as around a banner or flag (standard), and to *measure*. As rallying points, standards aim to articulate core educational values that teachers seek to manifest in their practice. Developers of professional standards will be guided by conceptions of learning and development; what they believe it means, for example, to educate a mind, to learn with understanding, and to think independently of the teacher. Standards, by definition, are statements about what is valued. As measures, standards will not only describe what teachers need to know and be able to do to put these values into practice, but standards will also describe how attainment of that knowledge will be assessed and what counts as meeting each standard. A standard, in the latter sense, is the level of performance on the criterion being assessed that is considered satisfactory in terms of the purpose of the evaluation.

It should be clear from this definition that teaching standards are not fully developed or defined until it is clear how they are to be used to judge teachers' knowledge and practice. When standards are used for professional certification, there are three essential steps in their development. These are:

1. Defining what is to be assessed; that is, what do highly accomplished teachers know and do? (This is what the National Professional Standards for Teachers in Australia aim to do. These are often called *content* standards.)
2. Developing valid and consistent methods for gathering evidence about what a teacher knows and is able to do in relation to the standards.
3. Developing reliable procedures for assessing that evidence and deciding whether a teacher has met the standard. (This will depend on developing *performance* in addition to content standards.)

The Olympic decathlon provides a good illustration of the steps involved in developing a standards-based system for assessing performance. The concept behind the decathlon is the "great all-around athlete." The origins of the decathlon go back to the early 20th century, when King Gustav V of Sweden told the American Jim Thorpe, "You, sir, are the world's greatest athlete."

People used to argue, apparently, about what makes a great all-around athlete, just as they still argue about what makes a good teacher. The International Olympic Committee realized the concept needed definition. What should all-around athletes be able to do? After a lot of debate, they decided that the main elements of what constituted a great all-around athlete were *strength, speed, stamina, endurance*, and *perseverance*. In other words, they defined what should be assessed—the *content* standards as it were—if one were to judge whether someone was a good all-around athlete.

The next step was to reach agreement on how to judge the all-around athlete; how to assess strength, speed, and so forth. What should an athlete be asked to do to provide evidence that he or she is a good all-around athlete? Ten events over 2 days were decided upon somehow, and the concept was thereby operationalized. On Day 1, the events are the 100-meter run, the long jump, the shot put, the high jump, and the 400-meter run. On Day 2, the events are the 110-meter hurdles, the discus, the pole vault, the javelin throw, and the 1500-meter run.

A set of 10 events was seen as a sufficient *sample* of evidence on which to make judgments about an athlete's overall ability as an all-around athlete. Of course, the choice of events has to be somewhat arbitrary (e.g., why 100 meters instead of 200?), but the events *as a group* must be selected to ensure that there is more than one kind of evidence for each of the elements (i.e., the standards). When evidence about each element is gathered in more than one way, the reliability of the assessment is increased, which is also a fundamental point to keep in mind when assessing teacher performance.

Finally, the International Olympic Committee needed to *set* the performance standards, which meant reaching agreement on the level of performance in each event that met the standard. So far as the decathlon is concerned, several "benchmark" levels have been set for each event. For example, running 100 meters in 10.395 seconds earns 1,000 points, 10.827 seconds earns 900 points, 11.278 earns 800 points, and 11.756 earns 700 points; so on for each event.

The overall level of performance is determined by weighting and combining the performance across all events. *Performance standards* not only need to specify how well an athlete must do in *each* event to qualify; the standards also need to specify how well the athletes must do across *all* events on the average to be rated good all-around athletes. Athletes must participate in the same set of events; there is no choice. However, a good performance in one event can compensate for a poor performance in another.

The decathlon example is a useful reminder that a full set of teaching standards must point not only to what will be measured but also to how evidence about capability and performance will be gathered and how judgments will be made about whether the standards have been met, as shown in Figure 20.2. Just as it is difficult to imagine a decathlon that would gain respect if each country decided on its own events and performance standards, it is difficult to see how a nationally consistent system that aimed to provide a widely respected certification to highly accomplished teachers could emerge if each state or local education authority developed its own assessment methods, using the national standards only as a framework. A professionwide certification system would need nationally consistent methods of assessment.

CHARACTERISTICS OF WELL-WRITTEN STANDARDS FOR ASSESSMENT PURPOSES

Standards need to be written at two levels. The first is the generic level, where they identify aspects of teachers' knowledge and practice that apply to *all* teachers, regardless of what or who they teach. The NBPTS, for example, has a set of five generic propositions about what accomplished teachers know and do. Second, standards writers then need to move to deeper levels, where they elaborate on what good teachers know and do in the many specialist fields that make up the teaching profession. The NBPTS has developed standards in 25 specialist fields of teaching,

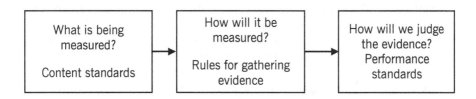

FIGURE 20.2. Conceptual framework for developing standards-based assessments.

in which practitioners in each field spell out in more detail what the five proposi-tions mean for their particular field of teaching. The NBPTS asks mathematics teachers, for example, to respond to questions such as, What do teachers need to know besides generic teaching skills to teach mathematics well?

These two steps in writing standards are important if they are to be useful guides for professional development. Teachers find generic standards of limited use in identifying what they need to know and to be able to do to promote student learning more effectively. Teaching standards need to identify not only what is com-mon to all teachers but also what is unique about good teaching in different fields of teaching.

Recent research indicates the importance of subject-specific pedagogical knowledge for student progress (e.g., Baumert et al., 2010; Goulding, Rowland, & Barber, 2002; Hill, Rowan, & Ball, 2005; Kelcy, 2011; Kersting, Givvin, & Thomp-son, 2012). Given its importance, this knowledge needs to be articulated in teaching standards in the relevant specialist field of teaching. For example, what an early primary teacher needs to know about learning to read is very different from what a secondary science teacher needs to know about helping students overcome mis-conceptions in learning physics. What a primary teacher needs to know about child development is different from what a high school physical education teacher needs to know about adolescent development. And so on. Similarly, if standards are to provide a clear guide for assessing professional knowledge and performance, they need to be elaborated for each field of teaching. This is just as true for primary teachers as secondary teachers.

Well-written standards for teachers are grounded in a clear understanding of what counts as quality learning for students in particular subject areas or at levels of schooling. Kennedy (2010) points out that standards need to be driven by a vision of high-quality learning *of something*, whether it is literacy, numeracy, art, or science, and why it is important for students to learn it. This contemporary vision of what learners need to know and be able to do will often be found in national curriculum statements.

Take, for example, this extract from one standard in a set of standards for accomplished teachers developed by the Australian Science Teachers Association (2002, p. 18):

> *Standard:* Accomplished teachers of science engage students in scientific inquiry.

> *Elaboration:* Their teaching reflects both the excitement and challenge of scien-tific endeavor and its distinctive rigor. They both teach and model practices that allow their students to approach knowledge and experiences critically, recognize problems, ask questions and pose solutions. They actively involve students in a wide range of scientific investigations. . . . (p. 18)

This standard goes on to describe an important element of what counts as quality learning *in a science classroom*. It invites the teacher to show how he or she engages students actively in *doing* science in their school. What kind of assessment does it call for? Clearly, not some kind of national achievement test; it calls for methods of assessment that reflect the complexity of what the teacher is trying to do. It calls for *evidence of what the students are doing as a direct result* of the teacher's teaching.

Several features of a standard such as this are noteworthy. The first is that it points to a large, meaningful, and significant "chunk" of a science teacher's work—it is an example of the challenging educational aims he or she is trying to achieve over an extended period of time. It is not a micro-level competency, or a personality trait. It is a valid thing to ask a science teacher to do to show that he or she is an accomplished teacher.

The second is that the standard is context-free in the sense that it describes a practice that most agree accomplished science teachers should follow no matter where the school is. By definition, a professional standard applies to all contexts in which teachers work (which is not to say context does not affect practice). No matter where a school is, engaging students in scientific inquiry is likely to be regarded as a core responsibility of science teachers.

The third feature is that the standard is nonprescriptive about how to engage students in "doing science" and "thinking scientifically"; it does not standardize practice or force teachers into some kind of straitjacket. There are many ways to engage students in scientific inquiry. Although the standard identifies an essential element of good science teaching, it does not prescribe how the standard is to be met. In this way, the standard also allows for diversity and innovation. Teachers are invited to show how they meet this standard; how they engage students in scientific inquiry.

The fourth feature is that, as a standard, it points to something that is measurable, or observable. It is possible to imagine the kinds of evidence that science teachers will assemble over time to show that they meet the standard, such as samples of students' work or videotaped segments over time provided by teachers. These features apply to standards in all teaching fields, whether primary or secondary or specialist subjects.

RECENT APPROACHES TO STANDARDS-BASED METHODS FOR ASSESSING TEACHER PERFORMANCE

The standards drive the assessment methods chosen. We know that this is important in assessing students. It is just as true when we come to assessing teachers. The standards should point to the kind of evidence that might be appropriate to gather about a teacher's performance.

Teacher evaluation is a large field of study, and it is only possible here to give a very brief overview of work in this area. The important point is that this field has reached the point at which there is confidence that teachers' performance can be assessed against standards in ways that are valid, reliable, and fair (e.g. Gitomer, 2009; Kennedy, 2010). Perhaps more important, it can be done in ways that teachers are very comfortable with, and in ways that have significant effects on their professional development.

A working example of this is the certification system developed by the NBPTS in the United States. The NBPTS has developed assessment methods that provide two types of evidence:

1. Demonstrations of teaching practice (by means of structured portfolio tasks). These demonstrations are based on three types of evidence:
   a. Samples of student work over time.
   b. Videotapes of classroom interaction.
   c. Records of contribution to the school and professional community.
2. Demonstrations of content knowledge and pedagogical knowledge. Teachers attend designated assessment centers where their knowledge is assessed by means of computer-delivered constructed response exercises.

The NBPTS assessment system builds on Shulman's 5-year long TAP at Stanford, which pioneered the development of a radical departure from previous approaches to teacher evaluation (Collins, 1991; Haertel, 1991; Shulman, 1991). Rather than attempting to identify standards as lists of competencies or duties, Shulman's team started by asking experienced teachers to identify tasks that accomplished teachers should be able to perform well, tasks that were fairly commonplace, tasks that posed difficult challenges for teachers, and tasks on which exemplary teachers were likely to distinguish themselves from novices or those of lesser competence. These tasks formed the basis for creating assessment methods that were capable of eliciting the kind of knowledge and skill that expert teachers possess.

The NBPTS built on the work of the TAP in developing assessment methods for each field of certification (Ingvarson & Hattie, 2008). Here is a set of portfolio entries that illustrate what a primary teacher was asked to demonstrate in applying for National Board certification.[1] (Full guidelines for these tasks are much more detailed.)

1. Provide evidence of a unit of work, with student writing samples, in which you have developed students' *writing* ability over time.
2. Develop an interdisciplinary theme and provide work samples that show how you engage students in work over time that deepens their understanding of an important idea in *science*.
3. Provide a videotape and commentary illustrating how you create a climate that supports students' abilities to *understand perspectives other than their own*.
4. Provide evidence, through a videotape, written commentary, and student work samples, of how you have helped build students' *mathematical* understanding.

---

[1] These tasks have been revised in recent years.

There are several things to note about such tasks. First, primary teachers, in collaboration with experts in educational measurement, develop them. They regard each task as a valid thing to ask them to do—as a way of providing evidence relevant to the standards. Although complex, these are authentic tasks; they are based on what most accomplished teachers normally do. Second, as a group, they provide evidence of teaching across at least four of the main areas of the primary school curriculum: literacy, mathematics, science, and social studies. This increases the validity and reliability of the assessment. The tasks cover most of what primary teachers are contracted to teach. Third, in contrast to merit pay schemes based on student test scores, they focus on what the students are doing and learning *as a result of the conditions for learning set up by the teacher*. Fourth, although they provide a common structure within which teachers have freedom to show how they meet the standard in their context, they do not prescribe how the teacher should teach or meet the standards.

EFFECTS ON PROFESSIONAL LEARNING

Few would argue that these are not valid things to expect an accomplished primary teacher to do well. There is now a substantial body of research indicating that the process of analyzing practice against the standards and preparing evidence has significant benefits for teachers' practice. The certification process is not only a tool for *identifying* accomplished teachers; it is also a means of promoting accomplished teaching and teacher leadership on a broader scale.

Unlike many traditional types of teacher evaluation, the genius behind this work was to put the teachers whose performance was being assessed in the *active* position of being asked to show how they met the standards. This was the reverse of the *passive* position typical of traditional approaches to teacher evaluation, such as classroom observations, student rating forms, supervisor reports, and national tests of student achievement.

When teachers engage with new forms of assessment such as portfolio tasks based on videos and student work samples over time, teachers necessarily become engaged in the kind of analyses and reflections of their own practice that are consistent with the most effective modes of professional learning (Hawley & Valli, 1999; Sato & Monte-Sano, 2002). A survey of 10,000 teachers who had been through the National Board certification process found that 92% reported that the process made them better teachers, and 89% said it equipped them to create stronger curricula and to better evaluate student learning (NBPTS, 2001a, 2001b). Nearly all said it was the best professional development experience they had ever had.

Other research has shown that the process of preparing evidence for certification has powerful effects on teachers' professional learning (Lustick, 2011; Lustick & Sykes, 2006; Tracz et al., 1995). Sato and Monte-Sano (2002) found that certification led teachers to engage more in teacher leadership activities. Sato, Wei, and Darling-Hammond (2008) found that this process led teachers to use a greater variety of assessment methods and to improve the way assessment information was used to support student learning. In states where it is rewarded, certification is also redefining the nature of university master's courses that teachers in the United States routinely take for salary progression (Browne et al., 1999; Unrau, 2002).

Much of this research has been summarized by the NBPTS (2007). National Board Certification is a "transformative experience" for many teachers, and they often apply in the classroom what they learn from the certification process—whether they achieve certification or not. The certification process itself improves teachers' ability to improve student learning. Research shows that teachers who gain professional certification are significantly more likely to remain in teaching. Independent studies show that students of National Board-certified teachers do better on standardized tests than students of noncertified teachers (*www.nbpts.org/promoting-student-learning-growth-achievement*). Increasing evidence shows that when groups of teachers within the same school prepare together for certification, it can make a significant improvement to student learning outcomes in disadvantaged schools (*www.mitchell20.com*).

On a second sabbatical to the United States in 1999, I took the opportunity to visit many teachers who were preparing for certification or who had been though the process. Universally, they said the process had had a greater effect on their teaching than any other professional development activity in which they had participated. One particularly persuasive experience came one late afternoon in a rather dingy room in the Detroit Federation of Teachers building, watching teachers discussing the NBPTS standards for their specialist field and the extent to which the evidence in their portfolio entries showed that they were meeting the standards. These meetings over time meant that teachers were looking at video clips and student work samples from each other's teaching and providing rich feedback to each other—a core requirement for growth. A couple of previously National Board-certified teachers were there to facilitate the discussion. One teacher seemed very *au fait* with the process, which wasn't surprising because she was going through it a second time in another field of teaching. "I got so much out of it the first time; I wanted to do it again." If ever there was a manifestation of the meaning of "professional learning community," this was it.

I interviewed about 25 teachers, most of whom had gained NB certification. Comments such as the following were common.

> "Never before have I thought so deeply about what I do with children, and why I do it. I looked critically at my practice, judging it against a set of standards developed by expert teachers in my field.... I am not the same teacher I was before the assessment, and my experience seems to be typical of the other Board certified teachers I have met."

I urged these teachers to be more explicit about just how the certification process had improved their teaching; however, they had difficulty with this. Few said that it led them to teach in fundamentally different ways. One teacher of English, whose students performed significantly better following her gaining certification, eventually articulated what most said—that she had learned to analyze what she was doing more insightfully. She talked about a heightened level of awareness of each student and a greater ability to involve her students in decisions about their own learning. Such comments bear a striking resemblance to those made in other fields about the experience of developing expertise (Berliner, 1992).

Given that the process of certification engages teachers' attention constantly and in unavoidable ways in receiving feedback and analyzing their teaching over a long period of time, such comments are unsurprising. The NBPTS standards provide teachers with reference points as to where they are in their development and where they might go. They lead teachers to seek the kind of professional development that will help them meet the standards. A well-rewarded standards-based professional certification system has the potential to create a professional learning system fit for a profession of teaching. Most professional development courses cannot do this.

RECOGNIZING AND REWARDING PROFESSIONAL CERTIFICATION: STANDARDS-BASED CAREER PROGRESSION

Debate has raged about how to strengthen links between pay and performance for teachers. The best reason for doing so is to improve incentives for teachers to develop their practice to the point at which they can demonstrate that they have attained high professional standards. The worst reason is to "incentivize" teachers through annual bonus payments to focus exclusively on improving scores on national tests, which has been happening with the Teacher Incentive Fund in the United States.

A certification system needs to provide strong incentives if it is to succeed in engaging most teachers in professional learning that leads to high standards. A critical issue in redesigning the teacher pay system, therefore, is to understand the kind of incentives that make a difference to teachers and their teaching (Johnson, 1984, 1986). Questions such as the following need to be addressed:

- What role do incentives play in the quality of teaching?
- What are the incentives that really motivate teachers?
- What kind of incentive system is most likely to lift the quality of teachers and teaching?

The past century is littered with failed merit pay schemes (Johnson, 1984; Murnane & Cohen, 1986). And a number of major studies have been completed in the past year or so showing that annual bonus pay schemes do not change teacher practices or improve student achievement in the long term (Glazerman & Seifullah, 2010; Marsh et al., 2011; Springer, 2009; Springer, Ballou, et al., 2010; Springer, Lewis, et al., 2010). They do not promote professional development and better teaching in the way that standards-based certification systems have been shown to do (National Research Council, 2008).

As Daniel Pink (2009) points out, bonus schemes work for simple routine tasks. But for tasks requiring even rudimentary cognitive skill, the higher the incentive, the worse the performance. The secret to high performance is not extrinsic rewards and punishment but the intrinsic drive to do things better because they matter. Pink identifies three important "drives" or incentives:

1. Autonomy—the urge to direct our own lives.
2. Mastery—the desire to get better at something that matters.
3. Purpose—the desire to do something in the service of something important, larger than ourselves.

Pink's work on incentives is very relevant to current discussions about how to link teacher pay to performance and the kind of incentives that matter to teachers. However, one more incentive might be added to his list. Based on many interviews I have conducted with teachers who had been through the process of preparing for certification by the NBPTS, the *power of professional recognition* for teachers' self-esteem and sense of personal agency were palpable. Most teachers want to teach well—to have a sense of increasing efficacy. They also crave public recognition for good teaching and greater understanding of the complexity of good teaching (OECD, 2009b). There are plenty of teachers who have reached high standards, but our current systems for providing them with recognition for their achievement are inadequate.

Bonus pay schemes do not work in professional organizations in which success depends on judicious use of professional expertise and values in dealing with complex, nonroutine problems. If ever there was such a job, it is teaching. The inherently competitive nature of bonus pay schemes also undermines the openness and collaboration characteristic of successful schools. In contrast, when schools and teachers support each other to gain certification, it leads to the most effective method of professional learning. The research indicates that a professionwide system for providing certification to highly accomplished teachers would have a greater impact on children's education than bonus payments based primarily on value-added measures based on national tests of student achievement.

Countries that are doing well in international assessments of student achievement are not doing it because they have bonus pay schemes. They are doing it because they offer salary progression and working conditions that attract the ablest graduates and keep them close to the classroom (Barber & Mourshed, 2007). Salaries rise to more than double the starting salary in Scotland, Singapore, and Taiwan, and to three times more in Korea. Performance pay schemes that link teachers' professional learning with rewards through reformed career structures are proving more durable than bonus pay schemes and are attracting increasing support (e.g., Johnson & Papay, 2009).

INTERNATIONAL DEVELOPMENTS

Increasing numbers of countries are introducing certification schemes for recognizing and rewarding accomplished teachers (Ingvarson, 2013; Ingvarson &

Kleinhenz, 2006a). However, they vary in the extent to which they can implement all four components. It is becoming clear that the independence of the certifying body and the rigor of the assessment are critical to their success. Some current examples of certification schemes include the following:

- The Chartered Teacher Scheme in Scotland (Scottish Executive Education Department, 2001, 2008).
- The National Board for Professional Teaching Standards scheme in the United States (NBPTS, 1989).
- The Certification of Teaching Excellence (Asignación de Excelencia Pedagógica) program in Chile (Araya, Taut, Santelices, & Manzi, 2011; Araya, Taut, Santelices, Manzi, & Miño, 2012; Manzi et al., 2007).
- The Excellent Teacher and "Advanced Skills Teacher" levels in England and Wales (Fuller, Goodwyn, Francis-Brophy, & Harding, 2010; Office for Standards in Education, Children's Services, and Skills, 2001).
- The Master Teacher career track in Singapore (Lee & Tan, 2010; Sclafani, 2008; *www.moe.gov.sg/careers/teach/career-info*).

Australia is currently attempting to introduce a system for the certification of teachers at two levels; the Highly Accomplished Teacher and Lead Teacher levels (Australian Institute for Teaching and School Leadership, 2011, 2012). Despite strong support in principle by the main stakeholders, implementation is proving difficult. In fact, attempts to introduce certification schemes for teachers have met with difficulties in most countries.

The NBPTS (1989) is arguably the most ambitious attempt by any country to establish a national system for the advanced certification of teachers. Its independence is a critical factor in its longevity, as well as its rigor. As of 2013 more than 200,000 teachers have applied for National Board certification in 16 different content areas across four developmental levels, totaling 25 unique certifications. As a result, 102,000 had been successful, a remarkable achievement. Yet, after more than 20 years, despite positive evaluations of its professional development benefits (NBPTS, 2001a, 2001b), its validity and the reliability of its assessment procedures (National Research Council, 2008), it has yet to become an integral part of career pathways for most teachers. The NBPTS operates in a large federal system with local school management and industrial bargaining. Persuading governments and 14,000 school districts to provide substantial salary recognition for professional certification has been a slow process. However, as states and school districts such as North Carolina (12% pay raise) provide salary increases for National Board certification, increasing numbers of teachers have applied.

The NBPTS certification system remains the most highly respected and longest-standing system for recognizing and rewarding accomplished teachers in the United States (National Research Council, 2008). It is no accident that practicing teachers play a major part in every level of its operation. In contrast, the English "threshold" scheme failed to engage teachers at any stage in its development or to ensure rigor in its standards and assessment process. It was more a performance management system than a professional certification system. Consequently, the scheme had little impact on professional learning and quickly lost respect (Wragg, Haynes, Chamberlin, & Wragg, 2003). The scheme has been discontinued. Like Australia, England demonstrates the importance of a national professional body being independent of governments and the changing political context.

Scotland, for example, got the recognition part of the system right in its recent Chartered Teacher scheme (Scottish Executive Education Department, 2001). They ensured strong buy-in from teacher unions, governments, and employing authorities, and all agreed to provide substantial incentives for teachers who gained certification (20% pay raise). It also mobilized the universities to provide an impressive professional learning infrastructure to support applicants (Forde & McMahon, 2011). However, the scheme has faltered, partly because the credibility of the assessment process for certification was not clearly established (Ingvarson, 2009). The scheme became vulnerable. A recent review of the Chartered Teacher scheme ("Advancing Professionalism in Teaching: Report of the Review of Teacher Employment in Scotland," 2011) claimed that

> while we received evidence that demonstrated the commitment and professionalism of many chartered teachers, the widely held view is that the existing cohort of chartered teachers does not singularly represent the best teachers in Scotland. (p. 29)

Insufficient attention was given to ensuring that the process for assessing teachers was rigorous—and therefore capable of withstanding criticism about its credibility. Consequently, the system has come into question recently as the economy has weakened. Proponents are struggling to provide good arguments for retaining the system as governments seek to cut costs.

In contrast, the NBPTS certification scheme carried out extensive research to ensure that its assessments met high psychometric standards before offering certification (Ingvarson & Hattie, 2008). It encouraged rigorous tests of the reliability and validity of its certification from leading figures in educational measurement (NBPTS, 2007). These studies provided convincing evidence that the assessment process was rigorous (National Research Council, 2008).

CONCLUDING REMARKS

It is an open question whether the professional model of certification can be applied to the teaching profession. However, what is becoming clearer from recent international research is the link between the professional status of teaching as a career and the quality of student learning. Recent OECD reports, for example, increasingly emphasize the central importance of building a high-quality teaching profession (e.g., OECD, 2009b, 2010, 2011). However, these reports rarely elaborate what it might mean to build a profession of teaching, or what the necessary conditions might be in raising the status of teaching to that of a profession. This chapter has argued that what it might mean is that the teaching profession builds its own independent professional learning and certification system, as other professions have done.

The basic rationale for such a system is to drive more effective professional learning and widespread use of successful teaching practices. Certification schemes for teachers, like those in other professions, aim to provide a service to the public and to employing authorities seeking assurances of quality. Governments and employing authorities must be convinced that certification is a guarantee of high professional standards if they are to recognize it in terms of higher salary and promotion. To be successful, certification schemes must therefore be credible, as well as independent. They must be based on a rigorous assessment of professional knowledge and performance, as defined in a set of professional standards.

In summary, if a standards-based certification system were working well:

- Teachers would regard the standards as challenging and worth pursuing as a guide to their professional learning over the long term.
- It would lead most teachers to seek professional learning experiences that helped them reach accomplished teaching standards and thereby improve learning outcomes for their students.
- Teachers would regard the assessment methods as valid, reliable, and fair.
- Employing authorities would regard certification as a reliable basis for recognizing accomplished teachers and providing salaries and career opportunities that retained the best teachers close to the classroom.
- It would lead teachers who could not attain the standards after a reasonable period of time to consider other occupations.

The concept of a standards-based professional learning and certification system is consistent with recent OECD reports on building a high-quality teaching profession (e.g., OECD, 2009a, 2010, 2011):

> to attract the best graduates to the teaching profession, these systems need to transform the work organization in their schools to an environment in which professional norms of control replace bureaucratic and administrative forms of control. (2010, p. 17)

This chapter illustrates how a professional certification system strengthens the role that teachers and their organizations play in setting the direction for their own professional learning system and ensuring widespread use of successful teaching practices.

The NBPTS represents a model of how the teaching profession in any country can gain greater control over the direction and quality of its own professional learning system and prove its credentials as a profession. Ron Thorpe (2013), president of the NBPTS, captures this aspiration well:

> As teachers express concern over how to get their voice, they need to look at the National Board for Professional Teaching Standards whose standards and certification processes were created by them and represent the bedrock of what their

work is. If Board Certification were the norm in education, rather than the exception, that voice would provide teachers with a prominence equal to their counterparts in medicine and law, and teachers would have a more compelling case to make for defining the key terms of their profession. (p. 3)

A mystery that remains for many outside the United States is why such a rigorous, profession-operated certification system with the capacity to engage all teachers in effective professional learning has yet to become the norm across most states and school districts.

QUESTIONS FOR DISCUSSION

For Teachers

1. Would professional certification linked to salary advancement be a more efficient way to promote effective professional learning for teachers than academic credits?

2. What roles can I play in supporting a national professional certification system for teachers such as that provided by the National Board for Professional Teaching Standards?

For Administrators

1. How can I organize professional learning in my school so that it supports groups of teachers who wish to prepare for professional certification?

2. Would professional certification linked to career advancement be a more valid and less divisive way to link pay to performance than annual bonuses or merit schemes?

For Policymakers

1. How can we promote the development of teaching as a profession with its own standards-based professional learning and certification system?

2. Are current salary structures and career pathways providing sufficiently attractive incentives for all teachers to work toward attaining professional certification?

REFERENCES

Advancing professionalism in teaching: Report of the review of teacher employment in Scotland. (2011). Edinburgh, UK: Government of Scotland.

Araya, C., Taut, S., Santelices, V., & Manzi, J. (2011). Validez consecuencial del programa de asignación de excelencia pedagógica en Chile [Consequential validity of the Certification of Teaching Excellence Program in Chile]. *Revista Estudios Pedagógicos, 37*(2), 25–42.

Araya, C., Taut, S., Santelices, V., Manzi, J., & Miño, F. (2012). Teoría subyacente del Programa de Asignación de Excelencia Pedagógica en Chile [Theory of action of the Certification of Teaching Excellence Program in Chile]. *Revista de Educación, 359*, 530–553.

Australian Institute for Teaching and School Leadership. (2011). *National professional standard for teachers*. Melbourne: Australian Institute for Teaching and School Leadership. Retrieved from *www.teacherstandards.aitsl.edu.au*.

Australian Institute for Teaching and School Leadership. (2012, April). *Certification of highly accomplished and lead teachers: Principles and processes*. Melbourne: Education Services Australia. Retrieved from *www.aitsl.edu.au/verve/_resources/Certification_of_Highly_Accomplished_and_Lead_Teachers_-_Principles_and_processes_-_April_2012_file.pdf*.

Australian Science Teachers Association. (2002). *National professional standards for highly accomplished teachers of science*. Canberra: Australian Science Teachers Association.

Baker, E., Barton, P. E., Darling-Hammond, L., Haertel, E., Ladd, H. F., Linn, R. L., et al. (2010). *Problems with the use of student tests scores to evaluate teachers* (EPI Briefing Paper No. 278). Washington, DC: Economic Policy Institute.

Baratz-Snowden, J. (1993). Assessment of teachers: A view from the National Board for Professional Teaching Standards. *Theory into Practice, 42*(2), 82–85.

Barber, M., & Mourshed, M. (2007). *How the best performing school systems come out on top*. London: McKinsey.

Baumert, J., Kunter, M., Blum, W., Brunner, M., Voss, T., Jordan, A., et al. (2010). Teachers' mathematical knowledge, cognitive activation in the classroom, and student progress. *American Educational Research Journal, 47*(1), 133–180.

Berliner, D. C. (1992). The nature of expertise in teaching. In F. K. Oser, A. Dick, & J.-L. Patry (Eds.), *Effective and responsible teaching: The new synthesis* (pp. 227–248). San Francisco: Jossey-Bass.

Browne, B., Auton, S., Freund, M., & Futrell, M. H. (1999). Meeting the millennium challenge: National Board for Professional Teaching Standards partnerships supporting the teaching profession. *Teaching and Change, 6*(4), 364–375.

Carnegie Forum on Education and the Economy. (1986). *A nation prepared: Teachers for the 21st century: The report of the Task Force on Teaching as a Profession*. New York: Carnegie Forum on Education and the Economy.

Cohen, D., & Hill, H. (2000). Instructional policy and classroom performance: The mathematics reforms in California. *Teachers College Record, 102*(2), 294–343.

Collins, A. (1991). Portfolios for biology teacher assessment. *Journal of Personnel Evaluation in Education, 5*, 147–167.

Darling-Hammond, L. (1992). Creating standards of practice and delivery for learner-centered schools. *Stanford Law and Policy Review, 4*, 37-52.

Darling-Hammond, L., & Baratz-Snowden, J. C. (2005). *A good teacher in every classroom: Preparing the highly qualified teachers our children deserve*. Washington, DC: National Academy of Education.

Dinham, S., Ingvarson, L., & Kleinhenz, E. (2008). Investing in teacher quality: Doing what matters most. In *Teaching talent: The best teachers for Australia's classrooms*. Melbourne: Business Council of Australia. Retrieved from *www.bca.com.au/Content/101446.aspx*.

Elmore, R. F. (1996). Getting to scale with successful educational practices. *Harvard Education Review, 66*(1), 1–26.

Fenstermacher, G. D., & Richardson, V. (2005). On making determinations of quality in teaching. *Teachers College Record, 107*(1), 186–213.

Forde, C., & McMahon, M. (2011). *Accomplished teaching, accomplished teachers in Scotland*. Glasgow, UK: University of Glasgow, Department of Education.

Fuller, C., Goodwyn, A., Francis-Brophy, E., & Harding, R. (2010). *Advanced skill teachers: Summary report.* Reading, UK: University of Reading, Institute of Education.

Gitomer, D. (Ed.). (2009). *Measurement issues and assessment for teaching quality.* Los Angeles: Sage.

Glazerman, S., & Seifullah, S.A. (2010). *An evaluation of the teacher advancement program (TAP) in Chicago: Year two impact report.* Washington, DC: Mathematica Policy Research.

Goe, L., Bell, C., & Little, O. (2008). *Approaches to evaluating teacher effectiveness: A research synthesis.* Nashville, TN: Vanderbilt University, National Comprehensive Center for Teacher Quality.

Goulding, M., Rowland, T., & Barber, P. (2002). Does it matter?: Primary teacher trainees' subject knowledge in mathematics. *British Educational Research Journal, 28*(5), 689–704.

Haertel, E. (1991). New forms of teacher assessment. *Review of Research in Education, 17,* 3–30.

Hawley, W., & Valli, L. (1999). The essentials of effective professional development: A new consensus. In L. Darling-Hammond & G. Sykes (Eds.), *Teaching as the learning profession: Handbook of policy and practice* (pp. 127-150). San Francisco: Jossey-Bass.

Hill, H., Rowan, B., & Ball, D. (2005). Effects of teachers' mathematical knowledge for teaching on student achievement. *American Educational Research Journal, 42*(2), 371–406.

Ingvarson, L. C. (1998). Professional development as the pursuit of professional standards. *Teaching and Teacher Education, 14*(1), 127–140.

Ingvarson, L. C. (2009). Identifying and rewarding excellent teachers: The Scottish chartered teacher scheme. *Professional Development in Education, 35*(3), 451–468.

Ingvarson, L. C. (2013). Reforming career paths for Australian teachers. In M. Akiba (Ed.), *Teacher reforms around the world: Implementations and outcomes* (pp. 237–273). Amsterdam: Emerald Books.

Ingvarson, L. C., & Hattie, J. (Eds.). (2008). *Advances in program evaluation: Vol. 11. Assessing teachers for professional certification: The first decade of the national board for professional teaching standards.* Amsterdam: Elsevier Press.

Ingvarson, L. C., & Kleinhenz, E. (2006a). *Advanced teaching standards and certification: A review of national and international developments.* Canberra: Teaching Australia, Australian Institute for Teaching and School Leadership. Retrieved from *www.teachingaustralia.edu.au/ta/go/home/projects/standards.*

Ingvarson, L. C., & Kleinhenz, E. (2006b). *A standards-guided professional learning system.* Melbourne, Australia: Centre for Strategic Education. Retrieved from *www.cse.edu.au.*

Ingvarson, L. C., & Rowe, K. (2008). Conceptualizing and measuring teacher quality: Substantive and methodological issues. *Australian Journal of Education, 52*(1), 5–34.

Johnson, S. M. (1984). Merit pay for teachers: A poor prescription for reform. *Harvard Educational Review, 54*(2), 175–185.

Johnson, S. M. (1986). Incentives for teachers: What motivates, what matters. *Educational Administration Quarterly, 22*(3), 54–79.

Johnson, S. M., & Papay, J. P. (2009). *Redesigning teacher pay: A system for the next generation of educators* (EPI Series on Alternative Teacher Compensation Systems, No. 2). Washington, DC: Economic Policy Institute.

Kelcy, B. (2011). Assessing the effects of teachers' reading knowledge on students' achievement. *Educational Evaluation and Policy Analysis, 33*(4), 458–482.

Kennedy, M. (1998). *Form and substance in inservice teacher education* (Research Monograph No. 13). Arlington, VA: National Science Foundation.

Kennedy, M. (Ed.). (2010). *Teacher assessment and the quest of teacher quality.* San Francisco: Jossey-Bass.

Kersting, N. B., Givvin, K. B., & Thompson, B. J. (2012). Measuring usable knowledge: Teacher's analyses of mathematics classroom videos predict teaching quality and student achievement. *American Educational Research Journal, 49*(3), 568–589.

Lee, C., & Tan, M. (2010, March). *Rating teachers and rewarding teacher performance: The context of Singapore.* Paper presented at the Asia-Pacific Economic Cooperation (APEC) Conference on Replicating Exemplary Practices in Mathematics Education, Koh Samui, Thailand.

Lustick, D. (2011). *Certifiable: Teaching, learning and national board certification.* New York: Rowman & Littlefield.

Lustick, D., & Sykes, G. (2006). National Board Certification as professional development: What are teachers learning?: An empirical investigation of the learning outcomes from the National Board for Professional Teaching Standards' certification process. Retrieved from *www.nbpts.org/sites/default/files/documents/research/LustickSykes_NBCasPD_WhatAreTeachersLearning.pdf.*

Manzi, J., Araya, C., González, R., Barros, E., Bravo, D., Peirano, C., et al. (2007, March). *Validity evidence for the certification of teaching excellence in Chile: A pioneer experience in Latin America.* Paper presented at the annual conference of the American Educational Research Association, Chicago.

Marsh, J. A., Springer, M. G., McCaffrey, D. F., Yuan, K., Epstein, S., Koppich, J., et al. (2011). *A big apple for educators: New York City's experiment with schoolwide performance bonuses: Final evaluation report.* Santa Monica, CA: RAND Corporation. Retrieved from *www.performanceincentives.org/data/files/gallery/ContentGallery/POINT_Report_Executive_Summary.pdf.*

McCaffrey, D., Lockwood, J. R., Koretz, D. M., & Hamilton, L. S. (2003). *Evaluating value-added models for teacher accountability.* Santa Monica, CA: RAND Corporation.

Murnane, R. J., & Cohen, D. (1986). Merit pay and the evaluation problem: Why most merit pay plans fail and few survive. *Harvard Education Review, 56,* 1–17.

National Board for Professional Teaching Standards. (1989). *Toward high and rigorous standards for the teaching profession.* Detroit, MI: Author.

National Board for Professional Teaching Standards. (2001a). *I am a better teacher: What candidates for national board certification say about the assessment process.* Arlington, VA: Author.

National Board for Professional Teaching Standards. (2001b). *National Board certification candidate survey.* Arlington, VA: Author.

National Board for Professional Teaching Standards. (2007). *A research guide on National Board Certification of teachers.* Arlington, VA: Author.

National Commission on Excellence in Education. (1983). *A nation at risk: The imperative for educational reform.* Washington, DC: U.S. Government Printing Office.

National Research Council. (2008). *Assessing accomplished teaching: Advanced level certification programs.* Washington, DC: National Academies Press.

Office for Standards in Education, Children's Services, and Skills. (2001). *Advanced skills teachers: Appointment, deployment and impact.* London: Author.

Organisation for Economic Cooperation and Development. (2005). *Teachers matter: Attracting, developing and retaining effective teachers.* Paris: Author.

Organisation for Economic Cooperation and Development. (2009a). *Creating effective teaching and learning environments: First results from TALIS (Teaching and Learning International Survey).* Paris: Author.

Organisation for Economic Cooperation and Development. (2009b). *Evaluating and rewarding the quality of teachers: International practices.* Paris: Author.

Organisation for Economic Cooperation and Development. (2010). *Strong performers and successful reformers in education: Lessons from PISA for the United States.* Paris: Author. Retrieved from *http://dx.doi.org/10.1787/9789264096660-en.*

Organisation for Economic Cooperation and Development. (2011). *Building a high-quality teaching profession: Lessons from around the world background report for the International Summit on the Teaching Profession.* Paris: Author. Retrieved from *http://fulltextreports.com/2011/03/16/building-a-high-quality-teaching-profession-lessons-from-around-the-world.*

Pink, D. (2009). *Drive: The surprising truth about what motivates us.* New York: Riverhead Books.

Rothstein, J. (2009, May). *Teacher quality in educational production: Tracking, decay and student achievement* (NBER Working Paper No. 14442). Cambridge, MA: National Bureau of Economic Research.

Sato, M., & Monte-Sano, C. (2002, April). *The National Board certification process and its impact on teacher leadership.* Paper presented at the annual meeting of the American Educational Research Association, New Orleans, LA.

Sato, M., Wei, R. C., & Darling-Hammond, L. (2008). Improving teachers' assessment practices through professional development: The case of National Board Certification. *American Educational Research Journal, 45,* 669–700.

Schochet, P. Z., & Chiang, H. S. (2010). *Error rates in measuring teacher and school performance based on student test score data.* Washington, DC: U.S. Department of Education, National Center for Educational Evaluation and Regional Assistance.

Sclafani, S. (with Lim, E.). (2008). *Rethinking human capital in education: Singapore as a model for teacher development.* Paper prepared for the Aspen Institute Education and Society Program. Retrieved from *www.aspeninstitute.org/sites/default/files/content/docs/education%20and%20society%20program/SingaporeEDU.pdf.*

Scottish Executive Education Department. (2001). *A teaching profession for the 21st century: The agreement following the recommendations of the McCrone Report.* Edinburgh, UK: Author.

Scottish Executive Education Department. (2008). *Report of the chartered teacher review group: Report of the review group.* Edinburgh, UK: Government of Scotland.

Shulman, L. S. (1991). *Final report of the Teacher Assessment Project.* Palo Alto, CA: Stanford University.

Springer, M. G. (Ed.). (2009). *Performance incentives: Their growing impact on American K–12 education.* Washington, DC: Brookings Institution Press.

Springer, M. G., Ballou, D., Hamilton, L., Le, V.-N., Lockwood, J. R., McCaffrey, D. F., et al. (2010). *Teacher pay for performance: Experimental evidence from the project on incentives in teaching.* Nashville, TN: Vanderbilt University, National Center on Performance Incentives.

Springer, M. G., Lewis, J., Ehlert, M. W., Podgursky, M. J., Crader, G. D., Taylor, L. I., et al. (2010). *District Awards for Teacher Excellence (D.A.T.E.) program: Final evaluation report.* Nashville, TN: Vanderbilt University, National Center on Performance Incentives.

Snowden, C. D. (1993, October). *Preparing teachers for the demands of the 21st century: Professional development and the NBPTS vision.* Paper prepared for the National Board for Professional Teaching Standards, Detroit, MI.

Sykes, G. (1999). Teacher and student learning: Strengthening their connection. In L.Darling-Hammond & G. Sykes (Eds.), *Teaching as the learning profession: Handbook of policy and practice* (pp. 151–179). San Francisco: Jossey-Bass.

Thorpe, R. (2013, February). *Teacher voice and teacher leadership.* Paper prepared for the Sustaining Teachers' Professional Growth Seminar, Cambridge, UK.

Tracz, S. M., Sienty, S., Todorov, K., Snyder, J., Takashima, B., Pensabene, R., et al. (1995, April). *Improvement in teaching skills: Perspectives from National Board for Professional Standards field test network candidates.* Paper presented at the annual meeting of the American Educational Research Association, San Francisco.

Unrau, N. (2002, April). *Lessons learned from MA candidates pursuing National Board Certification.* Paper presented at the annual meeting of the American Educational Research Association, New Orleans, LA.

Wilson, S., & Berne, J. (1999). Teacher learning and the acquisition of professional knowledge: An examination of research on contemporary professional development. *Review of Research in Education, 24,* 173–209.

Wolf, K., & Taylor, G. (2008). Effects of National Board Certification on teachers' perspectives and practices. In L.C. Ingvarson & Hattie, J. (Eds.), *Advances in program evaluation: Vol. 11. Assessing teachers for professional certification: The first decade of the national board for professional teaching standards* (pp. 381–412). Amsterdam: Elsevier.

Wragg, E., Haynes, G., Chamberlin, R., & Wragg, C. (2003). Performance-related pay: The views and experiences of 1,000 primary and secondary head teachers. *Research Papers in Education, 18*(1), 3–23.

CHAPTER 21

The School as a Center of Inquiry

BRUCE R. JOYCE
EMILY F. CALHOUN

Our purpose is to provide the basis for a dialogue to:

- Build cumulative knowledge about professional development.
- Gather ideas for integrating information and communication technology into professional development, classroom instruction, and curriculum implementation.
- Consider the components of a pervasive professional development system and create structures for supporting individual and collaborative learning.

Forty-seven years ago, Bob Schaefer (1967) produced a wonderful essay describing school as a place where the faculty continuously inquire into teaching and learning, thus modeling the same cooperative inquiry processes they are teaching students. Schaefer succinctly captured the school as a learning community, the process of continuous school renewal, and a model of professional learning that has not been surpassed. We suggest using Schaefer's concepts—along with the tools available from digital technology; research on teaching, learning, and professional development; and a half-century of experience on how to implement changes in education—to build a pervasive professional development system in every school. Let's design a system that improves the learning opportunities for both adults and children. Let's finally create the school as a center of inquiry.

We are in a period of great promise brought about by what might seem to be a crisis. In many settings, there is little evidence of the effects of professional development on student learning (Wei, Darling-Hammond, & Adamson, 2010). Many schools lag behind in integrating technology into learning in all content areas (Collins & Halverson, 2009; Partnership for 21st Century Skills, State Educational Technology Directors Association, & International Society for Technology in Education, 2007; Zhao, 2009). However, the new curricula being adopted in literacy and language arts, mathematics, and science have the potential for accelerating K–12 learning, if implemented. But education has long struggled with implementing promising practices (Fixsen, Naoom, Blase, Friedman, & Wallace, 2005; Fullan & Pomfret, 1977). Within this context, can we realize the promise, grasp these opportunities, and transform professional development? We believe we can.

The goal of professional development is learning. How can we use today's global access to information to support the learning of all within our schoolhouse? How can we unleash the potential for collaborative problem solving and working with each other, whether in the same building, state, or country, and whether 7, 14, or 64 years of age? Educators and students benefit from well-designed learning experiences provided to expand curricular and instructional practices. Let's think together about the problem and how to exploit these potential opportunities.

A GIFT OF RICHES

If we wish to turn criticisms and laments into pathways to learning, here are some of the riches we have:

- The capability to generate distance support for professional development that can reach every school—every professional learning community—every teacher.
- New core curricula that are generating real impetus for improving curriculum and instruction, particularly in literacy and language arts; science, technology, engineering, mathematics (STEM); and the social studies with interdisciplinary instruction, learning through inquiry, and application of knowledge and skill emphasized for the youngest children and throughout schooling. A strong civic and personal belief in the value of education that we can marshal in support of our own learning and that of our children.

Today, students, teachers, and school faculties have resources we could not have dreamed of just a couple of decades ago. In classrooms all over the world, we can look in on each other and study together, exchange information about our cultures, and respond to each other's questions in seconds using the global networks that are changing our world. Repositories are being developed as museums and libraries digitize their archives and collections. Just look at the U.S. Library of Congress with its remarkable collection of books, documents, and other materials online—more than a million photographs—along with lesson plans and tips and resources for teaching everything from immigration to political cartoons (*www. loc.gov/index.html*). The promise of the information and communication technology (ICT) revolution is not in simple online courses in the school subjects, nor in sitting at the kitchen table taking a graduate course, but in the massive resources available to students, teachers, and learning communities.

Even though we have all these resources, the conceptual/inquiry approach built into the new curricula presents a considerable challenge to educators at all levels—states, districts, schools, and individual classrooms—because curricula and instruction from K–12 will need to be redeveloped in many settings.

After decades of struggle to build a pervasive professional development system, it may be that a key has always been right under our noses: turning each school into a center for learning by the adults as well as the children. We can make a strong beginning by creating professional learning centers in every school—a place where all faculty members study teaching and curriculum, redevelop courses, and build their own backgrounds in content and teaching and leadership. Through ICT, combined with the movement toward elevated core curriculum standards, we can recreate our curricula and build a collaborative profession in which individuals and faculties are continuously engaged in action research to energize education in the schools where they work.

THE INFRASTRUCTURE: PROFESSIONAL LEARNING CENTERS IN SCHOOLS AND ICT EVERYWHERE

Imagine building into our schools—right in the middle of the first floor—a center for teachers to study, develop lessons and materials, and to learn the documented effective teaching strategies of our craft, which, if used extensively with fidelity, will bring almost all of their students into the world of literacy and independent learning. The equipment in our center will not be exotic. The center needs a couple of interactive whiteboards, several computers with optimum Internet connections, good graphic programs, decent printers, and educationally useful software for a range of purposes, from creating multimedia to assessing student learning.

All teachers will spend 5 or 6 hours each week in the center, rebuilding their lessons and courses, and they will participate in interactive distance-provided workshops to introduce them to teaching and learning strategies that will improve the pace and content of learning in the school. People now designated as coaches will have good work to do—stimulating the process, coordinating efforts and investigations, and providing onsite professional development. There will be inside-out experiences of the kind that the proponents of professional learning communities have envisioned and outside-in experiences as methods and products created in other settings are made available. In other words, rather than planning first how to bring technology to students, we need to plan how to integrate teachers with technology.

To build such a center in every school is within our grasp. The cost is not large, yet the payoff in learning can be. Professional development providers can reach thousands of educators at costs far below that of providing service in an agrarian fashion to just a handful of schools. Both from a distance and from within the school, providers can lead teachers to the best we know about teaching and learning and the ways of opening the world for their students.

In most developed countries there are populations that are underserved, such as schools that have students who are learning English as a second language. In U.S. schools there may not be enough bilingual teachers to support Hispanic students. However, we can provide instruction by experts in any language if we build the proper connections, online and in our local communities. We can actually take our *teachers* and paraprofessionals to school in the languages of the students they teach—if we build centers of learning to fuel our professional development.

The goals—better education for our children through better education for teachers, more powerful uses of our technologies, professional inquiry as integrated features of our schools, and equity of learning opportunities for our children—are within reach if we choose.

Cautions

Without powerful professional development, the new core curricula and ICT will simply wash past the schools, leaving them further and further behind the rest of the society and endangering the lead the United States has held for many years as a land of innovation and opportunity. A new generation of distance courses, workshops, and seminars is emerging for students from kindergarten through high school, college, and graduate studies. Super-courses that can be bounced to any classroom or student in any space or culture are appearing, and through them tens of thousands of people are involved in advanced study from our leading universities. Although the new and sometimes powerful courses will generate opportunities for our students, they will not generate the professional development to integrate ICT within schools unless educators choose to make it happen.

The education of many of our children is still taking place in old-fashioned environments in which teachers receive virtually no support. Even in some schools that have worked to provide Web access in every classroom, the connections are so slow that many teachers give up in frustration. If they could speak, the old buildings would cry out for teacher centers and high-quality networks that so many professionals take for granted in their workplaces. How have we ended up with an educational model that leaves out the continuing education of the staff?

Many advocates of No Child Left Behind gave outside-in professional development a bad name with their aggressive embrace of an obsolete way of teaching literacy and their possession of the hammers: withdrawal of funds and increases in high-stakes testing accompanied by increased penalties for failure. These misguided efforts at school improvement may still be around, but they will not be the focus of work in our professional learning centers.

THE DEVELOPMENT OF HYBRID COURSES AS A SERIOUS FOCUS

The workday for teachers moves from one demanding task to another, time to think and plan is in short supply. Policymakers at all levels literally bombard the schools with initiatives that are lightly funded and sometimes regressive. There may be computers and whiteboards, but little training on how to use them for instruction. Some of us are not so anxious to be "trained," feeling that training is an imposition on "professionalism." Many principals and central office folks seem to be almost wary—or maybe simply fatigued—by the demands of educational leadership. New content comes in cycles; teachers try to implement it. Today, some may secretly hope that the new curricula in literacy and language arts, mathematics, science, and social studies will pass on like many initiatives have. Before I go to the 40k network on the other side of the Styx, I want to see a real focus on getting our act together.
            —A friend who, as you can tell, has lived in this profession for a while

The policymakers do have to get their act together. As Richard Allington (2009) put it so pungently: "for fifty years Title I has managed to get kids about two months of growth a year while they are two years behind and sinking and that is better than special education has done after more than forty years." The personal computer is some 30 years of age, and, as Mario Cuomo put it at the Democratic Party National Convention in 1984, "in many of our schools the chief use of technology is the metal detector."

A major reason some good ideas fail to become reality in many schools is the *failure to focus strongly enough on the idea that change can actually happen.* Many districts, and even schools, kill their initiatives simply by making too many of them. The new core curricula can generate a blizzard if we are not careful. Given what we have said earlier in this chapter, we have to be bold and suggest a focus to guide the very complex tasks involved in building the professional development that capitalizes on digital technology and the promise of the new core curricula.

The development of "hybrid" courses is needed at elementary and secondary levels; that is, courses that use both campus instruction and inquiry and distance resources to support learning; courses that take advantage of the new digital libraries of the world and the communication avenues that are available, with new avenues appearing regularly. The concept of "hybrid" implies an integrated approach, not just going online once a week or blending resources casually (Joyce & Calhoun, 2012). Nor are the uses of digital libraries and distance resources only for secondary education. Teaching and learning in PreK, kindergarten, and the primary grades would follow the same path as would the upper elementary grades. The renewed courses would emphasize inquiry that draws on ICT. To make this possible, teachers would need to learn to build these hybrids and use them, and a key component would be in building learning communities on the campuses and teaching the students how to inquire productively. For the effective use of the Web lies not only in how to find information but also in how to organize and interpret it. Inductive inquiry needs to be central.

Imagine an art class on some aspect of sculpture that draws on the Louvre, the Metropolitan, the Uffizi, and the Museum of Modern Art. The amount of available material is dizzying to the person who has not learned to build categories and interpret them—in other words, studying with an inductive model of learning. The days of providing predigested material are about over, whether offered through lecture-recitation or "comprehensive" textbooks. The student will have to build high-level skills, those at the core of the 21st-century skills (Joyce & Calhoun, 2012; Kay, 2010), and at the center of the new literacy and language arts curriculum framework as well. Learning how to learn will empower students in school and beyond.

SCHOOL FACULTIES AND SUPPORT SYSTEMS: LEAD TEAMS, COACHES AND COACHING TEAMS, AND PROFESSIONAL LEARNING COMMUNITIES

The internal organization of the school will be critical, as will be the development of support for teachers in the school. Let's begin with the school. Within the school we find individuals, small study groups or professional learning communities (PLCs), and the faculty as a whole. All of these can be supported through a pervasive professional development system. Some individuals, some small groups, and some faculties are already doing a fine job of creating hybrid combinations, but they are not the norm. Generally, all three can use support as they begin to innovate in their work.

Organizationally healthy schools usually have committees of lead teachers who guide the action research process at the whole-school level and who support action research and development activities by individuals and PLCs. The lead team members go "in front" in development of the courses and in implementation in the classroom.

For our purpose here, let's imagine that a leadership team has led the faculty of a given school to assess needs and that they have come to the conclusion that a major need is to learn how to effectively combine campus teaching with support from the ICT "global library" and online and other distance offerings. Similarly, they have energized the PLCs, and several of those have come to believe that the overall faculty need is theirs also. A couple of individual teachers have done a good deal of self-study and organized their classes in a fashion similar to that of the art class mentioned earlier. Unfortunately, they are reluctant to get into the position of offering in-house professional development sessions because they feel too busy with their own teaching, and they also do not want to cope with a couple of staff members who have a history of resisting professional development in every form. This is a familiar problem. Lead team members and administrators will need to model distributed leadership and mediate the organizational climate so that these teachers, who have so much to offer, will feel that they can share their work and participate as leaders in the larger learning community.

The more deeply building administrators are involved, the better is the implementation. School-based administrators can facilitate the front-runners and first leaders mentioned earlier, possibly enabling them to offer service to their peers. In schools with more than 100 staff members, the chief principal may have little choice but to behave primarily as a manager, squeezing out time to meet with and support the lead team. Even working out regular short meetings and observations with a member of the lead team can provide him or her with a surprisingly large amount of information. In large schools, other administrative staff can take on the major instructional leadership responsibility. In smaller schools, the principal and assistant principal should be involved, usually as members of the lead teacher team. In our imaginary school, both administrators are part of the lead team, but decision making is a collective matter.

If we have a reasonably healthy school organization, then there is just one little problem with respect to learning to build hybrid courses: Most of the faculty will need support; the PLCs will need support; and individuals will need support. In fact, the leadership team will need just as much support as everyone else, perhaps more, if they are to stay a little "out front." Learning to teach inductive models of learning will be another sizeable challenge. Already some teachers and school faculties are doing a dazzling job. But most will say that they have a distance to go. Thus professional development is in order, but not just any variety of professional development.

This brings us to the intersection of the ICT revolution and professional development—*what we are talking about is utterly dependent on high-quality professional learning, supported by a very high level of professional development.* Therein lies the challenge. Neither ordinary PLC work nor sporadic workshops will do the job. Learning to incorporate ICT and building inquiry-oriented communities of students who can use inductive methods is a complex innovation.

Fortunately, we know something about the needs of teachers if they are to take on and implement complex curriculum and instructional models that are new to them. We learned many years ago that professional development that ensures high levels of implementation requires several elements that facilitate learning by educators (Joyce & Showers, 2002). The elements are:

- The study of rationale.
- Demonstrations—more than are generally used by the field.
- Practice with the companionship of peers. (Joyce and Showers termed this "peer coaching," but the media images of "coaches" screaming from the sideline and the history of structured clinical supervision confused people. It is better to think of a pair of colleagues planning together and trying to think out problems as equals—imagine a friendly study group or PLC.)

If these elements (study of rationale, lots of demonstrations, and practice with peer companionship) are combined, implementation of a new teaching practice is as high as 90% compared with 10–15% without any one of those components (see Figure 21.1). Essentially, teachers are very good learners, but they need several things: understanding of the model of teaching or instructional practice and understanding about why any new practice is useful (the study of rationale); good, practical demonstrations that are sufficient to see how the model or practice works; enough time so that they can develop skill in its use; and the opportunity to practice in the company of peers as they provide their own follow-up. We called the organization "study groups," currently called PLCs.

Elements	Effect on Knowledge	Short-Term Use	Long-Term Use
Rationale	+++	5–10%	5%
Rationale plus demonstrations	++++	5–10%	5–10%
Rationale plus demonstrations plus preparation time	++++++	80% and higher	5–10%
All of the above, plus peer coaching	++++++	90% and higher	90% and higher

FIGURE 21.1. Design elements.

The lead team or lead teachers organize coaching teams, but *they* are not the coaches for all teachers. Pairs and triads of teachers can help themselves just fine, "coaching" each other through mutual experimentation and companionable support when things get a little tough (Joyce & Calhoun, 2010, 2012; Joyce & Showers, 2002). Teachers prefer job-alike study, but cross-grade and cross-disciplinary groups do well where they are not resisted, and very small schools have no other option.

Where might this high-quality professional development come from, and what would it look like? We imagine hybrid courses again, this time for the adults. Lead teams, school faculties, and individuals look for help, and help needs to be available on the Web. But—from whom?

ORGANIZING TO PROVIDE SUPPORT DIRECTLY TO THE SCHOOLS FROM A DISTANCE

Hands-on, site-based, face-to-face, personal-consultant-driven service may not be practical, and that may be a good thing. Compared with the need, we have a scarcity of consultants and trainers who have done this work. Importantly, you cannot offer good professional development service in this area unless you have developed hybrid courses yourself. You can't work effectively from someone else's book. So, what to do?

We suggest that agencies at several levels create interactive courses that the schools can access. School districts, intermediate agencies, and states are well positioned to do this. A small group of developers can create a course that combines explanation with demonstrations, discussions and development activities on the campus, and provisions for questions and discussion. Probably separate courses for primary, elementary, middle, and high school levels would be more popular, although they might share modules on rationale both for hybrids and inductive inquiry. These courses would be delivered online. Regular times could be scheduled to answer questions and deal with implementation problems. If that development is accomplished, our school can reach to the Web for support.

It is not out of the question for development to be initiated at the national level. For example, Learning Forward (previously known as the National Staff

Development Council) could take the lead and involve some of the other curriculum area-oriented organizations. State education departments are well situated because of the emphasis on new state curricula and the purchase they have due to their position as conduits of federal funds. If good distance courses are created based on the needs of students in districts and schools, and if campus faculties include leadership teams and are organized for cooperative action research, we should have a winning learning community.

In a previous publication (Joyce & Calhoun, 2010), we described five approaches or models that are currently used to provide support to education professionals. One is providing support to the individual teacher or administrator, generally through the provision of stipends and paid leaves for a period of time. Unquestionably, an individual can engage in the kind of study outlined. Some can teach themselves if they have time and appropriate resources in the form of both hardware and software such as interactive whiteboards, well-equipped laptops, and access to resources ranging from TumbleBooks to Education Discovery. Individuals can also seek providers, looking for them where the theory–demonstration–practice paradigm is available to support their learning. If a component, such as demonstrations, is not available from a provider, then the help will be minimal. This model is a good avenue when a cadre of local support personnel is being developed at the district level. The district advertises for volunteers to serve on a cadre and accept training as a condition, selects a number according to the budget, and gets going.

The second approach consists of direct personal services, by which someone who is relatively expert in the content offers training and companionship as in individual practices, a version of what is often called "coaching." In the case of the content that is the subject of this chapter—the development of hybrid courses built around cooperative/inductive inquiry teaching and learning—personal service can work, but it requires the preparation of coaches in areas that will be new to most of them.

The third approach is through the organization of cooperative study groups—PLCs—whose members set goals for action research to improve the services they provide to their students. The most successful of these make changes in curriculum, instruction, or the social climate of the school and classroom. The content and approach to professional learning that we recommend here will probably require professional development through workshops led by professionals who have become expert in the content and the conduct of professional development. Importantly, many approaches to the organization of study groups assume that the group will decide what to study. If they do not address the incorporation of ICT into their curriculum areas, then what we are presenting here would have little pertinence to their directions.

Fourth, a school, district, or state decides to make a curricular or instructional initiative. If that initiative includes the content we are addressing, then it would fit nicely provided that the school, district, or state is not simply making a paper initiative but supports appropriate professional development as well as making and publishing documents and providing digital and media support. Video collections of demonstrations are very important in supporting schools in the acquisition of technology (see, e.g., *www.BooksendLabs* channel). Providing easy access to websites, such as Badgerlink in Wisconsin, make it easy for teachers to incorporate multimedia resources into their regular instruction.

The fifth approach is to provide service through professional development offerings during days or parts of days during the school day. The content and type of professional development we are describing can be nested into this type of offering, provided that the providers are expert in them, sufficient time is provided, and the teachers are organized to provide peer coaching.

HARNESSING THE WEB AND PRINT RESOURCES THROUGH INDUCTIVE INQUIRY: REVIEWING OUR POSITION AND PROVIDING A SCENARIO

The Web represents an evolution of the library (what we call *the great new library*) that enhances self-learning opportunities to a remarkable extent. How can we help teachers and students build the tools to organize and use the stacks of information they can retrieve? Because of the digital revolution, the possibility of elevating education has never been poised so well, but it may slip away if it is not accompanied by teaching students how to build concepts and organize their inquiries, essentially teaching students to engage in basic inductive work.

The proposition we rely on is that the model of inductive teaching and learning holds the key to capitalizing on the marvelous avenues to learning enabled through (1) the new electronic libraries, (2) the offerings of distance education, and (3) the transformation of campus courses into hybrids with instruction that capitalizes on both campus interaction and Web resources. Let's look at an illustration in which one elementary teacher learns to build a hybrid course. As we visit her, we provide commentary about the professional development and infrastructures that support her continued learning and that of her students.

This hybrid course is built on inquiry and uses both campus study and the resources of ICT, blending them together. The teacher leads the inquiry and helps students access multiple sources on the Web and organize information, ideas, and opinions as they build conceptual knowledge of a domain of study.

Ginny's Primary Students Ask, "What's Growing in Our Neighborhood?"

Let's imagine Ginny Townsend's second-grade students as they embark on a study of the vegetation in the neighborhood of their school. The inquiry stemmed from a discussion in which they realized that they had little knowledge of the growing things they pass every day. They had names for only a small proportion of the flora they live with and only superficial knowledge about how the vegetation they see every day gets nourishment, grows, and reproduces. Ginny knows that they begin with very little content knowledge, but they have experienced plant life all their lives and have more information than they realize.

Professional Development Commentary

Ginny and her grade 5 colleague, Traci, have been studying ICT and inductive science teaching together. They took advantage of a district program that provides stipends to a number of teachers for independent study and attended an International Society for Technology in Education (ISTE) workshop on locating Internet data sources and helping elementary students access them. They also took a distance course from the state university on experience-based inductive inquiry with K–12 students. The result was that Traci and Ginny agreed to begin building hybrid, inductive courses in which campus and distance experience are intertwined.

The campus dimension leads Ginny's students to work together and provides them with learning strategies. In this case they will be learning a cooperative/inductive way of educating themselves, beginning by collecting data from the living plant life in their neighborhood. Digital resources provide vastly more information on many topics than any human teacher could expect to have. Of course, print sources such as books, encyclopedias, and other references continue to be important.

Ginny's class is well equipped: a print library of relevant books, a dozen computers, e-mail, digital cameras and camcorders, and an interactive whiteboard. She has developed a class Web page on which she and the students can post ideas and information.

Professional Development Commentary

A windfall came when the company that had sold the district the whiteboards came to the school and provided a series of short workshops on how to use them for instruction.

Ginny knows that she will be leading her kids into relatively unfamiliar content and will have to help them learn to collect and classify information from print and digital sources (and from local experts). The students will need to learn to develop and test ideas and to generate attractive and accurate reports about the results of their inquiries, building general computer skills and Web skills as the inquiry proceeds. Their work will help them build content knowledge, as well as digital and media literacy.

Ginny decides to begin by having students collect information through observing the vegetation around them during the first week in September. Therefore, the inquiry opens with walks around the neighborhood, observing and taking pictures of the specimens as a whole and close-up pictures of their leaves. The pictures are printed and pinned up on a wall so they can be studied. She asks the students to look carefully at the leaves and classify them. They use the interactive whiteboard to display and explain their categories, moving the pictures around and talking about them. Some of the categories are "leaves that look like hands in gloves," "leaves come in sets along the sides of twigs," and "oval leaves." The students agree on those categories and reorganize the pictures to display them.

Professional Development Commentary

The companionship between Ginny and Traci is very important at this stage. Both notice that the students tend to rush through the tasks and use single attributes (such as obvious differences in color) to speed the process and don't take the time to use multiple attributes (such as color and size). They both have to slow the students down, have them look again at the samples, and learn that understanding is the goal, not just getting through a task.

In Ginny's class, she leads the students to examine the pictures of the plants, bushes, and trees and classify them, using the general categories and the attributes of the leaves to build more categories, again reporting and sharing by moving the pictures around on the whiteboard.

Gradually, they work out a terminology for the categories that most can agree on: tall trees with glove-like leaves, tall trees with oval leaves, and so on, and they reorganize the pictures to reflect the new categories.

Professional Development Commentary

Traci has a friend who teaches a botany course in the high school, and she asks him to visit Ginny's classroom and offer comments. He does so, is impressed, and also suggests that she and Traci check out www.knowplants.org, www.nsta.org, and www.exploratorium.edu.

A few days later, Ginny displays *knowplants.org* on the interactive whiteboard and leads the students to study the lists of databases and select ones that might provide descriptive information about vegetation in their area. She adds the link to *knowplants.org* to their Webpage, and, through it, students have access to more than 100 other databases. Teams are organized to search specific bases and particular species. Categories are redeveloped and named, such as "bushes that have flowers." Working in pairs, the students build PowerPoint presentations of categories they have generated, describing the items in the categories. They create a "virtual plant walk" and share it with other classes and with their parents.

Some students suggest that they label many of the things they have studied in their neighborhood with their colloquial and scientific names. Ginny leads them to the town council for approval. Their next discussion is over how much information to include on the labels. Providing just the names doesn't seem enough.

REFLECTING ON INDUCTIVE AND INQUIRY TEACHING

In the previous scenario, collecting information about the domain (local vegetation) being explored and categorizing the information (trees, bushes, types of leaves, plant structure, and so on) drives the unit. Students build knowledge and social skills as they generate questions and learn to work together productively. Digital pictures and displays support the categorization and clarification of attributes, and the Web-based data sources bring additional information from specialists into the inquiry. Being good citizens in the larger community also found its way into the process. Ginny and Traci are working on assessment tasks that can be used with investigation-oriented units in which the content emerges rather than being a set piece; they feel they are making progress but have much to learn.

Building concepts enables Ginny's students to manage information, retain it, and use it. There is a high probability that building concepts is the foundation for the 21st-century skills, for most higher-order thinking skills, and, probably, for most types of intelligence (see Joyce & Calhoun, 2012; Joyce, Weil, & Calhoun, 2009). The basic inductive, concept-building model can be used from nursery school through doctoral study, and the skills built are useful in almost every workplace setting.

We have attempted to use the scenario as a simple illustration of what is possible in most every setting. Although the example concerned only two teachers, it could have been a grade-level team or whole faculty learning together and modeling learning for their students.

AT THE CROSSROADS

If educational professionals do not take charge of the incorporation of technology, there is the frightening prospect that entrepreneurs will do so, and the result will be a desert of online courses that do not realize the promise of ICT to create a better education for all. Already many states are accrediting "cyber schools" and their courses. Already universities are offering to certify teachers through Internet offerings. An incredibly bleak prospect is possible unless we support teachers at every grade level in creating courses that combine face-to-face benefits with the new global digital libraries and the opportunities for distance communication. In many schools PLCs are floundering; principals struggle to provide quality leadership in curriculum and instruction; and school and literacy coaches do not have the inductive and inquiry approaches in their repertoires. Let us change this and create a healthier learning organization.

A focus on the development of hybrid courses can help with both the incorporation of ICT and the implementation of the new core curricula. Development can begin with building leadership teams or with the PLCs, as in the case of Ginny and Traci, who make a natural peer-coaching team. The work can be organized at the school level or at the district level.

We can build a professional development system that will transform the profession of education and simultaneously elevate student learning. We can capitalize on the ICT revolution and develop a high-quality delivery dimension of a pervasive professional development system in every school—if only we choose to do so.

QUESTIONS FOR DISCUSSION

1. How does your school or organization support continued learning by its members as individuals, small groups, and faculties? What structures support or could support

the creation of a pervasive professional development system, or, as Schaefer put it so eloquently, the development of the "school as a center of inquiry"?

2. How much inductive and inquiry teaching and learning is occurring in your classroom, school, or district? What data are you using as evidence? How is ICT incorporated into classroom learning experiences and into professional development inquiries?

3. What are the advantages and obstacles to overcome in placing a teacher center in your school(s)?

ACKNOWLEDGMENTS

This chapter rests on a base of research and concepts reported in *Realizing the Promise of 21st-Century Education* (Joyce & Calhoun, 2012), and *Models of Teaching*, 9th edition (Joyce & Calhoun, 2013). We thank Stephanie Hirsh and Shirley Hord of Learning Forward for taking the time to look over the manuscript and offer helpful suggestions.

We invite readers to share their impressions and interpretations of this chapter. We are particularly interested in your views on the idea of the school as a center of inquiry, the idea of a professional learning center in every school, and the use of distance education and digital media as part of the professional development delivery system. Feel free to contact us at brucejoyce40@gmail.com or efcphoenix@aol.com.

REFERENCES

Allington, R. L. (2009). *What really matters in response to intervention: Research-based designs.* Boston: Pearson.

Collins, A., & Halverson, R. (2009). *Rethinking education in the age of technology: The digital revolution and schooling in America.* New York: Teachers College Press.

Fixsen, D. L., Naoom, S. F., Blase, K. A., Friedman, R. M., & Wallace, F. (2005). *Implementation research: A synthesis of the literature.* Tampa: University of South Florida, Louis de la Parte Florida Mental Health Institute, National Implementation Research Network (FMHI Publication #231). Available at *http://ctndisseminationlibrary.org/PDF/nirnmonograph.pdf*

Fullan, M., & Pomfret, A. (1977). Research on curriculum and instruction implementation. *Review of Educational Research, 47*(2), 335–397.

Joyce, B., & Calhoun, E. (2010). *Models of professional development: A celebration of educators.* Thousand Oaks, CA: Corwin Press.

Joyce, B., & Calhoun, E. (2012). *Realizing the promise of 21st century education: An owner's manual.* Thousand Oaks, CA: Corwin Press.

Joyce, B., & Calhoun, E. (2013). *Models of teaching* (9th ed.). Boston: Pearson.

Joyce, B., & Showers, B. (2002). *Student achievement through staff development* (3rd ed.). Alexandria, VA: Association for Supervision and Curriculum Development.

Joyce, B., Weil, M., & Calhoun, E. (2009). *Models of teaching* (8th ed.). Boston: Pearson.

Kay, K. (2010). 21st century skills: Why they matter; what they are; and how we got there. In J. Bellanca & R. Brandt (Eds.), *21st century skills: Rethinking how students learn* (pp. xiii–xxi). Bloomington, IN: Solution Tree Press.

Partnership for 21st Century Skills, State Educational Technology Directors Association, & International Society for Technology in Education. (2007). Maximizing the impact:

The pivotal role of technology in a 21st century education system. Retrieved from *www.p21.org/documents/p21setdaistepaper.pdf*.

Schaefer, R. (1967). *The school as a center of inquiry*. New York: Harper & Row.

Wei, R. C., Darling-Hammond, L., & Adamson, F. (2010). *Professional development in the United States: Trends and challenges*. Dallas, TX: National Council for Staff Development. Retrieved from *www.nsdc.org/news/NSDCstudytechnicalreport2010.pdf*.

Zhao, Y. (2009). *Catching up or leading the way: American education in the age of globalization*. Alexandria, VA: Association for Supervision and Curriculum Development.

APPENDIX 21.1. RESOURCES

Curriculum Standards Documents

When discussing the challenges of implementing the new curricula, these documents contain much of the content the authors have in mind.

Achieve, Inc. (2013). *Next generation science standards*. Washington, DC: Author. Retrieved from *www.achieve.org/next-generation-science-standards*.

National Council for the Social Studies. (2010). *National curriculum standards for social studies: A framework for teaching, learning, and assessment*. Silver Spring, MD: Author. (See also *www.socialstudies.org/standards/introduction*)

National Governors Association Center for Best Practices and Council of Chief State School Officers. (2010a). *Common Core State Standards for English language arts and literacy in history/social studies, science, and technical subjects*. Washington, DC: Authors. Retrieved from *www.corestandards.org/assets/CCSSI_ELA%20Standards.pdf*.

National Governors Association Center for Best Practices and Council of Chief State School Officers. (2010b). *Common Core State Standards for English language arts and literacy in history/social studies, science, and technical subjects: Appendix A: Research supporting key elements of the standards and glossary of key terms*. Washington, DC: Authors. Retrieved from *www.corestandards.org/assets/Appendix_A.pdf*.

National Governors Association Center for Best Practices and Council of Chief State School Officers. (2010c). *Common Core State Standards for English language arts and literacy in history/social studies, science, and technical subjects: Appendix B: Text exemplars and sample performance tasks*. Washington, DC: Authors. Retrieved from *www.corestandards.org/assets/Appendix_B.pdf*.

National Governors Association Center for Best Practices and Council of Chief State School Officers. (2010d). *Common Core State Standards for English language arts and literacy in history/social studies, science, and technical subjects: Appendix C: Samples of student writing*. Washington, DC: Authors. Retrieved from *www.corestandards.org/assets/Appendix_C.pdf*.

National Governors Association Center for Best Practices and Council of Chief State School Officers. (2010e). *Common Core State Standards for mathematics*. Washington, DC: Authors. Retrieved from *www.corestandards.org/assets/CCSSI_Math%Standards.pdf*.

National Research Council. (2012). *A framework for K–12 science education: Practices, crosscutting ideas, and core ideas*. Washington, DC: National Academies Press. Retrieved from *www.nap.edu/catalog*.

National and International Assessments of Student Progress

Some of the sources and/or documents we look to regularly and had in mind in relation to comparative statements made about student performance.

Martin, M. O., Mullis, I. V. S., Foy, P., in collaboration with Olson, J. F., Erberber, E., Preuschoff, C., & Galia, J. (2008). *TIMSS 2007 international science report: Findings from IEA's Trends in International Mathematics and Science Study at the fourth and eighth grades*. Chestnut Hill, MA: TIMSS & PIRLS International Study Center, Boston College. Available from *http://timss.bc.edu/timss2007/intl_reports.html*.

National Center for Education Statistics. (2011). *The Nation's Report Card: Reading 2011* (NCES 2012-457). Washington, DC: U.S. Department of Education, Institute of Education Sciences. Available from *http://nces.ed.gov/nationsreportcard.pdf/main2011/2012457.pdf*.

Organisation for Economic Cooperation and Development. (2009). *OECD programme for international student assessment (PISA) 2009 results*. Retrieved from *www.oecd.org/edu/pisa/2009*. (The OECD library is a rich source for studying what 15-year-olds across countries have acquired academically: *www.oecd-ilibrary.org/education/pisa_19963777*.)

PISA 2006: Science competencies for tomorrow's world. (2007). *OECD briefing note for the United States*. Retrieved from *www.oecd.org/dataoecd/16/28/39722597.pdf*.

Further Reading

In terms of our purpose, we wish to connect readers to a diverse body of relevant literature. Here we suggest several additional sources useful for inquiring into teaching and its effects on student learning and into professional development and technology use in the schools.

Almy, M. (1970). *Logical thinking in the second grade*. New York: Teachers College Press.

Anderson, R., Kahl, S., Glass, G., Smith M., & Malone, M. (1982). *Science meta-analysis project*. Boulder: University of Colorado, Laboratory for Research in Science and Mathematics Education.

Anderson, R. D. (1983). A consolidation and appraisal of science meta-analyses. *Journal of Research in Science Teaching, 20*(5), 497–509.

Ball, S., & Bogatz, G. A. (1970). *The first year of* Sesame Street. Princeton, NJ: Educational Testing Service.

Barton, P. E., & Coley, R. J. (2010). *Parsing the achievement gap: II*. Princeton, NJ: Educational Testing Service. Retrieved from *www.ets.org/Media/Research/pdf/PICPARSINGII.pdf*.

Baumert, J., Kunter, M., Blum, W., Brunner, M., Voss, T., Jordan, W., et al. (2010). Teacher's mathematical knowledge, cognitive activation in the classroom, and student progress. *American Educational Research Journal, 47*(1), 97–132.

Bennett, L. L., & Berson, M. J. (2007). *Digital age: Technology-based K–12 lesson plans for social studies*. Silver Spring, MD: National Council for the Social Studies.

Bloom, B. S. (1984). The 2 sigma problem: The search for group instruction as effective as one-to-one tutoring. *Educational Researcher, 13*, 4–16.

Bonk, C. J. (2009). *The world is open: How web technology is revolutionizing education*. San Francisco: Jossey-Bass.

Bredderman, T. (1983). Effects of activity-based elementary science on student outcomes: A quantitative synthesis. *Review of Educational Research, 53*(4), 499–518.

Burns, M. (2011). *Distance education for teacher training: Modes, models, and methods.* Washington, DC: Educational Development Center. Retrieved from *http://idd.edc.org/ sites/idd.edc.org/files/Distance%20Education%20for%20Teacher%20Training%20 by%20Mary%20Burns%20EDC.pdf.*

Calhoun, E. F. (1994). *How to use action research in the self-renewing school.* Alexandria, VA: Association for Supervision and Curriculum Development.

Calhoun, E. F. (2004). *Using data to assess your reading program.* Alexandria, VA: Association for Supervision and Curriculum Development.

Dewey, J. (1916). *Democracy and education.* New York: Macmillan.

Dewey, J. (1937). *Experience and education.* New York: Macmillan.

Eysink, T., de Jong, T., Gerthold, K., Kolloffel, B., Opfermann, M., & Wouters, P. (2009). Learning performance in multimedia learning arrangements: An analysis across instructional approaches. *American Educational Research Journal, 46*(4), 1107–1149.

Fuchs, L., Fuchs, D., Hamlett, C., & Karns, K. (1998). High-achieving students' interactions and performance on complex mathematical tasks as a function of homogeneous and heterogeneous pairings. *American Educational Research Journal, 35*(2), 227–267.

Gagné, R., & White, R. (1978). Memory structures and learning outcomes. *Review of Educational Research, 48*(2), 137–222.

Goode, J., Holme, J. J., & Nao, K. (2008). *Stuck in the shallow end: Education, race, and computing.* Cambridge, MA: MIT Press.

Hirsh, S. (2013). Six "E" words essential to student success. Retrieved from *http://blogs. edweek.org/edweek/learning_forwards_pd_watch/2013/04/six_e_words_essential_ to_student_success.html.*

Hord, S. M., & Sommers, W. A. (2007). *Leading professional learning communities: Voices from research and practice.* Thousand Oaks, CA: Corwin Press.

International Reading Association's Literacy Leadership for Urban Teacher Education Commission. (2010). *Improving teacher preparation and development for promoting literacy achievement in high poverty urban schools: A systemic approach.* Newark, DE: International Reading Association. Retrieved from *www.reading.org/Libraries/ resources/LLUTE_WhitePaper_Final.pdf.*

Jacob, B. A. (2007). The challenges of staffing urban schools with effective teachers. *The Future of Children, 17*(1), 129–153. [Special Issue: Excellence in the Classroom: Policies to Improve the Teacher Workforce.] Retrieved from *http://futureofchildren.org/ futureofchildren/publications/docs/17_01_07.pdf.*

Johnson, D. W., & Johnson, R. T. (2010). An educational psychology success story: Social interdependence theory and cooperative learning. *Educational Researcher, 38*(5), 365–379.

Joyce, B., Calhoun, E., Jutras, J., & Newlove, K. (2006). *Scaling up: The results of a literacy curriculum implemented in an entire education authority of 53 schools.* Paper presented at the annual meeting of the Asian Pacific Educational Research Association, Hong Kong.

Killion, J. (2012). *Meet the promise of content standards: Professional learning required.* Oxford, OH: Learning Forward.

Klauer, K., & Phye, G. (2008). Inductive reasoning: A training approach. *Review of Educational Research, 78*(1), 85–123.

Knapp, P. (1995). *Teaching for meaning in high-poverty classrooms.* New York: Teachers College Press.

Knight, J. (2011). *Unmistakable impact: A partnership approach for dramatically improving instruction*. Thousand Oaks, CA: Corwin Press.

Learning Forward. (n.d.). Definition of professional development. Retrieved from *http:// learningforward.org/who-we-are/professional-learning-definition*.

Lee, J., Grigg, W., & Donahue, P. (2007). *The nation's report card: Reading 2007* (NCES 2007–496). Washington, DC: U.S. Department of Education, Institute of Education Sciences, National Center for Education Statistics. Retrieved from *http://nces.ed.gov/ nationsreportcard/pdf/main2007/2007496.pdf*.

Martin, W., Strother, S., Beglau, M., Bates, L., Reitzes, T., & McMillan Culp, K. (2010). Connecting instructional technology professional development to teacher and student outcomes. *Journal of Research on Technology in Education, 43*(1), 53–74.

McGill-Franzen, A., & Goatley, V. (2001). Title I and special education: Support for children who struggle to learn to read. In S. B. Neuman & D. K. Dickinson (Eds.), *Handbook of early literacy research* (Vol. 1, pp. 471–483). New York: Guilford Press.

Minner, D., Levy, A., & Century, J. (2009). Inquiry-based science instruction: What is it and does it matter? Results from a research synthesis, years 1984–2002. *Journal of Research in Science Teaching, 47*(4), 474–496.

Mouza, C. (2009). Does research-based professional development make a difference?: A longitudinal investigation of teacher learning in technology integration. *Teachers College Record, 111*(5), 1195–1241.

Novak, J., & Musanda, D. (1991). A twelve-year longitudinal study of science concept learning. *American Educational Research Journal, 28*(1), 117–153.

Organisation for Economic Cooperation and Development. (2009). OECD programme for international student assessment (PISA) 2009 results. Retrieved from *www.oecd.org/ edu/pisa/2009*.

Pasnic, S., Bates, L. Brunner, C., Cervantes, F., Hupert, N., Schindel, J., et al. (2010). *Ready to learn summative evaluation*. New York: Center for Children and Technology.

Peske, H. G., & Haycock, K. (2006). *Teaching inequality: How poor and minority students are shortchanged on teacher quality: A report and recommendations by the Education Trust*. Washington, DC: Education Trust. Retrieved from *www.edtrust.org/sites/ edtrust.org/files/publications/files/TQReportJune2006.pdf*.

Prensky, M. (2010). *Teaching digital natives: Partnering for real learning*. Thousand Oaks, CA: Corwin Press.

Puma, M., Karweit, N., Price, C., Riciutti, A., Thompson, W., & Vaden-Kiernan, M. (1997). *Prospects: Final report on student outcomes*. Washington, DC: U.S. Department of Education, Office of Planning and Evaluation Services.

Quellmatz, E. S. (2010). Assessing new technological literacies. In F. Scheuermann & F. Pedró (Eds.), *Assessing the effects of ICT in education: Indicators, criteria and benchmarks for international comparisons* (pp. 121–142). Paris: OECD.

Rao, K., Eady, M., & Edelen-Smith, P. (2011). Creating virtual classrooms for rural and remote communities. *Phi Delta Kappan, 92*(6), 22–27.

Scherer, M. (2011). Transforming education with technology: A conversation with Karen Cator. *Educational Leadership, 68*(5), 16–21.

Shymansky, J. A., Kyle, W. C, & Alport, J. M. (1983). The effects of new science curricula on student performance. *Journal of Research in Science Teaching, 20*(5), 387–404.

Sitzmann, T., Kraiger, K., Stewart, D., & Wisher R. (2006). The comparative effectiveness of web-based and classroom instruction: A meta-analysis. *Personnel Psychology, 59*(3), 623–664.

Stevens, R., & Slavin, R. (1995) The cooperative elementary school: Effects on students' achievement, attitudes, and social relations. *American Educational Research Journal*, 32(2), 321–351.

Tucker, M. (2011). *Standing on the shoulders of giants: An American agenda for education reform*. Washington, DC: National Center on Education and the Economy. Retrieved from *www.ncee.org/wp-content/uploads/2011/05/Standing-on-the-Shoulders-of-Giants-An-American-Agenda-for-Education-Reform.pdf*.

U.S. Department of Education, Office of Educational Technology. (2010). *Transforming American education: Learning powered by technology*. Washington, DC: Author. Retrieved from *www.ed.gov/sites/default/files/NETP-2010-final-report.pdf*.

U.S. Department of Education, Office of Planning, Evaluation, and Policy Development. (2010). *Evaluation of evidence-based practices in on-line learning*. Washington, DC: Author.

Wagner, T. (2008). *The global achievement gap: Why even our best schools don't teach the new survival skills our children need—and what we can do about it*. New York: Basic Books.

Wilkinson, L. C., Morrow, L. M., & Chou, V. (2008). Overview of policy, research, and sociocultural issues affecting the preparation of teachers of reading for urban settings. In L. C. Wilkinson, L. M. Morrow, & V. Chou (Eds.), *Improving literacy achievement in urban schools: Critical elements in teacher preparation* (pp. 1–11). Newark, DE: International Reading Association.

Windschitl, M., & Sahl, K. (2002). Tracing teachers' use of technology in a laptop computer school: The interplay of teacher beliefs, social dynamics, and institutional culture. *American Educational Research Journal*, 39(1), 165–205.

Zhao, Y., & Frank, K. A. (2003). Factors affecting technology uses in schools: An ecological perspective. *American Educational Research Journal*, 40(4), 807–840.

CHAPTER 22

Supporting Professional Growth through External Resources

DIANA J. QUATROCHE
KATHRYN L. BAUSERMAN
LEAH NELLIS

- Effective professional development is instructive, reflective, active, collaborative, and substantive.
- Schools provide their staff members with professional learning opportunities through a variety of delivery methods and external resources that meet local needs and requirements.
- The effective use of external resources to provide professional learning requires intentionality, sustainability, consistency, evaluation, and a focus on the corresponding desired outcomes for school staff members.
- Schools can use strategies to maximize external resources to meet critical professional development needs.

Learning Forward, formerly known as the National Staff Development Council, defines professional development as a comprehensive, sustained, and intensive approach to improving teachers' and principals' effectiveness in raising student achievement (Darling-Hammond, Wei, Andree, Richardson, & Orphanos, 2009). The professional development process as outlined in the definition

may be supported by activities such as courses, workshops, institutes, networks, and conferences that: (1) . . . address the learning goals and objectives established for professional development by educators at the school level; (2) advance ongoing school-based professional development; and (3) are provided by for-profit and nonprofit entities outside the school such as universities, education service

431

agencies, technical assistance providers, networks of content-area specialists, and other education organizations and associations. (Learning Forward, 2013, p. 1)

This definition, which is in the reauthorized version of No Child Left Behind (NCLB), also includes sustainability, collaboration, and job-embedded coaching.

The importance of leadership in the planning and design of professional learning opportunities for educators and specialized instructional support personnel, such as interventionists, counselors, school psychologists, and others, has been identified as a critical factor (Wei, Darling-Hammond, & Adamson, 2010). Having a comprehensive professional development plan is essential for designing models of professional learning that are ongoing and that lead to increased educator and staff effectiveness, as well as positive student outcomes. The focus of the plan should be informed by a number of factors, including local improvement initiatives, staff needs assessment and input, school and student data, and identified staff development needs. In this chapter we discuss (1) principles and traits of effective professional development, (2) factors that influence districts' needs to use external resources, (3) considerations for the use of external resources for professional development, and (4) strategies for maximizing the value of external resources for professional development.

TRAITS AND GENERAL PRINCIPLES OF EFFECTIVE PROFESSIONAL DEVELOPMENT

The view of professional development as a 2-hour "make-it-and take-it" workshop is a thing of the past. Effective professional development requires a much deeper investment in time and energy, as teachers reflect on their pedagogy and their instructional practice. Donnelly and colleagues (2005) speak of a process of transformative professional development that compels teachers to examine their teaching philosophy and challenge it. Teachers' learning can take place in their own classrooms, in the school community, and through professional development initiatives (Borko, 2004). Looking for commonalities in the research, we found the following five traits that describe effective professional development:

1. Professional development is instructive. It supports teachers as they gain content knowledge and acquire instructional strategies (Guskey, 2003; Long, 2012). Teachers need to build their knowledge base, too (Donnelly et al., 2005). In addition, teachers should do additional independent research to keep abreast of the latest research in their respective fields (Kedzior, 2004).

2. Professional development is reflective. Teachers need to reflect deeply, and they need to reflect over time (Donnelly et al., 2005). They also should reflect on theory-based practice (Brooke, Coyle, & Walden, 2005; Kedzior, 2004).

3. Professional development is active. Teachers are thinkers and intellectuals. They should be engaged in the learning process (Donnelly et al., 2005). Teachers

need to learn many instructional strategies so they have a large repertoire from which to choose (Darling-Hammond, 2000). Classroom action research projects are another important step in helping teachers become actively engaged in their own professional development (Kedzior, 2004).

4. Professional development is collaborative. It goes beyond the classroom and should focus on school improvement and/or district improvement (Donnelly et al., 2005; Guskey, 2003; Long, 2012). Teachers should be engaged in study groups to challenge themselves and expand their thinking (Hurd & Licciardo-Musso, 2005; Mahn, McMann & Musanti, 2005).

5. Professional development is substantive. It should be extensive and continuous. There should be significant hours from a minimum of 6, and for greater impact as many as 35 or more (Kedzior, 2004; Long, 2012).

When professional development is instructive, reflective, active, collaborative, and substantive, it will likely be more effective. This means that teachers and school staff are more highly qualified and, therefore, will have a positive impact on student learning.

Newer methods for the effective delivery of professional development may include coaching, webinars and seminars, mentoring, use of experts in the form of consultants, attendance at conferences, and participation in online networks (Darensburg, 2010). In the past professional development usually consisted of a staff development day that included an "expert" who delivered information related to curriculum or some other area a school district decided was of interest (Darensburg, 2010). However, rarely was the 1-day staff development presentation or workshop implemented in the classroom.

In one study Yamagata-Lynch and Haudenschild (2008) surveyed teachers regarding their preferred method for receiving professional development. They found that teachers preferred professional development delivered by their own schools because it was situated and met immediate classroom needs. The "overall finding...indicates that the delivery format of a professional development program does not matter in terms of teacher preparation regarding the success or failure of the program. What matters is how the identified barriers and aids of professional growth in professional development interact with the work-related activities of individual teachers" (pp. 99–100). Districts need to make efforts to develop teacher leaders who can lead professional development at the school level (Marrongelle, Sztajn, & Smith, 2013). One concern is that the intent of the professional development program may be compromised when it is adapted to the needs and conditions of a specific school (Borko, 2004).

Practice-based professional development has also been shown to be effective in improving student learning (Harris et al., 2012). Practice-based professional development is based on the needs of teachers, including content and pedagogy. It also includes modeling and supported practice with ongoing observation and support, much like coaching. Oftentimes, teachers have a need to become more knowledgeable and want strategies that can be easily implemented (Kragler, Martin, &

Kroeger, 2008). They need congruent messages, time to reflect, and lots of support for new information to become part of their practice.

We now know more about how adults learn and the importance of linking theory to practice. We also recognize the importance of coaching in helping teachers implement new practices in the classroom. Newer methods of delivery of professional development can involve collaboration, action research, and the elements of coaching, which include feedback and discussion or other types of follow-up activities. Some themes that emerged from principal interviews is that professional development needs to be ongoing, collaborative, data-driven, interest-driven, and interactive (Lutrick & Szabo, 2012).

Professional development delivered by technology offers some promise for districts that may not have access to other forms of delivery. A study by Fisher, Schumaker, Culbertson, and Deshler (2010) demonstrated that there was no difference in the results for teachers enrolled in a virtual workshop and teachers enrolled in an actual face-to-face workshop. The researchers measured teacher satisfaction, teacher knowledge, and student achievement. A follow-up study showed that computerized programs have the potential for changing teacher behavior but can also improve student outcomes and student satisfaction.

Online professional development provides convenience as there is no need to travel or to arrange for child care. It can also be more cost-effective. Some of the pluses for this type of professional development are that it can provide new ideas for instruction, have direct application to classroom instruction, and lead to the integration of course technology tools into teaching practice (Holmes, Signer, & MacLeod, 2010). A minus is that there need to be multiple forms of interaction included in the online format for it to be successful. Social presence and teacher presence are very important. Although there needs to be more research regarding the use of emerging technologies for professional development, it does offer the advantage of using nonlocal resources and aligning with teacher schedules (Marrongelle et al., 2013).

A general consideration for good professional development is how to deliver consistent messages when using various resources. How will all of the various sources be congruent, and what do we mean by effective professional development?

UTILIZING EXTERNAL RESOURCES FOR PROFESSIONAL DEVELOPMENT

External resources for professional development may include, but are not limited to, grants; state department of education websites, resources, and consultants; webcasts; professional organizations and conferences; commercial corporations; educational programs at museums; universities; and school consortiums. There are many factors that influence a district's need and decision to use external resources. Professional development from external sources may be utilized when there is a lack of expertise about a specific topic on the part of school district personnel. In such situations, a district may use Web-based resources, consultants, or professional conferences to increase the knowledge and skill of several or a few staff members who can subsequently train others. External resources may also be utilized when a district experiences staff turnover and needs to provide new staff training in a specific area. Webcasts, webinars, and resources on professional association or department of education websites can be accessed to prepare new staff members in a content area in which other staff members have already been trained. School districts may also identify a professional development-related need when the demographics of the student population change and faculty and staff need training to increase knowledge and skills to meet students' needs. External resources may be especially helpful in such situations when there is limited local expertise or experience with the student population.

External resources may also be called on to build district-level capacity to implement a new initiative or innovative program. Preparing a large number of educators, administrators, and specialized staff for such a change in practice often requires ongoing and varied professional development opportunities (Fixsen, Naoom, Blase, Friedman, & Wallace, 2005). Sending a large number of staff members to conferences or trainings may be cost-prohibitive in terms of registration fees, travel expenses, and substitutes. Thus using external resources such as a consultant to provide in-district training may be the most efficient and effective way to deliver the needed professional development.

Districts may also find themselves in the position of having to provide professional development to address a federal or state requirement or mandate. Such situations occur when there are identified performance or compliance issues that are determined to be related to staff training and practices. The required corrective action may specify the topics and/or providers for the needed professional development or technical assistance. When professional development is provided in this context, it is important for district leadership to connect the learning to district practices, initiatives, and needs so that faculty and staff understand the purpose for the professional development and are open to learning and applying the information discussed.

Utilizing external resources to address professional learning needs can be a highly effective and efficient strategy. However, it is important that district leadership is strategic about how external resources and sources supplement other forms of professional learning. Identifying the specific focus and purpose for which external resources are needed is critical. For example, if a topic or focus area is one for which internal capacity and expertise are needed, then external resources might be used to train a few key staff members who will facilitate and lead professional learning experiences for colleagues. However, if professional development is needed to update or provide technical assistance on a very specific practice or strategy, then using a Web-based module from a professional association during a staff meeting might be appropriate. Aligning the external professional development with the goal or purpose for which it is being utilized is critical for ensuring congruence and fit. Integrating external resources and sources of professional development can be challenging and requires planning, intentionality, coordination, and monitoring to ensure that the focus and outcomes are in alignment with school and staff needs.

CONSIDERATIONS WHEN UTILIZING EXTERNAL SOURCES FOR PROFESSIONAL DEVELOPMENT

Including external resources and sources as part of a comprehensive approach to professional learning can be effective but does require careful planning, intentionality, and leadership at the school/district level. Characteristics of effective professional development, as discussed previously in this volume by Long (Chapter 2), Mraz and Kissel (Chapter 9), Fisher and Frey (Chapter 11), and Firestone and Mangin (Chapter 17), and again in this chapter, also apply to professional development provided through external sources. However, utilizing external resources to provide professional development also presents unique issues and challenges. Following are four key issues that should be considered and addressed to maximize the impact and value of professional development provided by external resources.

Alignment with State Regulations and District Initiatives

Professional development that aligns with local initiatives and school improvement efforts has a much greater likelihood of being perceived as relevant to those participating and having an impact on practices (Darling-Hammond et al., 2009). When educators and specialized instructional support personnel feel a disconnect between what they are being asked or required to do on a daily basis and what is focused on in professional development activities, the potential impact of the activity is diminished. The impact of the professional development can even be negative if the activity encourages practices or actions that are inconsistent with local or state requirements and regulations.

Utilizing external resources and sources of professional development introduces, and potentially increases, the possibility that the message and recommended practice or strategy will be different from those that are being emphasized in the school or district. It is essential that district-level leadership ensures that the content of the professional development is in alignment with state regulations and district initiatives.

Consistency of Message and Recommended Practices

When external sources and resources are used as part of an overall professional development plan, it is important that the message and recommended practices are consistent with those being taught, modeled, and encouraged through other professional learning opportunities and daily work in the school. Furthermore, it is important that all groups of staff members (e.g., teachers, administrators, specialized support personnel such as counselors, school psychologists, and interventionists) are included in the professional development plan and receive professional development that emphasizes similar messages and practices. Too often the professional development plan addresses teacher professional development while other groups are left to obtain learning opportunities as individuals or subgroups. When this occurs, the potential for selecting external resources/sources is very high, and, if not well coordinated with the overall professional development plan, it brings the high likelihood of inconsistency of message and recommended practices. Thus it is essential that district leadership design comprehensive professional development plans for all staff members and that any external professional development resources are selected based on focus, purpose, structure, and fit with the district's needs and initiatives.

Planning for Sustainability

When part of a larger professional development plan and/or followed up with discussion, reflection, modeling, and feedback, professional development can have a significant impact on teacher practice and student achievement (Loucks-Horsley, Hewson, Love, & Stiles, 1998; Steiner, 2004). As stated previously in this chapter, professional development must be an ongoing initiative for schools because of the many changes taking place in terms of expectations for teachers to deliver quality instruction and for students to demonstrate high levels of knowledge and skills.

As Darensburg (2010) points out, teachers and specialized instructional support personnel are currently faced with an increasingly diverse population of students. In addition, technology is changing rapidly, and schools are now beginning to expect teachers to appropriately and effectively integrate this new technology into the classroom. Most states have adopted the rigorous new Common Core State Standards and expect schools and students to meet the goals included in the standards. Finally, the many school reform efforts and accountability initiatives have linked teacher evaluation to student achievement.

There are many challenges to sustaining professional development partnerships and initiatives. However, Bier, Foster, Bellamy, and Clark (2008) offer several principles to keep in mind that can help to foster sustainability. One principle is that basic agreements regarding the partnership need to be formed and sustained. All parties need to ensure that the various priorities of the partners and the commitment to the partnership can be mutually supportive. The partnership should be organized to support the expanded objectives of the partnership.

School principals play an essential and unique role in sustaining such partnerships. They are responsible for establishing and maintaining the structure of the partnership by involving individuals who represent both the school and the external partner. Additionally, the principal utilizes leadership skills to facilitate collaboration, coaching, discussion, and reflection among members of the partnership, as well as among school staff, to ensure optimal use of the professional development services being provided.

For sustainability of professional development to take place, districts must plan for duration of a project (Garet, Porter, Desimone, Burman, & Yoon, 2001). Teachers need time to try out new things in their classrooms, get feedback, and then engage in in-depth reflective discussions. New practices can be sustained over time when the focus of the professional development is a group of teachers from the same school.

In planning for sustainability, schools can opt for a train-the-trainer model. For example, the district may send a core group of teachers or staff members for professional development related to a schoolwide initiative. This core group, after their initial training, in turn becomes the professional development team for the district. They then plan, provide, and follow up with district teachers in implementing the required or desired model of instruction. The fact that the professional development is being delivered onsite by individuals who have a unique perspective on the school environment can help to ensure sustainability.

An example of the train-the-trainer model is Reading Recovery. In the Reading Recovery model, a district chooses someone who will be the Reading Recovery leader for the district. The leader receives training at a Reading Recovery training site, and the leader comes back to the district and trains the Reading Recovery teachers for the district. The Reading Recovery teachers are coached after the implementation of initial training. To ensure sustainability, the Reading Recovery teachers attend periodic follow-up meetings, the purpose of which is to maintain fidelity of the model.

Another option for sustainability is the use of coaching, which is now present in schools as a way to help teachers implement new materials, strategies, and practices. When Mouza (2009) investigated whether teachers could change their practice after initial learning, one component that was found to enable teachers to learn and change over time was the support of colleagues and administrators. Collaborative relationships in which teachers could practice their craft, reflect, and receive feedback helped to support sustainability.

Study groups, mentoring, and coaching are all described as reform types of professional development by Garet and colleagues (2001) and are supported when they take place during the regular school day during the process of classroom instruction or during teacher planning time, along with continuing support.

Evaluating the Effectiveness of Professional Development

Most professional development activities need an evaluation plan that demonstrates whether the goals and objectives have been met. The evaluation plan also needs to consider whether the professional development has included the five traits of effective professional development identified earlier in this chapter. Are the professional development activities instructive, reflective, active, collaborative, and substantive?

There are several reasons why an evaluation plan is necessary. First, an evaluation plan provides a measure of accountability. Second, it shows what has been accomplished in reference to the goals and objectives. Well-planned professional development activities with well-articulated goals should have some positive outcomes or results that demonstrate that the activities reached or partially reached several or most of the intended goals and objectives. Results can be used to inform future professional development initiatives.

The first step in the process of creating an evaluation plan is to determine who will do the evaluation (Mason, 2005). Most projects choose either an external or an internal evaluator. The evaluator should be involved in writing the evaluation plan and be responsible for planning the process of evaluating the professional development activity to make sure the design fits the goals and that the goals can be measured. The evaluator selected to implement the evaluation should have experience with collecting and analyzing various forms of data.

The next step in the process is to determine what kinds of evaluation tools will help measure the results of the activities (Mason, 2005). There are many evaluation tools that can be used to help determine whether or not the goals have been reached. Pretests and posttests are basic tools to measure whether there was an impact on participants. These can be used to measure whether the content was instructive and/or substantive. Attitude surveys can be used to measure participants' feelings and reactions to activities, causing participants to be reflective about the professional development activities. Individual interviews and conversations with focus groups on collaborative aspects are other methods of gathering data about all five traits. Additionally, open-ended questionnaires are a means to gather data on each of the five traits. The questionnaire itself would be a means of reflection. Example questions to cover the other traits might look like this: "What did you learn as a participant that you can use in your work?" (instructive); "What could we do that would improve the activity?" (active); "What are some ways we could increase the collaboration with peers?" (collaborative); "How could we improve the substance of the project and make it more useful to you in your classroom?" (substantive). Having participants keep journals is a great way to ensure that they are reflective. Pictures, testimonials, and anecdotes are other means of gathering data. If possible, it is best to use a variety of methods to collect data. It is important to keep everything that is collected during the professional development activities, as these materials may provide additional means for evaluating the outcomes of the professional development project. Keep in mind how the project will be sustained, especially after any funding is gone, because funding agencies want to know that the impact of the project will be sustainable.

The timeline for evaluation is another consideration (Mason, 2005). What is the length of the training? When should the evaluations take place? Should there be a midpoint evaluation? Formative evaluation would occur during the timeline of professional development activities, usually at the midpoint. It would help inform activities and determine whether any changes in the process might be necessary. Formative evaluation methods are usually based on qualitative tools such as surveys and questionnaires. It is important that such instruments do not ask questions about items that cannot or will not be changed. The summative evaluation, also called outcome evaluation, is completed at the end of activities. Summative evaluations are used to determine program effectiveness and the impact of the professional development activities on participants and their practice. Some questions that can be answered with a summative evaluation are as follows: What did the professional development accomplish? Did this professional development meet its goals and objectives? If applicable, were the results statistically significant?

Final reports are usually required as a means of validating the expense and time spent on a professional development initiative. These reports may be more informal to meet district needs or more formal to meet the needs of outside support from resources such as granting agencies or university researchers. Running analyses and reporting on the evaluation results is the final step in the evaluation process (Mason, 2005). Analyses should be appropriate to the instruments being used. The final report should include a summary and a full report. Links between activities and outcomes or goals should be very clear. Charts and other graphic displays of results have high impact and help administrations understand those results. Negative results can have as much meaning as positive results. Other questions to consider in the final report include: Were there unexpected events that had an impact on the project? Could the results be replicated? Are there some obvious next steps in the initiative? In addition to writing the final report, other means of sharing results include follow-up meetings, project results meetings, and press releases. Presentations at faculty meetings, school assemblies, or groups with similar projects are also a means of sharing what was accomplished and any new knowledge that was gained. Finally, journal articles and conference presentations are other traditional ways to share the results. See Guskey (Chapter 23, this volume) for more information on evaluating the effectiveness of professional development.

STRATEGIES FOR MAXIMIZING THE VALUE OF EXTERNAL SOURCES OF PROFESSIONAL DEVELOPMENT

The following strategies reflect the five traits of effective professional development and may be helpful for utilizing external sources of professional development in a focused manner. Strategies do not align directly with one specific trait but instead address multiple traits so that efforts to support staff professional learning are efficient and ensure consistency of message.

- In order to ensure that the professional development is instructive and substantive, identify the specific content focus, purpose, and staff members for which external sources of professional development are needed. Use the professional development plan as an overall structure for identifying where external sources and resources are needed.

- When selecting external resources, make sure that the professional development design and structure is in alignment with district-identified focus and purpose. If the external resource will provide awareness about a topic or skill, make sure that other professional learning opportunities will support skill acquisition and application. Failure to do so will likely limit implementation and thus have little impact on student learning and outcomes.

- Interview external consultants or trainers before entering into a contractual arrangement. Open discussions with consultants can ensure that both the content and the format of the provided professional development will be in alignment with the needs and preferences of the school staff. Specifying the professional learning goals and objectives that the trainer is being asked to address is helpful in that it connects the activity to the larger professional development plan and guides the trainer's preparation and focus.

- Carefully review resources (e.g., webinars, DVDs, books, training kits) to ensure that the content is consistent with local initiatives and direction for improvement. Marketing materials often highlight key features, but a thorough review is needed to ensure that all of the content is in alignment with local practices.

- Provide external consultants or trainers with information that they need to ensure alignment and consistency of message. Local guidelines or procedural documents, previously provided professional development materials, district professional development plans, and so forth will help the external consultant understand the needs of the local district and schools and prepare learning activities that are instructive, reflective, and substantive.

- Ask to review an external consultant's presentation agenda, materials, and handouts in advance of the professional development session. Working collaboratively with an external professional development provider to prepare training materials will help to ensure an alignment with local initiatives, practices, and learning needs.

- Ensure that the external resource or source is appropriate for the purpose(s) for which it has been selected. For example, if staff will need ongoing support and coaching to implement a specific strategy, it is important to make sure that the external consultant has the capacity to deliver. If not, then other external resources might need to be explored.

- If multiple external resources/sources are being used, ensure consistency of message across materials. This prevents confusion, a lack of understanding, and possibly negative impact on implementation.

- Collaborative professional development is important; however, if other staff members are responsible or permitted to select external resources for group professional development, use strategies to ensure alignment, consistency, and appropriate focus. Such strategies might include providing guidelines or criteria for selecting external resources and having resources reviewed and approved by leadership.

- Evaluating the results and outcomes of professional development is critical in general and especially when external resources are being utilized. External sources and consultants may collect evaluation information for their own use, but it is also important that the school district collect feedback from their staff to ensure that the learning opportunity has met the intended purpose and provided staff with the desired knowledge and skills.

- Districts should evaluate the impact of their professional learning activities and the impact on various stakeholders. Guskey (Chapter 23, this volume) describes five levels of evaluation that districts should consider when assessing the value of professional learning. At each level the stakes get higher. The first level that Guskey describes is to look at participants' reactions – did they like it? Level 2 considers participant learning—did they acquire the expected knowledge and/or skills that the professional learning activities were to deliver? Level 3 evaluates organizational support and change—was there an impact on the organization's goals and procedures as a result? Level 4 considers new knowledge and skills participants have acquired as a result of the professional learning activity. Ultimately, Level 5 considers whether student learning was affected as a result of the professional learning. (See Chapter 23, this volume, for more details.)

SUMMARY

It is important for schools to think about how external resources can be utilized to meet varying professional development needs at the school level, as well as for individual staff members. The variety of external resources available enables teachers and specialized instructional support personnel to focus on their own specific professional development needs. As school staff members reflect upon their own continued learning interests and feedback from performance evaluations, specific professional development needs are likely to be identified. These needs may not be universal across all staff members in the building, so the necessary school-based professional development may not be arranged or provided. Thus individual staff members may need to pursue other opportunities for their professional learning, and external resources may be the most cost-effective and efficient options. Regardless of whether professional development occurs at an individual or a school level, attention to the alignment between the identified topic and purpose and the outcomes achieved will be critical for ensuring continued professional growth for educators and positive outcomes for students.

QUESTIONS FOR DISCUSSION

1. As a teacher, interventionist, coach, counselor, or school psychologist, how do you ensure that your continued professional learning meets the needs of students? What resources (e.g., professional associations, state resources and guidelines, colleagues in neighboring districts or schools, etc.) are available to further develop your knowledge and skills, and how might they be used for development in areas that are necessary to support student learning and growth?

2. As a district leader, how are specific school and staff needs identified in light of the variety and ever-changing education initiatives, such as Common Core State Standards and Race to the Top? What external professional development will be needed? Which examples of external professional development would best meet the school's or district's objectives?

3. As a policymaker, how are educational initiatives and requirements used to make decisions about resource allocation such as grants and school funding that provide for professional development and technical assistance to schools and districts? What policies and guidance are needed to ensure that schools are able to access and secure the resources required to assist staff in meeting student needs and achievement outcomes?

REFERENCES

Bier, M., Foster, A. M., Bellamy, G. T., & Clark, R. (2008). Professional development school principals: Challenges, experiences, and craft. *School–University Partnerships: The Journal of the National Association for Professional Development Schools, 2*(2), 77–89.

Borko, H. (2004). Professional development and teacher learning: Mapping the terrain. *Educational Researcher, 33*(8), 1–49.

Brooke, R., Coyle, D., & Walden, A. (2005). Finding a space for professional development: Creating Thirdspace through after-school writing groups. *Language Arts, 82*(5), 367–377.

Darensburg, E. (2010, Fall). Professional development. *Teachers of Color*, pp. 60–62.

Darling-Hammond, L. (2000). Teacher quality and student achievement: A review of state policy evidence. *Education Policy Analysis Archives, 8*(1), 1–44.

Darling-Hammond, L., Wei, R. C., Andree, A., Richardson, N., & Orphanos, S. (2009). *Professional learning in the learning profession: A status report on teacher development in the United States and abroad.* Dallas, TX: National Staff Development Council. Retrieved from *www.learningforward.org/docs/pdf/nsdcstudy2009.pdf.*

Donnelly, A., Morgan, D., DeFord, D., Files, J., Long, S., Mills, H., et al. (2005). Transformative professional development: Negotiating knowledge from an inquiry stance. *Language Arts, 82*(5), 336–346.

Fisher, J. B., Schumaker, J. B., Culbertson, J., & Deshler, D. D. (2010). Effects of a computerized professional development program on teacher and student outcomes. *Journal of Teacher Education, 61*(4), 302–312.

Fixsen, D. L., Naoom, S. F., Blase, K. A., Friedman, R. M., & Wallace, F. (2005). *Implementation research: A synthesis of the literature* (FMHI Publication No. 231). Tampa: University of South Florida, Louis de la Parte Florida Mental Health Institute, National Implementation Research Network. Retrieved from *http://nirn.fpg.unc.edu/resources/implementation-research-synthesis-literature.*

Garet, M. S., Porter, A. C., Desimone, L., Burman, B. F., & Yoon, K. S. (2001). What makes professional development effective? Results from a national sample of teachers. *American Educational Research Journal, 38*(4), 915–945.

Guskey, T. R. (2003). What makes professional development effective? *Phi Delta Kappan, 81*, 581–584.

Harris, K., Lane, L., Graham, S., Driscoll, S., Sandmel, K., Brindle, M., et al. (2012). Practice-based professional development for self-regulated strategies development in writing: A randomized controlled study. *Journal of Teacher Education, 63*(2), 103–119.

Holmes, A., Signer, B., & MacLeod, A. (2010). Professional development at a distance: A mixed-method study exploring inservice teachers' views on presence online. *Journal of Digital Learning in Teacher Education, 27*(2), 76–85.

Hurd, J., & Licciardo-Musso, L. (2005). Lesson study: Teacher-led professional development in literacy. *Language Arts, 82*(5), 388–395.

Kedzior, H. (2004). Teacher professional development. *Education Policy Brief, 15*, 1–6.

Kragler, S., Martin, L., & Kroeger, D. (2008). Money down the drain: Mandated professional development. *Journal of School Leadership, 18*, 528–550.

Learning Forward. (2013). Definition of professional development. Retrieved from *http://learningforward.org/who-we-are/professional-learning-definition.*

Long, R. (2012). Professional development and education policy: Understanding the current disconnect. *Reading Today, 29*(3), 29–30.

Loucks-Horsley, S., Hewson, P., Love, N., & Stiles, K. (1998). *Designing professional development for teachers of science and mathematics*. Thousand Oaks, CA: Corwin Press.

Lutrick, E., & Szabo, S. (2012). Instructional leaders' beliefs about effective professional development. *Delta Kappa Gamma Bulletin, 78*(3), 6–12.

Mahn, H., McMann, D., & Musanti, S. (2005).Teaching/learning centers: Professional development for teachers of linguistically and culturally diverse students. *Language Arts, 82*(5), 378–387.

Marrongelle, K., Sztajn, P., & Smith, M. (2013). Scaling up professional development in an era of Common Core State Standards. *Journal of Teacher Education, 64*(3), 202–211.

Mason, L. (2005). *Evaluation programs for grant projects* [PowerPoint presentation]. Oklahoma City: Oklahoma State Regents for Higher Education, Oklahoma Summer Grant Writing Institute. Retrieved from *www.okhighered.org/grant-opps/ppt/beginning-grant-writing.ppt*.

Mouza, C. (2009). Does research-based professional development make a difference? A longitudinal investigation of teacher learning in technology integration. *Teachers College Record, 111*(5), 1195–1241.

Steiner, L. (2004). *Designing effective professional development experiences: What do we know?* Naperville, IL: Learning Point Associates.

Wei, R. C., Darling-Hammond, L., &Adamson, F. (2010). *Professional development in the United States: Trends and challenges*. Dallas, TX: National Staff Development Council.

Yamagata-Lynch, L. C., & Haudenschild, M. T. (2008). Teacher perceptions of barriers and aids of professional growth in professional development. *School–University Partnerships, 2*(2), 90–106.

PART IV

PULLING IT TOGETHER

Why have I lasted 40 years? Passion. . . . I kept looking for ways to excite me . . . to make teaching/learning better and to pass that love of learning on to my students...which is so much more exciting and rewarding than just giving knowledge. Professional development is a personal fit if it is successful. Each person has to be able to connect to the professional development. It can't be "canned" or one size fits all or the "buzz word" of the year. Teaching is a profession, not just a job.

—Shirley Thacker
National Board Certified primary-grade teacher
Wes-Del Elementary
Gaston, Indiana

CHAPTER 23

Measuring the Effectiveness of Educators' Professional Development

THOMAS R. GUSKEY

- How do we determine the effectiveness of educators' professional development activities?
- What are the purposes of professional development evaluation?
- What are the five critical levels of professional development evaluation?

The demand for accountability is the driving force behind nearly all reform initiatives in education today. Educators at all levels are asked to provide evidence to show that what they do makes a difference. In most cases this demand for accountability relates to the demonstrable impact of school leaders and teachers on student achievement. But increasingly, such demands are being extended to educators' learning as well. Legislators and policymakers want to know about the value of educators' professional development, the impact of those activities on their practice, and the effects of those practices on student learning outcomes.

Ensuring accountability in professional development poses new challenges for educators. Historically, educators have seen professional development as a right. Throughout the world, time for professional development is included in nearly all teachers' contracts for employment. In recent years, however, as economic conditions decline and education budgets grow tight, government officials and program funders concerned with accountability have begun to question that right. They look at what schools spend on professional development for school leaders and teachers and want to know what benefits it brings. Does the school's or school district's investment in professional development for educators yield tangible payoffs, or might that money be spent in better ways? Such questions highlight the importance of measuring the effectiveness of educators' professional development (Guskey, 1998, 1999).

The professional development experiences of educators cover a broad range of activities. Many of those experiences involve personal reflections on the everyday interactions between teachers and students. Teachers regularly try new approaches to teaching, gather information about how well those approaches work for their students, and then decide what changes need to be made or instructional alternatives added in order to improve students' learning success. Thoughtful deliberations on these ongoing classroom interactions are a vital component of every teacher's professional development.

In addition, school leaders and teachers also take part in a variety of more structured professional development activities specifically designed to enhance their knowledge and improve their professional skills. These experiences include not only the broad spectrum of seminars and workshops in which educators engage but also online programs, peer observations, professional learning communities, coaching or mentoring, university courses, conferences, and the like. In this chapter we focus primarily on measuring the effects of these more structured and formalized professional development activities.

THE LACK OF GOOD EVIDENCE

Educators generally pay scant attention to measuring the effectiveness of their professional development, even those activities that are more structured. When they do, their efforts tend to be restricted to descriptive accounts of what took place or surveys of participants' reactions to the experience. Rarely do efforts extend to consideration of the impact these activities have on teachers' classroom practices or resultant improvements in student learning. Two large-scale reports conducted in the United States point explicitly to the extent of this lack of well-designed evaluations.

In *Reviewing the Evidence on How Teacher Professional Development Affects Student Achievement* (Yoon, Duncan, Lee, Scarloss, & Shapley, 2007), a team of scholars from the American Institutes for Research analyzed the findings from 1,343 studies and evaluation reports published over a period of 20 years that potentially addressed the impact of educators' professional development on student learning outcomes. Using the U.S. Department of Education's *What Works Clearinghouse (WWC) Evidence Standards* (see *http://ies.ed.gov/ncee/wwc/overview/review.asp?ag=pi*) to judge the quality of evidence presented in these investigations, the team identified only *nine* studies of sufficient quality for drawing valid conclusions about the characteristics of effective professional development for educators (see Guskey & Yoon, 2009). All of the other studies and reports had significant design or methodological flaws that challenged the credibility of their findings.

The second report, *Does Teacher Professional Development Have Effects on Teaching and Learning?* (Blank, de las Alas, & Smith, 2008), came from the Council of Chief State School Officers' study of teacher professional development programs in mathematics and science sponsored by the U.S. National Science Foundation. The authors of this report reviewed evaluation studies from a voluntary sample of 25 professional development programs nominated by 14 states. Presumably, these programs represent the best of the best. Their analysis of study reports and papers from these nominated programs revealed that only *seven* program evaluations reported measureable effects of teacher professional development on subsequent student outcomes. No examination of the quality or validity of this evidence was conducted.

Some argue, of course, that significant progress has been made in more recent years and that our knowledge of effective professional development is improving. But even more current evidence indicates that much of the research on educators' professional development, as well as most evaluations of professional development initiatives, continues to be descriptive rather than quantitative (Sawchuk, 2010). Hard data on which professional development models lead to better teaching and improved student learning remain difficult to find (Viadero, 2011). In addition, new investigations employing rigorous methodological designs continue to yield uninspiring results.

Two recent, randomized field studies funded by the U.S. Department of Education, for example, investigated intensive professional development programs. Both studies found no effects on student achievement, even though the programs were generally aligned with the characteristics of effective professional development identified in the Yoon and colleagues (2007) review. In the first study, two professional development approaches based on a popular early reading program were found to increase teachers' knowledge of literacy development and their use of explicit reading instruction during the year of the intervention but had little effect on the reading achievement of second-grade students in high-poverty schools (Garet et al., 2008). In the second investigation, a professional development initiative focusing on secondary math was found to have significant effect on instructional practice but little impact on teachers' content knowledge or students' learning (Garet et al., 2011). The results from these recent studies and the earlier reviews show how few well-designed investigations and evaluation reports exist to adequately judge effectiveness or guide improvements in professional development programs and practice.

THE NEED FOR SOUND MEASURES OF RESULTS

We can only speculate as to why so little good evidence exists on the effects of professional development in education. It may be educators' commonly held perception of evaluation as a costly, time-consuming process that diverts attention from important planning, implementation, and follow-up activities. In addition, many educators undoubtedly believe that they lack the skill and expertise needed to become involved in rigorous evaluations. As a result they either ignore measurement and evaluation issues completely or leave them to "evaluation experts" who are called in at the end and asked to determine whether what was done made any difference. Sadly, these last-minute, post hoc evaluation efforts are seldom adequate in determining any activity's true effects.

Good evaluations build from reliable and valid measures of effects. They do not, however, need to be costly or complicated. What they require is thoughtful planning, the ability to ask good questions, and a basic understanding of how to collect appropriate measures in order to find valid answers. In many ways, good evaluations are merely the refinement of everyday thinking. They provide sound, meaningful, and sufficiently reliable information that allows thoughtful and responsible decisions to be made about professional development processes and effects.

In this chapter we explore the process of measuring the effectiveness of educators' professional development within the context of accountability. Three basic questions are addressed:

1. What does measuring the effectiveness of professional development mean, specifically in the context of accountability?
2. What purposes do professional development evaluations based on these measures serve?
3. What are the critical levels of professional development evaluation and what measures are essential at each level?

Finally, the implications of the answers to these questions are considered with regard to accountability issues.

WHAT DOES MEASURING THE EFFECTIVENESS OF PROFESSIONAL DEVELOPMENT MEAN?

Just as there are many forms of professional development for educators, there are also many forms of evaluation. Although experts may disagree on the best definition of evaluation, a useful operational definition for most purposes is: *Evaluation is the systematic investigation of merit or worth* (adapted from the Joint Committee on Standards for Educational Evaluation, 1994).

Each part of this definition holds special significance. The word "systematic" distinguishes this process from the multitude of informal evaluation acts in which people consciously engage. "Systematic" implies that evaluation in this context is thoughtful, intentional, and purposeful. It is done for clear reasons and with explicit intent. Although its specific purpose may vary from one setting to another, all good evaluations are organized and deliberate.

Because it is systematic, some educators mistakenly believe that professional development evaluation is appropriate only for planned seminars and workshops, but not for the wide range of other less structured, ongoing, job-embedded professional learning activities. Regardless of the form it takes, however, professional development is not a haphazard process. It is, or should be, purposeful and results- or goal-driven (Schmoker, 2004, 2006). Its objectives remain clear: to make a positive difference in teaching, to help educators reach high standards, and, ultimately, to have a positive impact on students. This is true of seminars and workshops, as well as study groups, professional learning communities, action research, collaborative planning, curriculum development, structured observations, peer coaching and mentoring, and individually guided professional development learning activities. To determine whether the goals of these activities are met, or whether progress is being made, requires systematic evaluation.

"Investigation" refers to collecting and analyzing appropriate and pertinent information. Although no evaluation can be completely objective, the process is not founded on opinion or conjecture. Rather, it is based on acquiring specific, relevant, and valid evidence examined through appropriate methods and techniques.

Using "merit or worth" in the definition implies appraisal and judgment. Evaluations are designed to determine something's value. They help answer questions such as:

- Is this experience or activity leading to the intended results?
- Is it better than what was done in the past?
- Is it better than another, competing activity?
- Is it worth the costs?

Answers to these questions require more than a statement of findings. They demand an appraisal of quality and judgments of value, based on the best evidence available. Such appraisals are the basis of accountability.

WHAT PURPOSES DO PROFESSIONAL DEVELOPMENT EVALUATIONS SERVE?

The purposes of evaluation are generally classified in three broad categories: *planning*, *formative*, and *summative*. Most evaluations actually fulfill all three of these purposes, although the emphasis on each changes during various stages of the evaluation process. Although this blending of purposes blurs their distinction, differentiating their intent helps clarify understanding of evaluation procedures (Stevens, Lawrenz, & Sharp, 1995).

Planning Evaluation

Planning evaluation occurs *before* a professional development program or activity begins, although certain aspects may be continual and ongoing. It is designed to give those involved in program development and implementation a precise understanding of what is to be accomplished, what procedures will be used, and how success will be measured and determined. In essence, it lays the groundwork for all other evaluation activities. Although some experts advocate an "evaluability assessment" prior to planning as a means of determining if a professional development experience or activity is "evaluable" (Wholey, Hatry, & Newcomer, 2004), others contend that planning evaluation done well makes such assessment unnecessary (Guskey, 2000a).

Planning evaluation involves appraisal of a professional development program or activity's critical attributes, usually on the basis of previously established standards. These include the specified goals, the proposal or plan to achieve those goals, the concept or theory underlying the proposal, the overall evaluation plan, and the likelihood that the plan can be carried out with the time and resources available. In addition, planning evaluation typically includes some measure of needs, assessment of the characteristics of participants, careful analysis of the context, and the collection of relevant baseline information.

Evaluation for planning purposes is sometimes referred to as "preformative evaluation" (Scriven, 1991) and may be thought of as "preventative evaluation." It helps decision makers know if professional development endeavors are headed in the right direction and likely to produce the desired results. It also helps identify and remedy early on the difficulties that might plague later evaluation efforts. Furthermore, planning evaluation helps ensure that other evaluation purposes can be met in an efficient and timely manner.

Formative Evaluation

Formative evaluation occurs *during* the operation of a professional development experience or activity. Its purpose is to provide those responsible for the activity with ongoing information about whether things are going as planned and if expected progress is being made. If not, this same information can be used to guide necessary improvements (Scriven, 1967).

The most useful formative evaluations focus on the conditions for success. They address issues such as:

- What conditions are necessary for success?
- Have those conditions for success been met?
- Can they be improved?

In many cases, formative evaluation is a recurring process that takes place at multiple times throughout the life of the professional development program or activity. Many program developers, in fact, constantly engage in the process of formative evaluation. They use evidence gathered at each step of development and implementation to make adjustments, modifications, or revisions (Fitzpatrick, Sanders, & Worthen, 2004).

To keep formative evaluations efficient, Scriven (1991) recommends using them as "early warning" evaluations. In other words, they provide an early version of the final, overall evaluation. As development and implementation proceed, formative evaluation can measure intermediate benchmarks of success to determine what is working as expected and what difficulties must be overcome. Flaws can be identified and weaknesses located in time to make the adaptations necessary for success.

Summative Evaluation

Summative evaluation is conducted *at the completion* of a professional development experience or activity. Its purpose is to provide program developers and decision makers with judgments about the program or activity's overall merit or worth. Summative evaluation describes what was accomplished, what the consequences were (positive and negative), what the final results were (intended and unintended), and, in some cases, whether the benefits justify the costs (Phillips, 2002).

Unlike formative evaluations that are used to guide improvements, summative evaluations present decision makers with the information they need to make crucial decisions about a professional development program or activity. Should it be continued? Continued with modifications? Expanded? Discontinued? Ultimately, its focus is the "bottom line."

Perhaps the best description of the distinction between formative and summative evaluation is one offered by Robert Stake: "When the cook tastes the soup, that's formative; when the guests taste the soup, that's summative" (quoted in Scriven, 1991, p. 169).

Unfortunately, many educators associate evaluation with its summative purposes only. Important information that could help guide planning, development, and implementation is often neglected, even though such information can be key in determining a professional development program or activity's overall success. Summative evaluation, although necessary, often comes too late to be much help. Thus, although the relative emphasis on planning, formative, and summative evaluation changes through the life of a professional development program or activity, all three are essential to a meaningful evaluation.

WHAT ARE THE CRITICAL LEVELS OF PROFESSIONAL DEVELOPMENT EVALUATION?

Planning, formative, and summative evaluation all involve collecting and analyzing information. Measuring the effectiveness of educators' professional development requires consideration of the five critical stages or levels of information, as shown in Figure 23.1 (Guskey, 2000a, 2002a, 2005). These five levels represent an adaptation of an evaluation model developed by Kirkpatrick (1994, 1998) for judging the value of supervisory training programs in business and industry. Kirkpatrick's model, although widely applied, has seen limited use in education because of inadequate explanatory power. Although helpful in addressing a broad range of "what" questions, many find it lacking when it comes to explaining "why" (Alliger & Janak, 1989; Holton, 1996).

Evaluation Level	What Questions Are Addressed?	How Will Information Be Gathered?	What Is Measured or Assessed?	How Will Information Be Used?
1. Participants' Reactions	• Did they like it? • Was their time well spent? • Did the material make sense? • Will it be useful? • Was the leader knowledgeable and helpful? • Were the refreshments fresh and tasty? • Was the room the right temperature? • Were the chairs comfortable?	• Questionnaires or surveys administered at the end of the session.	• Initial satisfaction with the experience	• To improve program design and delivery
2. Participants' Learning	• Did participants acquire the intended knowledge and skills?	• Paper-and-pencil instruments • Simulations • Demonstrations • Participant reflections (oral and/or written) • Participant portfolios	• New knowledge and skills of participants	• To improve program content, format, and organization
3. Organizational Support and Change	• Were sufficient resources made available? • Were problems addressed quickly and efficiently? • Was implementation advocated, facilitated, and supported?	• Minutes from follow-up meetings • Questionnaires • Structured interviews with participants and district or school administrators	• The organization's advocacy, support, accommodation, facilitation, and recognition.	• To document and improve organizational support • To inform future change efforts

454

Evaluation Level	What Questions Are Addressed?	How Will Information Be Gathered?	What Is Measured or Assessed?	How Will Information Be Used?
	• Were successes recognized and shared? • Was the support public and overt? • What was the impact on the organization? • Did it affect organizational climate and procedures?	• District and school records • Participant portfolios		
4. Participants' Use of New Knowledge and Skills	• Did participants effectively apply the new knowledge and skills?	• Questionnaires • Structured interviews with participants and their supervisors • Participant reflections (oral and/or written) • Participant portfolios • Direct observations • Video- or audiotapes	• Degree and quality of implementation	• To document and improve the implementation of program content
5. Student Learning Outcomes	• What was the impact on students? • Did it affect student performance or achievement? • Did it influence students' physical or emotional well-being? • Are students more confident as learners? • Is student attendance improving? • Are dropouts decreasing?	• Student records • School records • Questionnaires • Structured interviews with students, parents, teachers, and/or administrators • Participant portfolios	• Student learning outcomes: • Cognitive (performance and achievement) • Affective (attitudes and dispositions) • Psychomotor (skills and behaviors)	• To focus and improve all aspects of program design, implementation, and follow-up • To demonstrate the overall impact of professional development

FIGURE 23.1. Five levels of professional learning evaluation. From Guskey (2000a). Copyright 2000 by Thomas R. Guskey.

The five levels in this model are hierarchically arranged, from simple to more complex. With each succeeding level, the process of measuring the most pertinent factors and gathering relevant evaluation information requires more time and resources. And because each level builds on those that come before, success at one level is usually necessary for success at higher levels.

Level 1: Participants' Reactions

The first level of evaluation looks at participants' reactions to the professional development experience or activity. This is the most common form of professional development evaluation and the easiest type of information to gather and analyze.

At Level 1 the questions addressed focus on whether or not participants liked or valued the experience. Did they feel their time was well spent? Did the content and material make sense to them? Were the activities well planned and meaningful? Was the leader knowledgeable, credible, and helpful? Did they find the information useful?

Also important for some professional development experiences are questions related to the context, such as: Was the room the right temperature? Were the chairs comfortable? Were the refreshments fresh and tasty? To some, questions such as these may seem silly and inconsequential. But experienced professional development leaders know the importance of attending to these basic human needs.

Participants' reactions are usually measured through questionnaires handed out at the end of a program or activity or by online surveys distributed later through email. These questionnaires and surveys typically include a combination of rating-scale items and open-ended response questions that allow participants to provide more personalized comments. Because of the general nature of this information, many organizations use the same questionnaire or survey for all of their professional development activities, regardless of the format.

Some educators refer to these measures of participants' reactions as "happiness quotients," insisting that they reveal only the entertainment value of an experience or activity, not its quality or worth. But measuring participants' initial satisfaction provides information that can help improve the design and delivery of professional development programs or activities in valid ways. In addition, positive reactions from participants are usually a necessary prerequisite to higher-level evaluation results.

Level 2: Participants' Learning

In addition to liking their professional development experiences, participants ought to learn something from them. Level 2 focuses on measuring the new knowledge, skills, and perhaps attitudes or dispositions that participants gain (Guskey, 2002c). Depending on the goals of the professional development program or activity, this can involve anything from a pencil-and-paper assessment (Can participants describe the critical attributes of effective questioning techniques and give examples of how these might be applied in common classroom situations?) to a simulation or full-scale skill demonstration (Presented with a variety of classroom conflicts, can participants diagnose each situation, and then prescribe and carry out a fair and workable solution?). Oral or written personal reflections or examinations of portfolios that participants assemble also can be used to document their learning.

Although Level 2 evaluation information often can be gathered at the completion of a professional development program or activity, it usually requires more than a standardized form. And because measures must show attainment of specific learning goals, specific indicators of successful learning need to be identified *before* activities begin.

Careful evaluators also consider possible "unintended" learning outcomes, both positive and negative. Professional development activities that engage teachers and school leaders in collaboration, for example, can additionally foster a positive sense of community and shared purpose among participants (Supovitz, 2002). But in some instances, individuals collaborate to block change or inhibit advancement (Corcoran, Fuhrman, & Belcher, 2001; Little, 1990). Investigations further show that collaborative efforts sometimes run headlong into enormous conflicts over professional beliefs and practices that can impede progress (Achinstein, 2002). Thus even the best planned professional development endeavors occasionally yield completely unanticipated negative consequences.

If concerns arise that participants may already possess the desired knowledge and skills, some form of pre- and postassessment may be required. Analyzing this information provides a basis for improving the content, format, and organization of professional development programs and activities.

Level 3: Organizational Support and Change

At Level 3 the focus shifts from participants to organizational dimensions that may be key to the success of the professional development experience or activity. Organizational elements also can sometimes hinder or prevent success, even when the individual aspects of professional development are done right (Sparks, 1996).

Suppose, for example, that a group of secondary educators participates in a professional development program that acquaints them with the effective use of cooperative learning. Through the program they gain an in-depth understanding of cooperative learning theory and organize a variety of classroom activities based on cooperative learning principles. But then following their training, they attempt to implement these activities in classes in which students are graded or marked "on the curve," according to their relative standing among classmates, and great importance is attached to each student's individual class rank. Organizational grading policies and practices such as these make learning highly competitive and thwart the most valiant efforts to have students cooperate and help each other learn. When graded "on the curve," students must compete against each other for the few scarce rewards (high grades) dispensed by the teacher. Cooperation is discouraged, as helping other students succeed lessens the helper's chance of success (Guskey, 2000b).

The lack of positive results in this case does not reflect poor training or inadequate learning on the part of the participating teachers, but rather organizational policies that are incompatible with implementation efforts. Problems at Level 3 have essentially canceled the gains made at Levels 1 and 2 (Sparks & Hirsh, 1997). That is precisely why professional development evaluations must include information on organizational support and change.

Level 3 questions focus on the organizational characteristics and attributes necessary for success. Did the professional development activities promote changes that were aligned with the mission of the school? Were changes at the individual level encouraged and supported at the building and district levels (Corcoran et al., 2001)? Were sufficient resources made available, including time for sharing and reflection (Colton & Langer, 2005; Langer & Colton, 1994)? Were successes recognized and shared? Issues such as these often play a large part in determining the success of any professional development program.

Procedures for gathering information at Level 3 differ depending on the goals of the professional development program or activity. They may involve analyzing school records, examining the minutes from follow-up meetings, administering questionnaires that measure factors related to the organization's advocacy, support, accommodation, facilitation, and recognition of change efforts. Structured interviews with participants and school administrators also can be helpful. This information is used not only to document and improve organizational support for professional development but also to inform future change initiatives.

Level 4: Participants' Use of New Knowledge and Skills

At Level 4 the primary question is: Did the new knowledge and skills that participants learned make a difference in their professional practice? The key to gathering relevant information at this level of evaluation rests in specifying clear indicators of both the degree and quality of implementation. Unlike in Levels 1 and 2, this information cannot be gathered at the end of a professional learning program or activity. Enough time must pass to allow participants to adapt the new ideas and practices to their settings. And because implementation is often a gradual and uneven process, measures of progress may need to be gathered at several time intervals.

Depending on the goals of the professional development program or activity, this information may involve questionnaires or structured interviews with participants and their school leaders. Oral or written personal reflections or examinations of participants' journals or portfolios also might be considered. The most accurate information typically comes from direct observations, either by trained observers or through digital recordings. These observations, however, should be kept as unobtrusive as possible (for examples, see Hall & Hord, 1987).

Analyzing this information provides evidence on current levels of use. It also helps professional development leaders restructure future programs and activities to facilitate better and more consistent implementation.

Level 5: Student Learning Outcomes

Level 5 addresses the "bottom line" in education: What was the impact on students? Did the professional development program or activity benefit them in any way? The particular student learning outcomes of interest will depend, of course, on the goals of that specific professional development endeavor. In addition to the stated goals, the program or activity may result in important unintended outcomes. Suppose, for example, that students' average scores on large-scale assessments go up, but that the school dropout rate also goes up. Because mixed results such as this are so typical, evaluations should always include multiple measures of student learning (Chester, 2005; Guskey, 2007).

Because stakeholders vary in their trust of different sources of evidence, it is unlikely that any single indicator of success will prove adequate or sufficient to all. Providing acceptable evidence for judging the effects of professional development activities will almost always require multiple sources of evidence. In addition, these sources of evidence must be carefully matched to the needs and perceptions of different stakeholder groups (Guskey, 2012).

Results from large-scale assessments and nationally normed standardized exams may be important for accountability purposes and will need to be included. In addition, school leaders often consider these measures to be valid indicators of success. Teachers, however, generally see limitations in large-scale assessment results. These types of assessments typically are administered only once per year, and results may not be available until several months later. By that time, the school year may have ended and students been promoted to another teacher's class. So while important, many teachers do not find such results particularly useful (Guskey, 2007).

Teachers generally put more trust in results from their own assessments of student learning—classroom assessments, common formative assessments, performance demonstrations, and portfolios of student work. They turn to these sources of evidence for feedback to determine whether the new strategies or practices they are implementing really make a difference. Classroom assessments provide timely, targeted, and instructionally relevant information that also can be used to plan revisions when needed. Because teachers compose a major stakeholder group in any professional development activity, sources of evidence that they trust and believe will be particularly important to include.

Measures of student learning typically incorporate cognitive indicators of student performance and achievement, such as assessment results, portfolio evaluations, marks or grades, and scores from standardized exams. But in addition, affective and behavioral indicators of student performance may be relevant as well. Student surveys designed to measure how much students like school; their perceptions of teachers, fellow students, and themselves; their sense of self-efficacy; and their confidence in new learning situations can be especially informative. Evidence on school attendance, enrollment patterns, dropout rates, class disruptions, and disciplinary actions are also important outcomes. In some areas, parents' or families' perceptions may be a vital consideration. This is especially true in initiatives that involve changes in grading practices, report cards, or other aspects of school-to-home and home-to-school communication (Epstein et al., 2009; Guskey, 2002c).

Furthermore, Level 5 evaluations should be made as methodologically rigorous as possible. Rigor, however, does not imply that only one evaluation method or design can produce credible evidence. Although randomized designs (i.e., true experimental studies) represent the gold standard in scientific research, especially in studies of causal effects, a wide range of quasi-experimental designs can produce valid results. When evaluations are replicated with similar findings, that validity is further enhanced. One of the best ways to enhance an evaluation's methodological rigor is to plan for meaningful comparisons.

In many cases, evidence on outcomes at Level 5 is gathered from a single school or school district in a single setting for a restricted time period. Unfortunately, from a design perspective, such evidence lacks both reliability and validity. Regardless of whether results are positive or not, so many alternative explanations may account for the results that most authorities would consider such outcomes dubious at best and meaningless at worst (Guskey & Yoon, 2009).

It may be, for example, that the planned professional development endeavors did, indeed, lead to noted improvements in student learning. But maybe the improvements were the result of a change in leadership or personnel instead. Maybe the community or student population changed. Maybe changes in government policies or assessments made a difference. Maybe other simultaneously implemented interventions were responsible. The possibility that these or other extraneous factors influenced results makes it impossible to draw definitive conclusions.

The best way to counter these threats to the validity of results is to include a comparison group—another, similar group of educators or schools not involved in the current activity or perhaps engaged in a different activity. Ideal comparisons involve the random assignment of students, teachers, or schools to different groups. But because that is rarely possible in most education settings, finding similar classrooms, schools, or school districts provides the next best option. In some cases involvement in a professional development activity can be staggered so that half of the group of teachers or schools that volunteer can be randomly selected to take part initially while the others delay involvement and serve as the comparison group. In other cases, comparisons can be made to "matched" classrooms, schools, or school districts that share similar characteristics related to motivation, size, and demographics.

Using comparison groups does not eliminate the effects of extraneous factors that might influence results. It simply allows planners greater confidence in attributing the results attained to the particular program or activity being considered. In addition, other investigative methods may be used to formulate important questions and develop new measures relating to professional growth (Raudenbush, 2005).

Student and school records provide the majority of information at Level 5. Results from questionnaires and structured interviews with students, parents, teachers, and administrators could be included as well. Level 5 information is used summatively to document a program or activity's overall impact. But formatively, it can help guide improvements in all aspects of professional development, including design, implementation, and follow-up. In some cases information on student learning outcomes is used to estimate the cost effectiveness of professional development programs and activities, sometimes referred to as "return on investment," or "ROI," evaluation (Parry, 1996; Phillips, 1997; Todnem & Warner, 1993).

IMPLICATIONS FOR IMPROVEMENT

Three important implications stem from this model for evaluating professional development. First, each of the five evaluation levels is important. Although evaluation at any level can be done well or poorly, the information gathered at each level provides vital data for improving the quality of professional development programs and activities. And although each level relies on different measures and different types of information that may be gathered at different times, no level can be neglected.

Second, measuring effectiveness at one level tells little about the impact at the next level. Although success at an early level may be necessary for positive results at the next higher one, it is clearly not sufficient (Cody & Guskey, 1997). Breakdowns can occur at any point along the way. Sadly, most government officials and policymakers fail to recognize the difficulties involved in moving from professional development experiences (Level 1) to improvements in student learning (Level 5). They also tend to be unaware of the complexity of this process, as well as the time and effort required to build this connection (Guskey, 1997; Guskey & Sparks, 2004).

The third implication, and perhaps the most important, is that in planning professional development programs and activities to impact student learning, *the order of these levels must be reversed*. In other words, education leaders must plan "backward" (Guskey, 2001a, 2001b, 2003), starting where they want to end up and then working back (Hirsh, 2012).

BACKWARD PLANNING FOR ACCOUNTABILITY

In backward planning, educators first decide what student learning outcomes they want to achieve and what evidence best reflects those outcomes (Level 5). Relevant evidence provides the basis for accountability. School leaders and teachers must decide, for example, whether they want to improve students' reading comprehension, enhance their skills in problem solving, develop their sense of confidence in learning situations, or improve their behavior in class, their persistence in school, or their collaboration with classmates. Critical analyses of data from assessments of student learning, samples of student work, and school records are especially useful in identifying these student learning goals.

Next they must determine, on the basis of pertinent research, what instructional practices and policies will most effectively and efficiently produce those outcomes (Level 4). They need to ask questions such as: What evidence verifies that these particular practices and policies will produce the results we want? How good or reliable is that evidence? Was it gathered in contexts similar to ours? In this process, leaders must be particularly mindful of innovations that are more "opinion-based" than "research-based," promoted by people more concerned with "what sells" to desperate educators than with "what works" with students. Before jumping on any educational bandwagon, leaders must make sure that trustworthy evidence validates the chosen approach.

After that, leaders need to consider what aspects of organizational support are needed for those practices and policies to be implemented well (Level 3). Many valuable improvement efforts fail miserably due to a lack of active participation and clear support from school leaders (Guskey, 2004). Others prove ineffective because the resources required for implementation were not provided. The lack of time, instructional materials, or necessary technology can severely impede teachers' attempts to use the new knowledge and skills acquired through a professional development experience. A big part of planning involves ensuring that organizational elements are in place to support implementation of the desired practices and policies.

Then, leaders must decide what knowledge and skills the participating professionals must have in order to implement the prescribed practices and policies (Level 2). In other words, what must they know and be able to do to successfully adapt the innovation to their specific situation and bring about the sought-after change?

Finally, consideration turns to what set of experiences will enable participants to acquire the needed knowledge and skills (Level 1). Seminars and workshops, especially when paired with collaborative planning, structured opportunities for practice with feedback, and follow-up coaching can be a highly effective means of sharing information and expanding educators' knowledge. Action research projects, organized study groups, collegial exchange, professional learning communities, and a wide range of other activities can all be effective, depending on the specified purpose of the professional development.

What makes this backward planning process so important is that the decisions made at each level profoundly affect those made at the next. For example, the particular student learning outcomes being sought influence the kinds of practices and policies that need to be implemented. Likewise, the practices and policies to be implemented influence the kinds of organizational support or change required, and so on.

The context-specific nature of this work complicates matters further. Even if school leaders and teachers agree on the student learning outcomes they want to achieve, what works best in one context with a particular community of educators and a particular group of students might not work equally well in another context with different educators and different students. This is what makes developing examples of truly universal "best practices" in professional development so difficult. What works always depends on where, when, and with whom.

Unfortunately, professional development leaders frequently fall into the same trap in planning that teachers do when they plan their lessons. Teachers often plan in terms of what they are going to do, instead of what they want their students to know and be able to do. Similarly, those planning professional development programs and activities often focus on what they will do (workshops, seminars, institutes, etc.) and how they will do it (study groups, professional learning communities, action research, peer coaching, etc.). Their planning tends to be "event-based" or "process-based." This not only diminishes the effectiveness of their efforts but it also makes evaluation much more difficult.

The most effective professional development planning begins with clear specification of the students' learning outcomes to be achieved and the sources of evidence that best reflect those outcomes. With those goals articulated, school leaders and teachers can then work backward. Not only will this make planning much more efficient, but it also provides a format for addressing the issues most crucial to evaluation. As a result, it makes evaluation a natural part of the planning process and offers a basis for accountability.

CONCLUSION

Many good things are done in the name of professional development. One could argue, in fact, that no significant educational improvement effort has succeeded in the absence of high-quality professional development for educators. Unfortunately, many rotten things also pass for professional development. What leaders in education have not done well is provide evidence to document the difference between the two. The new demands for accountability today make measuring effectiveness and presenting that evidence more crucial than ever.

Evaluation provides the key to making the distinction. Making the systematic gathering and analysis of crucial evaluation evidence a central component in planning all professional development programs and activities will enhance the success of professional development endeavors everywhere.

QUESTIONS FOR DISCUSSION

1. In what ways are the demands for accountability benefiting professional development in education? Are there potentially negative consequences of those demands?

2. Are there forms of professional development for which consideration of their impact on student learning outcomes would not be essential or appropriate?

3. In what ways might the backward planning process improve the impact of professional development activities? How difficult would it be to make backward planning the typical way we plan professional development at all levels?

REFERENCES

Achinstein, B. (2002). Conflict amid community: The micropolitics of teacher collaboration. *Teachers College Record, 104*(3), 421–455.

Alliger, G. M., & Janak, E. A. (1989). Kirkpatrick's levels of training criteria: Thirty years later. *Personnel Psychology, 42*(2), 331–342.

Blank, R. K., de las Alas, N., & Smith, C. (2008). *Does teacher professional development have effects on teaching and learning? Analysis of evaluation finding from programs for mathematics and science teachers in 14 states.* Washington, DC: Council of Chief State School Officers. Retrieved from *www.ccsso.org/projects/improving_evaluation_of_professional_development.*

Chester, M. D. (2005). Making valid and consistent inferences about school effectiveness from multiple measures. *Educational Measurement: Issues and Practice, 24*(4), 40–52.

Cody, C. B., & Guskey, T. R. (1997). Professional development. In J. C. Lindle, J. M. Petrosko, & R. S. Pankratz (Eds.), *1996 review of research on the Kentucky Education Reform Act* (pp. 191–209). Frankfort: Kentucky Institute for Education Research.

Colton, A. B., & Langer, G. M. (2005). Looking at student work. *Educational Leadership, 62*(5), 22.

Corcoran, T., Fuhrman, S. H., & Belcher, C. L. (2001). The district role in instructional improvement. *Phi Delta Kappan, 83*(1), 78–84.

Epstein, J. L., Sanders, M. G., Sheldon, S. B., Simon, B. S., Salinas, K. C., Jansorn, N. R., et al. (2009). *School, family, and community partnerships: Your handbook for action* (3rd ed.). Thousand Oaks, CA: Corwin Press.

Fitzpatrick, J. L., Sanders, J. R., & Worthen, B. R. (2004). *Program evaluation: Alternative approaches and practical guidelines* (3rd ed.). Boston: Pearson Education/Allyn & Bacon.

Garet, M. S., Cronen, S., Eaton, M., Kurki, A., Ludwig, M., Jones, W., et al. (2008). *The impact of two professional development interventions on early reading instruction and achievement.* Washington, DC: U.S. Department of Education, Institute of Education Sciences. Retrieved from *http://ies.ed.gov/ncee/pdf/20084030.pdf.*

Garet, M. S., Doolittle, F., Warner, E., Wayne, A. J., Stancavage, F., Taylor, J., et al. (2011). *Middle school mathematics professional development impact study: Findings after the second year of implementation.* Washington, DC: U.S. Department of Education, Institute of Education Sciences, National Center for Education Evaluation and Regional Assistance. Retrieved from *http://ies.ed.gov/ncee/pubs/20114024/pdf/20114024.pdf.*

Guskey, T. R. (1997). Research needs to link professional development and student learning. *Journal of Staff Development, 18*(2), 36–40.

Guskey, T. R. (1998). The age of our accountability. *Journal of Staff Development, 19*(4), 36–44.

Guskey, T. R. (1999). Making the most of professional development. In J. H. Block, S. T. Everson, & T. R. Guskey (Eds.), *Comprehensive school reform: A program perspective* (pp. 417–430). Dubuque, IA: Kendall/Hunt.

Guskey, T. R. (2000a). *Evaluating professional development.* Thousand Oaks, CA: Corwin Press.

Guskey, T. R. (2000b). Grading policies that work against standards...and how to fix them. *NASSP Bulletin, 84*(620), 20–29.

Guskey, T. R. (2001a). The backward approach. *Journal of Staff Development, 22*(3), 60.

Guskey, T. R. (2001b). Backward planning: An outcomes-based strategy for professional development. *Curriculum in Context, 28*(2), 18–20.

Guskey, T. R. (2002a). Does it make a difference? Evaluating professional development. *Educational Leadership, 59*(6), 45–51.

Guskey, T. R. (2002b). *How's my kid doing?: A parents' guide to grades, marks, and report cards.* San Francisco: Jossey-Bass.

Guskey, T. R. (2002c). Professional development and teacher change. *Teachers and Teaching: Theory and Practice, 8*(3/4), 381–391.

Guskey, T. R. (2003). Scooping up meaningful evidence. *Journal of Staff Development, 24*(4), 27–30.

Guskey, T. R. (2004). Organize principal support for professional development. *Journal of Staff Development, 25*(3), 8.

Guskey, T. R. (2005). Taking a second look at accountability. *Journal of Staff Development, 26*(1), 10–18.

Guskey, T. R. (2007). Multiple sources of evidence: An analysis of stakeholders' perceptions of various indicators of student learning. *Educational Measurement: Issues and Practice, 26*(1), 19–27.

Guskey, T. R. (2012). The rules of evidence. *Journal of Staff Development, 33*(4), 40–43.

Guskey, T. R., & Sparks, D. (2004). Linking professional development to improvements in student learning. In E. M. Guyton & J. R. Dangel (Eds.), *Teacher education yearbook XII: Research linking teacher preparation and student performance.* Dubuque, IA: Kendall/Hunt.

Guskey, T. R., & Yoon, K. S. (2009). What works in professional development? *Phi Delta Kappan, 90*(7), 495–500.

Hall, G. E., & Hord, S. M. (1987). *Change in schools: Facilitating the process.* Albany: State University of New York Press.

Hirsh, S. (2012). Student outcomes are the driving force behind professional learning decisions. *Journal of Staff Development, 33*(5), 72.

Holton, E. F. (1996). The flawed four-level evaluation model. *Human Resources Development Quarterly, 7*(1), 5–21.

Joint Committee on Standards for Educational Evaluation. (1994). *The program evaluation standards* (2nd ed.). Thousand Oaks, CA: Sage.

Kirkpatrick, D. L. (1994). *Evaluating training programs.* San Francisco: Berrett-Koehler.

Kirkpatrick, D. L. (1998). *Evaluating training programs: The four levels* (2nd ed.). San Francisco: Berrett-Koehler.

Langer, G. M., & Colton, A. B. (1994). Reflective decision making: The cornerstone of school reform. *Journal of Staff Development, 15*(1), 2–7.

Little, J. W. (1990). The persistence of privacy: Autonomy and initiative in teachers' professional relations. *Teachers College Record, 91*(4), 509–536.

Parry, S. B. (1996). Measuring training's ROI. *Training and Development, 50*(5), 72–75.

Phillips, J. J. (1997). *Return on investment in training and performance improvement programs.* Houston, TX: Gulf.

Phillips, P. P. (2002). *The bottom line on ROI: Basics, benefits, and barriers to measuring training and performance improvement.* Atlanta, GA: CEP Press.

Raudenbush, S. W. (2005). Learning from attempts to improve schooling: The contribution of methodological diversity. *Educational Researcher, 34*(5), 25–31.

Sawchuk, S. (2010, November 10). Proof lacking on success of staff development. *Education Week.* Retrieved from *www.edweek.org/ew/articles/2010/11/10/11pd_research.h30.html.*

Schmoker, M. J. (2004). Tipping point: From feckless reform to substantive instructional improvement. *Phi Delta Kappan, 85*(6), 424–432.

Schmoker, M. J. (2006). *Results now: How we can achieve unprecedented improvements in teaching and learning.* Alexandria, VA: Association for Supervision and Curriculum Development.

Scriven, M. (1967). The methodology of evaluation. In R. E. Stake (Ed.), *Perspectives of curriculum evaluation* (pp. 39–83). Chicago: Rand McNally.

Scriven, M. (1991). *Evaluation thesaurus* (4th ed.). Newbury Park, CA: Sage.

Sparks, D. (1996, February). Viewing reform from a systems perspective. *The Developer*, pp. 2, 6.

Sparks, D., & Hirsh, S. (1997). *A new vision for staff development*. Alexandria, VA: Association for Supervision and Curriculum Development.

Stevens, F., Lawrenz, F., & Sharp, L. (1995). *User-friendly handbook for project evaluation: Science, mathematics, engineering, and technology education*. Arlington, VA: National Science Foundation.

Supovitz, J. A. (2002). Developing communities of instructional practice. *Teachers College Record*, *104*(8), 1591–1626.

Todnem, G., & Warner, M. P. (1993). Using ROI to assess staff development efforts. *Journal of Staff Development*, *14*(3), 32–34.

Viadero, D. (2011, June 29). Professional development. *Education Week*. Retrieved from *www.edweek.org/ew/issues/professional-development/*.

Wholey, J. S., Hatry, H. P., & Newcomer, K. E. (Eds.). (2004). *Handbook of practical program evaluation* (2nd ed.). San Francisco: Jossey-Bass.

Yoon, K. S., Duncan, T., Lee, S. W. Y., Scarloss, B., & Shapley, K. L. (2007). *Reviewing the evidence on how teacher professional development affects student achievement* (Issues and Answers Report, REL 2007 No. 033). Washington, DC: U.S. Department of Education, Institute of Education Sciences, National Center for Education Evaluation and Regional Assistance, Regional Educational Laboratory Southwest. Retrieved from *http://ies.ed.gov/ncee/edlabs*.

CHAPTER 24

Sustaining Teacher Professional Development

LAURA M. DESIMONE
DANIEL STUCKEY

- Effective and sustainable professional development programs share certain core features.
- Accountability related to the quality of professional development and classroom monitoring and support is crucial for driving improvement.
- Professional development should be targeted to teachers' individual learning needs.
- Professional development works best in an environment of coherent policy.
- School administrators should have realistic expectations about what professional development is likely to do and when.

SUSTAINABILITY IN PROFESSIONAL DEVELOPMENT

To identify sustainable practices in teachers' professional development, we first identify the characteristics of high-quality, effective professional development. Second, we discuss how and why implementation of professional development in the classroom may vary, as well as challenges to measuring and studying professional development's effectiveness. Last, we discuss how to sustain models of high-quality professional development over time, at both the district and school levels.

Defining High-Quality Professional Development

A growing body of empirical research suggests that effective professional development programs share a core set of features (e.g., Desimone, 2009; Garet et al., 2010;

Penuel, Gallagher, & Moorthy, 2011). These core features include the following: (1) *content focus*: activities focused on subject matter content and how students learn that content; (2) *active learning*: opportunities for teachers to observe, receive feedback, analyze student work, or make presentations, as opposed to passively listening to lectures; (3) *coherence*: content, goals, and activities that are consistent with the school curriculum, teacher knowledge and beliefs, the needs of students, and school, district, and state policies; (4) *sustained duration*: professional development activities that are ongoing throughout the school year and that include 20 hours or more of contact time; and (5) *collective participation*: groups of teachers from the same grade, subject, or school participate in professional development activities together to build an interactive learning community.

Over the past 5–8 years, several rigorous, randomized controlled trials (RCTs) have attempted to build off of the correlational and observational studies of professional development, experimentally testing the importance of some or all of these features of high-quality professional development. We draw on these recent RCTs on professional development to forward thinking about what works and how to sustain what works.

First, we discuss the role of implementation fidelity. Second, we discuss how different types of professional development (e.g., activities targeted to knowledge, behavior, curricula, or a combination) present different challenges and expected benefits. Third, we highlight the importance of furthering our understanding of how teachers vary in participation and response to learning activities. Fourth, we propose the policy-attributes theory as a way to organize thinking about what needs to be in place in the policy environment to sustain models of high-quality professional development. Finally, we consider the results of recent professional development interventions and make preliminary conclusions about the type of outcomes we expect and how we might improve them.

Although the RCTs we discuss here are more rigorous than previous research, they are not perfect. They do not measure outcomes as often as we might like (e.g., once a year instead of periodically throughout the year); the control group is not "pure," because teachers in the control group are usually engaged in alternative learning experiences; and the studies are usually underpowered (i.e., enrolling too few teachers to detect small effects). Nevertheless, the findings from this recent and developing rigorous knowledge base point to several key areas we think hold promise for improving our understanding of how to achieve quality and sustainability in teachers' professional development.

Theory of Change and Instruction: The Role of Implementation in Effects and Sustainability

Sustainability relates to whether both the theory of instruction and the theory of change work. That is, when implemented well, (1) does the new content or pedagogy learned in professional development improve student learning (theory of instruction), and (2) how well do the professional development activities elicit improvements in teacher knowledge and instruction (theory of change; Wayne, Yoon, Zhu,

Cronen, & Garet, 2008)? If the intervention causes teachers to implement better instructional practices, then the intervention should be sustained. Positive effects on teaching and learning are probably the most powerful mechanism for institutionalizing an intervention because positive effects foster teacher buy-in and motivation (Desimone, 2002).

There is a substantial literature on instructional best practice, but identifying aspects of professional development that reliably change teacher behavior has been more elusive. Barriers to teacher implementation of instructional best practice include professional development that falls short on the core features (e.g., too short, not enough practice, not coherent with other initiatives, no opportunities for feedback, not integrated into the curriculum). We would expect that all the core features need to be in place for a reform to last in a school. For example, in an RCT of reading comprehension and vocabulary instruction in first grade, Gersten, Dimino, Jayanthi, Kim, and Santoro (2010) hypothesize that their professional development would have been more successful in changing practice if the professional development had been enacted for the duration that was originally planned; school officials allowed teachers to participate only during their planning time "due to scheduling constraints" (p. 731).

Even professional development with all the core features of quality sometimes does not have the strong effects on teachers and students that we might hope for. One way to further our understanding of why this might be is to examine effects across different teachers, which we do next.

Variation in Implementation

In their simplest form, most theories of professional development boil down to this: Professional development alters teacher classroom behavior, which in turn alters student performance (see Yoon, Duncan, Lee, Scarloss, & Shapley, 2007, p. 4). Therefore, we expect that student outcomes will be heavily influenced by the degree to which teachers actually alter their behavior vis-à-vis a professional development intervention. In other words, fidelity of implementation plays a key role in determining whether professional development's effects on teachers and students will be realized.

Recent RCTs have shown that intervention models often include models of change that work for *some but not all teachers* and that student outcomes are higher for teachers who have higher fidelity of implementation, meaning that their execution of the desired instruction is closer to the ideal envisioned by the designers of the intervention. For example, Davidson, Fields, and Yang (2009), in a study of preschool phonological awareness, found no significant main effects for student performance but did find higher outcomes for the students of teachers who showed higher fidelity to the intervention. Thus the intervention failed to boost average student performance, but when teachers changed their behaviors to better align with the intervention, student performance did improve. When student outcomes are better for high-fidelity teachers, there is evidence that a professional development's theory of instruction is sound, even if its theory of change is not able to transform all teachers into "high implementers." This idea is consistent with past findings that a key driver of student improvement may be increasing teacher fidelity to interventions (e.g., Desimone, 2002). Professional development can be successful for subsets of teachers even when it does not seem to be successful on the whole. Understanding why professional development is successful with some teachers and understanding how to expand that subset is crucial for improving overall student achievement.

But how does this help us learn how to foster more widespread high implementation? The experimental literature on professional development tends to focus on average effects across teachers and students, and the experiments are designed and randomized to test these average effects. However, we suggest that professional development affects teachers differentially, depending on their previous knowledge, their level of experience, and other factors.

Of course, teachers differ from one another in many ways. Although this may seem obvious, Piasta and colleagues (2010) stress that teacher variability is a "major finding" and encourage future research to explore "teacher × professional development interactions" (p. 369). We have not reviewed any study that incorporates teacher variation on key factors such as experience or a priori knowledge into the design of the experiment to see which teachers are most likely to take up the professional development. However, it is common to conduct exploratory or post hoc analyses to try to understand why some teachers became high implementers and others did not. These suggest that particular teacher characteristics do matter.

Experience as a Key Source of Variation. Five recent RCT studies explored whether professional development affected novice and veteran teachers differently. Of these five, three found no differences—Garet and colleagues (2010), Gersten and colleagues (2010), and Sailors and Price (2010). Of the two other studies, one found that veteran teachers had higher fidelity, whereas the other found that novice teachers were the ones with higher fidelity. Davidson and colleagues (2009) found that veteran teachers were stronger implementers of a program in phonological awareness. On the other hand, Borman, Gamoran, and Bowdon (2008) found a significant interaction effect between years of experience and professional development around inquiry-oriented science teaching in the fourth grade. On average, the Borman and colleagues intervention had significantly negative main effects on students' elementary science skills. However, when the researchers looked only at students who were taught by teachers with fewer than 3 years of experience, the intervention had positive effects on student science achievement. Based on this finding, they conclude that "it appears that students of new teachers did benefit to a greater extent than students of more experienced teachers from their teachers' exposure to professional development in science inquiry" (p. 255).

One explanation of these mixed results may be that, in certain circumstances, veteran teachers have higher uptake of more "traditional" practices (e.g., phonological awareness), whereas novice teachers might be more adept at reform-oriented professional development. It might also be that novice teachers are more open and flexible about new approaches, whereas veteran teachers are less likely to change easily because they have ingrained, established practices. Future studies could use block designs to explore the differential effects of professional development on novice versus veteran teachers, as well as other potentially influential characteristics.

Content Knowledge as a Key Source of Variation. The relationship between teachers' content knowledge and their fidelity of implementation is mixed, but it seems like a potentially important variable to consider. From Davidson and colleagues (2009), we see evidence that teachers' content knowledge matters very little: "there was not a relation between teacher scores on the [teacher knowledge test] and child performance on the outcome measures. The anticipated moderating effect of teacher knowledge did not occur" (p. 195). On the other hand, in a study of sixth-grade teachers' ability to teach fractions, ratios, and equations, Santagata (2009) reported higher student outcomes when teachers' math content knowledge was higher. To explain this result, Santagata suggests that teachers have difficulty focusing on intervention strategies or curricular changes when they do not understand the content well. In our own forthcoming randomized study (Desimone, Covay, & Caines, 2013), we witnessed similar trends. Some teachers with low content knowledge made use of the materials of the intervention without giving deep attention to the scientific principles behind the intervention, whereas other teachers indicated that they thought the best aspect of professional development was an opportunity to improve their content knowledge, even though this particular intervention was not set up for that purpose. Teachers also may react differently to each other and to professional development providers based on content knowledge differences. For example, Yoon, Liu, and Goh (2010) describe how members of a professional development team shunned another member seemingly *because* he had higher content knowledge.

Thus variation in implementation due to teacher characteristics is a critical area of attention for schools and districts interested in sustaining the effects of professional development for all of their teachers. One powerful way for districts and schools to increase the effectiveness and sustainability of their professional development efforts is to acknowledge the way that professional development affects teachers differentially and to adjust it accordingly. This may mean adding additional supports for certain types of teachers, focusing professional development efforts on those teachers that they are most likely to work for, or choosing professional development programs that are best suited to the faculty of a particular school or district.

The Role of Teacher Buy-In

Although it was not an explicit focus of any of the RCTs we surveyed, a synthesis of findings and previous research suggests that strong teacher buy-in goes a long way to improving implementation and facilitating sustainability (Desimone, 2002). We hypothesize that voluntary interventions have higher initial buy-in than mandatory interventions. If we use voluntary as a proxy for high buy-in, we see that when interventions are voluntary, student outcomes are improved. Of the twelve recent experimental studies, three were mandated, and of those three, one (Borman et al., 2008) had negative effects on student outcomes and the other two (Garet et al., 2010; Santagata, 2009) had no effects on student outcomes. In contrast, of the three professional development opportunities that were clearly voluntary, one (Gersten et al., 2010) had no effect on student outcomes, but the other two (Penuel et al., 2011; Sailors & Price, 2010) had significantly positive effects on student outcomes. Districts will frequently want to provide professional development to all of their staff, not just to those who are willing to volunteer, but the importance of fostering buy-in should not be ignored.

Implementation Dip

Another issue related to implementation is the "implementation dip," noted in many circumstances in which new knowledge and behavior are asked of teachers (Fullan, Cuttress, & Kilcher, 2005). Teacher and student performance can get worse before it gets better. Because studies usually last only 1 year, we do not have a good understanding of the ebb and flow of teacher learning or the way that implementation of new instruction continues into year 2, year 3, and beyond as a result of high-quality professional development. Borman and colleagues (2008) hypothesized that an implementation dip was responsible for the negative results of their professional development experiment, but it would take further years of study to determine whether that was actually the case. Dips in implementation (and in standardized test scores as a result) can be catastrophic for schools and districts because such dips are often used as reasons to abandon the reform before it has had a chance to take hold. Thus it is helpful to take a longer-term view of a teacher learning intervention and to establish reasonable expectations about when effects might occur (e.g., in year 2 rather than year 1).

Depth of Implementation Measures Vary

Another complication in studying implementation is how we measure it. Methods range from checklists (Davidson et al., 2009) to observations (Gersten et al., 2010; Piasta et al., 2010; Sailors & Price, 2010) to surveys (Santagata, 2009), with each method offering advantages and disadvantages. There is also the possibility that the instruments used to measure implementation are not sensitive to differences among treatment and control (e.g., Kim et al., 2011). To address these possible weaknesses, any professional development intervention should have a comprehensive system of evaluation, which includes observations, self-reports, opportunities for feedback, and practice. These mechanisms help ensure that teachers will have the continuing monitoring and feedback shown to be necessary for teacher learning to transfer to institutionalized classroom instruction change (Cohen & Ball, 1990).

The Interaction of Dosage and Substance: Are We Aiming to Change Knowledge, Behavior, or Decision Making?

Beyond teacher characteristics and the ebb and flow of change represented by the implementation dip, the extent to which a professional development intervention is successful depends on both its duration and its focus. Unless teachers receive a certain "dosage" of hours or sessions, it seems unlikely that professional development will be effective. In the experiments reviewed by Yoon and colleagues (2007), for example, teachers experienced 49 hours, on average, and students performed significantly better whenever their teachers experienced at least 14 hours of professional development.

In the more recent experiments, teachers have received as many as 114 hours (Garet et al., 2010) without significantly influencing student outcomes. On the other hand, professional development was sometimes effective even at a low dosage. In particular, the preschool literacy intervention studied by Piasta and colleagues (2010) is good news for those hoping to implement sustainable professional development programs. The researchers deliberately examined a program that fit within the resources that schools and districts usually have available to them. The professional development took only 11 hours, the teachers missed little teaching, and the curricular materials were relatively inexpensive. Monitoring, accountability, and feedback were accomplished through a pattern of submitting videos and receiving letters, thereby obviating the need for expensive coaching.

Why would an 11-hour professional development produce student achievement gains, whereas a 114-hour professional development failed to? Clearly, factors besides dosage contribute to an intervention's effectiveness. One possible explanation is that the 114-hour intervention focused on content, whereas the 11-hour intervention focused on changing specific instructional behaviors.

As we reviewed 12 recent RCTs, we noticed that interventions tended to fall into one or more of these three categorizations: (1) examining academic content, (2) changing specific teacher behaviors, or (3) improving teacher decision making. The 114-hour mathematics intervention studied by Garet and colleagues (2010) focused primarily on content. First, it aimed to improve teachers' content knowledge of rational numbers, and second, it aimed to help teachers deliver more "precise definitions...explain rational number concepts and procedures, identify and address persistent student misconceptions...and use representations of rational number concepts in teaching" (p. xvi). Through deep engagement with content, developers hoped to improve teachers' understanding of rational numbers and their ability to explain the content to students. However, teachers who received professional development scored no better than control teachers on tests that measured their "common knowledge (CK) of mathematics and specialized knowledge (SK) of mathematics for teaching" (p. 14).

Content Knowledge

This pattern was common across the studies that examined teacher content knowledge. In four out of five studies (Davidson et al., 2009; Garet et al., 2010; Neuman & Cunningham, 2009; Santagata, 2009), teachers experiencing professional development showed no significant improvement in content knowledge. In the fifth study (Gersten et al., 2010), teachers showed significant improvement in knowledge for teaching vocabulary, but not in knowledge for teaching comprehension. Though common sense tells us that improving teachers' content knowledge is a good idea for improving student outcomes, the studies demonstrate how hard it is to improve teachers' content knowledge.

Pedagogy

A second approach to professional development focuses less on content and more on curricular, pedagogical, or behavioral changes. This type of intervention provides teachers with additional materials or suggests specific instructional strategies that teachers should use. The Piasta and colleagues (2010) study is emblematic. Teachers in the treatment group were asked to read a specific book to preschool students four times a week; the books included inserts alerting teachers to how they might explicitly make "print references when reading" (p. 353). Similarly, Sailors and Price (2010) studied teachers who were asked to teach a discrete set of cognitive reading strategies to students in grades 2–8. Coaches helped these teachers to modify the curriculum and sometimes engaged in team teaching of the cognitive strategies, leading to significant positive effects.

On the other hand, Borman and colleagues (2008) found significant *negative* effects for a professional development intervention meant to transition teachers into a new elementary science curriculum based on inquiry-oriented practices. These negative effects may be due to the relative complexity of inquiry-oriented practices compared with the relative simplicity of reading strategies such as *ask questions* and *make predictions*. The negative results may also be due to the inadequacy of a train-the-trainer model; in the Borman study, only one teacher from each school received the training, and that teacher was then responsible for training the other teachers.

Together, the Piasta and colleagues (2010), Sailors and Price (2010), and Borman and colleagues (2008) studies suggest that simple behavioral changes can be effected by professional development and can have positive effects on student achievement but that more complicated behavioral changes are less tractable. Of course, professional development is likely to focus on content *and* instructional behavior. Neuman and Cunningham (2009) write, "professional development that contains both content and pedagogical knowledge may best support the ability of teachers to apply literacy knowledge in practice" (p. 534). Santagata (2009) suggests that the superficial changes brought about by these pedagogical interventions are necessary for establishing more transformative change.

Decision Making

A third approach focuses on teacher decision making, which has received less empirical attention. If some researchers hypothesize that the key to improving professional development outcomes is increasing fidelity to a set program, Penuel and colleagues (2011) hypothesize that teachers will always adapt curricula and professional development to suit their own settings and needs. Therefore, Penuel and colleagues attempt to build an adaptive professional development program that helps teachers make better decisions about content and pacing, helping teachers to see how to use both "expert- and teacher-designed activities" to teach earth science to students in grades 6–8 (p. 1018). The students of teachers receiving such development—focused on decision making and adapting materials—had significantly higher science achievement than the students of teachers who received only a new curriculum. Ultimately, the key to sustainable professional development might not be putting stable practices in place but rather helping teachers become adaptive planners capable of making good decisions over time.

The Policy-Attributes Theory

Now we take a step back to consider the broader organizational and policy context that facilitates implementation and sustainability. Recent studies of professional development (and previous research on reform) have identified several organizational variables that are strongly linked with the initial success and sustainability of reform focused on teacher learning. These organizational variables can be described by a policy-attributes framework, which identifies authority, power, coherence, and specificity as key factors in determining the effects and longevity of a reform (Desimone, 2002). The recent RCT studies of professional development that we review here shed light on which aspects of these attributes may be most important for the sustainability of high-quality professional development.

Authority

As with most reform efforts, professional development interventions rely to a great extent on the leadership support at the school and district levels. Although some studies are not clear on how leadership influenced the implementation and success of their professional development interventions (e.g., Borman et al., 2008; Davidson et al., 2009), others emphasize the crucial role that principals can play in structuring time for teachers to participate in professional development (Gersten et al., 2010). Santagata (2009) provides an example of how tension between teachers and the district can cause teachers to view a professional development program unfavorably if teachers associate the professional development with the district. The influential role that support and backing from authority figures can play in improving initial implementation and increasing the longevity of an intervention is well documented in the broader school reform literature (e.g., Desimone, 2002).

Power (Accountability Pressure)

Previous studies have shown that power exerted through the pressure of rewards or sanctions can alter teacher behavior, but such changes are usually not as long-lasting as behavior changes that result from self-motivation or buy-in (e.g., Desimone, 2002). One critical question is, To what extent should we encourage districts and schools to use accountability pressures to motivate teachers to adopt practices encouraged in professional development?

It seems possible that teacher change is highly mediated by power, or accountability pressures. For example, Santagata (2009) found that when observed, teachers "treated" with professional development spent significantly more time working on assessment problems than did control teachers, but that treated teachers did not increase the cognitive demand on their students. This may suggest that teachers felt pressure to comply but did so in a superficial way, rather than deeply changing their underlying behaviors in ways proposed by professional developers. Garet and colleagues (2010) hypothesize that one reason their professional development on teaching rational numbers to middle schoolers may not have had strong effects was that there was no pressure from the district or school for teachers to change what they were doing.

Further support for the possible effects of accountability comes from Neuman and Cunningham (2009), who found that when preschool child-care workers received a course on preliteracy skills, the teachers did not change their practice, but that when the course was paired with coaching at the child-care center, workers *did* significantly change their practice. In this case, we might construe coaching at least in part as an accountability mechanism—when teachers know they will be observed by experts looking for particular teaching behaviors, they may be more likely to adopt those new behaviors. Videotaping and feedback may work similarly (Piasta et al., 2010). In this way, accountability mechanisms can be considered a type of "implementation driver" (Hulleman & Cordray, 2009).

Coherence

The extent to which the professional development is compatible with the curriculum and standards the teacher is using can play a substantial role in influencing a teacher's willingness and ability to adopt new content or practices. Penuel and colleagues' (2011) elegant study was set up for success. The participating district was engaging in large-scale change, and the professional development intervention was intentionally integrated with the more holistic change that was occurring across the district. In contrast, when districts communicate competing priorities, creating an incoherent environment for teachers, we would expect implementation to be weak (e.g., Santagata, 2009).

Another dimension of coherence may be autonomy; in Neuman and Cunningham's (2009) study, in which teachers had autonomy to change, there was little chance the professional development was incoherent with demands on them because teachers did not have many rules and regulations to abide by. Perhaps the most troubling circumstance occurs when we are asking teachers to change inside a system that is not itself changing, or at least not openly supportive of change. Thus it is important for districts and schools to align their teacher learning initiatives with other reforms that teachers are being asked to follow.

Specificity

Previous research has demonstrated that when a policy or intervention clearly states the activities and behaviors that are the target, teachers are more likely to show higher implementation. We read the recent professional development literature as coalescing on a similar finding: The more concrete the behaviors asked for in the professional development, the more likely teachers are to be high implementers.

For example, teachers are more likely to be able to implement a concrete, specific task—such as more use of phonological exercises (Davidson et al., 2009)—than to engage in a more nuanced, complicated task, such as inquiry-oriented science practices (Borman et al., 2008). This is likely because more conceptual teaching requires a complex knowledge base and sustained practice (Cohen & Ball, 2002), whereas more process- or pedagogically oriented behaviors are likely much easier to implement. Similarly, interventions are more likely to find effects on more proximal outcomes specific to the intervention rather than on more broad measures such as standardized tests.

DISCUSSION: WHAT RECENT INTERVENTION RESEARCH TELLS US ABOUT THE SUSTAINABILITY OF PROFESSIONAL DEVELOPMENT

Given contemporary reform pressures, professional development programs are likely to be sustained only if they can show results. Ultimately, "showing results" may require improving student achievement on the state's standardized tests, but districts seeking sustainability should first look for more gradual or proximal signs of success. When developing and evaluating professional development programs, districts should remember several lessons about how professional development affects student outcomes: (1) Professional development is likely to improve some teachers' instruction more than other teachers' instruction; (2) teacher behaviors are likely to change before student achievement changes; (3) it may take a while for student improvement to occur; and (4) student improvement may be too narrow to register on state tests.

Teachers First

Improving student achievement is difficult to do, and even when student achievement is accomplished, it may be difficult to measure or confirm. However, the recent batch of RCTs demonstrates that professional development is good at eliciting some kinds of behavioral changes in teachers. Professional development interventions can seek to affect teacher behavior, teacher knowledge, or both. Nine of the recent studies measured whether teacher behaviors or practice changed as a result of the professional development, and in seven of them, researchers found significantly positive behavioral changes. In these seven cases, researchers thought that teachers who experienced professional development acted in ways more in line with best practice.

Of course, best practice is always theoretical unless empirical support shows that such behaviors lead to improved student outcomes—but the important lesson is that professional development gets teachers to change. If the professional development is based on an appropriate theory of instruction, it should get student outcomes to improve if given enough time.

On the other hand, increasing teacher content knowledge seems more difficult. We identified four studies (Garet et al., 2010; Gersten et al., 2010; Neuman & Cunningham, 2009; Santagata, 2009) in which the researchers attempted to improve teacher content knowledge and also provided a posttest of content knowledge in order to test significant differences between teachers in the control and treatment groups. Three of these studies showed no significant effects, and the fourth (Gersten et al., 2010) showed increased teacher knowledge of best practices in vocabulary instruction but not best practices in reading comprehension instruction. These studies are the most recent evidence that building teacher content knowledge is complicated and requires sustained, ongoing, high-quality supports throughout a teacher's career (Cohen & Ball, 1990).

Teacher Variability

As discussed earlier in this chapter, professional development programs have variable effects on teachers and their students. Although professional development seems to change teachers' behaviors *on average*, it does not change all teachers equally. At the inception of professional development programs, districts may want to focus on the teachers who stand to benefit the most from development, either because they are the teachers in the most need of improvement or because their characteristics imply that they are most likely to change their behavior. As professional development continues, districts may want to add additional supports or accountability pressures in order to further the development of teachers who have shown the least behavioral change during the early stages of the professional development efforts. Another idea is to structure and plan professional development targeted to teachers with different levels of classroom experience or content knowledge.

Time

Ideally, professional development programs would have immediate impacts on student achievement, but because improving student achievement is difficult, professional development is unlikely to have immediate effects and may even have initially negative effects. As mentioned, Fullan and colleagues (2005) calls this the implementation dip, referring to the ways teachers stumble as they first experiment with new practices.

The recent RCTs fail to show the longitudinal effects of professional development programs. None of the 12 recent interventions engaged teachers for more than 2 years, and none of the interventions measured students for longer than 1 year. Thus it remains unknown how teacher or student outcomes persist over time. Although several studies reported teachers changing their behaviors during an intervention, it is unknown whether teachers maintain new behaviors once the intervention is over. (In light of concerns that teachers are really responding to accountability pressures—not professional development—we might be especially worried that teacher behavior would not persist absent ongoing development or accountability pressure.) In a similar vein, we do not know how student outcomes are affected over time. Because none of the trials tracks student achievement in subsequent years, we cannot know whether student gains persist or fade away, nor whether there are any latent effects on student achievement. All of these questions are worthy of investigation.

Narrow Success

Yoon and colleagues' (2007) meta-analysis of high-quality professional development studies found that across nine interventions, student outcomes improved on 18 out of 20 measures, and for the RCTs, the average effect size was 0.51. However, the RCTs since 2007 imply that professional development is considerably less successful at effecting student achievement gains. Of the nine studies that report student outcomes, one reports negative effects on fourth graders' performance on an elementary science benchmark (Borman et al., 2008). Four studies report no effects on tests that measure either elementary math or literacy (Davidson et al., 2009; Garet et al., 2010; Gersten et al., 2010; Santagata, 2009), and only three demonstrate significant positive results. Kim and colleagues (2011) find that Latino English language learners in grades 6–12 get better at writing text-based, analytical essays. Sailors and Price (2010) find that students in grades 2–8 improve their reading comprehension. Penuel and colleagues (2011) find that students in grades 6–8 have higher achievement on a test of earth science knowledge.

Although we often hope that professional development will improve student achievement across a content area, professional development is more likely to improve student achievement on some narrow skill. For example, Simmons and colleagues (2010) found that fourth-grade students of teachers receiving professional development did significantly better than their peers on an achievement test that closely matched the content of the intervention. However, gains were washed out on a broader test of reading comprehension and vocabulary. The researchers note that this finding is consistent with earlier research on professional development; it seems easier to effect change on targeted content than to effect the generalized improvement necessary to improve state test scores. If policymakers and school leaders are interested in using professional development to improve achievement, they should target their professional development to the skills students are most lacking or to the skills that are most generalizable.

Districts should keep these lessons in mind. Lack of results can cause a district to abandon professional development, but districts would be wise to look for proximal results in the short term. If teacher behaviors are changing, or if student scores are changing on more narrow measures, these proximal results can be the flywheel of continued improvement, and they can provide an argument for sustaining current professional development activities.

RECOMMENDATIONS AND FUTURE DIRECTIONS

From our reading of recent rigorous causal studies of professional development, we draw several conclusions and suggest several ideas that may be helpful in designing sustainable professional development.

First, for practices to become institutionalized, professional development must have the core features of quality—content focus, active learning, coherence, sufficient duration, and collective participation.

Second, we emphasize the importance of ongoing support and monitoring of implementation. This includes comprehensive assessment, which might include videotaping instruction, observation, feedback, discussion, practice, and modeling.

Third, districts seeking sustainable and effective professional development programs should keep in mind several lessons about teacher variation. Teachers vary in their ability and their responses to professional development. Even when professional development programs boost average student outcomes, the effects are likely to be uneven. In light of teacher differences, districts might consider differentiating professional development according to teacher characteristics. In order to maximize effects, districts might match teachers with development opportunities most likely to suit their knowledge, experience, and learning needs.

Fourth, teachers are more likely to implement professional development interventions with fidelity when the policy/organizational environment has the following attributes, integrated and in balance: accountability mechanisms in place to motivate implementation; authority in the form of support and buy-in from school officials and teachers; coherence in terms of integration with curriculum, standards, assessments, and other demands on teachers; and specificity, in terms of identifying specific activities and behaviors to be targeted by the professional development intervention.

Last, this most recent set of RCTs allows us to see both strengths and weaknesses in the way we support teachers. They provide evidence that well-structured, relatively short professional development can change specific behaviors, but changing underlying content knowledge in meaningful ways is much more challenging. Links to student learning are often tenuous and are most easily demonstrated by tests that measure narrow content. The field needs more longitudinal and in-depth studies of how professional development affects individual teachers and also how professional development affects the trajectory of teacher practices and student learning over time. We can only learn to sustain high-quality professional development by sustaining our studies of it.

QUESTIONS FOR DISCUSSION

1. What evidence should school administrators collect to help them evaluate whether professional development is successful? What counts as success?

2. What strategies can administrators use to increase the chances that professional development will be successful for their teachers?

3. How might administrators decide which type of professional development is most appropriate for their teachers—for example, professional development targeted to using a particular curriculum, adopting a specific type of pedagogy, building content knowledge,

or training teachers to make better decisions about how to adapt materials to their students?

4. What is the boundary between teacher professional development and the rest of the work that teachers do? Is professional development best conceived of as a "program" or an "intervention," or does the goal of sustainability require some other characterization?

5. What should we make of the discrepancy between the large and consistent effects on student achievement found by Yoon and colleagues (2007) and the more muted and inconsistent effects of the RCTs completed since 2007?

ACKNOWLEDGMENT

The research reported here was supported by the Institute of Education Sciences, U.S. Department of Education (Grant No. R305B090015) to the University of Pennsylvania. The opinions expressed are those of the authors and do not represent views of the Institute nor the U.S. Department of Education.

REFERENCES

Borman, G. D., Gamoran, A., & Bowdon, J. (2008). A randomized trial of teacher development in elementary science: First-year achievement effects. *Journal of Research on Educational Effectiveness, 1*(4), 237–264.

Cohen, D., & Ball, D. L. (1990). Relations between policy and practice: A commentary. *Educational Evaluation and Policy Analysis, 12*(3), 249–256.

Davidson, M. R., Fields, M. K., & Yang, J. (2009). A randomized trial study of a preschool literacy curriculum: The importance of implementation. *Journal of Research on Educational Effectiveness, 2*(3), 177–208.

Desimone, L. M. (2002). How can comprehensive school reform models be successfully implemented? *Review of Educational Research, 72*(3), 433–479.

Desimone, L. M. (2009). Improving impact studies of teachers' professional development: Toward better conceptualizations and measures. *Educational Researcher, 38*(3), 181–199.

Desimone, L. M., Covay, E., & Caines, J. (2013*). Implementation of a middle school science curriculum intervention: Teacher challenges* (Working paper). Philadelphia: University of Pennsylvania.

Fullan, M., Cuttress, C., & Kilcher, A. (2005). Forces for leaders of change. *Journal of Staff Development, 26*(4), 54–59.

Garet, M. S., Wayne, A. J., Stancavage, F., Taylor, J., Walters, K., Song, M., et al. (2010). Middle school mathematics professional development impact study: Findings after the first year of implementation (NCEE Publication No. 2010-4009). Washington, DC: U.S. Department of Education, National Center for Education Evaluation and Regional Assistance.

Gersten, R., Dimino, J., Jayanthi, M., Kim, J. S., & Santoro, L. E. (2010). Teacher study group: Impact of the professional development model on reading instruction and student outcomes in first-grade classrooms. *American Educational Research Journal, 47*(3), 694–739.

Hulleman, C. S., & Cordray, D. S. (2009). Moving from the lab to the field: The role of fidelity and achieved relative intervention strength. *Journal of Research on Educational Effectiveness, 2*(1), 88–110.

Kim, J. S., Olson, C. B., Scarcella, R., Kramer, J., Pearson, M., van Dyk, D., et al. (2011). A randomized experiment of a cognitive strategies approach to text-based analytical writing for mainstreamed Latino English language learners in grades 6 to 12. *Journal of Research on Educational Effectiveness, 4*(3), 231–263.

Neuman, S. B., & Cunningham, L. (2009). The impact of professional development and coaching on early language and literacy instructional practices. *American Educational Research Journal, 46*(2), 532–566.

Penuel, W. R., Gallagher, L. P., & Moorthy, S. (2011). Preparing teachers to design sequences of instruction in earth systems science: A comparison of three professional development programs. *American Educational Research Journal, 48*(4), 996–1025.

Piasta, S. B., Dynia, J. M., Justice, L. M., Pentimonti, J. M., Kaderavek, J. N., & Schatschneider, C. (2010). Impact of professional development on preschool teachers' print references during shared read alouds: A latent growth curve analysis. *Journal of Research on Educational Effectiveness, 3*(4), 343–380.

Sailors, M., & Price, L. R. (2010). Professional development that supports the teaching of cognitive reading strategy instruction. *Elementary School Journal, 110*(3), 301–322.

Santagata, R. (2009). Designing video-based professional development for mathematics teachers in low-performing schools. *Journal of Teacher Education, 60*(1), 38–51.

Simmons, D., Hairrell, A., Edmonds, M., Vaughn, S., Larsen, R., Willson, V., et al. (2010). A comparison of multiple-strategy methods: Effects on fourth-grade students' general and content-specific reading comprehension and vocabulary development. *Journal of Research on Educational Effectiveness, 3*(2), 121–156.

Wayne, A. J., Yoon, K. S., Zhu, P., Cronen, S., & Garet, M. S. (2008). Experimenting with teacher professional development: Motives and methods. *Educational Researcher, 37*(8), 469–479.

Yoon, K. S., Duncan, T., Lee, S. W. Y., Scarloss, B., & Shapley, K. L. (2007). *Reviewing the evidence on how teacher professional development affects student achievement.* Washington, DC: U.S. Department of Education, Institute of Education Sciences, National Center for Educational Evaluation and Regional Assistance.

Yoon, S., Liu, L., & Goh, S. (2010). Convergent adaptation in small groups: Understanding professional development activities through a complex systems lens. *Journal of Technology and Teacher Education, 18*(2), 319–344.

CHAPTER 25

Lessons Learned

What Our History and Research Tell Us about Teachers' Professional Learning

SHERRY KRAGLER
LINDA E. MARTIN
RUTH SYLVESTER

- The perception of the teaching field has changed over the decades.
- Research has revealed the complexity of the act of teaching.
- Different methods and models of staff and professional development have been refined over decades that align with the research of each era.
- Professional learning of educators takes time and is an ongoing process.
- Often, implemented educational policies do not contribute to teachers' learning or school improvement.

Letter to the President (now and future):

We recognize that you as well as other citizens (business leaders, parents, politicians, educators) are concerned about the education of our children. This is seen in the decades of legislation that is intended to increase student achievement through professional development of teachers. However, there is little evidence of any impact from this legislation, as seen in the recent NAEP results.

We know that most legislation includes language that focuses on the quality of teachers and the quality of instruction students receive. But, again based on various test results nationwide, it is clear that some of these directives are not getting the intended results. One reason is that the methods suggested in the legislation are not aligned with how teachers learn and grow professionally.

From our perspective as educators, we have found that most choose teaching because they want to work with children and older students. In the process, these individuals devote time and money to go to school to become teachers. Most graduate from high-quality, accredited, nationally recognized programs. Thus, they are well prepared to teach. However, in many cases these teachers must teach in ways that are driven by written directives or interpretation of educational policy rather than best practices. First, these directives can influence a district's decision regarding instructional materials purchased for teachers and pedagogy expected of teachers. As a result, some schools may have mandated curricula, many with scripted texts, without regard for the schools' student population.

Next, these directives overemphasize preparing students for various tests required by the district and/or state, leaving little time for teachers' instruction that has been practiced and learned in their preparation programs. In addition, there can be a directive that all students are to be doing the same thing at the same time, even though this might not address the students' needs. Finally, teachers are required to attend staff development meetings and other inservice workshops, even if these sessions do not address their professional needs. In conclusion, we hope these issues will be considered when developing future educational policies.

Sincerely,

Sherry, Linda, and Ruth

In this chapter, we identify four different eras that reveal beliefs about teachers' learning and how instructional changes take place, as well as the lessons learned along the way. Each section begins with a vignette that gives you a "picture" into a classroom of that specific era, followed by the historical context—social, political, and theoretical—and a review of pertinent literature. Finally, the chapter ends with several important topics that need to be considered when planning professional learning opportunities for educators.

INSERVICE ERA

Inservice Workshops for Teachers

Citrus Elementary School (CES) was located on the fringe of a suburban neighborhood in a southern state. The school had been built recently following the open-classroom model. Students from several neighborhoods in the city were bused in as the school district's solution to segregation issues. Approximately 25% of the students were receiving free or reduced-price lunches. Mr. Fine had been leading the school for 2 years. While he was a fifth-grade teacher from 1958 to 1966, he drove an hour each week to take courses at the state university to obtain an MEd in educational leadership. The teachers at CES not only liked him as a person but also liked his leadership style. The students respected him as the disciplinarian and grinned from ear to ear when he greeted them by name as they stepped off the school bus.

Teachers at CES participated in a variety of inservice opportunities. According to the teachers, the 1-week voluntary workshop they had attended the previous summer, in which they intensively studied the scientific method, was their favorite. The school district emphasized a focus on "back to basics." To assist teachers with the grading of multiple-choice quizzes and tests, the principal accepted an invitation by a Scantron sales representative to demonstrate the Scantron machine during the upcoming faculty meeting. Although the teachers acquiesced because of Mr. Fine's position and their fondness for him, the teachers in the upper grades were not confident that their students would be able to fill in the bubbles in the manner required to score the scan cards accurately, and the teachers in the primary grades were annoyed by the requirement to attend a demonstration of a product that would not benefit them or their students.

As seen by the vignette, teachers' inservice training was offered as short (at times, a one-shot occurrence) opportunities to give teachers the training needed to implement new instructional methods (Lambert, 1989). As a result of the various trainings, it was hoped there would be increased student achievement. Thus, the focus was on students' learning, and changing teachers' behaviors was a way to accomplish this (Flanders, 1968; Moore & Schaut, 1976).

To understand this era, we need to examine closely how teachers' learning was envisioned and what was happening with schools and society. At this time, teaching was not considered a "profession" because the knowledge base the teachers had acquired in the teaching field was considered to be minimal in contrast with those of other professionals, such as doctors or lawyers (Benveniste, 1987). Because of this perception, teachers themselves were not considered learners (Sprinthall & Thies-Sprinthall, 1983), and therefore teachers were under constant pressure from others who had a vested interest in their classrooms for one reason or another, such as parents, administrators, and politicians (Benveniste, 1987). They had to be trained to follow a scripted pattern. This behaviorist theoretical model aligned nicely with the prescriptive way that instruction was commonly delivered to students (Lovell, 1968). Students (across learning levels) were at the same stage and teachers all followed the same procedures (Lovell, 1968). The results of this perception of the teaching field were low salaries and poor working conditions.

At the same time, there were changes in the field. First, teachers were beginning to come together as a profession. They did this by forming unions, such as the American Federation of Teachers, and by striking. At the same time, the National Education Association also attempted to raise the profile of the professional, but in less confrontive ways (Urban & Wagoner, 2009). Next, there was also conflict regarding curriculum. A push for more vocational training and less focus on a child-centered approach was supported, as well as a rigorous curriculum in the public schools. As Urban and Wagoner (2009) point out, there was disagreement between those who thought there was a decline of traditional academic curriculum and those who favored courses that helped students function in society. So, as teachers were coming together as a group, there was disagreement about what schools should be teaching.

Even though our society was facing several different issues, two will be mentioned. One is *Brown v. Board of Education*, which looked at the role of schools in addressing social conflict (Urban & Wagoner, 2009). The second is *Sputnik*. Because of the Russians getting into space before the Americans, the federal government pushed for legislation that would increase teachers' knowledge in math and science (see Long, Chapter 2, this volume). The idea that teachers and schools should address social issues arose, which brought about the need for increased teacher learning through inservice workshops.

The impact of inservice workshops on teachers' instruction was limited (Harris, Bessent, & McIntyre, 1969). This could be due to the fact that, in general, inservice workshops were planned "for the teacher rather than with the teacher" (Ainsworth, 1976, p. 107). In a survey given to teachers, Ainsworth found that most teachers desired workshops on instructional methods for their area and teaching level. Teachers mentioned the need to be involved in the planning of the workshops (Ainsworth, 1976). Howey (1976) mentioned that teachers need to know why they are learning new strategies, and he believed that "inservice should be seen as a natural concomitant of any professional endeavor—an activity which can be engaged in a variety of settings at a variety of times" (p. 105). Unfortunately, in general, teachers "redefined inservice in terms of its irrelevancy, ineffectiveness, and inefficiency" (Mangieri & McWilliams, 1976, p. 110).

Even though the effectiveness of inservice workshops was not investigated holistically (Joyce & Showers, 1980), researchers examined various aspects of inservice, such as minicourses, microteaching, and simulations to increase various skills of teachers. For example, Borg, Langer, and Kelley (1971) studied the effectiveness of minicourses as a way to increase teachers' skills and teaching behaviors. These 15-day minicourses had the following basic characteristics by which the teacher: "(a) studies a specific teaching skill, (b) applies the skill in a short videotaped lesson, (c) watches replay of lesson with a supervisor, and (d) replans, reteaches, and receives further feedback" (p. 233). Borg and colleagues (1971) found that the minicourses helped teachers become more proficient in a variety of skills, such as clarifying, redirection, and other skills. Similar to the minicourses, Young and Young (1968) found microteaching effective in changing particular teachers' skills, for example, teachers' responses to students' questions and comments. Young and Young found the use of videotaping helpful; teachers and supervisors could both view and discuss the video. Simulations were also effective in helping teachers to study classroom behavior by allowing them the opportunity to practice specific behaviors in a supportive environment (Cruikshank, 1968).

As teachers implemented new techniques from the training, they commonly received feedback that focused on the observed behavior, which was compared with a standard for what should have happened (Flanders, 1968; Tuckman, McCall, & Hyman, 1969). Flanders's (1962) work highlighted the importance of helping teachers look carefully at their teaching. He did not think teachers had the tools for "gathering information systematically" (p. 314). There were four assumptions underlying Flanders's work. They were: "(1) only a teacher can change his/her own behavior; (2) changes in teaching behavior are personal, they involve feelings as well as knowledge; (3) no one pattern of teaching can be adopted universally by all teachers; and (4) the most effective environment for change provides freedom to express both feelings and ideas, encourages self direction, and is free of coercion" (p. 315).

Dissonance was found to play a role in teacher change (Cohen, 1959; Festinger, 1957; Tuckman et al., 1969). Tuckman and colleagues investigated whether or not teachers' behaviors and perceptions of themselves would change if the teachers' views of themselves differed from an observer's perceptions of them (1969, p. 607). They studied 24 high school teachers and found that teachers' behaviors and self-perceptions can be changed by invoking a discrepancy between their self-perceptions and feedback from others.

Even though research has shown that inservice workshops did not produce instructional changes in teachers and that many teachers considered inservice workshops a waste of time (Ainsworth, 1976; Harris et al., 1969), various lessons can be derived from research during this time: (1) teachers can learn and need to be involved with their own learning (Knowles, 1970); (2) teachers should be actively engaged in planning for their professional needs (Howey, 1976; Mangieri & McWilliams, 1976; see also Lieberman & Miller, Chapter 1, this volume); (3) teachers like ideas that address their content areas and the level of their students (see Merriman, Chapter 19, this volume). Consequently, inservice workshops should be differentiated to align with teachers' goals as they teach their content areas. From the implementation of workshops it was learned that: (4) videotaping and providing feedback to teachers were instrumental in improving particular teachers' skills (Borg et al., 1971), and (5) teacher dissonance appears to play a role in changing behaviors and self-perceptions (Tuckman et al., 1969). When teachers receive specific verbal feedback that is not consistent with their perceptions of their teaching, teachers will change. As this era ended, we were beginning to understand some of the complexities of learning and teaching. Gage (1968) states, " We shall have to continue to grapple with the problems of cognitive complexity and individualization through the medium of the live, human, teacher even in the realm of the well-formulated cognitive objectives" (p. 124).

STAFF DEVELOPMENT ERA

Staff Development for Teachers

Having taught sixth-grade math for a decade at CES before moving into the principal position, Mr. Watson was intimately familiar with CES. He had recently attended an annual conference for educational leadership at which the keynote speaker addressed the theory of learning styles. Research findings and humorous anecdotes riddled the presentation, convincing Mr. Watson that if teachers considered the various learning styles represented by the students in their classrooms and planned lessons with this in mind, students would experience greater achievement.

On a whim, he contacted the local university to ascertain whether anyone was knowledgeable in this area. To his amazement, a professor in the educational leadership department had just written a paper on the topic and was willing to give a presentation at the next faculty meeting. The school secretary created a flyer to promote the meeting, made copies on the ditto machine, and then distributed the flyers to the teachers' boxes.

The teachers were curious about the topic but were secretly wishing the scheduled faculty meeting had been canceled so that they could finish students' report cards rather than attending staff development training.

The hour presentation by Dr. Moore from the university was informative and engaging. He clearly depicted different types of students in the classroom, which demonstrated that he had been a K–12 teacher at some time. Toward the end of the presentation, he passed out an inventory for teachers to complete to determine their own learning preferences.

Mr. Watson was quite pleased with the staff development on learning styles. The teachers appeared to be engaged, they completed the inventories, and some asked a few mindful questions. During a faculty meeting a few weeks later, he asked the faculty to share any changes in their pedagogy based on the presentation by Dr. Moore. No one said anything. Feeling the awkwardness due to the silence, Ms. Fields explained, "We really liked Dr. Moore and the topic, but we don't know enough about it to make any changes just yet."

It became apparent that inservice workshops were not effective, and change was needed regarding continued teacher learning. This in part occurred because we began to realize that learning extended past adolescence into adulthood (Knowles, 1970; Lambert, 1989; Sprinthall & Thies-Sprinthall, 1983). These theorists suggested that adults learn somewhat differently than their students do and that they therefore required a different approach. As a result, teachers needed to be self-directed, to set their own learning goals that are practical and relevant, and to be able to base new learning on their experiences. We began to examine how to engage the teacher in learning through staff development.

Although there was a concern regarding evaluating the process of staff development, more research was needed to determine the impact of staff development on teacher change (Valsame, 1977). Researchers began to investigate the qualities of effective staff development (Showers, Joyce, & Bennett, 1987; Sparks & Loucks-Horsley, 1989; Wood, McQuarrie, & Thompson, 1982). From these investigations, general patterns of effective staff development emerged. First, staff development should be aligned with goals to improve the school program for all the children in the school (Wood et al., 1982), and clearly defined needs should be determined for any staff development (Bentley, 1972; Nagle, 1972). Next, teachers should participate in any decisions regarding staff development programs (Lambert, 1989; Sparks, 1983). Teachers reflect regarding the effectiveness of their instructional practice, and this "allows teachers to make active, conscious decisions" (Martin & Kragler, 1999, p. 313). As Hunter (1979) points out, teaching is a process of making decisions "before, during, and after instruction" (p. 62). These decisions will affect teachers' involvement in any staff development program. Because of this, staff development should be differentiated so that both teachers' and students' needs are accounted for (Howey & Vaughan, 1983).

Another attribute of effective staff development is that time is allowed for teachers to collaborate with one another (Little, 1981). Poole (1995) highlights the importance of collaboration in creating an atmosphere in which teachers can develop a common voice regarding their schools' programs. Coaching is seen as one means of effective staff development for teachers, and it is one way to support teachers as new instructional practices are implemented (Showers et al., 1987; Thomas, 1979). Adult learning theory, knowledge of the principles of learning, knowledge of effective instruction, and supervision/feedback to the teacher played key roles in effective staff development programs (McCormick, 1979; Wilsey & Killion, 1982). Finally, the teachers' context plays a critical role in the success of any staff development program (Joyce, 1980). Goodlad (1972) considers the "culture of the school as basic and central to the processes of educational change" (p. 210).

In an effort to align research regarding the qualities of effective teacher learning, researchers generated models of effective staff development (Sparks, 1983; Wood et al., 1982). Sparks and Loucks-Horsely (1989) list five different models of staff development, each with its own activities and assumptions: (1) individually guided, in which teachers guide their own development by reading, attending conferences, discussions, and trying new ideas; (2) observation–assessment, in which teachers are observed and receive feedback from others, that is, coaching; (3) involvement in a development/improvement process, in which teachers are involved in systematic programs to solve a particular need in a school; (4) training, which has been synonymous with staff development and in which teachers attend workshops to watch an expert; and (5) teacher inquiry, which can take various forms.

Two staff development models that were predominant were the observation–assessment model and the training model. Joyce and Showers (1983) referred to the observation–assessment model as a way to create opportunities for teachers to reflect and converse in an organized frame about their instruction. Important elements of successful coaching included a significant amount of practice of the desired instruction. However, Wade (1984/1985) found that coaching did not always lead to changes in teachers' instruction.

There were two predominant training models during this time. One was Madeline Hunter's Mastery Teaching, and the other was Oregon Direct Instruction (Rosenshine & Meyers, 1978). Hunter (1979) recognized the importance of teachers reflecting on their own practice to make adaptations in their instruction. Therefore, she created four components necessary to guide teachers' professional development: "a) identification of the decisions a teacher must make in any given situation, b) inservice which enables the teacher to combine science and art in teaching, c) films and videos which provide opportunities for teachers to observe exceptional teaching, and d) a diagnostic-prescriptive instrument which provides knowledge for the teacher of the results of their professional performance" (p. 67).

The Oregon Direct Instruction model (Rosenshine & Meyers, 1978) comprised a number of procedures for teachers to follow and, as seen by the scripted nature of the program, was aligned with Bloom's Mastery Learning (Bloom, 1976). During the training workshops, teachers learned the various procedures that were allotted to specific activities and times. In addition to the procedures, teachers were given materials to use when teaching. By having teachers following this program, it was assumed that all children would learn these skills. Although not advocating for either the Hunter or the Oregon Direct Instruction models, Wade (1984/1985), in her meta-analysis, found that training models could lead to changes in teachers' instruction.

In addition to the aforementioned models, Guskey (1986) generated a model to evaluate the impact of staff development programs on teacher change. Within the model, four different aspects of teacher change were identified. The aspects are: "(1) the staff development program; (2) change in the teachers' classroom practice; (3) change in student learning outcomes; and (4) change in teachers' beliefs and attitudes" (p. 7). The value of this model is that it begins to examine teacher change as a process that needs to be looked at more broadly than is possible by just looking at teachers' views of the staff development program. In his model, Guskey highlights the role of student learning outcomes on teachers' continued growth. As he points out, "practices that help students attain desired learning outcomes are retained; those that do not work are abandoned" (p. 7).

Even though there was evidence of what constituted effective staff development, many of these programs did not influence teacher change (Lambert, 1989). Furthermore, several issues became clear. First of all, the terms "staff development" and "inservice workshops" were often used synonymously. Dale (1982) suggested that clarity of the terms is needed and that staff development be the "totality of educational and personal experiences that contribute toward an individual's being more competent and satisfied in an assigned professional role" (p. 31).

Next, in many cases staff development programs had a top-down structure, that is, administrators determined what the programs would be without teacher input (Guskey & Peterson, 1995–1996). Because of the structure, a deficit model regarding teachers was predominant (Katzenmeyer & Moller, 2001). As in the previous era, teachers were viewed as not being competent, so administrators planned programs for their teachers. Wood and Thompson (1980) stated that many administrators thought teachers needed to be required to participate in staff development. Therefore, a districtwide focus on staff development was a problem in that this focus did not allow schools to develop their own programs. They concluded that, in general, most staff development programs did not model the kinds of practices teachers were expected to show in their classrooms.

Finally, we were learning new lessons. One was that teacher instructional change takes time and is sometimes a difficult, yet constructive, process (Guskey, 1986; Katzenmeyer & Moller, 2001; Sarason, 1997). Because teachers are not all at the same stage of learning, any professional growth opportunities need to account for this with differing levels of support (Diamond, 1993; Oja, 1991). In reality, teaching and learning are not activities that can be perfected but are processes that continually grow and change (Diamond, 1993; Regan, Anctil, Dubea, Hofmann, & Vaillancourt, 1992). Next, schools need to be a place where students, teachers, and administrators can all learn (Lewis, 1996; Louis, Kruse, & Raywid, 1996). Although the teachers are the focus of most staff development programs, it is important for principals to consider their own learning and to stay close to their teachers (Evans & Mohr, 1999). Finally, creating coherent staff development programs that are based in strategic decision making by a school faculty are critical to ensure that any staff development is interconnected and is aligned with the school's strategic plan (Guskey, 1994). These coherent plans become the "basis for all activities within the school, and provide a vision that helps the school focus its efforts, engage teachers in their work, and build strong parent and community support" (New American Schools, 1995, p. 7).

PROFESSIONAL DEVELOPMENT ERA

Professional Development of Teachers

With the advent of the national math standards, the principals at several schools, along with Ms. Bradley of CES, contracted two elementary math teachers turned consultants from another state, Mary and Martha, to provide professional development to teachers at their schools. Mary and Martha's students showed significant achievement, and within a short period of time, news of the teachers spread like wildfire. The consultants claimed that students' astounding math achievement was due to the students' extensive use of manipulatives to solve problems and requiring them to explain their processes for solving problems in a written format. Several schools attended professional development for 6 weeks for 2 hours each week. In addition to the 6 weeks' training, the teachers attended two sessions on Saturday that were held at CES. To entice teachers to attend the Saturday trainings, teachers were given a stipend for their attendance. Primary-grade teachers met in an all-purpose room with Mary, while the intermediate-grade teachers met with Martha in another room. Both presenters were quite entertaining, especially Martha. The 6-hour session was interrupted by a 1-hour lunch for teachers to get a bit of nourishment and a slight reprieve from the arduous task of using manipulatives to divide fractions. The professional development did not end with the six 2-hour trainings or the two Saturday trainings. Mary and Martha were contracted to visit classrooms of those who attended the sessions for consultation and coaching. Although Mary and Martha preferred to consult in classrooms to which they were invited by the teachers, several principals insisted that they observe and consult all teachers who attended the training.

As it turned out, telling teachers what and how to teach was not working. Teachers remained passive, with little involvement in their learning. As seen earlier, teachers were still not treated as professionals (Lambert, 1989). Even though an attempt was made to align staff development with adult learning theory, not all that encompasses this theory was addressed (Lambert, 1989). As Goodlad (1983) pointed out, staff development for teachers and administrators focuses

> largely on the improvement of individual skills. Collaboration with others on a faculty to determine school-wide goals, for example, is an exceedingly arduous activity and appears not to be commonly attempted. Indeed, the school as an institution may well be the most inactive and ineffective part of the decision-making structure that includes classroom, individual schools, district, and state. (p. 38)

Therefore, a new era began as we looked more deeply at how teachers learn in their classrooms and better ways to obtain their full engagement in the learning process. Engaging teachers meant allowing them to have options, choice, authority, and responsibility for their learning, as well as supporting their peers' learning (Benveniste, 1987; Swan Dagen & Bean, Chapter 3, this volume; Lambert, 1989). This new view empowers teachers by considering them as professionals in that they have the knowledge base and expertise to engage in and to facilitate school reform movements (Benveniste, 1987). Teachers not only could focus on their personal learning but could openly participate in school reform movements using that expertise (Hughes, 1967).

Professional development at this time was guided by various theories besides the adult learning theory. The constructivist theory, founded by Dewey (1916), supported the idea that learning was internal and controlled by the learner through inquiry. It is demonstrated by the different experiences that one has and the inferences that are made as one learns new teaching techniques (Tracey & Morrow, 2006). A branch of this theory is the social constructivist movement. From this perspective, learning is a personal and a constructive process (Standerford, 1997; Vygotsky, 1978). Bandura's (1969, 1986) social cognitive theory stresses the need for adults to focus on their individual goals, to reflect, and to collaborate with others as they learn from their attempts, successes, and failures. Later, Bandura (2000) examined the role of self-efficacy in learning, that is, whether one believes that he or she possesses the ability to obtain new learning. Bandura believed that learning is affected by one's understanding of the value of a task. Teachers may be cautious in making decisions about the implementation of a new task, or teachers may feel confident in their ability to implement it. The result is that some teachers may feel it is too hard, whereas others endure. Bandura also examined the importance of collective efficacy, in which adults' shared beliefs in their power to act collectively will in the end produce the desired results.

Professional development research is focused on its effectiveness and on the impact of these programs on student achievement (Desimone, Porter, Garet, Yoon, & Birman, 2002; Wayne, Yoon, Zhu, Cronen, & Garet, 2008). In the results of a survey of math and science teachers, Garet, Porter, Desimone, Birman, and Yoon (2001) found that teachers reported the following attributes of professional development that made an impact on their teaching: (1) focus on content knowledge; (2) active learning; and (3) coherence with other learning (p. 916). The duration of the professional development also seemed to be a factor. A longer time period and more contact hours for the professional development seemed to create more teacher growth than shorter programs. Besides the attributes mentioned by Desimone and colleagues (2002) and Garet and colleagues (2001), Ingvarson, Meiers, and Beavis (2005), in a survey of teachers, found that the following were helpful when attempting new strategies: (1) receiving feedback; (2) working with peers as they examined student work; and (3) follow-up. Teachers mentioned that support was needed once the professional development program was finished.

The school culture seems to have an impact on the effectiveness of professional development (Darling-Hammond & Richardson, 2009; Donaldson, 2007; Sarason,

1997). Research has shown the importance of the school culture in supporting students' and teachers' learning (Hord, 1997; Louis, Marks, & Kruse, 1996). Much of this depends on the school leadership's being part of the learning community and developing a collaborative environment (Martin, Shafer, & Kragler, 2009). Teachers and school leaders work together to develop common goals for their schools (Guskey, 2003) and create plans to achieve these goals (Anders, Hoffman, & Duffy, 2000). In these schools, time is allotted for teacher reflection, inquiry, and collaboration (Vandeweghe & Varney, 2006). This allows teachers and school leaders to "raise issues, take risks, and address dilemmas in their own practice" (Darling-Hammond & Richardson, 2009, p. 48).

As we began to realize the complex nature of the learning process of individuals and the interaction of the school culture, there was a subsequent change in the models and conceptions of professional development. Desimone (2009, 2011) suggests that the aforementioned attributes can be used as a way to shape professional development programs. Using the core features of professional development will lead to increased teacher knowledge and a change in instruction (Desimone & Stuckey, Chapter 24, this volume). The end result should be an increase in student achievement. Borko (2004) suggests the following elements of professional development: "the program, the teachers, who are the learners, the facilitator, who guides the teachers, and the context" (p. 4). Other models are centered in school-based learning communities (Thompson & Goe, 2009; Wilson & Berne, 1999).

Clarke and Hollingsworth (2002) developed an interconnected model of professional growth that is based in research. Their model has four different domains of teacher learning: "the personal domain (teachers' knowledge, beliefs, and attitudes); the domain of practice (professional experimentation); the domain of consequences (salient outcomes); and the external domain (sources of information or support)" (p. 950). This particular model addresses various facets that all affect teachers' learning and possible change and that have a "non-linear structure that provides recognition of the situated and personal nature, not just of teacher practice, but of teacher growth" (p. 965).

However, even considering this, as Guskey (2003) points out, much of what we know about effective professional development is not completely settled. One example is the research pertaining to the need for a content focus in professional development. These studies were done with math and science teachers. Little research has been done in other academic areas. Guskey continues, stating that collaboration works well under certain conditions but that collaboration can also work against professional development of teachers. It is important to remember that professional development is complex and that "it may be unreasonable to assume that a single list of characteristics leading to broad-brush policies and guidelines for effective professional development will ever emerge" (p. 750).

Wilson and Berne (1999), in an analysis of several research studies pertaining to professional development, found challenges to be considered regarding professional development. One is that we cannot "mandate" learning. Although teachers may be required to attend professional development programs, each teacher comes with a perception of his or her professional knowledge and teaching behaviors.

They may not be open to learning new strategies or see the need to do so. There-fore, Wilson and Berne suggest that constant negotiation between the teachers and those who will be implementing the professional development is critical. Finally, they suggest that it is important to recognize how difficult the learning process is and that there are many setbacks as one learns new strategies.

In a report on the status of professional learning of teachers, Darling-Ham-mond, Wei, Andree, Richardson, and Orphanos (2009) found that many attributes of professional development were in place, such as teachers being involved in pro-fessional development of some type and teachers having the opportunity to be engaged in a wide variety of activities. There was also a focus on the development of subject-matter content. However, there were some issues in what they found. One is that teachers were disappointed in many of their activities. Also, there was little support for teacher collaboration to discuss curriculum, policies, or other deci-sions regarding their schools. The authors conclude that there is a "growing body of research on effective professional development for a new paradigm of teacher professional learning, one based on evidence about the kinds of experiences that appear to build teacher capacity and catalyze transformation in teaching practice resulting in improved student outcomes" (Darling-Hammond et al., 2009, p. 27).

PROFESSIONAL LEARNING ERA

Professional Learning of Teachers

Ms. Bradley has witnessed a range of professional development experi-ences throughout her career as a teacher and principal at CES. One expe-rience that, she believes, not only views teachers as adult learners but also honors them as professional is the concept of learning communities. These communities ranged from successful and more experienced teachers men-toring novice teachers to a group of fourth-grade teachers who regularly met after school to review students' writing for the future statewide writing test. Whereas these junctions were driven by grade level, a book club spans across all grades. Ms. Fields, a second-grade teacher, approached Ms. Brad-ley about the prospects of initiating a book club for teachers at the school after she had attended a session on guided reading at the International Reading Association's annual conference. She immediately purchased the book online. She read through the book with a highlighter and pencil in hand to mark salient points in the text. She believed the book and discus-sions about the book would be a meaningful professional development opportunity for all teachers at her school. Anyone could join, but she knew that, in order for the professional development to be successful, at least two teachers from each grade level or content area should attend together. Collaborating professionally with a peer provides space for growth and creativity. Ms. Fields scheduled the volunteer book club for after school on Tuesdays, as the majority of interested teachers indicated they were avail-able then. Consistent with research, the book club would extend across the semester. She hoped the interactive and meaningful conversations that began during the book club meeting would continue and that results of the conversations would appear in their teaching practice.

With the various theories that encompass a social constructivist view of learning, we have finally reached a time when our scope of learning has broadened to include various facets involved in the learning process (see Rohlwing & Spelman, Chapter 12, this volume). And as such, our perception of learning is changing rapidly. As Sarason (2004) states, "Learning is not a thing. Learning is a process that occurs in an interpersonal and group context, and it is always composed of an interaction of factors to which we append labels such as *motivation, cognition, emotion* or *affect*, and *attitude*, as we broaden our scope of how learning takes place at school. It is not something that just happens" (p. vii).

We also have more information about what makes up effective professional learning (Darling-Hammond et al., 2009; Desimone, 2009; Jaquith, Mindich, Wei, & Darling-Hammond, 2010; Mindich & Lieberman, 2012) that can be sustained over time (see Raphael, Vasquez, Fortune, Gavelek, & Au, Chapter 8, this volume). As Mindich and Lieberman (2012) state, "effective professional learning enables educators to develop the knowledge, skills, practices, and dispositions needed to help students learn and achieve at higher levels" (p. ii). Glickman (1990) wrote that we cannot "pretend not to know what we know" (p. 4). From a review of the research of the field, several important topics that contribute to effective professional learning of educators are shared next.

The Impact of School Culture

One constant idea that runs through the literature is the impact of the school culture on teachers and students. Sarason (1996) found that schools are all unique, depending on the people who inhabit them. Therefore, each school may have different needs and different ways of taking care of their problems. In this case, teachers can and should be a part of the solution in reforming schools. Teachers know their students and they know the curriculum that is used. The perception of "teachers as learners" not only puts them in charge of the learning in their classrooms (in respect to their students, as well as their own personal learning) but also makes them responsible for the outcome. Thus teaching has evolved into a profession in which educators can identify the issues that affect their schools and organize and implement solutions, and the outcome will be not only a more productive learning environment for children but also an environment that inspires teachers' learning.

The impact of the school's culture cannot be understated. The work of Cobb, McClain, Lamberg, and Dean (2003) with middle school math teachers highlights this. In their article, they describe an analytical approach to investigating communities of practice. They found that even though these teachers may not have used instructional tools (e.g., interpreting test scores or adapting instructional strategies needed to teach their students), much of this was due to the constraints placed on them by the school setting. Without looking at the interconnections of the teachers and school culture, no real change can occur (see Firestone & Mangin, Chapter 17, this volume). Sarason (2004) asserts that "teachers cannot be expected to create and sustain a context of productive learning for children if such a context does not exist for teachers" (p. ix). In fact, Putnam and Borko (2000) contend that the situative perspective can provide an important basis for "exploring these complex relationships, and for taking them into consideration as we design, enact, and study programs to facilitate teacher learning" (p. 13).

Because of the role of the school culture, a current model of organizing schools for reform has emerged. We have moved away from the perception of teachers' learning as a training model to a *professional learning through practice* model (see Lieberman & Miller, Chapter 1, this volume). This stance situates the professional learning of teachers within their school setting (Katzenmeyer & Moller, 2001). The emphasis is on the continued growth of teachers and school leaders and is a later "evolution" from learning communities (Katzenmeyer & Moller, 2001, p. 45).

The learning community model, in which teachers focus on their professional needs (Sarason, 1971, 1996), is still relevant. The underlying concept of this model is that learning is dependent on the social situations in which it occurs (Firestone & Mangin, Chapter 17, this volume). This concept can be labeled as *community of practice* (Lave & Wenger, 1991), *professional community* (McLaughlin & Talbert, 2001), or *professional learning communities* (DuFour, 2004). The importance of the uniqueness of individual schools and of teachers actively engaging in their own learning, working in collaboration with others to solve problems, and being a part of the solution rather than the problem is a predominant theme in this model.

The Importance of Teacher Inquiry

Teacher inquiry plays a large role in professional learning. Teachers continually reflect and examine their practices (Carpenter, Fennema, & Franke, 1996) as they make decisions about instruction (Ball, 2009). Rather than having professional development be planned by the district or consultants, Jacobs and Yendol-Hoppey (Chapter 16, this volume) point out that teacher inquiry focuses on teachers' concerns. Cochran-Smith and Lytle (1993) see action research as a "systematic intentional inquiry by teachers about their own school and classroom work" (pp. 23–24). They argue that teacher inquiry is a "powerful way of articulating local knowledge and for redefining and creating a new knowledge base for teaching and learning" (p. 279). Through inquiry, teachers are asking their own questions, working through and determining their answers, and asking more questions (Richardson & Placier, 2001). As teachers collect data, observe, reflect, and make decisions about the results of their inquiry, they begin the cycle again. Therefore, teacher inquiry is recursive in that "inquiry is nested within cycles of deliberate, self-regulated attempts to advance their own learning" (Butler & Schnellert, 2012, p. 1208). This recursive cycle of teacher inquiry can lead to transformation of teachers' practice as well as the school culture (Pine, 2009).

The Heart of Professional Learning: Transformation

Professional learning is an ongoing and messy process. As teachers critically reflect on their practices and thinking, cognitive dissonance emerges (Festinger, 1957; Wheatley, 2002). Even so, this examination allows transformation of beliefs and practices (Donnelly et al., 2005). Mezirow (2003) defines transformative learning as "learning that transforms problematic frames of reference—sets of fixed assumptions and expectations (habits of mind, meaning perspectives, mindsets)—to make them more inclusive, discriminating, open, reflective, and emotionally able to change" (p. 58). Whereas individual transformation is at the heart of Mezirow's theory, others contend that individual transformation may be difficult if one is in a dysfunctional social setting (Brookfield, 2000; Servage, 2008).

Mezirow (1994) stresses the role of dialogue and engagement among learners. During these conversations, it should be recognized that dissent is a natural part of the dialogue (Hargreaves, 2004). Servage (2008) suggests that conversations be open-ended and centered around "foundational" educational concerns rather than immediate issues. One such foundation concern would be the impact of policies on their school. Servage is concerned that, with the current emphasis on "data driven" conversations held in most schools, there will not be time for true reflection or dialogue.

The Stages of Development

In reality, as with other professionals, there is a range of abilities and professional knowledge among teachers. Not all teachers are at the same stage of development at the same time. It is important to recognize the stages of development in order to better plan professional learning opportunities for teachers. The stages shared here are related to literacy instruction. However, these stages would be similar for other fields. Snow, Griffin, and Burns (2005) describe five levels of increasing teacher knowledge and possible career progression (p. 6). The levels are

> (a) declarative knowledge, which is the foundation of disciplinary knowledge relevant to success as a teacher. One is learning about child development, instructional strategies, and content; (b) situated, can-do procedural knowledge, which means teachers have the routines to teach a strategy or skill. Teachers can also use them effectively; (c) stable, procedural knowledge, which means some teaching routines have become fairly automatic for the teacher. Teachers can also adapt the routines to fit their particular students' needs; (d) expert adaptive knowledge, which is teachers begin to see the strengths and weaknesses of different programs and routines; and (e) reflective, organized, analyzed knowledge, teachers can use their knowledge to critically analyze programs and methods to predicting which might work best with their students. (p. 217)

At the last two levels, teachers will be involved with leading professional development at their schools and engaged in more districtwide activities. The upshot of these levels is that professional learning programs should focus on "expectation of and the skills required for continuous learning" (Snow et al., 2005, p. 212). Thus each level helps set the stage for the next level. Therefore, professional learning is instructive (Long, 2012), as teachers develop in-depth and relevant knowledge that they can use with different students and in different contexts (Snow et al., 2005).

The Role of District and School Leadership

School and district leadership play a large role in creating positive learning environments (see Tallerico, Chapter 7, this volume). With all the recent federal policies, many teachers face multiple demands from the state, local government, business leaders, and others. Many of these demands result in policies and practices that are inconsistent and lack coherency, which may lead to lower student achievement (Allington, 2009; see also Jaquith, Chapter 5, this volume). Honig and Hatch (2004) highlight the role of the district and school leadership to "work together to help schools manage external demands" (p. 26). In other words, school leaders and teachers should take a prognostic view toward addressing the multiple demands (Coburn, 2006). School leaders and teachers examine issues related to the mandated policy to build a school vision and set goals to guide them (Leithwood, Harris, & Hopkins, 2008; Thessin & Starr, 2011). It also means that the school leadership is aware of specific practices, such as the role of teacher collaboration, providing teacher support, and others that make for a positive school culture (Leithwood et al., 2008), which should have a positive impact on students' learning (Guskey, 2003). The outcome is a schoolwide plan that is focused on fewer instructional issues while aligning to a new method of implementation, for example, coaching, professional learning communities, or book studies (Swan Dagen & Bean, Chapter 3, this volume; Knight, 2009; Semadeni, 2010). As Jaquith and colleagues (2010) point out, "when decision making on professional development and other school improvement policies is shared among a broader group of professionals, the strategies look quite different from those designed purely from the top down" (p. 6).

CONCLUSION

The expectations and responsibilities that are placed on teachers have grown over the decades, many of them mandated by federal legislation (Long, Chapter 2, this volume). Mandated federal policy can lead to a disconnect between what is known about teachers' professional learning and how professional development is implemented at the local level (see Reutzel & Clark, Chapter 4, and Jaquith, Chapter 5, this volume). We know that teachers are learners and that they need to be actively involved in decisions pertaining to their development (Rohlwing & Spelman, Chapter 12, this volume), although not all forms of activity to promote teachers' learning "will necessarily be relevant for all teachers" (Postholm, 2012, p. 423). In addition, it is important to recognize the various factors—emotional factors; beliefs about one's teaching; motivational, cognitive, and other factors—that affect the professional development of teachers (Postholm, 2012; Tschannen-Moran & Chen, Chapter 13, this volume). We know the school culture plays a large role in teachers' professional development and student achievement.

Finally, we also know that the training model of staff development as we presented it does not work. Often, at this time, educational policy (federal, state, and local) does not consider the individual differences of schools and the needs of the teachers and their students. In addition, the training model of staff development is what many of the mandated policies suggest. Amazingly, as seen by the examples given in the appendix to this volume, there are schools across the country and around the world that manage to succeed. These schools have strong and supporting leadership who work with the teachers to learn and to solve problems within their school communities.

In closing this chapter, we have reflected on the different eras across decades of research to remind us of what we have learned about teacher professional development and of the importance of using what we know to support teachers and ultimately their students. As demonstrated in the quotation from Shirley Thacker at the beginning of Part IV in this volume, the payoff is tremendous. She considers teaching a lifelong passion in which one eagerly engages in different projects to learn. The result is amazing when you step into her classroom and see first graders engaged in tasks that some think are impossible. She, like millions of other teachers, is doing so because she wants to make a difference (Benveniste, 1987). Teachers are professionals who deserve our respect for their lifetime of service, work, and dedication to our children of all ages.

QUESTIONS FOR DISCUSSION

For Teachers

1. Reflect on your own classroom and practices. What issues do you feel you need to examine? Why?

2. You are a learner, and it is personal! How can you accomplish this task with the resources you have available?

For Administrators

1. Think about the role you play to support not only individual teacher's needs to learn but also whole-school concerns. Develop a plan to work *with* all your teachers.

2. In what ways can you facilitate individual and group learning that aligns with what is known about adult learning—that is, that learning needs to be reflective, collaborative, personal and motivational and include active participation in decision making by all involved?

3. How can you develop a prognostic stance with your teachers as you implement practices to address various policies?

For Policymakers

1. Considering the work of scholars over decades and what has been learned about effective school reform, how can you develop a mechanism to give teachers and administrators an active role in the creation of educational policy?

2. How can you develop policy that ensures the implementation of effective professional development of educators?

REFERENCES

Ainsworth, B. (1976). Teachers talk about inservice education. *Journal of Teacher Education, 27*, 107–109.

Allington, R. (2009). Literacy policies that are needed: Thinking beyond "No Child Left Behind." In J. V. Hoffman & Y. M. Goodman (Eds.), *Changing literacies for changing times: An historical perspective on the future of reading research, public policy, and classroom practices* (pp. 247–265). New York: Routledge.

Anders, P., Hoffman, J., & Duffy, G. (2000). Teaching teachers to teach reading: Paradigm shifts, persistent problems, and challenges. In M. L. Kamill, P. B. Mosenthal, P. D. Pearson, & R. Barr (Eds.), *Handbook of reading research* (Vol. III, pp. 719–742). Mahwah, NJ: Erlbaum.

Ball, A. (2009). Toward a theory of generative change in culturally and linguistically complex classrooms. *American Educational Research Journal, 46*(1), 45–72.

Bandura, A. (1969). *Principles of behavior modification.* New York: Holt.

Bandura, A. (1986). *Social foundations of thought and action: A social cognitive theory.* Englewood Cliffs, NJ: Prentice Hall.

Bandura, A. (2000). Exercise of human agency through collective efficacy. *Current Directions in Psychological Science, 9*(3), 75–78.

Bentley, E. (1972). Comprehensive staff development. *Theory into Practice, 11*, 262–266.

Benveniste, G. (1987). *Professionalizing the organization: Reducing bureaucracy to enhance effectiveness.* San Francisco: Jossey-Bass.

Bloom, B. S. (1976). *Human characteristics and school learning.* New York: McGraw-Hill.

Borko, H. (2004). Professional development and teacher learning: Mapping the terrain. *Educational Researcher, 33*(8), 3–15.

Borg, W., Langer, P., & Kelley, M. (1971). The minicourse: A new tool for the education of teachers. *Education, 90*(3), 232–238.

Brookfield, S. (2000). Transformative learning as ideology critique. In J. Mezirow & Associates, *Learning as transformation: Critical perspectives on a theory in progress* (pp. 125–148). San Francisco: Jossey-Bass.

Butler, D., & Schnellert, L. (2012). Collaborative inquiry in teacher professional development. *Teaching and Teacher Education, 28*, 1206–1220.

Carpenter, T., Fennema, E., & Franke, M. (1996). Cognitively guided instruction: A knowledge base for reform in primary mathematics instruction. *Elementary School Journal, 97*, 3–20.

Clarke, D., & Hollingsworth, H. (2002). Elaborating a model of teacher professional growth. *Teaching and Teacher Education, 18*, 947–967.

Cobb, P., McClain, K., Lamberg, T., & Dean, C. (2003). Situating teachers' instructional practices in the institutional setting of the school and district. *Educational Researcher, 32*(6), 13-24.

Coburn, C. (2006). Framing the problem of reading instruction: Using frame analysis to uncover the microprocesses of policy implementation. *American Educational Research Journal, 43*(3), 343-379.

Cochran-Smith, M., & Lytle, S. (Eds.). (1993). *Inside/outside: Teacher research and knowledge.* New York: Teachers College Press.

Cohen, A. R. (1959). Communication discrepancy and attitude change: A dissonance theory approach. *Journal of Personality, 27,* 386-396.

Cruikshank, D. (1968). Simulation. *Theory into Practice, 7*(5), 190-193.

Dale, E. (1982). What is staff development? *Educational Leadership, 40* (1), 31.

Darling-Hammond, L., & Richardson, N. (2009). Teacher learning: What matters? *Educational Leadership, 66*(5), 46-53.

Darling-Hammond, L., Wei, R., Andree, A., Richardson, N., & Orphanos, S. (2009). *Professional learning in the learning profession: A status report on teacher development in the United States and abroad.* Dallas, TX: National Staff Development Council.

Desimone, L. (2009). Improving impact studies of teachers' professional development: Toward better conceptualizations and measures. *Educational Researcher, 38,* 181-199.

Desimone, L. (2011). A primer of effective professional development. *Phi Delta Kappan, 92*(6) 68-71.

Desimone, L., Porter, A., Garet, M., Yoon, K., & Birman, B. (2002). Effects of professional development on teachers' instruction: Results from a three-year longitudinal study. *Educational Evaluation and Policy Analysis, 24*(2), 81-112.

Dewey, J. (1916). *Democracy and education.* New York: Macmillan.

Diamond, C. T. (1993). In-service education as something more: A personal construct approach. In P. Kahaney, L. Perry, & J. Janangelo (Eds.). *Theoretical and critical perspectives on teacher change* (pp. 45-69). Norwood, NJ: Ablex.

Donaldson, G. (2007). What do teachers bring to leadership? *Educational Leadership, 65*(1), 26-29.

Donnelly, A., Morgan, D., DeFord, D., Files, J., Long, S., Mills, H., et al. (2005). Transformative professional development: Negotiating knowledge with an inquiry stance. *Language Arts, 82,* 336-346.

DuFour, R. (2004). What is a "professional learning community"? *Educational Leadership, 62*(8), 6-11.

Evans, P., & Mohr, N. (1999). Professional development for principals. *Phi Delta Kappan, 80,* 530-532.

Festinger, L. (1957). *A theory of cognitive dissonance.* White Plains, NY: Row, Peterson.

Flanders, N. (1962). Using interaction analysis in the inservice training of teachers. *Journal of Experimental Education, 30*(4), 313-316.

Flanders, N. (1968). Interaction analysis and inservice training. In H. J. Klausmeier & G. T. O'Hearn (Eds.), *Research and development toward the improvement of education* (pp. 126-133). Madison, WI: Dembar Educational Research Services.

Gage, N. L. (1968). An analytical approach to research on instructional methods. In H. J. Klausmeier & G. T. O'Hearn (Eds.), *Research and development towards the improvement of education* (pp. 119-125). Madison, WI: Dembar Educational Research Services.

Garet, M., Porter, A., Desimone, L., Birman, B., & Yoon, K. (2001). What makes professional development effective?: Results from a national sample of teachers. *Educational Research Journal, 38,* 915-945.

Glickman, C., (1990). Pretending not to know what we know. *Educational Leadership, 48*(8), 4–10.

Goodlad, J. (1972). Staff development: The league model. *Theory into Practice, 11,* 207–214.

Goodlad, J. (1983). The school as workplace. In K. J. Rehage & G. Griffin (Ed.), *National Society for the Study of Education Yearbook: Staff development* (Vol. 82, Issue 2, pp. 36–51). Chicago: University of Chicago Press.

Guskey, T. (1986). Staff development and the process of teacher change. *Educational Researcher, 15,* 5–12.

Guskey, T. (1994, April). *Professional development in education: In search of the optimal mix.* Paper presented at the annual meeting of the American Education Research Association, New Orleans, LA.

Guskey, T. (2003). What makes professional development effective? *Phi Delta Kappan, 84*(10), 748–750.

Guskey, T., & Peterson, K. (1995–1996). The road to classroom change. *Educational Leadership, 52,* 14–19.

Hargreaves, A. (2004). *Teaching in the knowledge society: Education in the age of insecurity.* New York: Teachers College Press.

Harris, B., Bessent, W., & McIntyre, K. (1969). *In-service education: A guide to better practice.* Englewood Cliffs, NJ: Prentice-Hall.

Honig, M. I., & Hatch, T. C. (2004). Crafting coherence: How schools strategically manage multiple, external demands. *Educational Researcher, 33*(8), 16–30.

Hord, S. (1997). *Professional learning communities: Communities of continuous inquiry and improvement.* Austin, TX: Southwest Educational Development Laboratory.

Howey, K. (1976). Putting inservice teacher education into perspective. *Journal of Teacher Education, 27,* 101–105.

Howey, K., & Vaughan, J. (1983). Current patterns of staff development. In K. J. Rehage & G. A. Griffin (Ed.), *National Society for the Study of Education yearbook: Staff development* (Vol. 82, Issue 2, pp. 92–117). Chicago: University of Chicago Press.

Hughes, H. H. (1967). Measurement of the attitudes of teachers toward "teaching as a profession." *Journal of Educational Research, 60*(6), 243–247.

Hunter, M. (1979). Teaching is decision making. *Educational Leadership, 37,* 62–67.

Ingvarson, L., Meiers, M., & Beavis, A. (2005). Factors affecting the impact of professional development programs on teachers' knowledge, practice, student outcomes, and efficacy. *Education Policy Analysis Archives, 13*(10), 1–26.

Jaquith, A., Mindich, D., Wei, R., & Darling-Hammond, L. (2010). *Teacher professional learning in the United States: Case studies of state policies and strategies (Summary report).* Stanford, CA: Stanford Center for Opportunity in Education.

Joyce, B. (1980). Learning how to learn. *Theory into Practice, 19,* 15–27.

Joyce, B., & Showers, B. (1980). Improving inservice training: The messages of research. *Educational Leadership, 37*(5), 379–385.

Joyce, B., & Showers, B. (1983). *Power in staff development through research on training.* Alexandria, VA: Association for Supervision and Curriculum Development.

Katzenmeyer, M., & Moller, G. (2001). *Awakening the sleeping giant.* Thousand Oaks, CA: Corwin Press.

Knight, J. (2009). What can we do about teacher resistance? *Phi Delta Kappan, 90*(7), 508–513.

Knowles, M. (1970). *The modern practice of adult education: Andragogy versus pedagogy.* New York: Association Press. (ERIC Document Reproduction Service, No. 043812)

Lambert, L. (1989). The end of an era of staff development, *Educational Leadership*, 47(1), 78–81.

Lave, J., & Wenger, E. (1991). *Situated learning: Legitimate peripheral participation.* New York: Cambridge University Press.

Leithwood, K., Harris, A., & Hopkins, D. (2008). Seven strong claims about successful school leadership. *School Leadership and Management, 28*(4), 27–42.

Lewis, J. (1996). *What every principal should know about transforming schools: The mandate for new school leadership.* Westbury, NY: National Center to Save Our Schools.

Little, J. (1981). *School success and staff development: The role of staff development in urban desegregated schools* [Executive summary]. Washington, DC: National Institute of Education.

Long, R. (2012). Professional development and education policy: Understanding the current disconnect. *Reading Today, 29*(3), 29–30.

Louis, K., Kruse, S., & Raywid, M. (1996). Putting teachers at the center of reform: Learning schools and professional communities. *National Association of Secondary School Principals (NASSP) Bulletin, 80,* 9–21.

Louis, K., Marks, H., & Kruse, S. (1996). Teachers' professional community in restructuring schools. *American Educational Research Journal, 33,* 757–798.

Lovell, K. (1968). Developmental processes in thought. In H. J. Klausmeier & G. T. O'Hearn (Eds.), *Research and development toward the improvement of education* (pp. 14–21). Madison, WI: Dembar Educational Research Services.

Mangieri, J., & McWilliams, D. (1976). Designing an effective inservice program. *Journal of Teacher Education, 27,* 110–112.

Martin, L., & Kragler, S. (1999). Creating a culture for teachers' professional growth. *Journal of School Leadership, 9,* 311–320.

Martin, L., Shafer, T., & Kragler, S. (2009). Blending together, step by step. *Journal of Staff Development, 30*(5), 20–24.

McCormick, W. (1979). Teachers can learn to teach more effectively. *Educational Leadership, 37*(1), 59–60.

McLaughlin, M. W., & Talbert, J. E. (2001). *Professional communities and the work of high school teaching.* Chicago: University of Chicago Press.

Mezirow, J. (1994). Understanding transformation theory. *Adult Education Quarterly, 44,* 222–232.

Mezirow, J. (2003). Transformative learning and discourse. *Journal of Transformative Education, 1*(1), 58–63.

Mindich, D., & Lieberman, A. (2012). *Building a learning community: A tale of two schools.* Stanford, CA: Stanford Center for Opportunity Policy in Education.

Moore, J. W., & Schaut, J. A. (1976). Stability of teaching behavior, responsiveness to training and teaching effectiveness. *Journal of Educational Research, 69*(10), 360–363.

Nagle, J. (1972). Staff development: Do it right. *Journal of Reading, 16,* 124–127.

New American Schools. (1998). *Blueprints for school success: A guide to new American schools designs.* Arlington, VA: Educational Research Service.

Oja, S. N. (1991). Adult development. In A. Lieberman & L. Miller (Eds.), *Staff development for the '90s: New demands, new realities, new perspectives* (pp. 37–60). New York: Columbia University, Teachers College.

Pine, G. (2009). *Teacher action research: Building knowledge democracies.* Los Angeles: Sage.

Poole, W. (1995). Reconstructing the teacher–administrator relationship to achieve systematic change. *Journal of School Leadership, 5*(6), 565–596. (ERIC Document Reproduction Service No. 384127).

Postholm, M. (2012). Teachers' professional development: A theoretical review. *Educational Research, 54,* 405–429.

Putnam, R., & Borko, H. (2000). What do new views of knowledge and thinking have to say about research on teacher learning? *Educational Researcher, 29*(1), 4–15.

Regan, H., Anctil, M., Dubea, C., Hofmann, J., & Vaillancourt, R. (1992). *Teacher: A new definition and model for development and evaluation.* Philadelphia: Research for Better Schools.

Richardson, V., & Placier, P. (2001). Teacher change. In V. Richardson (Ed.), *Handbook of research on teaching* (4th ed., pp. 905–950). Washington, DC: American Educational Research Association.

Rosenshine, B., & Meyers, L. (1978). Staff development for teaching basic skills. *Theory into Practice, 17,* 267–271.

Sarason, S. B. (1971). *The culture of the school and the problem of change.* Boston: Allyn & Bacon.

Sarason, S. B. (1996). *Revisiting the culture of the school and the problem of change.* New York: Teachers College Press.

Sarason, S. (1997). *How schools might be governed and why.* New York: Teachers College Press.

Sarason, S. B. (2004). *And what do you mean by learning?* Portsmouth, NH: Heinemann.

Semadeni, J. (2010). When teachers drive their learning, *Educational Leadership, 67*(8), 66–69.

Servage, L. (2008). Critical and transformative practices in professional learning communities. *Teacher Education Quarterly, 35*(1), 63–77.

Showers, B., Joyce, B., & Bennett, B. (1987). Synthesis of research on staff development: A framework for future study and a state-of-the-art analysis. *Educational Leadership, 45*(3), 77–87.

Snow, C., Griffin, P., & Burns, M. (Eds.). (2005). *Knowledge to support the teaching of reading.* San Francisco: Wiley.

Sparks, D., & Loucks-Horsley, S. (1989). Five models of staff development for teachers. *Journal of Staff Development, 10*(4), 40–56.

Sparks, G. (1983). Synthesis of research on staff development for effective teaching. *Educational Leadership, 41*(3), 65–72.

Sprinthall, N. A., & Thies-Sprinthall, L. (1983). The teacher as an adult learner: A cognitive-developmental view. In K. J. Rehage & G. A. Griffin (Ed.), *National Society for the Study of Education yearbook: Staff development* (Vol. 82, Issue 2, pp. 13–35). Chicago: University of Chicago Press.

Standerford, N. S. (1997). Reforming reading instruction on multiple levels: Interrelations and disconnections across the state, district, and classroom levels. *Educational Policy, 11*(1), 58–91.

Thessin, R. A., & Starr, J. P. (2011). Supporting the growth of effective professional learning communities districtwide. *Phi Delta Kappan, 92*(6), 48–54.

Thomas, D. (1979). Staff development through inquiry, observation, and feedback. *Clearing House, 53*(1), 11–13.

Thompson, M., & Goe, L. (2009). *Models for effective and scalable teacher professional development* (Report No. ETS RR-09-07). Princeton, NJ: Educational Testing Service.

Tracey, D. H., & Morrow, L. M. (2006). *Lenses on reading: An introduction to theories and models.* New York: Guilford Press.

Tuckman, B. W., McCall, K. M., & Hyman, R. T. (1969). The modification of teacher behavior: Effects of dissonance and coded feedback, *American Educational Research Journal, 6*(4), 607-619.

Urban, W., & Wagoner, J. (2009). *American education: A history* (4th ed.). New York: Routledge.

Valsame, J. (1977). Accountability and staff development. *High School Journal, 60*(4), 184-187.

Vandeweghe, R., & Varney, K. (2006). The evolution of a school-based study group. *Phi Delta Kappan, 88*(4), 282-286.

Vygotsky, L. (1978). *Mind in society.* Cambridge, MA: Harvard University Press.

Wade, R. (1984/1985). What makes a difference in inservice teacher education?: A meta-analysis of research. *Educational Leadership, 42*(4), 48-54.

Wayne, A., Yoon, K., Zhu, P., Cronen, S., & Garet, M. (2008). Experimenting with teacher professional development: Motives and methods. *Educational Researcher, 37,* 469-479.

Wilsey, C., & Killion, J. (1982). Making staff development programs work. *Educational Leadership, 40*(1), 36-38, 43.

Wilson, S., & Berne, J. (1999). Teacher learning and the acquisition of professional knowledge: An examination of research on contemporary professional development. *Review of Research in Education, 24,* 173-209.

Wheatley, K. (2002). The potential benefits of teacher efficacy doubts for educational reform. *Teaching and Teacher Education, 18,* 5-22.

Wood, F., McQuarrie, F., & Thompson, S. (1982). Practitioners and professors agree on effective staff development practices. *Educational Leadership, 40*(1), 28-31.

Wood, F., & Thompson, S. (1980). Guidelines for better staff development. *Educational Leadership, 37,* 374-378.

Young, D., & Young, D. (1968). The model in use (Microteaching). *Theory into Practice, 7*(5), 186-189.

APPENDIX

CASE STUDIES: SUCCESSFUL SCHOOLS THAT HAVE SUPPORTED TEACHERS' PROFESSIONAL DEVELOPMENT

Rhoades Elementary and Ball State University Working Together to Impact Student Learning

KAREN BOATRIGHT
Principal, Rhoades Elementary Schotol, Indianapolis, Indiana

JILL C. MIELS
Ball State University

MARY HENDRICKS
First-grade teacher, Rhoades Elementary School, Indianapolis, Indiana

In order to know where you're going, you have to know where you've been. . . .
—Staff professional development meeting (fall 2007)

In April 2002, the evening news and local newspapers announced that Rhoades Elementary School was among the first schools in Indiana to be identified through No Child Left Behind (NCLB) as a failing school. Although this was not good news to the Rhoades community, the school and district had already taken action to improve teaching and learning by embarking on a professional development school (PDS) relationship with a nearby teacher- preparation institution during the 2000–2001 academic year. As part of this partnership, the school intentionally adopted a structured approach to goal setting, data analysis, and focused teacher professional development.

The school reaped the rewards of the PDS partnership in the fall of 2004 when Rhoades had a visit from Brian Jones, general counsel for the U.S. Department of Education, and was publicly congratulated by the State Superintendent of Public Instruction for being nationally recognized as a model school for student achievement and school improvement. In September 2005, Rhoades was one of the annual recipients of the NCLB Blue Ribbon Schools Award.

A DESCRIPTION OF THE SCHOOL ENVIRONMENT

Rhoades Elementary School serves 854 PreK–6 students from a large metropolitan school district in the Midwest. The school is set on the western edge of the state's largest urban area, and the Rhoades population increasingly reflects the ethnic and cultural diversity of the area. Eighty percent of the students receive free or reduced-price lunches, and the school qualifies for full Title I funding. The student body is 60% European American and 17% each Latino and African American. Furthermore, 12% of the students receive English-as-a-second-language (ESL) services, and that number continues to grow as more Latino families move into the area each year. Approximately 70 students receive special education services, the majority of whom have primary placements in inclusive classroom settings.

At this time, certified staff includes teachers with experience between 1 and more than 20 years, with the majority falling into a category of 10 years or less. In addition to certified classroom teachers, there is also a full complement of resource staff (Title I, special education, counselors, etc.); a full-time nurse; a media specialist; art, music, and physical education teachers; a parent liaison; a principal; and an assistant principal. Because Rhoades is also a PDS, a Ball State University (BSU) faculty member is assigned time in the building each week, acting as liaison between the two stakeholders and as the university supervisor for teacher candidates.

The atmosphere is positive and welcoming. Hallways feature student work projects, and outside of each room academic data and learning-outcome statements alert visitors to what is going on inside each room. Schoolwide routines and procedures are followed for moving around the building, for arrival and dismissal, and for recognizing positive behavior. In addition to individual class achievement displays, there is a schoolwide data board and an area that features pictures of individual students as they progress through the "levels" of demonstrating positive behaviors. The classroom teachers, using engaging and relevant instructional strategies, positive classroom management strategies, and implementation of classroom routines and procedures, address inappropriate behaviors themselves. In other words, children are given the opportunity to be successful learners and collaborative classmates. When removal from a class is required, each teacher is paired with a companion teacher for support at a different grade level. Seldom do students require intervention by an office administrator.

PROFESSIONAL DEVELOPMENT AT RHOADES ELEMENTARY

Professional development has become part of the culture at Rhoades Elementary. There is an ongoing commitment to professional development for inservice teachers, high-quality clinical placements for teacher candidates, enhanced student learning, and research pertinent to the needs of the school. Professional development is planned at the building level, with input from district administrators and supported through district policy. Although the state department of education recently eliminated paid professional development days for teachers, the reallocation of district funds continues to provide time for professional development at the beginning of each semester; a full day of districtwide sessions, each presented by district faculty and staff; and release time for team-level and grade-level planning.

Professional development at the building level is organized by the principal and school leadership team, which is composed of grade-level team leaders and area representatives (specials, special education, and Title I). There are multiple layers to professional development at Rhoades, all with a focus on improved student learning. On the first day of the 2012 school year, the Rhoades teachers were presented with three priorities that would drive professional development for the year and beyond. The three priorities were districtwide initiatives. Priority 1 was to create a coherent, content-rich curriculum in the form of English/language arts (E/LA) units of study allowing teachers to make instructional decisions based on their own teaching preferences and the needs of their students. The second priority was extended periods of time for students to read, write, and discuss from a variety of text materials. Finally, the third priority focused on lesson design and consistent delivery of instruction.

The school leadership team put together a calendar of goals, but teachers have input into how the goals are achieved. They also worked cooperatively on action research plans of their own design. One fourth-grade teacher reflected, "I was thinking about the importance of 'teacher choice' in professional development. Back five or six years, we had book studies, and we got to choose a book provided by Karen [the principal], and we guided our own learning. We were all at different levels of professional development and what we knew about those topics."

Professional development at Rhoades is a multilayered process. School goals become the focus of district professional development days, monthly schoolwide meetings, and weekly grade-level meetings, with support from a building staff developer and "compelling conversations" between administrators and teachers. There have been book studies, action research projects, professional development focus groups, and the opportunity for the development of teacher leaders. The culture and language of the school promote teaching for learning, and this is done from a strong belief in the efficacy of effective professional development for teachers.

Working Together to Create Effective Professional Development

Professional development at Rhoades Elementary is not so much unique as it is effective. The content of this volume on effective professional development, of course, addresses the many things we know about effective professional development. Those same characteristics can be seen at Rhoades. Professional development is part of the fabric, the culture of the building. New teachers are hired based in part on their ability to work within a community of professional educators.

Although there have been changes to the PDS partnership over the years, the underlying principles include improvement of preservice teacher clinical placements, increased inservice teacher growth, student learning, and research in fields of interest to the school site. Teacher candidates work collaboratively with individual teachers and as participating team members throughout their experience in the school. This includes full participation in all school activities and initiatives. As a result, the student teachers are learning about effective professional development from the school faculty.

Just as teachers know the expectations for their performance, they are also given significant support to achieve their efforts. Administrative "walk-throughs" help to keep the professional development efforts on course. A staff developer works in classrooms as needed and also provides additional inservice support for new teachers, those in their first 3 years of teaching. In addition, the staff developer designs and develops professional development for three different schools.

For weekly grade-level meetings, a structure has been established to make the time productive and focused on student learning. Pre- and postassessments for each E/LA unit allow teachers to collect and chart data; analyze data and prioritize needs; set, review, and revise incremental goals; select common instructional strategies; determine results indicators; monitor and evaluate results; and submit recording forms for accountability.

Working Together to Ensure Professional Development Success

Many external factors can be identified as factors in successful implementation of professional development at Rhoades. There are also internal, personnel factors that strongly influence the success of professional development. Teachers at Rhoades are totally committed to being the very best they can be. They are eager to be "effective" teachers and understand that change is part of their responsibility in serving children.

The formal partnership with BSU is also critical to success. With the growth of this partnership, teacher leaders have emerged based on their ability to supervise and to modify their own practice while mentoring teacher candidates. The student teachers are expected to participate as part of the learning community. The university supports a coteaching model in supervision of student teachers and requires that classroom performance be supported by student success using a teacher work-sample model.

Strong administrators have been a critical piece of successful professional development at Rhoades. It takes vision, long-term goal setting, and a focus on establishing a learning environment for staff and students. In the case of Rhoades Elementary, the importance of effective school leadership can be clearly identified. Students have flourished under two principals who demonstrated the ability to establish and sustain a safe and orderly environment, expectations for success, and a clear focus, time on task, data-driven decision making, and home–school relationships.

SUMMARY

There is an excitement, a synergy, connected to the work occurring at Rhoades Elementary. Teacher leaders emerge, many of whom are "graduates" of the Rhoades PDS experience. Others serve as models of best practice in the content areas or demonstrate specific teaching strengths in strategy implementation. Regardless of the positions of the people involved (teachers, administrators, candidates, practicum students, observers, BSU faculty), everyone in the building knows they have a responsibility to enhanced student learning. It is this focus that makes the school successful.

Professional Development at Bay–Arenac Community High School, Michigan

RYAN DONLAN
Indiana State University

The mission of the Bay–Arenac Community High School is to provide a positive community for up to 150 at-risk students each semester in which to learn the skills necessary for attaining personally meaningful lives that are economically productive and socially responsible. As director, I had the responsibility of ensuring that all professional development was planned, organized, and implemented with that mission in mind. Now a faculty member in higher education, I realize how deeply the ongoing, targeted professional development that we were involved in was embedded into the school's culture.

Student learning in our academy required vigilance in teaching students how to address life's challenges without resorting to violence. This was incredibly challenging for students to learn, as violence made up most of what they had been taught from an early age. Compounding this challenge was the fact that our school also provided services to pregnant teens, infants, toddlers, and other medically fragile persons. Because ensuring safety was a preeminent concern, our school operated for years with a zero-tolerance policy that provided that students who used physical force on others were removed for the remainder of any given semester on first offense. As the Bay–Arenac Community High School was a "last-chance educational option" for many of our students who had been removed from other schools, it was incredibly important that we provided an environment that offered both conflict prevention and conflict resolution each day.

Meaningful professional development in conflict prevention helped ensure that our instruction minimized student distress through its relevance, differentiation, and creativity. Staff focused on a variety of pedagogical topics at weekly staff meetings, sharing contextual best practice and demonstrating instructional techniques that worked to minimize student distress. We brainstormed options for colleagues having difficulty. To a large degree as a result of this classroom engagement, our teenagers learned without fear, engaged with interest, and performed academically.

Professional development in conflict resolution was also ongoing and included both students and staff. Training and team-building activities were held at whole-school meetings each week. Veteran students demonstrated techniques to new students. Staff participated as well. These activities involved a number of topics, which provided to us a focused training regimen. We would focus first on what it meant to have a safe community. We shared the history of the school and why students themselves made the decision to work alongside others in peace. We taught the skills of positive communication—how to disagree agreeably, and why it was valuable to learn new ways of solving problems.

We involved academics in these training experiences, using the sciences of biology and physiology to teach what happens inside human beings when perceptions lead to anger. We taught students about the limbic system's function as our organism's gatekeeper to higher-order thinking and how "fight or flight" was brainstem-related. We also reinforced how a structured process of conflict resolution could encourage participants into higher levels of thinking, allowing all to "save face." The ongoing topics were broad and deep. Networking and social capital were integral to our philosophies of professional development, as experts from within were valued, as were those from without.

Ongoing weekly dialogue, training, implementation, and reflection were key in what made professional development unique to our school. We "lived" our professional development each day. With a 100% at-risk student population, we were given many new and exciting situations in which to practice our skills. In our weekly staff meetings, faculty and staff would bring up specific instances from the week prior in which conflict prevention and resolution worked and in which they didn't. We would then perform blameless autopsies, as we called them, on the situations shared. Critical questions, such as "What could have been the result if...?" and "Were other avenues available for...?" were posed. Staff members were encouraged to reenact "teachable moments" for review, analysis, and reflection. Our meetings were like learning laboratories, in which practitioners shared new and unique ways of addressing students' instructional and social-emotional needs.

When we were exposed to new opportunities in professional development, we examined them for alignment with our mission, yet, at the same time, we were open to new ways of thinking. As director, I served as the staff-appointed "guardian of mission," yet encouraged all to help extend the boundaries of what would fall under our umbrella. One such opportunity came to us a few years ago as a model through which we could better understand our students' personalities. It was based on many years of clinical psychology and had been applied in myriad settings. Not only did we find that the concepts and practical applications fit what we were doing, but we also found that the new learning allowed us to improve our conflict resolution processes.

Our lead interventionist, Rick Sochacki, was sent out of state for 10 days of training to develop his expertise. He became a "train-the-trainer" and offered training to our staff, students, and parents. Within minutes of meeting another person, Rick could predict with accuracy his or her preferred learning style, emotional needs, and predictable ways of behaving while under stress. What incredible information for a school community!

Unique was the fact that our school operated under a consensus-building model in planning most new topics for professional development. The principal rarely made the decisions alone; the same could be said for our curriculum committee. All staff members were encouraged to participate in decisions on professional development through a consensus process. In these conversations, everyone had a voice, as a staff member other than the principal facilitated the conversation. Consensus was reached when all faculty members answered that they could "live with" a particular decision or direction.

An example of how this worked involved the amendment of a strategy of helping staff members handle students who were misbehaving and interrupting instruction. A particular model was piloted in which teachers helped and supported other teachers. At the conclusion of the school year, however, staff reached consensus that this new model was not a fit and that other approaches needed to be investigated. The school's leader and my successor, Erin Sullivan, supported staff consensus of perspective and is currently utilizing new approaches and professional development opportunities that are a better fit.

I hear often of this staff's continued good work in professional development. Erin has worked to provide even more consensus-driven opportunities for teachers to find curricular and pedagogical solutions to conflict prevention and resolution through professional development and training. I commend all at the Bay–Arenac Community High School in moving forward under new leadership to even greater successes with at-risk students. Such strong support for consensus-driven professional development exists that it has become deeply embedded in school culture, with behaviors, beliefs, and values reflecting the way business is done, even with a change in leadership.

The Bay–Arenac Community High School continues to this day with a high level of trust, as staff members have professionally developed together and, through this, have grown in their performance capabilities for many years. The school is much like a hospital, with clinicians continually "on rounds," learning from each other. Even the school leader directly applies her professional development while facilitating conflict prevention through instructional leadership and conflict resolution through building management.

Professional development is successful in the Bay–Arenac Community High School because it is mission-driven, planned through consensus, organized according to current and future needs, implemented continually, and reinforced in partnership with students. It is successful because all are involved. Students are involved as they build skills, help others, and reflect deeply during the weekly, whole-school gatherings. Faculty members enhance their own efficacy through sharing, training, implementing, exploring, diagnosing, and reflecting as well. To that end, the Bay–Arenac Community High School builds community by sharing what it believes and values and acting upon what it learns. This focus has, over time, allowed professional development to ensure that the Bay–Arenac Community High School drives its mission toward its vision of guiding its children and young adults from where they are in life to a better place.

Professional Development at Schaumburg School District 54, Illinois

NICK MYERS
Superintendent, Schaumburg School District 54, Schaumburg, Illinois

THE DISTRICT 54 LEARNING ENVIRONMENT

Schaumburg School District 54 is the largest elementary school district in Illinois, with 14,000 students in prekindergarten through eighth grade in 27 schools. Three years ago, District 54 became a majority minority district, meaning less than 50% percent of students are white. District 54 serves families that speak 84 different languages. The district's ethnic diversity is expected to increase in the years to come.

During the 2005–2006 school year, District 54 began a systemwide implementation of the professional learning community [PLC] framework advocated by Dr. Richard DuFour and Rebecca DuFour. The district provided initial training to all stakeholder groups and adopted the following Board goals for student achievement:

- Students who have attended District 54 schools for at least 1 year will read at grade level upon entering third grade.
- Each school will close the achievement gap for all students in reading and math as measured by both district and state assessments.
- At least 90% of all students will meet or exceed standards in reading and math as measured by both district and state assessments.

At the time the goals were adopted, 76% of District 54 students were meeting state standards in reading, and 80% were meeting state standards in math. Dramatic gaps in achievement levels existed among demographic subgroups. No school had 90% of its students meeting state standards in reading and math.

Within 7 years of implementing PLCs, academic performance in District 54 has improved dramatically. During the 2011–2012 school year, 91.6% of students met or exceeded state standards in reading, and 95.4% met or exceeded state standards in math; 19 of the district's 27 schools met the district's 90% goal in both reading and math. Six of these schools achieved at the 95% level in both reading and math.

KEY COMPONENTS OF PROFESSIONAL LEARNING PROGRAMS

District 54 places a priority on developing and refining the teaching skills of its employees as it strives to ensure student success. A range of professional learning opportunities is available to staff, all of which support the Board's student performance goals. Bruce Joyce and Beverly Showers (2002) note that effective teacher professional development programs are anchored by the following principles: (1) They are focused on student learning outcomes; (2) they are focused on and embedded in daily teacher practice; (3) they are informed by the best available research on effective teaching and learning; (4) they are collaborative and involve opportunities for teacher reflection and feedback; (5) they are evidence-based and data-driven to guide improvement and measure impact; and (6) they are ongoing, supported, and fully integrated into the culture and operations of the system. Joyce and Showers emphasize that effective teacher professional development programs focus on how to create classroom environments that support student learning and on knowledge of subject area content and of how students best learn that subject matter. District 54's professional development offerings support all of these components.

PROFESSIONAL DEVELOPMENT MODELS

District 54 relies on four key models to provide powerful, professional learning experiences to staff: professional learning teams, mentoring, instructional coaching, and in-house staff development programs. Each of these models enables teachers to remain current in their understanding and use of best instructional practices, as shown next.

Professional Learning Teams

District 54 uses the PLC framework to guide improvement efforts in its schools. School PLCs are responsible for collectively improving instructional practices to achieve gains in learning for all students. Team meetings focus on identifying the skills and competencies students are expected to master in each subject at each grade level; on developing common assessments to measure student mastery of essential learning outcomes; on analyzing assessment data and work samples; on sharing effective instructional practices; and on designing intervention and enrichment experiences to enhance student learning. Effective team processes have reduced variations in student learning outcomes between classes as teachers now support each other.

Mentoring

District 54 provides support to new hires through its three mentoring programs.

1. Release-time instructional mentors are assigned to teachers with fewer than 4 years of teaching experience. Release-time mentors establish strong working relationships with the teachers assigned to them by conducting weekly or biweekly classroom observations, taking part in debriefing meetings, providing classroom management strategies, and coplanning lessons and analyzing student work samples with the teachers.

2. One-on-one mentors are assigned to new staff members in specialized positions, including occupational therapists, physical therapists, psychologists, social workers, and speech and language pathologists. One-on-one mentors facilitate induction week sessions and remain an ongoing resource to new hires through their first 2 years in District 54.

3. Building operational mentors are building-based mentors assigned to support all new teachers at a given school. Building mentors serve as a resource for cultural and procedural questions and meet monthly with all new hires to share timely information, answer questions, and direct new teachers to best resources as needed.

Instructional Coaching

District instructional coaches provide support to schools refining instructional practices in specific subject areas (literacy, math, English language learning [ELL], and special education). Support is customized to the needs of each of the schools and teachers and may include coplanning lessons, participating in team meetings to analyze student work samples and discuss effective instructional practice, modeling best instructional practice, sharing research, and providing buildingwide staff development connected to the goals noted in a school's integrated school improvement plan.

Each school also has at least one literacy coach who provides similar supports. Literacy coaches work with teams to analyze assessment data, develop quality lesson plans for literacy instruction, develop intervention and enrichment lessons, share research, coteach and model lessons, and provide authentic feedback on ways to continue to refine instructional practice.

In-House Staff Development Programs

A wide range of in-house staff development programs also build the capacity of teachers.

- In 2009, the district began a summer professional development series, which is organized around key instructional initiatives in the district and taught by District 54 teacher leaders and district-level content area directors. Salary credit is provided to teachers who participate. More than 750 teachers attend each summer.

- In June 2011, District 54 held its first professional development symposium, which included more than 30 sessions facilitated by teacher teams representing schools around the district. Presentations related to how teachers used PLC processes, as well as other instructional and cultural strategies, to impact student learning. Sessions were designed for teachers by teachers. More than 500 employees attend the annual event.

- Each August, District 54 offers an induction week for new hires. The sessions are differentiated to meet the needs of new hires and to provide an understanding of the district's mission, vision, and goals. Sessions include overviews of the PLC framework and mentoring programs, time with principals to discuss the appraisal processes and building procedures, workshops on the district's curriculum and bilingual and special education programs, and time with the Schaumburg Education Association's board.

- District 54 teachers can also enroll in salary lane credit courses offered year-round by teacher leaders and district-level content directors. The courses align to the district's student achievement goals. During the 2010–2011 school year, the district launched a salary lane credit Literacy Academy focused on effectively implementing the district's balanced literacy model. Participants explored each component of balanced literacy in depth, videotaped their literacy lessons, and shared these videos with the group for discussion and reflection. A similar course structure has been introduced in math. More than 110 teachers have attended these academy offerings in each of the past 2 school years.

SUMMARY

In their 2011 book *Leaders of Learning*, Richard DuFour and Robert Marzano assert that "the best school systems focus their school improvement initiatives on creating conditions to improve the professional practice of educators." District 54 is committed to providing a wide range of professional development opportunities that enable this to happen. From the district level to the building level to the team level, District 54's teachers are highly engaged in substantive, job-embedded professional learning activities that enhance students' learning experiences each day.

REFERENCES

DuFour, R., & Marzano, R. (2011). *Leaders of learning*. Bloomington, IN: Solution Tree Press.
Joyce, B., & Showers, B. (2002). *Student achievement through staff development*. Alexandria, VA: Association for Supervision and Curriculum Development.

Supporting Teacher Researchers in a Rural PreK–5 School, West Virginia

AIMEE L. MOREWOOD
West Virginia University

A DESCRIPTION OF THE SCHOOL ENVIRONMENT

This rural, PreK–5 Appalachian school's population was just over 350 students, and received Title I benefits. It is important to note that this school is a professional development school (PDS) partnering with the local university. The mission of the university is to serve the people of the state, and this PDS partnership allows for the education faculty to be highly involved in local schools. The PDS collaboration has been in existence for nearly 15 years between this school and the university, which demonstrates the commitment of the school and university to the concept of school–university partnerships. This partnership laid the groundwork for this unique professional development experience because it provided the necessary time required to build trusting, collegial relationships that are necessary for effective professional development.

The participants who engaged in this specific professional development opportunity were experienced educators: The most novice member had 8 years of teaching experience, most had been teachers in different grade levels, and they all held various degrees within education. In addition to four classroom teachers, this group also included a Title I teacher, one teacher who held dual roles as a Title I teacher and technology integration specialist, the academic coach for the school, the media specialist, and various preservice teachers. This range of roles strengthened the professional development work as it became more inclusive of all educators within the school.

PLANNING, ORGANIZATION, AND IMPLEMENTATION

Teacher research was a useful methodology through which the educators could look critically at the connections between their learning and their instruction and how this learning affected student achievement. These educators participated in every aspect of teacher research, including identifying a problem or question, implementing a plan of action, collecting data, analyzing the data, evaluating students' learning, and disseminating the findings.

During this 2-year teacher research project, the university liaison and the school-based professional development coordinator (PDC) worked together to develop meaningful and effective teacher research projects that addressed the needs of the participating educators and the needs of the school. In order to do this, these two people reviewed the school's strategic plan and investigated resources that were available for this project. They also asked the participating educators to provide feedback about what they would like to focus on during all aspects of the professional development sessions. In other words, the educators had voice and power in their learning. A literacy focus emerged and guided the internal grant proposal, which outlined the plan for this teacher research.

During the first year, the focus was on fluency instruction. An internationally known literacy researcher, Timothy Rasinski, was presenting locally on fluency instruction, so to kick off this professional development, every member of the group attended this presentation. After this presentation, the group members participated in focused conversations that discussed literacy research. These conversations occurred within the professional learning community (PLC) created by this group. At the conclusion of the PLC, all of the educators engaged in reflective practice through a lesson study approach. Each educator selected a specific aspect of fluency instruction (i.e., prosody, accuracy, or rate) to focus on and videotaped three different lessons that they planned and implemented. Upon completion, each educator reviewed her video and completed a lesson study form, which guided and captured her critical thoughts about her pedagogy and her students' learning.

The professional development focus in the second year, comprehension instruction, emerged from the group's study of fluency instruction during year 1. Reviews of the lesson study forms and transcripts of the PLC conversations revealed that group members repeatedly identified learning more about comprehension instruction as a critical need. Although the teacher research process in the second year was similar to that in the first, it did contain some different elements. For example, in the second year the group decided to read *Reading with Meaning: Teaching Comprehension in the Primary Grades* (Miller, 2002). Another change from year 1 was the way the PLC conversations were held; instead of a face-to-face PLC, the participants engaged in an online blog to share their thoughts about the readings for year 2.

An additional difference was that the group participated in 3 days of professional development at the university. University faculty members who specialized in literacy instruction led the sessions, and the sessions provided the educators with information related to comprehension instruction (e.g., making inferences, using twin texts). At the conclusion of the university-based professional development, the teachers again began to engage in reflective practice through lesson study, which focused on comprehension instruction. Once the videos and lesson study forms were complete, the group reconvened for data analysis.

UNIQUE PROFESSIONAL DEVELOPMENT

This professional development was unique because it effectively wove two different forms of professional development together: teacher research and PLCs (in face-to-face and online formats). This group was able to fully engage in all aspects of teacher research with a collaborative supportive group. The educators worked together to formulate an area of focus, systematically collect data, analyze the data in multiple ways, and disseminate the findings. This procedure provided this group with ownership over their learning.

In addition to participating in teacher research, these educators also worked collaboratively as a PLC so that they could learn more from one another through critical, yet supportive, face-to-face or online conversations. Through these conversations the group members deepened their content knowledge of fluency and comprehension instruction.

SUCCESS OF THE PROFESSIONAL DEVELOPMENT

This teacher research was successful in three distinct ways and illustrates how the educators were actively involved in their learning. First, it was successful because it provided the educators in this group a way to systematically study their pedagogy. This systematic approach to professional learning gave the educators a way to reflect on their instruction during group conversations that focused on individual and group analyses.

Second, this professional development was effective in that the educators were able to explore student learning through their pedagogy. Instead of the teachers' assessing student growth and then placing the students into a specific learners' category, they were able to look at their instruction while simultaneously looking at the student data to better understand the alignment between what they did and what the students learned.

Finally, this professional development series was successful because the educators who participated in this teacher research became models of reflective practice for other educators and for the preservice teachers who were assigned to this school. The work of these teacher researchers is important and should be shared with other educators, as well as with preservice teacher candidates; this aligns well with the mission of partnership work at a PDS. For example, different members of this group have worked together to disseminate the findings of this teacher research through presentations at state and international conferences, as well as in writing for publication.

SUMMARY

Overall, through teacher research and the organization of a PLC, this professional development opportunity allowed each group member to better understand the connection between their instruction and their students' learning. This was accomplished because the educators actively engaged in critical, collaborative conversations while using a teacher research framework to study their instruction. The teacher research framework allowed these educators to control their learning within a guided professional learning environment. This is important so that educators feel respected as professionals and motivated to build content and pedagogical knowledge.

REFERENCE

Miller, D. (2002). *Reading with meaning: Teaching comprehension in the primary grades.* Portland, ME: Stenhouse.

Successful Staff Development Transforms Writing Instruction in an Oklahoma School

PRISCILLA GRIFFITH
University of Oklahoma

AUDRA PLUMMER
*Codirector for Inservice, Oklahoma Writing Project;
Principal, Oklahoma Virtual Charter Academy*

LORI CONNERY
Principal, Monroe Elementary, Norman, Oklahoma

SHARRI CONWAY
Third-grade teacher, Monroe Elementary, Norman, Oklahoma

DEB WADE
*Teacher–consultant, Oklahoma Writing Project;
fifth-grade teacher, Pioneer Intermediate School, Noble, Oklahoma*

Melanie arrived at the Jimmy Carter Elementary School to teach a demonstration lesson on writing "found poetry." In this particular lesson, Melanie wants to show teachers how she helps students integrate reading and writing with information text. This is a lesson she has successfully taught in her own fifth-grade classroom in a neighboring school district. Melanie is a teacher–consultant with the local writing project, and she is working with the writing project's director to provide 45 hours of classroom-embedded professional development in writing instruction to the teachers in grades 3–5. The professional development at Carter has been guided by the National Writing Project's belief that "teachers teaching teachers" is a powerful model. Linda, the principal at Carter, agreed to provide substitutes so that all the grade-level teachers could observe Melanie's demonstration lesson.

Melanie had helped design and had read the teachers' responses to a survey conducted during the planning of this professional development project; however, she felt she needed more specific curricular information to help her plan the demonstration lesson. Thus, prior to her visit, she conferred with classroom teachers to determine what topics were being covered in the curriculum, as well as to get an understanding of the students' prior knowledge about the writing process. She wanted to use the same instructional language the teachers used with students and to create a focus for students that could be integrated into daily lessons. In addition, this prior contact helped Melanie determine how she could help the classroom teachers incorporate new strategies into existing frameworks. She wanted to emphasize the importance of the process with content that was applicable to district and state lesson objectives.

Melanie began her day at Carter by teaching the lesson to third-grade students. During the demonstration, the third-grade teachers actually participated in the lesson with their students, and Linda was there observing and participating with the teachers. Melanie provided teachers with a graphic organizer to help structure their note taking, along with handouts connected to the lesson they were observing. Following the third-grade demonstration, Melanie moved to the fourth grade and then on to the fifth grade, each time teaching a version of the lesson. She adapted to accommodate the development levels of the children at each grade level, but for the most part the structure of her lesson was similar across grade levels.

Immediately after each lesson, she met for an hour with the grade-level teachers as they deconstructed the lesson step by step. Melanie guided the teachers through the lesson chunks with questions such as "How did I begin this lesson?" "What did I do next?" "And then what did I do?" These questions involved the teachers in the deconstruction process and helped them identify the intricacies of procedural information so important to the successful execution of the lesson. An observer would have heard comments such as "Wait, didn't she have the students underline some parts in the article before she wrote down their ideas?" Through this deconstruction, Melanie recorded the teachers' comments in a chart similar to the one in Figure A.1.

Melanie's purpose was to motivate the teachers to think closely not only about what she did but also how and why she did it. The purpose of the close examination of her lesson with the teachers was to draw attention to understated details that were important to student learning. Melanie's goal was for the teachers to be able to carry this level of reflection on lesson details over to their thinking about their own instruction.

After the lesson deconstruction, Melanie asked them to write for a short period of time (approximately 7 minutes) about something from her lesson that they could implement during the next week. She followed up this quick write with sharing and discussion. Melanie realized some teachers might feel comfortable duplicating exactly what she had done today but with different content. Others might identify several aspects of her lesson and plan a different lesson around those individual strategies, for example,

LESSON CHUNKS What did I do?	HOW How did I do it?	WHY Why did I do it this way?
You had the students write down information from the text that describes nocturnal animals.	The students did this independently. They wrote their information on 3″ × 5″ note cards. You told them they would write for 2 minutes.* *Across the three grade levels, teachers noted differences in how long their students wrote.	This would generate their thinking about what they might include in their found poems. The note cards were less threatening because the students did not have to fill in a large sheet of blank paper. They knew how long they had. The short time frame was also less threatening. The students would see this as manageable—something they could do.

FIGURE A.1. Lesson deconstruction chart.

finding ways to make prewriting activities seem less threatening. During the upcoming week, teachers would plan and implement a lesson.

Melanie would return in a week for an after-school meeting with all the teachers together to help them reflect on their classroom experiences. She asked them to bring their work samples to share and discuss. For this upcoming meeting, Melanie's goal would be to help them talk in terms of their successes and roadblocks. This discussion would involve a level of lesson deconstruction with a focus on what each teacher had done and how the students had responded. During the discussion with all teachers, staff members would be able to see what objectives may be reinforced in a future grade and what skills would need to be mastered before going on. This discussion, informed by student work-sample data, would help teachers prioritize skills and would add validity to the upcoming model lessons.

Melanie's demonstration lesson was the first of six provided by writing project teachers over the course of the school year. Carefully chosen topics for these demonstrations represented goals for developing students' informational and opinion writing skills. Among the lessons were writing beginning and closing paragraphs, developing claims and supporting evidence, using transition words—the intricacies of good informational and opinion writing.

Melanie's lesson occurred in October after planning and launching of this professional development project. In fact, planning had begun the spring before, when the local writing project learned of a grant opportunity through the National Writing Project (NWP) to provide professional development at a high-needs school. With 57% of the children in the school eligible for free or reduced-price lunches, Carter is a high-needs school. Linda indicated that the goals of the grant matched the school's intent to focus on writing during the upcoming school year, and there was a fit between the expertise that the writing project offered and the goals the school wanted to meet. The two entities created a planning team consisting of Linda, Carrie (a lead teacher from Carter), Angela (the writing project director), and Melanie. As part of the grant, this team attended an NWP meeting of all writing project grant recipients. At this meeting, the team developed a strong working relationship that enhanced their ability to find collaborative solutions to challenges.

Linda knew she wanted the professional development to be classroom embedded. Both Carrie and Melanie wanted to be sure the teachers would not think the professional development was a waste of their time. Together, the group developed a logic model of outcomes for students and teachers (see Figure A.2). The premise of their logic model was that professional development implemented with fidelity should have a positive impact upon teachers' knowledge, classroom skills, and feelings of efficacy, as well as on student achievement. Based on their goals, they outlined the content and structures of the professional development. The content in the logic model was refined using the teacher survey data collected during the initial planning of the project. Incorporated into the logic model were the resources each entity contributed to the project. The planning team decided on three professional development structures: workshops, demonstration lessons with follow-up implementation assignments, and teacher inquiry groups. The workshops would be primarily for providing teachers with information about writing instruction. The inquiry groups would engage the teachers around a question related to their teaching. The demonstration lesson cycle would take content from the workshops and inquiry groups to an implementation level in a classroom with students.

Although the grant funded professional development only for teachers in grades 3–5, Linda wanted all the teachers in the school to participate. The writing project accommodated this request. Teachers from grades K to 2 and the special staff attended all meetings that were held during the teachers' contract day. This schoolwide participation unified the staff in their understanding of the important role writing has in learning across all curriculum areas.

Respect for the teachers' professional knowledge and consideration of their time were critical to the planning of the workshops. Carrie helped the team consider the needs of the community of teachers. For example, she interjected comments such as, "That might be too much to do in December. It is a busy month!" Subtle details, such as food and the principal's door prizes, contributed to the positive environment at these meetings. The teachers received a loose-leaf notebook in which to keep materials they received as the professional development progressed through the year. Typically, workshops lasted 3 or 4 hours. Some were on district staff development days, but some had to be held on Saturdays. Those on Saturdays were strategically scheduled so they would not conflict with football games in this university town. The grant budget included stipends for teachers to compensate for Saturday meetings. The team recognized the importance of making every workshop interactive and of allowing plenty of time for the teachers to talk among themselves in horizontal and vertical grade-level groups.

The first week they were back to school in the fall, Angela and Melanie met with the teachers at a "launch" meeting for the professional development project. They shared the results of the online survey and the logic model. Their intent was to paint a clear picture of the goals and activities for the project. In September, after the launch of the project, Linda polled the teachers again. She asked three questions: What is one idea you took away from the workshop that you will implement in your writing instruction? When thinking about writing instruction, what are your teaching and classroom goals for this school year? What supplies and materials do you need to implement ideas

Resources → **Professional Development** → **Outcomes** →

Resources

School
- Administrative support
- Literacy coach
- District support
- School-level focus on professional development

Collaborative Solutions to Challenges

Writing Project
- Teacher consultant expertise
- Knowledge of CCSS, teacher evaluation system, and tiered instruction
- Staff support
- Expertise providing ongoing professional development

Professional Development

Content
- CCSS
- Information and opinion writing
- Writing process
- Traits of good writing
- Shared and interactive writing
- Conferencing: peer and teacher
- Analyzing student work samples
- Evidence-based instructional strategies

Structures
- Workshops
- Demonstration lessons and implementation assignment
- Inquiry groups

Outcomes

Teacher
- Efficacy
  o as a writer
  o as a teacher of writing
- Content knowledge
  o CCSS
  o writing process
  o traits of good writing
  o structures of information and opinion text
- Classroom practices
  o a community of writers
  o celebrate students' and teachers' writing
  o data-informed instruction
  o scaffolding student efforts
  o multiple writing opportunities throughout the day and across the curriculum

Student
- Confidence as a writer
- Awareness of task, purpose, audience, and role as a writer
- Clear and coherent writing
- Apply traits of good writing across all genres of writing
- Automaticity with basic writing skills: conventions, handwriting, keyboarding, spelling, and sentence construction
- Recognize and incorporate writing as a lifelong practice in academic and nonacademic settings

FIGURE A.2. The logic model for professional development at Jimmy Carter Elementary School.

for writing instruction this year? Using the information from this poll, she was able to provide ongoing support for the teachers.

In an early workshop, Angela and Melanie wanted the teachers to think about the unique skills they brought to work with children in this high-needs school. Angela introduced the teachers to the concept of "funds of knowledge" (Gonzalez, Moll, & Amanti, 2005) by showing a video of Luis Moll discussing his work. Then, individually, the teachers developed maps of their funds of knowledge. These maps were displayed around the room, and the teachers made a gallery walk. As the teachers viewed each other's maps, they learned new information about their colleagues. "Roger, I didn't know you were an expert on barbecue sauces," one teacher said to her colleague. Following that, the teachers at each grade level mapped and discussed what they perceived might be their students' funds of knowledge. They extended this activity into the classroom by having students make maps of their funds of knowledge. Angela and Melanie believed this classroom activity was valuable because it would increase the teachers' knowledge about their students' lives and it would make students aware of the information from their lives that they could bring to their writing.

In subsequent workshops, Angela and Melanie used multiple types of activities (e.g., videos, modeling, discussions) to provide the teachers with direct and vicarious experiences, to make the workshops interactive and hands-on, and to blend theory with practice. Every workshop offered teachers the opportunity to write, reflecting Angela and Melanie's belief that teachers of writing should be writers themselves.

As an introduction to the Common Core State Standards (CCSS), each teacher received a placemat-sized, laminated sheet with all the language arts standards for his or her grade level. The teachers appreciated these because they were able to see the relationship between the anchor standards and their specific grade-level standards. At this same workshop, Angela and Melanie had the teachers look closely at the application of the anchor standard for writing opinions at each grade level. Teachers highlighted key words and phrases to see the change in focus at each level. Finally, they examined their curriculum materials and discussed how they could apply opinion writing across the content areas.

The inquiry groups involved the teachers in a sustained focus on an area of their teaching. During one inquiry group, teachers examined student writing samples to identify areas of emphasis for their instruction. Among the student outcomes in the logic model was automaticity with basic writing skills. Working in grade-level groups, the teachers determined their goals for basic writing skills. They displayed these lists, noting overlaps in content across grades. Fifth- grade teachers were amazed at what was expected in third grade, yet they were not seeing those expectations manifested in their students' work. One teacher remarked, "I should see more complete paragraphs than I am seeing." By critically making a list of teaching objectives, teachers were able to see the overlaps as well as the gaps. Their conversations led to a vertical alignment of goals and instructional foci. The teachers analyzed their student writing samples using this new alignment of goals to identify emphases for instruction at each grade level.

Midyear, the planning team attended a second NWP meeting at which they reflected on and discussed the progress of the professional development.[1] One concern

---

[1]We acknowledge and gratefully appreciate the information about professional development structures received at the two NWP meetings we attended.

Linda and Carrie expressed related to the multiple mandates at the district and state levels. Linda said, "This is almost like a perfect storm." In addition to making the transition to the CCSS, the state introduced a new teacher evaluation system, and the district began requiring tiered instruction as part of the identification process for special education placement. In Carrie's words, "The combination of these three initiatives is stressing out the teachers." The planning team realized how important it was for the teachers to see the professional development as a scaffold to support these mandates. Subsequently, at each workshop, Angela and Melanie provided them with the content goal and an explanation of how the content was tied to the CCSS, teacher evaluation, and tiered instruction. As a result of this reflective meeting, the team was able to fine-tune the professional development.

During this project, the teachers shifted instruction from assigning writing to teaching children how to be writers. This was professional development that "worked," but what components made this project successful? First, the project had support and leadership from the principal. She was intricately involved in the planning, attended every meeting interacting with the teachers, and provided ongoing support to the staff as they became teachers of writing. Second, the professional development was classroom-embedded, represented what the teachers viewed as important, and blended theory and practice. Teachers saw how the content fit their curriculum goals. Third, the team evaluated the progress of the professional development at midpoint in the school year and made adjustments. Finally, the content of the professional development had credibility to the teachers. From the inception of the project, a teacher from the school was a member of the planning team. The faculty understood that the professional development was not just something the principal or someone external to the school had planned for them. The professional development, provided and led by teachers from the local writing project and the school, valued the voice and the professional knowledge of the participants.

REFERENCE

Gonzalez, N., Moll, L. C., & Amanti, C. (2005). *Funds of knowledge: Theorizing practices in households, communities, and classrooms.* Mahwah, NJ: Erlbaum.

Professional Development at Candeo Peoria, Arizona

MICHELE HUDAK
Dean of Academics, Candeo, Peoria, Arizona

CANDEO'S SCHOOL CUTURE

Candeo Peoria is an independent charter school in the northwest valley of suburban Phoenix. Candeo, a young school, opened in 2008. Currently, 480 students are enrolled in kindergarten through grade 6. Our population includes the following students: 87%

European American, 1% African American, 4% Latino, 1% Native American, and 7% Asian. Candeo does not participate in the free and reduced-price lunch program, nor do we receive Title I funds. Candeo has 20 classes, with 19 general education teachers, 4 special-area teachers, 1 special education teacher, 1 schoolwide enrichment specialist, a dean of academics, and a head of school/executive director. All general education and special education teachers are certified and highly qualified. Most teachers have less than 10 years of teaching experience. Five teachers have between 11 and 19 years of experience, and two teachers have over 20 years of experience. Since opening, Candeo has earned the highest rankings from the Arizona Department of Education for superior student achievement results.

We subscribe to a whole-child philosophy. We recognize the importance of a healthy lifestyle and promote that lifestyle on campus through our wellness policies. We provide a learning environment that is physically and emotionally safe for students. We engage our learners with curriculum and methodology that is guided by research and best practice. We provide rigor and challenge in a learning environment that is supported by highly qualified professionals.

To guide instruction, Candeo utilizes Core Knowledge, a classical curriculum, in conjunction with the Arizona and Common Core State Standards. Our goal is to deliver the curriculum in innovative ways using research-based methods. We utilize a comprehensive approach to literacy instruction—recognizing the importance of targeted whole-group, small-group, and individual instruction. We value the importance of strong, well-developed content-area instruction and subscribe to a philosophy of deep conceptual understanding of mathematics.

CANDEO'S PROFESSIONAL DEVELOPMENT

At Candeo, we believe that continuous job-embedded professional development is a key to increased student achievement. Currently, our professional development framework includes 7 full days of development prior to beginning the instructional year. Within those 7 days, 2 days are dedicated to individually assessing all students in reading so that strengths and needs are targeted prior to the school year beginning. New teachers to Candeo participate in 5 days of inservice prior to the full week with returning teachers. Each Wednesday 2 hours are set aside specifically for professional development purposes, for a total of 8 hours each month. This is possible because the students are released 1½ hours early that day.

Planning and organizing professional development is done in four main ways. First, teachers are surveyed both formally and informally near the end of the school year to determine areas of strength, areas for improvement, and desires for professional learning. Because we strongly regard within-school expertise, we ask teachers what they are willing to offer the staff in terms of development. Second, teachers, grade-level teams, teacher leaders, and building administrators analyze both internal and external summative data of student achievement to determine where needs may lie for professional development. Third, because we value the importance that practitioner research holds, we ensure that researching real problems of practice is incorporated in our model of professional learning for teachers. Finally, we recognize the need for professional development to be flexible and responsive to the unique needs of our teachers and learners. Although the framework remains relatively the same, the content changes and may be differentiated based on the needs within the building each year.

CANDEO'S UNIQUE CHARACTERISTICS

The dean of academics' role was added in Candeo's fourth year as a response to the need for one individual to focus on the continuous development of teachers and their impact on students' learning. The role is unlike that of an assistant principal, as the position solely focuses on teachers, their learning and continuous improvement, and the students they serve.

In essence, Candeo's professional development model is unique in three ways. First, because we value within-school expertise, teachers are invited to share their professional expertise with staff. Thus, prior to the beginning of each school year, teachers plan and offer differentiated sessions that serve to enhance teaching and learning specific to Candeo. When planning for these sessions, teachers and administrators work together to determine student and teacher needs. The sessions must strongly align with our curriculum and instructional practices. Thus, teachers must make a case for why such a session is deemed necessary before the session is offered. For example, new teachers to Candeo participate in sessions that often include new or unfamiliar practices (i.e., using formative literacy assessment to inform instruction, developmental spelling, reader's and writer's workshop, Singapore math, and response to intervention at Candeo). On the other hand, returning teachers participate in sessions that provide more depth to their practice (i.e., using primary-source documents to enhance content-area instruction, using mimeo technology in the classroom, Cornell note taking and the elementary student, using Socratic circles to enhance students' abilities to cite textual evidence). Teachers who are new to Candeo and unfamiliar with our core practices are required to attend various sessions. Veteran Candeo teachers are always welcome to attend basic sessions if needs are warranted (as determined by the teachers themselves or administration) and are invited to present to either new or veteran teachers or to attend sessions that serve to enhance their practice. Through these sessions, all teachers delve more deeply into practices deemed important at Candeo, identify building experts who serve as resources and mentors throughout the school year, and dialogue with professionals within and across grade levels.

Second, we incorporate systematic practitioner research as a focal point of our Wednesday professional development sessions. In 2013, one Wednesday each month is dedicated to learning the systematic process of practitioner inquiry. On the following Wednesday, teachers are provided time to identify their own problems of practice, seek professional literature to support their need for change, determine a course of action to change or enhance their professional practice, and measure the effects of student learning that may result from the actions taken. Important to note is that teachers who are new to Candeo are provided the opportunity to meet with the head of the school, the schoolwide enrichment specialist, and/or the dean of academics in a mentoring capacity, rather than researching a problem of practice during their first year. The content of these sessions is either predetermined by administration or determined by feedback provided by the teachers.

Third, we value the importance of teacher collaboration by ensuring that horizontal and vertical collaboration are embedded within our model. In addition to weekly team planning sessions during common preparation times, one Wednesday of the month is dedicated to reflecting on what was taught during the previous month. Grade-level curriculum maps are updated to accurately reflect the instruction that occurred. This time is also utilized to review the maps in preparation for the following month. During this reflective process, if a teacher determines a specific need for support, the dean of academics is contacted and plans for support are made. Coteaching, model teaching, observing other teachers, and planning meetings are examples of support that teachers might receive.

Professional development at Candeo has been successful because we place the teachers at the center of their professional learning. As we move out of our developmental phase as a school, we have become much more targeted in our needs for development. Our approach is collaborative rather than top-down, which teachers appreciate.

In the planning stages of professional development, we take feedback from our teachers seriously. We also consider both internal and external school data and student needs. In our organization and implementation phase, we recognize the expertise that our teachers bring to our learning community and ensure that they have a forum through which to share that expertise. Most important, we provide time for teachers to systematically study their own problems of practice, rather than mandating schoolwide goals that may or may not apply to particular teachers or grade levels. In our reflective phase, we celebrate our successes and make plans to address our challenges. Overall, teachers have choices for their learning, as well as opportunities to take an instructional lead.

SUMMARY

Because Candeo Peoria is a charter school, we have the autonomy and flexibility to determine professional development that is directly linked to the specific needs of our teachers and students. We value teaching as a learning profession and capitalize on the strengths of the professionals by whom we are surrounded. We recognize that not all teachers have the same professional learning needs and attempt to differentiate our professional learning opportunities to accommodate for the unique needs of the teachers. We rise to the challenges of teaching and learning as a group of professionals who collectively and passionately desire to make a difference for children.

Professional Development
at Peachtree Presbyterian Preschool, Georgia

JANE MONTGOMERY

Executive Director, Peachtree Presbyterian Preschool, Atlanta, Georgia

Peachtree Presbyterian Preschool is a large incorporated nonprofit half-day preschool located in the Buckhead area of Atlanta, Georgia. The preschool was established in 1959 to provide an early childhood education program of the highest quality and serves approximately 425 children annually. Central to the mission of the preschool is its community outreach, which supports children with special needs and Latino children in an inclusion model. The student population is mainly a reflection of the neighborhood demographics, with children coming from homes with two college-educated parents. In most school years, there are 25 children with special needs and 6 Latino children.

Currently, the preschool is inspired by the preschools of Reggio Emilia, Italy. The staffing model is based on two coteachers in the classroom with an additional support teacher assigned to classrooms with children with special needs. The school has several resource educators who work with all age levels.

Professional development has always been a strong value and priority for teachers at Peachtree. Early childhood program accreditation standards mandate that educational staff have a minimum number of annual clock hours of professional development, and generally the school's offerings were based on meeting the minimum number of hours with little regard for the development of the educator. In most early childhood professional development, a speaker lectures the teachers in a "tourist" approach on a specific topic or presents a "make and take" workshop. This factory approach to teacher learning returns teachers to classrooms with little or no dialogue or continuation of their professional development. After attending a conference at the National Association for the Education of Young Children (NAEYC) in 2004 and hearing Amelia Gambetti and Lella Gandini speak, the Director became inspired to make some changes to the pedagogy and hired a Director of Educational Practices to facilitate this process, which quickly became a journey! The staff spent the next year studying early childhood research, attending conferences, and visiting other schools.

In 2006, the Peachtree staff began to look within the school using a critical eye and to question why things were done the same way each year. Our school was a traditional, theme-based early childhood program with top-down leadership. The Director and the Director of Educational Practices met with small groups of teachers to reflect on the program. Using these reflections and the information gleaned from an internal accreditation review by stakeholders, including parents, the Peachtree staff initiated a pedagogical master plan. Part of the plan was to form a professional learning community within the school. Accordingly, a pedagogical steering committee of 17 educators was organized and began monthly meetings to engage in a process of self-reflection and self-discovery in collaborative meetings. The steering committee included members of the administration (Director, Director of Educational Practices), as well as classroom teachers. The school made a commitment to provide substitute teachers to allow teachers to attend the monthly meetings.

This was a new style of working together for us; educators were not accustomed to others' questioning their practices and sometimes took offense. Learning to collaborate was a slow and arduous task, with the challenge to slow down and wonder about the work of early childhood education. What should the first experience of children and school be? Questions arose about our lengthy (although very well-written) curriculum at Peachtree. There was a slow paradigm shift from this traditional "curriculum" to offering the children an environment with rich and stimulating experiences to learn concepts and skills in different ways. The dialogue regarding the changes in pedagogy slowly pollinated in our school, and as a result educators began to see the value in shifting to a collegial group of educators united in their commitment to children.

At some of the first collaborative meetings, educators were challenged to examine their own ideas regarding the philosophies of early childhood education. The meetings allowed needed time to go deeper with the dialogue regarding values—the underlying beliefs of the educators. Another topic of the group became: What does literacy look like in early childhood? These meetings became more interactive as the participants began to feel more comfortable with questions.

This model of professional development that emerged was different from the notion of learning from an expert because in a professional learning community, members learn and reflect with each other. However, this style requires structural changes within the school that affect policies, procedures, budgets, rules, and relationships. The school budgeted 2 hours of additional time into each educator's salary for weekly collaborative meetings. This extra time allowed coteachers to meet weekly in small groups, as well as whole age-level groups, focusing on the work of the children. This was a large cultural change in the school climate, moving from work in isolation to work in collaboration, and was difficult for some of the educators who were so immersed in their own work. Examining their conventional practices from a critical perspective was threatening. The conversations and dialogue were crucial as we developed a common understanding of our purpose, priorities, goals, and expectations.

The staff began to perceive documentation as a process of learning. Although it was complex and required a great deal of effort and practice, teachers began to see the value of observing the children, in addition to carefully listening to the children. Sharing this information with the professional learning community allowed the group to engage in building a shared knowledge regarding essential curriculum. Participants can't sit and just listen!

The school quickly realized that additional resources were needed to support the transition to working in this manner, as well as to change the pedagogy and school culture. Some of the staff attended an "Educator Exchange Day" at Saint Anne's Day School and became interested in the work of Project Infinity, a group of nonrelated schools working in collaboration. As a result, Peachtree became official member of Project Infinity in 2009. Project Infinity is a larger professional learning community that supports collaborative learning within and between ordinary schools in order to strengthen their depth and quality. Participating schools are asked to make two main commitments: a genuine, schoolwide interest in analyzing the experiences and philosophies of Reggio Emilia and an active commitment to the welfare of the other schools in the project. Experiences within the project include ongoing collaboration meetings, group visits to other schools in the United States, readings, discussions, conversations with visiting professionals, study weeks in Reggio Emilia, and restructuring the way professional time is invested at work. Schools within Project Infinity actively embrace the struggle of designing experiences born from ongoing research tempered by systemic professional collaboration. As of 2013, there are seven schools in the project.

There are approximately 200 educators in the project who meet together twice annually for whole-group professional development. A smaller Project Infinity steering committee meets four times a year for conversations regarding the work of the Project, professional development, systems of support, and pedagogy. Additionally, each participating school hosts two Educator Exchange Days, which offer visiting teachers an opportunity to formally share experiences within a reciprocal exchange, as well as tours of the school environment. This unique style of professional development has schools working together instead of in competition.

Intentional professional development has affected the school culture greatly, as a professional learning community provides deep, thought-provoking growth and development for educators that are imbedded each day in the work. As a result of these experiences and exchanges, Peachtree has adopted a more intentional professional development model with the assumption that learning is relationship based. We have continuing dialogue on the following questions: Is our staff willing to sustain a genuine interest in studying, researching, and analyzing the schools of Reggio Emilia? Can we work together on challenges? Can we have open attitudes to welcome all sorts of possibilities? Are we too attached to one way of doing things?

To make a transition of this magnitude, a commitment from 100% of the staff and parents is necessary. The Director and the Director of Educational Practices, with the support of Project Infinity schools, guided the change process. Some educators, however, were so entrenched in traditional methods and isolated work that they could not make the cultural and pedagogical transition, nor could they work in collaboration with colleagues, parents, and children. Accordingly, the staffing profile incurred some changes as the model shifted to coteaching.

Parents have always been involved as "volunteers" at Peachtree, for example, organizing holiday parties or the annual Spring Fling. Looking at parents as part of the triangle (teachers, children, parents) of a professional learning community is an uncommon practice for most schools. Our school transitioned from seeing parents only in the carpool line to welcoming parents to participate in the classroom experiences either through sharing a particular skill, reading to children, or working in the studio. Parents are included in the professional development, some even serving on a panel at Educator Exchange Day.

An unusual strategy for collaboration of the professional learning community was the development of a website for the Peachtree educators to use for exchange, inspiration, and communication. Technology allowed educators to expand collaborative methods beyond just weekly meetings. The website allows exchange using a message board and provides inspiration through recommended websites, professional readings, and photographs. The preschool also participates in a larger professional learning community through shared webinars and video sharing. Collaboration is no longer just a weekly mandated time—it is part of the life of the educators!

At Peachtree, educators had to shift from the "industrial" model to a different model that is relationship based and enables them to function as professional learning communities. We have discovered that our journey is a slow but rewarding experience. The impact on the school has been great, with teachers having a renewed passion for their profession. Additionally, the leadership model is transformational, as the school works together on a journey with the support of a professional learning community within our school and of the Project Infinity professional learning community to change from a focus on teaching to a focus on learning.

Professional Learning at The Hamilton and Alexandra College, Australia

BRUCE SIMONS
Principal

DAVINA MCCLURE
Director of Teaching and Learning

IEVA HAMPSON
Head of the Junior Campus
All at The Hamilton and Alexandra College, Hamilton, Victoria, Australia

BACKGROUND AND CONTEXT

The Hamilton and Alexandra College is an independent, coeducational school that educates 3-year-old preschool children through to the final year of secondary schooling. The College is associated with the Uniting Church in Australia, is a member of the Victorian Ecumenical Schools System, and is located in rural Victoria, Australia. Many students come from farming backgrounds and travel up to 100 kilometers (over 62 miles) to school each day. There is a current enrollment of approximately 520, with more than 70 secondary school boarders, including 25 international students from mainland China, Hong Kong, South Korea, and Japan.

Students at The Hamilton and Alexandra College are educated on two campuses. The Myrniong Junior Campus houses preschool and primary-age students, and the Chaucer Street Senior Campus (approximately 1 kilometer [three-fifths of a mile] away) houses students in the secondary years. The school employs approximately 50 full-time equivalent teaching staff members with the ideal that educators teach only in their areas of expertise. Specialist teachers in the areas of the arts, sports, languages, mathematics, English, science, and information services teach across both campuses. The school dates back to the early 1870s and prides itself on providing a blend of traditional and innovative educational approaches.

Until recently, approaches to professional learning in the College were largely focused on the perceived needs of different faculties in each of the primary and secondary areas, which were determined by the Head of the Junior Campus (primary) and the Director of Teaching and Learning (secondary). In 2010, the principal of the College proposed an initiative based on "capacity building" using the Canadian model of systematic education reform outlined in *Realization: The Change Imperative for Deepening District-Wide Reform* (Sharratt & Fullan, 2009). The emphasis of the initiative was on educating through best practice. The aim was to achieve significant improvement in student learning and embed across all areas of the curriculum high-quality instructional practice that would be implemented, supported, monitored, and deepened through professional shared practice and a common vision.

A high priority within the initiative was the improvement of literacy across the curriculum. For this purpose, "learning walks" were introduced for staff members to observe and support literacy learning beyond their own classrooms. Staff members were encouraged to observe each other's teaching and to engage in professional dialogue reflecting on their practice related to literacy teaching and learning. For this to be purposeful, the Director of Teaching and Learning and the Head of the Junior Campus recognized that teachers' professional learning at the College needed to:

- Encourage staff to focus on strategic vision of "capacity building."
- Ensure ownership by all stakeholders.
- Break down the "faculty mindset."
- Utilize the expertise of leading teachers.
- Engage staff in meaningful professional dialogue cross-faculty and cross-campus levels.
- Develop shared understandings of practice to improve student learning outcomes.
- Encourage staff to participate openly in the observation of colleagues' teaching practices and move beyond the "black box" mentality (Black & William, 2001).

THE PROFESSIONAL LEARNING INITIATIVE

Inspiration and Directions

In early 2011, the Director of Teaching and Learning and the Head of the Junior Campus decided to use John Hattie's (2010) work as a catalyst for refocusing the staff to develop a common understanding of what "capacity building" entailed. At the first professional learning session for the year, they highlighted evidence-based "best practices" from Hattie's research and the related effect sizes of each influence, which could be used by the staff to develop shared notions of effective "instructional practice." The relevance of the professional learning session content to day-to-day teaching practice ensured that the session was embraced by staff across the College. Teachers identified with specific influential effects, such as "teacher clarity," "teacher–student relationships," "self-verbalization/self-questioning," "worked examples," and "study skills."

Soon after the professional learning session, the Director of Teaching and Learning and the Head of the Junior Campus attended a professional learning conference led by a well-known U.S. educator, Charlotte Danielson. Danielson was visiting Australia to share insights into the use of classroom observation as a means to school improvement. Danielson's framework for observing and enhancing elements of professional practice provided a way forward in addressing the needs of the College's professional learning model, strategic vision, and shared understanding of best practice. During the conference, they met Melbourne University lecturer Hilary Hollingsworth, who had been working on the Third International Mathematics and Science Study (TIMSS) Video

Study project. Hollingsworth agreed to act as a consultant, over 2 years, for the College to assist in developing the desired professional learning model and culture.

Stage 1: Strategic Focusing of Instructional Improvements

The Director of Teaching and Learning and the Head of the Junior Campus considered it important to identify some of the school's potential change agents to drive the development of the school's professional learning model and culture. These staff members were invited to a think-tank meeting facilitated by Hollingsworth, with the understanding that they would become integral in promoting and leading the way forward. In preparation for the meeting, which was held mid-year, the think-tank members were given preliminary reading by Danielson (2008), Marzano (2007), the Australian Institute for Teaching and School Leadership (AITSL; 2011) and Clarke and Hollingsworth (2000). At the meeting, they considered what excellent teaching looks like and the suitability of the teaching and learning frameworks of Danielson and Marzano, as well as the draft Australian National Professional Standards for Teachers developed by the AITSL (2011), for the College's context. The team decided to select specific foci from Danielson's framework to share with the whole staff and to elicit interest and buy-in with regard to engagement in professional learning. The importance of shared ownership by all teachers was the impetus for planning the new strategy for subsequent professional learning sessions at the College.

The following month, all staff members were given the first six pages of *Enhancing Professional Practice: A Framework for Teaching, Second Edition* (Danielson, 2008) to read in preparation for Hollingsworth's second visit, at which she was to work with the whole school staff. Hollingsworth invited the staff to examine international examples of instructional practice in classrooms using video footage from the TIMSS Video Study project. Her aim was to convey the virtues of using classroom video as a tool for professional reflection and to promote the effectiveness of classroom observation as a professional learning experience. Hollingsworth set professional protocols for viewing classroom video:

- Focus on *the teaching*, not the *teacher*.
- Focus on what *could* have been done, not what *should* have been done.
- Value the professional contribution of the individual.

Utilizing Danielson's framework, *Enhancing Professional Practice* (2008), staff viewed several clips applying different elements from the components of practice to focus their discussion, for example, "Engaging Students in Learning: Structure and Pacing" (Danielson, 2008, p. 82). Following the video observation exercises, the teachers were asked to identify three components of instructional practice from Danielson's framework that they sought to refine or develop within their own practice. This excluded components from the domain of professional responsibilities, as these generally took place beyond the classroom and the focus of the initiative was on classroom observation. The three identified components were then recorded by teachers onto separate Post-it notes, which they stuck on to a prepared wall chart displaying the components of Danielson's framework. During a short break, the think-tank team members worked to review the professional learning needs identified by the staff. They looked for trends and collated the staff data to form teams based on shared instructional practice foci. This ensured that each individual could focus on a component that he or she had identified to be of interest. The think-tank "drivers" were strategically allocated to lead these teams. This process ensured relevance and immediate ownership of the direction forward for each and every staff member. Team members were given specific reading from the Danielson text outlining the breadth and depth of their component focus. They participated in a group discussion related to their focus and were invited to:

- Share individual reasons for selecting their focus area.
- Identify professional learning needs related to this focus area.
- Brainstorm and discuss desired outcomes that could be achieved by pursuing professional learning in this focus area.
- Set and prioritize achievable and measureable instructional goals to be worked on as an action research team project over the next semester.
- Create an action research project plan outlining each task (e.g., team meetings, class trials, shared professional reading, class observations), professional reading materials needed, other resources required, and who would be involved in each task.

Following the professional learning session, the team leaders were responsible for sharing their plans with the Head of the Junior Campus and the Director of Teaching and Learning. Once collated, the plans were made available to all staff via the College intranet and also with Hollingsworth for support and facilitation of each team, as required. Over the next 3 months, allocated common professional learning time, in conjunction with team-initiated meetings, helped each project progress. The Director of Teaching and Learning and the Head of the Junior Campus witnessed authentic and meaningful collaboration in the professional learning interactions of staff. It was evident that common language, vision, and understandings across faculties and campuses were developing. A further professional learning day was scheduled to report the work of each team and to seek feedback from colleagues. Through this sharing time, every staff member contributed to, and was accountable for, the team's project work and presentation. All groups brought along resources, strategies, and recommendations to contribute to the wider staff. Following this sharing day, each staff member was invited to complete a survey to provide feedback regarding the value or effectiveness of the new professional learning model. The survey revealed that the power of the team action research model, focusing on shared instructional practice within the context of the school, was that it had enabled collegial refinement of practice and produced learning outcomes that could be scrutinized, understood, and adopted by all. Staff members had valued the opportunity to drive and work on a pertinent project while drawing on the collective expertise of their colleagues.

Stage 2: Next Steps—Video Observations and Analysis of Classroom Practice

To maintain the momentum of the new professional learning model developed in 2011, the Director of Teaching and Learning invited Hollingsworth to return to the school to facilitate its direction for the 2012 school year. It was felt that the teachers were ready to take on the next step of the model: video recording and analyzing their practice with their colleagues. In order for staff members to be able to video students in their classrooms, the College obtained permission to video from parents with the sole purpose for staff to share their teaching with each other while working collaboratively to build on instructional techniques and teaching methods to improve student learning.

Once permission had been granted, the Director of Teaching and Learning and the Head of the Junior Campus approached experienced, confident teachers to record and then select video excerpts of their teaching practice to share. These excerpts were viewed by the whole staff, facilitated by Hollingsworth, as a means of establishing a culture for engaging in professional dialogue about shared instructional practice. Teachers used the protocols, introduced by Hollingsworth in the previous year, and were given a Classroom Observation Dimensions and Descriptors template (Hollingsworth & Kusznirczuk, 2012) to pinpoint how their colleagues

- Communicate expectations for learning.
- Utilize questions and discussions for learning.
- Develop tasks for learning.
- Build understanding for learning.
- Use assessment for learning.

Following this, teachers were encouraged to video, view, and reflect on their own practice using the Classroom Observation Dimensions and Descriptors template. They were invited to select an excerpt to share in a supportive and professional environment with their colleagues at a faculty or small-group level. Using video observations, teachers have begun to focus on elements of practice such as learning intentions, high expectations, offering feedback, cognitive demand, and allocation of time for topic depth and student thinking. The intention is to build on this work as a tool for professional reflection, in which staff revise questions about the consequences and influence of their instructional practice.

Key Features of the Initiative

The key features that contributed to the success of the professional learning journey at The Hamilton and Alexandra College included:

- Acknowledging the need to establish a framework to guide the delivery of professional learning.
- Bringing a consultant on board to facilitate the process.
- Identifying and engaging change agents from within the school to drive the process.
- Promoting professional learning as an opportunity to refine or develop (rather than "improve") professional practice.
- Ensuring the relevance of professional learning to all staff by offering ownership, through elements of choice and opportunities to steer the direction of the learning.

- Drawing on the collective expertise of the staff.
- Valuing and improving shared instructional practice by establishing protocols for viewing and discussing specific elements of practice.

In moving forward at The Hamilton and Alexandra College, the professional learning vision needs to be continually revisited to reinforce purpose, to maintain momentum, and to ensure that teachers are still "coming on board" and teachers new to the school are not left behind.

REFERENCES

Australian Institute for Teaching and School Leadership. (2011). *Australian professional standards for teachers*. Carlton South: Education Services Australia.

Black, P., & Wiliam, D. (2001). *Inside the black box*. London: Kings College.

Clarke, D. J., & Hollingsworth, H. (2000). Seeing is understanding. *Journal of Staff Development, 21*(4), 40–43.

Danielson, C. (2008). *Enhancing professional practice: A framework for teaching* (2nd ed.). Heatherton, Australia: Hawker Brownlow Education.

Hattie, J. (2010). *Visible learning*. New York: Routledge.

Hollingsworth, H., & Kusznirczuk, J. (2012). *Classroom observation dimensions and descriptors template*. Unpublished manuscript, University of Melbourne, Melbourne Graduate School of Education, Victoria, Australia.

Marzano, R. J. (2007). *The art and science of teaching: A comprehensive framework for effective instruction*. Alexandria, VA: ASCD.

Sharratt, L., & Fullan, M. (2009). *Realization: The change imperative for deepening district-wide reform*. Thousand Oaks, CA: Corwin Press.

Author Index

Subject Index

Page numbers followed by *f* indicate figure, *t* indicate table